M000317352

Our
Elders
Teach Us

Contemporary American Indian Studies

Series Editor

J. Anthony Paredes

OUR
ELDERS
TEACH US

Maya-Kaqchikel Historical Perspectives

Xkib'ij kan qate' qatata'

DAVID CAREY, JR.

En paz y solidaridad,

David Carey

THE UNIVERSITY OF ALABAMA PRESS
Tuscaloosa and London

Copyright © 2001
The University of Alabama Press
Tuscaloosa, Alabama 35487-0380
All rights reserved
Manufactured in the United States of America

2 4 6 8 9 7 5 3 1
02 04 06 08 09 07 05 03 01

Typeface: AGaramond and Frutiger

∞

The paper on which this book is printed meets the minimum requirements of American
National Standard for Information Science–Permanence of Paper for Printed Library
Materials, ANSI Z39.48-1984.

Library of Congress Cataloging-in-Publication Data

Carey, David.
Our elders teach us : Maya-Kaqchikel historical perspectives xkib'ij kan qate' qatata' /
David Carey, Jr.
p. cm. — (Contemporary American Indian studies)
Includes bibliographical references and index.
ISBN 0-8173-1119-X (pbk. : alk. paper)
1. Cakchikel Indians—Ethnic identity. 2. Cakchikel Indians—Historiography.
3. Cakchikel philosophy. 4. Oral tradition—Guatemala. 5. Guatemala—History.
6. Guatemala—Ethnic relations. 7. Guatemala—Politics and government.
I. Title. II. Series.
F1465.2.C3 C37 2001
972.81' 00497415—dc21
2001002652

British Library Cataloguing-in-Publication Data available

To the Kaqchikel
Matyox chiwe iwonojel

Contents

Preface

What would the history of Guatemala, or for that matter the history of the Americas, look like if the basic concepts were taken from Mayan oral tradition rather than European-dominated historiography? This remarkable book gives the answer. Centered on the lives and thoughts of the people in a Kaqchikel-speaking region in the western highlands of the country, this extraordinary book is a new history and a new historiography of Guatemala. It is a history and theoretical perspective of a Native American culture, American Indians who share the history of the Americas with other groups. And today, when as many as a million Maya have migrated to the United States, settled down, and sent their English-speaking children to schools and universities, this is a history that is shared between the United States and Guatemala. History is more than a relating of past events; it is also a conceptual and analytical approach to understanding the past, or historiography. The theory of history proposed in this book is also a perspective that other American Indians share. This thorough presentation of the narratives of the Kaqchikel elders is not just something that is useful for Guatemala specialists. It is a book for anyone interested in both the approach and the details of the history of the Americas as seen through the living narratives, conversations, and anecdotes of those who have most lived it.

Mayan oral histories are alive today in Mesoamerica. Sometimes elders sit and patiently tell a portion of their history, but more often history lives through phrases, references, and allusions to events long ago dropped into everyday conversations. In this way people growing up in Mayan villages hear history and understand it as part of the unconscious fabric of everyday life. History can be seen inscribed in a traditional dance, in the route a Mayan priest takes to arrive at a sacred place, or in the particularities of landscape: trees, streams, hillsides. The metaphors used in a customary matchmaking discourse suggest social contracts that go beyond individual families to clan groups, communities, and ethnic alliances. Formalized declarations of Mayan history are presented during disputes, during occasions of celebration, and during moments of political change. Oral histories are interwoven with the new literature of "testimonials" put on paper by Mayan leaders like Victor Montejo or Rigoberta Menchú—where traditional village life becomes interrelated with the atrocities of the recent decades of violence in Guatemala—and in the interviews given to human rights commissions and to asylum courts in other countries. Oral histories are found in people's names, in the names of their towns, in the names of parts of their houses. Roof rafters, for example, are "the way of the mice," recalling scenes from histories about the origin of corn. Oral histories among the Maya are found in both simple and complex grammatical constructions of the Mayan languages themselves.

These are some of the features of a Mayan historiography that are developed in this book. Carey approaches the histories of the area on solid ground: he learned Kaqchikel and carefully recorded the anecdotes, proclamations, references, and comments that make up the web of talk in the villages today. He gained the confidence of Kaqchikel people through four summers and over a year of concentrated fieldwork. He became a local historian himself, adding his skills and knowledge to the emerging educational projects in the area.

Carey is also an academic historian trained in the careful search of collaborating sources. He puts the Kaqchikel narratives in a context of oral and written documents from surrounding towns and from archives and compares Kaqchikel perspectives with those of Guatemalan and other non-Mayan historians. And because Kaqchikel history lives through everyday speech, it contains contradictions, disagreements, and mistakes. Mayan villagers throughout Mesoamerica enjoy a good argument; some of the most sacred ceremonies I have attended have included loud arguments by participants about the number and characteristics of the guardians of the forests. Carey presents Kaqchikel history as a tapestry of different threads and colors, not all of them in harmony. Points of contention and difference serve to ground contemporary declarations of history in the emotional investments of those people who believe strongly in what they are saying. It is far easier for a listener to remember a historic event that is related with strong language and disagreement among people than as an uncontested narrative.

The last half-century in Guatemala has seen increases in population, an increasing concentration of land in the hands of a few, and increasingly bitter and violent confrontations between many Mayan groups and non-Mayan people, or "Ladinos." It is not a great surprise, then, that a theme running through the oral traditions of the Kaqchikel is the division between these two groups. Part of that division is based on the unequal place Ladino history has had in schools, in professional literature, and in the arenas of popular culture and everyday worldview. Carey writes that this volume is designed as a "forum for contemporary Maya to share what is important to them about their past and talk about how they apply it to their lives" (23). But a Kaqchikel ethnohistory is more than just a look at themes not treated by Western academic history. It is also an orientation toward the connection between people and place, between the dramatic and uncontrollable forces of earthquakes and the controllable forces of oppression and exploitation. Carey's account is powerful because it does more than recount history from a local Kaqchikel point of view. There is also a theory of history, an analytic framework that Kaqchikel people use to organize what they talk about and how they talk about it. Chapters on the pre-European history of the area, leadership and political alliances, the military, education, and ethnic relations show that Mayan history is ever conscious of the holistic interconnections of time, place, and people.

This Kaqchikel perspective on their own history is especially apparent in chapters 3 and 4, which focus on the history of epidemics and natural disasters. Here the Kaqchikel (and larger Mayan) interest in the dialogue of history is especially apparent. The epidemics of cholera, smallpox, and influenza are seen in Kaqchikel history as intimately tied to the poverty that enveloped their history. One teacher told Carey, "My parents taught me about the tough times the Mayan people faced a long time ago: sickness, hunger, slavery, discrimination" (115). Interwoven through their accounts are the possibilities that the chemical warfare of poisoning wells with cholera-infected clothing made some of these epidemics yet another tool of Mayan oppression. And even when Ladinos do not help with the fury of the natural disasters, they use disaster recovery in dangerous ways. The 1976 earthquake that devastated Guatemala is a case in point. Villagers told Carey that they opened their homes to relief workers from the United States and elsewhere only to find their hospitality used against them. Villagers remember the violence against the Maya during the 1980s and 1990s as a result of earthquake relief: relief workers are said to have been preaching antigovernment lessons in return for their work. Even if this were only a belief—and their beliefs—it was a belief that government forces acted upon during the 1980s by systematically murdering those who opened their homes to relief workers.

The population of Guatemala is overwhelmingly Mayan, especially when those Maya who have adapted to urban contexts with city clothes, knowledge of both Spanish and English, and nonagricultural jobs are counted as Maya. And at the same time, available historic materials from the Mayan point of view have often been relegated to collections of folktales or colonial documents such as the *Popol Wuj*. Carey's book changes that by taking seriously the sociolinguistics of historical discourse in Mayan communities. But Carey does more than recount anecdotes and historic references that permeate village discourse. He has looked for and found an internal logic to these accounts, and within that logic he has started a dialogue between the perspectives honed through years of telling and retelling and the perspectives found in the official history and records of Guatemala.

This book is a modern-day chronicle, one that will be treasured as a source document for Kaqchikel and other Maya who are increasingly lending their voice to the academic discussions of history and culture of the Mayan world. It is also a chronicle of how people think and present information in the Mayan world at the beginning of the new millennium. And while portions of the book are already being translated into forms useful in the villages of Guatemala, this presentation in English will be read by the children of the almost one million Maya who have migrated to the United States to become the newest Indians in the United States. And the book will be a touchstone for American Indian historians as well, as they increasingly appreciate that Maya are native peoples of the Americas, from the Arctic Circle to the southern tip of South America.

Allan F. Burns
University of Florida Department of Anthropology

Acknowledgments

First and foremost I want to thank the people to whom this work is dedicated—the Kaqchikel. This work would not have been possible if they had not allowed me into their world. Lamentably, for reasons I will explain, I am unable to name them. I especially want to thank my host family in Comalapa who accepted me as their own. A number of other families in Comalapa opened their hearts to me, and I have many fond memories of the times we shared. I am also indebted to my host families in Poaquil and Tecpán for the generosity and kindness they showed me during my stays in their towns. In all the towns where I worked and lived, I always felt welcomed by the Kaqchikel community.

I am also grateful to the interlocutors and assistants who helped me gain access to informants and who made my research an insightful and joyful experience. The research was clearly not conducted in a vacuum; the informants themselves merit recognition for their contributions and openness. I regret not being able to mention them by name. All of these Kaqchikel individuals tremendously enriched my life, and I thank them for making my stays in Guatemala fruitful and rewarding well beyond my research.

Kaqchikel Cholchi' strongly supported my work on a Kaqchikel history textbook. Kaji' Kawoq deserves special thanks for his untiring assistance in the transformation of the document into a book. He quickly became one of my closest friends. Kab'lajuj Tijax also provided invaluable assistance in the textbook project.

A number of other people assisted my research in Guatemala. Edgar Esquit and Enrique Gordillo were especially helpful in my use of the Archivo General de Centro América (General Archives of Central America)(AGCA). I am grateful to the Kaqchikel family who graciously hosted me while I conducted my archival research in Guatemala City. Likewise, the de León family always welcomed me into their home during my infrequent stays in Antigua.

I sincerely hope that the many unnamed Kaqchikel whose individual and communal insights and efforts made this work possible can recognize their contributions to this attempt to record and represent their history.

I developed my research ideas and language skills in Tulane University's Kaqchikel language and culture course in Antigua, Guatemala. Directors Judith Maxwell and Robert McKenna Brown have created an environment there that allows students to share profoundly in the lives of native Kaqchikel speakers. Their work and dedication go well beyond the language and cultural parameters of the course. They exude a love and respect for the Kaqchikel people, and their positive energy is contagious. Likewise, the corps of native Kaqchikel instructors are to be commended for their teaching ability and their openness to outsiders. The Centro de Investigaciones Regionales de Mesoamérica (CIRMA) hosted the course in Antigua, and its staff facilitated my use of their library.

The Center for Latin American Studies at Tulane University granted me the opportunity to pursue doctoral studies and to write this manuscript. The former director Richard Greenleaf and his staff were always supportive. Tulane University's Latin American Library and Bill Nañez provided invaluable resources for this research.

My dissertation director and adviser, Ralph Lee Woodward, Jr., first inspired me to study Guatemala and has always been a source of guidance and inspiration. Judith Maxwell dedicated much of her time to revising this manuscript and contributed enormously to my understanding of Guatemala, Maya, and Kaqchikel. Furthermore, her sincere, reciprocal, and life-giving relationship with Kaqchikel piqued my interest and demonstrated a way that academics can have a positive impact beyond the university. In addition, Roderic Camp's commitment to academic rigor and excellence set a high standard for my own work. All three of my mentors emphasized the importance of making research and writing available and understandable to a wider audience. I also want to thank David Conrad, Christopher Lutz, Todd Little-Siebold, Douglass Sullivan-González, Kristin Harpster Lawrence, and Rosemary Mosher for their contributions to this book. Finally, I wish to thank the two anonymous reviewers from the University of Alabama Press for their constructive criticism.

The funding specific to this research was provided by the Fulbright-Hays scholarship. I greatly appreciate this financial support for my 1997–98 year in Guatemala. The Tinker Foundation and the Foreign Language and Area Studies Fellowship generously funded my enrollment in Tulane University's Kaqchikel summer program in 1994 and 1995.

I also need to express my thanks and love for the most constant and unwavering source of support: my family. My parents and my brother, Bob, have always encouraged me to pursue my goals of higher education and development as well as my intent to have a positive impact on those with whom

I work and live. In many ways they instilled the values that motivated my studies and research and that continue to challenge me to improve.

Finally, my wife, Sarah Johnson, profoundly knows this manuscript. She accompanied me for a month during my research in Guatemala and edited numerous versions of this text. Beyond her academic and editorial contributions, she also provided emotional support. My words fail to express my gratitude to her, but my thanks, respect, admiration, and undying love for her continue to grow.

Even with these contributions, the work is my own and I accept full responsibility for any shortcomings or failures.

Our
Elders
Teach Us

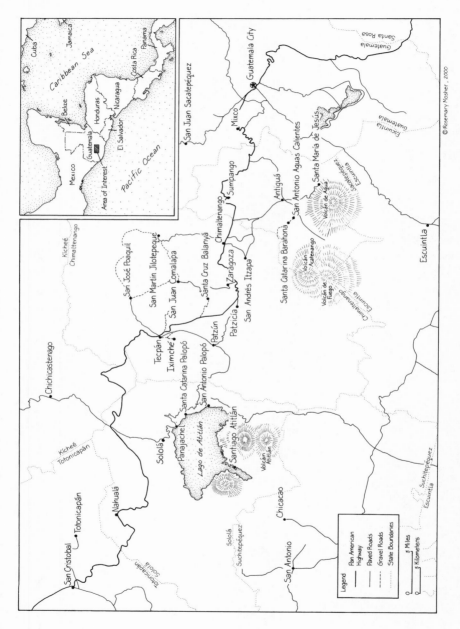

Map of Kaqchikel and surrounding towns in the central highlands of Guatemala

© Rosemary Mosher, 2000

Legend

——	Pan American Highway
——	Paved Roads
- - -	Gravel Roads
....	State Boundaries

0   5 Miles
0   5 Kilometers

Methodology

My research began in 1994, when I enrolled in Tulane University's Maya-Kaqchikel language and culture class in Antigua, Guatemala. The teachers were native speakers who lived in the surrounding area, and the class was sometimes held in their respective towns, which allowed further insight into Kaqchikel lifestyle and culture. As my personal relationships developed, some of the teachers invited me to stay at their homes on weekends and then after the end of the six-week course. Beyond being rewarding on a personal and emotional level, these relationships were invaluable to my research. The more my friends shared with me, the more I realized how little I had read about their ideas on Guatemala's present and past through conventional historical resources. I began to formulate some ideas about how I could better understand Kaqchikel approaches to history and reality and make it my research.

I returned to Guatemala each summer from 1994 to 1997 to expand my knowledge of Kaqchikel and to develop personal relationships, and I maintained correspondence with my Kaqchikel friends when I was in the United States. In fall 1997 I began a one-year residence in Comalapa. I returned again in summer 1999. That I returned each summer convinced people of my commitment to Guatemala and to the Kaqchikel people in particular. After studying the Kaqchikel language for four summers and taking classes at Tulane University with a native speaker and a North American linguist fluent in Kaqchikel, my communication skills were good enough that I could spend a year in Comalapa.

The research design was twofold. First, I lived in the community to hear oral traditions and histories of Kaqchikel. All of my interviews and informal conversations with Kaqchikel speakers were conducted in Kaqchikel. Second, I researched documentation in the AGCA to compare to and complement oral histories. It was imperative that I conduct the research in this order: living in the community prior to researching documentation allowed me to frame questions from oral histories, not from histories in the archives. To understand Kaqchikel historical perspectives and worldviews, I needed to know from the community's point of view what constituted an important event or person. Only after learning what constituted Kaqchikel viewpoints did I go to the archives to search for information that would support, conflict with, and supplement the data I acquired during my fieldwork. The combination of the two sources provides a more holistic and critical understanding of Kaqchikel reality and history.

Of the two aspects of the research design, the more challenging was earning confidence and trust. However, years of learning the language and developing relationships with Kaqchikel allowed me access to their historical perceptions. The barriers imposed by my not being a Kaqchikel native dissipated as my command of the language and commitment to the people became clear. As Chippewa Indian Duane Champagne states, "I do not believe that Indian scholars have a monopoly on Indian Studies. As in all human groups, culture, institutions, and social and political processes are usually understandable to most anybody who is willing to learn and who at least may observe, if not participate, in the process."[1] The longer I lived in these Kaqchikel communities the more capable I became of understanding what was important in their history and how best to access their worldview. In order to study oral traditions, the researcher must live in, actively participate in, and acculturate to the community. A thorough understanding of the language is critical to entering the community on a deep level. A complete study of oral histories requires more than simply listening to and analyzing stories; oral traditions cannot be studied if the researcher is oblivious to or distanced from the social and cultural context in which the information is communicated.

Only my five years of living in and returning to these towns provided me with an understanding of the context and reality of Kaqchikel and allowed me the opportunity to learn about historical perspectives and relevant events in Kaqchikel history. This understanding enabled me to formulate relevant questions in interviews. One of my Kaqchikel assistants, Oxlajuj Kan, taught me that it is helpful to recognize important events in local history in order to encourage people to talk. Asking a general question about history often does not evoke a response from interviewees. The best approach is to allow the conversation to flow so that the interviewee is not aware that he or she is being interviewed.[2] Oxlajuj Kan had mastered this technique, and observation of his work was instructive. One must listen attentively and know how to facilitate informative conversations.

Most importantly, my research could not have been conducted without advanced language skills. Many of my informants either only spoke Kaqchikel or did not feel comfortable expressing themselves in Spanish. Others only granted me access because I spoke Kaqchikel.[3] Kaqchikel do not tell the same stories in Spanish that they do in Kaqchikel. In her collaborative study of the villages around Lake Atitlán, Perla Petrich attests to the importance of using Kaqchikel because of the different versions of the same history. She found that when someone told a story in Kaqchikel, he or she included details and happenings that they omitted in the Spanish version, and vice versa.[4] Linguist and anthropologist Judith Maxwell also asserts that because languages encompass cultural values, a cognitive gap exists between Maya and Spanish languages.[5] Kaqchikel recognize this condition. They stress that if they lose their language, they will also lose their spirit or character (*na'oj*). Kaqchikel worldviews are not comprehensibly expressed in Spanish. Rigoberta Menchú, the 1992 Nobel Peace Prize Laureate, explains the depth of her Maya-K'ichee' language: "Our languages express our culture, and speaking and understanding them means learning about a new world, and thinking about things in a new way."[6] According to Menchú, Spanish fails to capture the essence of the K'ichee' language and therefore the K'ichee' culture and history.

Speaking Kaqchikel enabled me to gain confidence, trust, and recognition from the people with whom I was living, working, and interacting on a daily basis. At times, that I spoke Kaqchikel was enough to elicit an invitation from someone to visit them at their home and talk about history.

Case Studies

After learning about and living with Kaqchikel for four years, I decided to focus my study on five Kaqchikel towns and make occasional visits to other Kaqchikel areas. My goal was to gain insight beyond a single community by conducting research among different groups of Kaqchikel. I performed a total of 414 interviews.[7] I usually resided in the town of San Juan Comalapa, where I performed 222 interviews in the main town and its outlying villages and hamlets. In San José Poaquil and Tecpán, I performed 60 and 44 interviews, respectively, and in the smaller towns of San Antonio Aguas Calientes (henceforth referred to as Aguas Calientes) and Santa Catarina Barahona (henceforth referred to as Barahona), I (with Kaqchikel assistants) performed 23 and 21 interviews, respectively. I conducted two more confined studies in San Martín Jilotepeque and Santa Catarina Palopó, where I performed 17 and 7 interviews, respectively. Lastly, I conducted a number of isolated interviews in the Kaqchikel towns of Santa Cruz Balanya', Patzicía, San Antonio Palopó, Santa María de Jesus, and Sumpango, as well as in Chimaltenango and Guatemala City. An in-depth study of five Kaqchikel towns in two departments and additional research in other Kaqchikel towns and Guatemala City allowed me a broad view of Kaqchikel historical perspectives.

I decided on these five towns because from 1994 to 1997 I had developed close relationships with informants from each. Furthermore, I wanted to acquire information from a wide range of the Kaqchikel population, and the towns I chose vary in population, size, urban-rural locations, population concentration, proximity to major means of communication, Ladino influence, employment makeup, and education levels.[8] Education seldom went beyond the primary level, and the majority of informants were agriculturists who owned their land. Some owned enough land to provide for their basic needs, while others, especially the landless, had to seek agricultural employment to support themselves and their families. Other informants worked as bakers, barbers, restaurant and store owners, artists, bus and truck drivers and assistants, weavers, vendors, domestic servants, nurses, technicians, security guards, teachers, administrators, and mayors. In general, teachers, nurses, technicians, administrators, and mayors had received education beyond the secondary level. Clearly, this exposure allowed them access to sources of knowledge beyond oral traditions and provided an environment in which to apply their analytical and comparative skills. Each informant's distinct background colors the information he or she shares. Likewise, Mayan intellectuals consisting of university professors, authors, and leaders and their employees in Mayan organizations generally have some university education and in many cases a political agenda of improving Mayan rights. I point out the distinct employment and educational background of some informants because it affects their historical perspectives. However, in this study more than 75 percent of the informants are manual laborers whose education does not exceed the primary level. Regardless of education levels, nearly all informants said that their knowledge of history came from their elders, not from schools or books.

The towns of Tecpán and Comalapa are similar in that a significant number of Kaqchikel in these municipalities work and study outside the community. These residents tend to have more interaction with Ladinos, Kaqchikel from other areas, and other Maya than do the people who seldom leave, and these diverse experiences color their perspectives. These towns also contain the two largest municipal populations in the study. Despite their similarities, one difference is immediately evident: except on market day, Tecpán appears to be a Ladino town in which the preferred language is Spanish. In contrast, Comalapa is clearly a Kaqchikel town in which the dominant language and dress is Kaqchikel. The two towns provide an interesting contrast because one is more affected by Ladino influences.

Where the relative isolation of other communities affect their residents' historical perspectives, Tecpán's Ladino influence is due in part to its proximity to the main thoroughfare in Guatemala. Comalapa, especially its villages, and Poaquil provide excellent case studies of communities isolated from constant outside interaction. Aguas Calientes and Barahona are similar to Tecpán in terms of their level of daily contact with noncommunity members. Residents of Aguas Calientes and Barahona also have significant interaction with tourists, as the towns are popular tourist attractions, and many residents work in Antigua, a town with a considerable number of international travelers. Distinct levels of interaction with people outside local communities provide a variation in Kaqchikel historical perspectives.

It is important to look at the ways oral histories vary in different towns and in what ways they remain constant. The five towns I studied are located in two different departments (Chimaltenango and Sacatepéquez) and consequently have different local events. National policies are uniform, but their implementation can vary depending on local leaders. Furthermore, natural disasters, such as the 1976 earthquake, affect some regions more than others.

I chose to live with a Kaqchikel family in Comalapa because 95 percent of its 27,287 inhabitants are Maya, I had already developed close relationships with a number of residents, and it is centrally located within the Kaqchikel-speaking region of Guatemala.[9] While it is a predominantly agricultural area, 57 percent of the population lives in the municipal capital, and the other 43 percent are dispersed in some twenty-five agricultural communities associated with Comalapa. The town is 2,150 meters above sea level, twenty-eight kilometers from the department capital of Chimaltenango, and eighty-two kilometers from Guatemala City.[10] To a certain degree, Comalapa is isolated by its location in the highlands. The quickest outlet is a seventeen-kilometer road that until 1999 was treacherous.[11] Comalapa is a predominantly Kaqchikel town; women wear intricately woven Comalapa po't (traditional hand-woven blouse) marked by two red stripes on the shoulder. Kaqchikel dominate the town in all aspects: politically, economically, socially, culturally, and linguistically. Their control of the area represents an important shift in their history that occurred in the 1970s when Kaqchikel retook the town from Ladinos, who until then controlled the town center, along with the political and economic life of Comalapa. Kaqchikel take pride in this power shift.

The second town in my study is Tecpán. I lived here for two different three-week periods with a Kaqchikel family and made various weekend visits. Tecpán contains the largest population in the area outside of Chimaltenango. Tecpán has 41,152 inhabitants, 89 percent of whom are Maya. Unlike Comalapa, the majority of residents live in rural settings outside the city limits; only 22 percent of Tecpán's population live in the municipal capital.

The area is predominantly agricultural, but the town boasts a number of different industries, shops, restaurants, and even a few hotels. Ladinos dominate most political and economic activity even though they comprise a small percentage of the population. Thirty-four kilometers from Chimaltenango and eighty-eight kilometers from Guatemala City, Tecpán is located off the Pan-American Highway, which makes it more accessible to outside influence. Every Thursday, Tecpán is home to the largest market in the area, which provides an opportunity for interaction among people from different regions. The climate is cooler than Comalapa's, as it is 2,313 meters above sea level.[12]

The final town in the department of Chimaltenango is Poaquil, where I stayed with a Kaqchikel family for more than a month and made overnight visits to throughout the year. Poaquil has a population of 15,808, of which 93 percent is Maya. This municipality borders Comalapa. The rural population dominates Poaquil, as 75 percent of its people live outside the municipal center. The town is noticeably smaller than either Tecpán or Comalapa, boasting only seven streets crossing seven avenues. Forty-seven kilometers from the department capital and 104 kilometers from Guatemala City on a well-maintained dirt road 14 kilometers from the Pan-American Highway, Poaquil is even more geographically isolated than Comalapa.[13] Furthermore, due to limited bus service (the last bus departs the town at 2 P.M.) more people remain in their respective communities than in the other towns in the study. Poaquil is situated fifteen hundred meters above sea level. Like all of these municipalities, many of the villages of Poaquil are located in areas quite distant from the main town, some as many as 18 kilometers away. Some of these communities are considerably lower in altitude and experience coastal climates. The worst years of Guatemala's civil war, which for Poaquil was the early 1980s, devastated much of the town's male population. Consequently, many families are predominantly female. In comparison to the other towns, Poaquil presents an interesting case because it is smaller, more self-contained, and historically Kaqchikel-dominated.

Even though Poaquil is the most geographically isolated town in the study, some of its residents are intimately connected to national and international arenas. A small percentage of the population has studied at the university level in the capital or in the United States. Others commute to Tecpán or the department capital to work. Even though a smaller portion of this population has constant interaction with people outside the community than individuals in the other towns in the study, the impact of Ladino or foreign influence is evident. At the same time, due to its geographic isolation and Kaqchikel-dominated history, Poaquil has the least Ladino presence and influence of the communities in the study. The contrast between Poaquil's rural, insulated population and its more cosmopolitan members who interact significantly with people outside the community adds to this town's complexity.

The final two towns in the study, Barahona and Aguas Calientes, are located in the department of Sacatepéquez. I had Kaqchikel assistants in both towns but often made day trips from Comalapa and for this reason did not live in either Aguas Calientes or Barahona. These are the two smallest towns in population. Barahona has 2,323 inhabitants, 94 percent of whom are Maya. Likewise, 93 percent of Aguas Calientes's population of 6,740 is Maya. Both Aguas Calientes and Barahona are overwhelmingly urban; 83 percent of the population of Aguas Calientes lives in an urban setting, and Barahona has no rural residents. Aguas Calientes is 1,530 meters above sea level, and Barahona is 1,520 meters above sea level.[14] The towns share a border in the Quinizilapa Valley and are separated only by a street. These two towns present interesting cases because they are located close to Antigua, Guatemala, the department capital (10 and 11 kilometers, respectively). This proximity provides much interaction with Ladinos and even North American and European tourists. In fact, in addition to agriculture, the predominant economic activity is the creation of artisan products to sell to national and international tourists.

In an attempt to ensure a comprehensive view of Kaqchikel history, I performed limited case studies in two other communities. I stayed for one week in Santa Catarina Palopó, a town on Lake Atitlán in the department of Sololá, to investigate historical perceptions. Palopó is a town of 1,527 inhabitants, 96 percent of whom are Maya and who are mostly agriculturists and fishermen. Palopó's men and women continue to wear their traditional dress.[15] This commitment to their traditional dress might affect their historical perceptions and worldviews; they maintain a strong adherence to oral traditions, and their oral histories are very much present and relevant in their lives. Kaqchikel is the preferred language in Palopó, and 84 percent of the residents live in the center of town. Palopó is more removed from Guatemala City than the rest of the towns in the study; however, it is close to the tourist town of Panajachel.

The most geographically isolated community I studied was Rosario Canajal, an *aldea* (hamlet) of San Martín Jilotepeque, the municipality that borders Comalapa to the northeast. This aldea provides an interesting case study because it is composed of a mix of about one thousand Kaqchikel and K'ichee' speakers who settled there to work for a large landholder. The community is located twenty kilometers from San Martín Jilotepeque on a dirt road riddled with holes. Only two buses access the community, both passing through town before the break of dawn. This study was conducted on two different occasions, a day trip and an overnight stay. My assistant had been a teacher in the local school for three years and had developed an extensive network of relationships, which made the collection of oral histories possible.

Sampling Method

Gathering information from both urban and rural sources was an important aspect of this study. Except for Barahona, all the municipalities have aldeas connected to the municipal center. These aldeas are predominantly agricultural communities located as far as twenty kilometers from the municipal capital, thus allowing easy access to the residents' farms. The populations range in size from fifty to twenty-five hundred people. I gained access to these communities through the assistant mayors of the communities and through people I knew in the main town who accompanied me to see their families in the aldeas. In these cases, assistants chose further informants for me based on their perception of who would be good sources of knowledge. It was consequently imperative for me to become known in these communities and get to know people better, because then I could establish interviews on my own with people whom the informants may not have viewed as especially good sources of history, specifically women. I visited all the aldeas associated with the town of Comalapa; in Poaquil I visited seven and in Tecpán only two. These interviews and relationships allowed me to sample the differences between rural and urban perceptions.

To move toward a comprehensive understanding of Kaqchikel oral traditions and ways of remembering the past, I incorporated interviews with people of all generations, professions, education levels, and both genders. One of my objectives was to understand how much history was transferred from one generation to another. Despite my efforts to interview an equal number of people in all these groups, the largest core group and the most knowledgeable about history was the older generation. Anthropologist Carol Hendrickson also noted this source of abundant knowledge in her work in Tecpán: "As repositories of knowledge and wisdom, *ancianos* [the elderly] . . . are consulted as prime sources of historic knowledge. . . . [A]s *ancianos* a person is a living link to the Maya ancestors and a focus of respect that derives partly from his or her personal contact with the relatively distant past. . . . The strength and contribution of the older generations lie in their ability to preserve and perpetuate the links with the past."[16] Older generations are the keepers of history, and they gradually share this information with younger generations.

My goal was to follow oral traditions through different generations. I interviewed people of all ages and both genders to develop a more comprehensive understanding of their oral histories. I was successful in this goal to a certain degree; however, the largest interviewee population was elderly men. My greatest limitation in the interviewee selection was my inability to access females, especially older women. Whenever I explained my project to assistants they invariably responded that I must want to talk to the *ri'j chïk achi'a'* (elderly men). They seldom suggested talking to older women. My access to elderly women was further limited by my own gender and by the women's humble self-perceptions and adherence to Kaqchikel propriety. Although women possessed vast historic knowledge, they often deferred to their husbands when they learned the nature of the interview or claimed they did not know any history since they had not attended school. In general, Kaqchikel consider older men to be the keepers of history. Fortunately, through the help of the family with whom I lived, through my own persistence, and because I asked other women to perform interviews for me, I was able to acquire data from this elusive group. When I did have the opportunity to share and learn from older women, I found them quite insightful and knowledgeable about history.

The interviewing technique I employed consisted of network sampling: a process of arranging and developing interviews through personal connections. The development of future interviews spreads through this personal network.[17] This connection is essential in Guatemala because Mayan communities tend to be closed to outsiders. Fortunately, my ability to speak Kaqchikel allowed me easier access to people. The longer I lived in Comalapa, and to a lesser degree in Poaquil and Tecpán, the more people became comfortable with my presence and the more they understood my work. As time passed, I became known as the local historian. As my reputation spread, people began to refer me to local experts in history of their own volition, or they offered their own accounts.

I arranged interviews in a number of ways. As network sampling implies, I began doing interviews through contacts I had developed over the previous four years. Teachers were a wonderful source of information and a valuable connection to the community. The community respected local teachers for their education and work and were always willing to assist them in any project. The organizational system of the municipality also provided an important source of connections. Each week the mayor met with the *alcaldes auxiliares* (auxiliary mayors) from each of the outlying communities. The mayor supported my work and allowed me to talk with the auxiliary mayors to arrange meetings in their respective communities. Predominantly, meetings were with male elders and/or leaders of the communities. The presence of an assistant provided a good source of new questions. Particularly in the beginning of my research, native speakers phrased questions more appropriately or asked more poignant questions than I would have. As my proficiency in the language and understanding of historical perspectives and relevant questions increased, I established and performed interviews alone. Since questions condition answers, I gathered some of my best data when I simply listened to people talking about history.

Assistants were essential conduits to people in rural areas. I could not have realized my research project without the aid of assistants who introduced me to members of different communities and facilitated people's increased confidence in me. In most cases, as a foreigner[18] I would have had no access to these communities due to their closed nature and to *la violencia,* the thirty-six-year civil war (1960–96), and consequent fear of anyone outside the Kaqchikel community.[19] Most Kaqchikel consider foreigners and Ladinos catalysts of la violencia. As a result, they receive strangers with trepidation. My recurrent presence in Comalapa, Tecpán, and Poaquil since 1994 helped to placate these tensions. At the same time, the fear of foreigners was not as pronounced in the municipal centers as it was outside city limits. The reality of the more remote communities necessitated that I have some connection to the rural villages I visited.

The nature of interviews established by assistants varied. In some instances, assistants would accompany me to one or more of the interviews. At other times they would arrange a meeting in a common building, such as a school. Assistants often organized a number of people to be interviewed at the same time. Interviewees appeared comfortable with this arrangement as it more closely simulated how they were accustomed to talking about history: in a group environment. Kaqchikel talk about history during any number of quotidian activities such as working in the fields, eating meals, or during ceremonies. In short, history topics inevitably arise when Kaqchikel are gathered in groups, small or large. They enjoy sharing different aspects of their past with each other. While most people participate in these conversations, statements from elders are generally respected as the most definitive historical contributions. One technique these interviewees employed was to refer to or ask someone, whom they perceived to have detailed knowledge about a certain event or trend, to describe it. Historian and anthropologist Jan Vansina argues that group interviews are not desirable because interviewees tend to limit information, sharing only what they can all agree on. However he concedes that "group testimony may also be customary and a guarantee of truth."[20] In my experience, instead of limiting the information they provided, informants sought to expand upon others' input. This format not only elicited more information but also established a consensus through discussion.

The interaction of the interviewees with each other and with me allowed me an in-depth look at how they approach and discuss history. On one occasion, an assistant mayor from Pawit, Comalapa, talked to different people from the community about history before I arrived and then relayed the information to me. The historical research he conducted was done independently and was therefore a perspicacious way for me to observe the historical process without influencing it. His means of collecting information, the questions he asked, as well as the data he received gave me an understanding into how people define history. A native idea of history came from responses not prompted by questions. Sometimes I would arrive at an interview where the interviewee knew I wanted to learn about history and would share his or her ideas prior to any questions.

Another phenomenon occurred when elders recounted history: children entered the room to listen. Kaqchikel pass on oral traditions to younger generations, thereby preserving them. I appreciated the extent of this transfer of information when I was working in an aldea school and some of the students related to me oral histories they had heard from their parents and grandparents.[21]

While multiple-person settings were common, many of my interviews were one-on-one. One of my goals was to develop substantial relationships with some of the interviewees. On most occasions, after the interview the interviewee invited me to visit him or her in the future. I also offered to take photographs of all my interviewees as a way to thank them for their time and knowledge, since my friends and assistants advised me that money was not a proper exchange for time and conversation. It was better to give a gift than to pay people.[22] Taking pictures was an excellent way to give interviewees something they appreciated and in most cases could not obtain themselves. Furthermore, delivering the photographs on another occasion gave me a pretext for returning. The second meeting allowed me the opportunity to ask follow-up questions and/or listen to additional historical perceptions that developed as the conversation flowed. In some cases a return visit led to regular meetings and a more rewarding and enlightening relationship.

In the interviewing process, I also targeted certain groups that I suspected had a broad base of knowledge about history. For example, I attempted to interview current and former mayors of the towns. Another group I interviewed was painters from Comalapa who are known internationally for their artistic ability and who often portray history in their paintings. Teachers were enlightening sources of historic knowledge that they derived from their own education and their interaction with members of the communities where they teach. The annually crowned daughters or queens of the towns underwent instruction sessions about town history during their reign.[23] On two occasions, dressed in traditional Kaqchikel male attire, I was fortunate to escort the Kaqchikel queen of Comalapa to regional celebrations. At these events, I observed elders or teachers sharing different aspects of their history and culture with the young women. Finally, intellectuals also provided valuable insight that did not deviate significantly from their counterparts who had never attended school. Focusing on certain groups, in addition to tapping the general population, allowed me to take a comprehensive approach to learning about Kaqchikel historical perspectives.

I was also curious how responses to different interviewers would vary. Assistants performed interviews in my absence, and their findings provided a valuable source of information. My goal was to compare these data to information I had collected to ascertain any differences in oral histories when no foreigner was present. I did not, however, find that oral accounts collected by my Kaqchikel colleagues were drastically different from those recounted in my presence. In some cases, interviewers accompanied me on a number of interviews to get a sense of the kind of free-form conversation I sought. These informants also transcribed their interviews, which provided me with additional insight as to how they translated Kaqchikel into Spanish. One of the main advantages of these interviews was that assistants collected information without the biases of a North American researcher. In some cases, the assistants' approach to the interviews was different from mine, and the conversation they yielded proved an enlightening complement to my own data.

In addition to asking friends to perform interviews for me, I also asked some members of a nongovernmental organization called the Kaqchikel Linguistic Community (KLC), which represents Kaqchikel speakers, to transcribe some of my tapes and then to translate them into Spanish. These transcriptions allowed me to check my work, as the tapes were from interviews I performed and had taken notes on. I felt confident in my Kaqchikel language skills, but these transcriptions verified my work. I especially assigned tapes for transcription if I did not comprehend certain words or phrases during the interview. This interaction also served as another source of information, since those who transcribed interviews commented on their interpretations of history.

My connection to the KLC enabled me to substantiate my research. I worked at Kaqchikel Cholchi', a branch of the KLC, each Thursday.[24] Linguists there helped me to understand nuances of the language and how the language affected Kaqchikel oral histories. During this time, I compiled oral versions of Kaqchikel history to develop a sixth-grade-level Kaqchikel history textbook. This project, supported by KLC, was an interactive process by which I put oral accounts in a written format and showed it to people who then helped me to refine it. The readers helped me to produce an accurate amalgam of Kaqchikel oral histories and to understand what people ratify as accurate description. This process tested the validity of arriving at a Kaqchikel oral history. The feedback from people at Kaqchikel Cholchi', teachers, and others with whom I shared the work proved invaluable to my comprehension of oral history. This interaction was also a good way to verify the accuracy of my research. The main goal of the textbook project was to give something back to the community that played a crucial role in my research. The book will be used to teach Kaqchikel students about Kaqchikel history and life in their own language. In addition to being a valuable resource for the community, the book offered me a platform from which to discuss my research and test my analyses and emphasis.

That I worked at Kaqchikel Cholchi' each Thursday provided a bridge for people in the community to better understand my work. I explained that I was a historian gathering information for my thesis and working on a textbook written in Kaqchikel to be used in community schools. These were concrete descriptions of my work. If people were not familiar with the work of Kaqchikel Cholchi', they had at least heard about the group. That I was employed in a comprehensible manner made my transition into the community smoother than if I had been simply a foreign researcher.

Manual labor was an indispensable means of connecting with people and provided opportunities for a natural communication of oral histories. When individuals invited me to work in their fields with them, I readily accepted. I also performed voluntary communal labor on roads, assisted in the construction of a school and homes, gathered firewood in the surrounding hills, and did other daily chores. In addition to performing this manual labor, I assisted a teacher in one of the aldea schools, teaching English through Kaqchikel. Other friends asked me to speak at their respective schools in Comalapa, Poaquil, Patzicía, and other Kaqchikel communities. A temporary health clinic in Poaquil required my services in translating from Kaqchikel to Spanish or English so that doctors could communicate with elderly female patients. All of these labors provided an opportunity to learn more about people's work, daily lives, and worldviews without asking questions. Comments were not staged but simply what people happened to be thinking at the time. As Vansina states, "Unintentional materials are often the most trustworthy."[25] Some of the most honest comments surfaced when people were most comfortable with their environment. Conducting interviews in people's homes put interviewees at ease, but accompanying people in their daily lives and working alongside them provided an even more comfortable setting for conversation and allowed me to develop even stronger bonds with them.

The head of my host family's household in Comalapa was Ixq'anil, a sixty-five-year-old widow. Like many of the women in Comalapa, her husband was killed in la violencia of the early 1980s. Her friends, women of her age and status in the community, often visited, and they inevitably invited me to share in their conversation as we drank coffee or *saavada* (an herb used to make hot tea) and sat around the open fire of the cooking hearth. This interaction provided historical input from older females. Unfortunately, my access to elderly women did not expand considerably beyond these friendships. The information was deep, however, as I shared much time with these women and especially with Ixq'anil.

Living with a family connected me to the community. Kaqchikel, in the areas where I lived and worked, live in extended family housing. It clearly is not desirable to live alone. A strong sense of family and camaraderie is an important facet to Kaqchikel culture. As a result, living alone would have distanced me from the community. The importance of living with a family was also evident in Tecpán and Poaquil. Having the support of a family gave me a more immediate and significant association with the community. The families with whom I lived also provided a valuable source of network sampling. Beyond this advantage, local residents felt more comfortable knowing that I was part of a familial unit in town.

Because of my relationship with Ixq'anil's family and friendships I developed over the years, I received numerous invitations to *K'utunika*,[26] weddings, baptisms, Mayan ceremonies (such as *oyonik*),[27] graduations, road and school inaugurations, and other family and community celebrations. Conversations at these events often flowed naturally toward history, providing me the opportunity to hear people's thoughts on history without any prodding. Some of my assistants asserted that the best way to learn about Kaqchikel history was not to ask questions but to share time with people and listen to their stories in a natural setting.[28] I found the content of history in natural conversation to be significant, which is why I always accepted invitations to people's homes for familial or communal celebrations. The spontaneous nature of these conversations, the varied voices, and the different expressions of affective and emotive response to the content allowed me to understand which facts and interpretations were the most salient to Kaqchikel.

For them, the tendency to talk about history at community and family gatherings was a form of entertainment and education. Some of the interviewees stated that they heard history from people at social events, such as meetings and funerals, especially the latter.[29] These dialogues were an invaluable source for understanding what was important in Kaqchikel history and why. Being present while people spoke freely about historical facts and perceptions prevented a problem normally encountered during interviews: the influence of interviewer's prejudices on the information offered. Learning through these informal interactions enabled me to better adjust my interviewing techniques. I adapted my interview questions accordingly so that the questions themselves could provoke responses relevant to Kaqchikel history. I collected some of my most enlightening data in these informal settings.

One of the keys to understanding Kaqchikel worldviews is accepting and even enjoying the pace of life. I sought to have as little impact as possible on the towns in which I lived. My physical stature and appearance made that difficult, since not many six-foot-tall white males arrived in Kaqchikel communities speaking Kaqchikel. However, doing simple things such as maintaining the local schedule by waking early and going to bed early, eating with tortillas instead of silverware, and using a bike instead of a car as my means of transportation helped to ease my transition. Not everyone in the community lived in this manner, but it helped me to communicate better with some residents. I also participated in many of the local activities in an attempt to allow people to get to know me and become comfortable with my presence. I frequented a local barbershop for fifty-cent haircuts, for example. As I had suspected, the barber was a valuable repository of information and a good liaison to the community. Being an active participant in the community allowed me access to people and hence Kaqchikel history.

Other valuable sources of information included trips to surrounding areas. People requested that I accompany them to visit such important places as Iximche', the first Kaqchikel capital; Paminix, a Kaqchikel mine; Pan Ul, the site where Justo Rufino Barrios ordered his soldiers to kill Jun Tz'ikin; and San Antonio, the former site of two hospitals built to house the sick during the Spanish influenza and cholera epidemics. I was also brought to cemeteries and less-well-known historic markers. Visits to historic sites inevitably elicited detailed accounts of their significance. These excursions confirmed that Kaqchikel oral histories are alive and still relevant to the Kaqchikel.

Kaqchikel have various methods of maintaining their history beyond oral traditions. Dance is one way through which Kaqchikel relate their history and communicate lessons applicable to their daily existence. As a result, dances performed during ceremonies and celebrations are important repositories of history. Their dances illustrate that while oral traditions are the predominant means of maintaining the vitality of their past, other approaches for teaching history exist.

Most people I interviewed did not include dates in their oral accounts, though most recalled the 1976 earthquake and the 1944 democratic revolution. Even when asked when a certain event happened, they often could do little more than approximate, and many declined to do this. Exact dates of events are generally not recorded in oral history. In most cases, however, informants could determine when events occurred relative to other events. Part of truly understanding oral traditions is working within what Western researchers may perceive as limitations in order to access a potentially more expansive source of knowledge. Scarcity of dates is an obstacle the researcher must overcome to learn what is important to oral societies.[30]

The very nature of recording oral histories requires the presence of an interviewer. I am aware that my participation may have altered in some way the stories speakers shared or the details they emphasized. The observer's paradox is that any interaction among people necessitates that the parties accommodate one another. As much as possible, I attempted to be a conduit of history—simply observing, listening, not reacting. I broached new topics with open-ended questions and as much as possible allowed informants to structure the content of their accounts. Still, the nature of my questions influenced oral accounts: how a question is phrased tends to privilege one viewpoint while sanctioning another.[31] Nonetheless, as I spent more time in these villages, I asked fewer questions and could listen more to the spontaneous and natural communication of oral traditions.

Presenting history through oral sources means reconciling variations in oral accounts. Kaqchikel historical perspectives are fluid, not constant or monolithic entities. I do not wish to exclude individual voices, but in an effort to relay a manageable amount of information I had to generalize to a certain extent. In my presentation of Kaqchikel historical perspectives, I provide the histories that best encompass oral traditions and include the significant variations from those versions. Variation reflects competing social realities, not just creativity or deception. It represents negotiable parts of history. As anthropologist Dell Hymes states, "Each telling makes use of common ingredients, but it is precisely in the difference in the way they are deployed and shaped that the meaning of each is disclosed."[32] The incongruities are a valuable source of information and insight. Vansina notes that "to a point all memory is collective, but memories of traditions are especially so since different people hear a single rendering and may or may not render it later themselves."[33] He goes on to state, "irregularities survive and are indications that certain anecdotes may well have a foundation in the past."[34] People are selective in what they choose to share, and anomalies can be valuable data for analyzing oral traditions. Variations give an indication of what is crucial in oral histories and what can be emphasized or altered according to a person's preference.

Despite certain differences, oral traditions are maintained within certain boundaries that tend to reinforce their content. Vansina observes: "A neat single line of transmissions simply does not often exist, rather most oral tradition is told by many people to many people. . . . The information coming from more people to more people has greater built-in redundancy than if it were to flow in one channel of communication. Multiple flow does not necessarily imply multiple distortion only, rather perhaps the reverse."[35] Vansina recognizes that the nature of oral traditions is repetition and that oral cultures therefore build up a core of transferable stories that in peripheral ways may be altered while general accounts and ideas are preserved. Oral histories play a paramount role in forming the collective identity and worldviews of people in oral societies.

One challenge in researching oral histories is transcribing and translating; here I must mention the problem with quotations and paraphrasing. My quotations are translations from Kaqchikel and therefore are approximations of the content of utterances since translations cannot be exact; nor can the Kaqchikel turn of phrase or worldview be literally rendered comprehensible in English. I have tried to maintain the flavor and rhythm of Kaqchikel oral traditions through the quotations and paraphrases. One of my goals in writing this book is to allow Kaqchikel voices to speak.

Written Accounts

There are few written accounts by Kaqchikel in their own language. The *Anales de los Kaqchikeles* (henceforth referred to as the *Anales*), the Xahil family document that dates to 1524 (completed in 1605), is the best example of a Kaqchikel-authored historical source we have.[36] The Xpantzay documents and the Título de los del pueblo de San Martín Jilotepeque are some of the other surviving colonial documents. Kaqchikel voices are also evident in legal sources such as land documents and wills, but none are abundant.[37] The few written accounts available help to supplement Kaqchikel oral histories.

Most Kaqchikel record their history through oral accounts, but some are able to read and write about past events. Not until I had gained the trust of certain individuals did they give me access to their written accounts. One man had a history of his aldea that a family member had written in the 1980s;

two men who worked for the Catholic Church had short histories of the town and important recent events; another man shared with me his "libreto," a book in which he jotted down happenings and thoughts. Monographs about the aldeas—primarily the political, economic, social, and cultural conditions of the schools and communities—written for each of the rural schools provided me with additional sources of Kaqchikel history. The monographs reflect a combination of oral and written research on the village's past reality and offer the historical perspectives of the Kaqchikel teachers who wrote them.

Another valuable source was *Comalapan,* a monthly periodical that ran for a short time in the mid-1960s and included articles written by Kaqchikel journalists. Municipal monographs, while in some cases authored by Ladinos, also offered Kaqchikel perspectives of Comalapa's history. Local health clinics had unpublished typescripts that included short histories of the area. Kaqchikel proposals for community development projects usually included some historical references. These local monographs are problematic, however, because the authors do not provide evidence for their claims; they seldom cite sources or clarify their political agenda, and at times the author is unknown. While researchers must be critical if they use these monographs to purport historical fact, these monographs certainly provide valuable insight into historical perceptions. Each of these documents reserves a section for history. This emphasis attests that history is an important aspect of Kaqchikel worldviews and reality.

A newspaper written, edited, and produced bimonthly by Mayan journalists in Spanish and Mayan languages since 1993 provides a good idea of Kaqchikel worldviews. The paper, called *Rutzijol: Periódico Maya Independiente, por la autogestión del Pueblo Maya* (Rutzijol: Independent Mayan Periodical for the Self-Development of the Mayan People), targets all Mayan-language groups. Kaqchikel speakers dominate the staff, however. The journalists consistently write about historical events and how Mayan perceptions differ from Ladino perceptions, especially concerning the official history of the independence movement.[38] Edgar Esquit Choy, a Maya-Kaqchikel historian from Patzicía, has written adeptly on Guatemalan history from a Kaqchikel point of view. His most influential work concerns the Patzicía massacre in 1944.[39] His writings illuminate the fact that Kaqchikel history is not restricted to oral traditions. Additionally, a number of Kaqchikel participate in what has come to be known as the Pan Mayan movement *(movimiento Maya)* which consists mainly of Mayan public intellectuals. These authors, scholars, students, and activists challenge official Guatemalan history and write about the past from Mayan perspectives.[40]

Unfortunately, written accounts of Kaqchikel ideas and perceptions tend to be more contemporary. The municipal archives of the towns where I conducted my research were limited. The 1976 earthquake, followed by intense violence in the early 1980s, depleted, if not decimated, archival records. Some records remain, such as birth and death certificates, marriage licenses, and *cédula* number registration (Guatemalan identification cards), but these documents provide little insight into historical perceptions of Kaqchikel. This lacuna of written information prompted me to visit the archives in Guatemala City to search for Kaqchikel voices.

In Guatemala City I conducted research in three main sources: Archivo General de Centro América ([AGCA] General Archives of Central America); Hemenoteca Biblioteca (Hemenoteca Library), which held periodicals; and César Brañas Biblioteca (César Brañas Library). Mayan input was not common in the archives, but it did exist—letters written by Kaqchikel in the land documentation section, for instance. The AGCA houses the records of the National Ministry of Gobernación y Justicia (Government and Justice),[41] which includes its correspondence with other governmental departments. Unfortunately, sources for the twentieth century were neither organized nor cataloged, and much of the documentation was not at the national archives but either held in the local communities or lost. However, in some departments, such as Sacatepéquez, the correspondence collected by the Government and Justice Department was more complete. After I examined the archival evidence for Mayan perceptions at the time, I turned my efforts to exploring Ladino accounts of different happenings.

I used annual reports of government ministries to check Kaqchikel oral histories against what Ladinos recorded. No complete set of these annual reports exists, but the years that were available provided some substantive proof of Kaqchikel history. The ministries I researched included Public Health, Agriculture, Government and Justice, National Police, Development, and Education. Their annual reports were located both in the AGCA and the César Brañas Library. Accounts recorded by ministers of these departments and other key actors provided a sense of what the important circumstances were at the time. Some departments had journals associated with them that presented more detail about the nature and motivation of the work of different ministries. Newspaper accounts also provided valuable sources, some of which included input from correspondents in Kaqchikel towns. Newspapers were available in the AGCA and Hemenoteca Library. Piecing these contributions together helped me to develop an understanding of the circumstances and trends that paralleled Kaqchikel oral histories.

Physical evidence was another source. Municipal and national buildings carried plaques that gave their construction date. The names of roads, fountains, bridges, schools, and other physical structures also provided valuable insight into historically important figures. In general, Kaqchikel tend to name towns and streets after climatic, topographic, and geographic features, and in some cases a descendant lineage, but not after individuals. Linda Asturias de Barrios confirms this naming tendency in her study of Comalapa.[42] A person's being awarded a name on a piece of public property was a significant statement. The only two roads in Comalapa that have names other than the number of the street (e.g., First Avenue, Third Street) are named after local historical figures: Rafael Alvarez Ovalle and Andrés Curruchich.

To understand what Kaqchikel emphasize and why, my research had to begin in and be focused on the communities. I employed different approaches to gain information, the most insightful and least meddlesome of which was to share time with people in varied circumstances ranging from work to celebration to mourning. It was important to have as low an impact on the community as possible, to assimilate through the language and customs, and participate actively but not intrusively in daily life. People's oral histories can only be accessed over time by gaining the confidence of the community. Language and good listening skills, as well as an openness to new worldviews, are imperative. Coming to an understanding of different perceptions shared through oral histories can only be achieved by nurturing relationships through respectful participation and genuine interest in the community.

A final note about this manuscript: I suppressed some privileged information that was too private, too personal, or too politically dangerous. I have intentionally excluded Kaqchikel perspectives on the thirty-six-year civil war because stories and statements shared during interviews and daily interactions could jeopardize the safety of my assistants and interviewees. I also respected people's wishes not to share or publish certain information. More important than the research is the safety and security of my informants and assistants. I explained to each informant that the information he or she shared with me would be used to write history books in Kaqchikel, Spanish, and English. Kaqchikel informants understood that diverse audiences would read these works and, in the politicized context of Guatemala, were aware of the potential negative reactions from people who did not agree with their point of view or believe it should be expressed. The murder of Guatemalan bishop Juan José Gerardi, the coordinator of the Catholic Church's truth commission project (REMHI), midway through my fieldwork on April 26, 1998, reinforced the potential dangers all too clearly. Nonetheless, all the informants whose reflections appear in this book consented to these conditions, and the majority of them asked that I identify them so they could be associated with the project. The overwhelming majority of informants expressed a great sense of pride in participating in a project that would record their history from their people's point of view. Unfortunately, since the political situation in Guatemala remains volatile, for the well-being of my informants and assistants I use pseudonyms and hope they can recognize their contributions or at least know they are part of this collective project.[43]

Introduction

Ütz ipetik

About two months after I began my fieldwork in Comalapa, a town nestled in the western highlands of Guatemala, my Maya-Kaqchikel brother,[1] Jun Ajpu', returned for the weekend from his work in the neighboring department (state) of Acatenango. The town in which he worked was predominantly Ladino,[2] in stark contrast to his community. He was beaming with pride as he told me that he was selected as one of the best teachers in Acatenango. We sat around the hearth, sharing beans and tortillas and basking in his glory. His mother reflected on how times had changed from when she was young and Mayan children were afraid to attend school, let alone become teachers. Jun Ajpu' contemplated this thought and then solemnly explained: "The Ladinos in town did not like the fact that I won. I am Maya, and they did not think a Maya deserved to win." The room became silent as he continued: "They take things too seriously. I do not view it as the Maya winning. I just see it as a benefit to the town and the school."[3] This twenty-nine-year-old teacher refused to enmesh himself in the racial divisions and hatred of his country. He was proud of his award because it recognized his contribution to the people of Guatemala, regardless of their ethnicity.

The civil war period (1960 to 1996), in which the military was pitted against insurgency forces and in some cases the general population, was among the most violent in a five-hundred-year history of ethnocide in Guatemala. The United Nations Truth Commission concluded that two hundred thousand people were murdered or "were disappeared" and that close to one million people were displaced from their communities and country during the thirty-six-year civil war. Maya, the majority (60 to 70 percent) of Guatemala's approximately eleven million people, bore the brunt of la violencia. Kaqchikel are the third-largest Mayan-language group in Guatemala, and ethnocide struck them most severely in the late 1970s and early 1980s. Many Maya rejoiced in December 1996 when the government and the guerrilla forces (Unidad Revolucionaria Nacional Guatemalteca [URNG]) signed the Peace Accords to end the fighting. Unfortunately, communication between Ladinos and Maya remains strained. Today, Guatemala is trying to rebuild itself and implement a democratic government. However, tensions and fears are obstacles to convivial relations among Guatemala's diverse ethnicities. The peace process suffered a significant setback when on May 16, 1999, a mere 18 percent of Guatemala's registered voters turned out and rejected constitutional reforms that would have greatly expanded the rights of indigenous people. The "yes" vote won in most rural Mayan departments, but Guatemala City dominated the national vote, and it decided against ethnic, linguistic, and cultural pluralism. The 1999 presidential elections evidenced a further shift to the political right as Alfonso Portillo and the Guatemalan Republican Front (FRG) defeated the incumbent party with 68 percent of the votes cast in the runoff election. The founder and spiritual and political leader of the FRG, former military dictator José Efraín Ríos Montt, engineered some of the nation's worst genocidal violence against the Mayan population as president from 1982 to 1983. Peace remains tenuous in Guatemala. The stage is set for conflict or resolution.[4]

State policy toward Maya has fluctuated between isolation, eradication, and assimilation; however, it has always been biased. Some governments, such as the democratic ones from 1944–54, clearly sought to benefit Maya, but the approach was through incorporation into the national culture, not acceptance of their distinctions. In general, political and economic elites, who are heavily influenced by Western values and education, have infringed upon, exploited, attacked, and killed aborigines since the time of the Spanish invasion. Many Ladinos have never respected Maya as an inherently equal segment of the population. Certainly, some Ladinos accept the Mayan population and appreciate their differences. They criticize the inherently unjust social system and work to eradicate racism at all levels. Efforts range from writing about la violencia and injustice to learning Mayan languages and living and working alongside Maya. Maya recognize and appreciate these efforts but lament that these people do not represent the majority.

This book provides a forum for contemporary Maya to share what is important to them about their past and talk about how they apply it to their lives. It renders an in-depth view of Guatemalan history, as explained to me by present-day Maya. In it Kaqchikel express what past happenings they think about, discuss, and incorporate into their current reality. They share their opinions, interpretations, and analysis of their own history. It allows Maya to be participants, not simply subjects, in Guatemala's written history.

Societies incorporate what is important to them in their histories, whether written or oral. Kaqchikel histories are present in their oral traditions. Kaqchikel oral traditions span a vast historical period from before the arrival of the Spanish to contemporary events. Their oral histories do not present past circumstances in a chronological manner, however. This book attempts to remain true to Kaqchikel presentations of history by presenting them thematically, but, more importantly, it allows contemporary Kaqchikel voices to be included in Guatemala's national history. The strength of this work is in allowing Kaqchikel to tell their own history, rather than attempting to interpret their thoughts through documents or non-Kaqchikel speakers.

I do not present oral histories alone but rather contextualize them with references to written sources. Written sources can help explain the content and circumstances surrounding past events and people, and at times their comparison provides insightful juxtaposition to oral accounts. My goal is to provide a more holistic presentation of Guatemala's national history than has heretofore been presented by Ladino and Western scholars. This book is not a complete history of Guatemala but rather a look at what Kaqchikel consider the most relevant occurrences of the past and how their interpretations of these events compare to the presentations of the same happenings in archival documents and historical literature.

Ladinos and Maya seldom agree on each other's view of history, nor do they possess similar methodological, analytical, and theoretical tools to describe their realities. Nonetheless, history is an essential part of both cultures and a powerful tool. An axiom of occidental cultures holds that people who do not know their history are doomed to repeat it. A motto of the Guatemalan organization Maya Decenio para el Pueblo Indígena (Maya Decade for the Indigenous People) is that people who do not know their past cannot build a future.[5] These populations must reconcile their past to develop a peaceful, coherent, and united nation.

Kaqchikel histories contrast sharply with Ladino histories in their content, form, and perspective. In general, for Kaqchikel history is transferred orally from one generation to the next. Elders teach their children and grandchildren about past events and trends in settings that range from funerals and familial and communal ceremonies to meals around an open fire and tilling soil and harvesting in the hills. For example, the local barber, baker, butcher, store owner, and other proprietors naturally create environments where people share history and life experiences. Kaqchikel carefully guard their past and worldviews because it teaches them lessons and strategies for their lives today. In addition, they know their stories are not included in Guatemala's "official" written, national history. For this reason, many Kaqchikel do not give much attention to Guatemala's official history, but they know they have been incorrectly and racistly portrayed in it, and they resent that.

Official history can define a nation. Benedict Anderson refers to nations as "imagined communities" that attempt to create a pervasive sense of belonging or identity. He asserts that "as with modern persons, so it is with nations. Awareness of being imbedded in secular, serial time, with all its implications of continuity . . . engenders the need for a narrative of 'identity.'"[6] This narrative, however, must include, or at least reflect, all populations within a nation, or it creates a false or incomplete national identity. History written only from the perspective of a dominant group is myopic. Kaqchikel historical perspectives encourage a more holistic approach to its content.

The majority of Kaqchikel do not seek exclusivity; rather, they want all of Guatemala's populations to enjoy equal representation in Guatemala's official history and equal access to Guatemala's resources. They pride themselves on being Guatemala's aboriginal population but do not claim exclusive rights to the country's riches. They do, however, insist that their contributions to its past and present be recognized. Furthermore, they refuse to be viewed as passive participants in Guatemala's history. Their forebears were willing to share with the Spanish when they first arrived, and contemporary Kaqchikel seek to peacefully coexist with Ladinos in a way that would be mutually beneficial to the populations and the land.

North Americans, Europeans, Mexicans, and Ladinos have historically controlled the political, economic, social, and cultural policy in Guatemala. As Maya begin to play a larger role in the national life of the country, however, it is imperative that Ladinos and Maya develop a common ground upon which to work together. Jorge Solares makes a valuable contribution in this respect with his book *Derechos humanos desde la perspectiva indígena en Guatemala* (Human Rights from the Perspective of Indigenous People in Guatemala). He argues that Mayan perceptions of human rights are focused on respect for authority and the culture of their ancestors and, surprisingly (in contrast to Western thinkers), only to a lesser extent on the life and integrity of a person. For example, he notes that widows of the violence were as intent on demanding that the government find the remains of their loved ones so they could provide a proper burial as they were with demanding human justice. Solares has found that they were as concerned, if not more so, with cultural issues as they were with issues of violence, exploitation, and poverty.[7] Likewise, Salvadoran peasant organizer Miguel Marmol notes that worldviews in Guatemala are distinct: "At first it was difficult to understand the Indians, because though they may speak Spanish, their way of thinking is different from that of Ladinos, and their interests aren't the same as those of other Guatemalans."[8] An understanding of each other's ideas and goals will allow decision makers to formulate policies that will facilitate peaceful relations with the Mayan population and encourage them to be open to feedback and critiques by Maya.

Kaqchikel input elucidates a number of important historical questions. It reveals how Kaqchikel talk and think about history and what events, people, trends, and interactions have been significant for them throughout their history. Their viewpoints show how national policies were received at the local level and how they affected the population. Conversely, this study also explores how local reactions affected national leaders and policies. Why did national policies, such as acculturation, fail or succeed? How do Kaqchikel perceive ethnic relations and Ladino institutions? Furthermore, how do Kaqchikel historical perceptions compare to those of Ladino historians?

Kaqchikel oral traditions present vivid historical analysis of Guatemala and the reality of Kaqchikel. Oral histories reveal a number of central themes in Kaqchikel worldviews and historical perspectives. The most important theme that develops is security. The Kaqchikel hierarchy of rights and needs asserts personal security as the top priority. Consequently, they are willing to make many sacrifices for the assurance of both personal safety and national stability. They are not concerned solely with personal or communal well-being, however; they also seek fortitude for their nation. While they hold democratic beliefs and appreciate liberty and freedom, these ideals do not replace personal security or national stability.

Important aspects of this emphasis on security are a focus on equal justice and on leaders and administrations who provide clear rules and agendas. They historically judge actors and events from a perspective based upon their impartiality and equality. The legal system has seldom granted equal rights and representation to Maya, so they depend on strong leaders to guarantee justice. A clearly defined and explained legal system and leaders who uphold the laws are crucial for Kaqchikel. They want to understand the rules of the larger society in which they live so that if and when they choose to abide by them, they will be free from persecution. Even if the legal system discriminates against them, they will be better prepared to live peacefully and self-sufficiently if they understand the rules of the game and have confidence that the rules will not be constantly altered to assist the economic and political power holders. Oral histories relate the evils of leaders who act capriciously.

When Kaqchikel evaluate national policies, they judge critically the degree to which the state includes and informs them of its actions. Governments that fail to explain their policies or to develop good relations with Maya are met with resistance and, in some cases, rebellion. Kaqchikel want to be informed not only because it gives them a sense of security but also because the national stability and economic development of Guatemala are important to them. They desire equal opportunity to exploit economic resources. Their oral traditions portray Kaqchikel as having contributed more to the national economy than they have benefited from it. Today, as in the past, Kaqchikel accept hard work but not abuse.

Despite the benefits of outside facilitators of employment and trade, work on one's own land continues to be highly regarded. Kaqchikel prefer and have petitioned governments to maintain their right to work for themselves. They value land and self-employment and are willing to make sacrifices to maintain them.

Kaqchikel women have had and continue to have significant involvement with the cash economy as weavers, marketers, and factory laborers. The cash-income contribution that independently employed women make to family livelihood is an important aspect of Kaqchikel reality and worldviews because it increases the level of respect for women. In other communities the onset of the cash economy decreased the value of women because their work was in the unpaid sector, and therefore they did not augment the family income. Kaqchikel women's traditional and paid labor supports a Kaqchikel gender balance. Kaqchikel worldviews express the duality of male and female powers in the universe. Furthermore, Mayan women in Guatemala are viewed as the moral fiber of their people. They continue to wear their *traje* (indigenous dress) in the face of discrimination. Men recognize women as the braver gender because of this explicit expression of their identity. Kaqchikel differentiate between themselves and Ladino society because they perceive that many Ladinos fail to respect women. In fact, disrespect is a greater failing within the Mayan community than outside of it. Hence, the total disrespect with which many Ladinos treat Maya is a great barrier to rapprochement or collaboration.

A recurrent theme that runs through Kaqchikel oral traditions is the value of and the need to protect their wisdom, culture, language, dress, and spirit. Kaqchikel values include the beliefs that everything is alive, the universe is animate, women and men should be treated equally, elders and those who work hard should be respected, and wealth is not inherently good or evil, but it makes life easier. Kaqchikel react most strongly when they feel their personal or group safety threatened, but they also vehemently resist intrusions that threaten their distinct lifestyles and worldviews. They do not wish to isolate themselves from Guatemala or the rest of the world. However, they will not work within a government or system that fails to respect, or even attacks, their essence until they have developed means to stave off such potential infringements. They believe their contributions are essential to the development of a better nation and world, and they are committed to such improvement. Kaqchikel identify with the state but wish to increase their sense of ownership through increased and efficacious participation. Ideally, they would interact in a world where their differences, ideas, and approaches are valued. In the current less-than-ideal situation, Kaqchikel seek to have a positive impact on their environment.

However, Kaqchikel set parameters on the amount of impact it is desirable to have on their surroundings and the larger society. Kaqchikel worldviews present guidelines to strategies of interaction. In oral traditions, for example, wealth and power are often interrelated. While Kaqchikel respect people who acquire wealth and power, if these individuals do not share these benefits and contribute to the community then Kaqchikel discount them. If Mayan power brokers act like Ladinos, then Kaqchikel associate them with the out-group and they become Ladinos. Individuals can lose their group identity if their actions violate the norm. On the other hand, Kaqchikel extol local leaders, who, with few resources except for their intelligence, emerge victorious against national leaders who have the ability to kill them. These characters are analogized through the trickster tales of the rabbit and coyote prevalent in oral traditions.[9] The rabbit, although smaller and weaker, outsmarts the coyote and emerges from perilous situations unscathed. Similarly, Kaqchikel utilize various "weapons of the weak."[10]

Kaqchikel oral traditions teach peaceful strategies of resistance. For instance, when Kaqchikel parents did not want to subject their children to the state's attempt to assimilate them into Ladino culture and society through the schools, they simply hid their children or pretended they were ill. At the same time, oral histories relate that when young men could not avoid military conscription, they took advantage of the military's provision of Spanish-language classes and other skills but left after their required service to avoid assimilation into Ladino ways. Kaqchikel guard their language as a cultural marker but also utilize it as a means to communicate without Ladinos understanding them. Kaqchikel have been able to point out injustices or incongruities of state systems without directly threatening or challenging Ladino leaders and, in many cases, have circumvented state structures because they cannot achieve their needs through the system. Despite these forms of resistance, oral traditions teach adaptability, not isolationism: stories tell, for example, that Kaqchikel initially resisted Western medicine but have become more open to it. The success of Kaqchikel strategies of resistance against incursion gives them confidence to interact in the national society without sacrificing their ethnic identity.

Through oral traditions Kaqchikel guard their remarkable resilience in the face of intrusion. Kaqchikel construct their oral histories around the importance of their identity as the Mayan aborigines of Guatemala. The histories about town origins in chapter 1 elucidate a Kaqchikel view of legitimacy. For Kaqchikel, the legitimacy of their communities resides in their Mayanness, a connection to the original Kaqchikel inhabitants. The legitimacy of their towns also comes from the way Kaqchikel constructed their existence as a social unit prior to the Spanish arrival. Maya and their presence determine the viability of the unit, maintaining social organization even when physical displacement occurs. Thus in some ways Spanish forces applied to Maya are extraneous to their identity.

Diverse sources of conflict emanate from Kaqchikel oral traditions. Spaniards used force, war, forced labor mechanisms, and trickery to deceive and exploit Kaqchikel. Spanish military leader Pedro de Alvarado killed their leaders, traded them mirrors for their gold, burned Iximche', and forced them to build Tecpán. Spaniards took advantage of the inability of Maya to speak Spanish in order to deprive them of land, labor, and other valuable resources. Consequently, a basic pattern of distrust began at the time of Spanish contact and never underwent significant realignment. Constant infringements and attacks on Mayan communities and culture, however, do not eradicate Kaqchikel.

An important element of Kaqchikel worldviews is the malleability of the concept of "us and them." Kaqchikel apply the term *qawinäq* (our people) to indigenes of the same village, town, department, language group, other Mayan-language groups, nation, and world. As a result, anyone who is an indigenous person is qawinäq; *mo's* (Ladinos) clearly are not. Solidarity for Kaqchikel includes all indigenous people, while they depict Ladinos as "other."

The complexity of ethnic relations pervades Kaqchikel oral traditions. Kaqchikel see a clear distinction between themselves and Ladinos even though they share the same nation and in many cases towns and communities. The intricacy of these relations stems from the tremendous diversity of both populations. Kaqchikel oral histories abound with stories that depict Ladinos as abusive and exploitative controllers of social, economic, and political resources. Oral accounts portray Ladinos as having marginalized Kaqchikel. However, some oral traditions illustrate Ladino leaders who have treated Kaqchikel with respect and even made positive contributions to their communities. Kaqchikel individuals recount positive personal relationships with Ladinos. Kaqchikel of San José Poaquil, for example, appreciate local Ladinos who have made the effort to learn their language. Kaqchikel also appreciate Ladino anthropologists and linguists, such as Sergio Romero, who have learned Mayan languages and offer their services to the Mayan community. Furthermore, Mayan public intellectuals and Ladino leaders, such as

Marta Elena Casaús Arzú, have been collaborating to develop better communication and understanding between Maya and Ladinos.[11] Nonetheless, the overarching relationship between Kaqchikel and Ladinos is one of animosity.

Despite the recognition of a common adversary and the valuation of their ideas, Kaqchikel and other Mayan groups recognize some strains in their own internal relations. Tension over land and resources exists among and within Mayan communities, but internal group conflicts do not destroy a sense of shared heritage, institutions, and values. While relations are not idyllic, Maya are still intimately connected. Conflict between Maya and Spaniards and Ladinos is distinct from conflict among or within Mayan groups.

Kaqchikel recognize, however, that divisive conflict can arise within their own community. They cite religious competition—especially between Catholics and Protestants—as one source, but religion is not the only external source of conflict. Kaqchikel are suspicious of people's motives when they do not know the outsiders' families, because they have no common history or relationship with them. They have no background on which to build a level of trust. Kaqchikel are leery of foreigners until they can develop strong relationships. Outside actors potentially introduce uncontrolled factors that alienate people and wreak havoc in communities. Kaqchikel fear division could destroy their communities, so they develop strategies to maintain strong links among their people and prudently accept (or reject) foreigners.

Kaqchikel mind-set and psychology can be tapped through oral traditions. Claudia Dary asserts, "Oral archives permit us access to the internal cognition of societies."[12] As Vansina puts it, "History in the telling like history in the writing is often the teacher of life."[13] David Cohen comes to the same conclusion in his study of the Busoga in Uganda: "Tradition in Busoga is much less the arcane survival of an oral past than the lively and ever-functioning intelligence upon which society and man rest. The transmissions of historical information is not along orderly chains of transmission but across and through the complex networks of relationship, association, and contact that constitute life."[14] Similarly, in his study of the Saramaka oral tradition, Richard Price observes: "First-Time [history prior to 1800] ideology lives in the minds of twentieth-century Saramaka men because it is relevant to their own life experience—it helps them make sense, on a daily basis, of the wider world in which they live."[15] Vansina, Cohen, and Price agree that history is inextricably tied to the present. Kaqchikel also clearly value history for its applicability to the present. In her study in Tecpán, Carol Hendrickson notes this connection in Kaqchikel history: "The past is seen as the past only insofar as it lives at the moment, and the new makes sense only insofar as it relates to, builds on or contrasts with the old or traditional."[16] For oral societies, history is manifoldly connected to the present.

Kaqchikel oral histories contain different perspectives, are constantly changing, and remain applicable to the present. Therefore, only events, characters, and trends that are relevant to their lives today are recorded and transferred from one generation to another. Kaqchikel guard stories about national leaders such as Jorge Ubico (1931–44), Justo Rufino Barrios (1873–85), and Juan José Arevalo (1945–51) because they relate to current politics. Likewise, town residents keep alive histories of the origins of their towns because they are an integral part of their identity. Furthermore, historical accounts that transmit information about past ethnic relations teach lessons about inter- and intra-ethnic relations today. Oral histories remain relevant and alive because they teach lessons and strategies for today and tomorrow.

Maya emphasize the role of history in their communities. As Kan B'alam, a Kaqchikel journalist, states: "It is of the utmost importance for us, the Mayas, to know our true history to be able to pass it on to our children. . . . History has among its merits that it registers all the happenings of a community: its past and its present."[17] Consequently, Maya seek to restore and expand their historical cognition.

Kaqchikel are aware of how national leaders and institutions affect their communities. One method that Kaqchikel employ in their presentation of history is to personalize the acts of these leaders and institutions, thus keeping them vital. The personalization of history is not limited to indigenous groups, however. People in the United States, for example, say that President Lincoln freed the slaves; even though Lincoln did not remove the shackles of each slave, U.S. history associates him with this act. The personalization of history helps to maintain history's relevance in the present.

There is no monolithic, united Kaqchikel oral tradition or oral history. Oral histories vary over time and among informants and will continue to adapt to changing realities to remain relevant for the future and present. As reflected by the diverse array of perspectives found in archival records and their multiple interpretations, Kaqchikel are not one entity with a singular viewpoint. Kaqchikel oral traditions vary depending on regions, communities, neighborhoods, families, and individuals. Nonetheless, central themes emerge throughout Kaqchikel oral traditions. Similarly, certain events, personages, and trends receive considerable attention in Kaqchikel oral histories. I try to present and understand larger themes, ideas, and trends and focus on the past happenings that receive disproportionately significant attention in Kaqchikel oral histories. At the same time, to prevent a generalization of Kaqchikel oral history, I present contrary and minority historical perceptions and interpretations among Kaqchikel. My goal is to accurately present a version of Kaqchikel history and an appreciation for its nuances without overwhelming the reader with exceptions.

Kaqchikel historical perspectives are valuable contributions to Guatemala's national history, historiography, and the history of indigenous people. Guatemala is a nation made up of twenty-one different Mayan-language groups, Garífuna (an African-Arawak population on the coast), Xinka indigenous group, and Europeanized Ladinos. It is a country made up of four distinct nations, all of whom contribute to Guatemala's cultural richness. Some Ladinos, however, have written non-Ladino populations out of their national history. In fact, Ladino writers Antonio Batres Jáuregui, José Antonio Villacorta Calderón, and Miguel Angel Asturias have argued that Maya are the cause of Guatemala's uneasy economic and social conditions. They assert that Maya must become more like Ladinos, while suggesting miscegenist policies and encouraging European immigration to positively influence the Mayan population.[18] Anthropologist Robert Carlsen notes:

> Throughout much of the post-Columbian period a predominant bias represented in the literature on Mesoamerica reflects Hispanic myths of lazy and childlike Indians. These self serving and ethnic myths have contributed to the assumption that Indians are incapable of taking meaningful and significant action. As a result, the huge indigenous population has, until recently, been highly conspicuous in its near absence from the pages of historical literature. When Indians have appeared on the printed page they have typically been presented either as the targets of charges of mindless "paganism" or as subjects of paternalistic claims promising to advance them towards a "civilized" state.[19]

Ladino and Western researchers have misconstrued historical presentations in part because they write about Maya without consulting them.

History taught in Guatemalan schools still contains inaccurate depictions of Maya. Primary school textbooks exalt ancient Maya but assert that this indigenous group has degenerated since the arrival of the Spanish. One such textbook teaches children that precontact Maya "worshiped . . . some animals such as the coyote, raccoon and tapir." It also purports that Maya received Spanish priests with "special attention given as a result in grand part because of the little culture that they already had."[20] Misrepresentations continue in secondary-level textbooks. One such textbook asserts that when the Spanish imposed Catholicism on Maya, "A new religion full of love and peace" replaced "the sanguine rites that the native practiced to please their multiple gods."[21] Maya-K'ichee' speaker Luis Enrique Sam Colop adeptly points out this biased teaching in Guatemala's public school system at all levels (universities included). He also criticizes attempts by Ladinos to deny Maya their heritage, one being the claim by Rigoberto Juárez Paz, a university vice chancellor, that the *Popol Wuj* (authored by K'ichee') is a mestizo not a Mayan document. Sam Colop notes that some mestizos recognize this injustice and quotes Luis Cardoza y Aragón as saying, "We have deprived [the Indians] of even their past, exploiting it as our past."[22] Kaqchikel scholar and activist Demetrio Cojtí Cuxil agrees with this assessment: "Today, Maya culture, history, art, and grammar are proscribed from school teaching. The educational system continues to deny the Maya knowledge of their own history and ethnic reality. . . . The school continues to operate as a state organ par excellence in charge of the ethnocide of the Maya."[23] Cojtí continues: "The official education system transmits . . . erroneous facts, and prejudices and distortions about Mayan history, culture, civilization, art, and sciences that are at times offensive and insulting. . . . The contents of its teaching do not even point out Mayan contributions to the region, country, or humanity, nor do they point out the traits and components of Mayan life that could be useful . . . such as relations with the environment and the capacity for physical and cultural survival."[24]

This book is not an attempt to argue that the body of historical research on Guatemala is wrong but rather to show where it is lacking and shortsighted as a result of its ethnocentric nature. It is a contribution to, not a complete refutation of, scholarship on Guatemalan history. As anthropologist Kay Warren observes, "A daunting project is the writing of a Mayan history to counter official histories that justify Ladino domination. Mayan scholars see this as a critical project and local populations . . . are now aware that existing histories teach children ethnic inferiority. Many histories effectively end their portrayals of Mayas as historical agents at the Spanish conquest. . . . Mayas are erased from the historical creation of the modern nation-state."[25] Some colonial histories and recent documentation of the travails of Maya during the civil war have provided more accurate and inclusive representations of Maya in history.[26] Furthermore, Cojtí, Sam Colop, and other Mayan intellectuals in the pan Mayan movement challenge national histories with their own historical writings that reassess and include Mayan contributions and actors in Guatemala's nation building both before and after the Spanish arrival. The Mayan writings critique the erasure of indigenous agency in Guatemala's history.[27] Despite these efforts, most Ladino and Western historians who write about Guatemala fail to incorporate Mayan viewpoints. Consequently, the history of Guatemala is incomplete and biased. Kaqchikel, and

Maya in general, have been excluded from national history, and as a result misperceptions and inaccuracies abound in the representation of Guatemala's past.

As scholars such as Robert Carmack and Robert Carlsen point out, history and historical perspectives are dynamic. Both changes and consistencies must be examined and recognized as integral to historical analysis.[28] Kaqchikel oral histories reveal the flux and continuities throughout their past and Kaqchikel perceptions of it. History is a record of the effects of large forces at work combined with the impact of smaller entities working within and affecting these forces. For example, capitalism has played an integral role in shaping history at the macro and micro level, but at the same time, national, regional, and local conditions and peoples have affected the implementation and results of capitalism. Eric Wolf and Carol Smith both recognize the interplay between global historical processes and local indigenous societies.[29] Warren argues that the main historical processes interacting with local communities are not necessarily global, but national. She sets her study in the framework of injustice that the Guatemalan Ladino society imposes on local communities (in her case Kaqchikel of San Andrés Semetabaj).[30] Anthropologist Diane Nelson proficiently asserts that, "Neither the state nor transnational capital is a monolithic power that always gets what it wants. . . . Power works in multiply territorialized interstitial places. . . . Ethnic, gender and national identifications are produced through mutually constitutive and always contingent relationships."[31] She states that these are "not cause and effect relation[s]" but rather that these "multiple sites of power" all contribute to Guatemala's complex history and present.[32] Likewise, historian Greg Grandin points out that popular classes are neither "autonomous nor powerless in the face of economic and political transformation."[33] But how do Kaqchikel assess and analyze the past as one of these "sites of power?"

I show how the interplay between global, national, and local actors, events, and realities have affected Guatemalan history by presenting Kaqchikel perceptions of these interactions. Grandin adeptly shows that "an examination of the long term historical role [of] popular classes" is essential "for an integral analysis of how power functions and change occurs."[34] Scholars such as Nancy Farris and Carlsen argue that the central core of Mayan culture and history predates the Spanish arrival and thus Ladino oppression. In fact, Carlsen asserts that these consistencies are essential for understanding their lives today.[35] Likewise, ethnohistorians Robert Hill and John Monaghan show that present-day social organization in the Mayan town of Sacapulas can be linked to their precontact ancestors, not simply Spanish impositions.[36] Contemporary Maya maintain physical, intellectual, and emotional connections with their ancestors. However, Mayan history and reality today is a complex mix of autochthonous roots and regional, national, and global pressures. Most importantly, as Sherry Ortner explains, "A society, even a village, has its own structure and history, and this must be as much part of the analysis as its relations with the larger context within which it operates."[37] She and Grandin stress that researchers must explore the internal divisions, competitions, and resistance within communities to avoid the pitfalls of presenting groups as monolithic.[38]

This book extends the idea that history can be examined at the local level by allowing local people to tell their own history. Kaqchikel oral traditions illustrate their in-depth comprehension of history. Their oral histories provide the framework for this book. This book's organization and content is built on my attempt to maintain the topics, the flow of conversation, and the emphases as presented to me by Kaqchikel. This project provides a forum for Kaqchikel to define the important historical markers and their effects and to explain how, to a certain degree, they have charted their own historical course. It reveals what Kaqchikel recognize as the forces affecting them historically, such as the Spanish invasion, capitalism, and Ladino society, and it looks at how Kaqchikel perceive their effect on these larger historical forces. As Davíd Carrasco adeptly illustrates, Maya have survived the construction of their image and their history according to Spanish and Christian cultural and theoretical conceptions.[39] Instead of assigning interpretations of these perceptions from outside, this book complements and corrects much of the historical literature by giving Kaqchikel the opportunity to define their history, historical perspectives, and historical import.

Kaqchikel historical perspectives can best be attained through oral accounts because modern Kaqchikel have little written history (see Methodology). As one Kaqchikel exile explains, "My grandfather told me much of our history is not in the *Anales*. The secret of the Mayan world is in our language."[40] Oral history is as valuable and legitimate a source as archival evidence; it is a different type of knowledge. The two sources complement each other to provide more insightful historical interpretations. As historian Joe Lunn notes in his study of Senegal, "The testimony of a peasant from Khinine, for example, was usually as reliable about events witnessed in his village as that of a Governor General reporting to the Minister of Colonies."[41] Kaqchikel oral history also possesses distinct degrees of authority in its citation of knowledge. When a Kaqchikel informant says, "Our ancestors said long ago" (*Qati't, qamama' [qate', qatata'] xkib'ij kan*), there is no authority beyond that, and the statement has the highest degree of validity. In contrast, "He [or she] told me" (*Rija' xub'ij chwe*) or "I heard" (*Xinwak'axaj*) do not hold the same degree of validity as the former, although they may also be accurate. The statement "I read in a book" (*Xinsikij pa jun wuj*) is another way of knowing, but the most powerful source of knowledge about the past begins "Our elders teach us" or "Our ancestors said long ago."[42] Generally, Kaqchikel also place a high degree of validity on eyewitness accounts (with a few exceptions based on the speaker's character). The varying degrees of the validity of knowledge can be likened to historical revisionism. Only the most valid accounts and those that remain relevant today survive in oral tradition. In an attempt to understand Kaqchikel historical perspectives at the end of the twentieth century and beginning of the twenty-first, I will explore the most valid canons of information within a Kaqchikel system of knowledge: oral accounts passed down through generations and eyewitness accounts. Mayan oral history is knowledge and history, just as Ladino and Western history is knowledge and history.

History that ignores oral traditions sacrifices vast amounts of knowledge and wisdom. As Vansina states, "Without oral traditions we would know very little about the past of large parts of the world, and we would not know them from the inside. We also could never build up interpretations from the inside."[43] Oral history expresses a past that written history is unable to discover; it expands the limited nature of histories written only by the victors. Vansina continues, "By collecting oral traditions and studying them, by internalizing remembered ethnography . . . interpretations become more culture specific, less anachronistic and ethnocentric."[44] More egalitarian historical accounts that accurately depict the past at all levels of society can be compiled through the combination of written and oral sources. James Axtell notes that the challenge of ethnohistory "is to ensure that each culture is treated with equal empathy, rigor and discernment."[45] While history reflects the biases of its authors—written and spoken—the inclusion of oral sources provides a more balanced approach by allowing the interpretations and perspectives of nonliterate people to influence historical presentations.

The challenge in presenting any history is reconciling disparate accounts and, in this case, combining two distinct historical approaches. When written and oral history converge, the task is allowing both approaches to contribute in the telling of history. When they disagree, the methodology of combining sources is more problematic. Diverse accounts of the same event do exist within these distinct sources: Kaqchikel sources present contrasting depictions of the same occurrence, and archival records and historical monographs vary and thus allow multiple interpretations. When contradictions arose, I corroborated accounts by investigating other oral histories, archival documents, unpublished monographs, and historical literature. Only equal consideration and careful examination of both oral and written sources will result in an inclusive history. History will always carry some bias, but a presentation of differing and at times contradictory accounts will allow for a representative description and analysis of past events.

Just as Ladino and Western historical accounts fail to accurately describe all facets of Guatemalan history, so, too, Kaqchikel oral histories contain misconstructions or factual errors. Consequently, a combination of the two versions provides a more accurate presentation of Guatemalan history than has been previously presented.[46] Vansina notes, "Wherever oral traditions are extant they remain an indispensable source for reconstruction. They correct other perspectives just as much as other perspectives correct them."[47] Likewise, anthropologist Victoria Bricker asserts: "People who consider themselves to be of Spanish descent and Western culture are today politically dominant throughout the Maya area, as they have been since the conquest. They call their written descriptions of ethnic conflict 'history' (*historia*). Indian accounts of the same events are called 'legends' (*leyendas*), or 'stories' (*cuentos*), even though . . . they are often no less accurate factually than the 'history' of the other group."[48] Distinct historical perspectives and sources must be allotted equal and judicious consideration in the final presentation of history.

A fundamental difference in Mayan and Western historical methodology is that Maya relate their history in a cyclical, not a linear, pattern. Kaqchikel oral histories seldom connect past events to exact dates, although informants can ascertain the relative occurrence of an event as compared to other happenings. Informants do not tell history chronologically; they use a thematic approach. Consequently, although each theme may span hundreds of years, Kaqchikel tell the stories that relate to a particular theme and then move on to another theme (always with the possibility of returning to a theme already touched on). Bricker asserts that for Maya, events "are lumped together in terms of dramatic categories instead of being differentiated in terms of temporal provenience."[49] She refers to this methodology as the "telescoping of time." Bricker emphasizes that "the modern Maya still have a cyclical notion of time, but it is based on the repetition of natural and cultural events rather than on the ancient calendar."[50] A number of other anthropologists have discovered that the indigenous conception of time is cyclical and for Maya each year follows a pattern.[51] A society with a nonlinear view of time will have a different view of history than people who study in Western educational programs.

Kaqchikel envision a pattern for history. Bricker states, "The Maya believed that history was repetitive, that the events in one cycle would be repeated in all successive cycles as they had been repeating since time immemorial."[52] Consequently, oral history allows Maya not only to recount the past but also to develop strategies for the present and future. In this way, oral history provides a sense of security for Maya.

Oral history is also an essential base to the development of a collective identity. As Vansina states, "Most of what people hold to be true about reality is common. . . . [O]ral tradition is part of the process of establishing collective representations."[53] Collective identity is how a group of people think about themselves—how they perceive themselves in their own circumstances and relate to a larger context. The study of this collective identity or culture through oral tradition allows for a greater understanding of a group's worldviews.

Maya of Guatemala are aware of both the importance of their contributions to Guatemala's national development and the impending danger of the loss of their culture, language, and wisdom. Warren notes that "Mayan languages, calendrics, priest-diviners, and community elders' authority antedate the Spanish conquest; they are examples of Mayan cultural genius that were not completely eroded with the passage of time or with Spanish and later Ladino domination. Mayan scholars are arguing they must be revalued and revitalized before the past slips beyond the grasp of memory."[54] Many Ladino scholars have defined Maya by conquest rather than allowing Maya to define themselves through their own historical agency. Maya, though, refuse to allow misconstructions of history to erase their contributions and subordinate their identity.

The study of Kaqchikel oral histories contributes to more than just Guatemalan scholarship, however. It also advances the understanding of indigenous and of world history. As Champagne states, "Certainly, the study of Indian peoples, like other human groups, contributes to greater understanding of human culture in general, and Indians should be glad to contribute to this knowledge and welcome the contributions of non-Indian scholars."[55] Indigenous societies have significant contributions to make to an understanding of the world.

This book is an attempt to allow Kaqchikel to tell their histories and share their historical perspectives. It presents Kaqchikel oral histories and compares them to written accounts to arrive at a more holistic and inclusive presentation of Guatemala's history and national identity. The content of this work is thus designed to present Kaqchikel historical perspectives through a combination of Western and Kaqchikel approaches. I will use written sources to provide a time frame (Kaqchikel do not specify dates) and a general context for Kaqchikel oral histories. Oral traditions recall the establishment of their communities before the Spanish invasion, but the bulk of their oral histories focus on the nineteenth and twentieth centuries. As Vansina insists for historians of Africa, we "should all be writing our major works for an African public."[56] Likewise, this book seeks to appeal to Kaqchikel and Mayan audiences by adhering to their historical methodologies and presentations.[57] The chapters follow central themes in Kaqchikel oral histories: town origins, labor and land, epidemics, natural disasters, education, the military, President Jorge Ubico, other national and local leaders, and finally ethnic relations. These themes have all had a formative impact on Kaqchikel development and reality. If I have been successful, the flavorful and rhythmic articulation with which Kaqchikel present their oral histories will not be lost in my translations and presentation. I have sought to convey and examine the "significant past" of Kaqchikel as remembered by them.

The study of Kaqchikel historical perspectives is important on a number of different levels: it helps to present a more complete historical account of Guatemala's past through the incorporation of previously ignored or silenced yet valid and essential voices, and it adds to the understanding of indigenous approaches to history and presents distinct worldviews. Kaqchikel oral histories are an inherently valuable repository of knowledge that will aid Guatemala's understanding of its history and identity and will provide wisdom in the larger context of world history from local perspectives.

1
Town Origins

Ri laq'ab'enïk

Kaqchikel use their oral traditions in part to preserve the stories of how their towns were founded. One Kaqchikel ethnohistorian argues that "our people were the first ones to inhabit this land and that is important for our identity."[1] The actors in and the circumstances involved in settling communities are integral to Kaqchikel identity and are therefore essential components of oral traditions. Residents express a sense of ownership and autochthonous roots when they highlight who established the original community. K'ichee' speaker Menchú also recognizes the strong connection to place and land among American indigenous peoples: "Attachment to the land is common to indigenous populations throughout the continent."[2] According to Menchú, community and physical spaces are basic elements of the Mayan world. Angela Cavender Wilson, a Wahpetunwan Dakota Native American, concurs and notes that in Native American history, "Notions of place and homeland are given primacy, as it is this connection that is closely linked with our sense of identity."[3] Maya develop their identity from the history of their community. As anthropologist John Watanabe argues: "'Community' in the Mayan highlands . . . begins with two irreducible realities: first, 'place' as a physical locale with a given populace and resources; and second, 'premises' as the conventional strategies for surviving in that place."[4] Maya are inscribed in that "place" physically, mentally, and emotionally. Kaqchikel oral traditions encompass these realities. Kaqchikel inhabited Guatemala long before the Spanish arrived, and no attempt at assimilation with Ladinos can erase that from their identity or history.

For more than five hundred years, Maya have resisted Spanish and Ladino efforts to encroach upon their land, culture, and community. Protection and development of their culture and community has always been important for Maya, who can be identified by their language, dress, and customs. People show their solidarity to the region through similarity in dress. Many Maya preserve their culture by maintaining their traditional health practices, education, humility, harmony, solidarity, and understanding of each other and their surrounding environment.[5] Today, most Kaqchikel towns are divided into territorial sections called *cantones* that can be traced back to the residents' ancestors' principles of social units prior to Spanish arrival.[6] Kaqchikel communities are organized in such a way that those who live there experience continuity and a connection with their forebears. The connection to community and land and the great intrusions upon their culture and community are apparent in Kaqchikel oral traditions.

Attachment to community and place has led to a local identity but has not precluded a sense of connection with other indigenous groups. Maya also feel a connection to the nation, even though a national identity, subsumed by Ladinos, means little to them. Maya of Guatemala identify beyond their community, language group, and national borders. However, many Western scholars fail to recognize a broader indigenous identity among Maya. For example, in her study of Totonicapán, Guatemala, anthropologist Carol Smith argues that Mayan identity is rooted in the community, not in a larger ethnic group. She observes: "The Totonicapán Indians focused upon their Totonicapán identity, rather than their general Indian identity."[7] As a result of their distinct characteristics, according to Smith, no central bond ties Mayan communities together to act as a united force. Nevertheless, Kaqchikel do identify with members of different communities within and beyond their own language group.[8] Smith acknowledges that "what Indian communities generally share is their tradition of acting as corporate units in political struggles with the state—despite the fact that they may have different economic and political reasons for those struggles."[9] Identity and ways of interaction with others emanate from the community, but these perceptions extend well beyond individual communities.

Today Kaqchikel speakers number about 450,000 and live primarily in the departments of Chimaltenango, Sololá, Sacatepéquez, and Guatemala. The precontact population was most likely much greater, encompassing a larger geographic area.[10] Kaqchikel originally allied with K'ichee' to undertake the conquest of territories that had been seized from old Mayan and non-Mayan occupants. Kaqchikel were under the K'ichee' dominion through the reign of K'ikab in the fifteenth century. The alliance did not last long, however. Kaqchikel established their capital of Iximche' in 1463 but did not formally end their alliance with K'ichee' until K'ikab's death in 1475. The name Iximche' derives from the Kaqchikel words *ixim* (maize) and *che'* (tree). The Kaqchikel reign at the beginning of the sixteenth century encompassed a significant geographical area in the western highlands, but caustic relations between Kaqchikel and K'ichee' led to endemic war characterized by brutal and bloody periodic battles. Pedro de Alvarado, the leader of the Spanish military expedition into Guatemala, would later use this rivalry to his advantage to divide the most powerful Mayan groups.[11]

Kaqchikel remained in control at Iximche' for about sixty years, until the arrival of Alvarado's forces in 1524. At first, Kaqchikel leaders were loyal to Alvarado. In February, Alvarado defeated the K'ichee' (with the aid of Kaqchikel men), burned their leaders, and destroyed their capital, Utatlán. By April 1524, Alvarado set his sights on Iximche' and its Kaqchikel inhabitants. The leaders of Iximche', B'eleje' K'at and Kaji' Imox, had heard of the atrocities committed against the K'ichee'. To avoid further bloodshed, these leaders prepared a warm welcome for Alvarado's Spanish forces and their Tlaxcalan allies, who had accompanied them from Mexico. They offered the Spanish troops shelter, food, gold, men to fight in the army, and even some women. The beautiful Kaqchikel artisan work of gold and copper vessels and crowns especially appealed to Alvarado, and his demands increased. Relations quickly deteriorated, and by August most Kaqchikel had fled Iximche' to escape torture and cruelty at the hands of the Spanish forces. They retreated to the hills to wage war against Alvarado's troops. Spanish troops continued to battle K'ichee', Tz'utujil, and Kaqchikel groups into the 1530s.[12]

When the Spanish first arrived, Kaqchikel at Iximche' were in control of many Mayan groups, and Kaqchikel aided the Spanish to subdue these communities. One group that resisted Kaqchikel and Spanish intrusion was the Sacatepéquez. The Sacatepéquez began a war against their neighboring communities in 1524–25. Mayan leaders from the area appealed to Alvarado to quell the Sacatepéquez warriors, whose number was more than eight thousand. In 1526 Alvarado sent his army, led by Pedro de Portocarrero and Sancho de Barona, to "reduce to obedience" the Sacatepéquez rebels. The Sacatepéquez were fierce fighters and refused the Spanish offer of peace. Consequently, the Spanish, with the aid of some Kaqchikel, defeated the Sacatepéquez and gained control of the region.[13]

Alvarado and his forces took advantage of this victory to establish themselves in the area (known today as the department of Sacatepéquez). However, no clear evidence proves that indigenous groups inhabited the Valley of Quinizilapa, where the towns of Aguas Calientes and Barahona are located, prior to Spanish invasion in 1524. Alvarado did not found Santiago de Almolonga (Ciudad Vieja, a town neighboring Aguas Calientes) until 1527, about three years after Kaqchikel rebelled. Kaqchikel had withdrawn from the valleys and taken refuge in more inaccessible areas, and Spaniards therefore came upon no inhabitants when they entered the Valley of Quinizilapa. Alvarado quickly divided the rich agricultural land among his military leaders, two of whom, Juan de Chávez and Sánchez Barahona, held the communities known today as Aguas Calientes and Barahona. As a result of the population dearth in the area, Spaniards captured and purchased Maya to occupy and work their land grants.[14] Whether Spaniards formed these communities or if Kaqchikel lived there prior to the Spanish arrival continues to be debated among scholars and Kaqchikel. Archeologist William Swezey argues that a valley of such agricultural abundance would have to have been inhabited well before the Spanish arrival. Sheldon Annis suggests that the original settlers may have died or fled in the wake of Spanish control.[15] Some scholars argue that Spaniards founded the towns to provide a labor pool for their agricultural endeavors. The Spanish and the Catholic Church commonly established communities called *congregaciones* to concentrate dispersed groups into a central location and thereby provide a controlled source of labor for their agricultural estates.[16] Because of the lack of archeological evidence, the question of indigenous populations in the region remains murky. The Spanish, however, made an indelible mark on the communities of Barahona and Aguas Calientes.

In 1526 Hernán Cortés recalled Alvarado to Mexico. Alvarado left his brother, Gonzalo, in charge of the continuing battles. In February of that same year, Spanish troops burned Iximche'. After the arson, many Kaqchikel took refuge in Comalapa. The ravaged Maya took more decisive action against their aggressors. In 1526 the Kaqchikel nation rebelled to terminate the extortion and torture to which Gonzalo de Alvarado subjected them. Kaqchikel and K'ichee' then united the communities of Comalapa, Sololá, Chimaltenango, and Xilotepeque to form an army of more than thirty thousand to challenge the Spanish warriors. Kaqchikel fought valiantly, setting up stake pits to kill the soldiers and horses. The worst killing began on March 27, 1527, when the Spanish reorganized under the leadership of Pedro de Portocarrero and established a fort near Chi Xot (Comalapa). A prolonged war ensued, and Kaqchikel were proud that they did not pay tribute. This immunity to tribute did not last long, however.[17]

By January 1528 some Kaqchikel made peace and agreed to pay a tax to the Spaniards, as the Spanish abandoned the site near Comalapa. Although B'eleje' K'at and Kaji' Imox continued to resist the Spanish army into the middle of 1529, by May 1530 the remaining rebellious Kaqchikel surrendered to Alvarado and submitted to his demands for goods and labor. Spanish soldiers quelled a second insurrection between 1532 and 1535. Kaqchikel rebels sporadically led small uprisings against Spanish forces, but for the most part Alvarado won the political and military battle for Guatemala. Alvarado executed Kaji' Imox on May 26, 1540, and the remaining leaders from Iximche' by March 1541. Nature exacted justice upon the Spanish when later that year, on September 10, the Junajpú volcano erupted and the water from the interior flooded the surroundings, killing many Spaniards, including Alvarado's wife (Alvarado had been killed in June fighting in the Mixtón War in Mexico).[18] The termination of the military battles did not conclude the Spaniards' attempts to force Maya to acculturate to Spanish norms.

Spaniards forever changed these communities, but oral traditions preserve the details of these Kaqchikel places of origin. Kaqchikel residents of the towns of Tecpán, Comalapa, Poaquil, Barahona, and Aguas Calientes all have a strong sense of community and place. Oral traditions of each town retain the specifics of how, where, and, in some cases, when these communities developed. Iximche' will be the first town we will examine, because it was (and is) the Kaqchikel capital. Kaqchikel are proud of the accomplishments of their ancestors at Iximche'. Tecpanecos, especially, have a heightened sense of respect for their town and a keen awareness of what life was like prior to, during, and after the Spanish invasion.

Iximche', Tecpán Guatemala

People from Tecpán stress that their ancestors predated the Spanish arrival. Their town is located a mere five kilometers from Iximche'. Most Kaqchikel from Tecpán understand the significance of the name *Iximche'*. They know it is a combination of *maize* and *tree*, or *stick,* in their language. Many recognize the tree as the giver of life (and rain).[19] Jun Aj and his wife, Ix'ik', recount a popular version of the origin of the name in oral traditions: "A long time ago when people first settled in Iximche', there was a tree that bore corn cobs as its fruit. This tree was essential, especially when the cold frost came early and killed the farmers' corn crops. The tree provided food for the people, thereby preventing starvation. The tree was located at Iximche', and people ate of it to live."[20] Junlajuj Iq', a thirty-nine-year-old Mayan priest who has performed many ceremonies at Iximche', insists that *ixim* is the seed of corn.[21] Ixsu'm, a sixty-nine-year-old Catholic woman, says, "Indians were born here so they gave it the name Iximche'."[22] The different variations on the etymology of Iximche' all emphasize the life-giving and sustaining aspect of the Kaqchikel capital, the very center from which the Kaqchikel population emanated.

Oral traditions recognize Iximche' as the first civilization in Guatemala. One agriculturist, whose education was limited to second grade, states that Iximche' was the capital of Central America before the Spanish arrived.[23] Kaqchikel are aware that Tecpán was the capital for only a short time, as the

Spanish moved the capital to Ciudad Vieja and then Antigua, where it remained until an earthquake buried it. Kaqchikel also point out that the
Spanish then moved the capital to the Valley of Ermita, where Guatemala
City is located today.[24] Kaqchikel are proud that their towns were two of the
first capitals and thus integral in the founding of the country.

In contrast, local written accounts by Ladinos do not elaborate on the
Kaqchikel precontact society. The focus is on the arrival of Alvarado and
his troops and how they founded Tecpán. Tecpán's municipal monograph
purports Tecpán, not Iximche', to be the first capital of Guatemala.[25] The
monograph refers to Iximche' only as "The archaeological center 'Ruins of
Iximche' ' that in 1524 was the scene of important happenings . . . being this
place the capital and court of the Cakchiqueles."[26] The Ladino author rele-
gates Iximche' as an archaeological site with no relevance to the present. According to the monograph, Iximche' was the Kaqchikel capital, but nothing
important happened there prior to the Spanish arrival in 1524. Even though
Kaqchikel are the majority of the population, the author writes them out of
local history.[27]

Kaqchikel know that before the Spanish arrived Iximche' supported a
thriving society that was strategically located to protect and house Kaqchikel
leaders such as Kaji' Imox and B'eleje' K'at. They also assert that their ancestors had a palace to honor Tekun Uman, the K'ichee' warrior from Xelaju'
(Quetzaltenango).[28] Kaqchikel claims that a palace for Tekun had been at
Iximche are most likely inaccurate, since Kaqchikel and K'ichee' had been
involved in prolonged and bloody wars. The inclusion of Tekun at Iximche'
reflects the fact that Tekun has become a pan-Mayan hero. In this example,
Kaqchikel oral tradition has replaced historical accuracy to identify with a
uniting symbol of Mayan strength and courage. The inclusion of Tekun at
Iximche' also downplays the historical animosity between Kaqchikel and
K'ichee'.

Kaqchikel recognize Tekun as the supreme leader of Maya in Guatemala.
Many from Tecpán state that Kaji' Imox and B'eleje' K'at served under Tekun
and advanced to become kings only after Tekun died. They proudly assert that Tekun was an excellent fighter and difficult to kill. According to
Kaqchikel oral traditions, only the arrow made from the feather of the
quetzal could kill him.[29] Menchú observes that "the spirit of Tucum Umán
can never be captured or imprisoned."[30] Tekun is a powerful figure for Kaqchikel and other Maya of Guatemala.[31]

Kaqchikel oral traditions also assert that the Spanish invasion precipi-
tated exploitation, trickery, abuse, and death. Oral traditions emphasize a
precontact life based on agriculture and weaving and a population that had

minimal impact on the environment and that shared the land and other resources without internal unrest. This assessment contradicts the *Anales,* which describes constant turmoil and struggles among Kaqchikel and with other Mayan groups, especially the K'iche'.[32] Again, Kaqchikel oral traditions exaggerate the portrayals of an idyllic world prior to the Spanish arrival. A simpler, more tranquil life did exist before the Spanish invasion; however, it was not devoid of conflict, violence, and suffering. One reason Kaqchikel oral traditions paint a utopian picture of precontact life is to establish a starker contrast to life under Spanish rule. Oral traditions emphasize the decrease of the quality of life due to Spanish abuse and exploitation. Ethnic conflict between Maya and Spanish begins immediately upon Spanish arrival, and this has important implications in Kaqchikel perceptions of ethnic relations.

Kaqchikel histories of Iximche' and its surroundings describe efficient production and freedom of labor. One elder, whose age is estimated at more than one hundred, relates the history of his town: "A long time ago there was no owner of the land. People just planted where they wanted and whatever work the people wanted to do, they just did it. . . . This was a time of only *naturales*—there were no foreigners or Ladinos."[33] People from Tecpán develop a detailed image of this civilization through their oral traditions. They assert that communal ownership of the land eliminated the need for prices and money. Some informants point out that people did not wear clothes and that no one married through the Catholic Church because no Spanish priests were present. They attest that in this society, people treated each other with more respect and that younger generations respected their elders. Informants boast that the first generations were intelligent and used only organic medicines to cure the sick.[34]

Kaqchikel leaders selected the location of Iximche' for strategic and spiritual reasons. When Spanish historian Francisco Antonio de Fuentes y Guzmán first noted Iximche' around 1680, he admired its location because the surrounding canyons provided great protection.[35] Jun Tzinik'an, a Kaqchikel bus driver who farms on his free days, explains the importance of the location: "My grandmother and grandfather told me about the first pueblo here. They built the temples on a hill surrounded by canyons so the caretakers could detect invaders from a distance. The location also coincides with the four cardinal points, which were very important to our ancestors. Tekun Uman arrived here from K'ichee', but there was already a Kaqchikel leader here when he came."[36] Jun Tzinik'an's sixty-nine-year-old mother proudly says, "Iximche' was the heart of all places, and it was ours."[37] According to oral traditions, Kaqchikel decorated many of the structures with gold, especially the palace of Tekun. Their ancestors are also said to have made beautiful gold and silver jewelry, some of which locals discovered in the 1960s.[38]

This heightened awareness of the most significant Kaqchikel community provides people from Tecpán with more detailed oral histories surrounding Iximche' than their counterparts in other Kaqchikel towns. Tecpanecos have an acute understanding of Kaqchikel leaders and their roles. Kaji' Imox and B'eleje' K'at receive the most attention in oral traditions. A teacher, and advocate of Kaqchikel education, shares what she heard from her grandparents: "Kaji' Imox worked with B'eleje' K'at and helped our people, but when the Spanish came, they killed them by burning them alive."[39] Nearly all the Tecpanecos I interviewed recognized Kaji' Imox as an important player in Kaqchikel history, but they also mentioned B'eleje' Na'oj, Jolom B'alam, Ixmukane', and others. In contrast, people from other Kaqchikel areas seldom recalled these leaders. Tecpán's oral traditions opine that B'eleje' K'at was the secretary of Kaji' Imox before becoming king when Kaji' Imox died. Informants boast of the intelligence of these leaders who did not have any Western education. Some say that as many as ten different Kaqchikel "kings" existed at the time.[40] Even those who did not know the history of these figures could at least recognize the names of Kaji' Imox and B'eleje' K'at. The proximity of Iximche' sharpens Tecpanecos' memory of its history.

Daniel García López, a local historian and Ladino Tecpán native who writes for the annually published magazine *Revista Tecpán Guatemala,* uses documents from the AGCA and oral accounts from local Kaqchikel inhabitants to explore his municipality's history—"where the fusion of two cultures, the Old Continent and the New World, originated, giving origin to our *guatemalaness.*"[41] He stresses the significance of Iximche': "The meaning of Tecpán denotes a place inhabited by important people, by nobles . . . as Iximche' was the capital of the Kaqchikel Reign, one of the most important kingdoms in the time of the Spanish invasion of Guatemala. Belehe Cat [B'eleje' K'at] and Cahi Imox [Kaji' Imox] were the kings who governed the city. . . . Alvarado considered the Kaqchikel the most important indigenous nation of the territory and their capital the best geographically situated for his goals."[42]

Another Ladino author recognizes that Kaqchikel had developed a successful civilization well before the Spanish arrived. He asserts that Kaqchikel were descendants of the "Old Mayas and inherited the blood of the culture of that great American community."[43] Bernal Díaz del Castillo, who traveled through Iximche' in August 1526, had previously been awed by the magnificent splendors of the Aztec capital, Tenochitlán. His writings show that the wondrous beauty and artisan talents that Kaqchikel relate in their oral traditions were not exaggerations: "The rooms and houses were fine, and the buildings as luxurious as those of chiefs who ruled all the neighboring provinces."[44] In the late 1960s Swiss archeologist George Guillemín excavated Iximche' and asserted that Díaz's claims were justified. The walls and doorways of some of the once-luxurious buildings displayed remains of impressive paintings. In one grave Guillemín discovered "a headband of gold and a necklace of ten gold jaguar heads as well as forty small gold beads."[45]

Kaqchikel's detailed recollections of a history more than five hundred years old distort past relations between Maya. Kaqchikel of Tecpán are more aware than their neighbors of the historically antagonistic relations with K'ichee'. While the motives for the warring factions may vary, oral accounts do not obscure the rivalry. Some people attribute the caustic interchange to a difference in customs; competition over the rich resources of Iximche', such as gold, silver, and land; or just their desire to conquer each other.[46] Even though most people today are aware of tense relations, they assert that current relations are supportive and conciliatory and ascribe little import to the old rivalry today.[47] Like residents in other Kaqchikel towns, some people from Tecpán insist that the Spanish were the source of all evil and gloss over tensions between their Kaqchikel and K'ichee' ancestors. One eighty-seven-year-old farmer who never attended school and speaks no Spanish does not remember any problems between Kaqchikel and K'ichee'. According to him, the Spanish were the only ones with whom Kaqchikel fought.[48] The constant oppression by Spaniards and Ladinos have relegated struggles between Kaqchikel and K'ichee' to the background.

Oral traditions of Kaqchikel from Tecpán and other towns preserve Tekun's fate at the hands of the Spanish. A forty-three-year-old man who knits sweaters in his family's business explains that "Tekun Uman did not understand Spanish so he could not communicate with Pedro Alvarado. As a result, Pedro became upset and declared war on Tekun. While Pedro's men had horses, guns, and shields, Tekun's army was limited to bows and arrows. Consequently, the Spanish forces were victorious."[49] Another popular story in oral traditions, which Kaqchikel incorporated from the official history taught in government schools, is that Pedro Alvarado killed Tekun because he could not distinguish between a horse and a man. Tekun assumed that the horse was an extension of Alvarado. As he thrust his lance into the horse, Tekun believed he was killing Alvarado. Alvarado took advantage of this blunder to dismount and kill Tekun. People who have never attended school tell the same story.[50]

A sixteenth-century K'ichee' land-claim document similarly describes Tekun's battle with the Spaniards. According to this account, after Spanish troops had killed three thousand of Tekun's soldiers, they asked Tekun if he would like to agree to peace. Tekun refused, and the battle ensued. Tekun charged Alvarado in an attempt to kill him and instead beheaded his horse. In Tekun's second charge Alvarado was prepared and impaled him with his lance. Alvarado recognized Tekun as a noble and valiant warrior and protected his body from attacking dogs. The document concludes that Spaniards killed so many Mayan soldiers that there formed a "river of blood."[51] The *Anales* does not mention the specific battle between Alvarado and Tekun except to note that the Spaniards killed many K'ichee'.[52]

Many teachers and other highly educated Kaqchikel do not accept this version of the fight between Alvarado and Tekun. They view it as an attempt by the Ladino power structure to usurp and demean an important historical figure for Maya of Guatemala. They point out that Maya had cared for the horses before the break with the Spanish, so, clearly, they knew the difference between a horse and a man.[53] Despite this distortion, the story remains in Kaqchikel oral traditions. Tekun's loss to the Spanish forces does not tarnish his image, because Kaqchikel do not respect Spaniards as honorable soldiers.

Kaqchikel oral traditions portray Spaniards as conniving and abusive men of ill repute whose ideas, customs, and religion were supported and aided by the Catholic Church. Ka'i' Aq'ab'al, a sixty-eight-year-old Catholic agriculturist, animatedly passed down the history from his elders:

> When Christopher Columbus and Pedro Alvarado came over on boats in search of a new nation, the indigenous people in Central America did not meet them with open arms. Their food had run out so they returned to Spain several times. On return trips they gathered up prisoners to join them on the trip and work for them when they arrived in the new land. The Spanish sailed with new vigor because they were anticipating a battle. They also brought with them Jesús de Poroma on the boat. When the Spanish arrived they asked for peace in the name of God. They immediately assumed witches performed our religion. The Spanish fought the Kaqchikel and then forced them to carry their gold and silver on their backs to be shipped to Spain. Pedro Alvarado was a fine Christian; he raped young women and had children with them . . . [and took] their fathers' supply of gold and silver.[54]

Ka'i' Aq'ab'al argues the Spaniards made no effort to understand Mayan religion and that priests and soldiers combined efforts to subdue Maya.

Kaqchikel oral histories are more critical of the arrival of Spaniards and

Catholicism than most Ladino histories. Kaqchikel oral accounts attest that Spanish priests and the archbishop of Spain brought the "language of God" with them to teach "the doctrine of God" to Maya.[55] As one man points out, "We had to learn their language," not vice versa.[56] They note that in addition to the teachings, "The Spanish assigned us a saint—San Francisco." Kaqchikel recount that shortly after the Spanish arrival Alvarado and his soldiers forced Kaqchikel to build the Catholic Church.[57] The municipal monograph of Tecpán provides a different emphasis, proudly stating, "Tecpán was founded by the conqueror Pedro de Alvarado on July 25, 1524, where Iximche' was located, but Mexican Indians gave it the name Tecpán. On this day the first mass was celebrated by Father Juan Godinez, chaplain of the army commanded by Alvarado."[58] The Ladino author recognizes the close relationship between the Spanish invaders and the Catholic Church but not the negative connotations of this union.[59] In contrast, a Kaqchikel man concludes that "the Spanish came with their ideas and wanted to replace the ideas and character of our ancestors, calling their customs witchcraft (black magic). These accusations were false. Alvarado killed the people who did not change their ways and conform to Spanish thinking."[60] Oral histories ensure that Kaqchikel always know that their character and ideas are distinct from the ones that the Spanish soldiers and clerics imposed upon them.

The role of the Catholic Church and its missionaries among Kaqchikel is complex. While Kaqchikel informants focus on negative aspects of priests' role in the colonization process, some priests did make positive contributions. Francisco Ximénez, a Dominican priest who arrived in Guatemala in 1687, learned a number of Mayan languages, including Kaqchikel, translated the *Popol Wuj,* founded a hospital, and sought to discover herbal cures for diseases. He developed a great respect for Mayan customs, ceremonies, and general approach to life. He even encouraged his compatriots to learn from and adopt Mayan customs. Furthermore, not all Maya were unwilling converts to Catholicism. Some supported the church with food, services, and money, and, in some cases, Maya willingly donated labor to build churches.[61] Scholars argue that some Maya sincerely incorporated Catholicism into their religious practice and point out that in cases where priests failed to show up for religious celebrations, Mayan leaders performed masses themselves.[62] Nonetheless, the situation in Guatemala in the eighteenth century led Archbishop Pedro Cortés y Larraz to question the sincerity of Mayan Christianity. He noted that local leaders often told people that the Mayan religion was the only true religion and that Spaniards were deceivers.[63]

Kaqchikel oral traditions and some local Ladino literature emphasize that Kaqchikel resisted the Spaniards and their religion. One eighty-year-old

Kaqchikel Catholic who never attended school depicts the horrors of the Spanish invasion and the courage of his ancestors:

> The Maya were working and living all over Central America before the Spanish thieves and murderers arrived to threaten, rob, and kill our ancestors. They came to take our gold. They used guns that were no match for the bows and arrows of our people. They lied and tricked us and abducted our daughters and took them to Spain. They destroyed our cornfields and were killing our people. Two Mayan priests looked for a large rock to roll down the hill at the oncoming Spanish thieves. The plan was temporarily successful, as the Spanish soldiers screamed and ran away. Our people were strong and smart but eventually were overpowered and abused.[64]

Some Ladino authors concur with the oral descriptions of Kaqchikel valor and tenacity in warfare.[65] Furthermore, Díaz del Castillo attests that he had to "battle his way through into the city, as the Cakchiquel squadrons, hiding in the canyons, fought to keep the Spaniards from entering."[66] García López's written history also recognizes Kaqchikel resourcefulness and bravery:

> Initially the Kaqchikel feared the Spanish because of the reports about the cruel treatment they imposed on the Quichés, whose kings they had killed and how [the Spanish] proceeded to burn their capital. However, this fear turned into action as the Kaqchikel rebelled and fled the city. Alvarado pursued them in order to capture them, but the Kaqchikel became more hostile and set traps by digging holes in which they planted stakes to kill the horses and men. The war lasted until September 1526, when Alvarado returned to burn the city [Iximche'].[67]

García López glosses over the caustic relations between Kaqchikel and K'ichee', focusing his history on the strife between Spaniards and Maya. He notes that the Spaniards won not as a result of their superior strategic abilities but because they burned the Kaqchikel and K'ichee' capitals. Respect for Mayan resistance to the Spanish invasion is present in both Kaqchikel oral traditions and Ladino and Spanish written accounts, but most Kaqchikel oral traditions maintain that the Spaniards were criminals who used deception to defeat their ancestors.

Using a mirror as a form of trickery is one example. Oxi' K'at, a seventy-nine-year-old evangelical farmer, states, "The Spanish deceived two young girls with a mirror. The Spanish showed the mirror to the girls [so the girls would] show them where their king was. The girls took them to Tekun. That is when the war began, and it lasted thirty-five years. It was not a quick war."[68] Some oral accounts portray Maya as having traded their gold and silver for mirrors and uphold this as a deception because the two items were not of equal value.[69] Spaniards used mirrors to beguile Kaqchikel in other Kaqchikel towns, not just Tecpán, according to oral traditions.[70] (Archeological evidence does show that Maya possessed mirrors made of iron pyrite plates prior to the Spanish arrival.) As a result of Spanish trickery and unfair trade with mirrors, oral traditions teach that Spaniards were not to be trusted. For many Kaqchikel, this lesson holds true when applied to Ladinos today.

Chi Xot, or *Chi Q'a'l,* San Juan Comalapa

The people of Chi Xot, or Chi Q'a'l, San Juan Comalapa,[71] pride themselves on originating from the same population that existed at Iximche'. The founders of Comalapa were originally from Iximche', and their history is as rich as that of the people from the Kaqchikel capital. Comalapa predates the arrival of the Spanish. The carved stone feline heads in the town plaza and nearby artifacts prove that Comalapa was well established before the Spanish arrived. The original community of Comalapa was called Chuwi' Tinamït, which means "above the town."[72] People tell of a time before Spanish arrival that was peaceful and productive: when men farmed and women wove, and a thriving mine, named Paminix, produced gold and silver for church bells and clay for roofing tiles, pots, and other beautiful artisan works.

According to oral traditions, Kaqchikel worked the mine both before and after the Spanish arrived. Informants assert that workers forged different materials into practical tools and instruments, such as nails, and produced the gold chalice and other items that are the fame of the Catholic Church in Comalapa. Kaqchikel produced only what was needed and did not exhaust the mine. One of the clearest memories among informants is of the church bells that Kaqchikel workers forged at Paminix; they were not only beautiful but also produced an angelic sound. Kaqchikel recount that the bells impressed Ladinos in the capital, who borrowed the bells for their patronal feast and forced Kaqchikel to transport and hang them in the Guatemala City cathedral. When the festival ended, the same Kaqchikel carried the hefty bells back to Comalapa to reinstall in their own church. After three or four years of this cycle, these Ladinos began to feel remorse for the suffering bell transporters. As a result, they forced some Kaqchikel men to install the bells permanently in the Guatemala City cathedral. Kaqchikel emphasize that these Ladinos robbed the Comalapa bells. However, they note that some of the smaller bells are still used in the parochial church in Comalapa.[73] Many people from Comalapa, when in Guatemala City, frequent the Catholic cathedral to view its bells.[74]

Oral traditions further assert that at Paminix, Kaqchikel produced the gold and silver that decorated Tekun's palace at Iximche'. Informants name Tekun as the overseer of Paminix because it was located on the route between the Kaqchikel cities of Iximche' and Mixco Viejo.[75] They also note that when the Spanish forced Kaqchikel into more intense labor, the reserves were quickly depleted. Oral accounts attest that the Spanish shipped gold and silver back to Spain.[76] Portions of a structure built over the river to help mine workers look for gold are still in existence. Waqi' Q'anil, the auxiliary mayor of Simajulew, an aldea of Comalapa, formed a committee to take me to what remains of Paminix. They asked if I could put them in touch with an archeologist who would excavate the site and verify that it was once a thriving mine. These men told me that their ancestors constructed the walls and tunnels, some extending as far as a kilometer. They said that local people used the tunnels as escape routes in the 1980s, the worst years of the civil war. Waqi' Q'anil proudly stated, "This [Paminix] is not in any book. It only belongs to us."[77]

To my knowledge, no documentary evidence of Paminix exists. Nonetheless, oral histories about the mine correlate with numerous histories that show Spaniards as having quickly depleted the mineral wealth in highland Guatemala. Gonzalo Alvarado required young Kaqchikel boys to work gold deposits near Iximche'. K'ichee' documents reveal Pedro Alvarado's insatiable appetite for gold and other mineral riches.[78] Kaqchikel emphasize that Spaniards not only abused their ancestors but also failed to maintain a harmonious relationship with the environment.

The story of how Comalapa arrived at its current location illustrates a diligent and intelligent people. A former mayor recounts the history he heard: "A long time ago our ancestors made a town in the hills and called it Chuwi' Tinamït. In those days the men worked with a hoe and farmed maize, beans, wheat, lima beans, and the land was free. There was no owner of the land, so you could farm where you wanted. People only farmed small plots of land; they were not large landholders like those who came from Spain. The Kaqchikel preferred to have small landholdings. But as the population grew, the town was not big enough so they came here to Comalapa."[79] One of Comalapa's renowned painters says the community moved because Kaqchikel *caciques* (local leaders) engaged in land disputes that led to envy, rivalry, and the eventual disunion of the group.[80] Oral accounts of Comalapenses contain a number of different motivations for the move; however, all agree the new location was better suited to a larger population.

Some oral accounts imply that Kaqchikel moved to Comalapa after the Spanish established Antigua as the capital of Guatemala. Others state that the town was founded at the same time as Iximche' or that the original settlers came directly from Iximche'.[81] In any case, the accounts insist that Kaqchikel founded the town and do not acknowledge a Spanish presence.[82] One version states:

> Despite the fact that the people had already begun to gather large rocks to make a church at Chuwi' Tinamït and it was located close to Paminix, the townspeople decided they were too far from Antigua, where they went to buy and sell goods. It was also a problem when someone became infirm, as they could not get to Antigua in time to get to a doctor or medicine. They wanted to be able to make a round trip from their community in one day. The people had a meeting and agreed it was too far, there was not enough water, and it was very hilly. The inhabitants appointed a group of two or three men to set out early in the morning for Antigua, have lunch there, and then start back after lunch. During this time there were no cars so the men traveled on foot. The plan was to set up camp and sleep at the place they arrived when the sun set. This area would be the location of the new town. They made a sign where they would build the church and town. After sleeping in what would become Comalapa, a relatively plain and heavily forested area, the men arrived at Chuwi' Tinamït to inform the townspeople where their new village would be located.[83]

One of the reasons they moved the town was the same reason that Poaquil, formerly a Comalapa village, wanted to form its own town: the distance from a municipal center.

For some people, Chuwi' Tinamït was the name of the first community in Comalapa, and it was located where Comalapa is today, never in the hills. They assert that at first the town was just an overgrown forested and mountainous area, with only two roads and no light, so people always went to bed early. They say the town grew slowly and people began to farm more land.[84] The name of the first town survives in different ways today. For example, a development organization funded by *Christian Children* calls itself Chuwi' Tinamït.

Written sources express the pride that Kaqchikel of Comalapa feel as belonging to one of the first communities in the area. Problems among leaders caused the separation into different towns as Kaqchikel dispersed from Iximche'. In his interpretation of the *Anales,* Guatemalan anthropologist Adrián Recinos recognizes Comalapa as a pre-Hispanic seat known as Chi Xot or Ruyal Xot.[85] A monograph from the department of Chimaltenango claims that before the conquest, Comalapa was the capital of the Kaqchikel empire. The document lacks a specific founding date but asserts that the towns Iximche' and Comalapa date back millennia.[86] The author's failure to cite sources and his vague approximation of time periods for the founding of these towns limits its historical contribution, but it provides valuable insight into a Ladino historical perspective of these towns. The *Diccionario Geográfico de Guatemala* states that Comalapa existed "during the indigenous period" in a different spot than its current location.[87] In her study of Comalapan weavers, Asturias Barrios states that the original location of the town has changed but attributes the town's move in 1547 or 1549 to Spanish priest Diego de Alvarez.[88]

The fertile and beautiful location helped to motivate the move. One author describes Comalapa as "one of the most important municipalities of the department of Chimaltenango, of rich and historic Kaqchikel origin, an agricultural population, a fountain of riches, more than its silver mines, beautiful panorama, fertile and fecund lands, it rests in its spiritual purity."[89] One of the few local histories written by a Kaqchikel—in this case a fifty-two-year-old former photographer and part-time farmer and handyman—likewise praises the original location of the town: "It was an attractive place, surrounded by tall and mountainous hills, grand, fertile and beautiful plain, and enviable vegetation."[90] Comalapa has some of the most abundant natural resources in the department.

Local documents concerning the establishment of the first community by Kaqchikel are not as elaborate as oral traditions. The municipal monograph of Comalapa states that the Nahuatl (Tlaxcalan) Indians who accompanied the "conquerors" named Comalapa. The monograph, however, does not explore the preinvasion period other than to say that Comalapa was an important town in the Kaqchikel reign.[91]

Kaqchikel informants assert that their ancestors founded Comalapa between 1350 and 1400. They attest that one of the first things their forebears did was to build a temple in the new town. Informants point out that no cemetery existed then so the dead were buried in the temple. Others claim that skeletal remains can still be found because the church was built on top of the old cemetery. Wild animals in the environs were one of the first challenges Kaqchikel faced. Stories recall that because jaguars attacked and ate people, Kaqchikel ancestors made a large drum and built an enormous fire.

Accounts attest that the beating of the drum and the bonfire intimidated the animals so they retreated deeper into the forest and stopped bothering people.[92]

Comalapenses' oral accounts are divided over whether or not the Spanish conquered Comalapa. One version explains that the Spanish burned the town to destroy Comalapa and its inhabitants and describes how the straw and bamboo houses ignited quickly and facilitated the Spanish conquest of Comalapa. The Mayan bimonthly magazine *Rutzijol* writes that on February 7, 1526, the Spanish burned Chi Xot in one of the first massacres they committed against Maya.[93] Some weavers say that the red band on Comalapa's *güipil* (hand-woven blouse) is there to recall this destruction.[94] Almost all the residents know the story of why Comalapa burned, but not all inhabitants attribute it to the period of the first Spanish contact. Regardless of the date, as a result of the destruction one of the Kaqchikel names for Comalapa is Chi Q'a'l, a word that derives from *aq'a'l,* meaning charcoal. Oral histories note that only ash was left of Comalapa. One thirty-three-year-old evangelical woman and talented weaver says, "At first there were only our people here and we held our land in common, but then the Spanish came and burned all our houses because they wanted to terminate our people; they proceeded to take our land and conquer our village."[95] Kaqchikel represent the Spanish as a destructive force, but the Spanish were not always successful in their goals.

In another version, the Spanish are unable to conquer Comalapa. Oxi' Iq', a former mayor and successful businessman in town, recounts the oral tradition passed down to him:

> The Spanish never conquered Comalapa because when the Spanish arrived there were no people here. The Kaqchikel had seen them coming and hid in the surrounding areas. Consequently, the soldiers only found houses with smoldering fires and ash, so when they reported back to their superiors they informed them there were no people in town, only ash. When the Spanish soldiers left, the people returned to their homes, ready to retreat again. It was not until there was peace that the Kaqchikel people of Comalapa presented themselves to the Spanish, but they were never conquered.[96]

Again, the name Chi Q'a'l applies. Oxi' Iq' and others take pride in the fact that their ancestors outwitted the Spanish troops.[97]

Local written accounts also attest to Kaqchikel resourcefulness and bravery in their interactions with Spanish troops. Comalapa's municipal monograph boasts that the "inhabitants displayed great ancestry qualifying them as a Noble race. . . . During the conquest (in 1526) the inhabitants of this region defended their territory with heroism, entrenched in the high and inaccessible mountains of Holom-Balam, [they] were finally conquered because they were alone, after all the other towns had fallen."[98] The Comalapa health center and municipal monographs assert that Kaqchikel, commanded by their kings and principals, rebelled against the Spanish because the Spanish did not respect their alliance with the Kaqchikel. Those who did not rebel in town retreated from Comalapa into the surrounding hills to defend themselves against the Spanish. These sources proudly state that Kaqchikel lasted longer than any other group and surrendered only when all hope was lost. Finally, after the Kaqchikel "suffer[ed] grave defeats," Pedro Portocarrero controlled the region.[99]

Whether people claim that the Spanish conquered Comalapa or not, no one remembers the name of the Spaniard who came to subdue the area. Only in Kaji' Kan's written history is Portocarrero recognized as conquering Comalapa in 1524. Kaji' Kan also writes that Alvarado established his first military quarters close to Comalapa in a place called Tasbalaj.[100] Kaqchikel oral traditions know Alvarado but do not recount any other antagonist.[101] Unlike in the towns of Barahona or Tecpán, in Comalapa, Spanish invaders are not given any specific recognition. Oral traditions emphasize respect and admiration for their Kaqchikel ancestors and at no point become entwined with details about the Spanish forces, even though some important antagonists led the Spanish.

In the colonial period, Catholic missionaries came to propagate their religion and put Comalapa under the name of Saint John the Baptist. Some local Kaqchikel teachers recognize that one of the goals and results of religious teachings was to have the Kaqchikel learn Spanish and abandon their own language.[102] According to one monograph, Bishop Francisco Marroquín congratulated the friars because they organized the town of Comalapa. In 1549, however, Comalapa was transferred and entrusted to "conqueror" Juan Pérez Dardón.[103] The religious order of the missionaries who played a major role in Comalapa remains unclear yet omnipresent. In his written history, Kaji' Kan, who served on a committee for the parochial church of San Juan, expresses the role of religion:

In 1541 Fray Diego founded San Juan Comalapa. During those years many arrived at the city of Santiago of Gentlemen, many among them were religious: nuns, monks, Bethlehems, Carmelites, Capuchines, Dominicans, Franciscans and Claritas, all of whom began to found convents and construct churches, but the Claritas wanted to extend themselves more . . . so they looked for a place and chose San Juan Comalapa. They founded their convent and in 1622 began to construct the colonial church in a baroque style that they finished in 1646. At the same time they founded the *cofradías* [sacred religious brotherhoods] that continue to serve the church.[104]

The colonial church continues to be central to the town in terms of both location and social relations. The *cofradías* which began at this time have since seen their prestige and power diminish but continue to have a role in the community.

Some works record and verify aspects of the rich history of Comalapa, but other written accounts attempt to denigrate its existence prior to Spanish contact. Most histories of the area written by Ladinos fail to mention Kaqchikel and what made up their society prior to Spanish contact. Instead, they begin with the Spanish arrival. Inocencio del Busto, a member of the Anthropology Society of Guatemala, wrote an article in 1961 that virtually ignored Kaqchikel in the history of Comalapa. He emphasized only the arrival and dominance of the Spanish.[105] Francis Gall, a Ladino who compiled short histories of all the towns in Guatemala, attributes little importance to the community until after the Spanish invasion. He says, "At the beginning of the Spanish period Comalapa acquired its historical importance when the Spanish established a military quarters there."[106] For Gall and many other Ladino writers, the Spanish give Comalapa its significance even though Kaqchikel were the founders and remain the overwhelming majority of its population.

Pwaqil, San José Poaquil

While the historical perspectives of Ladinos and Maya are predictably incongruous, the divergence of historical presentation within the Kaqchikel population is less expected. The formation of the municipality of Poaquil presents an interesting case because of its relation to Comalapa. About 120 years ago, a village that belonged to the town of Comalapa struggled for its independence and formed the municipality of San José Poaquil. This event resulted in a bitter dispute. Poaquil and Comalapa are inextricably related, and Kaqchikel recognize this interdependent relationship. Some Poaquil teachers write that "this information [common history] is easy to see by the similarity of the traditional dress that the indigenous women wear and the similarity of last names."[107] These two towns, only fourteen kilometers apart, share many characteristics, such as clothing styles, language, last names, history, and culture, but differ in their perception of one significant event in their history: the separation of the two towns.

Oral traditions surrounding Poaquil's secession differ significantly. Poaquilenos believed that Comalapenses infringed upon their rights and violated their dignity. Kaqchikel residents of Poaquil recount a precise and caustic account of the independence of their town, a version that more accurately coincides with archival evidence. Kaqchikel from Comalapa are aware that Poaquil was formerly an aldea of Comalapa that gained its independence in the late 1800s. Most, however, claim this separation was a calm and peaceful process. Comalapa was once a far-reaching municipality but lost much of its land to independence movements of smaller communities. Comalapenses remember Poaquil specifically in this process but also in the context of a larger theme.

Poaquil's Version

Poaquilenos share oral historical traditions that surround the independence of their town. While variations in the recounting of this event exist, the commonalties far outweigh the differences. B'eleje' Ey, a forty-four-year-old farmer and teacher, provides an elaborate account:

The first people to settle in this area came from Comalapa across the hills over one hundred years ago. They were herders sent out from Comalapa to take care of the cattle that belonged to the Parish of San Juan [Comalapa]. The area provided ideal conditions for grazing cattle. Two main large landholdings called Hacienda María and Hacienda Vieja pertained to Comalapa. What is now the municipal center was a large cattle range and had the name Pa chab'äq [in the mud]. The men who came to care for the cattle originally left their families behind for a number of weeks while they tended the livestock in this remote community. The men were a great distance from their families and the town both geographically and logistically. Eventually these workers brought their wives and children with them to settle in the area. This community of herders was small but over time began to grow into a larger community, as they farmed the land in addition to tending the cattle.

The considerable distance was a serious inconvenience for the pastoral community. While the community was growing, it had no religious or secular services. When members of the community died, the people had to carry the deceased on their shoulders for fourteen kilometers and bury them in Comalapa. Other types of religious and secular obligations also had to be performed in Comalapa, such as baptisms and marriages. The people of what was to become known as Poaquil became frustrated because their community was so far removed from the municipality. Hence, they decided to form their own town to provide these services for the community. Seven local leaders took it upon themselves to represent their community and ask the authorities of Comalapa for permission to break off from the main town.

These seven men met with the mayor of Comalapa to propose their idea. At the first meeting the mayor denied their request for independence. Upon returning to the pastoral community, the seven men conveyed their failure to the people who in turn promptly encouraged them to try again. But at the second meeting with the mayor the results were the same. They made numerous other unsuccessful trips. Around this time they heard that Gen. Justo Rufino Barrios was returning from battle in the K'ichee' territory [an area to the north of their community]. Barrios was running a presidential campaign in the upcoming elections.[108] On his route back to the capital of Guatemala he was going to pass through a town quite close to them. The seven men decided to meet with the general, state their case, and ask for his assistance. They invited Barrios and his soldiers to come through their community. When he accepted, they planned to impress him with their hospitality.

The day he arrived with his soldiers, the people killed several cows to serve the men a bountiful lunch. As he and his soldiers relaxed on full stomachs—a rare event during his military campaign—the people explained their plight. Barrios lamented that at this point he had no power to affect their situation but promised that if he gained the presidency he would grant Poaquil its independence. In exchange for this promise he asked some of the young men of the community to join his military unit. In the meantime, the seven men continued to solicit the mayor for their independence, but the more they pleaded, the more adamant the mayor became in not granting them their wish.

When Barrios entered the capital city he instigated an uprising and took over as president. The people of Poaquil were elated by this turn of events, and the seven men went to the national palace to meet with the new leader of the country and gently remind him of his promise. He assured them that he would keep his promise and grant Poaquil its independence. Barrios sent a message to Comalapa commanding the independence of Poaquil. The mayor of Comalapa resisted this mandate and consequently Barrios sent his soldiers and ordered that the mayor be taken out to the hills and shot. The soldiers carried out his command. This action frightened the people of Comalapa, and the subsequent mayor was happy to oblige the request for Poaquil's independence.

The representatives from Poaquil went to meet the new mayor of Comalapa who was willing to concede this territory of Comalapa to form an independent town. He wanted, however, to be sure they understood the arduous work and responsibility that accompanied the formation of a town. He noted they would need to construct a municipal building and Catholic Church, as well as provide other services such as roads and water. The men insisted they were capable of completing the task. The mayor closed the meeting by stating that since there were seven leaders, they had to finish the town within seven years or the seven of them would be killed. Despite the threat and the enormous task that lay before them, the men's spirits were not dampened and they conveyed this victory to an elated crowd that had awaited their arrival. The excitement was channeled into a powerful working community where all members—women and children included—contributed to the goal at hand.

The first decision was to determine the location of the town. Initially, they considered the community of Ojer K'ayib'äl (old market), the site of the old market. Due to the lack of accessible water there, they settled on Pa chab'äq. Naturally, an area that was named after its constant condition of mud would have plenty of water. Moreover, Pa chab'äq had the added advantage of being surrounded by forest, which provided a good source of wood for building materials. Since their lives were in jeopardy if the task was not completed on time, the seven men passed a law to punish any member of the community who did not volunteer his [or her] time. The community developed a rack of wood to punish the offenders.[109] The people began by cutting trees for wood and making walls of adobe, roofing materials, canals and tubing for potable water, and roads of stone (seven roads pointing east-west and seven roads pointing north-south were named after the seven leaders of the town). Everyone contributed to the effort. Slowly, the community developed into a town, as they constructed the municipal building, Catholic Church (finished in 1895) and central fountain for washing clothes. In 1890, before the seven years had expired, the town was complete with the essential buildings, roads, and water system, so the seven men became the first mayors of Poaquil and enjoyed a long life.[110]

B'eleje' Ey's version is representative of basic elements contained in other Poaquilenos' oral histories pertaining to their independence. They share a description of motivations, processes, and events, but there are a number of variations of the version presented by B'eleje' Ey. The number of founding fathers ranges from five to ten, but they are always Kaqchikel. The first location selected for the town varies among different communities. People from the aldeas of Ojer Caibal and Saqirtacaj both claim their hamlet as the original town. What Poaquil gave to Barrios in their agreement for independence is another point of contention in oral accounts. Some say that Barrios named the town Poaquil (*pwaq* is the Kaqchikel word for money) because it was a resource-rich area with an abundance of gold and silver. Others assert that the nomenclature derives from the town's gift of money to Barrios in exchange for their independence.[111] The San José Poaquil monograph adheres to the latter version.[112] These distinctions, however, do not detract from the sense of pride and hard work, as well as the escape from persecution and abuse, that the story portrays. The founding of their town is in the forefront of people's thoughts. Recently, a group of women insisted on writing the town's independence history into their proposal to fund a project for their organic farmers' organization.[113] These women see a clear connection between the past and the present.

The San José Poaquil monograph, located in the municipal office, concurs with much of B'eleje Ey's account and attests that the special meal locals prepared for Barrios was "an unforgettable moment for the Poaquilenos." It also claims that Barrios executed the mayor of Comalapa when he resisted Poaquil's independence.[114] The document lists six names as the principal leaders of the independence movement; one man named Placido Simón became the first mayor and directed the construction of the roads, public buildings, and "most importantly" the Catholic Church: "[The housing and buildings] were simple but reflected the tranquility of the inhabitants."[115]

Archival evidence supports much of Poaquil's oral traditions. Land disputes between Poaquil and Comalapa that concerned the border and territorial possessions persisted in the late 1880s and early 1890s and became so volatile that the government sent its minister, Juan Fran Rubio, to settle the problem. He recognized Comalapa as "the center of a great parish with many dependents."[116] Minister Rubio elucidates how the towns separated: "In San José Poaquil there were a considerable number of indigenous people who, all being dependents of Comalapa, wished to be legitimate owners of the lands that they had planted in common; this was the objective that they presented to General Barrios, asking him for the secession to constitute a town under the name of San José Poaquil. General Barrios conceded but prevented them from farming the land communally, as they had always done."[117] On April 4, 1883, Fernando Chacach wrote a letter representing the mayor of Poaquil in which he says, "The General President [Barrios] gave the pact in which we formed our town to be independent of Comalapa. . . . [I]t gave initiative to the construction of indispensable buildings for the population."[118] Granting the independence of Poaquil fit into Barrios's scheme of privatizing land to usurp the communal landholdings from Maya. Barrios sponsored liberal reforms, one of which was to privatize land for wealthy landholders who would exploit and produce great quantities of agricultural export goods, especially coffee. Furthermore, as Grandin points out, "the liberal state did not arrive unexpectedly in communities in 1871; it was invited in."[119]

Even though many of the liberal reforms attacked Mayan communities, most Poaquilenos welcomed the onset of Barrios's presidency. Barrios viewed Maya as little more than another Guatemalan resource and unscrupulously exploited their land and labor in the interest of Guatemala's development.[120] After their independence they remained relatively isolated and controlled the governance of their municipality. According to Poaquil's oral traditions, the Barrios government did not intervene in community affairs, and many Kaqchikel of Poaquil considered Barrios a benevolent leader. Their neighbors in Comalapa, however, more keenly experienced the extensive intervention of the Barrios government and its ominous character.

The exact date of Poaquil's secession is unknown. The Ministry of Education claims that a government accord signed on November 1, 1891, created the town and asserts that it took a long time to found the town.[121] However, there is no such accord in the *Recopilación de Leyes* for that year. Regional histories written by Ladinos also fail to establish the date of the town's founding.[122] The San José Poaquil monograph asserts that the town is "fundamentally pre-Columbian" and was founded in November 1891.[123] That the town was founded in the late nineteenth century contradicts the assertion that Poaquil is pre-Columbian. Most likely, the intention of the monograph is to stress that the town is fundamentally Mayan. More accurately, a letter written by Domingo Oxi on October 11, 1886, states that the town was founded in 1881 (ten years before most written accounts claim), "when the president passed through our town on his last trip to Los Altos." According to Oxi, 1878 was the first year that Barrios granted them their independence.[124] In 1871 a liberal revolt, led by Miguel García Granados (1871–72) and Barrios, overthrew the conservative government of Vincente Cerna (1865–71). By 1873 Barrios assumed sole control of the government.[125] The year 1878 would have fallen in the seven-year period during which Poaquilenos constructed their town following Barrios's official consent. This approximation supports Poaquilenos' claims that the town gained its independence during the reign of President Barrios.

The extent and description of Comalapa's abuse of those from Poaquil varies significantly among informants. Most Poaquilenos emphasize that people in Poaquil and Comalapa had ill feelings toward each other. One seventy-eight-year-old Catholic farmer pointed out that those from Comalapa were quite upset that Poaquil broke away from Comalapa.[126] One woman attributed Comalapenses' acrimony to the fact that the division of the towns caused Comalapa to lose buyers in their market.[127] In many of Poaquil's oral accounts, the sense of superiority exhibited by Comalapenses and their exploitation of Poaquilenos are important themes. A twelve-year-old boy who retold the history of Comalapa one day in his father's store stressed the abuse Comalapa imposed on Poaquil. He then showed me his school notebook in which he had written that Poaquilenos were treated like "slaves."[128] Poaquilenos consider their independence story important enough to include it in the school curriculum, thereby making it an authorized, or official, written history. In contrast, Comalapenses do not include this history in their curriculum and, likewise, Poaquil's independence does not play a significant role in their oral histories. For Poaquilenos, the independence story as part of the school curriculum does not necessarily add credibility to their history (oral history is credible because it has been passed down from the elders); rather, it provides another source with which to teach children about their background and show them the relevance of their history to their lives today. Written versions also ensure that histories will not be lost. The history will be passed down to younger generations and even taught in the schools, thus keeping all people aware of themselves as a once-maligned group.

Poaquil's municipal monograph guards these perceptions when it laments that while shepherds had to bring an animal to Comalapa for the mayor's consumption each week, "The herders did not even receive the hide, let alone a piece of meat; for all practical purposes they were slaves. . . . The inhabitants of the area were very discontented with San Juan Comalapa, it did not allow them to satisfy their material and spiritual needs, such as lending them the services of the cofradía or municipal employees."[129] The monograph expresses the angst felt by inhabitants of Poaquil before they gained their independence. Poaquilenos were frustrated with the challenges of living in such an isolated area with no municipal or religious services and with Comalapa treating them like second-class citizens, or even "slaves." For them, independence was more than the opportunity to escape from an autarchic situation; it was a chance to earn respect and fair treatment from their former despot. They apply this lesson to their lives today: as an oppressed people, they constantly struggle for equal rights. While the former mistreatment and indignity are not felt with the same intensity today, most people of Poaquil are aware that this malice did exist at one time.

Cantankerous relations were not one-sided. Minister Rubio asserted that the dividing line caused "continuous disturbances" between the two towns for several years. "Instead of protecting the good harmony that should exist between towns," he noted, "they are constantly promoting quarrels that develop a terrible hate between the inhabitants."[130] On October 25, 1886, Eusebio Chalí, a trustee from Comalapa, wrote that Poaquil gained its independence "for consequence of disturbances that the indigenous people from Poaquil provoked." He continued, "The indigenous people of Poaquil, like always, presented some objections to the way the land was distributed. . . . Despite the government agreement, those from Poaquil returned with new claims."[131] Chalí signed his name "in justice" and asked that the government hold the Poaquilenos responsible for their actions and expenses.

Comalapenses were upset because they believed their municipality had lost a significant portion of its population and resources. By 1886 Dionicio Salazar from Comalapa concluded that the split was a mistake. He wrote: "To populate is to govern and why provoke the disadvantages that occur . . . from converting a grand town into two towns weakened in population and resources? The indigenous people from the section of Poaquil insisted for a long time, in their tenacity, without being discouraged [by] the repeated negative responses from the government until finally the General President Rufino Barrios acceded to their desire . . . at a cost to both towns."[132] Salazar may have been correct, because in December 1886, at the request of Comalapa's mayor, the president suppressed the municipal status of Comalapa and appointed a judge to handle the administrative affairs of the mayor.[133]

Poaquilenos were also experiencing angst. Domingo Oxi wrote: "Those from Comalapa are protecting . . . the interests that favor them . . . because they are rich, but it is not just."[134] Poaquilenos were aware of the developing rancor and the danger of its consequences. In a letter dated November 19, 1886, the mayor of Poaquil, José Hilario Roquel, along with other members of the municipality, asked that the towns find a quick solution to the problem to prevent further "heated agitation." He warned that if the disputes were not resolved quickly "it would leave the source of a seed of dispute fed by hate, and . . . will give frequent place to continuous discord and disorder that could cause [problems] for both sides . . . that could result in the interests of the two towns forever opposing each other."[135]

The stories told by Poaquilenos emphasize the struggle to escape an oppressive situation. Comalapa did not treat them as equals but forced them to work under burdensome, severe conditions without showing any respect or kindness. Poaquilenos perceived these relationships as tyrannical and wanted to end them. Comalapa shunned Poaquil's numerous efforts at negotiation, so the seven men from Poaquil appealed to a higher authority. They made a great effort to show Barrios their respect and appreciation by honoring him with a banquet and gifts. In return, Barrios killed their despot and granted their independence. After independence, Poaquilenos needed to build their own town, so everyone contributed with a sense of mission to ensure their dream would be a lasting reality. Poaquilenos feel a strong sense of pride because they confronted their oppressive situation, strove to overcome it, and established a sense of permanent ownership over their own destiny through hard work and perseverance. Diligence and dedication remain integral to their society today.

Poaquilenos do not nurture rancorous feelings toward their former oppressors. It is apparent that relations between the towns were tenuous at the time of the division. However, it has been more important for Poaquilenos to preserve a sense of overcoming an oppressive situation to develop a positive living situation rather than focusing on who caused the previously unjust conditions. They derive a great sense of accomplishment from escaping a tyrannical situation and developing equal, peaceful, and productive relations with their former oppressor. Ixb'atz' is a fifty-four-year-old woman whose grandmother met General Barrios and conveyed to her granddaughter the animosity that existed at the time. Ixb'atz' is well versed in the antagonistic relations between the two towns in regard to their separation but insists that the towns now have a convivial relationship.[136] Intermarriage and friendly interaction in markets and social events are common. The historical focus is not intended as an attack on those of Comalapa but rather an illustration of how Poaquilenos rose above adversity to form a permanent and comfortable relationship. That relations are now peaceful makes the triumph sweeter.

Comalapa's Version

Very few Kaqchikel in Comalapa recognize any unrest or resentment left over between the two towns from when they divided. Even those who say there may have been some disturbances claim that they subsided quickly. Some of the events and characters coincide, but for the most part their accounts are less elaborate. Junlajuj Imox, a ninety-three-year-old elder from Comalapa who walks cautiously with a cane but continues to work in his cornfields, provides a concise account of the separation:

The community was originally formed to take care of the cattle where they grazed at Hacienda María and Hacienda San Juan. The original residents were shepherds from Comalapa. The haciendas were a long way from Comalapa so, as the community slowly grew, the people decided they wanted to separate from Comalapa. When General Justo

Rufino Barrios came through with his soldiers, the people of Poaquil killed two or three cows and made a beef stew to feed them. After that kind gesture, Barrios was willing to grant the people their greatest wish: their independence. There was no problem when the towns split, since both parties were in agreement. However, there was some unrest when the people from Poaquil claimed that Simajulew and Agua Caliente, two territories that belonged to Comalapa, should be conceded to Poaquil. Comalapa refused to surrender these communities, so they remain part of Comalapa today.[137]

Junlajuj Imox's memories are more comprehensive than those of most people (few had heard about the land issue over Simajulew and Agua Caliente),[138] but his version is generally the story told by Comalapenses. Most people know that Poaquil gained its independence about one hundred years ago. According to some Kaqchikel, shepherds also farmed maize and coffee because the land was abundant and the soil rich. During one of my visits for a haircut, the neighborhood barber explained that "during that time, unlike today, there was plenty of land so there was no reason for a dispute when the towns divided."[139] Many assert that the fact that the two towns have the same clothing markers and virtually no language variation is a result of and proves their common history. The majority of Comalapenses assume no problems ever existed.

Oral traditions of each town contain an autonomous history of their towns' establishment. However, the size and importance of Comalapa diminished as its communities began to break off into independent units. Many Comalapenses lament the loss of their vast land and valuable resources to territorial divisions and encroachment. Kaqchikel assert that other surrounding towns, such as Santa Cruz Balanyá, were part of Comalapa before becoming independent.[140] In the 1960s, a Kaqchikel man from Comalapa named Edwardo Otsoy researched the Santa Cruz Balanya Catholic Church Archives and proved this aspect of their oral history.[141] None of Comalapa's prior communities, however, live as vividly in the memory of Comalapenses as Poaquil.

One of the ways in which Comalapa residents remember their former village is through a dance they perform each year for seven days. The participants dress in costumes representing the commoners (Kaqchikel), a wealthy landowner and his wife, who wear blonde wigs to represent the Spaniards, and the cows, who also dance. This dance tells the story of the towns' separation: the distance from Poaquil to Comalapa, the cows, the rich Spanish landowners who overburden the workers, Poaquil's independence, the death of the landowners, and the celebration of Kaqchikel victory.[142] The dance celebrates the victory of Maya over Spanish landowners, thus focusing attention away from internal strife between Kaqchikel of the two towns. Kaqchikel from Comalapa converted an internecine struggle to a class and ethnic conflict. The relevance of this history as expressed through the dance is the Kaqchikel's ability to overcome oppressive Ladinos.[143]

By 1890, residents of Comalapa had focused their energy on the struggles with Ladinos. Kaqchikel leaders of Comalapa complained to the national government about Ladino encroachment upon their land. They wrote, "The Ladinos are taking our properties. The government accord of July 14th [1889] left us in peace to work our lots that according to the aforementioned accord pertains to each of us, but it has not occurred this way."[144] These men pointed out that the law was supposed to treat everyone equally but that "without a doubt it gives more guarantees to the Ladinos than the naturales."[145] These Kaqchikel resented the favoritism that the local officials showered upon Ladinos. As a result, they resumed peaceful relations with their neighbors of Poaquil and turned their efforts to the pursuit of justice in a Ladino-dominated country.

Comalapan oral traditions also portray Kaqchikel-Ladino conflict in the circumstances that surround the execution of their leader. Oral traditions of Comalapa recount that Barrios killed Jun Tz'ikin, a local leader, but not in the context of the independence of Poaquil. A seventy-seven-year-old painter who portrays history through his art relates:

> Jun Tz'ikin was a very intelligent man who was mayor a long time ago. In those days there were always two mayors: one Ladino and one indigenous man. When Barrios arrived here after he won the revolution, he asked the Ladino mayor who was the smartest man in town. The Ladino replied that Jun Tz'ikin was extremely intelligent, he knew Spanish and tried to help his people. Barrios went to the home of Jun Tz'ikin, asked him many questions, and ordered his soldiers to take him to the hill called María Pan Ul to have him killed. Barrios killed him because he was intelligent and he did not want intelligent Indians around.[146]

Likewise, the eighty-three-year-old grandson of the man Barrios executed asserts that Barrios killed his grandfather because he was a smart man who knew Spanish and therefore was a threat to local Ladinos.[147]

The motivations and circumstances surrounding Poaquil's independence vary significantly, even though some basic facts, including the time frame, are consistent among oral traditions of the two towns. While a few people from Comalapa express a certain amount of tension in the division of the two towns, most people believe that Poaquil gained its independence de facto without struggle or debate.[148] They also perceive that relations with Poaquil residents have always been positive, especially since the first inhabitants were originally from Comalapa. Archival evidence, however, indicates that oral traditions of Poaquilenos more accurately capture the essence of relations between the two towns.

Poaquil's independence had a greater impact on oral histories of Poaquilenos than on oral histories of Comalapenses. One reason historical perspectives surrounding Poaquil's independence are distinct is because Comalapa has its own oral accounts of its birth. Versions from Poaquil and Comalapa, combined with the archival evidence, show that historical veracity has been preserved in oral traditions of both towns but that Comalapa's version omits some circumstances. Poaquilenos feel a greater sense of ownership, and therefore a stronger penchant for detail, than those from Comalapa. Poaquilenos actively participated in the independence movement, whereas Comalapenses had a more passive role. Furthermore, Poaquil was the winner in a valuable battle: one over land and community. Thus the Poaquilenos' struggle to become independent plays a dominant role in their oral histories and their collective identity. In oral histories, as with written history, victors control historical perceptions. Comalapa had lost much of its territory and communities over the years, but oral traditions do not focus on any one village.

People from Poaquil like to point out that since they founded the town after the Spanish arrival, they were never "conquered" and do not suffer from a strong Spanish or Ladino influence. According to Poaquilenos, they feel a stronger sense of sovereignty over their municipality than other towns, such as Comalapa, whose residents had to deal with the influence of "foreigners" and their oppressive actions.[149] The town monograph also highlights that historically Poaquil has been free of Spanish or Ladino control. Poaquilenos do not maintain an air of superiority over Comalapenses; they are simply proud because they avoided Ladino domination. This interpretation resonates with oral histories of Comalapa that express the evil of the Ladino society that kills Maya simply because they are intelligent and therefore a threat. Barrios's order to execute Jun Tz'ikin represents the *kaxlan,* or foreigners' attempt to eradicate all that is good about Mayan culture and identity. When Kaqchikel from Comalapa dance and celebrate their victory over Spanish landowners and Ladinos, they are achieving one of their goals: to distance themselves and defend themselves from the malevolent behavior of tyrannical Ladino leaders. In this way, the collective identities and worldviews of Comalapa and Poaquil residents are similar. Poaquil defined and constructed its town after the Spanish arrival and even after Guatemala's independence from Spain; hence, Poaquil's inhabitants are not associated with this source of evil and maintain a more autochthonous approach to their local history. The oral histories are different, but the lessons they teach are the same. The lessons contribute to the worldviews that Kaqchikel from Comalapa and Poaquil share. These related worldviews form a bond that leads to a common collective identity strengthened by the interdependence of the two towns.

Meq'en Ya, San Antonio Aguas Calientes, and *Katal,* Santa Catarina Barahona

Oral accounts of the establishment of Aguas Calientes and Barahona, two adjoining Kaqchikel towns in the Quinizilapa Valley, in the department of Sacatepéquez, provide an interesting comparison to the Poaquil-Comalapa accounts. An antagonistic relationship and rivalry between the two towns has persisted throughout their history, especially over the issue of water. Despite past and current disagreements, the oral histories of these towns express similar origin. For the most part, oral histories agree with Ladino and Western researchers' accounts. They diverge significantly only when Barahona insists the community was present before the Spanish arrived in the area.

Origin stories of Aguas Calientes maintain that their ancestors lived in a canyon in another region but moved and settled in the town's current location. Ix'ey, one of the most respected members of the community (due to her crucial role in the establishment of one of the first schools in the community), provides one version of the town's origin:

The first people came from a canyon named Verapaz.[150] They came here in search of a new place to make their town and asked the mayor of Santa Catarina Barahona for permission to rent some land to set up their community while they looked for a permanent spot. The mayor granted them their request. The land was attractive because it was flat and fertile. The people from Verapaz did not look for another spot and simply settled there. When the community first arrived, they renamed their village San Bartolo and later changed it to Las Milpas de Juan [Juan's corn crops]. However, the true owner of the land was a Spaniard named Antonio Sanchez who gave them the land. To honor this owner they named the town San Antonio Aguas Calientes. Aguas Calientes derives from the nearby hot springs and the fact that previously there were hot springs in the town itself. At the same time, they changed their patron saint from San Francisco to San Antonio. Unfortunately, soon after their arrival, the Spanish forces abused and enslaved Kaqchikel. The Spanish later forced the towns of Santa Catarina Barahona and San Antonio Aguas Calientes to unite into one entity, and there have been problems ever since.[151]

Ix'ey recognizes that Barahona was the first pueblo established and that the history of Aguas Calientes is more recent.

A number of Kaqchikel from Aguas Calientes add that one of the reasons their forebears left their original location of Verapaz was that coyotes and/or tigers were attacking their chickens and even the people. The dangers these animals presented forced people to resettle in San Bartolo, about two kilometers from the valley where they now reside.[152] In oral accounts, the date of the migration ranged from the early 1500s to the 1700s. Remnants from the walled structure that surrounded the town are located at the site of San Bartolo. Informants state that the people looked for a place with level land that would be amenable to farming. At first it was just a village and had not yet gained town status.[153] One man claimed that the first people came from a nearby village called San Andrés Ceballos (the current location of the hot springs), and another says they came from Chichicastenango.[154] The majority recognize Verapaz as their place of origin. In all of these accounts, the interviewees recognize that the Spanish were in the area when the people descended from San Bartolo, but the current residents emphasize that the founders of the town were of Kaqchikel descent. The Spanish landowner simply gave them the land.

Ladino and Western accounts support most aspects of these oral traditions. In her master's thesis, Ligia Archila Serrano says that according to "popular tradition," the community began in Verapaz. Later they changed the name to San Bartolo, but in the mid-1530s they abandoned that site. They then moved to where the town is now situated ("La milpa de Juan Chávez"), where a Spanish man named Antonio lived, and that is where the name of the town originates.[155] A monograph about Aguas Calientes states the town was founded in 1530.[156] In the *Diccionario Geográfico de Guatemala,* Gall notes that in 1571 Aguas Calientes was called "The cornfields of Juan Chávez."[157] The most accurate secondary source for the history of these two towns comes from historian Christopher Lutz. Using documents from the archives in Guatemala City, he found that Juan de Chávez founded Aguas Calientes around 1530 and that the "Indians were slaves." Chávez ceded the lands of the milpa to his former slaves in 1550.[158]

Kaqchikel of Barahona recount a similar history of the birth of their town and the Spanish presence. They insist that Kaqchikel settled in the area well before the Spanish arrived. An important issue for the inhabitants of Barahona is that they were the first ones in the Quinizilapa Valley and allowed Aguas Calientes to form a neighboring town by indefinitely "lending" land. According to people from Barahona, the problems with Aguas Calientes arose and continue because they want too much and are never satisfied with the resources Barahona has already shared. In Barahona's view, Spaniards and Kaqchikel from Aguas Calientes abused them.

People from Barahona feel a powerful sense of ownership over the land and its resources. Jun Tojil, a teacher who has worked with the Kaqchikel language and history, shares a well-developed story that elders of the community taught him:

> Originally there were only three people here in this predominantly farming village. One was a woman named Katal from whom the Kaqchikel name for the town is derived. When the Spanish came they changed everything. They forced our people to work for them, and eventually changed the character of our people and slowly the children became more like the Spanish.[159] Sánchez de Barahona, one of Pedro de Alvarado's soldiers, came to the town between 1521 and 1524 and imposed the Spanish ways on our people. That is why the town carries the name Barahona. At this point San Antonio Aguas Calientes did not exist. The land was always part of Santa Catarina Barahona, but then a group of people came from the mountain because the coyotes chased them away. In 1718 this group from San Bartolomé asked the mayor for permission to construct their own town. So now they are the owners of San Antonio Aguas Calientes. While they have a larger population, they have less land than us.[160]

Some of the major issues between the two towns are land and water, but according to Jun Tojil, Aguas Calientes also intercepted money from Spain intended to fix the colonial church in Barahona. He claimed Aguas Calientes used the money to build a school in their own community and said that Barahona did not exist.[161]

Other Barahona oral accounts of the establishment of Barahona and Aguas Calientes contain these same elements, though some variations and additions persist. Some mention that before the Spanish arrived the center of town was a cemetery and that occasionally people still find bones there.[162] For them, the cemetery proves that Kaqchikel arrived before Spaniards did, as generations had already been buried there. Informants note that Kaqchikel did not operate a school in the community prior to the Spanish arrival, so the Spanish established one.[163] Archival evidence confirms the Spanish construction of a school in Barahona. In a pastoral visit between 1768 and 1770, the archbishop observed that there was no school in Barahona so he ordered that a teacher be put there to teach "the doctrine."[164] Informants say the school exposed Kaqchikel children to Spanish ways and emphasize that the Spanish forced their ancestors to construct the buildings and perform other services.[165] Western scholars concur and note that one of the Spanish strategies for increased wealth was to force Maya to work in their newly usurped agricultural estates.[166]

Kab'lajuj Kan, a seventy-year-old farmer and member of a cofradía who learned of this history from his grandparents, relates a different version of the founding of Barahona:

> Barahona was the first town here and originally inhabited by two tribes named Palax and Katal. They were the first people here and they settled in this specific area around 1400. These two groups mixed to form the community here. The first Spanish founder of Barahona was Ignacio Bobadillo in 1500, but Sanchez Barahona replaced him, hence the town name. Our ancestors made the roads and Spanish fountain in the center of town. The Maya did all the work here, but of course the Spanish took credit for creating the town. While the Spanish claim they founded the town, there were people here before they arrived, and those same people—the Maya—performed the manual labor necessary to develop this municipality. The people from Aguas Calientes descended from San Bartolomé to escape the tigers, and a man named Antonio was their representative. That is how the town derived its name.[167]

Kab'lajuj Kan also asserts that Kaqchikel from Barahona were the first inhabitants in the valley. He attests that the border between the two towns was not drawn until 1870, and then only because Barahona had water. Kab'lajuj Kan also emphasizes that the Spanish abused Kaqchikel through forced labor and that Aguas Calientes continued this abuse when they demanded more land and water than was originally awarded them.[168] Some Ladinos also recognize Spanish abuses. In a 1912 newspaper article about the department of Sacatepéquez, Victor Miguel Díaz eloquently describes the Spaniards' exploitation in Barahona: "Santa Catarina was founded by Ignacio Bobadilla [who] did not leave [them with] good memories because of his cruelty. One can say without exaggeration, that the Indians of Santa Catarina watered the lands of their ancestors with their tears."[169]

Western histories, however, contradict important aspects of Barahona's oral traditions. Lutz cites Sancho de Barahona as the founder around 1530 and asserts that people from Barahona came from different areas and were not just Kaqchikel.[170] Lutz cites a document that states indigenous people of Barahona "said they were *Oriundos* (those of the environs) of San Juan Chamelco, Utatlecas (Quichés), Atitlán (Tzutuhil), Chontales (Tabasco or Oaxaca) and Pipiles (Pacific coast of Guatemala)."[171] Lutz's sources challenge Kaqchikel assertions that they were the first inhabitants of Barahona.

A group of historical plaques in the town center contributes to the detailed accounts retold by the people of Barahona about their town. A monument built in 1943 states: "Santa Catarina Barahona, founded by Mr. Sancho Barahona, captain of Pedro Alvarado between years 1530–40." It also states that one of the principal buildings was the Catholic Church, dedicated to Santa Catarina. Despite these assertions, the pre-Spanish presence motif in oral histories remains strong. Another monument erected in December 1996 shows the importance residents of Barahona place on history: "To conserve the past, to construct the future, to make history . . . that is our reason for being."[172]

Another source of Barahona's history and identity is guarded in the municipal building: a document that defended Barahona in a land dispute with a nearby town called Parramos. It states, "When the Spanish conquerors came, Parramos and Santa Catarina were already towns, while San Andrés, San Antonio [Aguas Calientes], Santiago Zamora[173] . . . and Dueñas were raised and formed some years later. . . . [I]t is only good to justify those lands that are founded [before Spanish arrival], the other towns were from the Spanish conquerors."[174] The document recognizes Barahona as the first town in the area and, more importantly, that the Spanish formed other towns, not Barahona. According to the authors of this document, Barahona predates the arrival of the Spanish. For them, being founded by the Spanish negates some of a town's legitimate claims to land and resources. The document continues: "It appears that the said town of Santa Catarina Barahona is founded on the site and cornfields of Barahona where the source of water that bathes the entire town is [located]."[175] The documentation in the municipal office verifies oral accounts that the community existed prior to Spanish arrival and that Barahona was the Spaniard who assumed control of the area.

The most significant point of contention between the written and oral accounts is the recognition of an indigenous population in Barahona before the Spanish arrived. The Barahona municipal document and oral histories claim that Kaqchikel lived in Barahona before the Spanish invasion. Furthermore, pottery shards found in the valley indicate that the area was inhabited prior to Spanish arrival. However, colonial documents imply that the Spanish were the first to establish the towns of Aguas Calientes and Barahona.[176] While the debate continues among scholars, the assertion that the Spanish founded Barahona is dubious.

Kaqchikel have a strong sense of pride in their origins, and identification outside of the Spanish dominion is important. Residents of Barahona and Aguas Calientes had considerable interaction with Spaniards because they had to provide the food for the capital of Guatemala (Santiago de Guatemala), but these Kaqchikel continue to identify with a rich history independent of Spanish influence. In his study of Aguas Calientes, Sheldon Annis argues that Kaqchikel became the lingua franca because Kaqchikel had limited contact with Spaniards.[177] Oral traditions maintain that despite numerous Spanish intrusions upon their communities, Kaqchikel language, culture, and history have survived.[178]

Oral accounts refer to the homogeneous arrival of Kaqchikel in the area. Archival records indicate that the Spanish imported different indigenous people to Aguas Calientes and Barahona to form a pool of labor for their agricultural endeavors.[179] Some oral accounts recognize the influx of different language groups in the area.[180] Generally, when immigrants arrive in a new community they assimilate to the established language group even if the immigrants outnumber the original inhabitants. The dominance of the Kaqchikel language in the area strongly supports the assertion that Kaqchikel were the original inhabitants in the region.

Kaqchikel from Aguas Calientes are aware of a significant Spanish influence and presence from the point they arrived at their current home. At the same time, most residents of Aguas Calientes recognize that Barahona was the first town, settled before their arrival by a commander of the Spanish army, Barahona. Oral traditions recount that the Spanish formed the town as it is seen today. For example, they assert the Spanish constructed the church, albeit with unpaid Kaqchikel labor. Informants claim the local commander even drew the border between the two towns.[181] However, they also emphasize a history prior to Spanish contact and imply that it was more tranquil and productive. Unlike residents of Barahona, people of Aguas Calientes do not recall a period in the Valley of Quinizilapa without Spanish presence. This distinction adds to the tension between the towns because people of Barahona pride themselves on establishing the first community in the region.

People from Aguas Calientes also mention hostile relations with Barahona that resulted from the struggle over water. Residents of Aguas Calientes claim that Barahona continues to refuse them sufficient water despite its abundant water source. This disagreement has always been caustic, and years ago both sides prohibited intermarriages because of the water dilemma and other sources of discord.[182] In a 1948 anthropological study of Aguas Calientes, Antonio Goubaud Carrera recognized the ill feelings. He remarked that Aguas Calientes has good relations with all other towns except for Barahona: "On the contrary, the people of the municipality of Santa Catarina Barahona are held in lesser esteem by the neighbors of San Antonio Aguas Calientes for offensive disagreements over the lands which arose between the two towns."[183] Barahona's land document highlights that tense relations between the towns date to at least the 1700s, when a dispute arose over the ownership of the lake that borders Barahona and Aguas Calientes.[184] The document reveals: "The lake of Santa Catarina Barahona in actuality has remained in the hands of the Indians of San Antonio Aguas Calientes [who] only controlled it through fighting, and Santa Catarina Barahona has an appeal pending for this land inhabited by the Indians of San Antonio Aguas Calientes."[185]

Residents of Barahona emphasize antagonistic relations more than residents of Aguas Calientes do. A former Barahona mayor asserts that Aguas Calientes became a town in the 1700s, two centuries after Barahona, and that the original people were from Comalapa, Itzapa, the coast, and other areas. He insists they were from different "races," unlike Barahona, which contains a pure race. He added that Barahona has given Aguas Calientes free water since 1915, but they always want more.[186] The mayor's perception of history does not coincide with documentary evidence, but it strongly supports the collective identity of Barahona and the town's rivalry with Aguas Calientes. Others claim that people of San Bartolomé first came down to ask for lodging and, when the Barahona mayor obliged them, never left.[187] Barahona residents also point out that Aguas Calientes does not really have hot springs, implying that Aguas Calientes is not honest or that it portrays an attraction that no longer exists. People from Barahona insist that only San Andrés Ceballos has hot springs and that only it merits the name "Aguas Calientes."[188] Some women in a weaving cooperative, whose ages range from sixteen to sixty, claim that Aguas Calientes never had hot springs and also angrily accuse Aguas Calientes of stealing their potential customers.[189] People in Aguas Calientes do not boast of hot springs today, but their oral accounts say that a long time ago hot springs there inspired the name of the town.[190] A letter dated July 12, 1586, supports this assertion: in it the author notes that Aguas Calientes had a fountain of hot water in which the Spanish and Indians bathed.[191] Other informants from Aguas Calientes say that the Aguas Calientes name came from the presence of hot springs in the neighboring village of San Andrés Ceballos.[192] The derivation of the Aguas Calientes name and its authenticity are not important to the people of Aguas Calientes. For people from Barahona, however, the hot springs issue provides proof that the people of Aguas Calientes are deceptive and conniving.

Despite tensions, oral traditions of Barahona and Aguas Calientes support each other in most aspects and vary mostly in what people choose to emphasize. Both sides recognize Sancho de Barahona as the Spanish founder of Barahona. All recognize Barahona as the first town. All agree that the people of Aguas Calientes came from another area to form their town with land that Barahona donated to them. People from Aguas Calientes recount more of the journey and details about their formation of the town, while those from Barahona simply state that the forebears of Aguas Calientes came down from the hills for fear of wild animals and that the mayor gave them a place to stay. Kaqchikel inhabitants of Barahona are proud that they lived in the Quinizilapa Valley before the Spanish arrived. This autochthonous claim is an important part of their identity, and oral accounts from Aguas Calientes do not challenge this point. Naturally, the Aguas Calientes and Barahona ownership of these histories results in a different emphasis. The basic events, however, are consistent and therefore support their veracity.

The most significant divergence in the oral accounts surrounds the issue of water. Barahona residents see themselves as generous and those of Aguas Calientes as unappreciative, while Kaqchikel of Aguas Calientes accuse Barahona residents of acting selfishly. People from Barahona portray this antagonism in their oral traditions with accounts about the usurpation of loaned land, intercepted aid, ownership of the lake, and the misnomer of the hot springs. While the tension is not as intense today, and intermarriage between the towns is common, oral traditions of both towns emphasize persistent inimical relations. They also stress Spanish abuse of Kaqchikel. A harmonious relationship based on camaraderie between the two towns is unlikely to develop. The towns are united geographically by land and socially by language, but divisive fissures exist. A common linguistic group does not necessitate a united polity.

Conclusion

Kaqchikel have a strong connection to their origins because these origins are alive in their present world. Their histories provide an unbroken sense of being that constitute who they are. As the committee of one rural village thirteen kilometers from Comalapa explains, "It is important to know one's origin. Our ancestors had a great deal of knowledge that they did not write down, but we must always maintain our orientation."[193] These men value the lifestyle, struggles, and lessons of their predecessors. Kaqchikel are aware that since the *Anales* no book records the wisdom of their ancestors. Ladino accounts fail to capture the basics, and certainly the essence, of their forebears' lives. One member of the committee criticizes Fuentes y Guzmán:

"Fuentes y Guzmán did not get it right, at least for our people. He did not find out about our reality, land, work, or life."[194]

Kaqchikel are proud that their ancestors founded their communities. It is through their communities that they maintain ties to their forebears and history. What makes a community proud and legitimate is existing as a cohesive social organization independent of Spanish influence. For example, for residents of Aguas Calientes, an integral part of their identity is that their community in Verapaz was free from Spanish contact. Consequently, that they were not the original residents of their current location or that Spaniards may have played a role in forming the town does not detract from their identity as Maya and Kaqchikel. The same is true in Tecpán, where Kaqchikel recognize that Spaniards forced them to build the town; their pride and identity emanate from their intimate connection to their capital, Iximche'. Kaqchikel have been resilient in maintaining social cohesion despite physical displacement. They connect to the history of their community as people and/or place and keep it alive to legitimize their identity as Kaqchikel and Maya and therefore as the original inhabitants of Guatemala.

Oral histories are enriched with more detail than Ladino written accounts. They emphasize how Kaqchikel established their communities prior to the Spanish arrival and how they reacted valiantly to the intrusion. Kaqchikel do not say that Iximche' is merely ruins or part of a past civilization, as many Ladino accounts claim. Rather, the original inhabitants of Iximche' continue to influence Kaqchikel. Today, Mayan priests perform ceremonies at sacred spots in Iximche' to solicit the blessings, advice, and help of their ancestors. A coalition of Mayan priests convinced the Ministry of Sports and Culture to declare the back courtyard at Iximche' a sacred precinct, preserved for traditional observance. An unequivocal sense of the importance and beauty of the town that their ancestors established and inhabited permeates their oral traditions. Kaqchikel oral traditions of Iximche' are more acute in Tecpán than in other Kaqchikel towns, as a result of Tecpán's proximity to Iximche'. Nonetheless, residents of other towns understand its significance for their people and express pride in its being the Kaqchikel capital and first capital of Guatemala. In contrast, Ladinos are aware of the praiseworthy and productive living conditions at Iximche' prior to Spanish arrival but do not relate these idyllic conditions to the present. Most historians tend to glorify a former Mayan tribe extinguished by the Spanish and downplay the role of their descendants in last five hundred years of Guatemala's national history. They perceive the modern descendants as poor indigenous people, not Mayan in the sense of belonging to a brilliant culture.[195]

One reason for the dichotomy between Kaqchikel and Ladino historical perspectives is the nature of historical method. A written history will never die, so consequently many events not essential to the worldviews or reality of people may be recorded. In contrast, oral traditions can potentially die with each generation. Therefore, only events, characters, and trends that are contemporaneously relevant are recorded and transferred between generations. Oral histories do not have the luxury of recording extraneous or irrelevant material. The circumstances and leaders surrounding Iximche' live on in oral traditions because the tranquility, respect, and omniscience of their ancestors are continuously sought after and utilized today by Kaqchikel.

Inherent in town origin stories are the abusive and exploitative conditions Spaniards imposed on Kaqchikel. Initial interactions between Spaniards and Kaqchikel initiated distrustful relations that have remained part of oral traditions for more than five hundred years. Oral traditions recount that the first Spaniards killed their leaders, pillaged their goods, destroyed their capital, displaced them (in some cases), exploited them as a labor source, and imposed a new religion. Forced labor systems abound in Kaqchikel oral traditions. Kaqchikel benefit from the work of their ancestors because they reside in these towns; however, they do not forget the evils of the system. They resent that relations were not more egalitarian. For example, Kaqchikel had to learn Spanish, but few Spaniards attempted to learn Kaqchikel. Spaniards also attempted to inculcate Kaqchikel through schools and Catholicism. Spanish incursions were so traumatic that they virtually erased from oral traditions the struggles that Kaqchikel had with K'ichee' and other Mayan groups prior to Spanish arrival. The *Anales* describes caustic relations and battles with K'ichee', but oral traditions focus their animosity and mistrust on Spaniards. The theme of Spanish and Ladino desires to extirpate Guatemala's Mayan population permeates Kaqchikel history. Oral traditions apply this lesson to their current reality to ensure that Kaqchikel are cautious about potentially exploitative interaction with Ladinos who seek to change their Kaqchikel worldviews and lifestyle. Ideally, as in the case of Poaquil, Kaqchikel can minimize interaction with Ladinos.

Oral traditions imply that Spaniards could not themselves have produced the riches that Kaqchikel created. Spaniards did not possess the capacity to produce the beauty and wealth of Iximche' or Paminix. Consequently, they resorted to force and deception in order to plunder the resources and talents of Kaqchikel. Kaqchikel ancestors used their superior intelligence and talents to produce beautiful images of their society that subsequently appealed to Spaniards. When Spaniards coveted and stole these items, Kaqchikel maintained their sense of honor and dignity. Kaqchikel did not want to compromise themselves or descend to the Spanish level of debasement. Even Ladino attempts to defile the image of Tekun as ignorant did not affect Kaqchikel perceptions of their own intellect. While Kaqchikel incorporated the story of Tekun's failure to distinguish between a horse and a man into their oral traditions, they remember Tekun as a powerful, cerebral leader who fought heroically against insurmountable odds. Kaqchikel remain a proud people despite Spanish attempts to destroy their community and character.

Conflict with Spaniards is a central theme, but oral histories also recognize rivalries among Kaqchikel. Disputes between Poaquil and Comalapa over land and community led to the division of the towns. At the time, both groups harbored ill feelings and felt betrayed and abused by the other. Nonetheless, the important result for both groups is that eventually peaceful, productive, and benevolent relations developed between the towns. Their oral traditions emphasize the polarization of Kaqchikel and Ladinos, not internecine struggles. Kaqchikel do not trust Ladinos, but they are confident they can overcome the obstacles they construct. Oral traditions surrounding Poaquil's secession are distinct in Poaquil and Comalapa, but the lesson remains analogous and reinforces their shared worldviews.

Oral traditions also show that historical animosity among Kaqchikel can lead to insuperable tensions. While Comalapa and Poaquil have restored fraternal relations, Aguas Calientes and Barahona continue to suffer from a tumultuous interdependency. Disagreements over natural resources (land and water) dating back hundreds of years continue today. Relations also remain tense because of issues ranging from tourists to outside funding. Poaquil and Comalapa have congenial relations because they resolved their disputes, but relations between Barahona and Aguas Calientes are tense because these towns failed to settle their historical differences.[196] Oral traditions reveal a less than united linguistic group.

Oral traditions conveyed by Kaqchikel illustrate a great understanding and pride in the Kaqchikel history, a history less contingent upon Spanish actors and events than histories by Ladinos. Alvarado measured his success partly by the riches he carried back to Spain. Much of Guatemala's development, however, can be attributed to Kaqchikel physical and mental capacity. Oral traditions emphasize Kaqchikel contributions, whereas Ladino works circumvent Kaqchikel impact on Guatemalan history. Kaqchikel do not exclude Spaniards from their history; rather, they emphasize what they consider more important and are more knowledgeable about—their own society. Their perspectives emphasize a society focused on daily living through agriculture, interpersonal relationships, and an appreciation and cohabitation with the environment, not a culture based on conquests and battles.

Town origin stories provide a sense of grounding and teach valuable lessons. Each town formation highlights the success Kaqchikel ancestors achieved through hard work and intelligence. Even in communities where Kaqchikel were not free to make their own decisions, such as Aguas Calientes, the towns were built by Kaqchikel muscle and sweat. In other cases, such as Poaquil and Comalapa, Kaqchikel contributed both mental and physical resources to the towns' development. While Tecpán was built under Spanish direction, the pride of the town focuses on Iximche', a community built independently of Spanish contact. Town origin stories exemplify the creative capacity of Kaqchikel.

Kaqchikel recognize Spanish malevolences but do not allow them to dominate their oral traditions. Alvarado is the only Spanish conqueror whom Kaqchikel distinguish. Kaqchikel forgot other actors, such as Portocarrero, who led the military expedition to Comalapa. Residents of the town of Barahona identify Sancho de Barahona because his name survives in the town name, and his bust remains in the town center with a small plaque depicting his local importance. Even in their town, however, the focus of oral histories is that Kaqchikel constructed the church and water fountain which remain an integral part of the community. Oral traditions focus on Kaqchikel, not Spanish or Ladino contributions to local and national history.

Oral traditions prove that Spanish and Ladino attempts to force Kaqchikel to acculturate into national culture have been unsuccessful. The Spanish slowly imposed the privatization of land. Kaqchikel always had held land communally but over time conceded it to the Spanish system. Kaqchikel adapted to some intrusions but in many aspects did not forfeit their identity and lifestyle. As a result, Spaniards did not indoctrinate or subdue Kaqchikel as effectively as they had hoped. Kaqchikel found ways to coexist with Spaniards and maintain a strong connection to their communities. Oral histories project Kaqchikel ancestors as strong, intelligent, and diligent and keep vital the stories surrounding the original communities. For Kaqchikel, identity is integrally related to their ancestors and community, and they have been remarkably resourceful in maintaining their autochthonous identity despite five hundred years of overt and covert policies of forced assimilation. Land and labor are central to Kaqchikel identity, and Spaniards and Ladinos have attempted to usurp both. The next chapter will examine how Kaqchikel strategies have varied between resisting and adapting to intrusions on their approaches to land and labor.

2
Land, Labor, and Integration

Ri rach'ulew rik'in ri samaj

Kaqchikel are teachers, office employees, artisans, tradesmen, and factory workers, but in general their work is tied to the land. Kaqchikel oral histories record a period when the land no longer supported its population. Because people could not produce enough food to support their families, men migrated to the Pacific coast in search of employment. Often they contracted with intermediaries known as *contratistas* (often Kaqchikel themselves) to find work on one of the large agricultural plantations.[1] Once chemical fertilizer was available to them, Kaqchikel farmers could stay on their own land. Using chemical fertilizer increased production but was not totally beneficial. It is expensive and has had an adverse effect on the land and public health. Because the majority of Kaqchikel are agriculturists with a holistic approach to farming, the need to search for work outside their communities and employ chemical fertilizer significantly changed Kaqchikel communities.

The Kaqchikel relationship with land and labor is central to Kaqchikel culture. They consider land sacred. Before beginning a cycle of work in the fields, they make an offering to the *rajawal* (spirit of the land) and ask the spirit's permission to use the land. Agriculture is such an important part of their lives that their year is based on the cycle of planting and harvesting corn. Corn not only provides the main sustenance for their diet but also has a religious importance. Even Kaqchikel professionals who work in Guatemala City or other areas outside their communities insist on planting corn on a small plot of land in their communities to maintain their connection to the rajawal.

Kaqchikel oral histories recall that prior to President Barrios's reign, most Kaqchikel held land communally. Kaqchikel point out that in some cases a party interested in utilizing the land had to ask permission from the municipality, but they say this was never a problem. One elder claims, "Before Barrios, you could build a house and farm where you wanted as long as it was not otherwise occupied or claimed because there was no owner of the land. No markers or borders existed, so Barrios authorized written registers for properties."[2] Generally, oral accounts depict an idealized notion of land usage prior to the onset of liberal reforms in the late nineteenth century, whereas in practice not all land was held communally and many tracts had well-defined boundary markers. As Hill points out, landholding during the colonial period was complex, and competition for land between Spanish and Kaqchikel and among Kaqchikel grew as time passed. Maya had to employ a number of different strategies to maintain access to their land. Nonetheless, Hill notes, both Spanish and Mayan systems allowed for the occupation and use of unoccupied land as long as the individual(s) did not leave the land idle.[3] For the most part, however, Maya, especially in the western highlands, lived in the mountains and valleys and farmed land originally possessed by their ancestors. As late as the mid–nineteenth century more than one thousand villages controlled and farmed over 70 percent of Guatemala's best agricultural land. Scholars argue this was the case until Barrios's liberal government accelerated the long process (which began under previous conservative regimes) that weakened Mayan resistance to incursion upon their culture and means of production.[4]

After 1870, the development of coffee-export production greatly increased the demand for Mayan labor and land. At the same time, between 1871 and 1940 Guatemala suffered repeated corn shortages. One reason for these food shortages is that by the late nineteenth century the Mayan population began growing significantly. This population growth, partially due to increased access to and improved Western medicine, was especially dramatic in the middle third of the twentieth century. Some communities complained they no longer had enough land to support their populations. In sum, liberal policies designed to foment coffee exports, combined with population growth and decreased agricultural productivity, made Maya more dependent on the cash economy.[5]

The goal of liberal governments was twofold: to aid agricultural entrepreneurs and force Maya to become "productive" contributors to national progress. Barrios made these aims clear:

The President fully understands that if agriculturists are forced to depend solely upon their own resources, without the active cooperation of the Government, the negligence of the Indian classes, who are so prone to deceit, will wreck and abort all agricultural undertakings and will doom the economic development of the country. . . . The only way to improve the situation of the Indians, to bring them out of the state of misery and abject poverty in which they live, is to create needs for them by putting them in continuous contact with the Ladino classes, and to accustom them to work so that they will become a useful and productive force in agriculture.[6]

The state helped landowners find Mayan labor. The loss of Mayan communally and privately held land made subsistence farming less viable and forced many Maya to work outside their communities. In addition, Barrios sent Ladino settlers into Mayan communities to usurp their lands. Liberal leaders knew that few Maya could write, or even speak, Spanish and that they would therefore be unable to register their lands. As a result, communities lost some of their most productive landholdings, and many became victims of debt peonage on Ladino-owned plantations.[7] This phenomenon explains the importance Maya place on Spanish literacy as a means to maintain control over their land and labor.

The decrees and regulations established during the Barrios regime provided the means for commercial agriculturists to quickly acquire inexpensive land. When residents could not produce legal title documents for their land, the government sold it at a low cost to coffee planters. Carmack claims the government expropriated nearly all the fertile land from Maya during the Barrios regime.[8] Historian Jim Handy estimates that in the first year the government registered 23,427 lots. Furthermore, from 1871 to 1883 the government sold about 972,290 acres of common land. Handy states that "the result was a cataclysmic alteration of village land structure."[9] The law not only robbed rural inhabitants of their land but also forced them to work for large landowners in export production because their livelihood had been undermined.[10]

Kaqchikel recognize that many people lost land due to these policies. Generally, those who had enough money and knew how to speak, read, and write Spanish could take advantage of the land titles and acquire land. One farmer states, as he proudly handles his machete, "You could buy a *manzana* of land for a peso, so men with money could buy a lot of land because there was no owner when Barrios divided it."[11] Informants attest that in Kaqchikel towns Ladinos were able to buy much of the communally held land as a result of Barrios's land registration law. They traced their borders and established *fincas* (large, landed estates). Oral histories assert, however, that Ladinos eventually sold their land because they did not like to farm. Many Kaqchikel lament that Barrios gave the best land to foreigners. They cite the evidence of foreign control of the rich agricultural land on the coast as an example. They point out that many Germans acquired land in this manner. Some Kaqchikel opine that today most poor villages are located in the mountains and valleys instead of in plain areas because foreigners took the best land. They argue that Barrios excluded the poor from Guatemala's rich land resources.[12]

Kaqchikel preserve oral histories that emphasize how Barrios discriminated against Maya when he distributed land. They claim he used land to reward people who were loyal to him. Comalapenses recount that Barrios needed soldiers for his liberal revolution and knew that Ladinos from the northern coast of Guatemala liked to fight. He enlisted their services and, for helping him in the 1871 revolution, awarded them the land that now makes up the town of Zaragoza. This land had been part of Comalapa, and Comalapenses lament this loss, asserting that Barrios favored Ladinos in his land-distribution policies.[13] A document in the AGCA confirms that Barrios formed the town of Zaragoza when he gave a large tract of Comalapa's land to Ladinos who had assisted him in his liberal revolution of 1871.[14] This action was not exceptional. Barrios's government encouraged the resettlement of Ladinos into the western highlands to displace Mayan labor. Furthermore, local officials often forced residents to part with their land so Ladinos could have it. In 1890 Kaqchikel leaders in Comalapa complained that "the governor of Chimaltenango required us to gratuitously give forty-six manzanas of land known as 'el sachol' for the redistribution among Ladinos."[15] At all levels, the government helped Ladinos take land from Kaqchikel.

Kaqchikel oral traditions also portray Barrios as a president who did not hold the same respect for land as Maya have. They note he gave Guatemala's western territory to Mexico in exchange for arms for his military revolution; many claim he did not even need the arms but gave away the land for his own wealth.[16] B'eleje' Ey expresses with disbelief Barrios's sacrifice of land: "Barrios was a very difficult man. He took a large tract of land, including Chiapas, which belonged to Guatemala and gave it to Mexico for arms. We were not even involved in a war at the time. There was no reason to do it. He just gave away the land. He and his men got rich while the rest of us stayed poor."[17]

Maya did not always view the formalization of land ownership as an attack on their rights. Barrios selectively took action against Mayan communities and offered concessions to some. Governments and large landholders had been encroaching upon Mayan lands since the Spanish invasion. Prior to the Barrios regime, most Maya had no written record to prove their dominion over the land. In Poaquil, until Barrios's time, "The *ejidos* [common public land] had pertained to the indigenous community of this town without title."[18] The town had no legal proof, other than oral accounts, of the ownership of their land. Some Kaqchikel invited formalization of land ownership and became frustrated when the "legalization" of their land was delayed.

They stated that "the government accord of June 3 has induced in us the desire to acquire the respective document for our urban sites."[19] They viewed land titles as a way to ensure their control and ownership over land their families had worked for generations. Kaqchikel were willing to cede their traditional method of landholding for the security of land titles. When Barrios granted the residents of Poaquil independence, he "prevented them from farming the land communally, as they had always done,"[20] but they gained the guarantee of inalienable land rights. Today, families guard their land titles as proof of their land rights and ownership.[21]

Despite Barrios's discriminatory practices and distinct perspective on land, most Kaqchikel laud his efforts to assign land titles because they provided protection for their landholdings. A local barber asserts that land could support the small population prior to Barrios but that as the population grew and land became scarce, land titles were essential to maintaining social order and peace.[22] Poaquilenos and other Kaqchikel claim Barrios helped Maya maintain their land and in some cases even gave land to them. Residents of Poaquil fondly remember him for the allotment of their municipal land. Some people claim he was a good president because he organized registration for land titles. They assert that once he implemented this order, haphazard land claims subsided. They say land titles meant people could be secure in their land ownership, whereas before Barrios anyone could encroach upon any settled land.[23] One agriculturist points out that "Barrios did a good job because a long time ago the land had no owners. . . . Barrios gave security to families and their land. He had a good idea and did it well."[24] According to most Kaqchikel, Barrios's system guaranteed land ownership and thereby reduced land disputes. One man pointed out that the move to private ownership resulted in a decline in the number of people who hunted. Consequently, wildlife could recover because people did not hunt on private land.[25] Land ownership brought about a sense of tranquility and order.

Kaqchikel realize that Barrios's land reform was not simply a way to establish private ownership of the land, however. He wanted to ensure a large labor force for entrepreneurial *finqueros* (owners of large, landed estates). Oxi' Ajpu', whose community is connected to Comalapa by a fourteen-kilometer footpath that traverses mountains and rivers, explains Barrios's goals:

> In his liberal reforms, Barrios amplified the land available with a law called *Adquisición de las tierras osiosos* [Acquisition of idle lands]. A long time ago, there were no owners of the land, just open land. When Barrios came here there were *criollos* and coffee planters so the government gave them one hundred *cuerdas* that they could work. He wanted to

increase the production of coffee by using the manual labor of the indigenous people. He gave them more free labor. He made a law that said those who owned land had to work sixty days on the coast and those who owned no land had to work ninety days on the coast. You had to carry a work card and show you did your required work. The history books focus on his development of the railroad, but they do not talk about how he robbed our land. He did not help the Maya.[26]

Oxi' Ajpu' argues that through the usurpation of Mayan lands Barrios forced people to earn their livelihood elsewhere and did not attempt to improve their plight. Barrios's program to export coffee directly affected Maya, but they did not benefit from the profits. In addition, Maya had to transport goods to the ports, build roads, and contribute labor and/or monies to other public projects.

The liberal governments that began with Barrios and ended with Ubico's downfall in 1944 ensured a plantation workforce through forced labor, legalized debt peonage, imprisonment, fines, and vagrancy laws. Landowners literally exhausted this human resource. The highlands provided 78 percent of the total workforce in the coffee, sugar, and cotton plantations. In 1937, the governor of Chimaltenango reported that finqueros "did not suffer from a lack of manual laborers."[27] While cotton plantations paid better wages, the working conditions were worse than on the coffee and sugar plantations.[28]

Kaqchikel oral traditions are full of travails of working on the coast, but most do not recognize a causal relationship with forced labor mechanisms; rather, they attest that climatic conditions and population pressure motivated Kaqchikel migration to the coast. Oral traditions recount that when the land could no longer support the growing population, and economic opportunities in Kaqchikel communities were minimal, especially in the early twentieth century, Kaqchikel looked for outside sources of livelihood. While the need for coastal employment has decreased, some areas still suffer a significant seasonal exodus. Ka'i' Imox, an eighty-two-year-old rural farmer, states, "Men who do not have any land suffer."[29] Kaqchikel say the landless invariably lacked food and needed to escape the onset of famine. Informants said the majority of people migrated from September until Christmas but that some had to return to the coast in January. According to oral accounts, if Kaqchikel could have earned their living without coastal migration they would not have left, but they were always in search of ways to support their families.[30]

In some areas during harvest season entire villages would be abandoned by all but the old and infirm as families migrated to the coast. In 1937 the governor of Chimaltenango reported that a few people stayed behind to farm their own land or work for large agriculturists in the department but noted that the majority of residents traveled to the coast to work in fincas, to the detriment of their harvests at home. Some men did not farm all of their land.[31] The artificially maintained low wages on fincas resulted in a decrease in the rural standard of living, despite the prosperity of coffee production.[32]

Migration to the coast remains significant in some communities. Poaquil's most intense coastal labor period was in the 1970s.[33] Some Kaqchikel estimate that today in Poaquil as much as 60 percent of the population, generally the poor and landless, migrate to the coast.[34] The Poaquil health center monograph states: "During the summer, due to a lack of [employment] activity approximately 40 percent of the manual laborers emigrate seasonally to the coast to take advantage of the cutting of cotton and coffee. It is affirmed that 95 percent of the agriculturists that go to cut on the coast work to pay for their fertilizers or money that has been lent to them for the purchase of those goods. The salaries paid the agricultural peon fluctuate between 1.50 and 2.00 quetzals daily."[35] In the 1970s, nearly half the Kaqchikel population in Poaquil had to migrate to the coast because of a dearth in labor opportunities in their community. This migration reflected a nationwide trend: in 1970 municipal functionaries estimated that 60 percent of the Mayan population had to migrate to the coast in search of employment. The increasing price of basic foodstuffs such as beans and corn was one reason behind the emigration. Furthermore, many people needed to earn money to pay for chemical fertilizer they employed in their local harvests. The 1973 international oil crisis resulted in higher oil prices and higher-priced fertilizer. Many families who had become accustomed to using chemical fertilizer could no longer afford it. Consequently, Maya with sufficient land and cash resources could avoid coastal migration, while less fortunate laborers continued to work on plantations.[36]

Temporal emigration to the coast still permeates all aspects of Kaqchikel lives. Kaqchikel lament that because families emigrate in September or October, children do not finish school.[37] According to the Poaquil health center monograph, "In some aldeas one observes the phenomenon of school absenteeism because of the migration of the parents to the coast. They register their children [for school] but do not allow them to conclude the school year. Consequently, the children need to repeat the school year, which they also fail to complete because they dedicate themselves to the farmwork with their parents. In the economic conditions in which they live, the earnings of all family members is necessary."[38] For some parents, children's contribution to the family income takes precedence over education. Consequently, coastal migration denies many children educational opportunities.

Because of the adverse effects of coastal migration, some Maya have creatively circumvented forced labor. In 1898 several Tecpanecos complained to the Ministry of Agriculture that the local authority forced them to migrate to the coast. The ministry supported these Kaqchikel men and ordered the authority to leave them "in peace" to plant crops in their community.[39] In some cases, the courts protected Maya against this abuse. Some have reacted to excessive labor demands with flight and physical resistance. They have escaped to the protection of the surrounding environs, other communities, and even across borders into Mexico and Belize.[40]

Kaqchikel oral histories relate that some Kaqchikel avoided the perils of plantation labor by providing auxiliary services to large plantations on the coast. Oral traditions recall that some Kaqchikel carried goods to the coast for trade and sale. Some people transported limestone on horseback and returned to their communities with sugar. Other accounts note that entrepreneurs established their own businesses on the coast. Kaqchikel point out that these merchants had greater control over their working conditions and earnings than migrant laborers.[41] The state never completely eradicated Mayan ability to maintain an independent livelihood. These governments failed to vanquish Mayan labor and property. Because Guatemala's export economy relied on seasonal migration, many Maya maintained their land and some basis for livelihood within their communities. Consequently, as scholars have noted, Maya became involved in the production of small commodities to provide goods to plantations and urban centers.[42]

Oral histories also explain how some Kaqchikel avoided coastal work altogether through the development of alternative forms of employment. In the mid–twentieth century, men began to paint and sell their art, and Kaqchikel women, who had been weaving for centuries, began to sell these textiles outside their communities and significantly contribute to family incomes. Men who worked on foot looms could also avoid coastal migration.[43] These sources of income allowed them to avoid some of the treacheries of coastal labor, assert their authority in their communities, and protect their culture.

Unfortunately, these opportunities were limited. Prior to the introduction of chemical additives, the majority of Maya worked seasonally on the coast. Kaqchikel employed on large coastal plantations worked in coffee, sugar, or cotton. According to oral accounts, the work on cotton and sugar plantations was the most strenuous. On coffee plantations, guanacaste trees provided shade and a respite from the burning sun. Kaqchikel note that landowners generally paid workers according to the number of boxes of coffee they picked.[44] Iximnik'te', a thirty-year-old teacher and linguist, shared her father's impressions: "My father always thanked God he did not have to go to the coast, but his friend went each year. The workers suffered. Some brought their families, but the children became sick with malaria or fever. The insects carry diseases. The houses only had tin roofs . . . no walls. People had to go because they had no house or land to farm here."[45]

Oral histories recount deplorable housing for laborers. Informants recall that people slept poorly and ate food of low quality and quantity; invariably, workers suffered from malnutrition. They say that workers often had to eat in the fields and that in some cases German owners denied them evening meals. On some days people did not eat at all. Kaqchikel note that migrants were aware of these conditions and knew to bring their own food. Additionally, Kaqchikel recall that overseers did not allow any rest days and explain how this exploitation, on top of the others, rapidly resulted in the loss of the laborers' strength.[46]

According to oral histories, the climate added to the discomfort of migrant workers because they were not accustomed to the heat and humidity of the coast and because the work generally occurred during the rainy season. It rained every day, and by the end of the season workers' clothes had virtually disintegrated.[47] As Ka'i' Imox explains, "I liked it [the coast] for one month, but then after a month you get really tired and lose your strength because of the heat."[48] Likewise, Kaqchikel of Santiago Sacatepéquez claimed that because they were acclimated to the highlands, the coast was "deadly" for them.[49] Other Kaqchikel assert that some people despised the working and living conditions so much that they returned home within a week.[50]

Kaqchikel oral histories recount the lack of food in their communities that necessitated some families' traveling together to the coast. Kaqchikel recall that the less fortunate ones had to walk. They assert that once they arrived conditions were especially hard on young children and lament that many times children also worked. In some instances, they fell ill and died.[51] Children were not the only ones susceptible to disease, however.

Oral histories depict how vector insects and the change in climate quickly attacked Kaqchikel immune systems. Kaqchikel note that some people were afraid to go to the coast because of the germs and fatal diseases that mosquitoes, ants, and other insects carried. They lament that many people returned from the coast with malaria and lice. Oral traditions recount that Kaqchikel were also susceptible to high fevers. Informants note that some men in Comalapa formed a team to cure those who returned from the coast infected with malaria. Kaqchikel recall that migrants often used money they earned on the coast to cure themselves when they returned to their communities.[52] In 1931 the government reported an outbreak of malaria on the coast and noted that migrant workers were especially susceptible to the disease. Dr. Luis Gaitán reported that "individuals from the highlands on the coast have been dismantled by the effects [of malaria] without the provision by the land-owners of adequate means to protect themselves."[53] In fact, more than three hundred people died because landowners provided no protection, such as good housing or medication, against the disease.[54]

While working and living conditions were harsh, Kaqchikel appreciated the opportunity to earn money and support their families. One woman from Tecpán elaborates: "My father went to the coast for two months. That is how we bought corn, firewood and other things. It was tough, but it was good because it relieved us of our poverty. It allowed him to bring back money to buy fertilizer. There was a disease there, but people did not die of it."[55] An elder from Aguas Calientes agrees: "My father went to the coast. It was hard work, but not sorrowful because you had to earn a living."[56] One group of men noted the work was tough, but for many people it was their only source of income in the off-season.[57]

Grievously, owners did not compensate severe working conditions with just wages. Oral histories recount that wages in the highlands during the 1930s ranged from three to ten cents a day. In contrast, a daily wage on the coast could be as high as forty cents.[58] A seventy-five-year-old evangelical farmer explains his motivation to work on the coast: "I worked on the coast seasonally for twelve years. Here [in Poaquil] I was earning ten cents a day, only three quetzals a month. But on the coast they paid twenty quetzals for one quintal [of coffee]. So I went to the coast."[59] However, while wages on the coast were higher than those in the communities, families had to pay for their basic subsistence that their farms at home would have provided them for free. As a result, remuneration provided less than a decent standard of living and few people returned to their homes with a significant profit. Furthermore, many returned with illnesses and the expense of medical care often consumed their earnings. One migrant complains that in 1965 he worked for twenty-five days and earned only fifteen quetzals.[60] Fortunately, wages increased under the administrations of Juan José Arévalo Bermejo and Col. Jacobo Arbenz Guzmán (1951–54). Consequently, coastal landholders augmented their remuneration to compete with increasing wages in the high-lands. Waqxaqi' Ajpu', a seventy-year-old agriculturist, attests that at first "you earned eight cents a day from 7 A.M. to 6 P.M. Men with families earned fifteen or sixteen cents a day. When Arévalo came, the wage increased to twenty-five to forty cents a day. Then under Arbenz it rose to between sixty and seventy-five cents a day. Finally, today you can earn as much as twenty-five cents [*sic,* read quetzals] a day."[61] Kaqchikel assert that wages did not raise the migrants' standard of living above a subsistence level. Kaqchikel also recall, with horror, that some fincas and wealthy people branded their workers.[62]

Unfortunately, a trip to the coast did not always produce cash. Oral accounts assert that in some cases migrants received a portion or all of their pay before they arrived on the coast and that they then had to work off their debt. Informants recall other instances where the government picked out a certain number of men and told them they had to work on the coast.[63] Ka'i' Kan, a fifty-three-year-old rural farmer, elaborates on this exploitation, "I worked for eight years on the coast. I did not think it was bad. I picked cotton and sugar. It was really hot and the mosquitoes were bad, but the pay was okay, except when the government grabbed you, then you were not paid. This happened quite a bit."[64]

Labor arrangements on the coast varied according to patron-client relationships. Oral traditions explain how some people worked on large export plantations and others farmed maize. Kaqchikel recall that several German- and Ladino-owned fincas were operated in Kaqchikel areas and note that people who worked for these fincas generally had to donate time to their owners. According to Kaqchikel, this agreement was especially true for residents of San Martín Jilotepeque, Comalapa, and Poaquil. In fact, a number of Poaquil's aldeas had formerly been fincas.[65] According to oral histories, some men donated their labor in exchange for the right to farm a small plot of the company's land on which they could plant their own crops, such as corn, tomatoes, and chiles, to bring back to their community or to sell on the coast. Oxi' Kan, a seventy-four-year-old entrepreneur, explains this relationship: "I went to the coast with my father for three years. We worked on coffee for September and October. If we did five boxes of coffee, we could farm one cuerda of maize."[66] Another man, who migrated to the coast for eighteen years, points out that some people rented land from finqueros on the coast to harvest crops.[67]

Because plantation owners were not always exploitative, some people liked the coast. "My grandfather worked at the Santa Lucía finca called Chuchi Choy," Ixk'at, a twenty-nine-year-old accountant, relates, "He was in Aguas Calientes. His father died and his uncle was a bad man, so the owners helped him out. They provided clothes for him."[68] Another man asserts that Kaqchikel dealt with both good and bad landowners but that if owners fulfilled their obligations in the patron-client relationship, Kaqchikel were loyal to and appreciative of them.[69]

Contratistas

Those who could not establish their own opportunities for income relied on contratistas to arrange plantation labor. Oral accounts assert that contratistas helped Kaqchikel earn money or goods so they could maintain their farms and homes in the community.[70] Even though work on the coast was horrendous, contratistas maintained a good reputation. Reflecting on eight years of work on the coast, one elder said, "The coast was terrible. The work was practically a donation. You had to do fifty, sixty, maybe eighty boxes a day. You suffered from starvation at the coast. For eight years I went with the contratista Juan Quill. He was a good man."[71] Kaqchikel do not associate the arduous work with the men who brought them to the coast. Rather, they are appreciative that contratistas facilitated their employment at a time when they most needed it. Another rural farmer explains how these relations continue today: "The contratistas help people. They bring them to the finca, pay their transportation, and give them work for thirty days."[72] Kaqchikel note that if a migrant did not go with a contratista, he often had to contact one when he arrived at the coast. Oral accounts note that when migrants were operating independently, they usually arrived on foot and slept outside during the three-day trek. In some cases migrants could negotiate with the finca to secure their wages. However, self-representation did not guarantee just working conditions and wages. Consequently, informants assert, most people felt more secure accompanied by a contratista they already knew. Others insist they went with a contratista because they could not make all the arrangements on their own.[73] For many people, a trip to the coast would have been impossible without such help.

Oral histories assert that during the twentieth century most contratistas were Kaqchikel, not Ladinos. Informants say these contratistas secured a large number of men to work and that they served as liaisons between migrants and landowners. Oral histories recount that, originally, men had to make the three-day walk to the coast but that contratistas hired from two to four buses to take them to their temporary employment; some contratistas are said to have even ensured that workers received just wages. Informants note that at times, contratistas would serve as foremen on fincas because they knew the administrators and could ameliorate harsh working conditions. Kaqchikel express confidence in these contratistas because they were "our people."[74]

Most Kaqchikel preferred to work for Kaqchikel contratistas. In contrast, Tecpanecos had significant interaction with Ladino contratistas, and their oral histories recall them as fair. The majority of Kaqchikel oral histories assert that most Ladino contratistas did not like to interact with Kaqchikel and exploited them. Kaqchikel recount how Ladino contratistas paid workers a portion up front but then reduced their wages when they arrived at the coast. Informants also note that at times these contratistas even hit migrants.[75] For the most part, Kaqchikel oral histories maintain that Kaqchikel contratistas treated their people better than Ladino contratistas did.

To attract more people, contratistas sometimes deceived Kaqchikel by promising higher wages or better working conditions than what actually awaited them. When Jun Kame went to the coast his contratista promised a wage of twenty-five cents a day, but Jun Kame only earned eight cents a day.[76] An elder from Tecpán concurs:

> I worked on the coast for two months. I went with a contratista who was a good man. We did not have any money so we went to the coast. He told us it was good work and good pay. He gave us money up front so I bought a new shirt, but the wages were not as much as he had promised. It was a sad thing. There are large snakes there. The cleaning was tough. The foreman told me to repeat my work because it was not good enough. So I did not get any food. The mosquitoes buzzed around me when I tried to sleep. There are no mountains there and I missed my family. The contratistas were "naturales" who organized people to go to the coast.[77]

Even though contratistas often misrepresented the conditions and earning potential of a job, many retained good standing among Kaqchikel.

Contratistas charged a fee for their services, but the fee did not have to be paid up front. Kaqchikel point out that today contratistas earn ten quetzals for each worker they bring to the coast, whereas in the 1940s and 1950s they earned two cents per person. They note that sometimes contratistas loaned money, chemical fertilizer, or goods to workers. Kaqchikel recall that other migrants received an advance payment so that they could pay for such important things as a marriage ceremony.[78] One seventy-two-year-old agriculturist praises contratistas: "The contratistas did business with the finqueros. . . . They helped our people. The payment was not theirs. They just got a percentage according to the number of people they brought to the coast."[79] Many Kaqchikel viewed the fee as an extraction of the landowners' wealth, not their own. Waqi' Iq', a former mayor of Comalapa, concurs, in his assessment of contratista Solomay Tuctuc: "Solomay Tuctuc was a good man. He did not take advantage of people, he just took a percentage. He was honest and did not lie."[80] Most Kaqchikel opine that the contratistas' profit was not a form of exploitation.

Not all Kaqchikel perceive contratistas' fees as benevolent, however. They say contratistas made more money than migrants even though they did not perform any manual labor, and they argue that contratistas earned money for transporting people to abusive labor situations. A few informants lament that contratistas' main concern was their own financial status, not the welfare of migrants, and some assert that most contratistas did not provide food or shelter for the people they transported. Critics say contratistas took advantage of people who did not have any legislation to protect them. They assert that some contratistas continue to exploit people who do not know their rights.[81] One young Kaqchikel man who works for a Guatemalan human rights organization criticizes Kaqchikel contratistas: "Anselmo Son was a contratista. He was one of our people from Comalapa. He knew Spanish so he could talk to the 'fat fish' finquero who told him to promise a certain amount that they would not really pay when the people got there. He would get all the workers because he deceived the people. Contratistas always had big money because they knew Spanish."[82] A school principal concurs: "The contratistas took advantage of the people who went to the coast. The finquero paid them to look for a lot of people to work whom he did not have to pay well. The salaries were unjust. Now if you bring one hundred workers you get twenty thousand quetzals. Contratistas are Kaqchikel and Ladino. There is always injustice."[83] According to these critics, contratistas—both Kaqchikel and Ladino—directly and indirectly exploited Kaqchikel.

A vertical alliance between workers, contratistas, and, in some cases, foremen developed through ethnic identity. This alliance surely contributed to contratistas' good reputation among those who migrated to the coast. Most Kaqchikel migrants perceived themselves as allied to contratistas because they were "our people." Working together, or at least sharing experiences, on the coast helped to strengthen the bonds between migrants and contratistas. This vertical alliance ameliorated migrants' perceptions of exploitation by Kaqchikel and Ladino contratistas. The minority of Kaqchikel who criticized contratistas are generally from younger generations and had not migrated to the coast. As a result, they did not have an opportunity to form a sense of solidarity with contratistas or other migrants. This separation allows them a different perspective. They assess the pains of coastal migration and labor and contratistas' role in this injustice and conclude that they were (and are) exploiting their own people. Ethnic identities among Kaqchikel can be extremely powerful, yet Kaqchikel are not blind to faults within their own communities. They recognize that exploitation can come from Kaqchikel, not just Ladinos.

The days when nearly the entire male population in Mayan communities migrated to the coast ended in the second half of the twentieth century because of two main factors. The first was the democratic governments of Arévalo and Arbenz, and the second was the onset of chemical fertilizer use. The democratic administrations of Arévalo and Arbenz removed the last barriers to the free movement of labor and capital. Maya could choose where and how they wanted to work. However, many were still dependent on coastal migration as a source of employment, at least seasonally.[84] In fact, Marilyn Moors asserts that "by the time forced labor was abolished, the Indian population of Guatemala had increased to the point at which the remaining land base of many Indian communities could no longer support a large part of its population."[85] This relationship changed for many with the introduction of chemical fertilizer and an increased harvest. Nonetheless, prior to the use of chemical fertilizer, Maya seemingly had the opportunity to improve their plight and regain their ancestral land through the 1952 Agrarian Reform Law.

Land Reform and Arbenz

Although skewed land distribution was a major cause behind Maya having to seek work outside their communities, Kaqchikel did not necessarily welcome the attempt to correct this injustice. President Arbenz passed the Agrarian Reform Law in 1952 in an attempt to alter social and economic relations in rural areas. This legislation proposed to break up inefficiently used large landholdings and redistribute them to the people who worked the land. Arbenz's economic and political policies were pragmatic and capitalist in nature. He envisioned that agricultural production, equitable land distribution, and the standard of living of the peasants could all increase, thereby improving the Guatemalan economy. Furthermore, Arbenz proposed to better the infrastructure of the economy through the construction of new highways and ports, but without forced labor, a tactic used by most previous Guatemalan rulers. The government redistributed land to Ladino *campesinos* (rural farmers) first and then to Maya. As a result, Maya did not benefit as much as Ladinos did. At any rate, the Agrarian Reform Law represented an improvement and renewed hope for a better life under the new government, and living conditions did improve in some areas.[86]

Kaqchikel remember Arbenz most for his land reform and for the fact that he did not finish his term, because Col. Carlos Castillo Armas (1954–57) overthrew his government. Kaqchikel approved of many of Arbenz's policies, especially his decision to increase salaries. However, they are divided in their judgment of his land reform. Some view it as a good idea gone bad; others perceive it as a communist plot to destabilize the nation, a plot rightfully ended by Castillo Armas. Any policy that affects land rights and ownership elicits strong reactions from Kaqchikel, and Arbenz's land reform was no exception.

The Agrarian Reform Law sought to develop productive and equitable agricultural enterprises. The law abolished all forms of unpaid labor, defended the rights of workers, and favored Mayan communities in disputes over land. The law sought to give land to peasants, resident laborers, and agricultural workers who had too little or no land, introduce new methods of cultivation to peasants, and increase the amount of credit available to them. In the mid–twentieth century, land tenure in Guatemala was unproductive, and its distribution remained extremely skewed. Two percent of the farming units controlled 72 percent of the land, while half of the farming units (165,850 families) owned less than 2 manzanas (barely enough to subsist) and many rural families were landless. A 1950 census showed that Ladino farm operators averaged 35 manzanas, while Mayan farm operators averaged only 4.4 manzanas. Arbenz set out to both improve these disparities and augment agricultural production. He intended the law to foster the development of production in the countryside and improve the lot of individual peasants, rural workers, and Maya, in general.[87]

The law set in motion the implementation of social and economic reform in the countryside but did not intend to transform rural society. Western political organizations aided Mayan communities, but their primary goal was to encourage the assimilation of Maya. In 1951 Arbenz raised the minimum wage to $.80 per day (it had ranged from $.15 to $.55 per day), although many fincas continued to pay less. By June 1954, the government expropriated more than two million acres and redistributed land to more than one hundred thousand campesinos. More than five hundred thousand people, out of a population of three million, benefited from the reforms. Thousands of beneficiaries received small, but crucial, credit to begin the process of diversification and investment in their new landholdings.[88]

The Agrarian Reform Law encouraged peasants to organize to receive land and loans from the National Agrarian Bank. Land was not simply given out. Campesinos had to organize into leagues or unions and make a claim for the land. An important aspect of the law was the active participation of rural poor. Maya reclaimed land that had been lost to large landowners, neighboring communities, or local elites. The system was meant to function from the bottom up.[89]

Because of the coup d'état, the reform law lasted for only two years, not enough time to penetrate the highlands effectively, and consequently many did not benefit from its efforts. Robert Wasserstrom criticized the reform because Arbenz limited the expropriated lands to nonproducing farms and as a result grants involved lands that were of limited agricultural value and potential. He argued that Maya remained the poorest segment of the rural peasantry because they depended on the availability of rental lands and wage labor to eke out a meager existence on marginal plots.[90]

While the circle of economic and political well-being expanded slightly, Maya were dissatisfied with the inequity of the reforms. The government did not achieve its goals of equal distribution of land and the return of land to Maya. In many cases, even when Mayan communities benefited materially, the government had determined the reforms. The government did not necessarily respond to Mayan demands; rather, it attempted to tailor expectations to their own program. Furthermore, in some cases the amount of land distributed was minimal.[91] In essence, the government had mapped out a plan for the modernization of Guatemala and Maya to meet their ideal of Western progress, society, and culture.

Arbenz's land-reform policies directly affected Kaqchikel. Oral histories describe how he split up a finca in Poaquil and redistributed the land to Poaquilenos. Others describe how he carried out his reforms in some of the aldeas of Comalapa—namely, Agua Caliente and Kojol Juyu'—in the neighboring villages of Rincón Grande and La Joya, and in the municipality of San Martín Jilotepeque. Kaqchikel point out that he redistributed land to workers on the coast, an action they perceived as fair because he was returning land to the original owners, in many cases to people who were landless. Arbenz was the favorite president of a few Kaqchikel. Many believed he wanted to help the citizens of Guatemala through his land reform but that he was misunderstood. They recall how landowners especially became enraged. Kaqchikel conclude that Arbenz favored poor farmers and laborers over wealthy landowners and that this led to his downfall.[92] Many Kaqchikel opine that agrarian reform was too innovative for the population to grasp. Informants recall that in some cases workers did not understand that they needed a land title to assume ownership so they attacked landowners, and some deaths resulted.[93]

Agrarian reform brought about increased violence and unrest on many levels. Land reform intensified traditional racial conflicts between Ladinos and Maya because it treated them as equals. Landowners naturally opposed the reform and in many cases tried to intimidate peasants so they would not register a claim for land. One plantation owner even burned the shacks of his workers and drove them off his land. In another incident, peasants were found hanged. Local authorities often condoned these actions by landowners. In response to this violence, Maya formed self-defense committees. At times, peasants even took the offensive and attacked landowners. In some instances, peasants illegally occupied lands and burned pastures or crops to have land declared uncultivated and subject to expropriation.[94]

Violence and conflict were not confined to peasant-landlord relations. Violence broke out not only between towns in competition for land being expropriated from finqueros but also among various aldeas of the same municipality.[95] In many places, agrarian reform divided communities. Much of the tension that developed was a reflection of the conflicts that started long before the agrarian reform. Members of the Santa María Joyabaj comunidad indígena (a local Mayan organization) expressed their frustration after the agrarian officials forced them to allow two hundred Kaqchikel farmers from San Martín Jilotepeque access to their communal lands:

> Each one of the political changes that has occurred in our nation has filled us with anxiety and dread because we know that individuals who say they represent the interests of the state rush to our community to fill our peaceful existence as agriculturists with confusion and disorder. It would take a long time to enumerate all the material sufferings our fathers endured to defend our *ejidos* [communal lands] and to give us the happiness of feeling we are on our own land. It would take a long time as well to describe the vexation and disgust we felt when others planted among us constant conflicts and litigations to reduce the size of our land. Now . . . we are looking for the justice that is required to reach a solution to the numerous problems that arose with the implementation of the sadly famous Agrarian Reform Law.[96]

For many, the law caused contradictory and confused infringement upon their lands and community. The reform opened a range of dormant social and economic conflicts.

Most Kaqchikel argue that Arbenz wrongly changed the land laws and ownership. As one agriculturist succinctly states, "The agrarian law he passed was bad. He did not help the Maya with it."[97] Another elder adds:

Jacobo [Arbenz] did not last long because he did not get along well with the people. He brought the poor to the national fincas and gave them land, but he also split up lands that were not national fincas. These lands had owners. But he took a lot of land and gave half of it away to the poor. That was the agrarian law formed by Arévalo but implemented by Arbenz. He only touched a few private lands because the finqueros got upset when he confiscated their land. It was not good that he took their land, because the land had owners. That is not a good law. It was like communism.[98]

Kaqchikel in the aldea of Panabajal were especially upset, because Arbenz was taking away the land of their revered *patrón* (landowner) Nemesio Matzer. One resident of Panabajal remembers how police incarcerated workers who defended Matzer's land.[99] These Kaqchikel were willing to go to jail to defend the land rights of their patrón. Some Kaqchikel pointed out that it was acceptable for benevolent landowners to give away their land but not for Arbenz to "steal" it from them. Others complained that Arbenz should not have just given the land away. They argued he should have made the recipients work for it, because if they did not work for it they would get lazy.[100] For Kaqchikel, land ownership is an inalienable right. They believe that the possession and acquisition of land should not be treated lightly.

As seen with Matzer's finca, Maya resisted the reforms, many preferring to be left alone. Many Maya disliked the changes because they had lived under the old system so long. They did not want to challenge the patrón. In addition, because their goals did not conform to the needs of the rural population, many of the village schools, cultural missions, and other national organizations were unable to establish close working relationships with the communities they were trying to serve. Few public servants could provide effective service under the conditions in isolated villages. As a result, some Maya felt disconnected from the reforms and resented the intrusion into their lives and infringement upon their communities.[101]

Some oral accounts maintain that Arbenz was a communist because he wanted to redistribute land from its owners to peasants. They also say he gave money away. Others claimed that he brought money and ideas from Cuba. Some assert that Arbenz continued to establish good laws like Arévalo had done but that he followed an evil doctrine.[102] In this case oral histories have collapsed time: Arbenz would not have received money from Cuba for his reforms prior to Cuba's 1959 revolution. However, the claims that revolutionary ideas from Cuba infiltrated Guatemala are well founded. In December 1953 Ernesto "Che" Guevara arrived in Guatemala, where he and other exiled

Cuban revolutionaries took a special interest in the Arbenz government. Some of the assertions in Kaqchikel oral histories that Arbenz was a communist can be attributed to the propaganda campaigns that were carried out against him in Guatemala. The United States successfully infiltrated the country and tried to convince Guatemalans that Arbenz was a communist. As a result of this campaign and because of some other factors, Arbenz had lost much of his popular support by the time of Castillo Armas's invasion in 1954. This situation, in turn, facilitated a rapid military coup.[103]

Most Kaqchikel rejected communism's attack on private property. They point out that in some towns Arbenz formed political parties to distribute cows and money.[104] For B'eleje' K'at, a forty-two-year-old artist and farmer, oral histories refute any historical revision of Arbenz: "I read a book about Arbenz that said he was pushing for democracy and was not a communist, but my dad told me he was a Communist. There were members of the Communist Party here. Government representatives went around and took people's animals to the town hall and told people they were no longer their animals but everyone's animals. They also said that land was no longer personal but everyone's. He was really a Communist not a democratic president."[105] One rural agriculturist asserts that "Arbenz sowed the seeds of subversion."[106] Kaqchikel did not view this land reform as a desirable return to the Mayan tradition or practice of communally held lands. They respect their ancestors' system of communal land ownership and honor this approach in their oral traditions. However, they acknowledge that while that system was ideal five hundred years ago, the increased population, which competes for limited resources, has made it impractical. Kaqchikel have grown accustomed to the security of private property. As a rule, these Kaqchikel opposed communism, and since they associated it with Arbenz, they were glad that his political and economic experiment ended quickly.

Land reform exacerbated ethnic tensions in Guatemala and undermined the maintenance of peace and order. Fighting persisted between Maya and Ladinos, between different Mayan groups, and even within Mayan communities. Kaqchikel and other Maya resented and feared this instability. The Kaqchikel priority was security, and Arbenz failed to meet their expectations in this area. Furthermore, he did not listen to other Mayan needs and concerns. Consequently, many believed that the program primarily benefited Ladinos, and many Kaqchikel viewed Arbenz's government as another attempt by the state to impose foreign ideas and culture upon their community.

Those who appreciated Arbenz's efforts supported his attempts to redistribute land to both the landless and its rightful owners, but Arbenz forced his reform on a population unprepared for the consequences. Even Maya, who recognized themselves as the original and rightful owners, did not understand how the reform would be implemented. As a result, most Kaqchikel criticized Arbenz for his ideas, labeled him a communist, and claimed he did not respect land and private property. The application of the Agrarian Reform Law did not fit into a Kaqchikel view of justice, which holds that the possession of land must be respected. Kaqchikel supported the redistribution of land to poor people but only through legal means. In Panabajal, Comalapa, workers defended their patrón against the government's attempt to redistribute his land to them. In part, Kaqchikel criticize Arbenz because he failed to adequately inform the populace of the radical changes that would take place. As reactions to both Arbenz and chemical fertilizer will reveal, Kaqchikel adapt well but approach change cautiously.

Chemical Fertilizer

In one sense, Kaqchikel oral histories laud the arrival of chemical fertilizer because it enabled people to stop seeking agricultural employment outside their communities. Chemical fertilizer increased harvests, especially corn, in the highlands. One agriculturist observed that his harvest increased sevenfold when he used chemical fertilizer, because the fertilizer gave strength to the land. According to oral histories, farmers produced enough to support their families for a full year, and famines no longer plagued them. Kaqchikel say the quality of life improved.[107] Waqi' Iq' attests that "a long time ago our people suffered because the agriculture did not give enough to support us. . . . The people suffered until the chemical fertilizer came and [then] they did not have to go to the coast again."[108] B'eleje' K'at adds, "The most important thing for us was the arrival of chemical fertilizer so people could farm better. Now there is a good harvest, and you can even have laborers work for you. They can also farm in the hills where they could not before."[109] Kaqchikel landowners were not the only beneficiaries of chemical fertilizer; with the increased crops, landless Kaqchikel could find jobs in the highlands. Lajuj Kan, who at age seventy-one is too old to work his land alone, takes great pride in working alongside his assistants every day. The dark, coarse, and cracked skin on the soles of his feet, developed from years of walking and working barefoot, serves as a constant reminder of his bond with the land. He explains the symbiotic relationship between labor on the coast and chemical fertilizer: "We farmed four to six cuerdas, but it did not give much maize; of the forty *varas* we barely got one *costal*.[110] So around August through October, we went to the coast. But thanks to God, science, and studies—I do not know where it came from—the chemical fertilizer helped the harvest. Sincerely, since then there has been no hunger and now almost all the children eat well."[111] Farming with chemical fertilizer mitigated people's need to migrate to the coast because it created more jobs, provided abundant harvests, and eradicated famines. Research indicates that chemical fertilizer greatly increased agricultural production in Mayan communities.[112] Kaqchikel communities were no exception. One elder states, "Until about fifty years ago corn was always scarce. In June, people had to begin to buy corn and famines struck. But now, thank God, that no longer occurs because of chemical fertilizer."[113] Most people attribute the lack of food to the absence of chemical fertilizer. According to Ixwatzik', a sixty-year-old woman who works in the fields as well as her home, "Chemical fertilizer has helped us significantly. . . . Without it you cannot farm. If there is no fertilizer, then there is no food."[114] The majority of Kaqchikel claim the use of chemical fertilizer resulted in the community's self-sufficiency.[115] Another rural resident concludes that "chemical fertilizer gives us life."[116]

Agricultural entrepreneurs in Guatemala had promoted the use of chemical fertilizer since the turn of the twentieth century. In 1903 the *Boletín de Agricultura* reported that "all plants without exception need chemical fertilizer. Chemical fertilizer is essential to vegetable life."[117] By the early 1920s, the Guatemalan Ministry of Agriculture stressed the importance of experimentation with chemical fertilizer "to improve the land and augment and improve the harvests."[118] Annis suggests that fertilizer and pesticide arrived in Aguas Calientes in the 1920s when evangelical missionaries established an "agricultural store" in that community.[119] Aguas Calientes was the exception. Widespread use of chemical fertilizer did not catch on in many Mayan communities until the late 1950s. At first, most Maya rejected this foreign substance. Chemical fertilizer entered the community of San Antonio Ilotenango in 1959, but the majority of K'ichee' residents did not incorporate it into their farming techniques until 1965. Likewise, in Totonicapán, K'ichee' farmers did not introduce chemical fertilizer into their agricultural techniques until the 1960s.[120] Most Mayan agriculturists approached this new technical input with trepidation.

Kaqchikel oral histories date the arrival of chemical fertilizer between the late 1950s and early 1960s. One eighty-year-old farmer noted in his journal that chemical fertilizer arrived in Comalapa on January 22, 1956.[121] The Chuwi' Tinamït project monograph for Comalapa states that "the use of chemical fertilizers barely had been introduced in the decade of the 1950s."[122] By the mid-1960s, most Kaqchikel residents of Comalapa were familiar with chemical fertilizer. In 1966 the local newspaper *Comalapan* reported a program to "develop the use of fertilizers for the small agriculturist to counteract the low national . . . cultivation of basic foodstuffs."[123] Residents were initially reluctant to employ foreign inputs in their agricultural techniques. Agricultural promoters encouraged local residents in Comalapa to use chemical fertilizer to boost their harvests of corn, beans, wheat, potatoes, and garden vegetables. The Development of Indigenous Economy organization studied and analyzed new forms of fertilizer that would improve Mayan agricultural production. This group encouraged the widespread use of chemical fertilizer in an attempt to augment annual output. Comalapa was one of the towns where they focused their efforts.[124]

Some Kaqchikel made direct connections between chemical fertilizer and improvements in lifestyle. One man credited chemical fertilizer with his ability to send his children to school. He attributed his own failure to attend school to the fact that he had to work the land. But when fertilizer came, the land was more plentiful and he could allow his son to finish his studies and become a teacher.[125]

Despite the immediate benefits that chemical fertilizer had on Kaqchikel communities, many people refused to use it. Oral histories recall they had no confidence in this new product because they did not understand its effects.[126] As a result, only a few tilled their soil with chemical fertilizer; the rest criticized these trailblazers' foolhardy approach to agriculture. Furthermore, oral accounts in some communities recall men and women from the United States who ostensibly came to give classes about chemical fertilizer and who wanted to organize an "army of the poor"—this association also gave a bad name to chemical fertilizer. According to some informants, these people planted the "seed of subversion," and massacres were the result.[127]

The majority of Kaqchikel now claim their initial trepidation was warranted, as chemical fertilizer has had many negative effects on the land, community, and population. Menchú agrees with Kaqchikel warnings: "If you use chemicals on a cucumber or a merliton, they will certainly grow quickly, but the natural process will have been interfered with."[128] Other Mayan farmers found that eventually some vegetables, such as those in the squash family, would not grow without the assistance of chemical fertilizer.[129] Most Kaqchikel, especially in Aguas Calientes, assert that these chemicals adversely affect public health. Others attribute deadly diseases to pesticides needed to maintain the farm. Informants say chemicals are present in agricultural products and that when people eat this food they become sick. Oral accounts teach that in place of the healthy vitamins people formerly consumed in vegetables and fruits, they now ingest chemicals. Consequently, according to oral traditions, people are not as physically strong and resistant to disease as they once were and thus do not live as long. Some people attribute cancer and diabetes to the intake of these chemicals.[130] A bonesetter and artist explains: "A long time ago there was no chemical fertilizer and because of that men were tougher; they did not fall ill. They farmed and ate the pure strength of the land. Now chemical fertilizer weakens us. The corn is bigger but it has chemicals in it. The land is no longer strong. It has disease in it. Furthermore, the underground insect population and waste have increased. These insects and waste eat the harvest. When there was no chemical fertilizer, nothing hurt. My grandfather lived to be eighty-five and when he died he was never hurt. He had great teeth, but now people's teeth are worse."[131]

In addition to the adverse effects on public health, many Kaqchikel notice that the land is not as fertile as it once was. They claim chemical fertilizer has taken the natural nutrients and vitamins from the land. Consequently, they say, people can no longer farm off the fecundity of the land alone because the land and seeds have become accustomed to chemical fertilizer. Many farmers claim crops do not grow without the application of this external stimulant.[132]

At the same time that the land is losing its strength, increasing prices and decreasing effectiveness of chemical fertilizer further compound the problem of small-scale agriculture. A former Comalapa mayor observes that "each time, chemical fertilizer is more expensive and less efficient. People should use organic fertilizer."[133] Kaqchikel remember that a quintal of fertilizer cost about four quetzals when it first came out; now the price is one hundred quetzals per quintal. Many farmers argue it is too expensive and say they had to give up their land and farming as a result.[134] An elder from Aguas Calientes relates: "A long time ago no one used chemical fertilizer because the population was low and land was abundant so they did not need it. Now there are more people, so the land has to give more. Most people use chemical fertilizer and it really helps. But now that people need it, the price of chemical fertilizer has increased. Chemical fertilizer is very expensive. The poor cannot afford it, so they have to work in the factories."[135] Wuqu' Iq', a sixty-nine-year-old rural farmer from one of Comalapa's aldeas, recognizes the importance of chemical fertilizer and believes that the government should keep the prices down.[136] In addition to excessive costs, many Kaqchikel assert that chemical fertilizer is not as potent as it once was. Oral accounts describe that in the 1960s one could apply a small capful but that now large quantities are needed to bring about the desired effects. Some agriculturists claim that producers have extracted the important active ingredients from fertilizer.[137] Another rural farmer opines: "In 1955, when chemical fertilizer arrived it was stronger and gave a good harvest. One quintal provided for eight to ten cuerdas. Now it is not as strong. The Ministry of Agriculture analyzed the chemical fertilizer from 1965 to 1970. They said it was the same, but that is not really true. They were lying to us. The price increases but not the strength. Now you pay one hundred quetzals for a quintal and it only lasts for one cuerda."[138] The cycle of chemical fertilizer prices out small agriculturists and allows large ones to usurp land from Maya (much like the programs of the liberal dictators, such as Barrios).

The cost of additional inputs, such as pesticides, results from the use of chemical fertilizer. Many Kaqchikel farmers assert that fertilizer produces plant-eating insects and microbes in the ground. They say these destructive insects eat crops before they can be harvested. Consequently, Kaqchikel assert, agriculturists must purchase a poison to kill them, but fumigation costs are high. In addition, some Kaqchikel believe that chemical fertilizer brought a new strand of plague that kills crops.[139] "You need poison to keep your farm going," Wuqu' Iq' notes, "there is no harvest if you do not apply poison, but there is also much disease in this poison."[140] Furthermore, Kaqchikel complain that while the costs of fertilizer and pesticides increase, the price of corn remains stagnant and that profits therefore diminish.[141] Such circumstances have forced some farmers to give up their land.

Kaqchikel farmers were not the only ones to suffer from increased costs. A Mayan group explains:

> Small and medium agricultural production fundamentally based on the use of fertilizers was cut short when the price of fertilizers, derived from petroleum, rose from Q2.85 to Q18.00 per hundred pounds. This resulted in bankruptcy for thousands of farmers. . . . At the same time that cultivation of such crops ceased to be affordable, the crisis also reduced the national and Central American market for fruits and vegetables coming from the Guatemalan highlands. Thousands upon thousands of farmers were forced to migrate to the plantations and to the capital.[142]

Fluctuations in the price of chemical fertilizer and decreased demand for their products reduced Mayan self-sufficiency. Increased agricultural productivity failed to offset the rising price of chemical fertilizer, so people had to seek outside income to meet these expenses.[143]

In some instances, fertilizer killed crops. One family in Tecpán inadvertently killed their potato harvest with the application of chemical fertilizer. Another family said chemical fertilizer killed all their crops.[144] As a result of these negative consequences, many Kaqchikel farmers prefer natural fertilizer. One agriculturist from Aguas Calientes explains: "I use natural, not chemical, fertilizer because there are no costs. It is good for my corn, bean, and tomato harvest. I have not had a plague in a while. The chemical fertilizer brought the plague [of insects] so then farmers had to buy poison from the same people who make the chemical fertilizer. It was a way to deceive the people. If you buy chemical fertilizer, you can make big money; but it will catch up with you because each day you have to fumigate."[145] Using chemical fertilizer begins a vicious cycle of increased costs from which farmers cannot escape. Many Kaqchikel reflect on a time when agriculturists employed only natural fertilizer from feces of domestic animals, such as goats, sheep, horses, and cows. Some continue to use feces because it is better for the land. They argue that natural fertilizer replenishes, rather than eliminates, the land's fecundity and assert that their crops, produced with natural fertilizer, provide a healthier diet than those produced with chemicals. They say natural fertilizer produces a better harvest for some crops, such as potatoes. Natural fertilizer can be prohibitively expensive and difficult to locate, but for those who have access to the resources, natural fertilizer is cheaper than chemical fertilizer. Some farmers advocate a mixture of the two forms of fertilizer for best results.[146] Most Kaqchikel see the benefits of natural fertilizer and believe more people would employ it if they had the resources.

Despite the use of fertilizer and improved harvests in some communities, such as Poaquil, men continue to migrate to the coast. Ka'i' Kame, a fifty-year-old Catholic whose third grade education does not preclude his effectiveness as a facilitator of local development groups, explains:

Now about 10 percent of [Poaquil's] population goes to the coast. It used to be 60 percent with Juan Quill. Then chemical fertilizer came, but as the cost of fertilizer increased more people had to go to the coast to pay for it. The contratistas gave them fertilizer in exchange for work on the coast. They owed between five hundred and two thousand quetzals. The chemical fertilizer resolved one problem but then caused another. Forty years ago fertilizer cost five quetzals per quintal, but now it is one hundred quetzals per quintal. A long time ago the land was stronger. It was not yet ruined, but now the chemicals have burned the land. The animals in the land have died. The land has lost its life.[147]

Ka'i' Kame argues that chemical fertilizer replaced one form of dependency with another. Other informants agree that chemical fertilizer attacked the long-term sustainability of agriculture by destroying the land's nutrients and fertility. Kaqchikel recognize that other regions, such as San Martín Jilotepeque, El K'ichee', Huehuetenango, and Chichicastenango, are more dependent on coastal labor for a portion of their income than they are.[148] In fact, Carol Smith argues that the Kaqchikel department of Chimaltenango sends few people to work on the coast. Agriculturists from Chimaltenango take advantage of their proximity to Guatemala City to produce basic food-stuffs for national consumption, where, in contrast, much of the adult labor force in the peripheral areas of Huehuetenango, northern K'ichee', and northern San Marcos work on the lowland plantations from three to six months a year.[149]

The improved agricultural situation in the highlands means that coastal plantations must offer humane working conditions and increased pay to at-tract workers. People now can earn an average of about five quetzals a day more on the coast than the daily wage in their communities. As a result, coastal labor is not as exploitative as it once was. Kaqchikel say the work remains arduous, however, and that in many cases the pay does not ade-quately compensate for the manual labor. In 1998 the average daily wage on the coast was twenty-five quetzals, barely enough to cover the cost of living for a family with two children, let alone the expenses from agricultural inputs such as fertilizer and seed. Informants also deplore that many migrants con-tinue to return with diseases.[150] While coastal work conditions have im-proved, many Kaqchikel continue to suffer because they must uproot their lives and seek temporary employment outside their communities.

Factories

Another option, which has intensified since the 1970s, for those who could not earn a sufficient income in their communities and did not want to mi-grate to the coast—particularly women—was employment in small indus-tries. In her 1978 survey of three thousand highland households, Smith found that 41 percent of heads of households worked in manufacturing activity and 17 percent worked in trade.[151] This trend is especially present in the Kaqchikel communities of Aguas Calientes and Barahona, where many work on factory assembly lines. Kaqchikel say factories give people, especially women and young adults, the opportunity to earn money outside their community. This employment is the only way many can support themselves, since work is scarce.[152] Some people have had good experiences in factories. One twenty-seven-year-old praised his boss: "I worked in a factory and liked it. I had an excellent patrón. He was an engineer and a hard worker. He did all the work that we did, and I liked that."[153] Others lament that while factories provide valuable income, they also infringe upon Kaqchikel culture and lifestyle. A seventy-year-old woman expressed her concern: "The factories are good because people can earn good money. But they are bad when our people lose their customs, such as making tortillas and weaving."[154]

Similar to work on the coast, factory labor is exploitative. Many Kaqchikel claim administrators provide minimal salaries and treat workers poorly. They also lament that factories provide no job security; the manager or owner often dismisses workers without notice. Kaqchikel point out that owners are Asian and virtually enslave young women who work for them. Studies show that factory or *maquiladora* (export processing plant) owners in Guatemala prefer to hire young, unmarried women and often use "violent means to ensure that they remain productive."[155] Furthermore, Kaqchikel note, some people even become ill as a result of this employment. Consequently, some Kaqchikel conclude that people should dedicate themselves to traditional work, such as agriculture and weaving, even if factory work pays better.[156] Jun Tojil points out that the loss of culture goes beyond just outward appearances: "Only women go to the factories and it is not good because it is changing their character and their clothes."[157] According to Jun Tojil, factory work corrupts the identity and soul of Kaqchikel.

Kaqchikel are aware that employment in factories is a consequence of a larger problem. As Jun Kej, a fifty-year-old Catholic from Barahona, explains, "Factories are fine but they [the laborers] only work there because they are poor. They [the owners] turn them into slaves."[158] Jun Kej points out that Guatemala's economic system maintains a large underclass to provide inexpensive labor for foreign and domestic economic elites. This economic reality attacks Kaqchikel culture and heritage.

Laboring in the manufacturing and agricultural export economy is just one of the many ways that Kaqchikel actively participate in the national economy. Many people have developed cottage industries in their towns. In Tecpán families have purchased machines to knit sweaters to sell in Guatemala City and other surrounding markets.[159] One family in Comalapa utilizes indigenous fabric to fashion new textiles, such as hats, bags, and book covers, that appeal to tourists. They sell these goods in Antigua. This same family established a school to teach computer skills.[160] Kaqchikel have used their entrepreneurial spirit to take advantage of and contribute to the national economy.

Conclusion

Oral traditions guard the critical role that land and labor play in the lives of Kaqchikel. The spiritual relationship most Kaqchikel maintain with the land, along with their strong work ethic, results in an abundant representation of land and labor in oral traditions. In addition, oral histories reveal the distinct and often contradictory ways that coastal migration, chemical fertilizer, and factories have affected Kaqchikel. For some, coastal conditions were too harsh, but others appreciated the opportunity to earn money and support their families. Likewise, while Kaqchikel appreciate the arrival of chemical fertilizer because in many cases it saved them from continued migration to the coast, they are also critical of its long-term impact on their land and community. Chemical fertilizer initially increased harvests but eventually trapped farmers in a cycle of dependency. Finally, factories provide income but attack Kaqchikel culture and identity.

Kaqchikel oral traditions reveal the complex effects that outside forces have had on their communities. Kaqchikel recall their existence prior to the Spanish arrival as pristine: they farmed land communally and worked together to build communities and maintain their livelihood. Despite Spanish relocations of Maya and forced labor mechanisms during the colonial period, Kaqchikel oral traditions continue to assert that land was farmed and occupied communally and, for the most part, independently of Spanish influence. This situation continued through the early independence period until the onslaught of liberal regimes that began in the 1870s with President Barrios.

Kaqchikel most remember Barrios for his land policies. He forced everyone to register a land title with the government. Most Kaqchikel recognize the need to privatize land, as population competition for land was increasing. The majority of Kaqchikel welcomed the establishment of land titles because it meant they could attain private property that would be protected by the state (at least in theory). Land titles provided the security that Kaqchikel cherish. In fact, most Kaqchikel had so internalized this system that eighty years later they criticized Arbenz's attempts to redistribute land more equitably. While Kaqchikel respect their forebears' approach to communal property, they no longer consider it practical, and they resist attempts to attack private property. Even though Arbenz's reforms were capitalistic in nature and he wanted to return land to Maya, most Kaqchikel did not perceive his means to be just and therefore lost their sense of security under his regime. Even today, Kaqchikel use land titles to prove their ownership and right to farm their land. In this way they use the past to prove their legitimacy to land rights today, and this legitimacy gives them a sense of security.

At the same time that most Kaqchikel appreciate Barrios for providing an orderly and secure approach to land use, they also realize that his view of land as a commodity that could easily be sold or traded contrasted their view of land as inviolable. Kaqchikel criticize Barrios's lack of respect for land, citing his giving away part of Guatemala's land to Mexico. In many cases, Barrios gave the best land to Ladinos and foreigners. Kaqchikel also lament that his policy expropriated the communal land of many Maya who could not read, write, or speak Spanish. As a result of the usurpation of land, Maya were displaced and forced to work outside their communities. Kaqchikel appreciate the security Barrios provided for those who knew enough Spanish to attain land titles but realize he also expropriated much of their land and exploited their labor.

The Kaqchikel desire for security and stability surfaces in their analysis of Arbenz's land reform. Some Kaqchikel supported Arbenz's land reform and his work to strengthen workers' rights and weaken landowners' grips on laborers. Some Kaqchikel benefited from his land reform, but even those who did not appreciated his effort to aid the landless. Most Kaqchikel recognize that Arbenz's attempts to assist Maya were met with indigenous, national, and international resistance that eventually led to his overthrow. This resistance and the subsequent coup revealed Guatemala's instability, and Kaqchikel are critical of anyone who makes the nation weaker. Most label Arbenz a communist, and they want to avoid this political association. Even though many Kaqchikel had to migrate to the coast as a result of government policies to expropriate their land, most did not want to upset the stability of their nation and risk security in their personal lives to change this reality.

The majority of men and many families had to work on the coast to supplement their income prior to the introduction of chemical fertilizer. Kaqchikel oral traditions assert that plantation labor was a necessary response to unemployment and threat of famine in the western highlands. In fact, Kaqchikel reject claims that forced labor mechanisms sent them to the coast. One family became quite agitated when their daughter came home from school and told them her assignment was to write about their family history of forced labor on the coast. The family, both men and women, vehemently insisted they were not victims of forced labor on the coast.[161]

Maya did not migrate to the coast simply because of debt peonage or vagrancy laws—many needed the cash supplement to survive. Kaqchikel oral traditions portray coastal migration as a response to, among other challenges, famines, the dearth of economic opportunities in their communities, and the increasing population pressure on the land. Coastal migration continues today for some of these same reasons even though institutions of forced labor have been eradicated. Kaqchikel did not have to escape loan sharks or municipal officials to dedicate themselves to full-time agricultural labor in their communities. As soon as they reaped the benefits of using chemical fertilizer, their dependence on plantation labor ended (at least temporarily). Thus, forced labor mechanisms did not have a significant impact on Kaqchikel coastal migration.

Oral traditions describe coastal work as having decrepit boarding conditions, sparse food provisions, grueling manual labor, a dramatic climate change, and numerous health hazards that plagued workers even after they returned to the highland communities. However, seasonal labor provided a relief from the dearth of labor opportunities in their communities, and in most cases wages were higher on the coast than at home. While Kaqchikel lament the squalor and suffering they experienced during their stints on the coast, they recognize that it fulfilled a need for income. Consequently, oral traditions praise the men who arranged for their transportation to the coast and employment there.

Kaqchikel assessments of contratistas show the complexity of ethnic identity. This identity broke down class differences as migrants formed bonds with labor brokers. The majority of contratistas were Kaqchikel; however, even some Ladino contratistas received high accolades from Kaqchikel. While most Kaqchikel recognize that some contratistas exploited them, they insist that these men were the exception. Laborers had to pay a fee for the services of contratistas, but their employment was guaranteed. Consequently, because they were paying for a service, most Kaqchikel did not view this fee as exploitative, and in many cases they believed that plantation owners covered this cost. Furthermore, most contratistas were honest men who acted in solidarity with "our people." In a few cases, contratistas worked as administrators on plantations to ensure humane working conditions. As a result of their benevolent reputations, contratistas were not held responsible for the atrocious and exploitative conditions on the coast. Kaqchikel view them as valuable conduits to necessary employment opportunities. The fact that most contratistas were "our people" gave the majority of Kaqchikel confidence that they had their best interest in mind. This ethnic identity erased any animosity deriving from the relationship between migrant workers and labor brokers. Nonetheless, a minority of Kaqchikel not involved in this relationship criticize Kaqchikel contratistas for exploiting their own people. Ethnic identity alone does not guarantee praise or acceptance.

Not all Kaqchikel were dependent on migrant labor. Some developed skills, such as artisanry, in their communities that allowed them to earn a living free of seasonal labor. Others went to the coast and established a trade or provided a service related to the plantation economy but remained self-employed. These entrepreneurs included families who would trade goods directly with plantation owners or sell food to workers. Others avoided the perils of the coast through legal channels or flight. Kaqchikel contributed to the agricultural export economy as laborers, as labor brokers, and as entrepreneurs in its tangential markets. Individuals who survived outside of seasonal coastal labor, however, were the exception, not the norm.

Kaqchikel welcomed the development of chemical fertilizer as an escape from migrant labor. At first Maya approached this foreign input cautiously, but by the mid-1960s and 1970s most Maya were enjoying increased harvests as a result of chemical fertilizer. Many, especially Kaqchikel, no longer had to supplement their income with outside sources. Kaqchikel cite chemical fertilizer as the catalyst that ended migrant labor for a majority of the population.

Chemical fertilizer was not a panacea, however. Nearly all agriculturists lament that it has corrupted the natural fecundity of the land. Furthermore, the ingestion of chemicals in food has adversely affected the health of those who consume them. These deleterious effects include loss of strength and stamina, increased vulnerability to disease, and decreased life span. Moreover, although chemical fertilizer temporarily resolved the migration problem for Kaqchikel, it also caused long-term problems in agricultural sustainability. The production of export, domestic, and subsistence crops now requires increased supplements such as fertilizer and insecticide, and thus the cost of agricultural inputs has increased. The decreased effectiveness of chemical fertilizer and its increased price have caused many to return to the coast for supplemental income that is necessary to pay for their farming inputs. Improved working conditions and wages on the coast are little consolation for farmers who hoped to break their dependency on plantation labor.

Kaqchikel do not wish to exclude outside influences from their lives, but they feel they receive more honest and just treatment within their communities than outside them. They lament their need to seek exploitative employment outside of their communities. Most residents of Aguas Calientes and Barahona are critical of young members of their community who work in Asian-owned manufacturing plants, arguing that owners virtually enslave laborers. They rue the cultural erosion that results from younger people's aversion to traditional forms of employment, such as agriculture and weaving. For the majority of Kaqchikel, maintaining their ethnic identity is imperative to their survival. Kaqchikel are not opposed to using outside inputs or working outside their communities as long as the relationship is based on respect and equality. The majority of Kaqchikel pride themselves on hard work, but they reject abusive labor relations. An entrepreneurial spirit among Kaqchikel is strong, and many are content to interact with national and international markets, as seen by the economic endeavors of families in Tecpán and Comalapa who produce wares in their homes and sell them in Guatemala City, Antigua, and other markets outside their communities. The majority want to contribute to the national economy, but they want the freedom to choose how.

Kaqchikel oral traditions portray the reality of Mayan life in the face of Guatemala's major economic transformations. Liberal governments needed Mayan labor to produce agricultural exports, such as coffee, bananas, and cotton. According to Kaqchikel oral traditions, forced labor mechanisms were unnecessary because most people needed to migrate to the coast when labor opportunities in their communities ceased and their harvests could not support them for the entire year. Kaqchikel responded to their own needs as much as they did to the demands of the national economy. In many cases, the two coincided. Kaqchikel took advantage of fertilizer to increase their freedom from coastal migration, not from the national economy. Maya have been the main contributors of labor to Guatemala's economy and national development and have ascertained ways to take advantage of their participation and maintain their ethnicity. Kaqchikel do not want isolation from the nation; they seek an equal opportunity to exploit and benefit from the national economy and its resources.

The same desire for egalitarian inclusion and interaction is present in Kaqchikel historical perspectives. Kaqchikel reject others' attempts to portray them as passive actors in Guatemala's history. Oral traditions reveal that impulses and strategies among Kaqchikel, as well as local conditions, are crucial to understanding coastal migration. Histories that explore only policies of national economic development and the imposition of capitalism fail to understand important forces propelling seasonal coastal migration in Guatemala. Local forces and populations are essential elements in the historical analysis of migration patterns not only within nations but also on an international level. As the next chapter discloses, the importance of examining history from a local level is also underscored in histories of epidemics in Guatemala. In some cases, Kaqchikel historical perspectives starkly contrast Ladino representations of epidemics. An analysis of both representations reveals strategies for improved relations between government officials and Maya.

3

Epidemics

Nima yab'il

Guatemala has a long history of natural forces wreaking havoc on its population. As a result, happenings outside human influence are recurrent themes in Kaqchikel oral traditions. Family histories express emotional scars, while gravestones and pockmarked faces provide physical evidence of the decimation that epidemics have unleashed on the Kaqchikel population. According to Kaqchikel worldviews, natural disasters, epidemics, and other threats to Kaqchikel communities happen in cycles. No generation avoids the effects of these tragic occurrences whose causes and timing are unpredictable. The next two chapters will examine the circumstances and effects of epidemics and natural disasters.

In oral histories, people ascribe different causes to these tragedies. Ixtoj, a forty-six-year-old midwife aware of the effects of disease, recognizes the cyclical nature of her life and the history that her parents passed on to her: "Illnesses continue to return. There was one about seventy-five years ago; many died. A bad fever also killed many people because our town was growing and we were fighting so the sickness came and wiped people out. When the town begins to grow too much again, another sickness will return. The lack of food was also hard on our people. Then the earthquake came, followed by the violence. But now we have rebuilt our town so maybe another illness will come."[1]

Ixtoj explains natural disasters as a recurrent theme that consistently punishes her people. Forty-six-year-old van driver Waqi' K'at associates these miseries with different generations: "We have suffered from the earthquake and the violence, before that it was cholera and fever, and even before that it was the famine. Many died because of these problems."[2] Oral traditions pass on these memories because they are relevant to life today. K'ayb'il B'alam, a Kaqchikel teacher and accountant from Tecpán states: "My parents taught me about the tough times the Mayan people faced a long time ago: sickness, hunger, slavery, discrimination, and we still face many of these challenges today."[3] Sharing the trials of their ancestors is an important coping mechanism for seemingly insuperable peril.

Disasters and diseases are a significant part of Kaqchikel oral traditions because they are unforgettable aspects of their reality. These tragedies have decimated their communities' population and physical structures, and Kaqchikel realize they are, to a certain degree, helpless to prevent these occurrences. Even though cures have been discovered for illnesses, such as cholera, new diseases are always emerging. The onset of cancer and AIDS concerns Kaqchikel, but the circumstances surrounding these tragedies cause Kaqchikel the most anxiety. Natural disasters and epidemics often bring outside influence into the community. The repercussions of these intrusions, generally people who come to mitigate the disasters' effects, frustrate Kaqchikel because, unlike natural forces, the intrusions are explainable and avoidable.

The two worst epidemics etched in Kaqchikel oral traditions are cholera and the fever associated with the worldwide epidemic of the Spanish influenza in 1918–19. People mention other diseases—measles, smallpox, leprosy, pneumonia, malaria, typhoid, alcoholism, and sores—but the biggest killers among the Kaqchikel population have been cholera and influenza. During these epidemics, people were dying so quickly that residents had to construct halfway hospitals to house the terminally ill. They also had to build additional cemeteries to accommodate the corpses.

Kaqchikel oral traditions recount that their ancestors were stronger, healthier, and smarter than contemporary Kaqchikel. Kaqchikel boast their ancestors lived to be over 150 years old because they used natural medicine and ate what grew and lived in the area—food with high nutritional value. Oral traditions assert that Kaqchikel had a minimal impact on, and a productive relationship with, their environment and would have continued to thrive if not for the introduction of diseases by the Spanish.[4] In fact, Spanish epidemics advanced faster than the Spanish themselves.[5] According to the *Anales,* in 1520 (four years before the Spanish invasion of Guatemala) a plague ravaged the Kaqchikel population. The epidemic spread rapidly because there was no means of controlling the disease, and the number of deaths quickly mounted. Many people took refuge in the hills because the plague claimed so many lives. The *Anales* concludes, "We were born to die."[6] After this devastation, Kaqchikel recovered and for the most part enjoyed good health, as oral traditions portray. However, Kaqchikel healthy lifestyles, diets, and environments were little match for subsequent epidemics introduced by the Spanish.

The debate about the death toll from Spanish diseases continues. Woodrow Borah and Sherburne Cook estimate that as much as 90 percent of the indigenous population died in some areas of Latin America as a result of Spanish-born diseases. The rate of depopulation was not as high in the Andes region of South America as it was in Mexico and Mesoamerica. Research has revealed that the major cause of death was not the battles with Spanish invaders but the spread of epidemic diseases to which indigenous populations had no resistance. Smallpox and measles were especially fatal, and Kaqchikel oral traditions recognize their potency. Diseases spread faster than the Spanish armies and made the armies' work easier. Nearly two hundred years after the Spanish invasion, Tecpán and Comalapa had yet to achieve their pre-contact populations.[7]

Cholera

The epidemic that most gravely affected Guatemala was cholera. This disease, which caused havoc throughout Europe by 1831, ravaged Guatemala in 1837, with major political consequences for the Mariano Gálvez presidency (1831–38). In 1833, after the epidemic struck Mexico, Gálvez attempted to protect his country from the disease. He established sanitary quarters, opened new water supplies and sewage facilities, and prohibited burials inside churches. By April 1837 cholera was ravaging Guatemala, and the Gálvez government quarantined certain areas, tightened sanitary cordons, and increased the distribution of vaccines. However, Catholic priests informed their congregations that the medicine the government put into the water was designed to poison them, when, in fact, the "poisons" were water purification chemicals that the government used to fight cholera. These priests undermined the government's public health program in response to the liberal government's attack of the Catholic Church. Maya perceived this government action as an attempt to further eradicate their race. They accepted the church's interpretation and misinterpreted the Gálvez government's plan to protect its citizens. While communal land encroachment and the loss of political autonomy were also important factors in Mayan opposition to the Gálvez government, few Maya dismissed the possibility of a state-sponsored bane.[8]

The fear of genocide that resulted from this incident which occurred more than 150 years ago remains in Kaqchikel oral traditions. One thirty-year-old woman who worked on a project to learn from elders in Comalapa recalls that a long time ago "the Ladinos poisoned the water because they do not like us. We are so many in number and they do not like to look at us. They do not value us. Many died from cholera, almost all the people were wiped out. The people dug a huge hole in the hills to bury the dead, but no one was left to bury them."[9] Kab'lajuj Tijax, a university professor, asserts, "With cholera, the people thought the government poisoned the water in an attempt to terminate our people. Many people died."[10] Kaqchikel historical perspectives express that Ladino governments wanted to extinguish all Maya, not just Kaqchikel. In more recent outbreaks of cholera, however, oral histories do not associate the epidemic with a conspiratorial plot.

Cholera outbreaks persisted throughout the nineteenth and twentieth centuries. An 1857 cholera epidemic decimated the population and claimed more lives than the 1837 cholera outbreak. Newspapers attributed the 1857 epidemic to the infection of the Guatemalan military in Nicaragua, where they had joined in the defeat of mercenary William Walker. By July 1857 the disease was spreading in Guatemala. Cholera claimed more victims in 1889–90 but not nearly as many as the previous cholera epidemics. Cholera plagued the citizens of Guatemala throughout the twentieth century as well.[11] According to oral histories, other strains of cholera broke out in the late 1800s, early 1920s, and 1940s; it even remains a threat in some areas today. Kaqchikel assert that many people died in all outbreaks of cholera.[12] Oral histories recount desolation as residents closed up their houses, and domestic and farm animals roamed the streets.

As a result of these and other interactions with the government, Maya were hesitant to trust outside influences. Nonetheless, government efforts continued. In 1917 the government allocated funds for biological serums to prevent and cure cholera.[13] Later in the twentieth century, attempts to provide medicine against fatal illnesses were more successful. Oral histories note that in an attempt to stave off the pestilent effects of cholera, people ate lemons. Kaqchikel assert that lemons help them to retain more water and to thereby avoid the fatal effects of dehydration brought on by cholera.[14] Oral traditions maintain that people should boil their water to prevent cholera. Over time the devastating effects of cholera broke down Kaqchikel resistance to the state's efforts to help. While the first attempts by the government to distribute medication to Maya were met with suspicion and fear, many Kaqchikel now recognize that Western medication and vaccinations are an important part of preventing cholera and other sicknesses such as measles and smallpox.[15] While Kaqchikel have become comfortable with these remedies, they have not forgotten that diseases can be used by a dominant group to decimate an undesirable portion of the population. In spite of their differences, Kaqchikel and Ladinos agree that cholera was as notable, and nearly as ruinous, as the 1918 influenza fever.

Spanish Influenza

The Spanish influenza of 1918–19 devastated much of the world's population. While the flu has been researched on an aggregate level, little is known about what happened on a local level. One of the reasons the epidemic spread so rapidly in Europe was that the German advance on Paris diverted attention that could have been focused on controlling the disease. As a result, more people fell victim to influenza than died on the battlefields of World War I. Initially, the disease hit Europe, China, and India. However, by September 1918 the disease had propagated in the United States, Mexico, and much of Latin America.[16] The disease quickly spread to Guatemala. In his landmark study of the effects of influenza on Guatemala City, historian David McCreery argues that the epidemic entered Guatemala about the same time as Mexico and took root in the highlands from the Mexican border to Chimaltenango.[17] Oral histories of Kaqchikel from Chimaltenango remember this devastation and attribute the government's inability to respond effectively as a main cause for the rapid propagation.

Kaqchikel dissatisfaction with the government reaction was indicative of a national trend. President Manuel Estrada Cabrera (1898–1920) was already unpopular by the time the influenza epidemic hit Guatemala in 1918. He failed to take the epidemic seriously and therefore did not create a government agency to specialize in public health. As a result, the Ministry of Justice had jurisdiction over efforts to stamp out the disease. This unprepared and already burdened ministry did not have personnel specialized in health care. Consequently, the best organized relief came from the Asociación Nacional de Salubridad (National Association of Public Health), a group of civilian doctors supported by the government. Estrada Cabrera's regional and local officials were not only inefficient and incompetent but also corrupt. Moreover, Estrada Cabrera's inflexible government failed to effectively address the 1919 economic crisis in Guatemala. His inadequate response to these crises, coupled with the U.S. withdrawal of political support, led to widespread rebellion, and he was overthrown in 1920.[18]

The influenza epidemic affected Guatemala more gravely than the government admitted. The Guatemalan Ministry of Government and Justice estimated the total effects of the epidemic to be 325,220 cases and 43,731 deaths.[19] However, the total number of recorded deaths in 1918 and 1919 was 66,248 and 64,841, respectively, nearly twice as many people as had died in 1920 and 1921 (37,489 and 35,466, respectively). These conservative statistics reveal an increase of nearly 60,000 deaths for the two years combined.[20] While these additional deaths are not necessarily all due to influenza, McCreery and anthropologist Richard Adams estimate the total deaths to be between 100,000 and 150,000—more than two to three times the government estimate.[21]

The government's inadequate relief efforts centered on the capital even though the effects of the epidemic were much worse among the rural population. The towns of Tecpán, Comalapa, Poaquil, Patzicía, and Patzún were hit especially hard. Some areas reported that 50 to 60 percent of the population had died. Many fled to the hills to die in peace. In some cases, entire families died without a proper burial.[22] *La República* estimated that in the departments of Chimaltenango and Sololá those infected with illness ranged from 30 to 90 percent of the population.[23] The same newspaper reported that Chimaltenango was "completely desolate, as the effects were the same as war or other grand cataclysms."[24] Government estimates place the morbidity and mortality rates in Chimaltenango at 7,462 and 200, respectively. These statistics appear exaggeratedly low when one considers the high number of victims nationally and remembers that Chimaltenango was one of the areas most severely affected.

One reason the government estimates were low was the pressure on local politicians to downplay the effects of epidemics. During the influenza epidemic, Dr. P. Molina Flores reported an outbreak of smallpox in the departments of Sololá and Chimaltenango. Molina Flores believed the government was closing its eyes to a potentially devastating health problem. He warned that the ensuing warm months of February, March, and April would exacerbate the problem, and he appealed to the newsprint media of the country "to energetically protest the absurd and dangerous manner in which the small operation is being carried out." He wrote that "there are many [public officials] who try to avoid the problem."[25] A few days later, Augusto Rodríguez, the governor of Chimaltenango, responded that not a single case of smallpox existed in his jurisdiction and said that every town had received the vaccine. Local officials in Chimaltenango continued to deny any outbreak of smallpox in their region even though they recognized cases in neighboring departments.[26]

La República accepted Molina Flores's challenge to more closely examine the situation. This newspaper supported Flores's diagnosis and assessed Governor Rodríguez's response as such:

We figure that the public official has worked with considerable haste without the certainty that his delegates in the towns told him the truth. The custom of hiding damage to prevent possible reprimands is very common. The local commissioner tries to falsify the truth, so his immediate boss does not come down on him with accusations of leniency or carelessness. The high-level department officials turn a blind eye and send grand reports to the Government Ministry about the serene state [of affairs] that contradicts the reality. . . . The lie of the public official is the most painful of all.[27]

The newspaper also cited a recent outbreak of yellow fever to highlight the need for honest reports. *La República* had further opportunity to highlight the government's inability (or lack of desire) to address the smallpox problem.

About two weeks after the debate began, another doctor discovered a case of smallpox in the department of Chimaltenango. This news forced local officials to admit that "unfortunately, we can no longer maintain . . . that in this department there has never been that illness [smallpox] because we know . . . Patzún presented ONE SINGLE CASE in the person of an indigene."[28] Clearly, when public officials denied or downplayed the presence of diseases in their jurisdiction, residents in that area suffered from a lack of appropriate medical attention.

Local newspapers did not underestimate the effects of Spanish influenza either. According to newspaper accounts, the most virulent form of it attacked from November to February. One journalist noted that "at times this frightening epidemic has left homes deserted."[29] The *Diario de Centro América* recognized that influenza "leaves in its wake ruins, desolation, death, tears and in its final stages the influenza is the most lethal of the pandemics that has flogged the Republic, including the *cholera morbus asiatic* epidemic that hit sixty-two years ago."[30]

The areas hit hardest in Guatemala were the highland states predominantly populated by Maya. In December the *Diario de Centro América* reported: "In Sololá the little towns that surround the lake are the principal victims, the same of Pochuta in Chimaltenango, Tecpán, Patzún and some places of the highlands. . . . The ports are completely healthy."[31] Another article a month later observed that "truly anxious [and] dying of fear, the western populations live with the rapid propagation of the influenza epidemic in the cities and farms. The disease has taken the worst clinical and mortal effects . . . on the indigenous race."[32] Kaqchikel were situated in the middle of the outbreak. Kaqchikel oral histories emphasize the high death rate caused by Spanish influenza and acknowledge that individual towns suffered varying degrees of intensity. Tecpán was one of the towns most affected by the epidemic. Wuqu' Kan, an eighty-year-old Catholic, shares what his uncle told him: "An epidemic hit us at the end of the First World War. When the war ended the fever came here around 1916 or 1917. There were ten, fifteen, twenty deaths each day. In about fifteen days, Tecpán had nearly lost its population. My uncle told me this. 1918 was the worst year of the epidemic.

There were no beds at that time. I was a crawling baby when my mom died of the fever. I was close to her so I got sick later. Thousands of people died in Patzún and Patzicía. They took the dead away in wheelbarrows."[33] Oral traditions assert that entire families succumbed to the disease and that houses were abandoned.[34] Many people accurately date the epidemic to 1918, or estimate that it happened about eighty years ago, and assert that the illness nearly finished off the population.

The government assigned health commissions from the capital to combat the disease in heavily infected areas. The department of Chimaltenango was one of those areas. Dr. Rodolfo Robles headed one such commission for Tecpán. He noted that "the number of sick people is very large, almost half the population." In one day, he and another doctor attended 480 cases of influenza. Only midway through the epidemic, Tecpán had suffered 7,000 sick and 600 deaths.[35] These estimates surpass the final government statistics of sick and dead for the entire department. Robles asserted that the high death toll was due to a lack of attention from families, nurses, and doctors. He also observed that "children pay a large tribute to this disease because the manifestations are very rapid in them."[36] Another report to the Ministry of Government by Mariano López asserted that Tecpán was the source of the epidemic and had spread the disease to other towns because it was a large commercial center.[37] One newspaper account exemplifies how desperate the situation was: "In Tecpán a baby suckled the breast of his dead mother without the innocent creature realizing she was dead."[38]

Comalapenses assert that their residents were nearly wiped out also, because the disease was extremely contagious. One woman in Comalapa tells of her grandfather's family in which six of nine siblings were lost.[39] Oral histories recall that residents of Kaqchikel towns constructed special hospitals for the sick to isolate them from the healthy. *La República* reported that "in Itzapa [a Kaqchikel town in Chimaltenango] the Authority [governor] has begun to construct an Epidemic Hospital. . . . Comalapa also will construct an analogous building."[40] Kaqchikel note that these remote hospitals reduced the possibility of contagion, but in effect they served as halfway houses for the dead. Kaqchikel lament that no medicine existed to aid the sick. Oral histories recount how some tried using cow's milk, the local moonshine, or herbal medicines, but none of these remedies succeeded. They deplore the fact that no doctor was available to help them. Comalapenses claim that it took ten years for their town's population to recover. Some Kaqchikel estimate the high mortality rate necessitated the creation of three to four new cemeteries. Local residents were also aware of the international context of their disease; they noted that more people died from the epidemic than died in World War I.[41] Even though the consequences were devastating, Kaqchikel knew they were not alone.

Comalapa residents commemorate the deadly effects of the influenza epidemic through a festive market held annually on May 20. Ixq'anil and Ixtz'i', two widows from Comalapa, relate that the market was established to build the children's strength: "A long time ago a priest started the market for the children. The town was not as big then. But a bad fever struck the town and the children became sick and died. They had to be buried where the nursery school is. The priest set up the market to ensure that children were well fed. There was a chapel and a *kaj* [corn grinder made of stone] about where the health clinic is now. The people would give the children tortillas and beans and they would eat them by the chapel. Our people did this because of the bad fever."[42] The focus of the market remains on the children, as vendors sell games, toys, and foods that appeal to them. Asturias de Barrios notes that the *Placita de Mayo* (May marketplace) was instrumental in the town's defense against a plague in the early twentieth century.[43] The yearly market safeguards the memory of the influenza epidemic and the need to make special concessions for children an occasion.

Oral histories are relevant for people today, but many prefer to forget some incidents. One of the most frightening aspects of the epidemics was the overzealousness of Ladino government officials to bury people. Oral accounts attest that public officials forced Kaqchikel to carry their sick relatives to the grave before they were dead. Informants recount with horror that people wrapped in straw mats and presumably dead moved while lying in their grave.[44] A university professor and his seventy-year-old mother, who speaks only Kaqchikel, animatedly explain: "People hid their sick relatives in the sweat bath to protect them from the government officials. The mayor sent these Ladino officials to inspect each home for anyone who may be sick or carrying the disease. If they discovered someone, dead or alive, they immediately took the person to the cemetery to be buried. They said they had to do it quickly because the disease was contagious. They did not allow us any time for a proper burial."[45] The anxious public officials' insistence upon immediate interment denied an important burial ritual for Kaqchikel.[46]

Stories of people buried alive may seem surreal, but archival evidence supports these claims. *La República* reports: "In Patzún[47] they buried alive a young man named Juan Samayoa. . . . Apparently dead, the youth Samayoa was carried with urgency to the cemetery, as they had been ordered not to delay the burials, but when they had already lowered him into the grave they heard noises from inside the coffin. . . . It would be good to deposit the cadavers in adequate sites and bury them as the law demands, not until twenty-four hours after death, to avoid cases such as this one."[48] One reason live burials occurred was that the government pressured local administrators to carry out rapid interments in an attempt to prevent disease from spreading. The Superior Council of Health recommended the immediate isolation of all infected cases. In addition to employing hygiene inspectors, the government formed "health police" "to watch over the cities so that all effectively completed the orders of the health associations."[49] In increased numbers, officials roamed communities in search of contagious people who needed to be quarantined.

Unfortunately, live burials were not an isolated phenomenon. A fifty-six-year-old mother of ten shares what her uncle told her about the fever epidemic:

> More than seventy years ago there was a bad sickness like typhoid fever. My husband's father died from it and they rolled him up in a straw mat because in those days there were no coffins. They made a special hospital in the canyon for the sick. Many people died. Government officials just grabbed men to dig large holes and bury the dead. They buried many in the same hole. If you were just barely alive they buried you with the dead. My uncle told me that my father was buried before he died. The doctors came from Guatemala City and they did not respect our natural medicine. They just tossed the sick into the hole and said they were dead. At that time there was no [Western] medicine.[50]

Mariano López's health commission visited Tecpán, Comalapa, Poaquil, Patzún, Patzicía, and Santa Apolonia. In Comalapa, Mariano López observed that the death rate was high among Kaqchikel and that "the healthy population is very scarce, no one can even bring them [the sick] water." He asserted that the lack of auxiliary personnel "undoubtedly has been one of the causes of the numerous deaths."[51] Newspaper accounts also recognized that the lack of doctors and nurses needed urgent resolution. Reporters frequently heard people say, "we do not have any doctors."[52] Kaqchikel oral histories and health officials' reports both highlight a lack of medical personnel as a factor in the loss of life.

According to most accounts, the epidemic most severely attacked Maya. The *Diario de Centro América* observed: "There are few Ladino victims but numerous indigenous."[53] In San Marcos, the majority of victims were Maya. Similarly, correspondence from the department of Chimaltenango showed that the disease had little effect on Ladinos, while Kaqchikel suffered grave consequences.[54] None of the reports attributed the propensity for Mayan mortality to coincidence.

As oral histories attest, few Ladinos displayed empathy or attempted to understand Mayan reality. Ladino accounts insisted the disease spread among Maya because of their squalor and lack of hygiene. Mariano López claimed that the "Indians' vicious customs," such as their tendency to sleep huddled together on the floor surrounded by their "secretions . . . have been valid factors for the rapid propagation of the disease and greatly diminishes the success that the humanitarian efforts of the government should have."[55] In his medical commission, Dr. Robles made similar observations of the "terrible hygiene" and penchant for moonshine among Maya. He asserted that "the death toll can be attributed solely to the deplorable hygienic conditions."[56] Newspaper reports agreed with Mariano López's and Robles's assessments: "An efficacious prophylactic is absolutely necessary in the Indian housing. These dwellings are the most unhygienic that one can imagine. . . . What admirable land for the propagation of the bacillus that kills us!"[57] Ladinos faulted Maya for the augmentation of influenza. Another correspondent asserted: "The indigenes have paid a strong tribute to the disease. And it is very logical."[58]

In their assessment of other diseases, Ladinos continued to highlight the theme of poor Mayan hygiene. In 1940, Dr. Carlos Catalán Prem wrote an article assessing the history of typhoid in Chimaltenango. Between 1912 and 1940, Tecpán, Comalapa, Patzicía, and other Kaqchikel towns were among the most adversely affected by the disease. He noted that "almost all of the department has paid tribute to [typhoid], more than anything the indigenous class; the Ladinos of a different cultural level understand much better what hygiene means."[59] The *Diario de Centro América* opined: "The poor Indians are defenseless victims of the scourge. . . . [T]hese unhappy people die oblivious of any assistance and lead a miserable life to which they have been accustomed since time immemorial and that is the initial cause among this unfortunate race of certain grave and endemic diseases. . . . They are situated in the mountains and do not have plans to abandon their sites. That is how it will be with all the epidemics that appear in these places because the lack of hygiene aggravates the situation."[60]

Most Ladinos appeared more concerned for the general health of the economy than the health of Maya. As one correspondent noted, "The epidemic . . . has left deep injury . . . above all in the masses of our Indians who are so useful for the agriculture and trade in general."[61] The main concern of the government was the dearth of agricultural workers. The 1919 annual report stated that "the sad and lamentable consequences of the yellow fever and influenza epidemics . . . have flogged the country, subtracted many hands from the agriculture and produced an economic disequilibrium."[62] Landowners' and administrators' views of agriculture and labor were simple: "God gives it and the Indians work it."[63] One Ladino writer from Cobán explicitly stated: "Exploit the poor Indian until the last drop of blood."[64]

Perhaps the best summation of the epidemic from a Ladino point of view came in the form of an editorial written on January 1, 1919:

> [The influenza] has interrupted the agricultural and commercial movement, naturally causing the near paralysis of business, the epidemic or, better said, the plague that whips the world and has visited Guatemala ravaging a great portion of its populations, including . . . Tecpán, Patzún, Comalapa, Poaquil, Patzicía. . . . There will be an eternal memory of the Spanish influenza . . . for the many victims that have fallen to never rise again, despite the battle waged by the authorities. . . . There are plenty of homes in mourning for a lost loved one and to think of the irreparable loss of so many manual laborers so useful for agriculture causes great sadness. . . . Because of their lack of personal hygiene and their natural ignorance it is in the indigenous race where more havoc was caused due to the reigning plague. . . . In these places we lack doctors who come to combat the epidemic and stay in the towns to fight for the cure. . . . [T]he indigenous for their ignorance do a thousand stupidities for which they almost always pay with their lives.[65]

The author recognized the irreversible effects of the epidemic in the Kaqchikel towns of Chimaltenango. He also noted that the lack of medical attention was a factor in the high death rate. But in the final analysis, he blamed Maya for their own fate: if they were cleaner and more intelligent, they would have survived in greater numbers. The author also equated the loss that family members felt for their loved ones with the shock that rich landowners suffered due to the lack of farmhands. As expressed here, Ladino concerns are markedly different from those expressed in Kaqchikel oral accounts.

The Guatemalan government felt its efforts should be lauded. The 1919 annual report to Congress asserted that the government's efforts successfully combated the epidemics, with only a few cases of influenza remaining in some departments. In the departments of Chimaltenango, Sololá, and others, the government claimed to have sent "medical commissions with sufficient resources to achieve the immediate goal of their important functions."[66] De-

spite this self-congratulatory rhetoric, Kaqchikel oral histories, newspaper accounts, and medical commission reports refute the government's claims of
success.

A difference in perception regarding the Spanish influenza becomes clear
when one contrasts Kaqchikel oral histories with the written accounts of
Ladinos. Kaqchikel feared the epidemic that disproportionately affected
them, but they also noted the government's lack of effort to aid with medicine or doctors. When the government did intervene, it was to prematurely
seize and bury the sick. Government officials did not attempt to understand
Mayan natural medicine or approaches to health. This type of intervention
made Kaqchikel more anxious about interaction with Ladinos. Concurrently,
Ladinos blamed Maya for their plight. However, from Ladino perspectives
the only unfortunate result was the diminished labor pool. Adams points out
that the Guatemalan state learned from the experience that "to promote the
well-being of the indigenous was to promote the well-being of the state."[67]
Kaqchikel have never thought Ladinos were concerned for their welfare as
human beings, but during the influenza epidemic the state even neglected
them as a labor source.

When given the opportunity to address public health issues with Western
medicine in the 1940s, most Kaqchikel were open to it, even if they were
hesitant at first. President Arevalo recognized that a shortage of Western-
trained doctors, nurses, and dentists plagued rural areas. In response to this
problem, he constructed new hospitals and health centers and created the
Ministry of Public Health and Social Welfare, which established health units
in each of the twenty-two departments and three ports. The prevention of
disease was its first objective. In 1945 the public health department created a
division to fight typhus. They established a three-year plan to eradicate the
illness with the "Cox" vaccination and to disinfect homes, furniture, clothes,
and the sick with DDT to destroy the lice that caused typhus. On April 11,
1947, Arévalo passed a decree that required all citizens to receive the typhus
vaccination. The public health department focused its efforts in the highlands
and on "the indigenous race, because the misery and lamentable hygiene in
which they live" made them more susceptible to lice and typhus.[68] This campaign was largely successful: the number of deaths due to typhus quickly
decreased, and by 1954 typhus had been virtually eliminated. While some
argue that the government expenditure on health care was less than sufficient,
it did improve the health of rural poor.[69]

Oral histories recount that Arévalo assigned health commissions and established a number of different health clinics in previously neglected communities. Kaqchikel note that he also distributed vaccinations to children via the

school system. They also remember how Arévalo ordered everyone to maintain good personal hygiene and to change their clothes to prevent the recurrence of insect propagation. Oral accounts describe how Arévalo instituted a fumigation campaign against lice, cockroaches, and other parasitic insects that burrowed themselves in people's bodies, hair, clothing, and homes.[70] A seventy-year-old agriculturist who was a young man at the time enthusiastically explained that "Arévalo got rid of lice and fleas that lived in people's hair and on their legs. He went everywhere with poison to get rid of them. He sprayed it in people's houses. Now some are coming back but only a little, and it has been a long time. He killed the insects."[71] While Arévalo did not physically appear in everyone's homes, this personalization of oral history helps keep his role vital. Kaqchikel appreciate a personal connection with their leaders and can identify with them when they envision them performing acts. This portrayal also depicts Arévalo's respect for Maya and his willingness to interact with them directly. Kaqchikel are comfortable with outside interaction when respect and compassion are present. Although Arévalo did not actually visit Kaqchikel homes, this account implies that he would have been open to it and would respect the residents and their lifestyle.

Initially, Kaqchikel did not welcome the government's efforts to improve public health. They viewed it as an intrusion into their community. Jun Kan, a health promoter, recalls the reaction of his fellow Comalapenses: "In his third year as president, Arévalo sent the order to vaccinate all the people, but the people did not want it. I became a health promoter, but I did not yet know about vaccinations. I went to the people to explain the vaccination to them. They were all afraid, so a doctor came to give classes on it."[72] As in years past, Kaqchikel feared the government's plan to improve their health. The 1830s cholera epidemic had left bad memories. However, Arévalo's efforts to educate people on the process and reasons for the vaccination ameliorated their concerns. That Arévalo was thought to respect Kaqchikel and that he used Kaqchikel to disseminate information enabled him to win their trust. Arévalo's approach starkly contrasts with those of the Gálvez and Estrada Cabrera governments and helps to explain why Kaqchikel reacted so differently in these cases.

Kaqchikel fondly remember Arévalo's public health efforts in Chimaltenango. There, his efforts eradicated lice, fleas, and other insects, and he immunized the population. The result was a drop in the level of disease in the area. In Poaquil a mobile unit applied doses of DDT to "individuals' [heads], clothes, and homes as well as familiar and distinct contacts."[73] These brigades also operated in Tecpán, Patzún, Patzicía, and Zaragoza. The public health department also carried out intensive campaigns in the department of Sacatepéquez.[74]

The influenza epidemic severely affected the department of Sacatepéquez but not as gravely as it did Chimaltenango. By 1919 the epidemic subsided in Sacatepéquez. The daily death toll, which at the beginning of January reached a high of forty-eight, diminished to between one and five deaths by the end of the month. Concurrently, the high rate of infection fell to about one hundred a day, and by the end of February local officials reported that only six people were sick and that nobody had died.[75] Conservative government statistics estimate that 4,723 people fell ill to influenza and 1,036 died in Sacatepéquez.[76] The influenza epidemic had taken its toll on the people of Sacatepéquez, but not to the extent it affected those from Chimaltenango.

Kaqchikel oral histories show that Kaqchikel do not reject health institutions per se; they reject personnel who fail to treat them respectfully and effectively. Most Kaqchikel are open to Western health care but not to abuse from Western doctors who do not value Kaqchikel medicine and practices. When national leaders and professionals are open to Kaqchikel distinctions, Kaqchikel welcome their input. In general, Kaqchikel recognize the need for health clinics, hospitals, and other public health institutions, but they do not uncritically accept the people who staff them. Kaqchikel resistance to offensive and at times detrimental health workers should not be construed as a rejection of Western medicine or health care institutions.

Malaria in Aguas Calientes

Kaqchikel of Barahona and Aguas Calientes remember the influenza epidemic in their oral histories, but a local outbreak of malaria in the early twentieth century obscures it. Oral traditions assert many people died from influenza fever. Residents note that doctors from outside the community came to help the sick but that their ameliorative effect was minimal. They recall the large hole the community built to bury the dead.[77] According to oral accounts, the source of malaria was the mosquitoes breeding in the lake that bordered Barahona and Aguas Calientes. While the death toll was not as great as it was after the influenza epidemic, the circumstances surrounding the development and eradication of malaria were traumatic.

In the early 1900s, yellow fever epidemics killed as much as a third of the population. In early 1927 the Epidemic Hospital established in Antigua, the capital of Sacatepéquez, reported the urgency of the epidemic and the need to isolate victims. Once again, the government's major concern was the threat to the labor pool.[78] In May 1927, *El Día* reported that the lake in Aguas Calientes had to be drained because the malaria endemic was "lashing" the surrounding towns, but people from Aguas Calientes did not like the idea because the reeds in the water constituted the prime material for the fabrication of their straw mats.[79] In May 1928, the mayor of Santiago Zamora (at that time its own municipality but now a village under the jurisdiction of and bordering Aguas Calientes) responded that he could not fulfill the Sacatepéquez governor's request for laborers because his "population has been decimated previously due to malaria." The mayor also reported that people continued to die of malaria in February and June that same year.[80] Malaria continued to attack these populations to such an extent that it infringed upon their daily activities and sustenance. Oral histories recount this turn of events: The lake had no outlet, and the stagnant water was a breeding ground for mosquitoes that spread malaria amongst the townspeople. At first, five or six people died, but then many more contracted the disease and died. A hospital was located in front of the cemetery, but no doctors or medicine could combat the disease. Malaria was contagious, so the men buried those infected with the disease immediately upon death. In some cases the survivors brought the infirm to the cemetery before they were dead. The custom of a wake had to cease, because the disease was contagious. At this time no coffins existed, so people interred the corpses in straw mats from the lake. As a result of the epidemic, President Lázaro Chacón decided to drain off the lake and seal it with petroleum. People came from other towns to build trenches to drain the lake. The government drained the lake about sixty or seventy years ago.[81] The loss of the lake was a devastating blow to the community, but people knew drastic measures were necessary.[82] One woman adds: "When they lost their lake, people said they lost an important part of their culture and that the sickness was a sin."[83]

Lázaro Chacón's government (1926–30) was aware of the urgency of the problem and the need to dry the lake before the rainy season began. Chacón commenced the process of desiccation at the beginning of 1927. The project required many manual laborers. In January 1927 the secretary of state wrote a letter to department governors which recognized that the scarcity of laborers was due to the fact that many men had to attend to their own farms, but he implored local leaders to do whatever was necessary to drain the lake.[84] In April of the same year, Chacón wrote to the governor of Sacatepéquez: "It would serve you to put all your efforts into supplying the greatest number of people possible for the work of drying the lake of San Antonio. It is essential to conclude before the next winter."[85] Chacón took a personal interest in the effort. Workers came from many different municipalities in the area and from the department of Chimaltenango. However, the dearth of laborers persisted. In May of the same year, Fidel Castillo, the public works engineer, complained that he needed more men who could complete the fifteen days required of them.[86]

Workers, some of whom came from distances as far as two days by foot, became disgruntled because of the poor working conditions and the lack of compensation. *El Día* stated: "The Indians complain that they are not paid and they are obligated to bring provisions for one to two weeks for which it was advertised they would earn $15 daily."[87] In fact, Manuel Velásquez, governor of Chimaltenango, sent laborers from all over the department, including Tecpán, Comalapa, and San Martín Jilotepeque, and insisted that no payment for his representatives was necessary.[88] Castillo demanded that those who came from Chimaltenango should stay for fifteen days and provide their own food and shelter since he did not have the funds to provide these bare necessities. He concluded, "I do not believe it is humane that they work without eating."[89] When Governor Velásquez received this news, he informed the mayors of each town to advise families to send workers with the necessary provisions to eat for two weeks.[90] This proposition was difficult for families to fulfill in a country where few had the benefits of refrigeration or access to chemically preserved foods.

Inhumane working conditions were compounded by the threat of typhoid fever and malaria. The lake exacerbated the conditions that spread disease. *El Día* reported that "Indians from neighboring towns and even from the department of Chimaltenango come to consume energy and lose their health in that work [drying the lake], without making any great progress.[91] The municipal doctor of Antigua informed the government that the need for vaccination against typhoid fever was urgent, as it was claiming many victims in the area.[92] The combination of poor public health and abusive working conditions provoked Kaqchikel to seek redress against this exploitation.

Confronting forced labor through legal channels was one Mayan reaction, but it often led only to frustration.[93] As a result, another response to labor abuse was escape. In some cases individual workers had a reputation for escaping, so governors made a special note to those in charge to keep an eye on them. At times, Velásquez insisted that officials confirmed the arrival of all the men he sent to Aguas Calientes.[94] When the government captured the escapees, officials doled out harsh punishment. In response to one escape, Velásquez writes, "I have ordered the capture of the servants from Itzapa [a Kaqchikel town] that fled from us in Aguas Calientes; when they are captured their tools will be withdrawn and they will be obligated to pay."[95] Inevitably, after their capture, governors sent them back to work.[96]

Aguas Calientes oral traditions do not mention problems with laborers, most of whom spoke their language. One reason for this omission is that for Kaqchikel of Aguas Calientes, Barahona, and other neighboring towns who worked on the project, food and housing were not issues. They were located close enough to go home to eat and sleep. Furthermore, the work directly benefited them. As a result, their oral histories do not mark this specific event as characterized by labor abuse. However, their oral traditions portray labor abuse in other situations, such as where men had to travel long distances to transport personal items belonging to government officials or to work on roads. Kaqchikel of Comalapa and Tecpán, two towns that provided workers, do not specify the labor abuses in Aguas Calientes, but they maintain that in many other cases the government forced them to work far from home with no food, pay, or shelter. Archival evidence documents much of the abuse to which Kaqchikel refer in their oral traditions.

In spite of all the challenges, workers completed the trenches and drained the water. The final stages had a few logistical problems, but by mid-July the trucks delivered the oil to seal the lake.[97] Kaqchikel of Aguas Calientes were thankful that the threat of malaria had ended. The 1927 Aguas Calientes annual report praised the work of Chacón's government: "Thanks to the activity and patriotism of the Supreme Government with the drying of the lake, the endemic illness of malaria has completely disappeared. . . . No cases of this or any other epidemic disease were registered; [Aguas Calientes] enjoyed the existence of good health."[98]

Residents of Aguas Calientes did not want the lake to disappear without a ceremony. Ka'i' Kawoq, a seventy-one-year-old farmer and keeper of one of the town's most memorable moments, shares the story of Chacón's visit:

The people invited Chacón to come, and sit on the shore of the lake one last time. When the lake was dried it was all mud. But we served the president a nice lunch with drinks and marimba. He brought his bodyguards with him. President Chacón saw that we had tables and chairs set up for our invited guests, but he knew that Aguas Calientes was famous for making straw mats. So he suggested we eat on the straw mats. The soldiers did not like the idea but President Chacón taught them how to sit cross-legged on the ground with the straw mats under them. Lázaro Chacón was a good man. He stopped the plague, named a group of doctors [to work here], and told the authorities to check all the houses. He also built a hospital near the cemetery so that when people died they were close to the cemetery. That was the end of the lake, but also the end of the sickness.[99]

Many people from Aguas Calientes have great respect for Chacón because he put an end to the deadly disease and because he respected Kaqchikel. His appearance in Aguas Calientes and attempt to understand their culture made him a revered figure in their oral histories. As a result, Kaqchikel accepted his method to eradicate the epidemic, even though it meant losing their lake.

Residents of Barahona and Aguas Calientes, but especially the latter, remember the lake that provided a livelihood and brought their towns joy. The lake was a source of pride. Oral histories recount how residents dried the reeds that surrounded the lake and made them into beautiful mats. Informants attest that fish provided a source of income for the community and boast that fishermen could fill their baskets in an hour. Kaqchikel point out that ducks inhabited the lake year-round and that the setting enticed presidents, governors, and other important dignitaries to vacation there. They say small boats and canoes navigated the lake for entertainment and fishing. Chacón donated a marimba, which the town still owns, and musicians from the village performed every Sunday, to the delight of townspeople and visitors.[100]

Kaqchikel from Aguas Calientes reacted much differently to the government's strategy of epidemic control than their counterparts from the department of Chimaltenango. Kaqchikel from Aguas Calientes and Barahona accepted the drastic measures of Ladino officials. Certainly Chacón and other governors who visited the town allowed residents to develop a rapport with and sense of confidence in their national leaders. On the other hand, at the time of the influenza epidemic, people from Comalapa, Poaquil, and Tecpán were more geographically isolated from the capital and therefore had no daily interaction with government dignitaries that would allow them to build trust. Consequently, the government only took intrusive actions in these towns, such as removing sick family members from their homes. These actions led to Kaqchikel's greater distrust of state officials. In contrast, people of Aguas Calientes and Barahona had more daily interaction with national officials due to their proximity to Guatemala City. Although the lake was an integral part of their culture and community, Kaqchikel did not resist the government's intervention because they deemed the response appropriate. However, the government's approach in the highlands of Chimaltenango appeared to be one of agitation and ethnocide rather than assistance and solutions.

Another reason Aguas Calientes residents reacted positively to the government is that after the lake disappeared, the government split up the land into lots, which they then gave to townspeople. By December 1927, the government assigned an engineer to divide the land. In February 1928, Chacón signed a law that proportionately and legally (through land titles) distributed the land among the poorest families of Aguas Calientes. He recognized that residents had suffered for many reasons and would suffer future economic hardship from the loss of the tule plant that provided income.[101] In an attempt to compensate people for their loss, Chacón donated the land to the townspeople.

Oral histories credit the local government with the fair distribution of the land. One elder explains: "When only land remained, the mayor had an engineer divide up the land. Then he gave it away to the people in the town. A representative from each family was eligible for a lot. If your number was called then you got one. That is why that section of town is now called lots. However, the land is only good for farming before the rainy season, because during the rainy season it floods."[102] Annis confirms that the town held a lottery to determine the more than one hundred families who would receive a plot of land.[103] Kaqchikel from Aguas Calientes felt that the government acted competently and in the interest of the people.

Kaqchikel recognize Chacón as a champion of their cause, but they also acknowledge that he was unable to completely eliminate their lake. The lake water returned in 1929, in 1934, and even today to a lesser degree.[104] Kaqchikel point out that during the rainy season, the area fills with water and provides a light outline of where the lake was located. Because the identity and culture of Aguas Calientes residents was tied into the lake, they are proud that no one can erase it completely. The lake's resurgence represents their own resilience against a dominant political, economic, cultural, and linguistic entity.

The combination of oral accounts and archival documents provides a holistic understanding of why and how the lake in Aguas Calientes dried. Aguas Calientes accounts remember that men dug a trench to drain the lake and then covered the area in petroleum to ensure it would dry. Chacón was especially attentive to the problem, as he wrote personal letters to local political bosses to ensure the project was effective and quick. An obvious explanation for his concern was the malaria epidemic. He could have left even those details to local health and public officials, but the project was important to him. Chacón's personal attentiveness to the town's plight implies a strong relationship between him and Aguas Calientes.

Kaqchikel from Aguas Calientes reminisce about their lake, but some Kaqchikel from Barahona are still bitter and dispute the ownership of the lake. These residents claim that Aguas Calientes did not yet exist when the lake was dried, though more realistic accounts assert that before people from Aguas Calientes settled their community, the lake belonged to Barahona and rightfully was still Barahona's property.[105] Kaqchikel from Barahona believe that people from Aguas Calientes neglected the lake. They claim this imprudence caused malaria and the need to dry the lake. People from Barahona note how they had exploited the lake successfully for years but that when Aguas Calientes occupied the area they degraded the environment and disrupted the harmony maintained by previous generations. They argue that Barahona lost a valuable resource. One seventy-year-old Catholic farmer explains: "The lake provoked malaria and dengue so they built a trench to drain it. Now Aguas Calientes suffers from a lack of water, because their water has disappeared. It is their own fault."[106] As seen in chapter 1, the water issue has caused caustic relations between the two towns, and many blame Aguas Calientes for its inability to maintain water. Oral histories of Barahona emphasize these tensions and express no remorse that Aguas Calientes lost a valuable source of income.

Conclusion

In comparison to Ladinos, Kaqchikel have an autochthonous sense of the pandemics that have struck Guatemala because these pestilent forces discriminately have affected Maya. Kaqchikel do not imagine a time free of pestilence; rather, they recognize illness as part of the natural course of life. Even while medications and vaccinations combat epidemics, new diseases develop that cannot be cured. While Kaqchikel value nontraditional methods of achieving and maintaining good health, they desire a symbiotic relationship between traditional and Western health practices.

Epidemics and illnesses fit within Kaqchikel worldviews, but interaction with outside forces can bring misunderstanding and fear. Kaqchikel share stories that show threatening advances of foreigners into their communities. In the 1837 cholera epidemic, for example, Kaqchikel oral traditions characterized the government as an evil institution that attempted to poison Maya. The Gálvez government not only had little concept of Mayan reality and worldviews, but its failure to explain its health campaign to the intended population exacerbated fear and resistance among Maya. Likewise, in the description of the influenza epidemic in 1918–19, Kaqchikel oral traditions recall the public officials who ignored their traditional health practices, quarantined their sick relatives, buried them before they died, and refused proper burials. These overzealous government officials left as bad an impression in 1919 as the Gálvez government did in its attempt to mitigate the cholera epidemic in 1837. Naturally, Kaqchikel remain skeptical of foreigners and Ladinos.

Despite these repercussions, Kaqchikel refuse to isolate themselves from interaction with these dominant groups. Many Kaqchikel accept advances of modern medicine and vaccinate themselves and their children against diseases. Many recall how isolated from Western medicine or doctors they and their ancestors were when different epidemics struck Kaqchikel areas. This failure to provide adequate health care led to the deaths of entire families and decimated communities. As a result, Kaqchikel historical perspectives highlight the Ladino government's approach that sought to take lives away, rather than cure them. The government exerted more effort to build "halfway hospitals" and cemeteries than to provide medical personnel and supplies. The government underestimated the impact of the influenza fever and therefore the state claimed the insufficient supply of medical personnel and medication was adequate and even praiseworthy. The government failed to provide suitable health care in cholera- and influenza-infected communities and denied the existence of smallpox. In some cases, local officials intentionally ignored diseases and denied health care to individuals and communities in need. In contrast, doctors recognized a lack of health care as a problem. Kaqchikel are open to the curative and preventive measures of modern science, but they want the opportunity to choose from all options and not be subjugated to shortsighted government decisions.

As proven in the case of malaria in Aguas Calientes, Kaqchikel were open to outside interaction when granted attention and respect. The lake was a huge loss for the community, but residents endorsed the government strategy to eradicate the illness because Chacón took the time to interact with, understand, and respect their community and culture. Chacón knew how important the lake was to the residents' livelihood and identity, showed respect for that aspect of their lives, and mitigated the loss by dividing up the land among the members of the community. In this case, Kaqchikel oral histories recall a good government solution to eradicate an epidemic. One of the reasons for this success was the attempt to understand Kaqchikel and their reality through Chacón's visits.

Likewise, Kaqchikel were initially cautious of Arévalo's public health campaign, but he clearly explained the goals and processes of the government's actions and Kaqchikel accepted the merits of his plan. Arévalo used the strategy of disseminating information through local leaders to gain the confidence of Kaqchikel. Kaqchikel did not deny that health problems existed in their communities; they simply desired an efficacious manner to address the problems that respected their distinct lifestyle and culture. Kaqchikel laud Arévalo for killing insects that propagate disease and depict him as entering their homes and personally combating this public health threat. Kaqchikel personalize Arévalo's acts because they perceive that he had their best interest in mind and, through local representatives, listened to them and learned about them. Kaqchikel also depict a close personal relationship with Chacón because he acted in their best interest without ignoring their distinct culture and lifestyle. For Kaqchikel, open communication, clearly explained policies, and mutual respect are essential to their acceptance of national leaders and their policies.

Unfortunately, this respect for Kaqchikel culture and lifestyle was not the norm. Perspectives surrounding the influenza epidemic depict formidable ethnic relations. Most Ladino accounts paint Maya as destitute and ignorant. Health and public officials attributed the source of pestilence to their lack of hygiene. In some cases Ladinos blamed Maya for the propagation of disease. When Ladinos arrived in Kaqchikel communities, they did not ask what Kaqchikel needed or how best to combat their suffering. Rather, these outsiders imposed their views and strategies on communities that did not understand them. During the cholera epidemic of 1837 or the influenza epidemic eighty years later, most Ladinos did not learn about the Mayan communities with whom they worked. The government only wanted to eradicate the epidemics. They did not seek to bridge ethnic gaps or build positive relationships. Even the government's earnest attempts to aid a suffering population alarmed Kaqchikel because public officials did not comprehend Kaqchikel culture and lifestyle. These officials and doctors only wanted to teach public health concepts of hygiene and administer medication to the Kaqchikel population. They did not attempt to learn from or respectfully communicate with Kaqchikel on equal terms. These sorts of interaction perpetuated bad relations and Kaqchikel fears of outsiders.

For most Ladinos, economic implications overshadowed personal hardships of Maya. Their main concern was the abatement of exploitable labor. One Ladino author wrote sarcastically and insightfully about how most Ladinos viewed Maya:

The landowner, who before was niggardly and brutal, has become full of good will and affection; the death of a farmhand represents an immense loss and the mature coffee—that is worth 20 dollars each 100 pounds—stays on the branch. The local political bosses are indignant and cannot explain that you [Indians] have died without their authorization. . . . The *fendera* also laments your death because the consumption of moonshine has diminished 60 percent, and the *habilitador* [loan shark] because many of you have gone without canceling your debts, and the political commissioner, secretary of justice, the jail keeper, the sacristan and the priest of the church because they have lost their best clients. . . . Rest, rest you that only knew painful anxiety and anguish, Bartholomé de las Casas will receive you in his arms; and your tombs will be watered with the sincere tears of the local political bosses.[107]

The main lesson for Ladinos from these epidemics was that they needed to secure the health of the Mayan population to ensure the well-being of the economy. Government attempts to ameliorate the effects of epidemics upon Maya were not based on altruism.

As seen in chapter 1, Kaqchikel identity is inextricably attached to place. Residents of Aguas Calientes identify with their lake because it provided sources of livelihood and recreation. It gave them life and continues to inspire them. The lake remains alive in their oral histories today because it represents their own resilience against dominant powers. Just as the technology and manpower garnered by political leaders could not erase the lake, so too political and economic elites cannot eradicate the distinct ethnicity of the Kaqchikel people.

Kaqchikel strategies and perceptions are not incompatible with Western approaches to public health, but the two groups need to achieve mutual comprehension. Health care is important to Kaqchikel, but they do not believe it is necessary to sacrifice their values and identity to gain access to Western health care. Kaqchikel accept change and new ideas when they are presented with respect for their reality and worldviews. Furthermore, Kaqchikel recognize when the government's provision of health care is inadequate, regardless of its infringements. Oral traditions portray the failure of Ladinos to provide proper attention. At times, Ladinos became too intimately involved with too little understanding of the community. In other cases, the government fell short of meeting Kaqchikel needs and expectations. In both extremes, Kaqchikel perceive a lack of concern, at best, and genocidal campaigns, at worst. Despite many Ladinos' condescending impressions and exploitative treatment of Maya, Kaqchikel do not seek exclusivity. They view Ladinos as a threat but do not seek to prevent all interaction with them. Instead, Kaqchikel seek fair and humane treatment in daily interaction and especially during times of crisis. They desire a peaceful coexistence characterized by mutual respect. Communication between Ladinos and Maya remains negligent, despite the historical interdependency of Ladinos and Maya, an interdependence clearly evident in cataclysmic events that have struck Guatemala and Kaqchikel.

4
Natural Disasters

Nima'q taq k'ayewal

Much like epidemics, natural disasters and famines have decimated the population in the Kaqchikel region. This destruction has brought Ladino and Western personnel to Kaqchikel aid, a form of help that has at times worked to the detriment of the Kaqchikel. The worst natural disaster was the 1976 earthquake that especially struck the department of Chimaltenango. The earthquake of 1917 lives on in Kaqchikel oral histories as well. Likewise, famines hit the area, causing many deaths, especially among young children. Finally, many people characterize la violencia as causing the worst devastation. Kaqchikel work to prevent or mitigate the potential damage of natural disasters, but they are aware that they cannot win in a duel against nature.

Earthquakes

Earthquakes are common in Guatemala, and Kaqchikel have suffered the consequences of their powerful force. In the early twentieth century, one of the national government's main concerns was the dearth of agricultural production caused by earthquakes. The 1917 earthquake paralyzed all economic activity, killed many people in Guatemala City, and left few Kaqchikel homes standing in rural areas.[1]

The 1917 earthquake devastated the capital, but residents of the department of Chimaltenango suffered few deaths. Junlajuj Imox, who was twelve years old at the time, shares why the effects were more damning in Guatemala City: "In 1917 there was an earthquake. It was strong but not many people [here] died because of the material of the houses; but in Guatemala City many people died because their houses were constructed of adobe. Then, around 1952 another earthquake hit and more people here died because by that time some houses had adobe walls and clay roofs, but the worst was in 1976. In that year many people died because the housing materials were heavy and buried them alive. Now, with the block construction and metal frames, the houses will come down again."[2] Junlajuj Imox notes that the improvements in housing construction actually decreased the chances of surviving earthquakes. Waqi' K'at concurs that in 1917 most people lived in houses constructed of bamboo and straw.[3] Later, they built houses of adobe and clay, and recently they have come to prefer concrete blocks and iron frames. Some people argue that tin roofing material used today is lighter than clay roofing tiles and therefore will not cause a high mortality rate. Many Kaqchikel believe that steel and concrete houses are shockproof. When adobe is destroyed, it crumbles like dirt, but concrete better maintains its form when its surface integrity is breached. Still, concrete blocks can do more damage than adobe walls; when they fall on people, they are deadly. The comparatively benign effects of the 1917 earthquake live on in oral traditions as a deterrent to temptations of modernization.

The survival rate of the 1917 earthquake proves the wisdom of Kaqchikel elders. While most people know the 1976 earthquake was more powerful than the one in 1917, they attribute the increased death rate to the "Spanish construction" of houses.[4] The implication is that if people had stayed with the older style of housing, many deaths could have been avoided. Clearly, the simpler construction that Kaqchikel ascribe to their older generations saved lives. The son of the first Kaqchikel teacher in the region uses the Catholic church as an example of superior Kaqchikel workmanship. The church was one of the only buildings standing after the earthquake. He says, "The church was well built by the Kaqchikel with special wood. Instead of using nails, they used cows' tails. The *kaxlan* [Spaniards/foreigners] did not do any of the work, only the Kaqchikel. That is why it did not fall."[5] Until his death in the early 1990s, one man in Comalapa who feared the consequences of an earthquake insisted on living in his own structure of straw and bamboo separate from his family's more modern home.[6] Some people heed the underlying advice of oral traditions. Most, however, could not resist the desire to build with new materials and, as a result, the devastation of the 1976 earthquake was overwhelming. In most cases, the lures of modernization are stronger than the lessons from oral traditions. This trend continues today as most families who can afford it construct with cement block and steel rods. Furthermore, some of the wealthier families build three- or four-story houses with these materials. Many Kaqchikel believe these people will suffer in the next earthquake because they have not recognized the insuperable power of nature in oral traditions.

The 1976 earthquake leveled a number of towns in the department of Chimaltenango. More than 22,000 died in the earthquake nationwide, but Guatemalan newspapers agreed that Chimaltenango bore the brunt of the loss. One newspaper estimated the death toll in the department of Chimaltenango to be as high as 15,172, with 30,456 injured. Compared to Chimaltenango, Sacatepéquez did not suffer extensive damage—1,556 died and 8,793 were injured.[7] The *Diario de Centro América* reported that the earthquake struck on the morning of February 4 at 3:03:33. It registered 7.2 on the Richter scale and lasted twenty-five to thirty seconds. The paper reported that Chimaltenango and Sacatepéquez had a "painfully extended panorama of death and ruins."[8] The National Meteorological Observatory reported that the seismic vibrations remained active for more than a week after the fateful day. These tremblings caused panic because people feared a repeat performance.[9]

Residents of Comalapa, Tecpán, and Poaquil tell vivid accounts of the earthquake. Nearly all of the residents recall that the earthquake hit at 3 A.M. on February 4, 1976. They remember that the earthquake leveled the towns immediately, and they recall how cries for help broke the silence of the night. Informants assert that the next day it was impossible to distinguish where the roads had been, and no vehicles could pass through or enter the town. Kaqchikel lament that thousands of people died trapped and crushed under the adobe and clay debris of the houses. They convey that as the day continued, bodies were stacked up, later to be buried collectively in large holes dug by the men. Informants deplore the fact that some entire families were wiped out. Kaqchikel also point out that the terror surrounding the earthquake did not end on that first day. They describe how people's fear swelled as tremors continued for a long time afterward.

The Guatemalan newspaper *La Hora* asserted that the earthquake exacted the highest toll on Comalapa and Tecpán, with Poaquil also suffering gravely.[10] Its front-page articles featured the devastation in the department of Chimaltenango: "San Juan Comalapa, Saragoza [*sic*], Patzicía, Tecpán, San Martín Jilotepeque possibly are the most seriously affected; from our observations yesterday, we found these towns completely razed and without any hope that they can be reconstructed."[11] Destruction in Comalapa was so overwhelming that *La Hora* focused its reports on conditions there:

Comalapa presents a true national tragedy, 98 percent of the houses have fallen to the ground and the few that are standing will have to be demolished. . . . The four Catholic temples suffered greatly. . . . [The central parochial church,] a national monument, conserved half its structure, but the convent and main altar came tumbling down; it has survived 3 prior earthquakes. The dimension of the catastrophe in Comalapa is terrible, the streets are impassable and each instant one stumbles upon the injured and dead, . . . the streets were processions of death. . . . Because of the shortage of coffins they had to bury [the

dead] in . . . rustic boxes, sacks, straw mats and some without any protection, in pits of 2 by 3 meters deep. . . . Because of the lack of space,
they buried as many as eight people in one grave. . . . The town of
Tecpán is also on the ground, and without official confirmation they
calculate that over 3,000 people have died.[12]

The only building left standing in Comalapa was the Catholic church.
Miguel Angel Rayo, a Comalapense who worked in the capital as a journalist, wrote: "The scene makes one cry when contemplating one of the saddest
phenomena that this department has ever seen, worse even than when we
suffered Fuego's volcanic eruption."[13] This generation had never experienced
such intense loss.

Kaqchikel remember how most residents of Tecpán, Poaquil, and Comalapa united in an effort to help each other, forgetting past differences. As
one teacher recalls, "The people formed groups to gather food and water
for each other, but there were no Ladinos in these groups helping people
out."[14] According to informants, Kaqchikel worked together, while most
Ladinos remained disinterested. Kaqchikel note that aid and volunteers arrived from other towns within Guatemala and from other countries. Residents of Comalapa recall that the town built a hospital in response to the
earthquake.[15] Kaji' Kawoq, a Kaqchikel linguist from Patzicía, compared the
1976 earthquake to the 1998 Hurricane Mitch disaster in Nicaragua and
Honduras. He noted that international relief efforts in both cases were impressive. His people learned that hope and life could come from intense hardship, and he speculated that people in Nicaragua and Honduras experienced
the same phenomena.[16] Kaqchikel united to overcome adversity, and as a result they consider themselves stronger and wiser.

The earthquake has been incorporated into oral traditions and will therefore be shared with future generations. In Comalapa, while working on a
road, a twelve-year-old boy told me that the pieces of adobe and clay we were
digging up were ruins from the houses destroyed in the earthquake. He proceeded to give me a detailed account of the disaster, which occurred before
his birth.[17] Members of the community had made sure that younger generations would not forget the event.

The earthquake did not systematically destroy all Kaqchikel towns. People
of Barahona and Aguas Calientes have more benign memories of the 1917 and
1976 earthquakes. Neither one hit their towns with significant force. Residents assert that most houses fell in Aguas Calientes and Barahona but that
only between five and ten people died in the 1976 earthquake. Oral accounts
specify Chimaltenango, Comalapa, and Tecpán as the main victims. Infor-

mants attribute their high survival rate to two factors: the three epicenters of the earthquake surrounded Chimaltenango, not Sacatepéquez, and the homes in Aguas Calientes and Barahona were made of bamboo and straw, not of adobe and clay.[18] Kaqchikel of Aguas Calientes and Barahona are aware that the earthquake hit other areas harder than their towns. Still, some residents in Aguas Calientes and Barahona continue to live in homes made of bamboo, straw, and wood.

While most people in Aguas Calientes and Barahona survived the earthquake, a lack of basic amenities ensued. Ixtojil, a fifty-eight-year-old weaver from Barahona, describes the aftermath: "On Wednesday, February 4 at 3 A.M. all the houses and chapels fell. There was no electricity or corn grinders. People quickly ran out of gas and candles. The road was covered. No cars could pass; people could walk over it [the debris] but not carry heavy things. People slept, and prepared and ate food in the road. In other places many more died. Some people lived in the soccer field because all the houses fell."[19] Others recall that another effect of the earthquake was an increase in prices due to the scarcity of goods. Informants also note that housing material was especially expensive because all the homes had to be rebuilt.[20]

Amidst the death and destruction, Poaquil enjoyed the creation of a lake. According to oral histories, the earthquake caused a landslide that dammed a river and created a lake. Poaquilenos recall that Canadian relief workers promptly stocked the lake with fish. Informants note that today some farmers take advantage of the water source to irrigate their fields. The lake has been a source of income and entertainment, as residents enjoy fishing and swimming. (Kaqchikel also point out that few people in Poaquil know how to swim well and that about a dozen people have drowned since 1976.)[21] The lake is currently drying, and some predict it will disappear within ten years. In spite of this fate, Kaqchikel see the lake as a gift. Poaquilenos named the lake K'ak'a' K'aslem (new life). One woman explains, "The water [lake] gave new life to our town."[22]

The disaster ended the 1976 campaign of President General Kjell Eugenio Laugerud García (1974–78) to retake Belize (after 1976 the Guatemalan government made other attempts to invade Belize). Guatemalans claim that Belize is rightfully theirs because England did not fulfill its agreement to build roads in exchange for land. The Guatemalan army was on the Belize border poised to attack when the earthquake struck. Laugerud wisely withdrew the military forces and focused all government energies on relief efforts. The troops worked on the roads and in this manner developed some ties to Mayan communities. Despite feeling a just claim to Belize, Kaqchikel were thankful that the earthquake stopped a potential military conflict. As

B'eleje' Ey states, "Before the earthquake, Guatemala and England had problems over Belize. Troops and tanks were at the border ready to fight. But the
next day, the earthquake hit and [the government] pulled back the troops.
People were scared because [the government] was ready to fight."[23] The earthquake spared Guatemala a military conflict, but it accelerated the conditions
for internal military strife.

The disastrous results of the earthquake revealed the Guatemalan government's inability to handle a national crisis. Political and military leaders
fought for control of the National Reconstruction Committee because they
were attracted by the possibility of large amounts of foreign aid. These leaders hoped to follow the example of Nicaragua's dictator Anastasio Somoza
Debayle, who took advantage of international relief response to the 1972
earthquake in his country to augment his personal wealth and control over
the country. Studies of Nicaragua showed that 70 percent of the aid given
did not reach the people in need. Guatemala's devastation also attracted
many national and international aid organizations. However, the experience
of nongovernmental organizations following Nicaragua's earthquake caused
them to directly control their aid. Nongovernmental organizations made a
policy decision not to funnel aid through the Guatemalan government. Ox-
fam and World Friends, for example, worked directly with people at the local
level. As a result, the Guatemalan government's effort was inadequate because they did not have significant resources. Still, the relief effort was quick
and efficient thanks to the contributions of these nongovernmental organizations, the Catholic Church, and to a lesser extent various Protestant groups.
In most cases, aid had to arrive by helicopter since roads were impassable.
People within Guatemala responded generously to the crisis. A group of
Comalapenses living in Guatemala City formed a committee to facilitate the
donation of corn, beans, milk, blankets, clothes, provisions, cooking pots,
medicine, tools, and gasoline to those most in need.[24] The aid from both
inside and outside the country proved essential to people's ability to survive
and rebuild their communities in the midst of their government's impotence.
However, as oral histories recount, this aid did not come without a high price.

Some of the volunteers who offered their services had ulterior motives.
Evangelicals had been arriving since President Barrios's invitation in the
1870s, but according to Kaqchikel oral accounts, the process accelerated in
the late 1970s. Kaqchikel assert that Protestants strengthened their presence
through their generous response to earthquake victims.[25] A significant evangelical presence remains in most Kaqchikel towns; in fact, Guatemala is one
of the most Protestant Latin American countries today.[26] The Protestant presence affected the culture, religion, and interpersonal relationships of these

towns, but it proved more benign than other influences swept in by relief efforts.

The international response to the 1976 earthquake was not focused solely on emergency aid. Some volunteers played important roles in the civil war that intensified in the Kaqchikel towns of Chimaltenango shortly after the earthquake. People of Poaquil remember a Canadian who came under the auspices of offering relief to earthquake victims but who wanted to organize a paramilitary group to fight the government. These international actors left an indelible mark on Kaqchikel communities because of the wake of death they left.

Many Kaqchikel consider the earthquake and the subsequent violence the most difficult circumstances they have had to face. Kaqchikel in the department of Chimaltenango make a strong connection between the earthquake and la violencia. Kaqchikel were delighted to have volunteers who offered building materials, foodstuffs, water, and clothes, but they point out that in some cases aid was conditional. Some say they had to attend meetings to gain access to these donations. They note that during these meetings, organizers espoused Marxist ideology and made lists of names of people interested in obtaining materials. While many Kaqchikel claim they did not reflect on the Marxist teachings, the military associated those being "indoctrinated" as guerrilla sympathizers. Kaqchikel informants claim that the military later acquired these lists and killed people whose names appeared on them. They also note that those who housed volunteers/revolutionaries suffered a similar fate. The ideological teachings were irrelevant to Kaqchikel; most attended meetings only to get aid materials. In fact, most recipients felt no ideological connection to the meetings. Therefore they see no basis for the military's actions and perceive the military's use of these names as wanton and baseless. Kaqchikel in Comalapa remember that local leader Enemías Cúmez was the first murdered by the military as President Gen. Romeo Lucas García (1978–82) ushered in his program of genocide in 1978. Foreign and domestic personnel associated with aid campaigns caused further destruction. The earthquake and la violencia are always mentioned together because the former simply flowed into the latter.

In contrast to Kaqchikel historical perspectives, most analysts find a more indirect connection between relief organizations, subversive groups, and increased violence. These scholars argue that the government's failure to respond to the earthquake provided nongovernmental organizations the opportunity to work directly with local organizations, such as Christian-based communities (grassroots Christian organizations) and other cooperatives and unions. At a time when Mayan communities needed them most, young local leaders exceeded their expectations. Young, emerging leaders had a chance to prove their abilities and thereafter continued to make positive contributions to their communities. The military regime quickly responded to the success of local leaders and organizations. Two weeks after the earthquake, the army began a counterinsurgency sweep of northern Guatemala in which leaders of Catholic Action and Liberation Theology groups, peasant cooperatives sponsored by USAID (United States Agency for International Development), reconstruction brigades, and others who took responsibility for relief efforts were targeted by a campaign of terror and repression. Because their demands were increasingly met with increased repression from the state, many Maya began to see armed struggle as their only outlet. Some began to directly and indirectly support guerrilla organizations as a means to struggle as a community against the structure of domination inherent in the state. As popular mobilizations increased, so did the violence.[27]

Jan Flora and Edelberto Torres Rivas offer another explanation for the state's campaign of terror. They argue that the reason behind military repression was not the danger of the guerrilla forces, but the containment of salaries. They point out that the repression of the late 1970s coincided with the decline in export profits that accompanied the world economic slowdown.[28] Regardless of the different explanations for increased military activity, scholars generally agree that la violencia increased shortly after the earthquake and that Maya were the main victims. Because their suffering continued to grow, Kaqchikel attribute a causal relationship between earthquake relief efforts and la violencia.

Despite this connection in oral histories, the capacity to comprehend the two stages differs significantly. The earthquake, though a mysterious event, made more sense to Kaqchikel than the genocidal campaign carried out after the natural disaster. People could explain the earthquake as an act of God, but the violence was incomprehensible. One Kaqchikel man from Tecpán explains that "the earthquake was very difficult but it was the [will] of God so what could we do? But the violence was different because it was the [will] of man. You have to understand how it was. We assumed the soldiers were going to help us but they killed us."[29] That soldiers would kill innocent people was preposterous to the Kaqchikel sense of justice. While the end results were the same, the catalysts were distinct. In some instances, what appeared to be an assuaging factor after the earthquake brought increased anguish.

In contrast, oral accounts from Barahona and Aguas Calientes imply that the civil war did not sow the violence that other regions of Guatemala experienced. Furthermore, Annis noted that compared to the north and west of the highlands, Aguas Calientes suffered little direct persecution. However, in other ways effects of la violencia disrupted Aguas Calientes.[30]

Interactions with foreigners that prove detrimental to Kaqchikel are not uncommon in Kaqchikel history. For this reason, Kaqchikel remain wary of outsiders. Prior to the Spanish arrival, Kaqchikel had constant tensions with other Mayan groups. The Spanish invaders began a cycle of conflict with nonindigenous people that Ladinos have perpetuated. Even under the auspices of aid, contact with foreigners can be harmful. Consequently, Kaqchikel reserve their trust until they know individuals well. When Kaqchikel can develop common bonds and mutual comprehension with outsiders, they accept them into their community.

Famines

The forces of nature and Ladinos at times combined to impose famines on Kaqchikel. Oral traditions attest that famines are a phenomenon of the last 100 to 150 years. They claim their Kaqchikel ancestors did not face scarcity of food because they lived in harmony with nature and only consumed what they needed from the surrounding vegetation and animal life. Contemporary Kaqchikel assert that land and resources were abundant and that older generations knew how to best manage the environment. They say food became scant with the arrival of the Spanish and more recent increase of the Kaqchikel population.

Contrary to Kaqchikel oral traditions, the *Anales* recorded a significant frost that killed the maize crops before the Spanish arrived. Kaqchikel forebears wrote, "The famine is truly terrible and the people cannot take any more."[31] The *Anales* also mentions that locusts caused great alarm in 1513.[32] While Kaqchikel oral traditions relate a more recent phenomenon of famines, the *Anales* shows that agricultural failure due to adverse climatic conditions and locusts occurred before the Spanish arrived.

Kaqchikel oral traditions assert that many years ago a widespread famine affected the people. Informants say that crops did not grow; some were able to buy basic foodstuffs such as corn and beans, but most had to forage for food. They emphasize that it was a difficult time.[33] Ix'ajpu', a thirty-year-old who works for a women's development organization, shares what her grandfather told her about a famine: "The hardest time in our town history was around 1900–1910, when there was no work, money, land, or food. We did not even have land to farm on. The Ladinos took our land. We had to buy corn, but we did not have any money. People were forced to start trading because they did not have any cash. People would trade their po't for food.

Many people died."[34] According to many people, famines were the most difficult times for the Kaqchikel.

Kaqchikel were not the only Guatemalans to suffer from famines. McCreery asserts that many Mayan groups complained of crop damage and food shortages. Guatemala suffered repeated corn shortages from 1870 until 1940, and had experienced periodic scarcity of foodstuffs since the colonial period. In 1915, for example, a lack of rainfall and a locust invasion resulted in a shortage of corn. To fill the void, the government imported corn for the municipalities.[35] Unfortunately, this aid did not reach many of the areas in need. A Ladino author from Tecpán noted that while corn and bean production did not reach the degree of scarcity expected after the lack of rain, the rising prices led to a difficult situation; the shortage in the market resulted in expensive corn.[36] A decrease in production affected farmers directly, in their own fields, but also indirectly through rising market prices of staple goods. Subnormal harvests meant that many people could not afford to buy enough corn to supplement what their own fields failed to produce.

Most contemporary Kaqchikel have lived through, or at least heard of, one or more famines. The causes of famine varies in Kaqchikel oral traditions. Ix'ajpu' blames Ladinos for usurping Kaqchikel land and subsequently their source of livelihood. However, others recognize that climatic conditions also played a significant role in some famines. Tecpanecos remember a bad famine in the 1920s or 1930s when a frost came early in September and killed all the cornfields.[37] They say farmers attempted to protect their cornfields by covering them with straw mats but that their efforts were unsuccessful and, as a result, food aid was necessary. Tecpanecos recall that people formed a line at 2 A.M. to receive four pounds of corn distributed by the town council. Because tensions were so high, people fought while they waited in line. Tecpanecos also note that sparse food supplies forced them to eat weeds and ground corncobs. Kaqchikel lament that for many people a bloated stomach led to death.[38] Other Kaqchikel towns, such as Comalapa and Poaquil, recall an early frost that killed their agricultural produce and, subsequently, their community members. In 1933 the governor of Chimaltenango also reported that frosts caused considerable losses to corn and bean crops in the towns of Tecpán, Patzún, Patzicía, and Santa Apolonia (which borders Poaquil and Comalapa).[39]

Oral histories note that another cause of famines was a lack of rain. Rainfall usually begins in April—May at the latest—in the highlands of Guatemala. However, in the mid-1950s, as Kaqchikel recall, rain did not come until after June 24, the patron saint day of Comalapa. They deplore that by this time farmers were desperate and say that a less than optimal crop resulted. Oral traditions recount that additional reasons for crop failure were locusts and other insects.[40] The failure of their staples—corn and beans—meant harsh living conditions.

The Ministry of Agriculture recognized that drought and locusts were primary causes of agricultural shortages. The 1923 annual report stated: "A strong invasion of worms in September significantly impaired the sowing of wheat in the department of Chimaltenango. These worms, recognized as the larvae of *Ag frotis segetum,* reproduce with exceptional abundance when there is a long period of drought, as occurred this year."[41] In Chimaltenango, maize production in 1922 decreased nearly 6,000 quintals from the previous year. In 1923 maize production fell an astronomical 27,287 quintals, and bean production dropped 2,289 quintals.[42] Chimaltenango was hit hard by the adverse farming conditions, but the nation as a whole also suffered decreased production. The government recognized the reduced corn harvest as a serious problem. In 1923 and 1924, President José María Orellana (1921–26) passed bills that eliminated import taxes on maize "to prevent the scarcity due to the bad harvests."[43]

Impending food shortages forced the government to import and distribute corn to the areas most in need. The geography and topography of Guatemala, however, impeded the government's ability to supply the areas that most suffered from famines. The department of Chimaltenango was one of these areas. Kaqchikel from Comalapa and Poaquil remember only one time that food aid came from an outside source, and in that case the corn had already spoiled.[44] Tecpanecos, on the other hand, received a ration of corn from the municipality. Tecpán's location on the Pan-American Highway allowed easy access to distribution centers. The inaccessibility of Poaquil and Comalapa, and other Kaqchikel towns, exacerbated the suffering during periods of low agricultural production.

The downturn of production did not correct itself quickly. In 1926 the Ministry of Agriculture warned that there would be a shortage of maize because the combination of a locust plague and a lack of rain had devastated the harvest in the previous year. The locust plague intensified in 1926. The continued scarcity forced the government to import 10,000 quintals of corn, which it sold at cost to departments most in need. By late 1926, with the aid of natural parasites, agriculturists were winning the battle against the locust plague. Unfortunately, this gain was ephemeral; in 1928 maize production decreased 10 percent. This deficiency forced the government to import 411,436 quintals of corn. The eradication of locusts continued to be a concern for the Ministry of Agriculture into the 1930s. The ministry consistently mentioned Chimaltenango and Sacatepéquez as departments threatened by these destructive insects.[45]

By 1934, weather conditions and insects ceased to ruin crops. The governor of Chimaltenango wrote that people farmed more communal land in an attempt to compensate for the low production in previous years. Likewise, residents of Poaquil solicited the municipality to distribute more municipal land among individual farmers. Unfortunately, the solicitors were too poor to pay for a surveyor, so the municipality did not distribute the land. Eventually, the program to farm more land resulted in large dividends. The governor of Chimaltenango was proud to report that the intensified sowing allowed his department to supply all the basic necessities of its inhabitants and to assist neighboring departments.[46] The governor was pleased with the agricultural production under his reign, but at the same time he recognized the prolonged suffering that people of his region had experienced. He stated, "A great number of people are in bad conditions, but harvests were abundant and the price of grains is completely low, avoiding in this manner the hunger that the farming people have felt."[47]

Families had different means of surviving famine. Kaqchikel recall that some people ate only one tortilla or a few lima beans a day. They remember that women mixed a little corn meal with chicken feed or ground corncobs to make tortillas. Some searched for edible plants in the forest. Informants lament that children suffered the most and that many died of malnutrition. In an attempt to numb their children's hunger pains at night, mothers boiled rocks in a cooking pot over an open fire, as if in preparation for a meal. When their children cried for food, mothers replied that it would be ready shortly, stalling until the children drifted off to sleep. Informants deplore that in the morning, children awoke with hunger pains that could not be quelled.[48] While people were creative with their resources, at times solutions could not be found within the communities.

To alleviate the suffering, men searched for work outside the community. The governor of Chimaltenango noted that the majority of the residents went to work on the large farms on the coast.[49] Oral histories recount that while people had worked on the coast seasonally for years, famines increased the number of men who migrated in an attempt to feed their families. Kaqchikel recall that at their worst, famines affected even the coastal regions, and people could not find work there either.[50] Poor agricultural conditions forced people to abandon their connection to the land of their birth. As seen in chapter 2, Kaqchikel recognized that even though coastal migration was harmful to their health and family, they had to go for economic reasons. That migration was warranted suggests the extent to which Kaqchikel were suffering in their western highland communities.

In 1955 the Ministry of Agriculture initiated a "program for the intensification of corn cultivation, as a necessary measure to counteract the scarcity of this article of daily consumption." The annual report specifically mentioned Poaquil as a town whose crops suffered over the past year. The government again imported corn to distribute among several departments,[51] and once again the government tried to remedy the low agricultural production that persisted in Kaqchikel territories; however, this aid did not necessarily reach the areas most affected.

To combat problems of famine, Kaqchikel experimented with different options. Many Kaqchikel agree that the arrival of chemical fertilizer ended the recurrent famines and alleviated the need to work on the coast. They say that chemicals initiated more intensive and productive farming. They note that increased production allowed for some margin of error, as dried and stored produce lasted longer. Kaqchikel assert that since the arrival of chemical fertilizer in the 1950s, no major famines have struck these Kaqchikel towns.[52] During good years, chemical fertilizer increased production that would offset low output during below-normal production years. As seen in chapter 2, however, these fertilizers also had negative consequences.

Oral traditions in Barahona and Aguas Calientes do not mention famines. One reason for this omission is the rich agricultural area in which they live. Furthermore, that their location has been close to the governing capital (first Ciudad Vieja, then Antigua, and then Guatemala City) may mean that public officials lent special attention to ensure that an adequate production of agricultural goods was supplied to the capital. Due to their proximity to important political and economic centers, climatic advantages, and rich farmland laden with volcanic soil, Kaqchikel of Barahona and Aguas Calientes were spared life-threatening famines.

Conclusion

Kaqchikel oral traditions purport that natural disasters and the resulting deaths are part of the cycle of life. Kaqchikel realize that earthquakes, famines, and other forces of nature cannot be eradicated. At the same time, Poaquil's lake provides proof that the forces of nature also create new life. Modernization allows for new building materials, but few elders believe that cement and iron can withstand the force of a powerful earthquake. Even the solution for famines—chemical fertilizer—has brought new problems. Consequently, Kaqchikel oral traditions preserve these tragedies, as well as the responses to these destructive forces, as a way to minimize their future impact on the community. These memories encourage people to both enjoy their life now and to be aware of impending danger.

Not everyone heeds these warnings. Few people construct their homes with bamboo and straw to minimize the effects of another earthquake. The pressure to modernize has been too great on the community. Most Kaqchikel want to incorporate technological and scientific developments into their lives. Kaqchikel do not fear change; in most cases, they embrace it. However, they also realize the limitations of modernization, and lessons of how desperate times can become will never be forgotten. The 1976 earthquake, women who boiled rocks to fool their children into sleep, and men who migrated to the coast in search of work are sad reminders of their lack of command over their own destiny. Kaqchikel understand, though, that they must accept events beyond their control.

While forces of nature fit within their conceptual understanding, death and destruction caused by human actions remain incomprehensible to Kaqchikel. They seek to avoid these evils. Kaqchikel share stories that show the advance of foreigners into their communities. Kaqchikel aversions to medical personnel and relief workers are apparent. Some people attribute famines to Ladinos' voracious appetites for fertile land. These historical relations leave Kaqchikel tentative about accepting outsiders who could potentially breach Kaqchikel security. When Kaqchikel do not have established relationships with foreigners they have no way of developing trust and confidence in them. Because they do not share the same history or connection to the community as Kaqchikel, outsiders must prove their legitimacy. Therefore, Kaqchikel are skeptical of foreigners and Ladinos even when they come offering aid.

Kaqchikel oral traditions teach people to approach foreigners with trepidation. Since Spanish contact, examples of Spanish and Ladino abuse, exploitation, destruction, and murder of Maya abound. These teachings are not unique to people of Guatemala. Richard Price found a similar vein in oral traditions of Saramaka people in Surinam: "The fear of group betrayal, forged in slavery and decades of war, remains a cornerstone of the Saramaka moral system."[53] Many generations of suffering caused by outside forces taught Saramaka to distrust other people. Similarly, a perpetual cycle of forced labor and violence has caused Kaqchikel to withhold their trust in Ladinos and foreigners.

On the other hand, Kaqchikel accept natural disasters and epidemics. At times they rationalize these natural calamities as punishments for past transgressions. Some opine that the population or community was growing too fast or that people no longer respected the land or forces of nature.

Even when Kaqchikel cannot explain why natural disasters happened, they can comprehend them. In contrast, destruction caused by human forces—government officials burying people alive, soldiers killing people, or, to a lesser extent, chemical fertilizer adversely affecting people's health—have no rational explanation other than human malice and are therefore unnecessary. Kaqchikel do not accept these actions in their worldviews as part of the natural cycle of life. This distinction is also apparent in the way they analyze national and local leaders. Kaqchikel abhor politics that bring national instability and personal insecurity. A major challenge for Kaqchikel is that the majority want to be involved in national and international development and invite relations with foreigners they can trust. At the same time, they seek ways to filter out negative consequences and sources of conflict that emanate from these interactions, especially those that seem avoidable.

The most important lesson Kaqchikel learn from hardships, however, is that they can overcome them. Kaqchikel oral traditions express different ways to deal with natural disasters. Kaqchikel work together or seek solutions outside the community, as exemplified by their varied reactions to earthquakes and famines. As Kaji' Kawoq observed, often these struggles lead to a greater understanding and appreciation of life. Kaqchikel resilience in the face of natural disaster and foreign intrusion is essential to the maintenance of their cultural, linguistic, and communal vitality.

5
Education, Exclusion, and Assertiveness

Ri tijob'äl rik'in ri qetamab'al, man junam ta'

Kaqchikel have felt the extension of the state apparatus in their lives through education. Historically, the government has imposed education upon Maya to incorporate them into Ladino society. Kaqchikel have recognized these intentions and have taken action to minimize their impact. They have long respected the importance of both formal and informal education. Teachers, school administrators, and others associated with academic pursuits receive high accolades in Kaqchikel oral histories. As one teacher points out, "Education is fundamental."[1] Kaqchikel desire a learning process that includes, comprehends, and respects their culture and lifestyle. Kaqchikel have willingly participated in educational institutions when the schools are advantageous to them, and they feel a sense of ownership. They refuse, however, to allow state institutions to undermine their distinct identity.

Uninviting Policies and Schools

The goal of education in Guatemala since independence has been the acculturation of Maya. The 1824 Constituent Congress clarified the government's approach to Mayan languages and cultures: "The Constituent Congress of the State of Guatemala, considering that it ought to have one national language, and, while those [languages] still used by Indians are so diverse, incomplete, and imperfect, and are not sufficient to enlighten the people, does decree and declare that: The parish priest, in agreement with the municipalities of the people, should, through the most expedient, prudent, and efficient means, extinguish the languages of the Indians."[2] Public education did not cordially welcome Maya. Beginning in 1831 with Guatemala's first liberal leader, Mariano Gálvez, the goal was to Westernize Maya and break down their insularity, or "perfect the natural and social man." To wrest control of education from the Catholic Church, the liberals established lay, free, and obligatory public schools. Gálvez proposed the removal of Mayan children from their parents so they could be taught by wealthy Ladino "protectors." Gálvez intended his educational reforms to extend throughout the country but, in fact, the government's education program had little impact on the rural population.[3]

When liberals regained political power from conservatives in 1871, they made a more concerted effort to extend education to the rural population. Barrios blamed the Catholic Church for Guatemala's uneducated population. He considered education one of the government's principal responsibilities. In 1875 liberals passed the Organic Law of Primary Public Instruction, which called for a general and uniform education system that was obligatory, free, and civil in character. The law allowed children to dedicate a certain number of hours each day or week to assist their parents with domestic, agricultural, and industrial chores. Furthermore, if a family had several children, they could "take turns" to fulfill the school attendance obligation. The liberal government recognized the value of child labor for parents and sought to accommodate these demands. In an effort to reach a larger percentage of the population, Barrios constructed more schools. However, the government's resources were limited, and corrupt officials impeded the distribution of scholastic materials. The lack of resources such as books and other educational implements resulted in a dependence on the rote learning method. Furthermore, teacher training was inept and focused little energy on the needs of Maya.[4] The curriculum was largely irrelevant to Maya and remained that way throughout much of the liberal period. The government never attempted to incorporate Mayan ideas, authors, or concerns into public education. The liberal approach to education continued to alienate Maya into the twentieth century.

While public education was not inclusive, many Kaqchikel appreciated having the option to attend school. Kaqchikel oral histories note that President Barrios offered education to a wider range of the population than previous governments. They say he developed schools in some of the aldeas. Kaqchikel recognize that he brought the education system under the control of the state because he wanted to reduce the power and influence of the church, which had previously controlled the school system. They assert that as a result, more lay people attended school. Kaqchikel appreciate that Barrios wanted people to be able to read and write and thus established free education and passed laws that favored teachers.[5] A sixty-year-old soap and candle artisan praises Barrios for his educational reforms: "Barrios was a good president. He was our first really tough president. He established the schools. Prior to Barrios no one knew the letters, but he taught us all twenty-eight letters. All children had to attend school, and they all had a teacher."[6] Barrios's role in providing an education to a population that had previously been denied this opportunity is so crucial to Kaqchikel that they keep it alive in their oral traditions by personalizing his efforts. While Barrios did not personally teach Kaqchikel the alphabet, this depiction helps to keep his memory vital. Kaqchikel respect education as an ideal and appreciate Barrios's efforts to extend it to them.

Kaqchikel oral histories are more critical of the role of another liberal dictator, Jorge Ubico, in the provision of education. A minority of Kaqchikel credit Ubico with the effort to expand educational opportunities for Maya. They point out that he was the first to authorize the establishment of schools in all towns. They also note that Ubico obligated each finca to hire a professor to teach the children of their workers.[7] At the same time, most Kaqchikel opine that Ubico's goal was to build more schools and enforce mandatory attendance, not to impose quality control on the education itself. They say that the requisite education was Ladino and not relevant to Maya. They also assert that Ubico did not respect people in the education profession. One seventy-six-year-old agriculturist who had been a teacher elucidates that "Ubico made many schools, but he could not get teachers because the salaries were miserable."[8] His failure to provide adequate compensation for teachers indicated to most Kaqchikel that he was more committed to the imposition of education and the state in their lives than the provision of a quality education. Many Kaqchikel believed that Ubico did not want Maya to become too smart. Consequently, they resisted his attempt to steer them into this Ladino-dominated institution.

To extend education to isolated areas, Ubico passed legislation that established the state's and finqueros' responsibility to open rural schools in areas where more than ten children of school age lived. The number of rural primary schools in Guatemala increased from 784 in 1933–34 to 1,581 in 1938–39, and attendance nearly doubled. Ubico required that all teachers speak both Spanish and the local Mayan language (few actually learned a Mayan language). Guatemala suffered from a lack of resources, and the educational system was inadequate to fulfill the needs of children. Furthermore, most of the major changes occurred in urban, not rural, areas. The law that required attendance was more an expression of idealism than of expected compliance. In most cases, facilities were not conducive to learning. Schools were usually poorly equipped one-room buildings. It was not unusual to find one of these single-room buildings serving an area with a population of several thousand. Rural districts seldom boasted more than four grades and usually no more than two. Despite attempts to improve education, the number of schools was low (especially in rural areas), buildings and supplies were almost non-existent, teachers' salaries were ridiculously inadequate, few teachers had teaching degrees, and often teachers were unprepared for the work. As a result of these problems, the illiteracy rate in Guatemala during the Ubico regime remained one of the highest in Latin America.[9] In his study of the Guatemalan educational system, Carlos González Orellana concludes, "The Ubico period was a regression of the national pedagogical process and a paralysis of the general development of the culture."[10]

Most schools were an overt attempt to inculcate Maya with Ladino ideas. The curriculum included lessons on Spanish literacy, morality, natural history, grammar, arithmetic, and civic instruction. In his trips to the countryside, Ubico stressed that personal health care and hygiene should be part of the curriculum. He militarized all schools to ensure that children received proper instruction in obedience. Consequently, because public education was not geared toward villagers' lives, Maya did not see the need for it. The curriculum was based on memorization of ideas, not on functional problem solving.[11]

Even today, educational materials, methodologies, and subjects exclude Mayan reality. The curriculum teaches students about their Mayan heritage but claims that the powerful and intelligent Maya died when the Spanish "conquered" them. Consequently, the indoctrination insists, Maya should assimilate into the national culture and leave their language, dress, customs, and other cultural differences behind. Primary school texts present Mayan languages as "dialects." Furthermore, *Estudios Sociales,* a text for secondary students, disrespectfully characterizes Mayan custom, practice, and historical representations as "folklore," refers to its artists as "artisans," and labels autochthonous religious expressions as "superstition." One of the main books on Guatemalan universities' curricula is *La patria del criollo* by Severo Martínez Paláez, an author who asserts that the colonial system created "Indian" identity and that the indigenous culture is therefore illegitimate. He also argues that the maintenance of indigenous culture only serves to further oppress Maya.[12] Most Ladino curriculum and authors misrepresent and disrespect Maya.

Kaqchikel recognize the educational system as the continuation of Spanish attempts that began in the colonial period to eradicate their language and culture. One Comalapa school monograph observes:

The Spaniards . . . invaded not only the land and riches, but also the ideas and principally the language. Upon the arrival of the first missionaries that propagated Christianity in Guatemala, so the natives of this land could receive the gospel of God, they had to catechize in Spanish.

It was in this moment that the loss of native languages of these lands was initiated, complemented by the Education System that has been implemented in the country since the colonial period. Nevertheless, today there is an effort [to ensure] that everyone who inhabits these lands discovers and values their own roots, principally the language and customs of this town.[13]

For the most part, Ladino technocrats control the Ministry of Education, and their pedagogical approach appeals solely to urban and Ladino students.[14] Kaqchikel seek to liberate the public school system that denies Maya knowledge of their own ethnic histories, communities, worldviews, and languages.

Oral traditions point out that schools impose a new culture and worldview upon Kaqchikel. The curriculum is not relevant to the reality of Maya. Kaqchikel opine that the Spanish eliminated Mayan sources of knowledge. A Mayan daykeeper (*ajq'ij*)[15] elaborates, "Students are learning from foreign books, not our own. When the Spanish came, they killed us to shut us up, to close our mouths. A long time ago we used the book called *Popol Wuj*. It is like the *Anales de los Kaqchikeles*."[16] Kaqchikel lament that students are no longer learning about their own people. Waqi' Kan, a teacher and pedagogical advisor to DIGEBI (Dirección General de Educación Bilingüe [General Administration of Bilingual Education]), explains the implications of this curriculum: "The school is alienating us. We are in a very accelerated process of losing our identity."[17]

Kaqchikel resent Ladino domination of education. They perceive the Ladino education system as eroding the level of respect students once showed their elders. Oral traditions note that children no longer obey their parents and do not appreciate the sacrifices their parents make for them so they can study. Most Kaqchikel fear that students will acquire a Ladino character or personality in place of their own.[18] As Wo'o' Imox, a sixty-four-year-old agriculturist, says, "It is good that children go to school, but there is always good and bad. School has brought some bad things, but overall it is good. The bad part is that young men don't want to work, they just form gangs."[19] Ixpaläj, a seventy-one-year-old evangelical woman, is even more critical than Wo'o' Imox: "Before there was more respect and a lot of work. But now the school has brought evil."[20]

Oral histories reveal fear of Ladino intrusion. Many people resisted education at first. Kaqchikel assert that many were afraid to send their children to school because schools were devoid of Kaqchikel; only Ladinos taught and attended schools. They say Ladinos often hit Kaqchikel children. Furthermore, oral accounts attest to parents' beliefs that in schools Kaqchikel children would become lazy and frivolous and would learn how to steal because these were Ladino traits.[21] Oxi' Iq', a fifty-year-old tailor and farmer, further elucidates: "Our ancestors did not want us to go to school because then we would see how much the Spaniards killed us. They [the Spaniards] have a different character, a different way of thinking. They kill and steal and our parents did not want us exposed to that. The Spaniards have committed many problems. They grabbed and violated women and girls, so our ancestors would not accept the government school."[22]

In contrast, some Ladinos viewed education as a means to aid Maya. They believed that Maya had equal rights within the school system. Early in the twentieth century, Ladinos boasted about the school system's leveling effects. In his 1912 article about the department of Sacatepéquez, Víctor Díaz wrote: "In the schools many children attend, Ladinos and indios; there [in the schools] there are no distinctions of any kind."[23] According to some Ladinos, the state provided ample opportunity for Maya to improve their plight through education. A group of Guatemalan doctors informed the Congress of American Scientists at their 1940 conference in Washington, D.C.: "In our country a copious educational policy continues for our indigenous race. They [the government] have established schools in our military barracks that fight for the literacy of our young soldiers and the primary rural schools [that] carry the light of education, and instruction to all parts have multiplied."[24] This assessment is misleading, however. The main goal of the government was to develop the military. The government ensured that what little aid they did give to schools was publicized, but few attended the small number of schools that received aid.[25]

Kaqchikel are aware of the dangers of participation in Ladino institutions. Their culture coexists with a minority population that constantly attempts to inculcate them. Waqi' Kan warns of this interaction:

We are losing our language. It is an accelerated process of Ladinoization. When we speak of Ladinoization we are speaking of the Western culture that is implanting [itself] each time more strongly in our culture to the point that many people are embarrassed to be Kaqchikel. . . . It is like an inferiority complex because indigenous people try to hide their identity. In reality we have to deepen [our understanding of] our history and culture because we know so little about them. All of a sudden we are interested in more academic things, but we are abandoning the investigation of our own identity.[26]

Most people agree with this educator and lament that most schools only teach Spanish and that many children are neglecting Kaqchikel language and clothing. Kaqchikel want to be cognizant of the maintenance and continued development of their culture and identity.

Local Impediments to Schools

In addition to the fear of acculturation, oral histories show that socioeconomic realities were (and continue to be) conducive to aversion toward school. Kaqchikel point out that families could not afford to send their children to class because they needed them to contribute labor or income to the family. Kaqchikel also assert that others could not afford to buy their children notebooks, pencils, and other tools necessary for school.[27] In its 1948 study of Aguas Calientes, the Indigenous Institute noted: "Children could attend school for seven or eight years, or longer, but the school steals the help that these children can provide for their parents in the daily chores and occupations. Also there are very poor families who do not have the means to purchase the required clothing. Furthermore, the father needs the son to help him in his work in the fields to support the family."[28]

Kaqchikel understand the reciprocal relationship between the economy and education. As a teacher from Poaquil explains, "When children do not eat or do not have books, that hurts their education. When the economy is bad, it hurts education. For example, children who work on the coast miss school."[29] Many young children do not benefit from public education because their parents lack the resources to create an environment where education is the focus.

For some parents, education was not a high priority. Ixb'atz' explains why she had no formal education: "I never went to school because a long time ago you only went to school for two years. We went to the coast. We did not see the importance of school. We did not value education, especially if you were a young girl, but even my brother did not attend school. He took care of the animals."[30] People could see little practical application for Ladino education because it was so far removed from their reality. Furthermore, the demand for immediate tangible contributions to the family income took precedence over education.

A more recent phenomenon that inspired parents to remove their children from school was the fear of Communism. When parents in the Comalapa aldea of Xetonox learned that the government was providing breakfast for the children at school, many feared the program was a Communist plot and pulled their children from school. They were afraid that "Cuban ideas" were infiltrating the system and that the period of civil war would return.[31] Years of oppression and violence clearly had made Kaqchikel sensitive to change and Ladino interaction.

Social attitudes often precluded the formal education of girls. Most parents who did allow their children to attend school subscribed to traditional gender distinctions. Generally, girls were less likely to attend school than boys. Oral accounts point out that most parents told their daughters that school was not necessary for women because they were destined for marriage and domestic life. Informants recall that boys could receive a basic education, but for women it was extraneous information.[32] One sixty-year-old woman deplores: "I never went to school. I did not hear Spanish. When I did go to school they [the teachers] made me grind corn and weave. I was just in the kitchen so there was nothing in my notebook. I cannot read or write. They said it was important for boys to attend school, but the girl should just stay in the home. But that is not true. Girls and boys are equal and both need the school. If you do not know Spanish, it is sad."[33]

In some cases, children wanted to attend school, but parents denied them the opportunity. A baker, who struggles with the basic math skills necessary to attend his customers, adds, "A long time ago people did not like school. They did not allow children to go to school. I cannot even write my name because my dad brought me to the hills [to work], not to school. I cried in the hills. School is important."[34] Oral histories note that parents who allowed their children to begin school saw basic literacy as the desired end product. When children achieved proficiency in reading and writing, parents removed them from school. Informants recount that children, but not parents, recognized the utility of school beyond reading and writing skills.[35]

Even when Kaqchikel were open to the pursuit of education for their children, opportunities were negligible. Oral histories attest that many communities did not even have a school. They recall that some villages established schools in private homes, pointing out that even when villages had a simple school, teacher attendance was erratic. At times, they note, a member of the community with no educational training served as the teacher because the government never assigned an instructor to them.[36] One middle-aged woman describes her rural school: "I went to school for one year. It was not a school yet. It was just an adobe room. All we had was one notebook of manila paper for all our courses. And you never knew if the teacher would show up."[37] Informants assert that minimal resources, personnel, and conditions led many Kaqchikel to perceive school attendance as a waste of time. They argue that even rural communities with better educational facilities and resources only provided for a sixth-grade education and say that to send their children to another town to continue their studies was too great a sacrifice for parents. Some complain that teachers failed to challenge students scholastically. Some older Kaqchikel assert that their limited studies only taught them how to write their names.[38] One fifty-year-old informant concludes: "Certainly it is good that children attend school to learn something, but the Ladino teachers do not want to teach well, because they do not want us to learn and improve ourselves as indigenous people. They only want us to work."[39] His sentiments have been echoed by some finqueros, including, in 1927, Erwin Paul Dieseldorff:

> Of what value is it to a plantation hand to be able to read and write, or to know about history and geography? . . . Is it not true that giving the Indian classes a higher education than their social position requires only serves to disrupt their work? We know this for a fact, because we have learned from experience that the Indians who have learned to read and write are no longer useful as agricultural workers. We all want the economic advancement of the Republic, and the best way to achieve such progress is to increase the production of food staples and export crops. If we are to succeed in attaining this goal, however, we need workers that are contented with their social status, not an abundance of learned persons who look upon manual labor with arrogant disdain.[40]

The education of Maya was a threat to many landowners.

As a result of bad precedents, the push to develop rural schools met resistance in some communities. Junlajuj Kan, who at the age of ninety is legally blind, describes the situation in Simajulew: "People here did not want a school. In 1942 five of us asked Ubico for one. He established one here, but the people did not want it. He ordered them to send their children to school. School is good and back then only three existed in the area."[41] While some local leaders encouraged the establishment of educational facilities, many people opposed this intrusion. In other cases, Kaqchikel actually attempted bribery to prevent the construction of a school in their community. One agriculturist explains the reaction in his village, Nueva Esperanza: "I never went to school because I could not. People here said the school was for Ladinos, not for us. Our grandparents brought eggs and chickens to the government as a gift so they would not put a school here."[42]

Kaqchikel informants assert that in many communities the government established separate schools for Ladino and Mayan children, because Ladinos did not want to attend school with Kaqchikel. They point out that schools reflected the ethnic divisions in these towns. Kaqchikel lament that Ladino institutions received better-trained personnel and resources, whereas Ladino teachers in Kaqchikel-populated schools did not have teaching degrees. Comalapenses recall that children who spoke no Spanish had to go to *número dos* (number two), the school for Maya. Informants say that Kaqchikel children who spoke Spanish could attend Ladino schools, but Ladinos hit them.[43]

Outwitting Agents of Assimilation

In an attempt to increase Mayan incorporation into Ladino society, the government assigned the national police to rural towns to enforce school attendance.[44] Kaqchikel oral accounts note that public officials and teachers also walked the streets with a list of names and searched homes for school age children. Oral histories also affirm that these authorities grabbed children in the market and forced them to attend school.[45] Then they informed local political bosses who reprimanded the children and their parents for the infraction. In 1924, Daniel Hernández, the director of the national police, proudly reported:

> The constitution establishes that one of the principal prerogatives of the government is Public Instruction. . . . That is required of all children between six and fourteen years of age, and it is in this virtue that the police in its completion of its vigilant duty, because the law must be followed literally, has imposed a strict vigilance against minors and pursued without rest the "infant vagrancy," taking care that there is regular school attendance among children. . . . I order the pursuit of child fugitives who failed to attend their schools. The work of the police in the republic in 1924 was arduous but very fruitful.[46]

The national police branches that operated out of the departments of Chimaltenango and Sacatepéquez dedicated themselves to the eradication of school absenteeism. However, despite Hernández's claims of success, the battle against "infant vagrancy" was a constant challenge. In 1929 the government created a special force, called the school police, to deal solely with this problem.[47] Ubico reaffirmed the principle of obligatory attendance for all children between the ages of seven and fourteen.[48] Nonetheless, local officials noted that efforts to curb truancy were unsuccessful in many departments.

In 1935 the governor of Chimaltenango reported that "the public education of the indigenous people is greatly neglected; too few [indigenous children] attend the schools."[49]

Oral histories illustrate how Kaqchikel children eluded these officials. Informants recall that a frequent Kaqchikel response was to hide their children in the *tuj* (sweat bath) or the fields and inform officials that no children lived in the home. They also recount that if children met an official in the street, they were to tell the official that their mother was sick and that they could not attend school because they had to take care of her. Kaqchikel note that children feared these officials. They also point out that such sequestration attempts were especially common during the Ubico dictatorship. They remember that Ubico generally assigned this duty to Ladinos but that on occasion Kaqchikel men performed the service. Informants note that teachers would also snatch loitering children and take them to school. Kaqchikel attest that as recently as ten years ago, the government sent officials to enforce school attendance because they realized that many children were working in the fields instead of attending school.[50]

Efficacious Participation

A shift in Kaqchikel perspectives of state-sponsored education occurred in the mid 1940s. Oral histories recount that during the Arévalo administration, public officials gathered children in each town to ensure school attendance and fined parents who did not send their children. Nonetheless, Kaqchikel lauded Arévalo's efforts and welcomed mandatory attendance because they perceived that Arévalo increased the quality of education. They recall Arévalo wanting each town and village to have its own school. In 1948, for example, he established a school in the Comalapa aldea of Xenimaquín. Arévalo also supplied essential resources to these educational facilities. Kaqchikel appreciate that he increased the salary of teachers to attract and keep talented people. Some oral accounts hail Arévalo as a better president than Ubico because he improved the school system.[51]

Many scholars also credit the democratic governments of Arévalo and Arbenz with great strides in education for Maya. Arévalo inherited a disastrous educational situation. In 1947, for the first time in history, the government's expenditure on education was greater than its military expenditure, almost double what it was under Ubico. Expenditure on education increased 800 percent from 1944 to 1954. Arévalo expanded educational programs to attack Guatemala's 75 percent illiteracy rate. The democratic administrations dramatically increased both attendance and the number of rural schools. Furthermore, Arévalo provided better resources for these schools. Three-fourths of all teachers worked in the capital, in part because salaries were extremely low in rural areas. To combat this problem, Arévalo increased salaries from six to thirty quetzals a month. His government also improved teacher training and consequently the capacity of teachers. In 1945 the government established the Alameda, a rural school designed to instruct teachers about the Kaqchikel reality in the departments of Sacatepéquez, Chimaltenango, and Sololá. Unfortunately, many of the teachers did not focus on learning a Mayan language; only three of the thirty-two students who graduated in February 1948 spoke Kaqchikel. The rest studied English. Despite some minor setbacks, the school produced top-quality teachers who were more aware than their predecessors of the reality of rural life and its challenges.[52]

Arévalo provided teachers to areas that never before had their own instructor. Kaqchikel appreciate that he augmented the level of education in aldeas with educational facilities. For example, in Pamumus, Comalapa, Ubico provided only three grades, but in 1945 Arévalo raised the level to six grades, as it remains today. Furthermore, oral accounts attest that Arévalo provided scholarships to motivate people to study beyond the primary level of education. In the military, for instance, those who completed their primary education were eligible to win a fellowship to attend the Escuela Politécnica, the Guatemalan military academy.[53]

Despite improvements, the curriculum continued to focus on Ladinos and to ignore Mayan contributions to Guatemala. Arévalo wanted to utilize education to construct a modern nation and tie citizens to state institutions. Under Arévalo, the state changed its method of indoctrinating peasants and forcing cultural assimilation from military conscription to education.[54]

Oral histories attest that the government's education plan discriminates against Maya. One local leader asserts that the lack of education has hurt his people: "Children receive only three to four grades of education. I think it is a failure and the reason for our poverty. Now it is changing, but there are still problems because Comalapa does not have enough schools, and the government does not pay the teachers well."[55] Oral accounts note that unequal access to education remains a problem today. Kaqchikel assert that Ladinos continue to view Maya as inherently inferior. As a teacher from Poaquil opines, "The Ladinos say they are more intelligent than the Maya, but that is not true. We are capable also, but the opportunity is the key and that is not equal."[56]

Despite economic hardships and the state's efforts to exclude Kaqchikel culture and identity from public schools, many Kaqchikel perceive an inherent value in education. One innovative response to Ladino education was the formation of a Kaqchikel school. In the early twentieth century, Kaqchikel leaders of Comalapa petitioned the government of President Carlos Herrera (1920–21) for a Mayan school. On August 12, 1920, Herrera obliged, and the government created an indigenous and night school that was annexed to school number two.[57] Consequently, Kaqchikel gained control of the administration and curriculum of the Mayan school in Comalapa. Oral histories of Comalapa recount that a local leader named Ka'i' Tz'ikin led the charge to establish a Kaqchikel school and promote Kaqchikel teachers to provide a viable educational opportunity for Mayan children. He convinced the government to award six scholarships to indigenous men so they could study in Guatemala City and become teachers. Informants point out that Ka'i' Tz'ikin's school furnished an alternative to Ladino education and proudly state that eventually Ladinos in town realized that the education provided at the Kaqchikel school was of higher quality than their own. The indigenous men were better teachers than the Ladino men were because they had graduated with a teacher's degree. Oral histories note that some Ladinos petitioned to enter the Kaqchikel school, but Kaqchikel carefully chose the first Ladino attendees to ensure they respected the Kaqchikel people and culture. Eventually the Kaqchikel school dominated education in Comalapa and the two schools merged into one.[58] A Comalapa school monograph asserts that the two schools merged in 1958 and that the first class boasted twelve teachers and 320 students.[59] Through the Kaqchikel school, Oxi' Tz'ikin proudly asserts: "My father [Ka'i Tz'ikin] slowly woke up our people."[60] Another elder explains: "The *naturales* created their own school because the Ladinos were abusing them. They mistreated and hit the Kaqchikel children. They were in the center of town, and the indigenous people were on the outskirts, so [we] thought it was better we split up. Two young *natural* teachers came . . . to teach us. They had teacher's degrees, which was rare at that time. That is when the indigenous people moved up and the Ladinos stayed down. So in 1940, the Ladinos wanted to unite the two schools, because they saw how well we were doing."[61] Kaqchikel teachers empowered their people and forced Ladinos to respect their abilities.

Kaqchikel are proud of having developed their own school and curriculum. Comalapa's oral traditions even recall the names of the first Kaqchikel teachers from the community.[62] Kaqchikel note that they developed their own teachers who comprehended Kaqchikel reality. That Ladinos recognized the superiority of Kaqchikel education affirmed Kaqchikel confidence in their own endeavors. Jun Kan, a seventy-seven-year-old painter, remembers the unification of the two schools as a great moment: "When many Ladinos entered número dos, [school] discrimination ended. We were like brothers, a family. They no longer called us 'ixto.' . . . With education, theft and jealousy cease."[63] Ladinos respected Kaqchikel education, and according to Jun Kan racial prejudice decreased. An agriculturist concurs: "I was in school for four years. At that time there were no books, but there were two schools: number one was for Ladinos and number two was for naturales. There was a belief in those days: the Ladinos thought we were dumb. They said 'ixto' to us. But now we don't hear that and actually the Ladinos were thieves. Now the *natural* has improved. We are better because of education."[64] According to Kaqchikel, Ladinos never liked Maya, but at least now they seldom call them "indio" or "ixto" to their faces or hit them.[65] One man whose family owns three sewing machines, which they use to produce sweaters, explains the transformation in ethnic relations: "Over time we had to learn their language. Now we know it well and we earn titles, so it is more equal. Before we were not important to them because we are indigenes. Now we are more important. Now race is not important, everyone is equal."[66] The founding of Kaqchikel schools and the subsequent establishment of a less biased educational system has reduced explicit racism and improved relations between Ladinos and Kaqchikel.

Kaqchikel oral traditions preserve the evolution of formal education in their communities. Members of the community of Xenimaquín recall requesting that the municipality build a school in 1948. One sixty-year-old resident explains how the school began: "There was no school here a long time ago. Classes were in a private home. The teacher was only seventeen years old and had no formal training. The education provided only up to fourth or fifth grade. Then in 1950 they built a school here and later improved it. Now it is a good school with six grades."[67] The government made limited attempts to develop educational facilities in the department of Chimaltenango. They built schools in the main towns and in some villages. In 1917 the government constructed a new building to house the school in Panabajal, a village of Comalapa.[68] In 1920 the Ministry of Development made structural improvements to schools in Comalapa and built a school for music in Poaquil.[69] Despite (or because of) piecemeal improvements, Kaqchikel remain critical of education's instantiation through the national system. As one elder asserts, "In Guatemala we have the materials, but not the education or training. That is why we are not as developed as we should be."[70] Many Kaqchikel feel that Guatemala has not reached its potential because the quality and provision of education is so low. In response, oral histories note, some communities built their own schools. Residents of Pamumus remember how in 1962, their community split off from the village of Simajulew because they wanted to establish an independent school so their children would not have so far to walk. Likewise, in Palima, Kaqchikel boast they built their own school in 1990.[71] The initiative for educational development came from Kaqchikel. The majority of Kaqchikel value education and want their children to have access to it. Kaqchikel see a clear distinction between school as an institution and teachers. They value education but know that for it to be efficacious, schools must be staffed with qualified teachers. Most Kaqchikel are happy to pursue Western approaches to education as long as they are syncretized with their own approaches, contributions, values, and realities.

Today, there are a number of community-based Mayan schools in various departments of Guatemala that use Mayan languages and culture to teach children. Like the school in Comalapa eighty years ago, these schools developed in response to the tendency by Ladinos to misconstrue or omit Mayan contributions to Guatemala's past and present. In the 1960s, Guatemala's Ministry of Education recognized that Mayan children "were simply spectators [in public schools], which resulted in an absolute lack of interest in school on the part of those being educated, as well as their parents."[72] Mayan schools address this problem by providing an inclusive education that is relevant to Mayan children in rural areas.[73]

Kaqchikel understand that Maya have a vast array of knowledge that needs to be preserved and applied to their lives today. Many Kaqchikel intellectuals visualize the establishment of a Mayan university. The curriculum would include the Mayan alphabet, hieroglyphs, herbal medicine, and natural agricultural techniques. Kaqchikel recognize that their ancestors were intelligent people, and they wish to rescue some of that knowledge. They assert that their ancestors were not exposed to formal Spanish education, yet had tremendous wisdom. A former mayor of Comalapa wants to establish such a university in his town.[74] Kaqchikel strive to expound their ideas and approaches to life at higher levels of education.

Kaqchikel wish to establish ways to preserve their knowledge because they realize it is distinct from that of Ladinos. They assert that Ladinos wish to erase this wisdom and impose their own thought processes on Maya. Oxi' Imox, a sixty-eight-year-old evangelical farmer and barber, explains: "The Spaniards taught the Maya the Spanish language. The Maya were very intelligent so they learned it quickly. Then the Spaniards got nervous because they realized the Maya were powerful and good enough to rule. That is when they decided to fight them."[75] Even today, Kaqchikel recognize that people who have been denied formal education have a great deal of wisdom. One elder commends a man in Comalapa who had no Western education yet predicted when the 1976 earthquake would strike.[76] Jun Aq'ab'al, a twenty-year-old linguistic student, vehemently criticizes the subordination of informal education to formal education: "You think that after you read three to four books a day for a while that you know more than these people who are fifty to sixty years old and have experienced so much life."[77]

Kaqchikel support and encourage education when it does not exclude Mayan input and reality. Oxi' Tz'ikin says that when he was mayor he provided for the needs of schools whenever possible.[78] Kaqchikel oral histories note that people became accustomed to schools and appreciated the possibilities education opened up for them.[79] An eighty-six-year-old rural farmer explains: "A long time ago people worked only with a hoe and a horse. There were no floors. They just farmed corn and beans. But then the school arrived, and life began to change about twenty to thirty years ago."[80] Access to education changed the lives of many Kaqchikel. Oral accounts attest that in smaller communities with only six grades, Kaqchikel want to extend the level of education; they do not want their children to have to leave the community at a young age to attain a secondary-level education. Others note that some adults believe education will improve their quality of life and attend night-school classes to make up for education they did not receive as children.[81]

Oral histories note that schools were important in teaching Kaqchikel to read and write Spanish. Prior to the establishment of schools, few were proficient in Spanish. Kaqchikel recount that even as children, they dedicated their lives to manual labor. A seventy-one-year-old rural agriculturist asserts: "It is important that children know how to read and write Spanish, but we cannot. We are mutes. I never went to school. I just worked in the hills."[82] One woman explained that she had a different last name than her siblings because her father incorrectly filled out her birth certificate information.[83] Oral histories attest that most Kaqchikel were unable to communicate with Ladinos and often could not perform vital administrative tasks or adequately defend their personal and property rights. As seen in chapter 2, Kaqchikel recognize the importance of Spanish literacy in land titling. Those who could not write in Spanish lost their land; those who could were able to establish and protect their property rights. Kaqchikel proudly state that now more people can read municipal or official documents and write their name on them. They also say that Spanish fluency improved people's ability to find employment.[84]

Many people point out that the number of Kaqchikel professionals has increased as a result of education.[85] They say these positions translate into better representation by Kaqchikel in the national economy and society. Kaji' Kej, a seventy-nine-year-old farmer from Aguas Calientes, elaborates: "School is important. It is important that the students continue [to study] and go, hopefully, to defend the people of our race, because before, no one arrived at an office. They looked at you and saw that you were nobody and no one paid you any attention. But now wherever you go you hear of [indigenous] people who went [to work] in businesses or hospitals. That is a support for the people here."[86] Oral accounts attest that as Kaqchikel extend themselves in diverse employment opportunities, their rights and power expand. They assert that the increased number of Kaqchikel professionals facilitates better interethnic relations and opportunities for the rest of the Kaqchikel population, educated or uneducated. Kaqchikel point out that a minority of Maya now represent their constituencies in Congress. Most Kaqchikel assert that schools have helped increase the power of Maya in political, social, and economic spheres.[87] In Warren's study of San Andrés Semetabaj, Kaqchikel noted that improved education resulted in better (non-manual) employment, more efficacious relations with local and national leaders, and increased alternatives for social progress. One of Warren's informants states: "In the past, we were unaware that we could progress because we lacked the means, the opportunity. No people in my generation could prosper, although they had the intelligence, because they lacked the opportunity and approval. Now . . . we see that Indians are capable of studying widely, and the progress of our race is distinguished."[88] Kaqchikel recognize the connection between education and the realization of personal, communal, and national goals.

A transition from agriculture as a main source of livelihood to education as an avenue to success and wealth is occurring among Kaqchikel. As an evangelical farmer and store owner asserts, "The school is important. Children should no longer have to carry firewood. The best inheritance you can give your children is education, not land. Just give them education."[89] Another agriculturist laments: "None of my children are professionals. . . . I would have sold my land to put them through, but they did not want to study. Education is important."[90] Kaqchikel respect rural labor, but it is a hard life and they want better for their children. Many Kaqchikel perceive office employment in Guatemala City to be better than agricultural work in the countryside. One reason they encourage urban labor over rural labor is because of the limits of land tenure: landowners divide their land with each inheritance, so that eventually individuals will not have enough land to subsist.[91] This emphasis on education has improved opportunities for younger generations. Ix'aj, a sixty-eight-year-old expert weaver, opines: "Now young men do not know what hard work is like. The main reason for that is school. Now they get a good education and can find other jobs."[92] In spite of their appreciation of manual labor, the majority of Kaqchikel today want their children to attend schools, and they make the sacrifices necessary to bring about that reality.

Kaqchikel, especially those who live in rural areas, do not advocate the elimination of agriculture as a source of livelihood, however. One Tecpaneco points out that studies and agriculture are not mutually exclusive: "Both things are important, studies and our life. They help each other. We need our agriculture to live; we work it. If all we have is studies and money then there is nothing to buy, no food. It is the corn and beans that keeps us alive."[93]

Kaqchikel say it is imperative for them to have input into the educational system. The benefits of Kaqchikel influence in education have already been realized in many aspects of their lives. A teacher and former mayoral candidate explains: "Indigenous teachers came here to work with us. They helped us. It was like a new life. Now there are no more problems or jealousy. We work and do not drink. We are not afraid to go elsewhere to travel or work. Now almost all the teachers here [in Comalapa] are indigenous. They give value to our ways. As a result of the Peace Accords, there is a law to make a Mayan language official and there are more books in Kaqchikel. . . . The Peace Accords gave value to our people."[94] For many Kaqchikel, Mayan teachers vindicate their worldviews. Consequently, Kaqchikel have the confidence to work in other areas, knowing all the while that their ideas and lifestyle are inherently meritorious.

In many schools in Kaqchikel communities, the majority of teachers are Kaqchikel, and even the directors are Kaqchikel. Kaqchikel recognize these personnel as a vital link to the maintenance of their wisdom and culture.[95] As B'eleje' Ey states, "Now 'our people' are teachers, and that is important, because the exploitation [of Kaqchikel] is not as bad."[96] Kaqchikel have been empowered through their efficacious participation in the national education system. They have a sense of ownership in the system and no longer perceive education to be dominated by Ladinos. Kaji' Kej states, "It is important that [our children] go to school. . . . Hopefully, they will defend the people of our race."[97]

Kaqchikel control of and input into the national educational system has contributed to the advancement of Maya in Guatemala. Perhaps some of the most important contributions have come at the local and individual level. Informants point out that people have gained the confidence to explore new opportunities. As Waqi' K'at explains, "When the police came to the house to look for children to bring to school, the children hid in the tuj and put a b'ojo'y [large clay pot] over themselves. Then they went to the school and learned. The teachers taught us and our worth came from there."[98] Kaqchikel, who at first evaded public education, eventually utilized it for their own empowerment.

Kaqchikel have also realized an improvement in the provision of education by non-Kaqchikel. In one of the aldeas of Comalapa, Felipe, a Ladino from Comalapa, teaches alongside a Kaqchikel teacher. Felipe recognizes and appreciates the differences between him and his Kaqchikel students. He is trying to learn the language and always teaches in a manner that is inclusive and respectful of Kaqchikel. He displayed his openness when he married a young Kaqchikel woman from the aldea and observed Kaqchikel traditions in their courtship and wedding ceremony. Kaqchikel in the aldea and Comalapa thus respect him for his efforts and admire him for his willingness to teach in a rural area and learn about their reality. Likewise, in another Comalapa aldea, a Mam woman from Todos Santos Cuchumatán, Huehuetenango, speaks little Kaqchikel yet remains popular in the aldea and main town because of her ability to identify with and relate to Kaqchikel students. While Kaqchikel have become active participants in their education, they do not claim to have a monopoly on the provision of quality education.

Conclusion

The majority of Kaqchikel view education as essential to national and individual progress. They recognize that Guatemala is rich in natural resources but fails to develop its human capital. Consequently, the country has suffered from underdevelopment. A 1998 report by the United Nations Development Program agrees with this assessment and notes that unsanitary education conditions and a deficiency of teachers and resources were prevalent throughout the country. Haiti is the only nation in the Americas that invests less in education than Guatemala.[99] Warren further highlights Guatemala's educational deficiencies: "70 percent of the public schools offer only four years of classes and 92 percent of the population over fifteen years of age has never finished the conventional six years of primary education."[100] Moreover, the state does not provide equal levels of education for the Mayan and Ladino populations. A 1993 report confirmed that Maya receive fewer educational services from the state than Ladinos. Kaqchikel intellectual Demetrio Cojtí Cuxil argues that the educational system has attempted to carry out forced cultural assimilation at all levels. He cites the legislation, policies, institution, and content of the curriculum as an attack on the essence of Maya.[101] Public education initially had little to offer Maya and, consequently, until they could influence its direction and content, Maya maintained a distance from it. Despite these challenges, Kaqchikel view education as essential to personal advancement. Education can provide an escape from manual labor. The majority of Kaqchikel view education as a more valuable inheritance than land—a strong endorsement from people whose culture and identity is attached to the land. Kaqchikel who take advantage of education can obtain office jobs in an urban center or become teachers for their people. Kaqchikel increasingly interact with other Kaqchikel outside their communities. This transformation gives them confidence. Kaqchikel influence has increased in the national society, economy, and politics. Increased educational opportunities have led to the rise of Maya in national leadership positions. Consequently, Maya have a voice in national forums. These advances have facilitated better ethnic relations in Guatemala as Maya and Ladinos become accustomed to coexistence through daily interaction on equal terms.

Kaqchikel have always respected education but historically have had varying reactions to the state-sponsored school system. Ladinos have attempted to assimilate Maya into national society since the Spanish invasion. A more concerted effort to acculturate Maya took place under the liberal regimes, especially beginning with Barrios in the 1870s. Oral histories reveal that Kaqchikel attribute a personal and vital role to Barrios, who provided them access to education. This was the first opportunity for many Kaqchikel to get a formal education. Barrios's regime also insisted that people needed legal documentation to prove their ownership of land. Consequently, Spanish literacy became more important to Kaqchikel to protect their property and rights. They also needed Spanish proficiency to perform other tasks through the municipality. Nonetheless, Kaqchikel quickly realized that outside of Spanish literacy, the curriculum offered little to Maya in terms of representation or practical application. In many ways, Kaqchikel viewed this education as a weapon of the state to eradicate their distinctiveness. The government provided educational resources to Mayan communities on an individual basis, but national policy on rural education was inconsistent and resulted in facilities and personnel of poor quality in rural areas. In addition, when children attended school, Ladinos hit them and discriminated against them. Consequently, most Kaqchikel avoided the school system. They hid their children when government officials tried to enforce mandatory school attendance. Parents did not want their children exposed to the evils of Ladino thought and actions, namely, sloth, theft, and murder. Additionally, school-related costs prohibited some Kaqchikel from participation, and few Kaqchikel families could afford to sacrifice the labor source and income their children provided. Kaqchikel did not view schools as a place for an equal exchange of ideas but rather as an institution imposed upon them to demean their culture and force assimilation. Kaqchikel protected themselves against these incursions by the state. Nonetheless, as in the case with health care, Kaqchikel value education as an entity and separate it from the people who staff schools. In this way, Kaqchikel maintain hope for an educational system that reinforces their pride and contributions.

As Maya began to develop a greater sense of ownership of the educational system, they took advantage of it. Kaqchikel believed that education was important because it could provide them with not only Spanish literacy but also with better employment opportunities and a higher quality of life. They simply wanted to see academic institutions staffed by people who would provide inclusive and respectful instruction. Consequently, Kaqchikel leaders in Comalapa established their own school. They realized the state was not committed to providing them quality education, so they provided it for themselves. However, a shift in Kaqchikel perceptions of public education began in the 1940s, when they recognized that Arévalo was committed to improving education. Kaqchikel became more confident in the state's desire to provide them education because Arévalo built more schools, provided scholastic materials and resources, and attempted to make teachers more aware of Mayan communities and people. During Arévalo's presidency, the Ministry of Education designed educational programs that were applicable to Mayan realities. They established a school for teachers in the Kaqchikel region and taught other Mayan languages to teachers. The Ministry of Education attempted to prepare teachers for education in Mayan communities. Teachers responded to Maya when they could but for the most part remained largely external to these towns. Furthermore, the curriculum remained Ladino-dominated. Schools do not use Mayan books such as the *Popol Wuj* or the *Anales*. Instead, they use assigned textbooks that misrepresent and demean Maya. As a result, most Kaqchikel appreciate Arévalo's efforts but say that much more needs to be done to make Guatemala's public education inclusive of its distinct populations. Kaqchikel seek a holistic approach to education. For some, the only answer is to follow the example of Kaqchikel leaders in Comalapa and form their own school.

Today, as a result of Ladino-dominated education, many continue to fear the loss of Kaqchikel language, culture, and character. Most Kaqchikel desire an education system where their ideas, influences, worldviews, and lifestyles are incorporated into the national curriculum. They want more Mayan authors and materials in Mayan languages to be included in the education process. Kaqchikel will not sacrifice their identity to Western education. The government offered few benefits to Maya, but Kaqchikel quickly took advantage of the opportunity to establish their own school and acquire scholarships for Kaqchikel students to become teachers. These teachers evinced the inherent value of Kaqchikel wisdom and culture in schools. Kaqchikel views of education changed when Kaqchikel teachers took ownership of its provision. They formed a school that quickly became the best in Comalapa. People regained confidence and a sense of pride in their roots. This school established Kaqchikel representation in education and sought the protection of their identity and spirit.

Most Kaqchikel did not wish to exclude Ladinos, however. As Ladinos realized that the Kaqchikel education was superior, Kaqchikel slowly allowed egalitarian-minded Ladinos to enroll in their school. Eventually, the two schools merged. One result of this cooperation was the reduction of explicit racism. Many Ladinos no longer used racial slurs. In fact, some Kaqchikel viewed those who had been their longtime nemeses as new family members. Kaqchikel were proud of the development of their own educational facility and the fact that Ladinos recognized the Mayan system as superior to their own. However, they did not wish to hold this over Ladinos; rather, they were content to share their talents. Furthermore, they recognized that some Ladinos are good teachers. Kaqchikel sought not to dominate education but to provide equal opportunities and improve relations between Maya and Ladinos.

Ladino and Kaqchikel perspectives on public education differ drastically. Initially, many Ladinos did not want to educate Maya because they feared it would detract from their labor source. Later, some Ladinos presented the public school system as a viable means for Maya to accomplish Ladino goals and assimilate into national society. Today, many believe public education treats Maya equally and provides them the necessary tools to succeed in Western society. In contrast, most Kaqchikel, and other Maya, perceive education as based on Ladino views and misconstructions of Mayan history and reality. At the same time, Maya realized that education was the means to national influence, and they wanted to take advantage of that opportunity. As Kaqchikel increased their direct influence upon public education, they facilitated a system they could benefit from without losing their worldviews and characteristics. While the system remains prejudiced, Kaqchikel have leveled conditions enough that most feel comfortable partaking of it.

Kaqchikel recognize the benefits of education on a personal and national level. They appreciate the opportunity to participate in the national economy beyond their traditional agricultural labor roles. They see education as a means to bring about egalitarian relations in Guatemala. They resisted education for centuries because it attempted to acculturate them and eradicate their identity. They want education on their own terms, not assimilation.

Today, many more Kaqchikel actively participate in education because they have more input. Most Kaqchikel do not seek to segregate Ladinos but to provide an environment where distinct cultures, people, and ideas can flourish in an egalitarian manner. Kaqchikel realize that public education remains skewed toward Ladinos and continues to threaten Mayan languages, cultures, and identities. At the same time, they point out that a reduction in racism has led to more peaceful relations. Kaqchikel approaches to education changed from resistance to acceptance through efficacious participation. This transformation resulted in their empowerment and increased access to national sources of employment and wealth. Public education, however, is not the only Ladino institution in which Kaqchikel have overcome racist barriers.

6
Kaqchikel in the Military

Qawinäq pa ri ajlab'al

As in public schools, the central goal of the Guatemalan military has been to indoctrinate Maya in Ladino ways. Kaqchikel did not simply succumb to the pressure to change; instead, many took advantage of what the military offered (prior to the onset of the civil war). The Guatemalan government has conscripted young Mayan men into the military since José Rafael Carrera (1844–48; 1851–65) led a revolt in 1837. However, Barrios was the first president to professionalize the military. Mayan men had to complete at least one year of military service for the government. Kaqchikel in the army suffered due to poor living conditions and separation from their families, but they used the institution to empower themselves. For many men, the military provided access to education, and they learned how to speak, read, and write Spanish. The skills and experience they gained in the military gave them confidence to confront Ladinos in their communities. Today, however, most Kaqchikel avoid the military because it is more violent and attempts to change their character. This government institution, designed to force the incorporation of Maya into national society, resulted in the Kaqchikel gaining confidence to stand up to Ladino oppression.

Nascent Relations

Political leaders in Guatemala have long used the military as a vehicle to attain and maintain political power. In 1837 Carrera led a revolt to remove the national government and establish a conservative regime. The maintenance of a strong military was one of his goals. However, for the next fifty years the government mainly relied on decentralized independent militias for military support. Local *caudillos* (strong-armed, charismatic leaders) directed these militias and demanded their loyalty. To mobilize a strong military, the government had to win the support of these caudillos and enlist their militias. Conservatives depended on these militias for national defense and on the Catholic Church for the maintenance of social control.[1] This dependence upon decentralized forces undermined the conservative government's power.

The liberal government immediately broke with this strategy when they assumed power, because the liberal economic and political strategies necessitated a strong, centralized state. As a result, the liberal regimes that began with Barrios in the 1870s centralized power by professionalizing the military and replaced the church with the military as a means of social control. Barrios established a professionally trained and organized military that responded to the national government. This development reduced the government's dependence on and concern with local militias. A strong military was necessary to protect the interests of domestic and foreign investors.[2]

The larger implications of the foundation of a professional military as a stabilizing force are not lost in Kaqchikel oral histories. Oral traditions acknowledge that Barrios marginalized the role of the church in Guatemala and promoted the military. Kaqchikel assert that he developed the military to fulfill the void left by a weak church. They recognize that Barrios used the military and strict, centralized rule to maintain tranquility and discipline.[3] Some Western historians assert that Barrios's military could easily handle any rural uprising but that Barrios maintained enough control to prevent soldiers from looting, stealing, or abusing the local population.[4] This control provided the sense of security and justice Kaqchikel favored.

The liberal government originally attempted to utilize only Ladino and literate men in its army. In 1872 the government passed a series of laws that established obligatory military service for single men between the ages of eighteen and fifty. However, the following year the government passed a law that exempted most Maya.[5] Liberal governments did not deem Maya worthy of military service, either because they believed them incapable of arms training or thought they could not be entrusted with such training. One of the roles of the military was to contain social unrest, which Ladinos perceived to be predominantly of Mayan origin. Adams states that "the Indians were . . . an object of the army, not a subject."[6] However, only the poorest Ladinos, who were few in number, joined the military to become soldiers. During peacetime, the military rarely consisted of more than two to four thousand men. Furthermore, local militias continued to play a dominant role in the policing of rural areas. These militias often allowed Maya to become officers —and thus improve their status—and they respected Mayan political and religious structures.[7] The liberal dream of a military that could extend its presence nationally continued to be elusive.

Conscription and Uninviting Conditions

Beginning in the twentieth century, the military came to depend on Maya to make up the majority of the troops, achieving such support through conscription.[8] Oral histories recount that each male between the ages of eighteen and sixty had to perform at least one year of military service.[9] At the same time, Ladino images of the utility of Maya in the military began to change. Ladinos wanted to take advantage of Maya because the "tribes that anciently populated Guatemala were valiant and accustomed to war."[10]

Oral histories note that few men joined the military by choice. Local military commissioners organized a day (typically a market day when town squares were teeming with people) when officials would come to the communities and grab men as young as fifteen years old. Officials then sent the young men out in trucks destined for the military quarters. This happened so quickly that families were often unaware that their sons had been kidnapped.[11] Kaqchikel were also susceptible to this disregard for their rights when they visited other regions of the country. One Kaqchikel man was grabbed in Totonicapán, a K'ichee'-speaking area.[12] Oral histories attest to harsh treatment that ensued after such physical coercion. Kaqchikel assert that at times officials hit Mayan men during their training. According to some Kaqchikel men, discrimination against Maya was prevalent in the military. Some men viewed their military service as a punishment.[13]

Most scholars argue that few Mayan men looked forward to military service. McCreery writes: "The indigenous population with few exceptions abhorred service in the regular army and did all they could to avoid it. To be drafted into the army means brutal treatment under Ladino officers, poor food, harsh and humiliating living conditions, and, often, years away from one's home community and interests."[14] Abusive conditions, coupled with the loss of time with one's family and work, discouraged many Maya from joining the military. Adams asserts that despite improved racial relations in the barracks, many Ladino officers discriminated against Mayan soldiers because they found them to be ignorant, lazy, and miserable. He also notes that only on rare occasions did Maya become officers; the majority of Mayan men were soldiers.[15] Mayan men who advanced through the military ranks were paid less than their Ladino counterparts, and Mayan conscripts received less food and salary than their Ladino cohorts.[16] While ethnic relations in the military were better than in the communities, racism continued to surface.

Oral histories also recount that living conditions in the military were less than desirable and that food provisions were poor. Waqxaqi' Kawoq, a sixty-three-year-old agriculturist from Aguas Calientes, says, "We only got beans and half-cooked rice with no onions, oil or tomato in it."[17] In addition to less than palatable food, Kaqchikel assert many men suffered from insects in their clothes and mattresses. Others complained that some soldiers consumed excessive amounts of alcohol, which created an uncomfortable environment.

Kaqchikel recount that in some cases, men were either not paid, or that when they were paid, the salaries were too small to contribute to their families' income. Kaqchikel opine that many men suffered during their military service because the military did not take good care of its conscripts.[18] Western scholars concur that the allocation of resources to the enlisted troops was negligible. They received minimal—if any—pay, no uniforms or boots, and little education. The military provided limited social mobility, and generally this movement was restricted to Ladinos.[19]

Benefits

Despite the sacrifices, some men appreciated the opportunities provided through military service. Carmack points out that the military education included the Spanish language and the opportunities to travel, develop leadership skills, and become familiar with, and confident about, the Ladino culture.[20] Kaqchikel oral histories express that most men appreciated the experience because without their military service they would have been unable to communicate in Spanish. According to oral histories, the military offered Spanish classes for one and a half hours each day. Most men welcomed the opportunity to learn to read and write Spanish.[21] Ka'i' Imox, who at eighty-two years old stands at about four feet, nine inches tall, says: "I never went to school. I do not know the numbers, but I do know how to write because I did school in the military under Ubico."[22] Prior to Arévalo's administration, the only schooling most Kaqchikel received was through the military. Some men volunteered their services to receive an education. In some cases Mayan men younger than the eligible age volunteered to join the military.[23] An elder from Aguas Calientes states, "I was in the army in 1944. I went to the Matamorros [military quarters]. I was not grabbed. I wanted to go. We presented ourselves and I had to sell my machete to get a ticket to get there."[24] That this man was willing to sell an essential agricultural tool to pay for his transportation to the military shows that he was determined to gain some experience outside his community and to expand his knowledge. The military also appealed to some men's sense of adventure. Oral histories attest that through the military, enlisted men traveled to areas they had never been, in some cases to foreign countries. For this reason, informants point out, some men served in the military through the Ubico, Gen. Federico Ponce Vaides, and Arévalo administrations.[25] For these soldiers, the military offered an escape from the quotidian reality of their communities.

For others, the military offered a livelihood and a chance to set their lives in a new direction. One woman explains her father's experience: "When [my father] was fourteen, he went to the military. He was looking for work and did not know what to do. He was working in a small restaurant and earned only his food. He had to sweep and clean out trash, so then he decided to go to the military where he could sleep and eat well. He did that for six to eight years."[26] Some men joined the military because they had few other options. This Kaqchikel man used the military to bring stability to his life and later began a successful career as a painter.

Kaqchikel men learned skills beyond Spanish. The military educated some in the use of firearms that required an understanding of mathematics. As a result, they learned how to multiply and add. Some men were content with learning how to swim. In other instances, men learned a skill that allowed them to earn a living in their communities. Oxi' Imox, for one, learned how to cut hair in the military, and today he uses the same tools for his trade that the army gave him in 1944. The military gave some men musical instruments which they continued to use in their communities.[27] Kaqchikel men who already had some education were able to teach classes. Junlajuj Ajpu', an eighty-seven-year-old musician and farmer, explains: "I went to school and earned a third-grade education. I knew how to read and write. The army liked that, so I gave classes to others."[28] Oral accounts attest that during the Arévalo administration the military offered scholarships to talented soldiers to study in the military academy.[29]

In addition to intangibles, such as education and leadership, the military did compensate troops financially, and this satisfied many Kaqchikel. Oral histories note that in some cases, conscripts earned money for their service. Kaqchikel recall that during the Ubico regime, the military paid its con-scripts three quetzals per month, a daily wage of ten cents, which was on a par with their earning potential in their communities. They also note that wages were higher in the military than in the highlands during the Arévalo administration. They say this compensation provided a valuable contribution to their livelihood and point out that men could buy land or cows with their income.[30] Thus the military provided the means for some men to establish a source of income independent of what they derived through their family.

Most Kaqchikel also appreciated the military's emphasis on discipline. They reflect that their self-discipline made their transition into the military easier. Informants assert that they displayed orderliness in marching drills and other assignments. Some opine that young people today are not disciplined because they never served in the army when it was respectable (before the overthrow of Arbenz).[31] Kaqchikel appreciated the military's clear set of rules. As long as they adhered to the physical and mental demands, they were free from abuse and in most cases respected as soldiers.

Empowerment

The military also provided Kaqchikel with an escape from an oppressive situation in their villages. As one elder explains, "I went to the military in 1925. I liked it because here [Comalapa] was a big problem. We were abused by the Ladinos. They did not like us, so they fought us."[32] When Kaqchikel returned from the military, Ladinos knew they had received training and so left them alone. Oxi' Tz'ikin, an eighty-three-year-old former mayor and entrepreneur, shares his father's opinion:

> In those days the Ladinos did not like "our people" and they did not treat us well. You always had to walk on the side of the road. If you got in the Ladinos' way, or even if not, they would push you or hit you. You let them have the middle. Thirty years ago that settled down a bit, but the Ladinos are still bad people. My dad got people together and told them it was wrong what the Ladinos do to us. They kill us. We are dumb. Back in those days, there was no school. He told them not to be afraid. He said they should go to the military because it makes you tough. That is how we can rise up. Go to the military, because it is tough. When you leave the military you have changed from a boy to a man.[33]

The military provided a means for Kaqchikel to defend themselves against Ladino abuse. Waqi' K'at notes, "When studies and military service came, they gave value to our people. We fought Ladinos, and we could read. There was no more ixto."[34] Likewise, some scholars recognize the military as the only institution that offered an escape from the racist system that prevented Maya from achieving a better quality of life. Carmack asserts that "the military organization showed the least indigenous-Ladino caste stratification in comparison with any other formal institution of the community, and provided the Indian with the best opportunity to reach a high public position."[35] Oral histories note that Kaqchikel appreciated the military for its ability to level race relations. Junlajuj Ajpu' asserts, "That is what I liked about the military. Everyone was equal. We worked and stood side by side with the Ladinos. Justice and rights were equal with the Ladinos."[36]

Kaqchikel oral traditions recall military service during the Ubico regime most fondly. Kaqchikel note that Ubico's government constructed military quarters in Chimaltenango and assert that Ubico cleaned up the military because he took pride in it. They recount that prior to Ubico, lice and other vermin inhabited the uniforms but that Ubico burned all the clothes and ordered new ones.[37] Kaqchikel argue that his government valued conscripts and compensated them for their service. Furthermore, they opine that Ubico respected them as Maya. They point out that in some cases, he allowed them to wear their *xerkas* over their uniforms.[38] B'eleje' K'at argues that Mayan individuals gained self-esteem through military service: "Now military service is bad and repressive, but during the time of Ubico, it helped our people. For example, when a young man went to the army, he gained self-esteem. He had never been to school, but they taught him things, like how to write and speak Spanish. So he no longer was afraid of the Ladinos. During Ubico's time, Ladinos had to perform military service also. Now men are not required to enter the military, and only Maya go, so many people do not understand that it was a good thing under Ubico."[39] The military gave Kaqchikel the confidence to confront Ladinos and therefore helped to reduce the racial separation of Guatemalans. Oral histories note that prior to Ubico, only Ladinos achieved the status of officers in the military, but Ubico changed that and some Kaqchikel became officers.[40]

In some cases, Kaqchikel entered the military to provide support and manpower for the mobilization of the nation and were disappointed in the lack of leadership. Junlajuj Ajpu' did not respect the president during his service: "I went to the Honor Guard. I did the military from 1928 to 1929. Lázaro Chacón was the president. He was weak. He got so scared during the war in Xela (Quetzaltenango) that he urinated in his pants. In contrast, Ubico was very strong."[41] Because Chacón failed to inspire his men, Ubico was the leader of choice.

Ladino Goals

Oral histories recall that Ubico developed the Guatemalan military with limited national expense through military conscription. Oral histories also attest that Ubico designed volunteer companies to ensure military participation of all men in the community. Kaqchikel assert that when a man completed his military obligation in one of the regional military quarters, he had to "volunteer" each Sunday morning for local military drills called "the voluntary company." They point out that the voluntary company was a misnomer because Ubico required everyone to contribute time and effort; he wanted to have prepared soldiers.[42] Kaqchikel recall that even men who had not served at a military quarters had to volunteer. One man elucidates: "I participated in the voluntary company for four years beginning in 1936 during Ubico's time. It was pure instruction and mobilization of arms. We did not get paid, but I was good at it. I never went to school, but I learned how to read in the army. . . . Then I bought a dictionary to improve."[43]

Other men resented this obligatory service because it eliminated their only day of rest and because their only compensation was a signature on their "control card," a booklet used to prove their service. Oral histories show that most Kaqchikel believed they gained something from their one- or two-year stints in the military quarters but viewed the voluntary company as a waste of time. Kaqchikel assert they had to report at six o'clock and march until eleven o'clock each Sunday morning and said they could not miss sessions because of an illness. They recall that each Sunday officers stamped the men's books to prove they had participated. They also recount that if the men did not have their stamps, they would be incarcerated—and a jail term meant five days without pay. They point out that these voluntary companies essentially eliminated any respite they would have had from their week's work. They say Ubico did not allow relaxation.[44] One man, who always wears his traditional clothes, expresses a mixed reaction to obligatory military service: "I served in the army for one year. The lieutenant instructed us. We had to carry arms and we also learned Spanish. I liked the military, but it was also a loss of my own time."[45]

Ubico's volunteer companies and conscription were part of his attempt to incorporate Maya into the army and national life. He said, "They come [to the military] rude, brutish, and with a primitive nature, but they return learned, *desnados* [transformed from a donkeylike condition] with good manners and in a condition to face life with improved personal faculties."[46] Ubico viewed military training as an educational device. He wanted to militarize the society and make all men, especially Maya, soldiers. Consequently, Maya made up the majority of the troops in the military. Furthermore, the *intendente* (local governor) organized a group of men from the community to serve as the national police to keep order in the town. These men received no provisions or pay from the government. Local volunteer companies organized by the state replaced former militias led by local caudillos. Ubico's militaristic approach to governance extended throughout social relations, and his goal was to promote the integration of Maya into society through Ladinoization.[47]

Many Ladinos believed that military service would be a good influence on Maya. One author opines that "although the physical conditions promise great success, the Indian is extremely self-denied, malnourished, and underclothed," but he concludes that many Maya become good soldiers: "although the Ladino is much more intelligent, the Indian possesses some military qualities of a higher level than that of the Ladino."[48] Military education combated illiteracy and included reading, writing, basic math, grammar, geography, and other subjects.[49] Another author emphasizes the importance of the role of acculturation in the military: "Here is the principal and most useful part. The Indian in the army will have to abandon his primitive outfit to dress in uniform . . . sleep in a bed, in a room that is much better than the home he left, eat at a table and bathe in a bathroom, in the daily ablution, acquire the habits of an exterior that better conforms to civilization."[50] One goal of the military was to create a "new Indian" who conformed to Ladino lifestyles and worldviews. The state believed this goal would contribute to Guatemala's modernization plan.

The Guatemalan press praised obligatory military service for Maya. *El Imparcial* applauded the efforts of the government which resulted in "dignifying the life of the soldier."[51] Reporters noted "the obvious transformation" of Mayan participants. "Many indigenous troops have been educated by the military. . . . A beneficial change is reflected in their customs, clothing and self-identity."[52] *El Liberal Progresista* also recognized a transformation that occurred in Maya which would help them "to conduct themselves better in society." This newspaper reported that demand to join the military exceeded the number of spaces available.[53] During her travels through Guatemala, Erna Fergusson observed that through military conscription Maya gained a sense of nationalism that subsumed their ancient tribal allegiance.[54] Most Ladinos were not striving for a multiethnic and pluricultural country, and according to these authors the military facilitated the government's goal of incorporating Maya into national society.

The military's attempt at acculturation was only mildly successful, however. One female Kaqchikel activist from Poaquil explains that "the ideology of the military is very different from our own."[55] Many Kaqchikel observe that today when men return from military service, they have lost much of their respect for their culture and community; their character has changed.[56] In contrast, prior to the civil war, indoctrination was not as intense and few men remained in the military long enough to lose their attachment to their homes and people. Kaqchikel oral histories point out that as a result of their talents, discipline, and diligence, the military promoted them to sergeant. In fact, some Ladino officers preferred to work with Maya rather than Ladinos because they were better soldiers. Most Mayan men succeeded in this environment because they knew what was expected of them and, for the most part, as long as they accomplished their tasks, they were not victims of capricious acts. Kaqchikel oral histories assert that most Kaqchikel men gained confidence from their military service, but few accepted promotions that required a continuation beyond their stipulated time. Kaqchikel note that most men missed their families and community life. They point out some men viewed the military as a waste of time that took them away from their responsibilities at home.[57] One elder states, "I learned Spanish in the military. I did it for two and a half years. I was a first sergeant. They wanted to promote me, but I did not want to stay. I wanted to come back to Comalapa. It is better that I work in the fields."[58]

Violent Skills and Experiences

Kaqchikel benefited from military education, but they understood the real motivations behind this schooling. They assert that the military sought to train men for combat.[59] Junlajuj K'at, a seventy-year-old agriculturist, explains: "I just learned a little how to read in the military. There was a quarter hour of school, then a quarter hour of instruction. They do not teach you to read, they teach you more how to use arms."[60] A local painter takes it one step further: "I never wanted to be in the military, because they teach you how to kill people."[61] A store owner who served in the military for two years under Ubico at the Matamorros barracks said: "I hated it. They taught you how to kill. Some of my friends were even killed. I was [only] seventeen years old."[62] A rural farmer succinctly states: "Ubico sent men to the military to exploit them."[63] Military training starkly contradicted Kaqchikel upbringing and respect for life. Kaqchikel knew the government did not send them to the military quarters for their own benefit.

Some Kaqchikel men experienced combat during their military service. The 1944 revolution is a vivid memory in Kaqchikel oral histories. One Kaqchikel participant explains: "I joined the military because I was obligated to. At first I was in it for one and a half years. Then they grabbed me again and I did another term during the October Revolution in 1944. I was in the palace, but my barracks were San José Fort. In the palace nothing happened, shots just passed overhead, but hundreds died in [the military barracks of] Matamorros, Honor Guard, and San José Fort."[64] Oral histories recall many soldiers died in the 1944 revolution. A painter recounts what her father told her: "My father was in the military in 1944, when they revolted and took out Ubico. It was a war between military quarters, so he [my father] had to kill others. Many people died."[65] For some Kaqchikel, the military was not just training, but mortal combat. Kaqchikel were not opposed to weapons training, but few wanted to utilize these skills. Although most Kaqchikel thrived in the military because they could abide by its clearly defined rules of conduct and expectations, they did not agree with the military's agenda.

Kaqchikel lament that they had to participate in the death and violence associated with the military.

By 1944 the country was ripe for revolution. Labor unrest, middle-class pressures for democratization and reform, and a loss of U.S. support all weakened President Ubico's position. On July 1, 1944, faced with an extensive petition from some of Guatemala's most respected professionals and business people, in solidarity with striking workers, Ubico resigned and turned over power to a military junta composed of three generals. Gen. Ponce quickly dominated the junta and ordered Congress to appoint him provisional president (1944). He threatened to forestall the elections. In October, cadets from the Escuela Politécnica and progressive members of the military Honor Guard in Guatemala City joined students in a bloody battle that forced Ponce's capitulation and established a more democratic political system with Arévalo at the helm.

Kaqchikel oral histories recall that the democratic experiment in Guatemala began violently. The military agreed to help in the rebellion, but internally the military was divided between younger progressive members and older traditionalists loyal to Ubico. One forty-year-old Catholic from Barahona elucidates: "There was a war that began with the military barracks. It commenced with confusion when the Honor Guard military quarters provoked the Matamorros military quarters, and from there the war continued."[66] Others add that in October the San Rafael Matamorros and San José Fort military quarters both burned to the ground and all the soldiers present died.[67]

The transition from Ubico to Arévalo had left the country in chaos and ignited ethnic violence. Ladinos had always feared Mayan rebellion, and any kind of unrest fueled their fears and led to increased problems. A number of different uprisings began in 1944 in La Aurora, San Juan Ostuncalco, Patzicía, and Chichicastenango. Newspaper reports of these uprisings only served to increase Ladino fears.[68] The most shocking of these events was the massacre in the town of Patzicía. On the night of October 22, 1944, some Kaqchikel gathered outside Patzicía to support the new liberal party. Kaqchikel protests were a response to a minority of Ladinos in the area owning more land than all the Kaqchikel, dominating the local government, marketing, and credit arrangements, and controlling all municipal land. Some men began what *El Imparcial* described as a "horrifying massacre and pillage."[69] Newspapers did not present the Kaqchikel side of the story; they presented the incident as another example of the smoldering racial hatred that threatened to erupt in rural Guatemala. Further inciting the Ladino population, *El Imparcial* printed a graphic depiction of a Maya chopping off the head of a nine-year-old boy.[70] This image haunted many Ladinos long after the courts sentenced to death or imprisonment thirty-four Kaqchikel in the community.[71]

Kaqchikel remember that night distinctly. Oral histories focus on the killing as stemming from the fact that in Patzicía, the majority of Ladinos sided with Arévalo while most Kaqchikel remained loyal to Ubico and the Ponce Party. Informants recount that violence escalated shortly after military troops arrived to kill Kaqchikel, and Ladinos from the neighboring town of Zaragoza arrived in Patzicía to massacre the Mayan population.[72] Arévalo's reputation as a man of peace sheltered him from blame for the Patzicía massacre. Ixya', a sixty-year-old evangelical woman, recalls: "Many people died when Arévalo came into office. I was thirteen years old. In Patzicía, people were terminated. I was told not to leave the house, because the killers were coming. I saw one in a truck with a gun. But I think Ubico did it, not Arévalo. He [Arévalo] was a good man. Arévalo made peace. You did not hear about any more violence when he came in."[73] Ubico's harsh manner caused people to equate him with violence, whereas Arévalo's performance as president erased any connection he had to the violence surrounding his rise to power. This inaccurate perception is maintained in oral traditions because while Kaqchikel have not forgotten the violence that marked the transition from Ubico to Arévalo, they associate Arévalo with the democratic order he sought to institute. They do not link him to military maneuverings because he opposed a militaristic style of governance.

The subsequent democratic administrations of Arévalo and Arbenz curtailed the role of the military in society. They reduced both its size and resource allocation. During Ubico's regime, the military received 17 percent of the national budget, but by the end of Arbenz's administration, military spending made up only 10 percent of the national budget.[74] The democratic government was a reprieve from a militaristic society, but this opening did not last long.

Ten years after the October Revolution, military conscripts were involved in another internal military struggle. Arbenz's government came to an abrupt end when Castillo Armas led a group of Guatemalan exiles, supported by the CIA, to overthrow the president. The army refused to resist the invasion, and Arbenz resigned on June 27, 1954.[75] Junlajuj K'at, who was in the military when Castillo Armas invaded Guatemala, says:

Jacobo Arbenz was the president when I was in the military. Then one month later [Castillo] Armas came from Honduras to oust Arbenz.

Some people died. [Castillo] Armas had a lot of arms, but I do not know what nation they [the arms] came from. Arbenz did not have an airplane, but Castillo [Armas] had an airplane and flew it over the capital. Soldiers shot at his airplane but could not shoot it down. It was Arbenz's fault because he did not prepare to have an airplane and defend himself. I was in Matamorros and we had a gun there that shot across at the Honor Guard. We had weapons to kill each other.[76]

While Junlajuj K'at is critical of Arbenz, the Castillo Armas administration, and especially the subsequent military governments, began a period when military service lost its appeal to Maya.

Most Kaqchikel recognize that Arbenz lasted a short time in office because of the controversy that surrounded agrarian reform. They are also aware that the impetus for this coup d'état was both internal and external to the country. They note that Guatemalan landowners were unhappy with agrarian reform but say the United States also played a major role in ousting Arbenz.[77] One evangelical store owner explains:

Arbenz passed the 900 decree to give land to the people. He was a military colonel who wanted to help the indigenous people and farmers. He was concerned for the workers. He was a humanitarian, but the United States did not like that so they took him out. It hurts me to know that such a big nation as the United States did not want to help a humanitarian. The United Fruit Company was involved. They supported the invasion of Castillo Armas. Also the United States ambassador to Guatemala was Foster Dulles, and his brother John Foster Dulles was the secretary of state. So the United States looked for a caudillo, and it was [Castillo] Armas. He came from Honduras and made his way through the country until he arrived at the capital and ousted Arbenz. The United States terminated Arbenz and that hurts me. [Castillo] Armas was killed because he did not do good work. He was a traitor.[78]

A teacher and university student from Poaquil states: "The problem was not that Arbenz was a Communist, but that he took the land from the banana companies and he enraged the United States."[79] Kaqchikel recognize that the United States, the United Fruit Company (UFCO), the CIA, landowners, and Castillo Armas conspired to organize an army to overthrow Arbenz. Informants claim that Arbenz was exiled "in his underwear" to El Salvador. Ixtijax, a weaver and teacher of the Kaqchikel language, says, "If he had not helped our people he would have finished his term."[80] Kaqchikel are aware that Arbenz's attempt to aid Maya, rather than wealthy Ladinos and foreigners, resulted in his political demise. Some Kaqchikel assert that Arbenz had a good idea but could not complete his promise to the lower classes. Other Kaqchikel considered him a liberator for his efforts. Kaqchikel lament that Arbenz's overthrow began the period of civil war in Guatemala even more than they lament that Arbenz's overthrow caused a devastating loss of land.[81] They are quick to point out that Castillo Armas died because he "lived by the sword" and note that some of his own officials and soldiers killed him three years later out of vengeance.[82] The inability of political and economic powers, both inside and outside Guatemala, to comprehend the egalitarian goals of Arbenz instigated the retraction of Mayan gains and a period of brutal violence against Maya.

The perceived threat of Communism by the United States and UFCO's reaction to their loss of land in the land reform instigated the 1954 invasion. Internal unrest also contributed to Arbenz's downfall. As seen in chapter 2, many Kaqchikel were critical of Arbenz's land reform. Further, some Maya viewed Arbenz's government as an attempt to replace Catholicism with Communism, and they rejected the perceived substitution of a political commitment for a religious one. The Catholic Church fueled growing criticism when Archbishop Mariano Rossell y Arellano called for Guatemalans to oust Communists. In addition, the army's refusal to defend Arbenz facilitated a successful coup. Nonetheless, the main force behind the invasion came from the CIA. With only between 150 and 200 men, Castillo Armas's army would have failed miserably had it tried to invade Guatemala. Instead it remained just inside the border in Esquipulas. CIA airplanes bombarded Guatemala City and other cities, and as the pressure increased, the military backed down and Arbenz had to resign. He escaped to Mexico, not El Salvador as Kaqchikel oral histories claim, before he lived in Cuba and other countries. Meanwhile, a U.S. embassy plane carried Castillo Armas to the capital. After a few short-lived interim governments, Castillo Armas became president on July 8, 1954. He promptly returned land that had been distributed through decree 900 (see chapter 2) to its previous owners. As a result, Maya who had gained land through the program quickly lost it. In some cases, Castillo Armas jailed Mayan recipients.[83] After Castillo Armas's collaboration with the United States and UFCO and the army's acquiescence to the invasion, the military was no longer honorable in the eyes of most Kaqchikel, and its reputation continued to plummet as the civil war began.

Prior to the 1940s, the military served as a vehicle for Mayan males to acquire an education that the government otherwise denied them. In many ways, their experience in the military allowed them to achieve their goals in the national society. They learned how to read, write, and speak Spanish, do basic mathematics, interact more efficaciously with the state and with Ladinos, and perform a variety of technical and vocational skills. They were able to explore their own country and learn more about its geography, topography, and diverse population. Some Mayan men were able to use these new talents and skills to improve their economic situation.[84] Despite advantages, however, the military appealed to only a few Maya. Most Mayan men preferred to end their obligation quickly and return to their communities.

Even though many men benefited from their experience in the military, some Kaqchikel leaders opposed military conscription because it infringed upon their freedom and rights. Oral traditions share that in the early twentieth century President Manuel Estrada Cabrera conscripted Mayan men into his military. They describe how the military would arrive in a town and grab men and force them into a year or more of service. Kaqchikel assert that Ka'i' Tz'ikin, a local leader, wrote the president a letter to tell him that Comalapa did not approve of a military that accosted its men and boys and forced them into the military. They proudly recount that the president responded to this admonition and that while men did not escape forced labor, they no longer had to endure military indoctrination.[85] Kaqchikel lament that subsequent governments reinstituted military conscription in Comalapa and that the practice continued through the civil war. Finally, informants point out, in the early 1990s a Kaqchikel woman from Comalapa named Rosalina Tuyuc successfully pressured the government to end this intrusive process.[86]

The violent and aggressive actions inherent in military service led many younger Kaqchikel to oppose the military. A thirty-one-year-old evangelical teacher says: "The military is an institution that has nothing to do in Guatemala. . . . In a democracy it should not exist. Look at Costa Rica. They should invest the money into the country."[87]

Conclusion

Few Kaqchikel freely chose to enroll in the military. Nonetheless, from early in this century until the mid-1950s, Kaqchikel realized and took advantage of the benefits offered by this unavoidable military service. However, they did not seek to prolong their experience in this Ladino institution. They accepted their conscription into the armed forces as an inevitable obligation and willingly performed their service. Kaqchikel could operate within the clearly established parameters of military work and life. In fact, they thrived in a situation where they knew what was expected of them and where the simple completion of their tasks exempted them from unwarranted abuse (in most cases). Furthermore, most appreciated the opportunities for education, employment, and social empowerment that the military provided them. They gained respect and confidence and utilized these attributes to interact assertively and efficaciously with Ladinos in their communities. The military, however, clearly attempted to acculturate them. Consequently, Kaqchikel never felt comfortable in the military and refused to surrender their lifestyles and worldviews to military indoctrination. They made good use of the military's "benevolence."

Experience in the military improved the quality of life for many Mayan men. The military provided exposure to life outside their communities, as men were able to travel to other areas and learn more about their country. Kaqchikel learned Spanish and other basic subjects in addition to professional skills they could parlay into income. Others earned income to share with their family or to begin their own endeavors. More importantly, they earned the respect of their leaders and learned how to operate in a Ladino-dominated environment. While ethnic relations remained skewed, these interactions were more benign in the military than in their communities. In a nation wracked with racism, the military was the one institution that mitigated such discrimination. The majority of Kaqchikel felt they were treated on an equal basis with Ladino conscripts. Maya gained the confidence to confront Ladinos and interact with other actors in an environment foreign to their community. Exposure to outside influences, newfound respect and confidence, and Spanish-language skills resulted in more efficacious interactions inside and outside their communities. Their experience in the military enhanced their bargaining power vis-à-vis Ladinos. Maya could escape the racism of their own communities and return with an empowered perspective on their reality.

Both Ladinos and Kaqchikel perceived the military to be beneficial to Mayan men, but for distinct reasons. Ladinos believed Maya would incorporate into national society as a result of this influence. One of the government's goals was to change Mayan dress, language, and mentality through the military. Many Ladinos described Maya as subhuman and believed exposure to the military and Ladinos would improve their lot. Once in the military, Maya continued to face racism, but some officers appreciated Mayan conscripts for their ability to withstand harsh conditions and apply learned skills. These Ladino officers extolled Maya as better soldiers than Ladinos. Kaqchikel assimilated well to the demands of discipline and diligence. Consequently, the military promoted some Mayan men to officer-level positions and gave them the opportunity to continue their studies and military careers.

Ladinos respected these Mayan leaders. Still, few Maya chose to remain in this institution and pursue a career, because although the military mitigated racism, it was a Ladino institution that contradicted Kaqchikel lifestyles and worldviews. Kaqchikel and other Maya proved they could succeed in a Ladino setting and not become dominated by it. Maya and Ladinos had different goals and approaches to military service. For the most part, the government and Ladino goal of assimilation failed. Kaqchikel took what could best serve them from the military but maintained their distinct identity and connection to their communities. Most Maya simply utilized this institution to improve their quality of life back in their communities.

The military had to conscript Mayan men because the conditions were horrendous and, despite some advantages, the overarching relationship was exploitative. The food and living quarters were unhygienic, health hazards were abundant, and abusive relations were prevalent. Some Ladinos hit Mayan conscripts, and in many cases Maya were paid less than Ladinos and received provisions of both lower quality and lower quantity. Alcoholism was also a problem that exacerbated the already uncomfortable conditions. Furthermore, conscripts lost time they could have dedicated to their farms, and they missed their families and communities. Under Ubico, Kaqchikel men had the added obligation of the volunteer companies, which eliminated any time they had to relax. Many considered the volunteer companies a waste of their time. Kaqchikel remember how Ubico extended his control over them by forcing every man to participate in military service to the nation. Military service compulsions were disruptive intrusions into their lives.

The demand that they put their military training into practice by engaging in combat especially disturbed Kaqchikel. They detested combat experience in the 1944 political coup. They recall violent and bloody outcomes from military campaigns. Kaqchikel had hoped their weapons training never would be called upon, because they did not want to kill other people, especially their own countrymen. Shortly after the Castillo Armas invasion of 1954, as the military assumed control of the government, Kaqchikel willingness to participate in military training declined. They accuse Castillo Armas of being a traitor because he invited U.S. involvement in Guatemala, which led to instability. Because the military failed to defend the nation against this invasion, Kaqchikel stopped respecting it. Kaqchikel are aware that national stability and development are contingent on outside forces. For this reason, they are critical of actors who invite outside interaction that weakens the nation or who fail to defend their country. Today, some Kaqchikel fail to see the need for a military force in Guatemala.

Many Kaqchikel empowered themselves through military service. They took advantage of the training to improve their communication skills and increase their efficacy with Ladinos. The military served as a leveling institution while Maya were stationed in the barracks and also when they were reintegrated into their communities. Ethnic relations never became egalitarian, but they did improve. Kaqchikel fulfilled their obligations and in the process improved their plight. In the period before the civil war, the military failed to incorporate the majority of Kaqchikel conscripts into national society. Instead, it empowered them. Kaqchikel appreciated the discipline, order, and reduced capriciousness inherent in the military and, as we will see in the next two chapters, they also desire these qualities in their national leaders.

7
Ubico's Legacy

Achike rub'anikil ri champomal richin ri tata'aj

General Jorge Ubico is a central figure of Kaqchikel oral histories. He served as president of the country for fourteen years—from 1931 to 1944—during which time he had a significant impact on the political, economic, social, and cultural life of the country. Kaqchikel historical perspectives paint Ubico as a complicated figure; Kaqchikel revere, fear, respect, and in some cases despise him. Regardless of whether their opinions of him are positive or negative, Ubico's name evokes a strong reaction from Kaqchikel. The range of viewpoints about Ubico presented in Kaqchikel oral histories illuminates how Kaqchikel perceive national leaders.

Ubico ruled Guatemala with authoritarian control. Even though he was a dictator who demanded law and order, some historians depict his regime as beneficial to Maya.[1] These scholars view him as an ally to Maya, much like Carrera in the mid–nineteenth century. Ubico's trips to the countryside allowed him personal contact with Maya, whom his predecessors had neglected. He improved the road system in Guatemala (albeit with Mayan labor), which enabled him to arrive in isolated communities that had never been visited by a head of state. During these visits, he interacted with Maya and in many instances defended and aided them (on an individual basis) against abusive government officials and landowners. He employed social justice demagoguery and limited reform to secure mass support, through which he strengthened his personal position. He recognized Maya as the key to the economy because they provided the bulk of the agricultural workforce. Ubico wanted to extend services that would improve the lifestyle of the rural masses, but he also wanted to centralize control of the country, and making local visits helped him to attain this goal. The visits and his personal style of government had a positive effect on many communities, and some Maya affectionately referred to him as "Tata," a respected elder.[2]

Ubico believed the best way to manage Maya was to incorporate them into Ladino society and particularly into the economy, but he did not view them as inherently equal to Ladinos. In fact, in 1935 he revoked the San Pedro

Sacatepéquez Mayan inhabitants' status as Ladinos.[3] Furthermore, Ubico opposed the involvement of Maya in public affairs because he did not want them to have access to power. In the last year of his presidency, on a visit to Patzicía, Kaqchikel residents held signs declaring the formation of the Liberal Progressive Club of Indians to be allied with Ubico's liberal progressive party. He responded that he did not want Maya "to consciously poison themselves with politics."[4] Ubico also outlawed all civic organizations that were independent of the central government. His true attitude toward Guatemala's Mayan population is perhaps best represented by a statement he wrote in 1922 concerning Jorge García Granados's arrest for political agitation. Ubico told Granados in a letter that Maya understood only "the law of the whip."[5] Ubico virtually granted impunity to landowners so they could deal with "criminals" on their land, an act that resulted in increased abuse of Maya in some areas. In addition, Ubico utilized military conscription and education to control the Mayan population. Ubico's efforts to acculturate Maya were entrenched in his paternalistic attitude toward them.

Legislation passed during his regime was seldom intended to aid Maya. He abolished debt peonage only to replace it with the vagrancy law. This legislation freed Maya from the servitude of one finca but ensured that they worked for someone. He also instituted the *Ley de Vialidad* (road-building law) that required either an annual payment of one quetzal or two weeks of "volunteer" labor on the roads. Naturally, Maya had to work because they could not afford the tax. He instituted the intendente system to replace mayors. Since the limited power of Maya existed mainly at the local level this change gave Ubico more centralized control of the communities and took away what little input Maya previously had in politics. Ubico's unwritten agreement with the Mayan population was that he would work to help them at the individual and local level, as long as they did not involve themselves in national politics.

When Ubico became president of Guatemala in the uncontested elections of February 6–8, 1931, he clearly allied himself with the small upper-class community in Guatemala City and the landowning class, including U.S. and German businessmen. He had undertaken the presidency at a difficult time. A decline in export prices that accompanied the depression of the 1930s hurt Guatemala, whose economy was primarily based on exporting commodities. Guatemala had accumulated a debt of more than five million dollars in loans and unpaid bills, with interest payments that threatened to consume nearly all government income. In an effort to combat these challenges, Ubico fostered agricultural diversification, implemented a road-construction program to link previously isolated villages to the national economy, imposed new taxes, and gave generous concessions of land and tax exemptions to large landowners, especially the United Fruit Company.[6]

Ubico's discriminatory views and actions toward Maya did not preclude his assuming an omnipresent role in Kaqchikel oral histories. He is known as a benevolent father figure, a policeman and keeper of justice, a harsh patrón who exploited the lower classes, a builder of great public works, a financial wizard, and a military disciplinarian. As one man said, "He was everything."[7] Even though some scholars have portrayed Mayan perceptions of him as simple, Kaqchikel do not present a straightforward image of Ubico; rather, Kaqchikel critically analyze his impact on Guatemala.

Ubico's program of national development depended on the existence of a free source of labor. Kaqchikel respect Ubico's dedication to work but realize that their sweat built much of Guatemala's infrastructure. Nonetheless, most appreciate the safety his system provided and were willing to sacrifice individual freedom for personal security. Oral histories portray a president who had a hand in all aspects of Kaqchikel lives but in a bearable and predictable manner. A more detailed examination of oral histories reveals the differences of opinion about Ubico's ideology, methods, and results.

The two qualities that appear most often in Kaqchikel oral histories in regard to Ubico are his work ethic and his sense of justice. His government established a system that imposed strict parameters upon the population. While Kaqchikel did not always agree with his style of governance, they understood his rules and could operate within this arrangement.

Hard Work

Kaqchikel oral histories recount how Ubico insisted that each citizen work diligently and carry proof of his or her contribution to the nation. As Wuqu' K'at, an eighty-year-old evangelical, explains, "You had to carry many papers with you at all times including: your jornato, *vialidad* [card] for roadwork, *control de cita* [work card], vaccination card, and certification of your profession."[8] Men had to carry papers that showed they had worked at least 100 (and in some cases 150) days a year for someone else; Wuqu' K'at refers to this as the control de cita. The vialidad card proved they worked two weeks on the roads, and the jornato (work card) proved they worked two to three weeks for the community. The vialidad card and the jornato were books that reflected unpaid labor. Failure to comply with labor requirements resulted in incarceration—usually five days, according to Kaqchikel. Informants explain that supervisors of work or road crews signed the books and that workers had to show them to the municipal secretary. (Oral histories explain that as part of this labor, local officials could order people to perform any errands they wanted.) They say police arrested people who did not complete or carry their workbooks.[9]

The economic system was vulnerable to abuse by landowners and local officials. Local officials interpreted the law to their advantage. As the only alternative to prison, an individual arrested for vagrancy could be compelled to work at proffered terms. When local officials acted in collusion, unscrupulous landowners were given opportunities to gain wealth and labor.[10]

Many Kaqchikel saw this system as an extension of a long tradition of forced labor the government imposed on Maya. Oral traditions attest that prior to and during Ubico's reign, the government forced Kaqchikel to work for free. For example, when a teacher or municipal employee moved to a new location, local officials would gather up the men and force them to carry the person's belongings to the new location on foot. When officials selected men, they had to stop what they were working on and report to the municipal office. Often, the round trip would take more than a week. An elder from Aguas Calientes explains this recurring trend:

> Before the time of Ubico, my father told me that the people had more obligations, because, for example, the women had to cook and bring the food to prisoners. The poor people did not rest; they were obligated to work. Or if a teacher or secretary was moving to a new town they told the local officials, who then rounded up the men to carry their things. In those days the men suffered more because some had to go to Xela, Totonicapán, and Huehuetenango. Then in the time of Ubico, I did not see any of these orders, but the people were obligated to work. You could not leave, if you had not filled out your workbook.[11]

Conditions had changed. Clearly, Ubico's regime did not demand as much as previous governments.

Ten years before Ubico assumed office, the *Diario de Centro América* painted a severe picture of Mayan life:

> In consideration that *caciquismo* [local leadership] is the first and most important of the determinant factors of the "laborer problems" . . . If there are functionaries (*Jefe Políticos* [governors], commissioners, commanders, mayors, etc.) that traffic with the Indian; if the $15 day wage that they pay in actuality they split between the Indian and the Jefe Político, $5 for the first and $10 for the second;[12] if they persecute and

hunt the Indian with the pretext of the military quotas and lists, public works, etc., and forcibly take them to torrid climates, to work in what they do not want to do and without just compensation; if they do not allow him to farm their own cereals and choose their residence in the finca or town where they want to be; [furthermore] to better exploit them they corrupt with impunity and they plunder them with debts and advanced labor, that afterward they charge them ten times as much, without grievances to prosecute them before tribunals and authorities to the point that the laborer "has three patróns" with equal rights over him; if they do not regulate the work, the shortage and even the deficiency of indigenous workers, about which many agriculturists complain, will not disappear and neither will our agriculture escape the lamentable present condition.[13]

These are the abuses that Ubico eradicated to ensure a surplus workforce; the majority of Kaqchikel appreciated protection from exorbitant persecution by innumerable sources. Under Ubico, exploitation emanated from one source: the president. Many Maya felt this exploitation was less arbitrary under Ubico and therefore less destructive and invasive.

Most Maya saw Ubico's reforms as a big improvement over previous regimes. One Kaqchikel from San Andrés Semetabaj remarked, "Before the time of Ubico, Ladinos dominated Indians. For making a mistake, patróns beat workers and brought them to jail. [President Estrada] Cabrera did not care for the indigenous people, only for the Ladinos. He maintained Indians as slaves. When Ubico entered the government, there was a change because he created an article in the constitution which made work sacred. The worker is in a sacred position while he is working. If the patrón came to bother him, and the laborer retaliated, it was because the patrón deserved it. Patróns obeyed this, and there were no more offenses."[14] Ladinos and the government had previously worked together to exploit Maya, but under Ubico many Maya believed the government acted in their defense.[15]

For other Kaqchikel, however, changes in the forced-labor system do not obscure the end result. Kaqchikel oral traditions express that Ubico treated people like chattel. An expert weaver from Aguas Calientes explains the reality of Ubico's work ethic: "Ubico made our people suffer. Our grandparents did the work with their lungs because no machines or tractors were present. The government did not pay our people. My father worked for that government and suffered a great deal. We were always slaves. Ubico was a hard man."[16] A rural agriculturist shares what his parents told him: "On Saturdays and Sundays they handed out a list because every fifteen days men had to go to the mountains to work on the roads. They had to bring their own food and they did not get paid. They were very much enslaved."[17] Many Kaqchikel concur that Ubico viewed Maya as little more than laborers to improve Guatemala's roads and infrastructure. Others note that men fell ill during these forced-labor stints because working conditions were deplorable. Informants point out that everyone had to work for Ubico and that most Kaqchikel felt they surrendered their freedom to him. Many people refer to work under Ubico as a "gift" to the government because all they earned was a piece of paper—no money.[18]

Roads

Kaqchikel oral histories attribute much of Guatemala's infrastructure to Ubico. Those from the towns of Chimaltenango especially remember their efforts to build the military barracks in the department capital. They recall that men carried heavy rocks from distant towns to construct the barracks' foundations; they had only picks and shovels, no machines. Once again, they emphasize that this work was a gift to the government, as Kaqchikel received no payment. Likewise, residents of Comalapa credit Ubico with the construction of the road from their town to the Pan-American Highway but are quick to point out that their grandparents performed the manual labor.[19] As one teacher noted, "The Ladinos were too proud to do that type of work."[20] A Mayan priest and former mayor remembers that he was in school when Ubico arrived in Comalapa:

> When Ubico came to town he saw the need for a large road. He came to see what we were doing here, if we were working hard or not. He authorized the road to Zaragoza. He did this purely by the roadwork card. Everyone had to work for one week during a six-month period. When six months was up you got a new card. People from all over came to help. They had to do their service here. If you wanted, you could pay one quetzal and you did not have to work the vialidad. But in that time farmers earned 9–10 cents a day so that was ten days' work—pretty expensive.[21]

Few people could afford not to work. Kaqchikel recall that Ubico visited towns to inspect the work and encourage people to continue in their endeavors. Oral accounts share that he forced men to work in towns other than their own and that even though the government sent men great distances it did not provide housing or food. Kaqchikel assert that Ubico constructed all the roads in this manner and that each town had to contribute.[22]

In 1933, Ubico established the Ley de Vialidad. The municipalities took a census every six months to make sure people fulfilled their obligations. Through better administration and stricter requirements, the law nearly doubled the number of workdays on the roads: from 794,049 in 1932 to 1,314,908 in 1934. The highway department expanded and repaired the department of Chimaltenango's roads and bridges with unpaid Mayan labor throughout the 1930s. It took especially good care of Tecpán's roads because it recognized the town as a commercial center. Maya performed the majority of the labor, and local officials frequently forced them to do more labor than was required of them by law. When the government needed roadworkers, the police chief could tear up a man's receipt for the work done and force him to repeat the labor. Authorities often refused to sign the men's cards, which forced them to work more hours.[23] Mayan labor was essential to the national economy, and officials at all levels extracted as much as they could from this population.

As Kaqchikel recognized, their labor provided real benefits for Guatemala's road system. Ubico presided over more road construction than any other president. He personally supervised the roadwork to ensure the state was benefiting from its labor. One government report claimed that he visited sites daily and developed a new labor dynamic in these projects. The work depended on an "untiring vialidad" system.[24] The expansion of the road system made the regime popular in rural areas and extended its control to the hinterlands.[25]

Kaqchikel from San Andrés Semetabaj assert that the vialidad policy was egalitarian because everyone was liable for the road tax. They also heralded the vialidad law and Ubico's public works program because both improved communication and transportation facilities. They did not view the vagrancy law as discriminatory; rather, they saw it as a reinforcement of the high value they placed on work. These Kaqchikel perceived the reforms as a split in the ideology between the government and the local Ladino landholders. They believed the laws protected the rights of Maya from abusive landowners. Mayan laborers were no longer bondsmen who could be mistreated for mistakes or disagreements with the patrón. They believed the Ubico presidency created greater justice for Maya and better relations between ethnic groups.[26]

Other Kaqchikel also perceived the vialidad to be beneficial. Kaqchikel recognize that changes that affect their community and culture are necessary in some instances. Most Kaqchikel welcome the development of roads to facilitate the exchange of labor and goods outside their communities. In fact, in some cases, oral histories recall Kaqchikel petitioning the government to build roads in their community. Kaqchikel assert that people have easier access to the coast and other distant employment locations as a result of this infrastructure. The first inhabitant of his rural community, Oxi' Kawoq, explains the importance of the road for his rural village: "A long time ago we did not have a road here and because of that many people died. . . . The highway gives life because it brings the harvest. A long time ago there was no harvest here, but on the coast the harvest was abundant. However, they could not bring the harvest here."[27] An agriculturist from a nearby village concurs with Oxi' Kawoq's assessment: "The road came to our village about forty years ago. It gives life, and therefore it is important. Vehicles can transport goods to be bought and sold. If you can only transport [goods] on your back, you cannot trade that much."[28] Some Kaqchikel point out that people did not begrudge the required labor because roads are a basic necessity.[29] Most Kaqchikel desire interaction with the national and international economy because they view it as a means to improve their quality of life.

Not everyone unconditionally supports these road systems in Kaqchikel communities, and roads certainly do not benefit everyone equally. Jun No'j, a fifty-year-old farmer who speaks Mam and Kaqchikel, opines: "The road only helps the rich. Those with cars and trucks can take advantage of it. The merchants benefit, but the poor stay the same."[30] According to Jun No'j, the road system only serves to increase the economic disparity in these communities. Other people lament that roads bring evil influences as well as outside trade. One woman noted that her previously tranquil village was subject to thieves as a result of the road.[31] Finally, some Kaqchikel argue that their cultural strength will suffer because of the increased interaction with outside influences. One Mayan intellectual laments: "The new road is both good and bad. It will allow people to get around more easily and improve trade. However, there are some serious negative cultural consequences. More people will arrive here and bring on more changes, such as religion. Foreign people and ideas will chip away at our culture. One of the reasons Comalapa has preserved its culture so well is that it is more isolated than other villages. Progress has its drawbacks and [the loss of] culture is one of them. A new and better road is important, but it will have negative consequences."[32] He points out the complexities involved in analyzing the impact of roads on Kaqchikel communities. His argument parallels the cultural argument people of Barahona and Aguas Calientes make against employment in factories. However, most Kaqchikel realize that changes are inevitable, and in many cases necessary.

According to oral histories, Ubico's most impressive work was the national palace. Informants note that he spent 2.5 million quetzals on it. A former Comalapan mayor attended the inauguration and recalls: "He inaugurated the national palace on November 10, 1942. I went there to see it and it was pretty impressive."[33] The overwhelming impression of such a grand structure did not erase the bitter memories, however. Kaqchikel are proud that they built these grandiose public works but resent the government and Ladinos for failing to acknowledge their contributions. A Kaqchikel educator states, "Ubico is popular for building the national palace and roads, but he did it all with our labor."[34] Oral histories recount that to build the national palace, prisoners had to carry heavy rocks on their backs from their town to the capital. Prisoners had to make this round trip three times for their punishment. One informant explains what her father told her: "Ubico built the foundation of the national palace with the stones of the prisoners' guilt."[35]

No Vagos (No Vagrants)

One way Ubico maximized his resources was to ensure that the labor source was accountable solely to him. Most Kaqchikel appreciated that he consequently eliminated the debt peonage system whereby landowners trapped laborers in a cycle of debt. Prior to Ubico, landowners often paid laborers before they began to work and then falsified their work times to hold them in perpetual debt. Oral accounts assert that seven years into his fourteen-year term, Ubico passed a law that gave the landowners three months to end debt peonage and that he helped poor people take advantage of the law. Kaqchikel assert that as a result of this law, they only went to work on the coast voluntarily. They appreciate that he wanted people to work of their own accord, without any debt.[36] One rural inhabitant explains the trials between landowners and farmhands before Ubico intervened, "Before Ubico, the rich did not pay their farmworkers. If you asked for a five-peso loan, they would write down ten, and if you asked for a ten-peso loan, they would write down twenty. But Ubico put an end to all of that; afterward, working for the farm was voluntary."[37] Kaqchikel knew that Ubico transformed this freedom from landowners into his own labor supply, but they preferred to work for Ubico and the progress of the nation, rather than add to the personal wealth of economic elites. Kaqchikel felt a sense of affiliation with the state and consequently were willing to contribute to Ubico's roadworks program.

Prior to the abolishment of debt peonage on May 7, 1934, the state supported the system of independent *habilitadores* (money lenders). These habilitadores loaned money to Maya for their local fiestas or crops and then forced them to work off the debt to finqueros with whom they had contracted the labor. Workers also became indebted by using the credit available through the network of finca stores. At times, the only wages offered were in the form of credit notes to be used in these stores.[38] The abolishment of debt peonage freed laborers from these obligations.

Immediately following the abolition of debt peonage, Ubico decreed La Ley Contra la Vagancia (henceforth referred to as the vagrancy law). Ubico required authorities and agents to search for vagrants and bring them to local judges. Any citizen could denounce vagrants to the authorities. Violators could be punished by imprisonment, fines, and forced labor. The government did not accept unemployment as an excuse for vagrancy; the laborer was responsible for his gainful employment.[39]

Kaqchikel understood Ubico's basic premise that everyone must work. While they did not appreciate forced labor, Kaqchikel enjoyed the secure environment. They note that Ubico forced people to be honest and work for a living; no one had the right to be lazy. The majority of Kaqchikel also hail the results of his approach because he rid the country of vagabonds. He incarcerated those who did not work and, more importantly, ensured that everyone had a job and therefore income. They note that no one had to steal in order to survive and that crimes such as theft and public intoxication consequently decreased. Kaqchikel assert that Ubico made Guatemala a safe place to live.[40] A sixty-year-old Mayan daykeeper explains why most Kaqchikel understood and respected Ubico's style:

> Ubico was the best president for us. We, as indigenous people, like to work. We look for work and we do it well, so the vialidad and mandates were good for our lives. It was honorable. He was a strict man who eliminated thieves. You could leave your tools and belongings in the street and they were there when you returned. I once saw when a man stole money from the municipality. They made an example of him by burning his hands. Also under Ubico, the police hit drunkards between 150 and 300 times according to the severity of their crime. Ubico did not miss anything.[41]

Ubico forced people to perform at their maximum capacity. A seventy-four-year-old farmer opines: "Ubico was a powerful dictator. He obligated everyone to work. He was helpful in that way."[42] The Kaqchikel work ethic fit well with this system.

Ubico argued that the labor reforms would facilitate modest improvements in the wages and standard of living of peasants. In his annual message to Congress in 1937, he informed his colleagues that debt peonage and vagrancy laws were designed to liberate Maya from slavery and allow them to work with dignity.[43] However, as work was an obligation, citizens' "liberty" was not absolute; freedom lay only in the choice of work one wished to perform. The new freedom did not allow people to be idle or produce only what they needed for their own consumption. In fact, the transition from debt peonage to the vagrancy law provided cheaper labor for landowners. Under debt peonage, landowners had to provide workers and their families with housing, food, transportation, health care, schooling, and land to farm. In contrast, under the vagrancy law, workers assumed these responsibilities. Furthermore, the vagrancy law required the vast majority of laborers to work for at least three months, which allowed enough time to ensure laborers for the harvest. In a sense, this change was part of the process of proletarianization, which moved from feudalism to capitalism through the emphasis on wage labor. It was a structural and legal change that facilitated central government rather than local control. The new system allowed Ubico to extend his control over the country, but the government did not take specific steps to ensure just treatment of laborers.[44] The official government newspaper, *Díario de Centro América,* provided a realistic analysis of the vagrancy law: "If this law is judged to be a slavery measure, it can be criticized, but it merits only praise if analyzed from the point of view of the national economy."[45] The government became the patrón as the law transferred power from local landowners to the state.

The vagrancy law also provided labor for Ubico's public works projects. Peasants who did not work on private farms or who failed to fulfill their requirements worked on road construction and other tasks for the state. Ubico sought to build and improve government buildings and communication facilities and provide electricity to rural areas. By the 1940s, power lines or small generators brought power to some remote villages. The public works program reached virtually every area in the republic in some form, even if the impact in some towns was minimal.[46]

Through the expanded road system and his public works projects, Ubico sought to integrate Maya into the national economy. As seen in chapters 5 and 6, Ubico also used military and education conscription to incorporate Maya into Ladino society. Furthermore, he believed that an improved transportation and communication infrastructure would benefit Maya by making commercial production possible even on small plots of land in remote areas previously devoted to subsistence farming.[47] Ubico also sought to promote and protect small and developing indigenous economies. In 1936 he passed legislation that prohibited the importation of "cloth or cloth goods with typical indigenous characteristics and colors similar to those made in this country."[48] Ubico also promoted a national fair in which he highlighted Mayan textile work. As Ix'aj recalls, "The best president was Ubico. He really cared about and wanted to help our people. He put on a textile fair in Guatemala City. He paid us and fed us well. My grandfather went and told me about it."[49] In this instance, Ubico provided an additional source of income for Maya. Nonetheless, his main goal was to stimulate international tourism at the fair through depictions of Maya.[50] Ubico believed Maya needed some incentive to integrate themselves into the national economy and society.

Regulations stipulated that anyone who owned ten *cuerdas* (approximately ten acres) or more was required to work 100 days a year and that anyone who owned less or no land was required to work 150 days a year. The government exempted (from the required workdays) men who could pay an annual tax of one quetzal. Few Maya had access to such large amounts of land, and even fewer could afford to pay the annual fee. The law required all agricultural laborers who could not afford this payment to carry a *libreto* (workbook), renewable each year, to verify the number of days they had worked. The administrator or owner of the property noted the amount of labor performed every fifteen days. Once laborers completed their workbooks they brought them to the jefe político for approval.[51] Since it was the responsibility of the administrator to mark the number of days worked and of the jefe político to approve libretos, the system was susceptible to corruption. Legislation later required that all those between the ages of eighteen and sixty carry libretos.[52]

The forced-labor system was not the only means to ensure that large landowners would have a sufficient supply of labor. In some cases, Ubico negated local farmers' rights to work their own land. As one rural agriculturist explains, "Ubico would not let you farm your own land, so you had to go to the coast to work. He sent auxiliaries to inspect your land. If you were farming corn or coffee without a license, they took you to jail. If you did not work for the large landowner you went to jail. We were just laborers [to him]."[53]

While his labor laws focused on men, he also regulated female activities. Oral histories describe how Ubico refused to allow women to sell in the market because he wanted them at home to take care of their children.[54] Like many other dictators, Ubico wanted to control the family life in addition to all other facets of Guatemala.

Strict Justice and Security

Kaqchikel did not appreciate the restrictions Ubico placed on their labor or agricultural practices, but they seldom complained of his imposition of a strict system of justice. An aldea resident summarizes one basic premise: "Ubico was a good president because if you were guilty, then he punished you; but if you were innocent, you were not castigated."[55] Kaqchikel oral traditions relate a history of persecution at the hands of economic and political elites. Informants attest that prior to Ubico, leaders ignored the law and scorned justice.[56] Consequently, Kaqchikel welcomed a government that allowed them to live without fear of mistreatment.

Ubico applied his brand of justice at the local level and portrayed himself as a protector of Maya. When local officials abused Maya, Ubico came to their defense. In Comalapa, for example, an intendente threatened to kill people for no reason. Ubico came to investigate the incident. One Comalapense elaborates: "A group went to the judge to testify. They went in one by one. I was the last one and I had to identify the intendente. When Ubico came out, he told us it was not our fault. We were not guilty. He told us to return to our town and we would not have any more problems. He brought about justice. He investigated the issues and he did not lie."[57] Others concur that when Ubico intervened in community problems, he ensured that justice prevailed. Ubico invited complaints about local officials and often overruled officials' decisions. Ubico also allowed for leniency in his personal interactions. For example, when Kaqchikel leaders from Panajachel documented why intensive labor on their small cash-crop plots should exempt them from forced-labor laws, Ubico allowed them to bypass the law.[58] Kaqchikel note that people knew what to expect from Ubico because he was straightforward. In some instances, these actions earned him a reputation among Kaqchikel as a friend of Maya.[59]

Kaqchikel did not think he favored them, however. Most assert that he ensured the law treated Ladinos and Maya equally. As a Kaqchikel teacher opines, "Ubico was not a racist. He treated everyone equally. He meted out justice, so many liked him. He also sent Ladinos, not just indigenous, to jail if they committed crimes."[60] As one couple explains, "General Ubico did justice. For him, there were no Ladinos and no naturales, everyone was equal."[61] Furthermore, as many Kaqchikel point out, even when Ubico exploited people, he did not differentiate according to ethnicity. One rural farmer explains: "Ladinos and Indians both had to work on Ubico's road projects and no one was paid."[62] According to these informants, Ubico wanted a united Guatemala. Some Kaqchikel assert that Ubico was also one of the first presidents to give Maya the opportunity for an education so they could achieve equal status with Ladinos.[63] Kaqchikel from San Andrés Semetabaj believed that Ubico's concern was genuine and viewed his legislation as a liberating force. They characterized the Ubico period as a time of law and order during which legislation protected Mayan rights. They believed that courts applied the law universally to Maya and Ladinos.[64] Most Kaqchikel appreciated Ubico because he was the first president to treat them equally before the law.

This equality was conditional, however. A weaver and painter opines: "Our people say that maybe Ubico was good because he got rid of thieves, but if you know history, what he did was not good. He took our land and gave it to the Ladinos. The indigenous people lost their land. We were poorer after he left office. He gave all the land on the coast to the rich and there are big landowners there now because of Ubico. He looked for friends to give land to. He was a bad man. Barrios did the same thing; he gave land to the Ladinos."[65] Others claim that if Ubico thought individual Maya were becoming too intelligent or talented, he oftentimes forced them to stop their work or he killed them.[66]

Harsh retribution became known as the law of Ubico. As an agriculturist explains, "There was a great deal of respect during the Ubico regime. There were no thieves. If a person killed another person, then that person had to die. That was the law. That was a strict government."[67] Ubico's severe approach to the law meant that few people attempted to circumvent it. Kaqchikel oral traditions illustrate the fate of those who broke the law. In one story, a boy killed his father, and Ubico sent the police to investigate. The police grabbed the boy and paraded him through town and the market and then killed him. The people were scared because that is how Ubico applied justice, but they liked his justice.[68] Kaqchikel appreciate that Ubico castigated people according to their crime and that he held wrongdoers accountable for their actions. As one woman noted, "Ubico's justice was the same as God's."[69] Others add that he abided by the law in the Bible: an eye for an eye.[70] An eighty-seven-year-old blind man from Aguas Calientes expresses a common perspective: "Some people say Ubico was bad, but I believe he was bad for bad people and good for good people."[71]

Kaqchikel thrived in this situation because they knew the rules of the game and would be secure as long as they contributed positively to society. Kaqchikel are not intimidated by, and actually invite, strong-armed leaders. As a bus driver says, "We want a tough leader."[72] One woman, who lost her husband to la violencia, summarizes: "People say that the Ubico government was evil. It was not evil, it was just tough."[73] According to the majority of Kaqchikel, a firm leader is essential to the maintenance of a governable and just society.

Oral histories hail Ubico because he made their towns, and especially Guatemala City, safe to live in. Informants say it was safe to sleep in Guatemala City and that people felt comfortable when they traveled to different towns or the coast. They note that towns would put on night concerts because it was safe for people to go out. Most assert that people were happy because Ubico rid the country of delinquency, thieves, and murderers.[74] Ix'ey, an unassuming leader and teacher dedicated to the maintenance of her language and culture, explains this attraction to Ubico: "Ubico made our people suffer, but they like him because there was no robbery or laziness. He took care of our town."[75] A peaceful living situation is a top priority for Kaqchikel. As a Kaqchikel university professor asserts, "People are OK with exploitation, if they have security."[76] For Kaqchikel, freedom came from the ability to enjoy their surroundings without the fear of criminal activity. The majority say Ubico's government was strict and harsh but beneficial.[77] They were willing to allow an infringement of their individual freedoms to gain personal security.

Many oral accounts remember Ubico as a harsh, angry leader. He hit people to punish them and killed criminals. Many informants describe him as a demanding man who did not listen to others. They assert that most people were afraid of him. Oral histories relate that he created many problems for people and interfered in everyone's lives; people could not simply relax. Kaqchikel assert that Ubico was hard on the poor because he made them do most of the work.[78] Some claimed they had no freedom during the Ubico dictatorship.[79] One twenty-seven-year-old who had heard a great deal about Ubico says, "Ubico was strict, so for one part, there was justice, but on the other side, he was not just. He forced everyone to work, and he was a violent man."[80] This young man argues that a system of forced labor is inherently unjust. Waqi' Kan, who is thirty-one years old, examines Ubico's omnipotence in Guatemala: "Unfortunately, we know only negative things about Ubico—not negative in the sense of his authoritarianism. He was a despot who overwhelmed the society of Guatemala under a government of fear; a government in which the president was considered almost like God. And we know very well that he remained in power for many years. Of course it was unconstitutional. Nevertheless, he made the nation submissive, and they did not resist because they were afraid. He frequently used exploitation."[81] Many Kaqchikel, especially younger generations, remember Ubico as an acrimonious leader who imposed strict regulations that extended to every aspect of their lives.

Ubico's concern for alcohol consumption among Maya reveals the paternalistic attitude that permeated his relationship with them. "It is necessary to eradicate, to the maximum," he said, "the affection for liquor among the Indians. . . . Because the bootlegged liquor is cheap, its use is popular. When we achieve a reduction of alcohol consumption among the Indians we will have better workers and healthier generations."[82] In 1940 he passed a law that prohibited the sale of alcohol in finca stores because primarily "Indians" consumed alcohol.[83] He doubled the price of the liquor the state produced and outlawed locally made liquor. Kaqchikel recognize that this law was difficult to enforce and knew that some people continued to make liquor at home. David Ordóñez, the director of the national police, nonetheless boasted that his corps had reduced production of clandestine moonshine between 1937 and 1940, closing 243 stills.[84] Kaqchikel point out another possible explanation for this reduction: some people used the law as a means to frame their enemies. Informants recount how people would bury liquor on the property of their enemy and then report the person to the police. According to oral accounts, Ubico's effort to purge the towns of drunkards was more successful. Informants recall that he only allowed people to drink on Saturdays and Sundays. Consequently, on workdays police arrested drunkards in the street and punished them with 150 to 300 lashes and a jail sentence.[85] One middle-aged rural farmer explains the fate of inebriated men: "If people were drinking *aguardiente* [homemade liquor], they were sentenced to only three days in jail, but you would also get two hundred lashes . . . from a big stick with thorns. You were all bruised on the backside. Only three days, but two hundred hits."[86] Ubico's retribution intimidated even the most afflicted drinkers. Unfortunately, according to Kaqchikel, this vice began to proliferate again after Ubico left office.[87]

Many of the gains Ubico made during his tenure were lost when he left, and most Kaqchikel claim that Guatemala is in a dire situation today without the leadership of a strong president like Ubico. A farmer from Aguas Calientes states: "Ubico governed from 1930 to 1944. There was much peace and love. Not everyone understood it, so they thought they were slaves, but it was not true. He was true and correct; we would have failed without him."[88] A Kaqchikel teacher from Poaquil adds: "We need a dictator like Ubico today. He was good because there was peace. If you killed, then you died. The government needs to take care of the people."[89] Kaqchikel fault a weak and corrupt government for society's ills. Informants recall that Ubico told people what to do and they did it. They appreciate that he taught people discipline, because they insist that without discipline you cannot have progress.[90] People took pride in their country because, as one man notes, "Ubico made the country honorable."[91] The militaristic state that characterized Ubico's reign did not alienate him from maintaining a revered position in Kaqchikel oral traditions. In fact, Kaqchikel appreciate that system because today, according to the same sources, people do not respect the law as they did under Ubico.

Because of a lack of pride today, people often disassociate themselves from the needs of the country. In most Kaqchikel towns, voluntary communal labor persists, but because they are not obligated not everyone contributes. A group of men who repaired the road to their aldea lamented that many of their neighbors neglected to show up. They recalled that during the Ubico years everyone would have been there. The work was voluntary and no one recorded who contributed. One man recommended they use a ledger to keep track of who volunteered their time and labor.[92] Ubico's model of workbooks and his ability to garner laborers appealed to these men. Unlike Ubico's government, the democratic regime today does not ensure that national progress affects the local realm.

A Personal Touch

Ubico's model for Guatemala's development necessitated a hands-on approach. He thrived on personal interaction, and Kaqchikel appreciated his communication efforts. Ubico occasionally visited men who worked on the roads. He could not visit every town, so road laborers provided a good connection to the people. As one elder explains, "Ubico liked to talk to people. He would tell them not to be afraid when cars came to town. He was building a new road so cars would come. He never did visit here [Poaquil] though."[93] Poaquil was the only town in this study that Ubico did not visit. Oral accounts attest that when Ubico came to their towns, residents had a celebration and decorated the streets. Informants note that people came from rural villages to see him and that in some cases he arrived in isolated communities. Kaqchikel recall that Ubico shook hands with people and that those who spoke Spanish could converse with him. Oral histories relate that some people were always happy to see Ubico because they believed he truly cared about them.[94] One eighty-six-year-old woman elucidates the motive behind Ubico's visits: "He visited Comalapa to supervise the works. It gave him the opportunity to know the town."[95] Ubico impressed most Kaqchikel because he initiated communication and contact with them. An eighty-six-year-old *chirimía* (oboe) player summarizes why Ubico could connect so well with people: "When he came to Comalapa, I went to see him. He was just a regular guy."[96]

Ubico's visits to the countryside portray how his concessions to Maya often had ulterior motives. Federíco Hernández de León accompanied Ubico on many of his visits, and his accounts reveal that Ubico's frequent personal interventions in response to petitions from villages garnered significant support. Ubico would walk through the village, surrounded by the local populace, to talk with residents and to visit schools, public offices, army barracks, and other institutions. For Ubico, the importance of these visits lay not in effecting any significant change but in giving Maya a sense of participation and an impression that the president really did care for them. On a trip to Patzún, for example, a number of Kaqchikel were complaining about certain local Ladinos and, according to Hernández de León, Ubico felt obliged to respond: "The Ladinos have the bad custom of systematically bothering the Indians."[97] Hernández de León notes that Ubico invited people to voice their concerns and problems and encouraged villagers to seek presidential justice. Ubico claimed that his justice was more immediate and just than that of the courts because it bypassed local officials. He investigated working conditions and wages on fincas and sometimes issued orders for back pay. His personalistic style of government—the way he lent an ear to Mayan communities accustomed to hostile local and national officials—prompted admiration and loyalty from many Maya.[98]

Ubico's visits to Kaqchikel towns had a profound impact on their inhabitants. They had the sense that Ubico spoke directly to them and intervened in their personal lives. Ka'i' Imox excitedly expressed how Ubico affected him: "I did not have a mother or father, but there was the Ubico government. He taught me discipline, and that is important. If you do not have discipline, then you are in trouble. God and Ubico taught me, but Ubico died."[99] Although Ka'i' Imox never had a conversation with Ubico, the president served as a surrogate father. Clearly, Ubico's personal touch exponentially expanded his control and impact.

Intendentes

The geographic isolation of many towns made it difficult for Ubico to maintain constant surveillance himself, so beginning in 1935 he appointed intendentes to replace mayors and impose strict control in the communities. Intendentes were usually Ladinos from Guatemala City, and they did not remain in their posts for long terms. Their position of authority was absolute. They developed little appreciation for village concerns because their welfare depended on how well they served Ubico's interests, not on how friendly or popular they were locally.[100] Generally, Kaqchikel oral traditions do not recall intendentes fondly. Oral histories explain that people did not elect them and that generally, since they were Ladinos, intendentes only helped Ladinos in town. One elder explains the role of the intendentes: "Ubico gave them the law and ideas, and they carried them out. You could not talk to them; that was not good. But if they committed an offense Ubico removed them."[101] Most Kaqchikel appreciated that Ubico applied the same law to intendentes that he applied to the rest of the citizens.

Like Ubico, intendentes did not understand the native language, but unlike Ubico, they usually made little effort to communicate and interact with Kaqchikel. As a result, the intendentes' presence was not beneficial to Kaqchikel. Kaqchikel note that they just came and left, without a stake in the community, and without taking good care of the residents. Informants opine that intendentes simply imposed Ubico's law and incarcerated those who did not comply.[102] One man tells of his experience with the intendente of Comalapa: "The intendentes were very bad people. They were not from here. One day I did not have my jornato, so he grabbed me. He controlled the road. He put me in jail. If you did not have your papers in order, the intendentes grabbed you and forced you to work. At his inclination, we did the roads."[103] Intendentes were Ubico's eyes and ears (yet deaf to the language of the majority of their charges), and in most cases their application of the law was strict.

A former Kaqchikel mayor of Comalapa explains why Ubico replaced the mayoral system with intendentes and how the community reacted:

> During the time of Ubico there were no mayors, only intendentes who were Ladinos. Ubico did not want people from the town to be mayors, so he brought them from another town to implement justice. Because if the mayor was from the town, he had family, *compadres* [relations through godparenting system], in-laws, and friends all of whom he had to do favors for, so he could not guarantee justice. The intendente did not know anyone. He had no connections so his justice was level, equal. We had fourteen years of intendentes. The people did not like it, because the intendentes spoke no Kaqchikel and the Kaqchikel did not speak Spanish. The intendente would not pay attention or address your problem, if he did not know you.[104]

Ubico's intendente system eradicated much of the corruption inherent in the municipal system, but it alienated Kaqchikel because it severed their means of communication with local political leaders. Informants point out that intendentes had no local network. Consequently, because Kaqchikel share and interact through a network of interdependent relationships, intendentes could not involve themselves in the community. Ubico realized that communal law was stronger than legal law in Mayan communities and constantly moved intendentes around to prevent them from forming and involving themselves in these networks. However, his practice of arbitrarily replacing intendentes in response to complaints from local residents created the impression that he was prepared to respond to popular will. Ubico allowed only himself the opportunity to develop paternalistic relationships with people. He forced intendentes to implement all aspects of the law, especially those such as forced labor that were not favorable to Maya. Intendentes performed daily tasks that emanated from a tightly controlled political system. In contrast, Ubico had the advantage of making quick trips during which he could apply his brand of justice or law in favor of Maya. Consequently, Maya felt a closer connection to Ubico than to local officials.

Ubico's obsession with centralization reduced Mayan autonomy and further undermined the communal power structure in Kaqchikel and other Mayan communities. The alienation of Maya from the political system produced tension between Maya and local Ladinos.[105] Nonetheless, Kaqchikel maintained some representation in the intendente system. In Tecpán, for example, the judge who served under the intendente was Kaqchikel. An elder from Tecpán explains: "The judge was pure *natural* (indigenous person), an employee. He would tell the Kaqchikel people what to do. . . . The intendente was in another part of the building. One for Ladinos and one for Kaqchikel. The *natural* was the judge because in those days the naturales had more offenses. Each year it [the position] would change."[106]

On rare occasions an intendente received high marks from Kaqchikel. Some intendentes attempted to get to know the community and listen to and assess the needs of the people.[107] Nonetheless, language and cultural barriers were a challenge even for those men who sought to have a positive impact on the community. Kaqchikel who perceived the intendente system to be an extension of Ubico's penchant for law and order praised the system.[108] Oxi' Kej, a fifty-six-year-old farmer who attended school for nine years, tells of his father's experience with an intendente: "My father was living with a family in Zaragoza where he was a teacher. They were a rich family, but the son was lazy. One day he hit the son in class, because in those days teachers could hit us and that was OK. The mother complained to the intendente. When the intendente asked my dad why he hit the child, my dad told him that the boy was lazy. The intendente replied that he was happy we have teachers who are concerned for our students."[109] As with Ubico's judicial system, as long as the accused had abided by the established rules, honest intendentes exonerated them.

The intendente system was an ambiguous assault on Mayan society. New authorities sometimes proved more resistant to landlords' demands than those of Mayan leaders. The requirements of the finca were balanced with the need to protect the subsistence economy upon which the finca depended for labor and food crops. At times this created conflict between finqueros and intendentes. In practice, intendentes often found it easier to work through the political system already in place. When a Ladino authority needed Mayan labor and/or collaboration, he would discuss the issue with local Mayan leaders. In many cases, relations between Mayan and Ladino authorities would have deteriorated, and the maintenance of order and discipline would have been impossible without the collaboration of local Mayan organizations.[110] Ubico's reorganization of the political system had varying effects on Maya, depending upon the degree of isolation of the community and the individuals involved. For the most part, Kaqchikel trusted this brand of politics because they saw Ubico as an honest man who eradicated the corruption seemingly inherent in politicians.[111]

The majority of Kaqchikel also appreciate Ubico's efforts to transform Guatemala from an indebted country to one with surplus money in the national treasury. They note that he even eliminated the debt to the United States. Nonetheless, Kaqchikel point out that one reason Ubico was able to save money and instigate Guatemala's development was that he had no labor expenses. While Ubico did not use this money for social services, his successor, Arévalo, generally invested money in the human resources of Guatemala. Kaqchikel recognize that Arévalo achieved many of his good works through the money that Ubico left in the national bank. They assert that Ubico was a good financial manager who maintained the quetzal on a par with the dollar. Kaqchikel point out that although the average laborer did not earn much money (ten cents a day), he could maintain a subsistence level and support a family because the cost of living was low.[112] Kaqchikel hail Ubico because he put the money back into Guatemala; he did not fill his own coffers with the nation's profits.

Some Kaqchikel felt confident that Ubico had their best interests in mind. They opine that Ubico capacitated Maya through education and the military because he gave them the opportunity to improve their position. Others note that he wanted to help poor people, and one woman claimed he even distributed clothes to them. Many Kaqchikel had the sense that he truly cared about the citizens of Guatemala.[113] Ubico portrayed himself as a dictator who cared about his fellow countrymen even though he was tough.

Many Kaqchikel viewed Ubico as a godlike figure who was omnipotent and omnipresent. He visited small towns and doled out his brand of justice, often in favor of Maya. Magical things seemed to happen in his presence. One instance early in his presidency exemplifies Ubico's uncanny ability to provide assistance to those in need. On November 21, 1931, at 3:30 in the afternoon, a boat that was transporting fifteen people across Lake Atitlán, a Kaqchikel and Tz'utuj'il region, capsized. The president happened to be enjoying a ride in his boat when he spotted the accident and saved the victims from their fate.[114] Even when he was on vacation, Ubico managed to be a savior.

Conclusion

Kaqchikel are aware of the downsides of Ubico's reign. Policies and rural reforms under Ubico were not as humane and farsighted as some Western scholars have suggested. Ubico was more concerned with the economic interests of foreign and local elite than with improvement in the lives of the masses. His policies in the countryside were not intended to, and did not, effect social progress. Ubico focused on the economic, not the social consequences of his policies: the administration denied that the majority of the population lived in poverty and argued that the country's inhabitants were not bad off in comparison to North Americans or Europeans because aborigines had a greater capacity for self-sufficiency in food, clothing, and other necessities. Furthermore, it said, Maya did not need aid because they turned to their relatives for help. Harsh political repression, not co-optation of the masses through improved living conditions, was the basis for Ubico's retention of power.[115]

Ubico's system used Maya as a labor force to build roads and to work for large landowners. The means for extralegal control remained in the system, leaving Maya vulnerable to exploitation. Abuse of the vagrancy law by local employers and officials prevented the ability of Maya to exercise their freedom. The human costs of these policies were great. The government severely punished vagrants and treated Maya as bondsmen on road projects. The intendente system attacked the traditional religious-political system of Mayan politics and relations. Highly centralized political control was vested in Ubico and exercised through the hierarchical system of nationally appointed leaders. Scholars argue that political action initiated outside the communities and the denial of autonomous organizations brought about destruction and violent alterations in sociopolitical structures. As a result, Mayan resistance to cultural change began to disintegrate.[116]

Ubico presented his reform laws in such a way that they would appear to benefit Maya. His intervention in local affairs produced isolated benefits to individuals or small groups of Maya, but these benefits did not improve Mayan life on a national level. These interventions mainly served to enhance his image as a friend of Maya, but the negative effects of his paternalism were many. However, prior to Ubico's rule, an amorphous distribution of power resulted in multiple sources of exploitation. Ubico appeared to fight middle-level exploiters as he concentrated power in the state. Most importantly, Ubico's costs were predictive and uniform, not capricious. Mayan reality, while not ideal, had improved since the time Ubico assumed office.

The majority of Kaqchikel recognized the exploitation inherent in the forced-labor system but accepted it as a lesser evil than systems of previous (and subsequent) governments. Furthermore, Ubico clearly set out the regulations for society and provided a safe environment. Kaqchikel knew that if they abided by his rules, he would guarantee their security. They appreciated Ubico's straightforward and honest style of government. He was not an impetuous leader who surprised them with unexpected oppression or persecution, as were many of the leaders during the civil war. In fact, they encouraged his policy of punishment for murderers, thieves, drunkards, and others who undermined his system. The top priority for Kaqchikel was to live in a safe environment, and Ubico provided these conditions.

Most Kaqchikel especially appreciated Ubico's local approach to politics. He visited them in their communities, shook their hands, conversed with them, defended them against Ladino abuses, and inspired them to continue their work for the community and nation. Like Lázaro Chacón in Aguas Calientes (see chapter 3), Ubico respected and attempted to understand Kaqchikel lifestyle, culture, and livelihood. He expressed an interest in people and wanted to get to know them and their reality. As a result of these efforts, Ubico significantly affected the lives of Maya where it meant the most to them: in their communities.

Through these visits, Ubico communicated that he was a defender of Mayan rights and property. He arrived in town to enforce justice regardless of the offender's ethnicity. He appeared to treat Ladinos and Maya equally and alleviated workers of the great burden of debt peonage. According to many oral accounts, Ubico wanted to help the poor. He shifted the control of labor from the private sector to the state, but he did not eliminate the burden of perpetual labor. As a result, Kaqchikel were responsible only to his government and his work obligations. They were no longer victims of avaricious landowners. Consequently, Kaqchikel no longer had the sense that they were simply subjects of landowners. Ubico's visits, egalitarian rhetoric, and isolated acts in defense of Maya facilitated a personal identification between

Kaqchikel and the locus of state power. Kaqchikel prefer to contribute to national development through roads and public works rather than add to the personal wealth of the landowning class. They strongly identify with the nation and care about its livelihood and success, but they do not feel a connection to the rich, nonindigenous landowners.

The desire of Kaqchikel to connect themselves through viable national transportation routes is apparent in their historical perspectives of Ubico. The majority of Kaqchikel commend Ubico's dedication to the development of Guatemala's roads, even though Maya performed the majority of the unpaid manual labor to achieve this goal. Most residents of Kaqchikel communities hail the development of the road system because it facilitates increased trade as well as an exchange of ideas. At the same time, some recognize the disadvantages of this opening. They lament that it threatens their culture and increases economic disparity. Still, most people accept these challenges and emphasize the improvements such as better access to foodstuffs, employment opportunities, and increased trade with national and international markets. The majority of Kaqchikel are not closed to outside influences and interaction because the potential benefits of these are apparent. Furthermore, they perceive this infrastructure as essential to Guatemala's effort to become a modernized nation. Oral histories surrounding Ubico reveal that national development is important to Kaqchikel.

Kaqchikel did not blindly support Ubico's regime, however. Most realized that he was a severe leader who treated Maya as a labor source. He forced them to work for the government. They performed grueling labor for which they received no pay, food, or shelter; their only compensation was a signature on their work card. Nonetheless, most Kaqchikel hail his accomplishments in Guatemala's infrastructure. He significantly expanded the road system, built the national palace, which continues to be a source of national pride today, and constructed other public buildings, such as military quarters. However, they point out that he achieved these feats on the backs of Maya.

Kaqchikel oral traditions present both positive and negative aspects of Ubico's reign. Informants commonly stated: "Ubico's government was both good and bad."[117] He exploited Maya through forced labor and workbooks, but he freed them of their perpetual debts to landowners. He forced military and education conscription upon them, but he allowed them the opportunity to interact on equal terms with Ladinos. He doled out harsh punishment to offenders of all crimes, but he made Guatemala safe for its citizens. He instituted austere economic reforms, but he alleviated Guatemala of its debtor status and left funds in the national coffers for the Arévalo government.

Kaqchikel oral traditions critically assess the Ubico regime and conclude that the demands made upon their people did not exceed the benefits enjoyed under his reign.

Kaqchikel analysis of the Ubico regime elucidates their hierarchy of values. In exchange for personal security, they are willing to sacrifice personal freedom (work cards and military conscription), political representation (intendentes), the ability to earn money (vialidad and the prohibition of female vendors), and in some cases even the indoctrination of different worldviews and ideas. They accepted these infringements upon their individual freedoms and rights because they wanted to live in a stable environment under a government that did not act capriciously. Kaqchikel prioritize the social good of national stability and personal security over individual and collective freedom. An examination of oral histories surrounding other leaders, both national and local, further elucidates Kaqchikel values and worldviews.

8
Leaders

K'amol taq b'eya'

Looking at which leaders remain relevant in Kaqchikel oral histories elucidates the qualities Kaqchikel respect and seek to emulate and what qualities
they spurn. Ubico commands the most attention in oral histories, but other
leaders have certainly made an impact on Kaqchikel. Kaqchikel historical
perspectives of these leaders reveal how national and local policies have affected them. Their oral histories compare the leadership styles and effects of
different dictators and democratic presidents. Kaqchikel realize they are
not isolated from the rest of Guatemala, and their oral histories elucidate
their reactions to and opinions of the state's role in their life. Likewise, local Kaqchikel heroes present examples of efficacious ways to interact with
Ladinos and the government. These oral histories vindicate Kaqchikel culture and reality but emphasize that these representatives have succeeded in
Ladino-dominated spheres without sacrificing their Kaqchikel identities. In
fact, these leaders are heroes because they use Kaqchikel characteristics to
advance the cause of their people. Kaqchikel seek comprehension of and involvement in national policies, and they utilize local strategies to achieve their
goals without relinquishing their culture and worldviews.

Justo Rufino Barrios

President Justo Rufino Barrios is portrayed similarly to Ubico. Barrios was
one of many caudillo figures in Guatemala's history. As seen in chapter 2, he
ushered in the liberal reforms of the 1870s that required Mayan land and
labor to produce goods for export. Kaqchikel remember him most for his
implementation of land titles and the development of Guatemala's railroad,
communication, and school systems. They also credit him with the initiation
of Protestantism in Guatemala. Some Kaqchikel portray him as a benevolent
"reformer," while others assert that he infringed upon Mayan rights and culture. Either way, he made an indelible mark upon Kaqchikel history.

Oral traditions present different facets of Barrios's dictatorship. As with
Ubico, Kaqchikel critically assess Barrios's leadership and emphasize aspects

of his rule that were important to them. One educator from Poaquil states: "Barrios did many different things and different people remember distinct things. You can put it all together. People here [in Poaquil] love him because he gave us our independence. Barrios is like Ubico. Ubico made us work. He is popular for constructing the national palace, but he did it with our labor."[1] Even those whose towns benefited from Barrios's reign realize that he exploited unpaid Mayan labor to complete public works. A forty-year-old woman whose family named her after the late president expresses the contradictions of his rule: "He killed our people, but he also gave us independence. He was a good man."[2] Ix'ajmaq, a twenty-nine-year-old teacher studying to earn her history degree, counters: "Barrios did well here [in Poaquil] but not in other areas."[3] Many people believe he had some good ideas and instituted progress and justice in the nation, but by the end of his term he had committed too many abuses. As one rural inhabitant states, "At first Barrios did good things, but then he became evil so they killed him."[4]

Kaqchikel appreciate that Barrios provided personal security and national stability. They point out that he wrote a new constitution to provide a framework for political stability. Kaqchikel compare Barrios to Ubico because both men maintained power through military rule. They note that Barrios was Ubico's godfather and say their similar styles of government reflected this deep connection. For example, both leaders made people carry work cards, used forced labor, and ruled with strong-armed tactics. They also note that Barrios killed murderers and thieves. The majority of Kaqchikel appreciated the security that both Barrios and Ubico ensured and argue that these two leaders imposed law and order.[5] A barber describes life under Barrios: "Barrios gave security to the people. He inaugurated the law and people respected it. At that time, homes did not need a door. People just crossed two pieces of wood in the form of an 'X' across their front door, and that was enough because people respected the law. Barrios respected the lives of men and women."[6] Kaqchikel enjoyed the safe living conditions he provided, and they liken the peace, tranquility, and order to the conditions under Ubico's reign. Scholars note that other Maya respect him because he applied the law equally to Ladinos and Maya. In some cases he even respected Mayan traditions and used local leaders to achieve his goals.[7]

Much like Ubico, Barrios traveled to communities to mete out his form of justice and centralize control over the country. A father of ten shares what he heard about one of Barrios's visits: "When Barrios visited the town, they rang the bells and everyone came to the center of town. He asked people what they wanted and how they were doing. He asked how the priest was and the people said he was doing a good job. Then he asked how the mayor was doing and people complained about him, so Barrios brought him up to the mountains and had him killed. There was another man who hit his mother, so Barrios had him killed right behind the church."[8] According to this man, Barrios delivered his harsh justice personally. Kaqchikel appreciated both this personal contact and the attention he paid to their lives.

Kaqchikel also laud Barrios for developing the national infrastructure. They praise him as the father of the railroad and telecommunications, much as they hail Ubico as the builder of the national palace and road system. They point out that Barrios constructed roads in Guatemala and that he rode in the country's first automobile.[9] Lajuj Iq', a sixty-year-old craftsman and farmer, explains the reactions to this development: "One hundred years ago electricity arrived in Guatemala. Barrios brought it. During this time there were no cars here, so Barrios went to the towns and villages on his horse. But the U.S. sent him a car and people were really surprised when he showed up in a car."[10] The assertion that Barrios rode in a car is historically inaccurate, as Barrios's death in 1885 predated the arrival of the automobile in Guatemala (and the United States).[11] Lajuj Iq' collapses time, but his account expresses how Kaqchikel appreciate that Barrios visited people. Furthermore, Lajuj Iq' personalizes Barrios's role in "bringing" electricity to Guatemala, thereby keeping Barrios's contributions vital. While the account given by Lajuj Iq' contains some historical inaccuracies, his historical perceptions highlight Barrios's role in improving Guatemala's infrastructure.

Ladinos and Western scholars recognize that Barrios improved Guatemala's road and seaport systems, established the first railroad, introduced electric lighting, and pioneered new forms of communication, such as telegraph lines. Guatemala completed a marine cable in 1880 that provided direct international communication. Four years later, Guatemala City and Quetzaltenango proudly initiated telephone service.[12] Kaqchikel assert that Barrios's development of the telegraph, telephone, and mail systems facilitated small industry in Guatemala and increased trade.[13] While he engineered liberal reforms to increase Guatemala's export economy, Kaqchikel note, the local economy also benefited. According to some Kaqchikel informants, Barrios ruled during Guatemala's most transformative period.

Kaqchikel oral traditions also note that one of Barrios's main goals was to decrease the Catholic Church's economic, political, and social power. Informants point out that the government assumed control over the registration of births and marriages in place of the Catholic Church. As seen in chapter 5, Barrios sought to replace Catholic schools with public education. Kaqchikel attest he believed the church was too political and for that reason did not like Catholic priests. They point out that he exiled the Jesuits and greatly reduced the number of other Catholic priests in the country. Oral histories relate that his final attack on the Catholic Church was to counteract its influence by using another religion. According to Kaqchikel, Barrios introduced the Protestant Bible and missionaries to Guatemala. They say that he brought the first Protestant missionary, John Mills, from the United States and that now Protestantism has proliferated in Guatemala.[14] Kaqchikel reactions to the attack on the Catholic Church and the introduction of the Protestant religion differed according to one's preferred religion. Catholics criticize his attacks on the church, while Protestants hail him as the catalyst for their religion.

Barrios blamed the Catholic Church for Guatemala's uneducated and impoverished population. He said:

> It has been more than three centuries that [Guatemala] has been governed under the oligarchic-theocratic regimen. The government has been backward and despotic; the clergy has enjoyed the highest privilege and meddled in everything; it has been maintained in its opulence and in the enjoyment of luxury by the sweat of the people. And what have they [the people] been given in compensation for so much sacrifice? Nothing, absolutely nothing! Here are some eight hundred thousand men, women and children who cannot read or write, who cannot understand the religion they profess and that for them is reduced to mere superstitious formulas. They go without shoes, almost naked, and work transformed into beasts of burden.[15]

Barrios's attack on religious orders left many rural areas without priests. As a result, the church's influence over Maya waned. Barrios also established religious tolerance when he invited Protestant missionaries to work and live in Guatemala.[16]

Barrios intended his reforms to transform Guatemala into a modern society, but he placed a disproportionate amount of the burden of this development on Maya. The government constructed the infrastructure with unpaid Mayan labor, and transformation to a coffee-exporting country required the lands of the Catholic Church and Maya. As seen in chapter 2, most Kaqchikel feel they suffered disproportionately for the development of the export economy. They are proud to have contributed to the national development but did not want to become impoverished because of it. They do not believe that national progress and local prosperity have to be mutually exclusive. Most Kaqchikel also point out that Barrios did not treat everyone equally under his law. Many opine that he openly discriminated against Maya.[17]

Kaqchikel intellectuals are also critical of Barrios's rule. Many of these intellectuals studied Guatemala's history at the university level and combine this knowledge with oral histories in their communities. In some ways, their perspective is distinct from the majority of Kaqchikel who have not been educated beyond primary school. One such intellectual asserts:

> Barrios was known as "the reformer," but he did not reform anything for us. He just took away our land and kicked out the church to bring in Protestants because he thought the church was too powerful and had land. The government was also in charge of birth certificates. He took away church power. He made people register for their land—but, remember, in 1860 our people only spoke Kaqchikel, not Spanish. But all the papers were in Spanish, so many lost their land—especially the communal land. Before Barrios, there were no owners of the land. All could plant when and where they wanted. Also they could graze cows, horses and sheep, but he changed all that by taking away our land and forcing people to learn Spanish to survive. Barrios made us poorer.[18]

Regardless of the diverse opinions about Barrios, Kaqchikel recognize him as a pivotal figure in Guatemala's development and history. A former mayor of Barahona explains why his town center displays a bust of Barrios: "A long time ago a group of men brought back his bust in a sack. They carried it on foot with a *tapel* [tumpline] from Guatemala City. They wanted to honor him, but he did not help us much here."[19] Barrios's presence is felt even in areas he did not directly touch.

Barrios mitigated some of this criticism through personal contact. He knew this contact was essential to rural support for his government and to ensure that the population respected and obeyed his laws. Kaqchikel recognize that he used the military to maintain social control, but they also appreciate his visits to the communities. Poaquilenos revere him for his direct intervention in their independence movement. They gladly conformed to his liberal policies and privatized their lands in exchange for local sovereignty. Furthermore, oral traditions recall that Barrios traveled to rural communities to dole out his brand of justice, which in some cases ostensibly favored Maya against abusive priests or local officials. Kaqchikel praise his ability to ensure a secure society; under his rule, they did not fear criminal activity. Finally, Kaqchikel also appreciate that Barrios's policies contributed to Guatemala's development and stability. They recognize his constitution as an attempt to establish a blueprint for the governing of the nation, and they appreciate his efforts to improve the national infrastructure and economy. Kaqchikel recognize, however, that the labor of Guatemala's development was not distributed equally among its population. Kaqchikel appreciated the subsequent peace and order; however, most Kaqchikel believe that he, unlike Ubico, intemperately exploited Maya. His ends did not justify the excessive means.

Kaqchikel respect strong-armed leaders who can maintain peace and order; however, they insist these conditions be applied equally. Barrios failed to implement a system that treated Maya in an egalitarian manner, and consequently Kaqchikel oral traditions emphasize his exploitative and discriminatory approach to economic, political, and social development. Interestingly, leaders who espouse equal rights do not automatically gain approval in Kaqchikel oral histories. A leader whose style contrasts starkly with Ubico and Barrios also maintains an important position in Kaqchikel oral histories. Oral histories surrounding the government of Juan José Arévalo shed light on Kaqchikel perceptions of democracy.

Juan José Arévalo

Kaqchikel oral traditions credit Arévalo with establishing freedom in Guatemala upon his return from Argentina. Informants say he allowed people to make their own choices, eliminated the workbooks and control cards, increased workers' salaries and established the social security system, emphasized health and education for even the most remote communities, and reinstituted the system of elected public officials that Ubico had eliminated. They point out that because Arévalo was a civilian president, unlike Ubico, he established a new constitution. Some Kaqchikel even opine that Arévalo was Guatemala's best president because he was diligent and provided a good example for the country.

Arévalo won a democratic election and emphasized the importance of equal rights for Maya. Research indicates that at the time finqueros and local officials were no longer persecuting Maya as they had during the Ubico regime and that Maya felt as if they were respected more as workers. The government even duly punished those, including the police, who abused Maya. It also sought to extend an improved level of education to Maya, even publishing some materials in indigenous languages.[20] As with Ubico and Barrios, Arévalo has qualities and characteristics that Kaqchikel both laud and criticize.

When Arévalo assumed the presidency on March 1, 1945, he clearly stated whom he wanted his policies to affect: "In the past, there has been a fundamental lack of sympathy for the working man, and the faintest cry for justice was avoided and punished as if one were trying to eradicate the beginnings of a frightful epidemic. Now we are going to begin a period of sympathy for the man who works in the fields, in the shops, in the barracks, in the small businesses. . . . We are going to join justice and happiness to order, because order based on injustice and humiliation serves no one."[21] Arévalo sought to increase the economic and political power of the worker, expand education through the improvement of schools, and extend the social service projects network, such as health care and agricultural extension, in order to reach a larger proportion of the population. Unfortunately, Arévalo's rhetoric was stronger than his actions, and consequently the actual effects were not far-reaching. The majority of small landholders, tenant farmers, sharecroppers, and other members of the scattered agrarian community at the margins of fincas and commercial agriculture were unable to take advantage of increased bargaining power because of the government's restriction on forming associations and striking.[22]

While defense of Mayan rights was one of the stated goals of the Arévalo administration, the means to that end was assimilation without respect for, or recognition of, the value of Mayan culture. Consistent with nineteenth-century liberal ideology, the goal was to make Maya active and productive participants in national society. While the government promoted some Mayan languages, it expected Maya to learn and use Spanish as their primary language. Despite the revolutionary government's claims that it aided Maya, some anthropologists have found that many Maya believed their lives to be better under the dictatorship of Ubico.[23] Ubico made the effort to have personal contact with many Maya in their communities and did not attempt to incorporate them into national politics. In contrast, the democratic government attempted to alter Mayan lifestyles and cultures in order to improve the situation of the Maya. Even though they realized improvements in some aspects of their lives, many Maya felt threatened by the government's effort to assimilate them into Guatemalan society.

Assimilation was one of the characteristics of Arevalo's government; however, a strong minority of Ladinos within the constitutional assembly wanted to allow for ethnic distinctions. Despite strong opposition, two important provisions in the 1945 constitution portray the efforts by this minority in the constitutional assembly to respect the resources of Mayan civilization and consuetudinary law, rather than force Maya to adopt foreign ideas:

Article 83: "The development of a comprehensive policy for the economic, social, and cultural improvement of indigenous groups is recognized as being a benefit and in the interest of the nation. To this end, laws, regulations and special provisions may be drawn up for the indigenous groups based on their needs, conditions, practices, uses and customs."

Article 137, paragraph 15 states that the functions of the president include: "setting up and maintaining appropriate institutions or agencies to deal with Indian problems and to ensure an effective use of government resources in the solution of such problems."[24]

In response to this political and ideological current, the government created the Instituto Indigenista Nacional (National Indigenist Institute), which committed itself to the platform of the Instituto Indigenista Interamericano (Interamerican Indigenist Institute), an organization that called for governments to "conserve and fortify the social discipline existing in the Indian community and coordinate the common aspirations of the group with the national aspirations."[25] Unfortunately, few respected the intentions of this institution. Even the director of the Instituto Indigenista Nacional stated: "Indigenismo is the manifestation, the symptom, of a certain social ill-health."[26] These political leaders were not cognitively dissonant. They wanted to exalt and explore certain Mayan qualities and institutions; however, according to these men, an autonomous Mayan population would undermine their attempt to build a united nation. Consequently, in their quest for modernity, they could not support plurality and diversity.

Arévalo's good intentions had other negative consequences. Many Kaqchikel opine that as a population Guatemala was not prepared for democracy. They point out that Ubico had maintained such tight control over Guatemala's inhabitants that they did not know how to react to liberty. As a result, according to Kaqchikel, many turned to vices and crime. They lament that public intoxication, theft, and murder increased.[27] One group of men state: "When Arévalo became president he gave freedom. There was no pressure, so that is when laziness began. If you did not want to work then you did not, but with Ubico all had to work or they were punished. Laziness increased, and then came the time of violence."[28] As B'eleje' K'at explains, "Democracy is disorder. You need some time to develop it."[29]

Not everyone viewed Arévalo's liberty as an inevitable failure, however. The majority of Kaqchikel enjoyed the increased freedom and the opportunity to dedicate themselves to their own work as intensely as they wished. Oral histories attest that most men could better provide for their families because they, not the state or large landowners, reaped the benefits of their labor. As one elder asserts, "Arévalo was a good man. He gave freedom to work not to steal."[30] A former mayor of Comalapa, who reveres John F. Kennedy, observes: "Arévalo was the best president. He gave us rights, but then it fell apart. Too many thieves took advantage of it all."[31] In general, Kaqchikel were happy about the transition from a military to civilian government but lamented the fact that some people abused this freedom.[32]

Legislation passed during Arévalo's administration freed the rural population from working for free. This change empowered rural workers and caused conflict in the countryside because it ended the landowners' access to forced labor and because Maya no longer had to work outside their communities. The 1945 constitutional convention hotly debated this topic. Many argued that "the Indian" was lazy and would not work if not required to do so. While many Maya still found it necessary to work on plantations to subsist, the removal of the compulsion to work allowed them increased bargaining power and took on special symbolic significance. Peasants repeatedly told one commentator: "Now we are free. We are equal to Ladinos. . . . No one can force us to work on a coffee plantation far away against our will. We will go only if we want to."[33]

Arévalo established a democratic government which was the precursor to the government that exists in Guatemala today. Kaqchikel assert that Arévalo established a new constitution and passed good laws to replace Ubico's repressive legislation. Informants recall that he eliminated the intendente system and reinstituted the mayoral election procedure so that people could choose their leaders. As a result, they assert, many Maya returned as mayors of their communities. Naturally, Mayan mayors facilitated better communication between the populace and the local administrative branch. Most Kaqchikel fondly remember Arévalo as their first democratic president and the founder of Guatemala's democratic tradition.[34]

The move toward universal suffrage was another issue designed to empower workers, especially Maya. After a month of intense debate at the constitutional assembly, Congress allowed literate women to vote and permitted illiterate men a public oral vote. This suffrage was an important victory for Maya since a large percentage of their population was illiterate. In many cases, the vote allowed Maya to gain control of local government. Furthermore, political parties began to grow and compete for support. The parties listened to Mayan concerns and supported their views.[35]

Maya were becoming more involved in politics, but local and national officials often blocked access to real power. In some communities, Maya had no political representation in form or substance during the democratic government. Many Ladinos did not feel the 1945 constitution had any implications for Maya. In short, not much changed politically or economically in some Mayan communities.[36] Unlike Kaqchikel, some Mayan communities did not benefit from an open political system.

The Labor Code, passed in 1947 and amended in 1948, sought to improve the plight of workers. It allowed for collective bargaining and the right to strike (except during harvest), and it set minimum wages. The Labor Code restricted child and female labor, legislated working hours, established special courts to arbitrate disputes, and required employers to pay indemnity for fired workers. The increase in the number of cases against private employers during this time shows that workers took advantage of these rights. In fact, personnel who favored labor staffed most of the labor courts. In 1946 the Social Security Law established the Instituto de Guatemala de Seguridad Social (IGSS [Guatemalan Institute of Social Security]), which was aimed at many of these same issues. It provided compensation for workers hurt on the job, maternity benefits, and child care, among other provisions. Although it was a limited system, it was designed to help urban and rural poor.[37]

Kaqchikel appreciate that the Labor Code and IGSS defended and provided services and benefits to workers. They claim that under Arévalo, landowners no longer abused their workers and forced labor was abolished.[38] An elder from Aguas Calientes explains one aspect of this program: "When the liberator [Arévalo] arrived, he pressured the rich people. If someone broke a leg during his work, he had the right to be paid by IGSS. He created IGSS and that is one good thing that lives on. Unfortunately, now IGSS sees that you are poor and ignores you."[39] Kaqchikel also laud Arévalo because he increased the daily wage for roadwork from ten cents to eighty cents a day and augmented the salary for soldiers from three to ten quetzals a month. In fact, they assert that he increased the salary level of all workers.[40] Kab'lajuj Imox, an agriculturist with a passion for talking about international politics, compares the impact of Arévalo's policies to those of his predecessors:

When [Lázaro] Chacón was president, you earned five cents a day and one and a half quetzals a month if you were in the army. You could not support a family on that. When Ubico was president, you earned ten cents a day and three quetzals a month if you were in the army. You had to go to the coast to make money for your family because you did not earn enough to support them. This forced people to go to the coast, and it took them away from their families. Many died there. Then came Arévalo. He was a teacher who respected education and the people. He raised the salary of teachers from ten or fifteen quetzals a month to one hundred quetzals a month. He really made a change. His counterpart, Arbenz, also respected people and tried to help them. He gave people back their land. He really helped the workers because the big companies farmed only bananas, coffee, and other large crops. They treated their workers badly and paid little. Arbenz gave people land to have their own farms again.[41]

Kaqchikel insist that Arévalo extended workers' freedom when he eradicated all control and work cards (except the jornato, for which the government charged one quetzal a year). They point out that Kaqchikel could work for the state as paid laborers, or for themselves. They note that Arévalo invited people to form unions and meet as common employees. Kaqchikel appreciate that people were free to work where and how much they pleased. They insist that no one ordered them to work.[42] One fifty-seven-year-old farmer summarizes Arévalo's impact on labor as such: "Arévalo made a major change. He ended slavery and terminated the work mandates. Everyone worked of their own volition, and that has continued to today."[43]

Freedom and just wages did not preclude Arévalo's ability to continue Ubico's roadworks program. He continued to build the Pan-American Highway and roads to the Pacific coast and Puerto Barrios. Kaqchikel concede that roadwork under Arévalo did not progress rapidly because he could not employ as many people as Ubico. Kaqchikel express gratitude that Arévalo used machines to relieve some of the manual labor, pointing out that their use resulted in more humane working conditions than laborers had experienced under Ubico. Most importantly, however, they assert that the government financially compensated these men for their work. Kaqchikel appreciate that Arévalo also developed an infrastructure to support the distribution of potable water and electricity. Among Kaqchikel, he is famous for the construction of the national stadium in Guatemala City. One man asserted that during Arévalo's term, Guatemala City established traffic signals. Some people in Comalapa even attribute to Arévalo the completion of the road that connects them to Zaragoza and the Pan-American Highway. Moreover, Kaqchikel revere Arévalo because he favored poor people. They note that his policies helped farmers, teachers, and other laborers.[44] A thirty-one-year-old accountant states that "Arévalo set up the branches of health and education. He gave more to people."[45]

Arévalo's commitment to justice showed through his education and health care programs, two areas the government had largely neglected in the past, especially in the countryside. Although Arévalo utilized the school system to achieve his goal of assimilation, his contributions to Kaqchikel communities gave Kaqchikel the impression that he cared about their welfare. As seen in chapter 3, Arévalo's government disseminated information about health campaigns, and this contact helped to assuage Kaqchikel fears of Western medicine and doctors. Arévalo gained their trust, and Kaqchikel came to appreciate his plan to distribute vaccinations and eradicate vector insects.[46] Kaqchikel had previously resisted Ladino and government health campaigns, but under Arévalo they welcomed his intervention in their community.

Kaqchikel recognize Arévalo as a defender of education. He had a Ph.D. and had dedicated his life to education. Arévalo gave Maya a chance to constructively participate in the education system. While many of the education programs fell short of their goals, the government at least recognized the importance and relevance of Mayan languages. Most importantly, though, to a certain degree, the government listened to the needs and concerns of Maya and responded. As seen in chapter 5, Kaqchikel oral histories reveal an appreciation for Arévalo's efforts to provide education to the most remote areas of Guatemala so that all citizens would have equal opportunity.[47] A Kaqchikel daykeeper states: "Arévalo knew that the indigenous race did not have formal education. He gave schools to all the towns and aldeas. He allowed our children to study. He did us a great favor and helped our people."[48]

Kaqchikel do not dispute the positive impact Arévalo had on social services, although some people credit this success to funds Ubico had accumulated. Oxi' Tz'ikin cynically opines: "Arévalo was not that good. He was good because he had the money that Ubico gave to Guatemala. He came from Argentina and created the IGSS because he had the money. Ubico ended our four-million-dollar debt with the United States, but Arévalo used all that money and now we are in debt again."[49] Others recognize that Arévalo had funding from Ubico but respect him because he allotted it for the people, not himself. One of Oxi' Tz'ikin's mayoral successors notes: "Ubico had a lot of money, but he did not spend it on us. He never returned the money to us, he just kept it in the treasury. When Arévalo came, he raised the salaries of the military, teachers, and other employees. He did some good work, while other presidents just filled their own pockets."[50] Most Kaqchikel respect Arévalo because he redistributed the national wealth. Because he fixed the quetzal at ninety cents during his administration, some say Arévalo was a sound financial manager. For most Kaqchikel, that much of the funding for Arévalo's projects originated from Ubico does not diminish the importance and impact of his work.[51]

While Arévalo's policy of sharing financial benefits contrasted with Ubico's policy, Arévalo did apply Ubico's strategy of personal contact with and defense of Maya. He did not dedicate as much time to rural visits as Ubico had, but on occasion he attempted to meet people in their communities. Kaqchikel assert that Arévalo defended Maya against racist acts and words during his visits. They say he wanted to create an egalitarian society. According to some Kaqchikel, Arévalo even allowed people to meet with him in

Guatemala City, where he, more importantly, actually listened to them.[52] He was able to give Kaqchikel a sense that he cared about their well-being and respected them as Maya.

Many people lament that the good life enjoyed under the Arévalo government slowly slipped away. They appreciated the peaceful environment that Arévalo had facilitated and point out that he completed his term, while his successor, Arbenz, did not.[53] When Arbenz assumed the presidency, social unrest and political instability were augmented.

Democratic reforms sought to stimulate allegiance and nationalism. They resulted in less isolation but also increased autonomy of Mayan villages. Community members adapted to these changes because they had proven an effective way to deal with the national government. Another reason Maya were more open to these changes was that they perceived the government demands to be less rapacious than in the past. Political parties, labor unions, and other organizations provided Maya with a device to confront their employers and civil leaders directly. Maya realized that it was possible to seek out other authorities and sources of power rather than just the unitary *patrónal* system. A new range of choices was opened up beyond those of the farm domain.[54] Smith asserts that Maya were the big winners in the 1944–54 political struggles because they enjoyed continued political autonomy, expanded commercial freedom, and the growth of the domestic economy based on plantation exports.[55] Although Maya were still at the bottom of the social ladder, their status and prestige increased, and many realized that social change was possible.

Kaqchikel oral histories unanimously praise Arévalo's ideas and programs but criticize their rapid and forced implementation. Arévalo made the commitment to reach Maya through mediums they could accept: education, health care, local representation, and free labor. Most recognize that he used government funds on programs for the people. Arévalo continued to improve Guatemala's infrastructure, but without abusing Mayan labor. They also enjoyed some tangible benefits under Arévalo. Reforms implemented by Arévalo's government empowered Maya, who took advantage of this newfound efficacy by asserting their rights. Kaqchikel and other Maya had a sense of owning their communities again. Most Kaqchikel believed in Arévalo's democratic principles, yet his move toward liberty threatened their need for a safe environment. Kaqchikel point out that, as a country, Guatemala was not prepared for this freedom; the government had imposed it too quickly and without adequately disseminating information. They lament that people responded by abusing the privilege of liberty. A sense of justice remains intact throughout Kaqchikel historical analysis of Arévalo. They would have preferred a more controlled and gradual application of democracy.

Local Leaders

In addition to Kaqchikel assessments of national leaders, their estimation of local leaders provides invaluable insight to their worldviews. Kaqchikel highlight their local heroes in oral traditions. They laud those who have done well by the community and in some cases the nation. Generally, heroes are Kaqchikel who have achieved their success in spite of, not as a result of, Ladino institutions and society. In many cases, these role models never attended school but gained recognition by using wisdom passed on to them. The threat of Ladino society, which is inherent in oral traditions, seeks, at best, to assimilate Mayan leaders overtly or covertly and, at worst, to destroy Maya who show a desire to assert their talents. These Kaqchikel icons embody the hope of a marginalized people and provide an example of how to live within and beyond their conditions.

Kaqchikel are not blind to temptations of success, and their icons are subject to both criticism and failure. Their heroes' actions teach both goals to strive for and downfalls to avoid. Oral histories present the reality of these individuals. This balanced presentation makes the inspiration gained and lessons learned from these personages applicable to people's lives today.

Nemesio Matzer

Local politicians have made an indelible mark on residents of Comalapa. During the first half of the twentieth century a mayor named Nemesio Matzer Tuwac etched his place in Kaqchikel oral histories. Matzer was known as "our people." He is remembered as a Maya who spoke Kaqchikel and as a mayor who represented the Kaqchikel people. That effort alone was admirable during a time when Ladinos dominated the political sphere. Oral histories explain that many people could not speak Spanish and that this voiceless majority of Maya was left out of the Ladino-controlled system. Informants attest that before Ubico assumed the presidency in 1931, the local administrative structure allowed for a subordinate Mayan mayor to work alongside the Ladino mayor. They point out that at a time when even this small concession to Maya was negligible, Matzer gained some political, economic, and social control for his people.

Oral histories highlight Matzer because he wanted to improve living conditions in the main town and its villages. Many people credit him with the construction of a municipal building, school, and roads during his numerous terms as mayor.[56] A sixty-seven-year-old farmer from a Comalapan village explains why Matzer was so loved:

> Matzer was a *natural*. He was well liked by the people because he always had a party for the new year. He was a good patrón. The people asked him to be mayor. But when he was mayor, he let people off easy. All they had to do was pay a fine and they were out of jail, unless you killed someone, in which case you would be executed. He became mayor a second time and he worked with and listened to the local representatives. A long time ago there were only Ladino mayors, but they did not listen to people and if you did any little thing you went to jail. They gave you a big fine so you had to sell your land and cows. They made you poorer. They did not give you any advice. That is how the Ladinos are here.[57]

Kaqchikel insist that Matzer differed from Ladino mayors in many ways. Oral traditions hail him as an honest man. Matzer's reputation extended beyond Comalapa. An elder from Poaquil says, "Nemesio Matzer gave us good advice. He was a good *natural*."[58] Oral histories attest that in the first half of the twentieth century the mayor also served as the justice of the peace. Informants recall that in many cases Ladino mayors charged people for these services. Kaqchikel recount how Matzer insisted that no one pay for his services and refused any opportunity to use the office for his own financial advantage; he simply meted out justice. One man, whose eighty-six-year-old mother continues to run the family store, explains Matzer's reasoning: "If there was no money involved then he could not favor you [because of your wealth]. He wanted real justice."[59] Kaqchikel appreciated Matzer's approach to government because power and wealth did not provide an advantage. When the system discriminates against Maya or when the rules are malleable, Kaqchikel become frustrated. Matzer clearly set out fair and equitable rules, and Kaqchikel gladly abided by them.

Oral histories recount that he was a wealthy man who owned great tracts of land, as well as cows, goats, and farm equipment, both in Comalapa and its surrounding communities. He owned a finca called Panabajal outside of Comalapa. Panabajal is now an aldea of Comalapa, and most of its residents remember Matzer fondly. They recall that when he retired, he gave land to his family and to all the workers who had been loyal to him. They point out that this act opened the door for his former employees to be landholders.

Oral traditions note that he repeated this kind gesture in other areas where he owned and ran agricultural estates. However, if his workers were lazy or not trustworthy, they received nothing. Kaqchikel appreciate this keen sense of justice. Informants recall that his farms were successful agricultural endeavors and that Matzer worked his resident farmers hard but fairly and paid them well. They attest that in his traditional clothes he hoed, planted, and harvested alongside his workers. Furthermore, they emphasize, he was a good worker. According to oral histories, people came from all over the Kaqchikel area to work for Matzer because they heard he was a good patrón. Kaqchikel laud him as a rich man who wanted to help poor people.[60] Matzer did not make any distinction between patrón and worker, and he prided himself on working in the fields with his employees.

Matzer's desire to treat his workers fairly extended beyond the boundaries of his land. Informants recall that he wanted to build a road from Comalapa to Guatemala City—a three-day trip on horseback—so trucks, instead of people, could carry agricultural produce and other goods. Matzer did not want his people treated like animals. Oral traditions share that shortly after the dirt path to Panabajal crosses a river, Matzer painted the picture of a donkey with this heading: "Will it always be like this?"[61] Matzer's main goal was to improve the quality of life for Comalapenses.

Oral histories note that at a time when the government allocated few resources to Mayan communities, Matzer took it upon himself to build a road from Comalapa to the Pan-American Highway as well as a road to Panabajal and other surrounding villages. Kaqchikel boast that although Matzer had no formal instruction as an engineer, he was extremely intelligent and traced a road that successfully traversed the mountainous area between Comalapa and the main road. In fact, they assert that years later when government engineers came to build a new road, they were so impressed by Matzer's work that they simply expanded his design.[62]

The road construction began in the 1930s. An elder who accompanied Matzer on his quest to build the road explains:

Matzer was mayor when the old road was no good. It was very broken and no cars could pass. Matzer asked for an audience with Ubico. Ubico attended to us at 7 A.M. We told him we were sorry to bother him, but he replied that it was no bother; rather, we were helping him so he would be glad to help us. Ubico said, "You brought me work and I want to make all the country work." He gave us a note to give to the Chimaltenango governor. The work was not paid, rather it was *sipaj* [given, read unpaid]. Fifty men from each village would work for a week. Matzer had a good nature. He was not lazy. He did all the engineering and it was good work. This happened around 1935.[63]

People from Comalapa built the road, and Matzer supplied much of the labor since he had allowed men from his landed estates and other villages to work on the road. Kaqchikel recall the work as treacherous and backbreaking because no machines existed at that time. They note that the road crew had only shovels and pickaxes. Informants add that Matzer provided this service of building roads to other villages around Comalapa and never charged residents for his labor or expertise. Most Comalapenses agreed that the road was important to their livelihood and were happy that Matzer had taken the initiative because it improved their standard of living.[64]

Not all oral accounts agree that Matzer was Kaqchikel. Some state that he came from Xela or Chichicastenango to make his money in Comalapa, but the majority of Kaqchikel agree that he was Maya and had learned to speak Kaqchikel. They note that his first wife was Kaqchikel but that when she died he married a Ladino woman.[65] Most importantly, Matzer was a leader who wanted to benefit the community. He was Maya but could assert himself within the Ladino power structure, and he returned his successes to his people. His ability to move between these two worlds but never abandon his roots makes him an admirable figure in Kaqchikel oral histories. Matzer's specific ethnicity is not crucial for Kaqchikel. He spoke Kaqchikel, comprehended their lifestyle and culture, shared experiences with them, and contributed to the community. He was sincere in his actions and relations, so the fact that he may have been from another Mayan group was inconsequential.

The Tz'ikin Family

Kaqchikel have always realized the need for a facilitator to communicate with Ladino power structures. The Tz'ikin family[66] has played this role in Comalapa since the nineteenth century. According to oral traditions, Jun Tz'ikin was a defender of Mayan rights who attempted to use his Spanish-language ability to improve the plight of his counterparts. His son, Ka'i' Tz'ikin, also played an important role in the establishment of more equal conditions for Kaqchikel. Ka'i' Tz'ikin facilitated the conditions necessary to surpass local Ladinos in some areas. Ka'i' Tz'ikin's son, Oxi' Tz'ikin, served twice as mayor and imposed his judicial and administrative system in Ubico-like fashion. He wanted Maya and Ladinos to be treated equally. The subsequent generation of Tz'ikins rose to influential positions in the Catholic Church, the government, the military, and international organizations, albeit not necessarily with the good of their people in mind. The Tz'ikin family is known well in Comalapa because they are a powerful family with access to Ladino institutions and in many cases have attempted to use their influence to benefit the local Kaqchikel population.

Oral traditions begin with Jun Tz'ikin. Accounts recall him as a community leader in the late 1800s and as the first Kaqchikel mayor of Comalapa.[67] They note that his ability to speak Spanish allowed him to help contemporaries who needed to complete administrative or personal tasks in Spanish but did not know the language. Informants point out that Jun Tz'ikin assisted his people in the completion of marriage licenses and baptismal records and even represented them before Ladino judges. Kaqchikel recognize that his penchant for and ability to aid Kaqchikel threatened powerful local Ladinos, who accused Jun Tz'ikin of opposing President Barrios. As explained in chapter 1, Comalapa oral traditions maintain that Barrios killed Jun Tz'ikin because he did not fear Barrios and wanted to help his people.[68] Jun Tz'ikin's effort to mitigate Ladino exploitation and discrimination of Kaqchikel resulted in his death.

Jun Tz'ikin's demise, however, did not mean the end of his influence. His beliefs and actions motivated his son, Ka'i' Tz'ikin (1883–1961), to strive for a better reality for Kaqchikel. Oral histories show that Ka'i' Tz'ikin inherited his father's courage. He did not back down from even the most powerful leaders in the country. Jun Tz'ikin was not intimidated by Barrios, and Ka'i' Tz'ikin was not daunted by either Estrada Cabrera or Ubico. Ka'i' Tz'ikin stood up to Estrada Cabrera on the issue of military conscription (see chapter 5) and eventually helped to topple his oppressive twenty-two-year government.

Ka'i' Tz'ikin's influence in politics extended beyond his mayoral duties. A letter and a concise document authored by Kaqchikel note that Ka'i' Tz'ikin established the Kaqchikel Unionist Party in Comalapa to oppose Estrada Cabrera's dictatorship. These documents point out that he celebrated President Carlos Herrera's democratic victory in 1920 but also took advantage of the situation to obtain several scholarships for young Kaqchikel men to attend the Normal School and Institute of Indigenous People in Guatemala City. These authors assert that as mayor he also instituted "radical reforms" in the town.[69] His goal as a politician was to make changes to improve the community, and his efforts often displeased Ladinos of Comalapa.

According to oral traditions, Ladinos attempted on one occasion to eradicate Ka'i' Tz'ikin in the same manner that they instigated his father's demise. The dictator in this case was Barrios's godson, Ubico. Jun Kan, a local artist, explains:

Ka'i' Tz'ikin was a local leader in town. The Ladinos in town wanted to frame him and some other Indians. They accused Ka'i' Tz'ikin of leading about seventeen to eighteen men in a plot to kill Ubico. I was in school at the time. The Ladinos tied their hands behind their backs to a tree where they kept the cows. For three days they stayed there, then on the third day the men went to Guatemala to talk to Ubico, but the Ladinos invented the conspiracy story. Ka'i' Tz'ikin was the first to talk to Ubico. Ubico asked Ka'i' Tz'ikin why he wanted to kill him. Ka'i' Tz'ikin was not scared. He said, "Mr. President do you really believe that I would want to kill you? I have no grade [education], I only work in the fields with my hoe and machete. Why would I want to take you out? I am not a president, governor, or mayor. I have no education." Ubico just fell silent. He did not speak. The rest of the men were farmworkers also. On the second day all the men were set free.[70]

Jun Kan portrays Ka'i' Tz'ikin as an intelligent and courageous man. He did not beg for forgiveness. He simply presented a rational argument to gain his and his compatriots' freedom. Ka'i' Tz'ikin challenged the Ladino power structure and was able to ward off the attempts to curtail his activities. Kaqchikel recount their oral histories in a cyclical, not repetitive fashion. In this case, Ka'i' Tz'ikin evades the fate his father suffered. These oral histories express the strength of Kaqchikel resilience as Kaqchikel strive for better relations and realities.

Despite the obstacles Ladinos placed in his path, Ka'i' Tz'ikin did not want to separate the two ethnicities; rather, he preached a peaceful coexistence. One Kaqchikel author asserts that he encouraged people to learn Spanish and to put aside their traditional clothing to break down barriers with Ladinos. Ka'i' Tz'ikin also cultivated friendships with many well-educated and powerful Ladinos and foreigners in his effort to establish a Mayan school in Comalapa. One of his closest friends was Clemente Marroquín Rojas, the editor and owner of *La Hora,* a Guatemalan newspaper.[71]

Ka'i' Tz'ikin sought equal rights and opportunities for Maya. Education was fundamental to opportunity, and it needed to be improved. Kaqchikel point out that he wrote letters to the government to request scholarships for Kaqchikel boys to study in the capital and earn their teaching degrees. They proudly proclaim that his efforts were successful and that by the 1920s Comalapa could boast several Kaqchikel teachers from their own community. Informants note that these first teachers worked for free since they were so elated about teaching, and especially about teaching in their own town. As seen in chapter 5, Ka'i' Tz'ikin also established a school specifically for

Mayan children, since the Ladino school discriminated against Kaqchikel children and did not provide an appropriate education.[72]

Education was one of Ka'i' Tz'ikin's passions. In a 1975 letter, Juan Val Curruchich praised Ka'i' Tz'ikin for raising the intellectual level of Comalapa, which "extracted the ingratitude of the Ladinos with his ideas and struggles." While local Ladinos despised Ka'i' Tz'ikin, from the Kaqchikel point of view his efforts to bring equal education to all improved interethnic relations in the town. Kaqchikel point out that his ideas and his struggle to attain scholarships for Mayan teachers instigated the surge of Kaqchikel teachers in Comalapa. One Kaqchikel man, Juan Val Curruchich, wrote that he could not decide whether Ka'i' Tz'ikin should be considered the favorite son or father of Comalapa, but he concluded: "We can almost say that Ka'i' Tz'ikin was for Comalapa what Benito Juárez was for Mexico. . . . He was a man who fought for his town."[73] This analogy to Benito Juárez is surpassed only by another Kaqchikel author's comparison of Ka'i' Tz'ikin to Ghandi.[74]

Oral histories show that Ka'i' Tz'ikin's idea of law and justice allowed for the sacrifice of freedom if it attained a greater good. One of his biggest concerns, a preoccupation inherited by his son, was the evil of alcohol. This anecdote expresses Ka'i' Tz'ikin's view of alcohol:

> In Comalapa there existed a *chicharía* where, Sunday to Sunday, numerous farmers got drunk with the marimba . . . regretfully spending their last cents that they had saved with the force of sweat. With this disastrous situation among the indigenous masses, Ka'i' Tz'ikin terminated this ruling custom that slowly consumes the health, fortune, freedom and justice, with his persistent preaching in meetings. For this tenacious struggle, he was the object of scurrilous criticism, transgressions, and persecutions by the authorities and private men.[75]

Ka'i' Tz'ikin imposed his views on others because he believed liquor destroyed the community. The curtailment of consumption reduced sales, and consequently owners and public officials expressed their ire with Ka'i' Tz'ikin's actions. The attack on Ka'i' Tz'ikin may have been a result of this angst on the part of local Ladinos. While he befriended some powerful Ladinos, others would have preferred that he had met the fate of his father. Regardless, Ka'i' Tz'ikin believed in his ideals and would sacrifice anything to attain them.

Ka'i' Tz'ikin believed the system needed to be readjusted in favor of Maya. Oral histories depict that like his father, he aided people who did not know Spanish. As a seventy-three-year-old farmer states, "We did not speak or understand Spanish, just Kaqchikel. We were blind and deaf. Ka'i' Tz'ikin helped us to translate [documents] for our land or whatever other affairs we had with a public official."[76] Ka'i' Tz'ikin helped his community survive and, at times, benefit from daily tasks and interactions with Ladinos. He wanted the benefits and laws of his town to be equally accessible and applicable to all its residents.

Ka'i' Tz'ikin raised his children with these ideals in mind. Two of his sons were among the first Kaqchikel teachers in town. Another, Oxi' Tz'ikin, served as mayor on two different occasions and strove to run the town efficiently and fairly, as his father had done. Oral histories attest that as mayor, Oxi' Tz'ikin was always available to people who needed the services of the municipality. Kaqchikel point out that he wanted to ensure that the entire population enjoyed basic amenities. As one forty-six-year-old woman relates, "Oxi' Tz'ikin was the mayor who performed good work because he was indigenous and he always attended to the people who came to his office. He set an example with his own work, and he obtained more water for all the municipality because in the summer it was quite scarce."[77] Kaqchikel assert that he also provided sound advice and ideas to the community.[78] Furthermore, Oxi' Tz'ikin was an example for people of the value and benefits of diligence.

Many people compared Oxi' Tz'ikin's style of government to that of Ubico's. Ixno'j, a thirty-year-old teacher in a primary school, says, "I heard that Mayor Oxi' Tz'ikin was just like Ubico. He wanted everyone to work. He took all drunks to jail. People said he was like Ubico because you had to do what he said."[79] Oral histories explain that Oxi' Tz'ikin ran the town with a heavy hand. Kaqchikel recall that he woke up at two or three in the morning to bike around town and look for drunks whom he made sweep the streets or go to jail.[80] Like Ubico, he believed that people's time was better dedicated to work than drink. In general, people remember Oxi' Tz'ikin as a tough but fair and efficient mayor.

At eighty-three, Oxi' Tz'ikin is proud of his reputation as a tough leader. He is satisfied with the many goals he accomplished during his tenure. He facilitated the construction of a library, a central market, roads, schools, basketball courts, and the park at the town's center as well as the arrival of potable water. Oxi' Tz'ikin emphasizes that during his administration, rich and poor, Ladinos and Maya were treated equally. He admits to his authoritarian tactics and expresses doubts about the agenda of human rights groups, especially in areas where a dictatorial rule was needed to prevent thieves and murderers. Oxi' Tz'ikin is cognizant of his family tradition and proud to live it out and pass it on to his children and grandchildren. He boasts, "Barrios killed my grandfather, but the Tz'ikin ideas live on with me and my family."[81] These ideas are grounded in blind justice and the restriction of freedom to ensure security and productivity.

Some Kaqchikel do not hold Oxi' Tz'ikin's children in such high esteem. A twenty-six-year-old man who works for a Guatemalan development organization states:

> The Tz'ikin family was powerful, especially in the '60s and '70s, because they had a lot of money. But lamentably, their daughter Ixtz'ikin has become a Ladino and is a congressional member. She wore the traditional dress only to win the support of the people, and that is not good. It is good that she is a representative for us, but unfortunately she does not always represent us and she is not sincere. Their son was the vice-minister of defense. He rose up in the military ranks, but as a general in the K'ichee' military zone he killed many indigenous people. The Tz'ikin family benefited the Kaqchikel in the sense of education through scholarships, but now the line is with the military, anti-Communist, capitalist, and killing, and that hurts "our people."[82]

Two years later, in 2000, when the FRG selected Ixtz'ikin as an ambassador, the same young man discerns: "I don't think Ixtz'ikin can be a good representative of Maya in foreign countries. She did not wear Mayan clothing until she became a candidate for Congress, she does not speak the language very well, and because of her family who include Catholic priests and military men. I believe she is just a political prop for the FRG Party to show the world a different face and eliminate the image of people such as Rigoberta Menchú and Rosalina Tuyuc. I don't think she is smart to do that."[83] This critique of some members of the latest Tz'ikin generation exemplifies that people can lose their status as members of the community if they fail to uphold Mayan values or give back to the community.[84] According to other informants, Ixtz'ikin no longer shares the Kaqchikel value of helping people. Furthermore, they point out that she wears her Mayan dress only in certain situations, not as a constant identifying Mayan marker. For the majority of Kaqchikel, it is not enough for Kaqchikel representatives to be elected to Congress; they must also remain loyal to their people. Ixtz'ikin's brother also assumed Ladino values and structures and therefore violated the Mayan respect for life. As a result, his actions disenfranchised him from Kaqchikel. The Tz'ikins gave education to the community, protected people from dictatorial demands, and aided Kaqchikel through the use of Spanish; however, some members of the last generation undermined their Mayan identity and used Spanish to become part of the power structure. Kaqchikel, in turn, no longer count them as Maya. Maintenance of their values, such as respect for life, land, Kaqchikel culture, and worldviews, is paramount to most Kaqchikel. According to Kaqchikel, people who violate the precepts of their Mayan identity are no longer Maya.[85]

Rosalina Tuyuc

Rosalina Tuyuc is another member of the Kaqchikel community and native of Comalapa whose name appears often in oral accounts because she has maintained her Kaqchikel roots. Tuyuc was elected to Congress in November 1995 as a candidate from the Frente Democrático Nueva Guatemala (New Guatemalan Democratic Front) Party. She was also the former head of CONAVIGUA (Coordinadora Nacional de Viudas de Guatemala [National Coordinating Committee of Guatemalan Widows]), a political organization that represents women who were widowed during the violence. Kaqchikel are proud that a Mayan woman can aspire to a position of national prominence and maintain her Mayan identity. The stories of how she arrived at this position and the reviews of her impact on the community are mixed, however. Some people discredit her for her participation in the civil war. Others criticize her because she no longer maintains strong ties to the community. Still, for the most part, people praise her efforts and lament the fact that, as a Maya surrounded by Ladinos in Congress, she cannot implement more of her progressive ideas. As a local, born and raised in a Kaqchikel community, she inspires people to achieve their goals in a country dominated by Ladinos.

Kaqchikel commend Tuyuc because she comprehends their reality and can convey it in a national forum. A Kaqchikel member of a peace commission notes: "Tuyuc is conscientious. She knows the reality. She suffered in the civil war and understands social causes."[86] Tuyuc has lived in the same fashion as her Kaqchikel constituents in the department of Chimaltenango. As one teacher and university student points out, "Tuyuc helps our people. She is a congresswoman now but was also a guerrilla. She is a good person."[87] Tuyuc has struggled for the rights of Maya and poor in a number of different forums. Many informants opine that Tuyuc did not "sell out" like other politicians. People from Poaquil remember her visit to talk to them about women's rights and the land tax. They note that she even visited Poaquil's aldeas. Kaqchikel also point out that in Congress she continues to wear her Mayan dress, which proudly marks her as a Mayan woman.[88] As a result of her commitment and dedication to her people, Kaqchikel feel comfortable with her representation. A twenty-one-year-old woman who is studying to be a nurse extolls: "She speaks for us."[89] Tuyuc represents the Kaqchikel population in a forum previously denied to them.

Kaqchikel recognize Tuyuc as a national leader on a par with Rigoberta Menchú. A former mayor of Comalapa compares the two: "Tuyuc is like Rigoberta [Menchú] in that they both suffered from many problems and looked for a way to lead their people. Tuyuc's husband died. She entered Congress and formed CONAVIGUA, the widows' organization."[90] Many Kaqchikel associate Menchú and Tuyuc with the resistance movements against the military governments during the civil war. Because they believe they were both involved with the guerrillas who killed people, some Kaqchikel do not agree that Menchú should hold the Nobel Peace Prize or that Tuyuc should be in Congress. These critics do not believe people involved in war should hold positions of power in a society that is attempting to establish peaceful conditions.[91] Others counter that even if these two women killed some people, they helped others. They note that their overarching goal was to advance the cause of Maya.[92] Kaqchikel may not agree on the means employed by these two leaders, but few dispute the passion they feel for their causes.

Tuyuc protected Kaqchikel liberty through her efforts to end the military conscription that had been reinstituted despite Ka'i' Tz'ikin's efforts to eradicate it. Oral accounts assert that Tuyuc pressured the government to end this invasion into their communities and that now Kaqchikel are no longer subject to such exploitation.[93]

Kaqchikel residents of Comalapa credit Tuyuc for the government's work of paving the road that connects them to Zaragoza and the Pan-American Highway. The majority of residents welcome the improved transportation infrastructure, as it helps them trade in other communities and countries and extend their education and employment opportunities. The government had promised to build a road years earlier and never did it. The state claimed it had appropriated the money to the mayor of Comalapa but that he never invested it in the road, and the next administration refused to pay for the road twice. Kaqchikel recount Tuyuc's insistence that the government complete its promise. Some people point out that if Tuyuc were not in Congress, Comalapa would still be without a paved road.[94]

While the majority of people perceive the road as a benefit, some people in Comalapa criticize Tuyuc for the sacrifices she made to ensure its construction. One young man, whose studies have taken him to the United States, notes: "The road is the fruit of many forces, but Tuyuc certainly helped. Twice the government inaugurated the work here and they had the money but they never did it. So as the leader of CONAVIGUA, Tuyuc had to make a deal. She promised that her group would no longer protest the PAN [Partido de Avanzado Nacional (National Advancement Party)] government in exchange for the construction of the road. She did it. There is always good and bad in politics."[95]

Kaqchikel understand that politics is about trade-offs. For some, that Tuyuc is involved in politics discredits her. An eighty-seven-year-old farmer opines that "all she does is politics, not real work. Politics is dirty, but sometimes it can be good."[96] Many people have an inherent distrust of politics but realize that some benefits can result. Others claim that once "our people" enter positions of power they forget their origins. As a midwife from Comalapa explains, "Tuyuc does not do any work here. She does not provide us with favors, she just takes advantage of everything. When our people go to Congress, they do not work to help us, they just help themselves."[97] For many people, politics corrupts, and once people attain positions of power, they succumb to its temptations. According to some Comalapenses, once Tuyuc gained a position of power she ceased to maintain contact or help her people. They claim she uses her party for personal endeavors and argue she is aligned with the party, not with the people. Others complain that Tuyuc talks but does not act according to her word.[98] One woman opined that Tuyuc may help Comalapa and the main towns but that she has neglected the rural villages.[99]

The majority of people, however, support Tuyuc's efforts and approve of her contribution to Kaqchikel communities and Maya. However, another challenge Kaqchikel emphasize is that politics and Congress are dominated by Ladinos. They note that Maya have little voice in these positions of power. Kaqchikel lament that Ladinos often exclude Mayan representatives from the political process and point out that while Mayan members of Congress may have good ideas and intentions to support their people, they cannot implement the strategies because Ladinos block their efforts. Many people likened Tuyuc to Menchú in that many Ladinos despise Maya in positions of influence.[100] However, Kaqchikel assert even though Mayan representatives do not wield much power in Congress, it is important for them to speak and help Ladinos understand the issues relevant to the Mayan population. A former mayoral candidate and university student explains: "Tuyuc is good because when we participate in politics, it is not so important that we win, just what we say. If people understand you, then you have won. It is not about making laws or completing big works. It is a good thing that our people get to Congress and represent the Maya. They are only four now so they cannot make laws, but they can speak and that is important."[101] Kaqchikel view these small victories of representation as imperative to the establishment of more peaceful relations in Guatemala.

Local leaders revered by oral traditions share several characteristics. They remained loyal to their Kaqchikel identity and people through language, clothing, and benevolent acts. Many of them succeeded in a Ladino-dominated world without the assistance of a Ladino education. Even those who received a Ladino education and combined it with their Kaqchikel-based knowledge relied more upon their traditional knowledge and worldview for their success. In some cases, the combination of these two distinct learning systems led to efficacious interaction in both worlds. These role models worked through the Ladino system to implement respect, equal justice, and favorable administrative policies for Kaqchikel. They did not retreat in the face of obstacles and threats; rather, they confronted and overcame such challenges.

All of these local heroes produced impressive works. Ka'i' Tz'ikin constructed a Mayan school in Comalapa, Matzer surveyed and constructed the first road to Comalapa, and Tuyuc contributed to its paving. More importantly, all these leaders fought for the rights of their people. Over three generations, the Tz'ikin family aided Kaqchikel of Comalapa (especially those who were monolingual) through administrative, educational, and security measures. Matzer always strove for the improvement of the quality of life of workers and citizens in his environs. He knew that at times he must tap into Ladino power structures to achieve his goals, such as when he appealed to Ubico for support in the construction of Comalapa's road. Tuyuc continues this struggle today through CONAVIGUA and national politics. These champions of Kaqchikel and Mayan causes represent their constituents efficaciously in a society controlled by Ladinos.

The barriers to equality erected by Ladino society did not intimidate or discourage these personages. Barrios killed Jun Tz'ikin because he did not back down. His son, Ka'i' Tz'ikin, had more success in his confrontations with Estrada Cabrera and Ubico. In their interaction with Ladino power structures, these idols spoke Kaqchikel, and some wore their traditional dress. Their identity as Kaqchikel and their connection to the people were essential to their success and eventual enshrinement as role models.

These leaders also implemented a form of justice consistent with local ideas and wishes. Leaders such as Ka'i' Tz'ikin, Oxi' Tz'ikin, and Matzer were harsh but fair. Much like Ubico, they held people accountable for their actions and provided for the stability of the community and personal security of its members. They executed murderers and forced drunkards to work. They meted out justice equally, favored no one, and clearly defined and enforced the rules of the game. In some cases, such as when Oxi' Tz'ikin forced inebriated men to work for the community, they curtailed personal freedom to gain the security and progress of the community. Furthermore, neither Matzer nor the Tz'ikins gained their wealth at the expense of the people, and once they earned a powerful position in the community, they used it for the good of the town. Kaqchikel appreciate the fair and straightforward approach to justice taken by Matzer and the Tz'ikin family, especially since it ensured their safety and livelihood.

Kaqchikel oral traditions praise local heroes who interacted with Ladino society and at times took advantage of Ladino resources to improve the plight of Kaqchikel. These representatives refused to sacrifice Kaqchikel wisdom, community, or culture in their endeavors. Instead, they used these resources to succeed on a national level. Matzer, the Tz'ikins, and Tuyuc worked in political circles and asserted the value of Kaqchikel in the face of Ladino domination. Once these Maya achieved positions of political, cultural, and economic influence, they efficaciously represented their people and never forgot their origins. Kaqchikel insist that participation in national society and maintenance of one's distinct culture and worldviews are not mutually exclusive.

Conclusion

Kaqchikel assess leaders according to their ability to clearly communicate their goals and methods. When Kaqchikel agree with the overarching goals, such as creating a just and (at times) representative society, and when they understand the rules of the game, they abide by the laws and support the government. Kaqchikel commend Arévalo for his commitment to an equitable society and to the implementation of policies to bring about this reality. He clearly explained his goals and means. Matzer and Oxi' Tz'ikin had distinct leadership styles in their efforts to maintain a tranquil society, but Kaqchikel always knew what to expect from them. Conversely, while Kaqchikel welcomed the sense of security Barrios provided citizens of Guatemala, he did not treat everyone equally under his law. His capricious style combined with discrimination against Maya meant that regardless of how Kaqchikel acted, the system did not guarantee their freedom from whimsical exploitation and abuse. A top priority for Kaqchikel is a safe and just society. They also need to comprehend the political system. Thus, they prefer leaders who clearly outline the conditions for an ordered and peaceful society.

Some leaders, such as Barrios and Ubico, gave the impression that they cared about justice and equality when they visited communities. Kaqchikel appreciate direct contact with leaders. However, especially in the case of Barrios, many Kaqchikel understood that he did not implement justice on a national level. Most Kaqchikel lauded Arévalo for his ideals of equal rights but criticize him for pushing his program too fast and not being able to control consequences that led to increased crime and sloth. The combination of personal contact and the ability to maintain equal representation and rights at the local level elevated local leaders such as Matzer and the Tz'ikins to important positions in oral histories. Kaqchikel especially laud Matzer for working alongside his laborers. In addition, they appreciate that Tuyuc strives for equal rights in a national forum, but they realize that many Ladino legislators present obstacles to equal representation in Congress. Kaqchikel praise leaders who sincerely work for the good of the community and nation.

Kaqchikel seek freedom in their lives, but liberty does not eclipse security in their hierarchy of values. Consequently, they prefer firm leaders such as the Tz'ikins or Ubico to leaders who unleash forces they cannot control. While the Tz'ikins or Ubico may have infringed on personal freedoms, their abilities to maintain personal safety and local and/or national stability solidified their popularity. Most Kaqchikel are willing to sacrifice liberty for peace.

Paramount in Kaqchikel perceptions of leaders is a sincere desire for the development and stability of the nation. Furthermore, most Kaqchikel see a direct relationship between local and national realities. At the same time, national development does not warrant the exploitation of Mayan labor. Kaqchikel are aware that leaders such as Ubico and Barrios utilized their labor and land to develop the infrastructure and economy. Most Kaqchikel want to see road and communication systems developed, but they do not want to be unduly exploited. Arévalo continued roadworks programs, as well as other important infrastructure components, but by using machines and paid labor. Kaqchikel realize that this transition slowed development and drained the national economy, but it was more humane than previous systems. Kaqchikel are not adverse to hard work and are willing to sacrifice for the good of the community and nation, but they also recognize that their burden can be eased. Kaqchikel personalize the image of Matzer surveying the road to Comalapa in order to keep his contribution alive in their oral histories. Many contributed to Matzer's road project because it would alleviate carrying goods on their backs. Furthermore, most appreciated the connection to other local and national markets. They want to contribute to the national economy and they want access to goods, services, and ideas outside their community. Furthermore, Kaqchikel do not view an improvement in their quality of life as exclusive of the common good of the nation.

Kaqchikel understand that connections to national and international markets necessitate increased interactions with people outside their communities. They recognize the need to improve ethnic relations, and they respect leaders who strive for this goal. Ka'i' Tz'ikin's efforts to bridge ethnic divisions remain an important part of Kaqchikel histories. Kaqchikel also appreciate Arévalo's attempt to eradicate racism on a national level. Kaqchikel accept outsiders into their communities once they have developed a level of trust. For Kaqchikel, that Matzer was Maya but probably not Kaqchikel did not cause any tension. Even when he married a Ladino woman, Kaqchikel continued to laud him. They do not want the erasure of ethnic distinctions but rather that they be mutually appreciated. They praise Tuyuc for maintaining her Mayan dress and language alongside Ladinos in a national forum. As we will see in the final chapter, Kaqchikel seek to overcome ethnic animosity and work with others for the development of Guatemala.

9
Ethnic Relations

Qak'aslem kikin ri ch'aqa chïk winaqi'

Kaqchikel oral histories contain a plethora of information concerning ethnic relations. Most of these accounts pertain to interactions with Ladinos and commence with the Spanish invasion. Kaqchikel assert that antagonistic relations began because Spaniards abused them. This exploitation continued with their interaction with the state and Ladinos and remains the cornerstone of relations today. Kaqchikel appreciate exceptions to this rule and hope for improved relations, but their oral traditions teach prudence when dealing with Ladinos. Nonetheless, most Kaqchikel try not to harbor resentment because they realize amicable relations cannot be built on bitterness. They strive for equality and justice, rather than revenge.

Oral History and Identity

Kaqchikel elders teach younger generations about their history because it is relevant to their lives today. Elders emphasize patterns and themes in the oral histories they recount. These presentations of history provide a framework for understanding their world. Consequently, younger generations have a strong connection to the origins of their people and communities. They are also well aware of the tribulations their people have faced and continue to confront. They learn how to live in a Ladino-dominated society without succumbing to it. Finally, oral histories provide strategies and hope for the future. Just as written histories attempt to define nations and contribute to national identities, oral histories describe peoples and provide a sense of unity for them. For Kaqchikel, oral histories serve as a guide, not just of the past but also of the present and future.

Kaqchikel oral traditions present a vivid historical analysis of Guatemala and the reality of Kaqchikel people. Most Kaqchikel wish to participate in the national political, economic, social, and cultural spheres when they are able to do so in an egalitarian manner. Unfortunately, these opportunities have been negligible, and in most cases Kaqchikel have to be especially assertive to draw out fairer conditions. Kaqchikel also seek equal participation and representation in Guatemala's national history.[1] They want to present a history that represents all of Guatemala's populations. Kaqchikel historical perspectives emphasize security and justice; respect and preservation of their ideas, worldviews, language, and culture; and the holistic development of Guatemala. Most political, economic, and intellectual elites of Guatemala ignore many of these ideas in their policies and attempt to develop a national identity through an official history that places Mayan origins and realities in a halcyon past. Unfortunately, distinct goals, realities, and worldviews, as well as a lack of mutual comprehension, have bred ethnic conflict in Guatemala.

That ethnic conflict began immediately upon Spanish arrival has important implications for Kaqchikel perceptions of ethnic relations. They portray the contrasts between pre– and post–Spanish contact. They exaggerate an idyllic world prior to the Spanish invasion in which Kaqchikel shared resources and lived in harmony with their environment. Oral traditions also downplay conflict with K'ichee' and other Mayan groups. They present Tekun as a pan-Mayan hero and take pride in his courage against Spanish invaders. Historical animosity with K'ichee' present in the *Anales* is virtually nonexistent in oral histories. Oral accounts insist that Kaqchikel leaders such as Kaji' Imox and B'eleje' K'at had close relations with Tekun. Even those Kaqchikel who recognize rivalries with K'ichee' prior to Spanish arrival insist that relations today are amicable. In contrast, the Spanish not only declared war on Kaqchikel and took their women (which many Kaqchikel say produced an "impure mestizo race"), they also forced Kaqchikel to work for them. Most Kaqchikel recognize that Spaniards treated their ancestors as little more than a labor source. Kaqchikel oral traditions present interactions with Spaniards, and later Ladinos, as the dominant source of ethnic conflict, while downplaying tensions with other Mayan groups. Oral traditions inaccurately portray relations with Tekun and K'ichee', but this presentation reinforces the idea for Kaqchikel that they are in solidarity with other Maya. In Guatemala the clearest distinction is between Maya and Ladinos. As Oxi' Tz'ikin of Comalapa avows, despite Ladino efforts to eradicate Kaqchikel, Kaqchikel lineage and ideas live on. Kaqchikel defend a transtemporal and transgenerational continuance of their worldviews because lineage is central to their identity.

In addition to ethnicity and family, Kaqchikel identify with their communities. A connection to their ancestors provides legitimacy to their place, actions, and future. Oral histories recount the role Kaqchikel forebears played in establishing their communities. While the physical place of the community is important, the essential factor is the community's Mayan roots. Consequently, even when communities change locations, they are still valid social organizations. For example, when Kaqchikel moved from their precontact capital of Iximche' to Tecpán, their existence as an organic whole was not corrupted by the change of location. In the case of Aguas Calientes, the people had social cohesion prior to Spanish contact, and therefore the integrity of their community was legitimate even when the Spanish moved them to a new place. Although Kaqchikel of Aguas Calientes were not originally from their current locale, they developed an intimate connection with it. They came to see the lake as part of their community and were proud that outsiders could not eliminate it. That Kaqchikel decided to dry the lake made its eventual, apparent desiccation an important part of their self-image. The lake lives on in oral histories because it inspires Kaqchikel to continue their own struggle against Ladino and government attempts to demean them and extinguish their distinctions. An important aspect of Kaqchikel identities and worldviews is connected to the Mayanness of their communities.

Ethnic Language

Unfortunately, most Ladinos misunderstand and misconstrue Mayan worldviews and lifestyles. Kaqchikel lament that Ladinos use racial slurs to define and identify them. In Guatemala, *indio* (Indian), a term commonly used by Ladinos, is an insult that connotes ignorance, indolence, inebriation, and uncleanliness.[2] Many Ladinos also refer, paternalistically, to Maya of Guatemala as *nuestros indios* (our Indians). Furthermore, when someone says, "indio, indio," it means "You are ignorant by descent and therefore there is no teaching you," or "You are lazy and dirty by heredity and there is no changing you." The term *ixto* is an even greater insult: it means "stupid indio." These terms have not disappeared. A twenty-one-year-old Kaqchikel man from Chimaltenango explains: "I always had friends who were Ladinos, and right in front of me when they wanted to insult each other they would say 'indio,' they didn't care that I was standing right there."[3]

Kaqchikel also have terms to describe Ladinos, although they are not necessarily derogative. They use the term *kaxlan* to describe anyone or anything foreign. Kaqchikel primarily use this term for Spaniards or South Americans. At the same time, a kaxlan practice is often a Ladino practice.[4] Some elders also use *q'eqawinäq* (black people) to refer to Spaniards. The most common term for a Ladino, however, is *mo's*. Kaqchikel often use this term in a derogative manner, as some Kaqchikel harbor ill feelings toward Ladinos.

Others simply opine that Ladinos cannot be trusted. Nonetheless, Kaqchikel use the term *mos* to delineate a Guatemalan who is not Kaqchikel, Maya, or indigenous—in short, someone different from themselves. Kaqchikel do laud Ladinos who have earned their trust and who contribute to the community or the nation. Some presidents such as Arévalo and Chacón earned the praise of Kaqchikel, as did a Ladino teacher who lives in Comalapa and contributes to an inclusive education of Kaqchikel children. In addition, some Tecpanecos appreciated the efforts of Ladino contratistas who facilitated their labor on the coast.[5] Most Kaqchikel do not generalize Ladinos as evil, but they view the overarching ethnic relationship as exploitative and racist.

When referring to themselves, Kaqchikel use the term *qawinäq,* which means "our people," and *indígena* (indigenous person), or *natural* (native). Most Kaqchikel have a strong sense of connection with their own community, yet Kaqchikel use these terms to identify members of their own community, language group, other Mayan speakers, and indigenous people in other nations. People who seldom or never leave their community identify with other aboriginal groups. Many Kaqchikel asked me if there are qawinäq in the United States. Furthermore, Kaqchikel who have traveled and met with indigenous people in the United States refer to these people as qawinäq. They may not identify with Ladinos on a national level, but they have a strong sense of connection to other indigenous people beyond their local environs. At the same time, they distinguish between different Mayan groups. Many Kaqchikel asserted, for example, that Matzer was not Kaqchikel, because he was from a region that spoke another language, but that he was Maya. His identification as a distinct Mayan-language speaker did not ostracize him from the community. The same is true for the Mam-speaker who teaches in a Comalapa aldea. Residence in the community helped these outsiders gain acceptance from Kaqchikel (as it helped the Ladino teacher gain the trust of some Kaqchikel), but Kaqchikel do not limit their identity to their community or language group. They express a bond with other indigenous people that goes beyond their community and even their nation.

Kaqchikel concepts of "us" and "them" are fluid. For example, even though Kaqchikel of Poaquil and Comalapa opposed each other when Poaquil gained its independence, they have always presented a united force against the neighboring Ladino town of Zaragoza. Likewise, Kaqchikel and K'ichee' have a long-standing rivalry, but this division is subordinated in the face of Ladino threats or intrusions. When faced with the more common external threats and oppression from Ladinos, Kaqchikel emphasize their identity as Maya and indigenous people.

Change, Consistency, and Challenge

The adaptability of the term *qawinäq* presents a good analogy for the fluidity of Kaqchikel worldviews. As with Kaqchikel perceptions of those who are one with them, Kaqchikel historical perspectives have not remained static. They have changed in reaction to historical trends and to external and internal forces. Traditionally, Kaqchikel and other Mayan groups held land communally and believed this to be the most productive system of land tenure. However, as the population pressure upon the land increased, many Kaqchikel approved of the liberal regime's goal to privatize land in the late nineteenth century. They had internalized this concept to the extent that eighty years later most Kaqchikel vehemently opposed Arbenz's attempt to redistribute land more equitably because it infringed upon private land rights. Although Mayan campesinos may have been the primary beneficiaries of Arbenz's efforts, most Kaqchikel perceived his policy to be inherently wrong, and some laborers even fought to defend their patrón's land. They rejected Communism in favor of private property rights. These Kaqchikel worldviews have evolved over time, and they will continue to adapt to their environment.

Alongside the constant revaluations and openness to change, consistencies remain. For example, many Kaqchikel assert that Arbenz was a Communist. However, because they believe in a communal approach to living, this label is a political, not an ideological, critique. Consequently, the label, not the social practice, has negative connotations. Most Kaqchikel continue to act communally in many ways. In work and pleasure, for example, they share communal lunches. Everyone brings food and pools it for group consumption. In addition, the practice of *kuchb'al* continues today. The kuchb'al is a mutual aid fund donated to by members of the community from which the person most in need can borrow and pay back at a later date. Most Kaqchikel accept the validity of communal practices, much as their forebears did with land. However, they reject practices labeled as Communist because they perceive "Communist" governments as bringing instability. One reason they reject governmental forms with this label is because the United States does not support Communist regimes and seeks to undermine this political system, especially in the Western Hemisphere. Kaqchikel care about Guatemala's national identity and stability and know that a Communist government invites internal and external intervention aimed at destabilization. Nonetheless, they do not believe that the practice of their ideas and lifestyles is threatening, and they seek to promote Guatemala's progress and aplomb.

That Kaqchikel identify strongly with their community, language, and ethnicity does not preclude divisions. Oral histories provide examples of disagreements and fighting among Kaqchikel. In fact, caustic relations remain between Aguas Calientes and Barahona. Kaqchikel from Poaquil demanded independence from Comalapa because of abuse and exploitation. When famines hit, Kaqchikel in Tecpán fought each other to get access to emergency food aid. Furthermore, some Kaqchikel assert that contratistas exploited their own people and helped Ladino landowners, even though they were Kaqchikel.

Kaqchikel are aware of the dangers of such discord among Maya. Even though journalist Estuardo Zapeta is K'ichee', Kaqchikel accuse him of failing to support Maya. Some point out that he opposed the 1999 referendum that sought indigenous rights in Guatemala.[6] As one young man explains, "Estuardo Zapeta should be one of us, but he doesn't support us. He has a Harvard degree and then came back to Guatemala to contradict us. He writes against us and tries to bring us down, and that is a shame."[7]

Kaqchikel recognize that outside influences can cause divisive conflict within their communities. They remember that Barrios introduced Protestantism to Guatemala—an action that sowed the seeds of religious conflict. Kaqchikel worry about this development because it divides the community. Whereas past conflicts over land and resources did not irreparably rupture the community, religious splits undermine the community's shared values, limits, and practices. Furthermore, religious conflict has caused rifts in the family, which is a basic and sacred Mayan institution. Today, divisions can be seen clearly between Catholics and Protestants.[8] In part because of the existing religious strife, Kaqchikel are cautious of the consequences of foreign interaction in their communities. Kaqchikel draw a similar lesson from the 1976 earthquake relief workers who caused discord in the communities and later military reprisal. Outsiders appear without any common history or trust; hence Kaqchikel have no mechanism to gauge their motivations or intentions. Oral histories provide numerous examples of destruction caused by outsiders and continue to preach prudent approaches to relationships with foreigners.

Oral histories capture the increased role of the state in the lives of Kaqchikel and its concurrent racism beginning in the last third of the nineteenth century. Many oral accounts present Barrios as a leader who had no respect for Maya and who wanted to inculcate Maya with Ladino traits. Informants relate that when he went to the Kaqchikel town of Patzicía to give his cry for independence, he said: "The Indian has died." Most Kaqchikel assert that Barrios discriminated against Maya, and their oral histories record how in one case he took away their status as Maya. Oral histories attest that in San Pedro Sacatepéquez, San Marcos, Barrios declared that Maya were henceforth Ladinos. Kaqchikel lament that he forced them to change their last names to Ladino names and to wear Ladino clothing. Informants relate that Mayan residents did not like this change but could not outwardly oppose it.[9] For many Kaqchikel, this action proved he was racist, and oral traditions bitterly preserve this affront against their people. However, Barrios's effort may not have been motivated purely by racism. It may have been a misguided attempt to improve the social standing of Maya and their potential for economic progress. In fact, in 1876, Barrios signed a law that revoked the legal identity of Maya of San Pedro Sacatepéquez, but he asserted that this gesture was an expression of his gratitude for their aid in the liberal revolt of 1871.[10] Kaqchikel and other Maya who are critical of Barrios's rule cite the San Pedro Sacatepéquez legislation as an example of Barrios's disrespect and disdain for Guatemala's aborigines. Barrios tried to force Maya to assimilate into Ladino society because he viewed Ladino culture as inherently better; he stated: "One hundred foreign families were worth as much as twenty thousand Indians."[11] Furthermore, he eliminated any Maya who threatened Ladinos' position of power. Residents from Comalapa recall that he killed their leader, Jun Tz'ikin, simply because he was an intelligent Maya who wanted to help his people.[12]

Contested Identities

Oral histories record Kaqchikel struggles to teach others about them and earn respect for their distinctions and distinctiveness. Ladinos and Maya compete over icons and symbols of personal, social, and national identity. For example, both groups recognize Tekun as a national hero, but Ladinos denigrate his abilities as a war hero by claiming he could not differentiate between a horse and a human. Likewise, while Rafael Alvarez Ovalle (1858–1946) is a local role model—primarily for Comalapa—he provides a metaphor for ethnic relations. His story is the macrocosm made microcosm. He embodies two sets of features that often lead to struggles over averring icons and competing identities. Both Ladinos and Kaqchikel assert him as a member of their group. As the composer of the national anthem, he successfully interacted in Ladino circles. Nonetheless, his use of nature in music is rooted in the Mayan community. Alvarez's identity is disputed and debated, as are many Mayan identities and national roles. He is an excellent example of Kaqchikel self-valuation and the challenges of ethnic relations present in oral histories.

Alvarez was born in 1858 and raised by Rosendo Alvarez and Ildefonsa Ovalle in Comalapa. He worked to help support his family from a young age.

Alvarez learned to play the piano, flute, violin, and guitar. At age twenty-one he left Comalapa to enter a school of music in Guatemala City. By twenty-nine he had composed the music to Guatemala's national anthem.[13] Some oral accounts claim that although he began his career as a music teacher, he never attended school.[14] Furthermore, most Kaqchikel emphasize, he used the natural setting of Comalapa to write beautiful music. They say the sounds he heard when he walked in the forest inspired his music. Jun Kan, who befriended Alvarez toward the end of the musician's life, explains how he wrote such amazing music: "Alvarez Ovalle was a simple man. I spoke with him four or five times. He told me that he got his music from the animals in the hills and canyons. He was always in the hills and canyons. One bird called guarda barranca was what he used to begin the national anthem. He told me others but I have forgotten. He wrote musical notes in the hills."[15] As one local barber asserts, "He wrote the solemn hymn as our ancestors would have."[16]

Comalapa keeps Alvarez's fame alive in a number of different ways. The home where he was born has been converted into a House of Culture that contains a library, small rooms for classes, and a large salon for theater, art, and music shows. In 1982 the local government christened the main road in town after him (although most refer to it as "0" Street, not Alvarez Street). In addition, his bust and a plaque that describes his life and significance adorn the town plaza. Finally, each year on the date of his birth, the town celebrates Alvarez's accomplishments. Alvarez is ubiquitous in the daily lives of residents of Comalapa, and their oral histories preserve his influence.

Few dispute Alvarez's talents, but his origin remains contested. Many people claim he was Kaqchikel, while some Kaqchikel counter that he was Ladino. Most people say he spoke Kaqchikel, wore the traditional clothing of white pants and shirt, xerka, cloth belt, black jacket, and a hat. They also claim that his mother, if not both his parents, was Kaqchikel.[17] Dissenters claim that his parents were Ladinos; his last names, Alvarez and Ovalle, are both of Spanish origin, and his descendants are Ladinos. This group also points out that he lived in Guatemala City, not Comalapa, for many years of his life. Another group, who concedes that his descendants are Ladinos, maintains that Alvarez was Kaqchikel.[18] Nonetheless, even Kaqchikel who declare Alvarez was Ladino say that he was of good character and was not racist. They point out that he was a simple man who fit into life in Comalapa. Informants assert that he worked in his cornfields and enjoyed going to the hills.[19] The majority of Kaqchikel in Comalapa take great pride that the composer of the national anthem is "our people" and a product of Comalapa.

Most Kaqchikel from other towns know that Alvarez wrote the music to the national anthem and that he was from Comalapa. No consensus exists, however, on his ethnicity. People from Poaquil tend to say he is Kaqchikel, perhaps due to their proximity and former relationship with Comalapa. Other people in Kaqchikel towns are not as certain, and when they hear the name they assume Alvarez is Ladino. Beyond Comalapa and Poaquil, few people identify Alvarez as Kaqchikel.

The question of Alvarez's background is a sensitive issue because some Kaqchikel claim that Ladinos conscripted him as their own in order to stake a claim to the national anthem. Others point out that some Ladinos even claim that Alvarez was not the author. One story opines that he assigned some of his students to write the music and then took credit for it. A university professor taught his students (some of whom were Kaqchikel) that Alvarez plagiarized the music from France's national anthem. Even if most Ladinos concede that Alvarez is the author, they then purport that he was not Maya. One Kaqchikel woman points out that Ladinos have taken over the House of Culture because they believe that Alvarez was Ladino.[20] People who debate Alvarez's ethnicity and credibility present an example of Ladino society that attempts to deface or co-opt one of the Kaqchikel's most illustrious members.

Kaqchikel oral accounts describe his success despite prejudicial circumstances. They assert that Alvarez was intelligent and that even as a small child had a gift for music. Informants say Alvarez practiced many different versions of written music. They note that he had to win the contest for the national anthem twice because he was Maya. Kaqchikel assert that Alvarez won the first time he entered the contest but that the judges rescinded his victory because they did not want to bestow such a great honor on a Maya. According to Kaqchikel oral histories, his talent did not suffice; Alvarez had to fight the Ladino system to gain recognition for his work. These accounts explain that someone else wanted to appropriate his music, so Alvarez entered the contest a second time and won. Oral histories conclude that this time the judges could not ignore him. Kaqchikel proudly boast that his national anthem is one of the best in the world.[21] A recent book about Guatemala's national anthem, *Historia del himno nacional,* also recognizes that Alvarez had to win twice but does not say why. The book does not examine Alvarez's ethnicity, but some photographs show that his family did not wear Mayan clothing.[22]

This book also asserts that Alvarez maintained strong connections to his hometown until he died in 1946 at age eighty-eight.[23] Kaqchikel point out that although he moved to Guatemala City, he never forgot his roots. A fellow musician tells how Alvarez helped him and some friends:

I knew Alvarez Ovalle. He was a *natural* from Comalapa. In those days the mayor required that we play free concerts every Saturday and Sunday. He did not pay us; we did not even earn a work card. We went to the capital and asked Alvarez to help us. We arrived late so he invited us to stay in his home. The next day we went to the minister of the military, who knew Alvarez, but sent him to the Ministry of Government because this department was in charge of mayors. The minister of government also knew Alvarez, and he immediately sent a note to the Comalapa mayor that insisted he not force us to play. He told Alvarez that if there were any other problems, they should let him know and he would straighten them out.[24]

Oral traditions cherish Alvarez because he is a self-made man who succeeded in a Ladino world and used his power to assist his Kaqchikel counterparts.

Kaqchikel respect Alvarez because he used his talents to express the beauty of Comalapa. One Kaqchikel author recognized Alvarez as one of Comalapa's most illustrious figures.[25] A Mayan priest states: "He is a good memory for our people. He gave music to our town."[26] People outside Kaqchikel communities also recognize his extraordinary work. President Estrada Cabrera, for one, awarded him a medal for his music. Poets, musicologists, and other intellectuals praise him.[27] Alvarez's accomplishments continue to inspire Kaqchikel of Comalapa. He transformed their reality and environs into sounds that people outside their community and even outside their country could appreciate.

Alvarez remains alive in Kaqchikel oral histories because he inspires pride through his ability to resist Ladino intrusions and usurpations. Alvarez did not attend Ladino educational institutions, yet he succeeded in a traditionally Ladino-dominated field. Kaqchikel emphasize that he used local resources to succeed on a national level. Barriers to equality erected by Ladino society did not intimidate or discourage him. Alvarez continued to present his score until the judges publicly recognized his superiority. Likewise, Kaqchikel continue to fight Ladino efforts to co-opt his fame. For Kaqchikel, their efforts to defend Alvarez's ethnicity and honor are part of the cycle that Alvarez experienced when he had to contest the Ladino system because it did not want to bestow such a great honor on a Maya. As illustrated by Jun Ajpu' winning a teaching award, some Ladinos continue to resist bestowing honors on Maya.[28] Alvarez's success inspires Kaqchikel in their ongoing struggle, and oral histories concerning his life provide valuable lessons for Kaqchikel today.

While Alvarez's ethnicity is still debated, most Kaqchikel adhere to the belief that he was Maya and that his success was based in his Kaqchikel roots.

Even Kaqchikel who question his identity assert that he was a humble man who lived with and learned from the Kaqchikel community. In contrast, most Ladinos attempt either to discredit him or to claim him as their own. Most Ladinos insist that the national anthem is central to Guatemala's identity and therefore that the music must have been written by a Ladino.[29] Kaqchikel want to ensure that their surroundings and reality remain connected to the national anthem.

Ethnicity and National Development

Kaqchikel value the work ethic passed on to them by their ancestors. They are proud of the churches and other buildings their ancestors built hundreds of years ago and that are still standing. Kaqchikel commend local icons, such as Matzer, for their penchant for hard work. They do not attribute this trait only to Maya, however. National leaders, such as Arévalo and Ubico, also gained the respect of Kaqchikel because they were diligent and portrayed work as valuable. In general, however, Kaqchikel associate Ladinos with laziness and shoddy workmanship and perceive them as contributing little to the community in terms of communal labor. Kaqchikel accept the differentiation of wealth because its acquisition is an acceptable reward for diligence. In their view, rich people are not inherently evil; they should even be praised if their wealth is derived from hard work and especially if they extend the benefits back to their families and communities, such as Matzer and the Tz'ikins. Most Kaqchikel, for example, commended contratistas because they facilitated employment on the coast for those who lacked work. Kaqchikel did not begrudge these men their profit; they viewed this income as compensation for the service they provided. Moreover, contratistas tended to be Maya, which increased the level of trust in them among Kaqchikel. The evils on the coast did not stem from hard work but stolen pay, illnesses, beatings, denial of rest days, and lack of fulfillment of educational obligations. Kaqchikel have a strong work ethic but denounce exploitation.

Kaqchikel's desire to promote Guatemala's economic development is evident in their high regard for leaders who contribute to national development. Ubico, for instance, received praise for his sound financial management. He maintained the value of the quetzal to the U.S. dollar and eliminated the national debt. Kaqchikel opine that this economic stability lent prestige to their country. In contrast, they disapprove of Arbenz because he weakened the state. At the same time, many Kaqchikel are more critical of Arbenz's deposer, Castillo Armas, and judge him to be a traitor because he aligned himself with the United States and violated Guatemala's sovereignty. Even those who agree that Arbenz's reign had to be terminated disagree with Castillo Armas's means.

Kaqchikel oral histories also highlight where state institutions have failed to adequately provide for the development of the nation. Kaqchikel recognize that Guatemala has valuable resources but that its people lack proper education or training to fully take advantage of these resources. Today, the majority of Kaqchikel perceive education to be an integral part of national and personal development. Education has allowed them increased opportunities, but they wish to expand their portion of the benefits. For a long time Kaqchikel resisted and avoided education because of its discriminatory curriculum and actions, but as they gained some control over education, and as its provision and quality improved, they welcomed this opportunity. However, they remain aware of the assimilationist policies of the schools. Some Kaqchikel also express concern over the process of acculturation inherent in road construction, which allows outside forces easier access to their communities. As cultures mix, compromises are eminent. Kaqchikel recognize, for example, that modernization has overcome the lessons of oral histories that encourage people to build with lighter, simpler materials to ameliorate the potential damage of earthquakes. Kaqchikel lament that at times the state has been more concerned with assimilating Maya into Ladino society than with national development.

Acculturation is a sensitive issue for Kaqchikel. The majority of Kaqchikel invite modernization as a means to improve their quality of life, but they do not want to sacrifice their ethnic identity for it. By definition, attacks on their ethnicity decrease their quality of life. Nonetheless, Kaqchikel are aware that their culture (like all cultures) is constantly changing. Oral traditions teach them different strategies for negotiating these forces without losing the significance of their identity. For example, Kaqchikel are proud that Tuyuc outwardly displays her identity in Congress, while they are critical of Ixtz'ikin because she refuses to wear her traje or use her language in Ladino settings. Many informants mentioned the dangers of interacting in Ladino institutions because they attempt to acculturate Maya. Older generations lament that younger Kaqchikel do not evince the same respect they displayed toward their elders. Many parents regret that many younger Kaqchikel fail to speak their native tongue. They lament that Ladino institutions corrupt their children's na'oj—essence—with Ladino influences. For example, the Kaqchikel military general who engineered brutal attacks on Maya during the civil war clearly replaced his Kaqchikel na'oj for a Ladino one, and consequently Kaqchikel discredit him. Kaqchikel in Aguas Calientes lament that young people who work in factories are giving up their Kaqchikel language, dress, and na'oj. Kaqchikel recognize that cultural erosion has taken place as a result of internal and external pressures. Most stress that preservation of their language is one of the most critical issues. Only their language can record Kaqchikel oral histories and the lessons therein. Kaqchikel assert that if they lose their language many of their distinct ideas and worldviews will perish also. Many Kaqchikel attest that Spanish translations fail to maintain all the nuances of their stories and their na'oj. Oral histories may be the best defense against acculturation and the loss of their unique identity. While oral histories warn against the loss of cultural markers, they also provide a sense of efficacy and empowerment that encourages people to act against it. Oral histories highlight that Kaqchikel are not passive participants in the maintenance of their ethnic identity, the development of Guatemala, or its national history.

The majority of Kaqchikel maintain that national development and distinct ethnicities do not have to be mutually exclusive. They can contribute to and benefit from national economy and society, yet maintain their own cultural, linguistic, and social distinctions. The preservation of their ethnicity adds to Guatemala's richness. Kaqchikel want mutual respect because it is imperative to national development that distinct cultures flourish. They do not believe everyone should have to choose a dominant culture. Their oral histories affirm their desire to resist assimilation and their desire to contribute to and be part of the nation, desires that are not incompatible. Kaqchikel continue to maintain their ethnic allegiances in the larger national culture. One Kaqchikel author lauds Ka'i' Tz'ikin because "he fought for the cause of the race and the progress of the community, [which was] a national struggle."[30] The author draws an intimate connection between the community and the nation because the progress of the community affects the nation, and vice versa. Improved ethnic relations must begin at the local level, but they are an essential part of the development of both the community and the nation. In their interactions with biased institutions, Kaqchikel seek to improve ethnic relations.

Public education and the military are two examples of Ladino-dominated institutions that attempt to incorporate Kaqchikel into national society. Because of their conceptions of Maya, Ladinos have attempted to eliminate their cultural separateness. Many Ladinos believe acculturation is the only way to form a united, modern nation. Consequently, the state compels Maya to enter the military and the schools to force their incorporation into national society. Ladinos present these institutions as the state's efforts to save Maya from their miserable plight. While the military provides more egalitarian relations than the public schools, both institutions operate through a system that denies and denigrates Mayan characteristics. Western historians and anthropologists assert that military conscription destroyed communal harmony in the highlands; most older Kaqchikel, however, emphasize the benefits of their military service. Where Ladinos perceive the goal of acculturation to have failed, they accredit the failure to the low mental and physical qualities of Maya. Oral histories show that Maya took from these institutions what benefited them, yet retained their culture, ideas, and identity. In general, Ladinos underestimate the Mayan desire to maintain and expand their unique essence.

Kaqchikel separate education into three sources: traditional knowledge (in which mathematical skills are inherent), Ladino schools, and Mayan schools. Kaqchikel resisted Ladino education for a long time because it was irrelevant to their reality, inaccurately taught events, discriminated against them, infringed upon their familial pool of labor and income, and led to forced acculturation. Today, Ladino education continues its attempt to inculcate Western values and attack traditional and life learning. Most Kaqchikel believe that Ladino schools corrupt the Kaqchikel spirit and contradict their work ethic. Furthermore, at times, Ladinos physically abuse Mayan children at school.

In response to these attacks on their community and culture, Kaqchikel leaders in Comalapa created a school to implement their own ideas, hire their own personnel, and eradicate the negative characteristics associated with Ladino influences. Kaqchikel have always valued education, but one that is inclusive and not Ladino-dominated. They had always recognized its importance for national and self-improvement, so when Arévalo increased the access to and attraction of public education for Maya, they responded with increased attendance. Many people cited financial hardship as an obstacle to school attendance, but as the Kaqchikel increased their ownership of public education, the school became a viable way to escape economic oppression. In fact, Kaqchikel now use public education to improve their status. One of the main goals of education for Kaqchikel is to acquire Spanish literacy, which is imperative to their self-defense and self-respect in the face of Ladino affronts. They need to read Spanish documents to protect their land, labor, and other resources, and they need to speak and understand Spanish in order to interact in the marketplace, municipality, and national society.

Likewise, Kaqchikel utilized the military to their advantage. In the service, men learned Spanish and gained other skills that contributed to their livelihood, but more importantly they gained confidence and became accustomed to more egalitarian interaction with Ladinos. They learned how to defend themselves verbally, using Spanish, and physically. Their self-esteem grew as their skills, strength, and endurance increased. The idea of self-respect and respect for others is central to Kaqchikel worldviews, and their participation in the military contributed to this valued concept. Participation in the military translated into improved relations with Ladinos in their communities.

The military was the only Ladino institution that mitigated the effects of racism. Kaqchikel accepted the poor conditions of the military because it facilitated better ethnic relations. They benefited from the military and succeeded within its environs. Military officials respected Mayan soldiers, promoted them, and sought to interest them in military careers. Few Kaqchikel pursued a military career, however, because the military not only clashed with Kaqchikel worldviews and lifestyles but also attempted to indoctrinate them in Ladino thought. Kaqchikel especially rejected the lack of respect for life in the military—many became disillusioned when they had to kill in the army. The military began to lose its credibility when it failed to defend the nation against Castillo Armas's invasion, and most Kaqchikel perceptions of the military worsened as the civil war began and the military began attacking, rather than defending, the populace.

Kaqchikel remain skeptical of other Ladino institutions. While they praise Arévalo for establishing the social security system, they realize that the system has tended to exclude them. Kaqchikel appreciate Arévalo's ideas and his efforts to help the poor but recognize that subsequent government officials have eclipsed his intentions. To date, no Ladino institution has convinced Kaqchikel that it has their best interests in mind.

Kaqchikel are aware that the military and school system have attempted to acculturate Maya, but most Kaqchikel have utilized these institutions to their advantage and have avoided the attempts at domination. Kaqchikel perceive that their participation in both of these institutions has reduced racism—they seldom hear "ixto" and "indio" directed at them.[31] Most Kaqchikel do not seek to eliminate the military and schools altogether (although today a minority argue that the military should be abolished); rather, they want equal representation, influence, and opportunities within these institutions. Likewise, Solares found that Maya distinguish institutions such as schools and health clinics from their staff. While Maya were often critical of personnel, they did not want to eliminate the institution itself.[32] Kaqchikel see institutions as benign, but people who run them often use them as tools for assimilation.

In some ways, the Kaqchikel personalization of leaders facilitates their ability to separate individuals from institutions. Kaqchikel can maintain their identity with institutions while they praise or criticize individuals. For example, one man's statement that Barrios taught Kaqchikel all twenty-eight letters juxtaposes accounts of teachers hitting and abusing Kaqchikel children and illustrates the Kaqchikel recognition of the value of and need for education and schools. Likewise, oral histories describe Arévalo fumigating homes and distributing medication to rid the nation of lice. These depictions sharply contrast those of Ladino doctors disrespecting Kaqchikel medicinal practices and customs and burying their infirm before they die. This personalization of Arévalo not only keeps his historical role vibrant but also emphasizes the importance Kaqchikel place on public health and Western medicine. Lastly, oral histories include approval and reprobation of national leaders, but Kaqchikel always support the nation. In this way Kaqchikel identify with the nation, though not necessarily with those who control it.

Ladinos have sought to incorporate Maya into a national Eurocentric Guatemalan society since the colonial period. An essential part of their modernization plan is that Maya be citizens of Guatemala. However, Ladinos limit the ways Maya can become citizens by saying that they must be Ladino. Consequently, the state has developed Western political, economic, and social organizations in Mayan communities. These institutions take root ostensibly to aid Mayan communities, but the main goal is to acculturate the population. In fact, most aid the government offers is assimilatory. According to the government, it aids Maya by making them more like Ladinos. Ladinos are not cognitively dissonant. At times, they exalt certain Mayan institutions of the past, but they want to build a unified nation, and, according to them, autonomy would undermine this goal. They cannot conceive of autonomy with unity. Consequently, many Ladinos cannot support pluralism and diversity. Rather, most Ladinos approach "their" indigenous population with a strategy similar to that of museum conservation because they see Maya as people of the past. They are willing to allow survival of vestigial Mayan groups and practices as curious, living exhibitions of the past, and they compartmentalize Maya in this way to achieve modernity.

Historically, Mayan labor has been the cornerstone of Guatemala's development. Barrios utilized Mayan land and labor to develop coffee exports, Ubico relied on Mayan labor for his roadworks program, Arévalo sought to modernize Maya through improved access to education and health care, and Arbenz hoped to incorporate Maya into society through land reform. Ladinos perceive that Maya resist these programs because of their retrograde ways; however, many Maya participated in these modernization programs for their own and the nation's benefit. For example, Ladino and Western historians generally opine that the Guatemalan state imposed forced-labor mechanisms (to the detriment of Maya) because otherwise Maya would not work outside their communities. However, Kaqchikel conceived of the government's forced-labor mechanisms as unnecessary. As the population pressure increased in the twentieth century, many Maya voluntarily sought work outside their communities. Coastal migration and plantation labor presented such opportunities. Maya have developed other ways to contribute to the national economy and their own livelihood, such as through textile production, which contributes to the export economy. They also produce basic foodstuffs for national consumption. Unfortunately, most Ladinos want to position themselves between Maya and the profits that result from their entrepreneurial spirit and industriousness. Ladino presumptions about the complete opposition of Maya to standards of hygiene, education, modernization, and Western religion and belief systems are unfounded.

Most Ladinos tend to have presented Maya as a drag on the country's development. Adams's study of ethnic images during the democratic governments of Arévalo and Arbenz illustrates some of Guatemala's racist attitudes: Maya are low and despicable, incapable of self-direction, and when left to their own devices they spend their money on liquor. Many Ladinos concluded that Maya must be Westernized or destroyed because they weakened Guatemala.[33] One of the contributors to racism was that many Ladinos feared Mayan uprisings. By newspaper accounts, Mayan massacres always seemed imminent but seldom occurred.[34] Some Ladinos argued that Maya were equal human beings, but these progressives were the minority. Guatemala's Nobel literature laureate Miguel Angel Asturias stressed the importance of cultural and political assimilation to improve the situation of Maya and Guatemala. This could only be done biologically, through miscegenation, but the mingling of Ladino and Mayan blood threatened the "vigorous blood" necessary for the progress of Guatemala. He advocated the importation of Europeans to replace the inferior intellectual and cultural characteristics of the Maya.[35] Deeply entrenched racist attitudes held by many Ladinos toward Maya have intensified ethnic conflict.

Kaqchikel oral histories abound with examples of ethnic tensions. During the cholera scare in the 1830s Kaqchikel believed the Gálvez government wanted to poison them. Because Maya had more contact with the priests than with the president and were fearful of the national government, they believed the priests' claim and feared government officials. Likewise, during the influenza epidemic, the government failed to inform Maya of the rationale and intentions of its actions. They treated Maya as subjects, not citizens, imposing their foreign medicines on Kaqchikel and refusing to listen to their concerns. The Ladinos' imposition of Western medicine and their efforts to bury the sick alive undermined the development of Kaqchikel's trust in Ladinos. Ladino officials had not developed any relationship with the local population, and consequently Kaqchikel saw them as hegemonic threats. In addition, most Ladino accounts of influenza depict Maya as the source of the disease because of their unhygienic living conditions. The government imposed its policy without attempting to understand Mayan reactions and reality.

Distrust and misunderstanding of outside factors continues among some Kaqchikel. Oral histories about epidemics evince that Kaqchikel perceived hospitals as places of isolation and death, not recuperation. They believed that contagion, not poor hygiene, caused disease and therefore believed that the government established hospitals as places to quarantine sick people to die, as a means of preventing further propagation of the epidemic. While Kaqchikel enjoy greater participation in and ownership of local health clinics today, the lack of information about hospitals and their purpose led Kaqchikel to believe that they were virtual halfway houses to death. This perception perpetuated the fear of Western medical intervention. Furthermore, Kaqchikel point out that their ancestors lived longer because they did not employ Western medicines and did not ingest chemicals in their diet. Some Kaqchikel prefer to use natural fertilizer because it avoids the adverse health effects brought on by the ingestion of chemicals. The chemicals and technology needed to increase agricultural production and profit have created a dependency on these inputs and caused the deterioration of public health. Some Kaqchikel see this relationship between outside inputs and decreased health as a conspiracy.

Misunderstandings, or misinformation, about other government policies are evident in oral accounts. Kaqchikel reprove Arbenz because he failed to clearly explain his land reform policy to the population. While some Kaqchikel assert that he had good intentions, the implementation process was confused and led to violence. Consequently, many view his land reform as a Communist attack on private landholdings. Arbenz failed to establish a good rapport with the population, and this oversight, combined with baroque explanation and implementation, led to his downfall. Governments that fail to inform Maya about their policies and goals do not gain the trust and respect of Kaqchikel.

In contrast, when the state informs Kaqchikel of its actions and clearly defines its laws and agenda, most respond amicably. Ubico receives high accolades because he visited towns and maintained contact with the population. He did not limit his appearances to crisis situations, and he explained to Maya that he needed their labor to develop the roads of Guatemala, a goal they supported. Furthermore, he established and maintained clear rules for his government and the populace. He was not seen to act capriciously. On a local level, Kaqchikel recognize Oxi' Tz'ikin as a good mayor because, although he was harsh, he consistently enforced a rule of order they agreed with and understood. Kaqchikel prefer simple and straightforward guidelines over idealism, but most importantly they want a leader who sticks by his word.

Chacón also interacted constructively with Kaqchikel. During his visits to Aguas Calientes, he showed respect for and developed a familiarity with Kaqchikel. He interacted with the local population prior to the malaria crisis that necessitated draining the lake. He had already developed a relationship with the people and had therefore gained their trust. Furthermore, in a meeting with Kaqchikel, Chacón insisted that everyone sit on reed mats, thus showing respect for their culture and an understanding of their reality. Consequently, Kaqchikel accepted and agreed with his decision to eradicate an important source of their livelihood.

Finally, Arévalo made great inroads with Kaqchikel primarily through open communication but also through limited visits. Many Kaqchikel recall that Arévalo worked to reduce racism. One eighty-two-year-old farmer describes Arévalo's visit to Poaquil while walking to his fields one day: "Arévalo came here. He was a good man. He said that all of Guatemala was Indian. If you are Ladino, black, or Indian, we are all the same. Even foreigners who come here are Indians. It was good because before that Ladinos put us down, called us 'indio,' 'pig,' 'fertilizer,' but then they stopped. He did a good job."[36] Kaqchikel perceived that Arévalo not only saw them as equals but also recognized their central role in Guatemala's development. When he sent health brigades to rural areas to eradicate public health threats, the people did not view his policy as an intrusion or a threat because he had made the problem and goals explicit. Where resistance to his policies persisted, Arévalo sent doctors or established local Kaqchikel commissions to explain the situation to people. Kaqchikel then agreed the health and hygiene hazard needed to be addressed, because they did not possess the resources to combat the plagues. Despite Ladino perceptions that Maya were dirty, Kaqchikel welcomed the opportunity to maintain their cleanliness and hence their self-esteem. When given the opportunity to participate in Western medicine, as opposed to being treated as passive and ignorant victims, Kaqchikel are open to government intervention.

Kaqchikel trusted leaders whom they perceived to be explicit in their policies, open about explaining the Mayan role and the impact these policies would have on them, and who did not wait for a crisis to occur before they approached the communities. Kaqchikel appreciate national leaders who visit their rural communities and show concern and respect for them. A number of national leaders, even today, have used the strategy of personal visits to enhance the perception that their goals include the best interest of Maya. Constant and clear communication ameliorates Mayan fears and can win active support.

Conclusion

The majority population of Guatemala is Maya, and its national history and development must include this influence. The reactions of Maya to national trends, events, policies, and leaders are essential to understanding Guatemala's past and charting a course for its future. History must account for how national policies affected local populations and how local populations affected national policies. Kaqchikel historical perspectives are complex, and historians may be forced to incorporate different ideas rather than present Maya as an entity with a single perspective. In the analysis of Barrios's development of coffee exports, for example, despite his attacks on Mayan land and labor, some Kaqchikel benefited from the imposition of land documentation. This view contrasts with perspectives of Western scholars, such as Carol Smith, who argue that Maya lost ground and were most in danger during dictatorships such as Barrios's. While many Kaqchikel would agree with Smith's assessment, Kaqchikel oral histories portray both the exploitative and the benevolent nature of his regime. A cursory acknowledgment of the Mayan population corrupts Guatemala's national history.

Past happenings must be examined at the local level. For example, historical analysis of the influenza epidemic that ravaged Guatemala in 1918–19 must include the Kaqchikel accounts that etched this crisis in their oral histories. Their population suffered greatly, and the state's reaction varied between being inadequate and being offensively intrusive. Furthermore, fears of the government public health measures remained from the 1831 cholera epidemic. According to Kaqchikel, the state acted negligently toward them in regard to public health until Arévalo's campaign to eradicate vector insects. These opinions are integral to the comprehension of public health in Guatemala and to the development of viable government policies today.

Kaqchikel oral histories also provide a close examination of national leaders and their governing strategies. Western and Ladino historians, for example, attribute Ubico's popularity among Maya to his visits to the countryside. However, the most important aspect of Ubico's approach was not the visits themselves but his ability to communicate to the population, emphasize the importance of Maya in national plans, display respect for and understanding of their reality, and provide them with a sense of participation in Guatemala's development. Since Kaqchikel seek equal and fair treatment above all, stern measures are acceptable as long as they are unbiased in their application.

Maya think about Guatemala as a nation and care about it as an entity. This concept seems to contradict logic when considered in the context of the repression, exploitation, murder, and torture they have suffered since the Spanish arrival. Furthermore, Western scholars such as Carol Smith and Eric Wolf claim that Guatemalan indigenous groups identify only with their local community, not on a national or even regional scale.[37] However, Kaqchikel clearly identify with other Kaqchikel communities, Maya, and indigenous people. Moreover, if Kaqchikel criticize Arbenz for land reforms that violate private property or were implemented too quickly, even though they stood to benefit from them; criticize Castillo Armas for inviting outside forces that led to instability in Guatemala; work on the roads to improve national infrastructure and their connection to it; and actively participate in education to improve its quality and egalitarianism, then they clearly care about the nation. They contributed to Ubico's road-building program not only because the government forced them to work but also because they valued the development of infrastructure as a way to improve the nation's economic status. In addition, they have been disappointed in bad leaders because such individuals fail to make Guatemala a strong, respected, and prestigious nation, not because these leaders do not provide Mayan communities and people with special privileges and protection. Kaqchikel separate the nation as an entity from the people who run it. Although they may not identify with Ladinos, they feel connected to the country and are willing to work with Ladinos, on an egalitarian basis, to improve it.

As seen throughout this book, Kaqchikel want what is best for their community and the nation and are proud of their contributions to national development. They lament, however, that their efforts are not valued or, at times, even recognized. Oral histories emphasize that Kaqchikel contributions to national development far outnumber the benefits they have enjoyed from their efforts. Most Kaqchikel display an allegiance to the state, government, and national territory through their involvement with political parties, social reform, and educational structures. Kaqchikel lament national defeats in political and economic arenas and recognize the importance of national progress. They invite and contribute to the development of the infrastructure in Guatemala, such as railroads, roads, and public buildings, and they praise leaders for their efforts to develop these. Even though many of these developments, such as the railroad, did not directly affect Kaqchikel, most valued them because they resulted in access to domestic and international markets. The majority of Kaqchikel continue to encourage road construction to facilitate their interaction with larger markets. The majority also commend Arévalo for his construction of schools and his facilitation of access to potable water and electricity. They have benefited from economic development programs such as export agriculture and have consistently contributed to the national economy through the production of agro-exports, foodstuffs, and textiles. Some used their entrepreneurial spirit to provide their services to the capital and the coast. Kaqchikel have incorporated foreign inputs, such as chemical fertilizer, into their lives and economy to improve their financial situation. However, Kaqchikel are critical of forced labor, loss of their land, unequal access to and inadequate representation in education and health care, and general racism that prevents them from attaining better employment. Kaqchikel want to contribute to and benefit from Guatemala's national development, but they want equal opportunities to exploit economic resources. They participate in institutions that contribute to the progress, maintenance, and protection of the nation but resist national policies that seek to eliminate them as a separate cultural group. Kaqchikel have successfully integrated foreign technology and ideas into their communities while maintaining their ethnic distinctions, and their oral histories have played an integral role in this balance. They do not seek a separate nation but egalitarian treatment in the current one.

A sense of national security and personal safety is paramount for Kaqchikel. Ubico is a central figure in Kaqchikel oral histories because he provided the personal security most Kaqchikel value. He rid the country of criminals and drunkards, and as a result people felt safe traveling inside and outside their communities. Even though Ubico forced them to work to develop Guatemala's infrastructure, Kaqchikel accepted this arrangement. Likewise, to a lesser degree, some Kaqchikel recognize Barrios as a strong-armed ruler who maintained peace, though they point out that he was less egalitarian in his treatment of Maya. Most Kaqchikel are critical of Barrios because even though he maintained national stability, under his domain personal security was not an inalienable right. For Kaqchikel, human needs such as security, food, and shelter eclipse other rights.

In most cases, Kaqchikel are willing to sacrifice personal and national freedoms for security. At times their democratic ideals do not correlate with their sense of survival. A Kaqchikel hierarchy of values is evidenced by their assessment of the Arévalo and Arbenz administrations. Most Kaqchikel praise Arévalo for his rhetoric of equality and democratic principles, but they criticize him because he pushed reform too quickly and undermined internal security. Crime increased during his democratic experiment and eroded a

Kaqchikel sense of personal safety. Likewise, Arbenz had the best interest of Maya in mind through his land reform, but his policy induced civil war. These administrations, while they may have been well intended, undermined Guatemala's fragile balance and wreaked havoc on the country. Consequently, the loss of personal security and national stability outweighed any gains made in the area of personal liberties or wealth.

Kaqchikel have clear perceptions of justice that coincide with their sense of personal security. The legal system in Guatemala has seldom worked to the benefit of Maya, so Kaqchikel have often depended on assertive leaders to apply strict justice. Kaqchikel commend local mayors, such as Matzer and the Tz'ikins, who ignored financial influence or favoritism in their application of justice. Ubico's harsh rule also made no exceptions. Most Kaqchikel commend Ubico because he punished Ladinos and Maya equally. They condemned Barrios because he did not. Kaqchikel do not assess justice simply by whether it works in their favor. Many Kaqchikel viewed Arbenz's attempt to expropriate land as unjust even though they may have benefited from the reform. Kaqchikel seek a system of justice in which people's security and equality are upheld.

Historically, Kaqchikel have not consistently enjoyed security or justice in Guatemala. Consequently, they have utilized various "weapons of the weak" to achieve their goals and to resist intrusions and exploitation. Kaqchikel used the tuj to hide their children when officials came to take them to school and to hide sick family members when officials came to bury them alive. One can imagine the rabbit safely hiding from the coyote in the tuj. In a more positive response to education, Kaqchikel built and staffed their own school to provide an education that was inclusive and respectful for their children. Kaqchikel extol local leaders such as Alvarez, Ka'i' Tz'ikin, and Matzer who used indigenous resources to succeed in a society dominated by Ladinos. According to Kaqchikel oral traditions, these men succeeded even though—and in some cases because—they had not attended Ladino schools. Alvarez wrote the national anthem from his (and Kaqchikel) surroundings, Matzer surveyed and built a road from indigenous ingenuity and local labor, and Ka'i' Tz'ikin avoided sure death by clearly presenting his (and Kaqchikel) reality to Ubico. These Kaqchikel were efficacious by utilizing their own wisdom, resourcefulness, and diligence. Their successes reinforce Kaqchikel pride and desire to maintain their ethnic identity, not as a vestige of their ancestors but as a tool in their lives today to succeed against great odds. Oral histories prove that progress is not contingent upon Ladino traits.

Sources of their icons' success were independent of Ladino influence; success was derived from Kaqchikel knowledge and reality. Kaqchikel do not hold these accomplishments over Ladinos; rather, they are content to share their achievements equally. In contrast to Ladino pressures to abandon their ethnic distinctions, oral histories insist on the need to utilize the resources inherent in their ethnicity to improve their own quality of life and contribute to their nation's development. Oral histories teach Kaqchikel that at times they need to circumvent state structures to achieve their goals. This reality became clear once again when no Maya were invited to the negotiating table of the Peace Accords. Formal exclusion was reinforced in May 1999 when the Guatemalan populace rejected the referendum for indigenous rights in Guatemala. Nonetheless, Tuyuc's successes prove that Kaqchikel efficacy is not a thing of the past. Sam Colop asserts: "In this dominant [Ladino] ideology, pluralism and peaceful coexistence seem to commit outrage against the evolution of the state, but a 'national unity' cannot be constructed while denying an existent plurality. To do so is to construct a future while walking toward the past. The Maya, in contrast, do not base their future on the past; they add their future to their history and to the history of humanity."[38] The cyclical nature of oral histories provides Kaqchikel ways not only to survive but also to improve their situation when their larger reality is biased against them.

Remarkably, despite this history the majority of Kaqchikel do not seek revenge against their oppressors. Oral histories do not stress vindictiveness. Poaquilenos fought for their independence to escape oppressive conditions, but their oral histories express the peaceful and productive relations that resulted and continue today, not the former angst. Oral histories surrounding their independence express hope for turning animosity into convivial and productive relations. Despite Ka'i' Tz'ikin's clear understanding of unjust relations with Ladinos, he befriended Ladinos and encouraged Kaqchikel to break down barriers to communication. He emphasized Kaqchikel's need to empower themselves but also wanted his people to be open to fruitful relations. Certainly, my house brother Jun Ajpu' internalized these lessons from oral histories. Despite Ladino criticism of a Maya winning an educational award, he refused to demonize them. He continues to hope for more egalitarian and productive relations. Likewise, a young Kaqchikel man from Chimaltenango explains: "I fear today that we are losing our ethnic identity. So we formed a group in Chimaltenango. We talked to elders to learn about our culture and history. It is a group of young people and we do plays, dances, and music to rescue our history and culture, but we don't include the deaths [from the civil war] in our productions because we don't want to cause resentments. We want to bury those. We do our plays about peace."[39] One

Kaqchikel intellectual analogizes the situation of Guatemala: "It is as if you had guests over to your home and they locked you in the bathroom. We do not wish to remove the guests from our home, we simply want to be let out of the bathroom."[40]

Kaqchikel insightfully articulate the historical reality of Guatemala and the potential for reconciliation. Cojtí asserts: "It is necessary to reorient *mestizo* [mixed race, hybrid] education from different angles (educational materials, teachers' attitudes, educational content, etc.) to remove the mistaken conceptions, prejudices and erroneous and distorted ideas in relation to the Mayan community . . . [for] solidarity or brotherhood, between Maya and Ladinos."[41] Kaqchikel do not wish to exclude Ladinos, they simply seek to encourage them to be more pluralistic and accepting. Cojtí's statement reflects one of the early goals in Comalapa when Kaqchikel founded their own school and allowed some Ladinos to participate. Kaqchikel recognize a cycle of acceptance, understanding, and peaceful coexistence but lament that it is not the dominant paradigm.

Understanding Kaqchikel historical perspectives elucidates the importance of indigenous history as told by the actors. Indigenous historical perspectives allow native peoples to speak for themselves by contributing not only their reactions to past happenings but also their opinions about the significance of the events. Furthermore, they may have different methodological approaches and theoretical constructs for history. For example, Kaqchikel recount their oral histories in a cyclical, not chronological, manner. Consequently, they do not record exact dates in their oral histories. This approach reinforces the idea that their history is relevant to their present because it teaches them strategies they can use in the future. History is animate, not a thing of the past. Cavender Wilson points out that rarely are Native American historical perspectives concerned with dates and times:

Because many [oral] accounts cannot be placed within a chronological framework, it is often impossible to employ academic historians' usual means of corroborating sources. Within Native American oral traditions, different means of validation and verification are utilized. For example, collective memories are engaged to insure the accuracy of any given account, and those who are known to have been trained well are respected and sought out within the community for their knowledge, skill, and expertise. In terms of establishing credibility or validation, in many native communities, the words and the honor of the elders are sufficient.[42]

She also notes that for Native Americans, "History is important because it establishes our sense of identity and belonging."[43] Kaqchikel also use their oral histories to pass on to younger generations ideas about who they are and the history behind their ethnic pride. If indigenous viewpoints are not incorporated into national histories, significant approaches to culture, life, and the basis for future action will be missing. These ideas can expand our base of knowledge.

Kaqchikel historical perspectives presented here are an attempt to not only understand the people, events, and trends that are central to the Kaqchikel past but also to comprehend how Kaqchikel think about the past and their role in it. Most Ladino and Western scholars' presentations of Guatemalan history fail to incorporate Mayan historical perspectives and values. These ideas are important to an understanding of Mayan past, present, and future. The willful ignorance of indigenous past, conceptions of that past, and how it is integrated into the present condemns to failure any national project for joint participation between Maya and Ladinos. More peaceful relations must be predicated upon mutual comprehension, inclusion, and respect. Indigenous groups, as well as other historically voiceless people, have valuable contributions to make to our understanding of history, reality, and the future. Indigenous groups have a desire either to participate in societies equally and with mutual respect or to live in their own communities without outside interference. World peace must be built from the local level and through an adherence to the acceptance and celebration of distinct worldviews. The first step is to allow these different perceptions to surface in a friendly environment. Revisionist history must include indigenous influences. Societies that establish a holistic history will not be doomed to repeat their particularistic past.

Glossary

Kaqchikel words are italicized

aguardiente	moonshine, homemade liquor
ajq'ij	daykeeper, a Mayan priest who can interpret signs and dreams and cure people and who can read, interpret, and divine the 260-day Mayan calendar
alguaciles	sheriffs, leaders
aldea	hamlet, small community
b'ojo'y	large clay pot or vessel
cacique	local rural leaders
caciquismo	system of rural political leadership characterized by the domination of powerful local leaders
cafetaleros	coffee-plantation owners
campesino	farmer, rural inhabitant
caporal	headman on a ranch
caudillo	strong-armed, charismatic leader
cédula	official identification card
chicha	homemade alcoholic concoction made from fermented fruit
chicharía	local drinking establishment
che'	tree
chirimía	oboe
cofradía	sacred religious brotherhood
compadres	godparents
constancia	immutable document, letter
contratista	broker for plantation labor on the coast
control de cita	work card
costal	large sack used to transport goods
cuerda	4,810 square yards
ejidos	common public land

fabricas	manufacturing plants
fincas	large, landed estates
finquero	owner of large, landed estate
guardería	nursery school
güipil	hand-woven blouse, part of traditional dress for Mayan women
güisquil	merliton
habilitador	loan shark, agent
indio	Indian, generally used in a derogatory manner by Ladinos to mean ignorant, drunk, lazy, and dirty
intendentes	Ladino military leaders assigned under Ubico to act as local governors
ixim	maize
ixto	derogatory term Ladinos use to label Indians
jefatura política	government (at the local or state level)
jefe político	governor
jornal	day work/day wage
jornato	day work card
kaxlan	foreign, usually something or someone who comes from outside the community
kaj	corn grinder made of stone
kuchb'al	mutual aid fund/society
k'utunik	Kaqchikel tradition of a boy asking his girlfriend to marry him
Ladino	nonindigenous Guatemalan; the distinction is based more on cultural, social, and ethnic characteristics than physical appearance or genetics
Ladinoization	the process of becoming a Ladino
ley de trabajadores	law governing laborers
libreto (libreta)	work cards used to ensure individuals were completing state labor requirements
liga campesina	farmers league/union
mandamiento	mandate, generally for unpaid labor
manzana	1.73 acres
maquiladora	export processing and finishing plant
marimba	musical instrument that closely resembles a large xylophone
mestizaje	cultural and genetic race mixing
mestizo	a person of mixed racial blood
milpa	cornfields or corn crops

mo's	Ladino; sometimes derogatory term used by Kaqchikel
na'oj	spirit, being, essence, character
natural	native, self-identifying term for Kaqchikel meaning indigenous person
oyonïk	Kaqchikel soul-calling ceremony
patrón	landowner or boss
po't	traditional hand-woven blouse (güipil in Spanish)
principales	indigenous political and religious leaders
qawinaq	our people; used by Kaqchikel to describe indigenous people
quetzal	national bird and national currency
quintal	one hundred kilograms; Kaqchikel also use it as a unit of volume
rajawal	spirit of the land
regidor	alderman
reglamento de jornaleros	regulation of day laborers
sipaj	to give, given (*sipanik* is a gift)
tapel	tumpline
tierras osiosas	common lands
traje	indigenous dress
tuj	sweat bath
vara	measurement of length, about thirty-three inches
vialidad	highway engineering/road building
la violencia	the thirty-six-year civil war
wuj	book, paper, or work card
Xela	Quetzaltenango
xerka	knee-length cloth worn in front of pants, part of traditional dress for Kaqchikel men

Timeline of Guatemalan Presidents
from 1831

Mariano Gálvez	1831–38
Interim liberal government	1838–39
Mariano Rivera Paz	1839–44
José Rafael Carrera	1844–48
Col. Mariano Paredes	1848–51
José Rafael Carrera	1851–65
Gen. Vicente Cerna	1865–71
Gen. Miguel García Granados	1871–72
Gen. Justo Rufino Barrios	1873–85
Gen. José Maria Orantes	1882–83
Gen. Alejandro M. Sinibaldi	1885
Gen. Manuel Lisandro Barillas	1885–92
Gen. José María Reyna Barrios	1892–98
Manuel Estrada Cabrera	1898–1920
Carlos Herrera	1920–21
Gen. José María Orellana	1921–26
Gen. Lázaro Chacón	1926–30
Baudillo Palma	1930
Gen. Manuel Orellana	1930–31
José María Reina Andrade	1931
Gen. Jorge Ubico	1931–44
Gen. Federico Ponce Vaides	1944
Three-man junta (Arbenz, Arana, Toriello)	1944–45
Dr. Juan José Arévalo Bermejo	1945–51
Col. Jacobo Arbenz Guzmán	1951–54
Col. Carlos Castillo Armas	1954–57
Military junta (Mendoza, Gonzalez, Flores)	1957–58
Gen. Miguel Ydigoras Fuentes	1958–63
Col. Enrique Peralta Azurdia	1963–66
Julio César Méndez Montenegro	1966–70
Col. Carlos Arana Osorio	1970–74

Gen. Kjell Eugenio Laugerud García	1974–78
Gen. Fernando Romeo Lucas García	1978–82
Gen. José Efraín Ríos Montt	1982–83
Gen. Oscar Humberto Mejía Victores	1983–86
Marco Vinicio Cerezo Arévalo	1986–91
Jorge Serrano Elías	1991–93
Ramiro de Leon Carpio	1993–96
Alvaro Arzú	1996–2000
Alfonso Antonio Portillo Cabrera	2000–

Notes

Methodology

1. Champagne, "American Indian Studies Is for Everyone," in *Natives and Academics, Researching and Writing about American Indians,* ed. Devon A. Mihesuah (Lincoln: University of Nebraska Press, 1998), 182

2. Oxlajuj Kan, 3/8/98, 9/12/98, Comalapa.

3. During an interview with a man in Rosario Canajal, San Martín Jilotepeque, Oxlajuj Kan told me he had come a month or so earlier with another North American researcher but had been unsuccessful. The man refused to grant the researcher an interview because the researcher did not really speak Kaqchikel; he spoke mostly Spanish with a few Kaqchikel words interspersed (12/10/97, Rosario Canajal, San Martín Jilotepeque).

4. Petrich, *Memoria de Mi Pueblo Santa Catarina Palopó* (Guatemala: IRIPAZ Publicaciones, 1992), 1–2.

5. Maxwell, "Three Tales—Two and a Half Linguistic Systems," paper presented at the American Anthropological Association Conference, Philadelphia, 1986.

6. Menchú, *Crossing Borders* (London: Verso, 1998), 207–8. The reader should be aware of the differences between Menchú and the majority of my sources. As a K'ichee' speaker, Menchú's linguistic heritage is distinct from that of Kaqchikel informants, and her political objectives differentiate her and most of my Kaqchikel collaborators. I refer to her reflections nonetheless to compare them with Kaqchikel perspectives.

7. I also performed a number of interviews with Kaqchikel people residing in the United States (1995, 1996, 1999, 2000).

8. Another important distinction among Kaqchikel informants is religious preference. Catholics and Protestants do not necessarily have the same worldviews or historical perspectives. For an in-depth analysis of the effects of Protestantism in Guatemala see Virginia Garrard-Burnett, *Protestantism in Guatemala: Living in the New Jerusalem* (Austin: University of Texas Press, 1998). For further background to the Protestant evangelical movement in Guatemala see Virgilio Zapata Arceyuz, *Historia de la iglesia evangelica en Guatemala* (Guatemala City: Genesis Publicidad, 1982).

9. All census information is from 1994, the latest census taken. Instituto Nacional de Estadística X Censo Nacional de Población y V de habitación, published

by Instituto Nacional de Estadística (Departments of Chimaltenango, Sacatepéquez, and Sololá).

10. Jerson Alexis M. Gómez Salazar and Epitario Salazar Bal, "Municipalidad de San Juan Comalapa, Departamento de Chimaltenango," 2.

11. During my research the government was paving the road and was scheduled to finish in October 1998. Comalapa was experiencing the effects of this change. As the work progressed more Ladino tourists from Guatemala City were arriving in Comalapa for day trips. By my return trip in June 1999, the road was completed and transportation to Comalapa was expedient.

12. "Monografia del municipio de Tecpán, Guatemala, Departamento de Chimaltenango," 1.

13. Pablo Sut Cristal, "Monografia de San José Poaquil" (typescript, n.d.), 2.

14. Francisco Rodríguez Rouaret, *Diccionario Municipal de Guatemala* (Guatemala: Instituto de Estudios y Capacitación Cívica, 1996), 166, 172–73.

15. Few Kaqchikel men continue to wear traditional clothing. In the department of Chimaltenango, the population of Kaqchikel men who wear traditional clothing consists mainly of those over the age of sixty. However, around Lake Atitlán, the tradition of wearing indigenous clothing remains more strongly embedded in the communities.

16. Hendrickson, *Weaving Identities: Construction of Dress and Self in a Highland Guatemalan Town* (Austin: University of Texas Press, 1995), 136, 140.

17. The network sampling method (arranging and scheduling interviews through personal contacts) and the importance of interviewee anonymity are discussed in detail in Lesley Milroy, *Observing and Analysing Natural Language: A Critical Account of Sociolinguistic Method* (Oxford: Basil Blackwell, 1987). Also see H. Russel Bernard, *Research Methods in Anthropology: Qualitative and Quantitative Approaches* (London: Altamira, 1994). Additionally, Dennis Tedlock offers insight into recording, interpreting, and analyzing oral histories in his *Spoken Word and the Work of Interpretation* (Philadelphia: University of Pennsylvania Press, 1983).

18. *Kaxlan* is the word used to describe anything or any person foreign to the Kaqchikel community. Kaqchikel use the term *mo's* to describe Ladinos, people of Guatemala who are not Maya. *Mo's* is often a derogatory term. On occasion, when people learned that I spoke Kaqchikel they generously referred to me as *qawinäq*, which means "our people."

19. The perception of Spaniards and/or Ladinos as dangerous to Maya has been going on for more than five hundred years—since the Spanish arrival—but the pace of killing and destruction increased when the military assumed control of the government after the overthrow of Jacobo Arbenz in 1954. Many people refer to that period, beginning around 1960, as the thirty-six-year civil war, which ostensibly ended with the Peace Accords of December 1996.

20. Vansina, *Oral Tradition as History* (Madison: University of Wisconsin Press, 1985), 61–62. Linda Shopes also recognizes the rewards of group interviews, especially in family settings; see Shopes, "Using Oral History for a Family History Project," in *Oral History: An Interdisciplinary Anthology,* ed. David K. Dunaway and Willa K.

Baum (London: Altamira, 1996), 237–38. One drawback to the nature of group interviews is that it prevents more timid people from providing contradictory yet valid viewpoints. At times, the dominant personality of one or more members of the group may determine the historical presentation. To combat this shortcoming, I tried to return after a group interview to speak to people individually.

21. Pachitur school students, 9/23/97, Pachitur, Comalapa.

22. Oxlajuj Kan, Comalapa; Jun Tojil, Barahona; Waqi' Kej, Tecpán; Ix'ey, Aguas Calientes.

23. The term in Kaqchikel is *rumi'al tinamït,* which literally translated is daughter of the town.

24. Kaqchikel Cholchi' is a linguistic research organization that represents the KLC and is elected from the KLC. Their main office is in Chimaltenango, but research teams work in most Kaqchikel-speaking areas.

25. Vansina, *Oral Tradition as History,* 93.

26. *K'utunik,* known in Spanish as a *pedida,* is the Kaqchikel tradition of a boy asking his girlfriend to marry him. The event spans the course of a few weeks, with three different trips to the girl's house. On the last trip, the boy brings a gift of large baskets of food and drink from his family; the visit ends with a large meal and celebration at the home of the girl's family.

27. *Oyonik* is the Kaqchikel soul-calling ceremony. It is an important aspect of their psychophysiological approach to health.

28. Iximnik'te', 11/24/97, Tecpán.

29. Wo'o' Imox, 5/23/98, Comalapa.

30. For analysis and methodological approaches concerning the lack of dates or chronological presentation see Vansina, *Oral Tradition as History,* 173–201; David Henige, *Chronology of Oral Tradition: Quest for a Chimera* (Oxford: Clarendon, 1974); David Henige, *Oral Historiography* (London: Longman, 1982), 96–105; Satish Saberwal, "The Oral Tradition, Periodization, and Political Systems: Some East African Comparisons," *Canadian Journal of African Studies* 1 (1967): 159–62; and Alex Haley, "Black History, Oral History, and Genealogy," in *Oral History: An Interdisciplinary Anthology,* ed. David K. Dunaway and Willa K. Baum (London: Altamira, 1996), 270–71, 275.

31. For a discussion of oral history fieldwork techniques from different scholars see *In Pursuit of History,* ed. Jan Vansina and Carolyn Keyes Adenaike (Portsmouth, N.H.; Heinemann, 1996).

32. Hymes, "Language, Memory, and Selective Performance: *Cultee's 'Salmon's Myth' as Twice Told to Boas," Journal of American Folklore* 98, no. 390 (1985): 392.

33. Vansina, *Oral Tradition as History,* 161.

34. Ibid., 172.

35. Ibid., 31–32.

36. For a description and analysis of the *Anales de los Kaqchikeles* see Robert M. Hill, *Colonial Cakchiquels: Highland Maya Adaptations to Spanish Rule 1600–1700* (New York: Harcourt Brace Jovanovich, 1992), 129–31 and Kay Warren, *Indigenous Movements and Their Critics: Pan-Maya Activism in Guatemala* (Princeton: Princeton

University Press, 1988), 148–60. Guatemalan anthropologist Adrián Recinos translated the *Anales de los Kaqchikeles* into Spanish and English; see Recinos, *Memorial de Sololá, Anales de los Cakchiqueles* (México, D.F.: Fondo de Cultura Económica, 1950), and Recinos and Delia Goetz, *The Annals of the Cakchiqueles* (Norman: University of Oklahoma Press, 1953). Maxwell and Hill are currently working on a project with Kaqchikel speakers to transcribe the *Anales* into modern Kaqchikel and then translate it into Spanish and English; see Judith Maxwell and Robert M. Hill, *Kaqchikel Chronicles* (New Orleans: MesoAmerican Research Institute, forthcoming).

37. For examples and discussion of Kaqchikel colonial documents see Robert M. Hill's *The Pirir Papers and Other Colonial Period Cakchiquel-Maya Testamentos* (Vanderbilt University Publications in Anthropology, no. 37. Nashville: Vanderbilt University, 1989); "Land, Family, and Community in Highland Guatemala: Seventeenth-Century Cakchiquel Maya Testaments," in *Dead Giveaways: Indigenous Testaments of Colonial Mesoamerica and the Andes,* ed. Susan Kellogg and Matthew Restall (Salt Lake City: University of Utah Press, 1998), 163–79; and *Colonial Cakchiquels.*

38. September 15 is National (Ladino) Independence Day in Guatemala. *Rutzijol* generally runs articles around this time about how Ladino historians had written the movement's important indigenous actors out of the history. Furthermore, they assert that the Maya are not yet independent; see *Rutzijol,* September and October issues 1993–98.

39. Esquit Choy and Isabel Rodas, *Élite ladina-vanguardia indígena de la intolerancia a la violencia, Patzicía 1944* (Guatemala: Caudal, S.A., 1997). Esquit Choy's other works include *Yiqalil q'anej kunimaaj tziij niman tzij: el respeto a la palabra* (Guatemala: Centro de estudios de la cultura maya, 1995), with Carlos Ochoa García; "Relaciones de poder en Patzicía, 1871–1944," *Estudios Interetnicos: Revista del Instituto de Estudios Interetnicos* 4, no. 5 (1996): 55–75; "Impacto del movimiento cafetalero en la vida cotidiana del municipio de Patzicía a finales del siglo XX"; and "Proyecto Político Maya y Reconstructora de la historia."

40. See Warren, *Indigenous Movements and Their Critics* and *Maya Cultural Activism in Guatemala,* ed. Edward F. Fischer and R. McKenna Brown (Austin: University of Texas Press, 1996).

41. *Memoria de la Secretaría de Gobernación y Justicia* is also known as the *Jefes Políticos.*

42. Asturias de Barrios, "Mano de Mujer, Mano de Hombre: Produción artesanal textil en Comalapa Guatemala" (Ph.D. diss., State University of New York, Albany, 1994), 204.

43. For the most part, I have used names that derive from the Mayan calendar. However, there are a few exceptions (e.g., Iximnik'te, Ixsu'm, Ixya', Ka'i' Tojil, K'ayb'il B'alam), mostly in the case of women. Female names can be recognized by the "Ix" prefix to their one-word names. In contrast, male names have two words. Any correlation with informants and their real Kaqchikel names is coincidental. For Kaqchikel, using their Kaqchikel names is an important cultural and historic marker. Only since the 1989 Guatemalan constitution have Maya been allowed to register under their Mayan names. Even after this legal victory, Kaqchikel had to fight ad-

ministrative discrimination. State employees denied them the right to register under their Mayan names until they made copies of the aforementioned constitution to prove their rights (as recounted by Ka'i' Iq', 6/28/98, Comalapa).

Introduction

The Kaqchikel chapter titles are not literal translations of the English but rather pragmatic equivalencies.

1. I lived with a Kaqchikel family in Comalapa. They kindly and generously accepted me as part of their family and treated me, and referred to me, as their son and brother. Consequently, Jun Ajpu' was *nuchaq'* (my younger brother). All Mayan words, such as K'ichee' and Kaqchikel, are presented in the modern, standardized spelling as recognized by the Guatemalan Academy of Mayan Languages (AMLG). However, when I quote other works the spelling will remain as the word appears in the text.

2. A Ladino is a nonindigenous Guatemalan, generally of Spanish descent. In Guatemala ethnic identity can change from one generation to the next or even within a generation. Generally, a Ladino is a person who does not display indigenous cultural traits and does not self-identify as Maya. A Maya can stop speaking his or her native language, wear Western clothing, associate with other Ladinos, and identify himself or herself as Ladino. Some Maya moved to Guatemala City and made this ethnic transition during the civil war to avoid persecution. For a concise etymology of the word "Ladino" in Guatemala see Greg Grandin, *The Blood of Guatemala: A History of Race and Nation* (Durham: Duke University Press, 2000), 83–85.

3. Jun Ajpu', 10/24/97, Comalapa.

4. REMHI (Recovery of Historical Memory Project), *Guatemala, Never Again!: The Official Report of the Human Rights Office, Archdiocese of Guatemala* (Maryknoll, N.Y.: Orbis Books, 1999); United Nations Human Rights Report (on-line), *Guatemala: Memoria del Silencio* (Comisión para el Esclaracimiento Histórico [CEH], Http://hrdata.aaas.org/ceh/mds/spanish, 1999); *CERIGUA,* Nov. 19, 1999; "Segunda Vuelta: Elecciones 1999," *Prensa Libre,* Dec. 31, 1999; Eloy O. Aguilar, "Opposition Figure Wins in Guatemala," *Boston Globe,* Nov. 9, 1999, A4; "Guatemala: Rightist Wins Election," *New York Times,* Dec. 28, 1999, A6; "Spirits High and Turnout Low as Guatemalans Cast Ballots," *New York Times,* Dec. 27, 1999, A9. For an excellent analysis of the rejection of indigenous rights in the May 16, 1999, popular referendum see Susanne Jonas, *Of Centaurs and Doves: Guatemala's Peace Process* (Boulder, Co.: Westview, 2000), 189–213.

5. This motto was written on Maya Decenio para el Pueblo Indígena posters in Guatemala (author's observation).

6. Anderson, *Imagined Communities* (London: Verso, 1991), 205.

7. Solares, *Derechos humanos desde la perspectiva indígena en Guatemala* (Guatemala: FLACSO, 1995), 61–65.

8. Roque Dalton, *Miguel Marmol* (Willimantic, Conn.: Curbstone, 1982), 463.

Unfortunately, Marmol does not elaborate on what ways these different interests and ways of thinking manifested themselves.

9. For examples of rabbit and coyote stories and other Mayan trickster tales see James D. Sexton, ed., *Mayan Folktales: Folklore from Lake Atitlán, Guatemala* (New York: Anchor Books, Doubleday, 1992); Fernando Peñalosa, ed., *Tales and Legends of the Q'anob'al Maya* (Rancho Palos Verdes, Calif.: Yax Te', 1995); and *Sahil ch'oolej sa'li hoonal (momentos alegres) leyendas Q'echi'es de El Estor, Izabal* (Rancho Palos Verdes, Calif.: Yax Te', 1995).

10. For an analysis and examples of weapons of the weak see James C. Scott, *Weapons of the Weak: Everyday Forms of Resistance* (New Haven: Yale University Press), 1985.

11. Warren, *Indigenous Movements and Their Critics,* 65–66.

12. Dary, *Relatos de los Antiguos: Estudios de la tradición oral de Comalapa, Chimaltenango* (Guatemala: Universidad de San Carlos de Guatemala, 1992). 7.

13. Vansina, *Oral Tradition as History,* 93.

14. Cohen, *Womunafu's Bunafu: A Study of Authority in a Nineteenth Century African Community* (Princeton: Princeton University Press, 1977), 8–9.

15. Price, *First Time: The Historical Vision of an Afro-American People* (Baltimore: Johns Hopkins University Press, 1983), 12.

16. Hendrickson, *Weaving Identities,* 140.

17. B'alam, "Reflexión sobre la historia y la actualidad," *Rutzijol: Periódico Maya Independiente, por la autogestión del Pueblo Maya,* Oct. 16–31, 1993, 5.

18. Batres Jáuregui, *Los Indios, su historia y su civilización* (Guatemala: La Unión, 1894), iii–xii, 173–96; Villacorta Calderón, *Curso de Geografía de la América Central para uso de los Institutos y Escuelas Normales* (Guatemala: Tipografía Sánchez y de Guise, 1928), 73–74; Villacorta Calderón, *Prehistoria e historia antigua de Guatemala* (Guatemala: Impreso en la Tipografía Nacional, 1938), 7–8; Asturias, *El problema social del indio y otros textos* (Paris: Centre de recherches de l'institut d'etudes hispaniques, 1971), 72, 101–13. For analysis of the twentieth-century Ladino historiography on Guatemala's indigenous population see David Carey, Jr., "*Indigenísmo* and Guatemalan History in the Twentieth Century," *Revista Interamericana de Bibliografía* 48, no. 2 (1998): 379–408.

19. Carlsen, *The War for the Heart and Soul of a Highland Maya Town* (Austin: University of Texas Press, 1997), 67.

20. Gerardo Gordillo Barrios, *Guatemala historia gráfica* (Guatemala City: Editorial Piedra Sanata, 1987), 86, 167.

21. Ester S. Castañeda, *Estudios Sociales (primer curso)* (Guatemala City: Tallers Imprel, 1962), 141–42.

22. Colop, "The Discourse of Concealment and 1992," in *Maya Cultural Activism in Guatemala,* ed. Edward Fischer and R. McKenna Brown, 107–13 (Austin: University of Texas Press, 1996), 109.

23. Cojtí Cuxil, *Políticas para la reivindicación de los Mayas de hoy: (fundamento de los derechos específicos del pueblo maya)* (Guatemala City: Editorial CHOLSAMAJ, SPEM, 1994). 60.

24. Ibid., 65.

25. Warren, "Transforming Memories and Histories: The Meaning of Ethnic Resurgence for Mayan Indians," in *Americas: New Interpretive Essays,* ed. Alfred Stephan (New York: Oxford University Press, 1992), 211–12.

26. See J. Daniel Contreras R., *Una rebelión indígena en el partido de Totonicapán en 1820: El indio y la independencia* (Guatemala: Imprenta Universitaria, 1951) for an example from the independence period. See Ricardo Falla's works, including *Masacres en la selva: Ixcán, Guatemala (1975–82)* (Guatemala City: Editorial Universitaria de Guatemala, 1992), and Víctor Montejo, *Testimony: Death of a Guatemalan Village,* ed. Víctor Perera (Willimantic, Conn.: Curbstone, 1987) for examples of the civil war period.

27. For an insightful analysis of these writings see Warren, *Indigenous Movements and Their Critics,* 132–47.

28. Carmack, *Rebels of Highland Guatemala: the Quiché-Mayas of Momostenango* (Norman: University of Oklahoma Press, 1995), xv; Carlsen, *War for the Heart and Soul,* 8.

29. Wolf, *Europe and the People without History* (Berkeley: University of California Press, 1982); Smith, "Local History in Global Context: Social and Economic Transitions in Western Guatemala," *Comparative Studies of Society and History* 17 (1984): 193–228.

30. Kay Warren, *The Symbolism of Subordination: Indian Identity in a Guatemalan Town* (Austin: University of Texas Press, 1978).

31. Nelson, *Finger in the Wound: Body Politics in Quincentennial Guatemala* (Berkeley: University of California Press, 1999), 40.

32. Ibid., 349–50, 353–55.

33. Grandin, *The Blood of Guatemala,* 15.

34. Ibid., 12, 14.

35. Farris, *Mayan Society under Colonial Rule* (Princeton: Princeton University Press, 1984), 8; Carlsen, *War for the Heart and Soul,* 8, 49.

36. Hill and Monaghan, *Continuities in Highland Maya Social Organization: Ethnohistory in Sacapulas, Guatemala* (Philadelphia: University of Pennsylvania Press, 1987).

37. Ortner, "Theory in Anthropology since the Sixties," *Comparative Studies of Society and History* 26 (1984): 158.

38. Ortner, "Resistance and the Problem of Ethnographic Refusal," *Comparative Studies in Society and History* 137 (1995): 173–93; Grandin, *The Blood of Guatemala.*

39. Carrasco, "Religions of Mesoamerica: Cosmovision and Ceremonial Centers," in *Religious Traditions of the World: A Journey through Africa, Mesoamerica, North America, Judaism, Christianity, Islam, Hinduism, Buddhism, China, and Japan,* ed. H. Byron Earhart (New York: Harper and Row, 1993), 114, 215–17, 239–41.

40. Ka'i No'j, Tecpán, 6/4/00

41. Lunn, *Memoirs of a Maelstrom: A Senegalese Oral History of the First World War* (Portsmouth, N.H.: Heinemann, 1999), 4.

42. In his translation of the *Popol Wuj* Dennis Tedlock also recognizes this distinction for K'ichee' people. He notes, "What the authors propose to write down is what Quichés call the *Ojer Tzij,* the 'Ancient Word' or 'Prior Word,' which has prece-

dence over 'the preaching of God' " (Dennis Tedlock, *Popol Vuh: The Mayan Book of the Dawn of Life* [New York: Simon and Schuster, 1996], 30).

43. Vansina, *Oral Tradition as History,* 198.

44. Ibid.

45. Axtell, "Ethnohistory: An Historian's View," in *The European and the Indian: Essays in the Ethnohistory of Colonial North America* (Oxford: Oxford University Press, 1981), 15.

46. The most accurate presentation, of course, would include the historical perceptions of all Mayan-language groups, Garífunas, and Xinkas, in addition to Ladino perspectives.

47. Vansina, *Oral Tradition as History,* 199.

48. Bricker, *The Indian Christ, the Indian King: The Historical Substrate of Maya Myth and Ritual* (Austin: University of Texas Press, 1981), 5.

49. Ibid., 154.

50. Ibid., 8.

51. For studies on the Maya interpretation of time see Barbara Tedlock, *Time and the Highland Maya* (Albuquerque: University of New Mexico Press, 1992); Sol Tax, "April Is This Afternoon: Correspondence of Robert Redfield and Sol Tax, 1933–44," *Collection of Manuscripts on Cultural Anthropology Series* 63:330 (Microfilm, University of Chicago Library, 1980); Munro Edmonson, *The Ancient Future of the Itza: The Book of Chilam Balam of Tizimin* (Austin: University of Texas Press, 1982).

52. Bricker, *The Indian Christ,* 7.

53. Vansina, *Oral Tradition as History,* 124.

54. Warren, "Transforming Memories and Histories," 210–11.

55. Champagne, "American Indian Studies Is for Everyone," 183.

56. Jan Vansina, *Living with Africa* (Madison: University of Wisconsin Press, 1994), 221.

57. The next step in writing this book for a Kaqchikel, Mayan, Guatemalan, and Latin American public is to translate it into Kaqchikel and Spanish. A sixth-grade-level Kaqchikel textbook based on Kaqchikel oral histories that I collected has been distributed on a limited basis in the Kaqchikel region (see Methodology).

Chapter 1

1. Oxi' Q'anil, 6/26/99, Comalapa.

2. Menchú, *Crossing Borders,* 146, 151–52.

3. Cavender Wilson, "Educating America: The Historian's Responsibility to Native Americans and the Public," *Perspectives* 38, no. 5 (2000): 46–47.

4. Watanabe, "From Saints to Shibboleths: Image, Structure, and Identity in Maya Religious Syncretism," *American Ethnologist* 17, no. 1 (1990): 134. Barbara Tedlock touches upon the importance of place among the Maya in her book *Time and the Highland Maya.*

5. Kay Warren, *The Violence Within: Cultural and Political Opposition in Divided Nations* (Boulder: Westview, 1993), 26. For additional descriptions of indige-

nous culture and customs in Guatemala see Warren, *Symbolism of Subordination* and Hendrickson, *Weaving Identities*.

6. Hill and Monaghan, *Continuities in Highland Maya Social Organization*. Also see Robert M. Hill, "Chinamit and Molab: Late Postclassic Highland Maya Precursors of Closed Corporate Community," *Estudios de Cultura Maya* 15 (1984): 301.

7. Smith, *Indian Class and Class Consciousness in Prerevolutionary Guatemala* (Washington, D.C.: Latin American Program, Wilson Center, 1984), 25.

8. Kaqchikel use the term *qawinäq* (our people) to identify members of their own language group, other Mayan speakers, and indigenous people in other nations. They do not limit their indigenous identity to their community. Even people who seldom or never left their respective communities had a sense that they were connected to other aboriginal groups in and out of Guatemala through their identification as indigenous people. Kaqchikel identity will be further explored in chapter 9.

9. Smith, "Introduction: Social Relations in Guatemala over Time and Space," in *Guatemalan Indians and the State 1540–1988*, ed. Carol Smith (Austin: University of Texas Press, 1990), 18. For additional discussion of the nature of Maya and their communities and plight see Smith, ed., *Guatemalan Indians and the State 1540–1988*.

10. For a recent summary of the population estimates in precontact Guatemala see William M. Denevan, "Native American Populations in 1492: Recent Research and a Revised Hemispheric Estimate," in *The Native Population of the Americas in 1492*, ed. William M. Denevan (Madison: University of Wisconsin Press, 1992), xxii–xxiii.

11. Jorge F. Guillemín, *Iximche'* (Guatemala: Tipografía Nacional, 1965), 25; Jorge F. Guillemín, "The Ancient Cakchiquel Capital of Iximche'," *Expedition: Bulletin of the University Museum of University of Pennsylvania* 9, no. 2 (1967): 25; Adrián Recinos, *Cronicas Indígenas de Guatemala* (Guatemala: Editorial Universitaria, 1957), 137, 153; Recinos, *Memorial de Sololá*, 96–121; Francis Polo Sifontes, *Los Cakchiqueles en la conquista de Guatemala* (Guatemala: Editorial José de Pineda Ibarra, 1980), 27–34; Robert Wauchope, "Las edades de Utatlán e Iximche'," *Revista de Antropología e Historia de Guatemala* 1, no. 1 (1949): 21; Robert Carmack, *The Quiché Mayas of Utatlán: The Evolution of a Highland Guatemala Kingdom* (Norman: University of Oklahoma Press, 1981), 136–37; Oakah L. Jones, *Guatemala in the Spanish Colonial Period* (Norman: University of Oklahoma Press, 1994), 15–16.

12. Recinos, *Memorial de Sololá*, 124, 128; José Antonio Villacorta Calderón, "Conquista de los Sacatepéquez," *Anales de la Sociedad de Geografía e Historia* 1, no. 3 (1927): 184; Fray Francisco Vásquez, *Crónica de la Provincia del Santísimo Nombre de Jesús de Guatemala* (Guatemala: Tipografía Nacional, 1937), 1: 47; Jorge F. Guillemín, "Un entierro señorial en Iximche'," *Anales de la Sociedad de Geografía e Historia* 34 (1961): 89–105 (here p. 96); Guillemín, "Ancient Cackchiquel Capital of Iximche'," 24–25; Polo Sifontes, *Los Cakchiqueles en la conquista*, 37; José Milla y Vidaurre, *Historia de la América Central* (Guatemala: Tipografía Nacional, 1937), 260; Polo Sifontes, *Los Cakchiqueles en la conquista*, 74; Jones, *Guatemala in the Spanish Colonial Period*, 20–21.

13. Villacorta Calderón, "Conquista de los Sacatepéquez," 182–87.

14. Christopher Lutz, "Population History of the Parish of San Miguel Dueñas, Guatemala, 1530–1770," in *The Historical Demography of Highland Guatemala*, ed. Robert M. Carmack, John Early, and Christopher Lutz, Institute for Mesoamerican Studies, no. 6 (Albany: State University of New York, 1982), 123; Jones, *Guatemala in the Spanish Colonial Period*, 93–106.

15. Sheldon Annis, *God and Production in a Guatemalan Town* (Austin: University of Texas Press, 1987), 145–46n2.

16. Christopher Lutz, *Historia sociodemográfica de Santiago de Guatemala 1541–1773*, monograph series no. 2 (La Antigua, Guatemala: CIRMA, 1984), 122–27. See William Sherman, *Forced Native Labor in Sixteenth-Century Central America* (Lincoln: University of Nebraska Press, 1979), 20–82, for a detailed discussion of Spanish forced labor systems.

17. Domingo Juarros, *Compendio de la Historia del Reino de Guatemala 1500–1800* (Guatemala: Editorial Piedra Santa, 1981), 358–65; Francisco de Paula García Peláez, *Memorias para la Historia del Antiguo Reino de Guatemala* (Guatemala: Tipografía Nacional, 1968), 1: 66; Polo Sifontes, *Los Cakchiqueles en la conquista*, 86; Recinos, *Memorial de Sololá*, 128–31; Vásquez, *Crónica de la Provincia*, 33–34.

18. Polo Sifontes, *Los Cakchiqueles en la conquista*, 86–87, Recinos, *Memorial de Sololá*, 132–38; Jones, *Guatemala in the Spanish Colonial Period*, 28–29.

19. Jun Tzinik'an, 5/26/98, Tecpán; Ka'i' Aq'ab'al, 6/7/98, Tecpán; B'eleje' Kawoq, 6/9/98, Tecpán; Wuqu' Kan, 6/5/98, Tecpán; Ka'i' Tz'i', 5/26/98, Tecpán.

20. Jun Aj and Ix'ik', 6/6/98, Tecpán.

21. Junlajuj Iq', 5/31/98, Tecpán.

22. Ixsu'm, 6/1/98, Tecpán.

23. B'eleje' Iq', 6/4/98, Tecpán.

24. Oxi' Tz'i', 5/29/98, Tecpán; Oxi' K'at, 6/5/98, Tecpán; Jun Aj and Ix'ik', 6/6/98, Tecpán; Junlajuj Iq', 5/31/98. Some oral accounts attribute the destruction of Antigua to the eruption of Junajpu' (the volcano *Agua*) (Wo'o' Kame, 5/29/98, Tecpán).

25. "Monografía del Municipio de Tecpán," 1. The exact location of the first Spanish capital remains unknown.

26. Ibid.

27. The monograph recognizes that 90 percent of the rural population and 65 percent of the urban population is indigenous (ibid).

28. Many Maya continue to refer to Quetzaltenango by its shortened Mayan name: Xela (derived from Xelaju'). According to Adrián Inés Chávez, Xelajub' (*sic*) is short for the original Xe Lajuj No'j; see Chávez, *K'iche' Tz'ib': escritura K'iche' y otros temas* (Guatemala: Libreria, ca. 1991). There are a number of alternate spellings of Tekun Uman; I have chosen the one used by the Academy of Maya Languages of Guatemala (ALMG). In the K'iche' land document "Títulos de la casa Ixquin-Nehaib señora del territorio de Otzoya," the name is spelled Tecún-Tecum and later simply Tecum (Recinos, *Crónicas indígenas de Guatemala*, 86). Menchú spells the name Tucum Umán in *Crossing Borders*, 18. Other spellings include Tecum Umam (see Bricker, *The Indian Christ*, 39). I will refer to Tekun Uman as Tekun throughout this book.

29. B'eleje' Iq', 6/4/98, Tecpán; Ix'aj, 11/26/97, Tecpán; Ka'i' Tz'i', 5/26/98, Tecpán; Junlajuj Iq', 5/31/98, Tecpán; Wuqu' Kan, 6/5/98, Tecpán.

30. Menchú, *Crossing Borders,* 18.

31. Ladinos manipulate the symbol of Tekun by making him the defeated Mayan leader. He is portrayed in statues, the currency, and in the national bird (the latter of which are both called *quetzal*) as a symbol of Guatemala's indigenous and vanquished past. They do not use the symbol of other Mayan leaders such as Kaji' Imox and Kab'lajuj Tijox; nor do they make use of images of current Mayan leaders such as Adrián Chávez, Waqi' Q'anil, Gaspar Pedro González, or Rigoberta Menchú. The symbol of Tekun Uman is as important to Ladinos as to Maya of Guatemala but for diametrically opposed reasons.

32. Recinos, *Memorial de Sololá.*

33. Kaji' Q'anil, 11/19/97, Tecpán. *Naturales* is a self-identifying indigenous term.

34. Ka'i' Kan, 11/24/97, Chuwatz'unuj, Tecpán; Wuqu' Aq'ab'al, 11/25/97, Tecpán; Oxi' Tz'i', 5/29/98, Tecpán; Wuqu' Kej, 5/30/98, Tecpán.

35. Francisco Antonio de Fuentes y Guzmán, *Recordación Florida: Discurso Historial y Demostración natural, material, militar y política del Reino de Guatemala,* 1690, vol. 1 (Guatemala: Tipografía Nacional, 1932–33).

36. Jun Tzinik'an, 5/26/98, Tecpán.

37. Ixtzinik'an, 6/2/98, Tecpán.

38. Ka'i' B'atz', 11/26/97, Tecpán; Kab'lajuj Iq', 5/31/98, Tecpán; Ix'ajmaq, 6/2/98, Tecpán; Wo'o' Kame, 5/29/98, Tecpán; Wuqu' Kan, 6/5/98, Tecpán.

39. Ixmukane', 11/26/97, Tecpán.

40. Waqi' Imox, 5/3/98, Tecpán; Oxi' Tz'i', 5/29/98, Tecpán; Junlajuj Iq', 5/31/98, Tecpán; Kab'lajuj Iq', 5/31/98, Tecpán.

41. García López, "Valiosa Historia," *Revista Tecpán Guatemala* (1997): 12. García López's brother, the acting municipal secretary of Tecpán, explained García López's use of both written and oral sources.

42. García López, "Historia de la ciudad de Tecpán Guatemala," *Revista Tecpán Guatemala* (1997): 14.

43. José Alejandro de Leon Pérez, ed. "Tecpán Guatemala," in *Memoria de labores, municipalidades de Chimaltenango* (Guatemala: Editora Educativa, 1984), 36–37.

44. Guillemín, "Ancient Cakchiquel Capital of Iximche'," 27.

45. Ibid., 33.

46. Junlajuj Iq', 5/31/98, Tecpán; Kab'lajuj Iq', 5/31/98, Tecpán; Ixtzinik'an, 6/2/98, Tecpán; B'eleje' Iq', 6/4/98, Tecpán; Jun Aj and Ix'ik', 6/6/98, Tecpán.

47. Wo'o' Kame, 5/29/98, Tecpán

48. Kaji' Aq'ab'al, 6/8/98, Tecpán.

49. Kaji' Iq', 11/18/97, Tecpán.

50. Wo'o' Kame, 5/29/98, Tecpán. People in Comalapa, Poaquil, Aguas Calientes, and Barahona also expressed this aspect of Tekun's downfall.

51. Adrián Recinos, "Títulos de la casa Ixquin-Nehaib, señora del territorio de Otzoya," in *Crónicas indígenas de Guatemala,* ed. Adrián Recinos (Guatemala City: Editorial Universitaria, 1957), 86–91. For an in-depth analysis of this and other Mayan documents pertaining to the Spanish invasion see Bricker, *The Indian Christ.*

52. Recinos, *Memorial de Sololá.*

53. For a critique of this history from the perspective of Mayan public intellectuals see Warren, *Indigenous Movements and Their Critics,* 155.

54. Ka'i' Aq'ab'al, 6/7/98, Tecpán.

55. Jun Aj and Ix'ik', 6/6/98, Tecpán.

56. Kaji' Iq', 11/18/97, Tecpán

57. Kab'lajuj Iq', 5/31/98, Tecpán; Ixtzinik'an, 6/2/98, Tecpán; Kaji' Aq'ab'al, 6/8/98, Tecpán; Oxi' Tz'i', 5/29/98, Tecpán; Ixmukane', 11/26/97, Tecpán.

58. "Monografía del Municipio de Tecpán," 1. No author is attributed to the monograph, but the secretary and mayor in the municipal office of Tecpán informed me that a Ladino wrote it.

59. A document produced by the Franciscan order in 1948 recounts a similar history of Tecpán, and credits the Spanish with the construction of "the grand temple" of the parochial church; see Rafael Ramirez Arroyo, "Tecpán," *Revista Franciscana* 1, no. 1–2 (1948).

60. Wo'o' Kame, 5/29/98, Tecpán.

61. Marshall N. Peterson, *The Highland Maya in Fact and Legend* (Lancaster, Calif.: Labyrinthos, 1999), 23–27; Hill, *Colonial Cakchiquels,* 115–16; Jesús María García Añoveros, *Población y estado sociorreligioso de la diócesis de Guatemala en el último tercio del siglo XVIII* (Guatemala City: Editorial Universitaria, Universidad de San Carlos de Guatemala, 1987), 31–32; Carlsen, *War for the Heart and Soul,* 51; Jones, *Guatemala in the Spanish Colonial Period,* 123.

62. Fernando Cervantes, *Devil in the New World: The Impact of Diabolism in New Spain* (New Haven: Yale University Press, 1994), 67–69; Farris, *Maya Society under Colonial Rule,* 318. It is important to note that Cervantes's and Farris's studies deal with Maya in Mexico, not Guatemala.

63. García Añoveros, *Población y estado sociorreligioso de la diócesis de Guatemala en el último tercio del siglo XVIII,* 57, 94.

64. Wo'o' Q'anil, 6/7/98, Tecpán.

65. de Leon Pérez, "Tecpán Guatemala," 36–37.

66. Guillemín, "Ancient Cakchiquel Capital of Iximche'," 27.

67. García López, "Historia de la ciudad de Tecpán Guatemala," 14.

68. Oxi' K'at, 6/5/98, Tecpán.

69. Kaji' Iq', 11/18/97, Tecpán; Ka'i' Tz'i', 5/26/98, Tecpán; Ka'i' Aq'ab'al, 6/7/98, Tecpán.

70. Wuqu' K'at, 4/5/98, Comalapa. Archaeological evidence shows that Maya possessed mirrors made of iron pyrite plates prior to the Spanish arrival. See David Freidel, Linda Schele, and Joy Parker, *Maya Cosmos: Three Thousand Years of the Shaman's Path* (New York: Quill William Morrow, 1993), 53, 140; Eric Thompson, *The Rise and Fall of Maya Civilization* (Norman: University of Oklahoma Press, 1975), 20, 52, 214, 253, 254; Michael Coe, *The Maya* (New York: Thames and Hudson, 1999), 83, 86. Nonetheless, oral traditions imply that Kaqchikel had not seen mirrors of the Spaniards' quality.

71. The italicized words are the Kaqchikel names for Comalapa. San Juan Comalapa is the Spanish name for the town. Kaqchikel use both Kaqchikel and Spanish town names depending on the nature of the conversation and the audience.

Subsequent subtitles in this chapter provide both the Kaqchikel and Spanish names for these towns.

72. Kaji' Kame (3/4/98, Comalapa) said it was called *Pa Chaj* because pine trees were plentiful. *Chaj* is the Kaqchikel word for pine trees.

73. Kab'lajuj Ajpu', 11/14/97, Comalapa; Kaji' Tz'i', 7/12/98, Comalapa; Junlajuj K'at, 7/9/98, Comalapa; Kaji' Kan, 8/16/98, Comalapa; Oxi' B'atz', 4/26/98, Comalapa.

74. Oral traditions assert that the bells in the cathedral today are the same ones Ladinos stole hundreds of years ago, but my inspection of the bells in the cathedral bell tower did not reveal clear evidence. Talleres Gómez, Guatemala, forged some bells; the dates range from 1622 to 1952 (reforged); Julio Vassaux of Maquinista de la Casa de Moneda, Guatemala, is credited with the production of one bell in 1871. Other bells have no written evidence on them. Unfortunately, Agustín Estrada Monroy's *Historia de la Catedral* does not refer to the bells.

75. Wuqu' K'at, 4/6/98, Comalapa; Waqxaqi' Kej, 5/24/98, Comalapa.

76. Oxi' Imox, 9/14/98, Comalapa.

77. Waqi' Q'anil, Wo'o' Tz'i', and Kaji' B'atz', 4/24/98, Simajulew, Comalapa. Clearly, Waqi' Q'anil and his compatriots wanted someone to excavate the site to support their oral traditions, but economic motivations also played into their interest in uncovering more about the mine: they mentioned that it could become a tourist site and that gold might remain buried in the ruins.

78. Hubert Howe Bancroft, *History of the Pacific States of North America,* vol. 2: *Central America, 1530–1800* (San Francisco: A. L. Bancroft, 1883), 79–80; Murdo J. MacLeod, *Spanish Central America: A Socioeconomic History, 1520–1700* (Berkeley: University of California Press, 1973), 110, 148; Jones, *Guatemala in the Spanish Colonial Period,* 22; Recinos, "Títulos de la casa Ixquin-Nehaib, señora del territorio de Otzoya," 86–91.

79. Waqi' Iq', 4/22/98, Comalapa.

80. Kab'lajuj K'at, 6/27/98, Comalapa.

81. B'eleje' Imox, 8/9/98, Comalapa; Oxi' Kan, 8/19/98, Comalapa; Ixkik', 6/21/98, Comalapa.

82. Oxi' Kej, 6/14/98, Comalapa.

83. I selected this version of the town founding out of quotes and accounts from Oxi' Imox, 2/11/98, Comalapa; Kaji' Kan, 9/6/98, Comalapa; Jun Kawoq, 5/1/98, Agua Caliente, Comalapa; Jun Tz'i', 7/12/98, Pamumus, Comalapa; Kab'lajuj Ajpu', 5/5/98, Comalapa.

84. Waqxaqi' Kej, 5/24/98, Comalapa; Wo'o' Imox, 5/23/98, Comalapa; Ix'aj, 2/9/98, Comalapa; Waqi' K'at, 8/21/98, Comalapa.

85. Recinos, *Memorial de Solola,* 131–33. In *Los Cakchiqueles en la conquista de Guatemala,* Polo Sifontes also refers to Chi Xot (Comalapa) as forming part of the extensive Kaqchikel reign (34).

86. José Alejandro de León Pérez, ed., *Memoria de Labores, Municipalidades Chimaltenango* (Guatemala: Editora Educativa, 1984), 78.

87. Francis Gall, *Diccionario Geográfico de Guatemala* (Guatemala: Instituto Geográfico Nacional, 1976), 1: 471, 4: 47.

88. Linda Asturias de Barrios, *Comalapa: el traje y su significado* (Guatemala:

Museo Ixchel del Traje Indígena de Guatemala, 1985), 59. Dary makes the same assertion in *Relatos de los antiguos,* 18.

89. *Historia del himno nacional* (Guatemala: Tipografía Nacional, 1997), 55.

90. Kaji' Kan, "Chixot y Desde 1541 Asta Hoy San Juan Comalapa" (typescript, ca. 1980), 1.

91. Gómez Sálazar and Sálazar Bal, "Municipalidad de San Juan Comalapa," 1.

92. Oxi' B'atz', 4/26/98, Comalapa; Kaji' Kan, 9/6/98, Comalapa; Wo'o' B'atz', Waqi' B'atz', and Oxlajuj Aq'ab'al, 7/9/98, Comalapa. I wish to note a few challenges in translating this passage. The Kaqchikel word for temple, or a precontact church, is *koxtun,* whereas *rachoch Ajaw* refers to a Catholic Church. Kaqchikel refer to a temple when the town was founded ca. 1400 but when speaking of the current location of Comalapa refer to the Catholic Church. *B'alam* is the Kaqchikel word for jaguar in precontact times, but today *b'alam* means tiger. The story of animals attacking Comalapa dates to before the Spanish arrival, so I have chosen jaguar instead of tiger.

93. "Documentos para la historia," *Rutzijol,* Oct. 16–31, 1995, 6. Unfortunately, the article does not cite its source for the February 7, 1526, massacre.

94. In general, weavers explain the red on the güipiles as representing the fire itself or Mayan bloodshed at the hands of the Spanish.

95. Ixtijax, 8/17/98, Comalapa. Many others recount this story of the burning of Comalapa (e.g., Oxi' Kej, 6/14/98, Comalapa), but they attribute it to a time well after the first Spanish contact.

96. Oxi' Iq', 12/2/98, Comalapa.

97. Ixkame, 8/17/98, Comalapa; Wuqu' Kawoq, 1/29/98, Comalapa; Waqi' Kame, 5/3/98, Pamumus, Comalapa; Wo'o' Kawoq, 3/3/98, Ko'ol Juyu, Comalapa.

98. Gómez Sálazar and Sálazar Bal, "Municipalidad de San Juan Comalapa," 1. In *Memoria de Labores* de León Pérez also cites Comalapa's "brave warriors who opposed Alvarado's army in a fierce battle" (78).

99. Miguel Angel Sotz O., "Mongrafia de Comalapa, Diagnostico Comunitario 1994," Proyecto 2439 Chuwi' Tinamït, San Juan Comalapa (typescript, n.d.), 4; "Centro de Salud Monografía," San Juan Comalapa Health Center (typescript, Dec. 1994), 3.

100. Kaji' Kan, "Chixot y Desde 1541 Asta Hoy San Juan Comalapa," 1. Kaji' Kan does not list his sources. Despite the title, he clearly states that he writes about Comalapa's history only up to 1870, not to the present.

101. Bricker notes in her study that Maya recall Alvarado most clearly. In fact, they credit him, not Hernan Cortés, with the conquest of Mexico; see *The Indian Christ,* 39.

102. Gómez Sálazar and Sálazar Bal, "Municipalidad de San Juan Comalapa," 1; "Monografía de San Juan Comalapa, Chimaltenango," Escuela Urbana Mixta, Canton 8, San Juan Comalapa Administration Building (typescript, 1997), 2–3.

103. Sotz O., "Mongrafia de Comalapa, Diagnostico Comunitario 1994," 5.

104. Kaji' Kan, "Chixot y Desde 1541 Asta Hoy San Juan Comalapa," 1.

105. Inocencio del Busto, "San Juan Comalapa," *Antropología e Historia de Guatemala* 13, no. 2 (1961): 27.

106. Gall, *Diccionario Geografico de Guatemala,* 1: 471.

107. Ministerio de Educación, "Mapa Escolar, March 1996, San José Poaquil, Chimaltenango," Direccíon Técnica Regional Central V, Supervisión Educativa No. 95-16. San José Poaquil Municipal Building (typescript, ca. 1996), A1.

108. Justo Rufino Barrios was president of Guatemala from 1872 to 1885.

109. The Kaqchikel word B'eleje' Ey used was *totob'anik* and his description was similar to a medieval stretching rack. In other accounts, the first building constructed by the people was a jail where those who did not contribute would be put (B'eleje' Kej, 3/19/98, Poaquil; Wuqu' Q'anil, 3/21/98, Poaquil). The Poaquil health clinic document also refers to the construction of a prison: "Three men built a jail so that those who did not work had to be incarcerated" ("Diagnóstico de Salud, Distrito San José Poaquil, Chimaltenango," San José Poaquil Health Center [typescript, 1980], 1).

110. B'eleje' Ey, 11/15/97, 11/23/97, Poaquil.

111. Ixkan, 3/29/98, Poaquil; Wuqu' Q'anil, 3/21/98, Poaquil; Junlajuj Kawoq, 11/17/97, Poaquil.

112. "Monografía de San José Poaquil," San José Poaquil (typescript, n.d.), 1. The author of the monograph is not listed, but municipal employees claim the author is Kaqchikel.

113. APAOP (Asociación de Pequeños Agricultores Orgánicos Poaquileños), "Proyecto Caficultura Orgánica," San José Poaquil, Chimaltenango (grant proposal, ca. 1998), 1. The women's insistence on including the reference to Barrios was conveyed to me by Peace Corps volunteer Kate Gilroy, who was affiliated with their group.

114. The mayor's first name varies in oral accounts, but the last name is always the same.

115. "Monografía de San José Poaquil," 1. A literal translation makes the monograph incomprehensible, so the author has rendered a liberal translation.

116. AGCA (Archivo General de Centro América [General Archives of Central America]), sección de tierras legajo 6, expediente 12, 108b.

117. Ibid.

118. Ibid., 1

119. Grandin, *The Blood of Guatemala,* 135.

120. David J. McCreery, "Coffee and Class: The Structure of Development in Liberal Guatemala," *Hispanic American Historical Review* 56, no. 3 (1976): 457; Robert Carmack, *Historia Social de los Quichés* (Guatemala: Editorial "José de Pineda Ibarra," Ministerio de Educación, 1979), 248; Ricardo Falla, *Quiché rebelde: estudio de un movimiento de conversión religiosa rebelde a las creencias tradicionales en San Antonio Olotenango, Quiché, 1948–70* (Guatemala: Editorial Universitaria, 1978), 280–84; Jim Handy, *Gift of the Devil: A History of Guatemala* (Boston: South End, 1984), 60–70; Ralph Lee Woodward, Jr., *Central America: A Nation Divided* (Oxford: Oxford University Press, 1985), 154.

121. Ministerio de Educación, "Mapa Escolar, March 1996, San José Poaquil," A1. Three other sources provide this government accord as the day of Poaquil's establishment: "Monografía de San José Poaquil" 1; Gall, *Diccionario Geográfico de Guatemala,* 3: 344; and "Diagnóstico de Salud, Distrito: San José Poaquil, Chimaltenango," 1.

122. de Leon Pérez, *Memoria de Labores,* 47.

123. "Monografía de San José Poaquil," 1.

124. AGCA, sección de tierras legajo 6, expediente 12, 111.

125. Handy, *Gift of the Devil,* 60–61, 67; Woodward, *Central America,* 154.

126. Waqxaqi' Kan, 3/18/98, Poaquil; Waqxaqi' Aq'ab'al (3/17/98, Hacienda María, Poaquil) was among those who mentioned Comalapa's negative reaction to Poaquil's desire to be independent.

127. Ixche', 11/22/97, Poaquil.

128. B'eleje' Aq'ab'al, 3/14/98, Poaquil.

129. "Monografía de San José Poaquil," 1.

130. AGCA, sección de tierras, legajo 6, expendiente 12, 108.

131. Ibid., 113–14.

132. Ibid., 47b

133. Viviano Guerra, *Recopilación de las leyes en todos por el supremo gobierno de la República de Guatemala desde 10 enero 1886 a último día de este año,* (Guatemala: Tipografía de P. Arenales, 1893), accord 14, Dec. 1886, 5: 284. The request was made due to unrest in Comalapa not necessarily related to the independence of Poaquil, but clearly trouble persisted among people in the town.

134. AGCA, sección de tierras, legajo 6, expendiente 12, 111.

135. Ibid., 120.

136. Ixb'atz', 12/4/97, 3/10/98, Poaquil.

137. Junlajuj Imox, 5/23/98, Comalapa.

138. The struggle over Simajulew and Agua Caliente is well documented in AGCA, sección de tierras, legajo 6, expediente 12.

139. Oxi' Imox, 2/11/98, Comalapa.

140. Lajuj Ey, Comalapa, 9/19/98; Waqi' Tz'i', 4/22/98, Xenimaquín, Comalapa

141. Edwardo Otsoy, "Breve Historia del Antiguo Nombre de Comalapa," *Comalapan,* Oct. 1966, 10. Further written evidence supports this claim. A letter dated 1768 or 1770 cites Santa Cruz Balanyá as being an annexed town of Comalapa (Gall, *Diccionario Geográfico de Guatemala,* 1: 473).

142. Lajuj Kan, 12/20/97, Pachitur, Comalapa; Jun Ajpu', 12/20/97, Comalapa; firsthand account by author Judith Maxwell. Many towns perform this dance named *El baile de torito* (dance of the bulls), albeit not with the specifics of the relationship between Poaquil and Comalapa. Lise Paret-Limardo de Vela obtained a script for the Comalapa dance and published it in "Original del baile del torito," *Guatemala Indígena* 3, no. 2 (1963): 93–118. For an insightful and comprehensive analysis of the baile de torito see Servando Hinojosa, "Spiritual Embodiment in a Highland Maya Community" (Ph.D. diss., Tulane University, 1999).

143. For excellent analysis of histories of ethnic conflict and history encoded in dance see Gary H. Gossen, "The Chamula Festival of Games: Native Macroanalysis and Social Commentary in a Maya Carnival," in *Symbol and Meaning beyond the Closed Community: Essays in Mesoamerican Ideas,* ed. Gary Gossen (Institute for Mesoamerican Studies, Albany: State University of New York Press, 1986), 244–48; Victoria Reifler Bricker, *Ritual Humor in Highland Chiapas* (Austin: University of Texas Press, 1973), 110–14, 116–26; and Bricker, *The Indian Christ,* 138–54, 167–68.

144. AGCA, sección de tierras, paquete 8, expediente 2, 74.

145. Ibid., 71b.

146. Jun Kan, 8/19/98, Comalapa. Jun Tz'ikin is a pseudonym. The informant used the real name of the former Kaqchikel leader.

147. Oxi' Tz'ikin, 8/5/98, Comalapa.

148. An interview with a Kaqchikel informant performed by Claudia Dary in 1985 relates the same oral account of many Comalapenses but also mentions that there were problems in regard to the border measurement between the two towns; see Dary, *Relatos de los antiguos,* 43–44.

149. Oxlajuj Kawoq, 3/18/98, Poaquil; Waqxaqi' Q'anil, 3/21/98, Nueva Esperanza, Poaquil.

150. People in Aguas Calientes translate Verapaz to mean "true peace" or "to see the peace." Oral accounts convey a more peaceful and tranquil community. One reason for this utopian existence may be the absence of Spaniards or Ladinos.

151. Ix'ey, 10/20/97, 7/25/98, Aguas Calientes.

152. Informants vary between saying San Bartolo and San Bartolome.

153. Wuqu' Imox, 11/12/97, Aguas Calientes; Waqi' Kan (Ix'ey interview), 11/97, Aguas Calientes; Ixch'op, 1/18/98, Aguas Calientes; Ka'i' Kawoq, 2/7/98, Aguas Calientes; B'eleje' Kan, 11/9/97, Aguas Calientes.

154. Lajuj Aq'ab'al, 11/14/97, Aguas Calientes; B'eleje' Q'anil (Ix'ey interview), 1998, Aguas Calientes.

155. Ligia Archila Serrano, "La Penetración evangélica en Aguas Calientes, municipio de departamento de Sacatepéquez" (Guatemala, Universidad de San Carlos de Guatemala, escuela de historia, área de antropología, 1989), 8.

156. "Monografía de San Antonio Aguas Calientes" *El Pueblo,* Sacatepéquez, June 1968, 6.

157. Gall, *Diccionario Geográfico de Guatemala,* 3: 213.

158. Lutz, *Santiago de Guatemala, 1541–1773, City, Caste y Colonial Experience* (Norman: University of Oklahoma Press, 1994), 27.

159. He used the word *na'oj,* which does not have a direct translation but roughly means manner of being, character, or intangible sense of you are.

160. Jun Tojil, 12/1/97, 1/19/98, 4/8/98, Barahona.

161. Jun Tojil, 7/8/98, Barahona.

162. Ka'i' Tojil, 6/12/98, Barahona; Wuqu' Kame (Jun Tojil interview), 1998, Barahona; Po't, women's weaving cooperative, 2/7/98, Barahona.

163. Wuqu' Ajpu' (Jun Tojil interview), 1998, Barahona; Waqxaqi' Imox, 2/7/98, Barahona.

164. Gall, *Diccionario Geográfico de Guatemala,* 3: 554.

165. Jun Kej (Jun Tojil interview), 1998, Barahona.

166. Lutz, *Historia sociodemográfica,* 122–27; Sherman, *Forced Native Labor,* 20–82.

167. Kab'lajuj Kan, 2/15/98, Barahona.

168. Ibid.

169. Victor Miguel Díaz, "Sacatepéquez," *Diario de Centro America,* July 10, 1912, 4.

170. Lutz, *Santiago de Guatemala,* 27.

171. Lutz, *Historia sociodemográfica,* 108.

172. Author's observance.

173. San Andres [Ceballos] and Santiago Zamora are now aldeas of Aguas Calientes.

174. Santa Catarina Barahona Municipal document, "Certificación Extendida a favor de la Municipalidad de Santa Catarina Barahona de departamento de Sacatepéquez" (Jan. 5, 1950, Office of the mayor, Santa Catarina Barahona), 5. The original document was illegible, so the mayor allowed me to see the copy, which had been handwritten by lawyer and notary Adalberto Aguilar Fuentes in 1950. Unfortunately, Aguilar Fuentes did not transcribe the date of the original document, but he attests to its veracity.

175. Ibid., 6.

176. Annis, *God and Production*, 14; Lutz, *Santiago de Guatemala*, 27.

177. Annis, *God and Production*, 16–17.

178. Certainly, Kaqchikel are critical of the erosion of their unique characteristics over time, an issue that will be explored further in chapter 9. Robert McKenna Brown reveals a decrease in the use of the Kaqchikel language in his study of Aguas Calientes and Barahona. He argues that there is a "switch" generation of parents who are fluent in Kaqchikel but who choose to speak with their children only in Spanish; see Brown, "Language Maintenance and Shift in Four Kaqchikel Towns" (Ph.D. diss., Tulane University, 1991).

179. Lutz, *Santiago de Guatemala*, 108.

180. Ka'i' Tojil, 6/12/98, Barahona

181. Kaji' Kej, 11/12/97, Aguas Calientes; Waqxaqi' K'at, 11/8/97, Aguas Calientes; B'eleje' Q'anil (Ix'ey interview), 1998, Aguas Calientes.

182. Kaji' Kej, 11/12/97, Aguas Calientes; Waqxaqi' K'at, 11/8/97, Aguas Calientes; B'eleje' Q'anil (Ix'ey interview), Aguas Calientes.

183. Goubaud Carrera, *San Antonio Aguas Calientes, Síntesis socio-económica de una comunidad indígena Guatemalteca* (Publicaciones Especiales del Instituto Indigenísta Nacional, no. 6, Guatemala: Instituto Indigenísta Nacional, Ministerio de Educación Pública, 1948), 29–30.

184. Santa Catarina Barahona Municipal document, "Certificación Extendida," 17–18.

185. Ibid. This quotation was brought to my attention by Jun Tojil, a research assistant who had the opportunity to view the document.

186. Ka'i' Tojil, 6/12/98, Barahona.

187. Waqxaqi' Ajpu' (Jun Tojil interview), 1998, Barahona; Ixtojil, 2/7/98, Barahona.

188. Waqxaqi' Kej, 2/7/98, Barahona; Kab'lajuj Kan, 2/15/98, Barahona; Ka'i' Tojil, 6/12/98, Barahona.

189. Po't, women's weaving cooperative, 2/7/98, Barahona.

190. Jun Ey, 11/12/97, Aguas Calientes; Kaji' Kej, 11/12/97, Aguas Calientes.

191. Gall, *Diccionario Geográfico de Guatemala*, 3: 213.

192. Waqxaqi' Kawoq, 11/8/97, Aguas Calientes.

193. Jun Imox, Ka'i Ajpu', and Oxi' Ajpu', 12/2/97, Panicuy, Comalapa.

194. Oxi' Ajpu', 12/2/97, Panicuy, Comalapa.

195. For an analysis of this trend in Guatemalan historiography by historians such as Batres Jáuregui and Villacorta Calderón see Carey, "*Indigenísmo* and Guatemalan History in the Twentieth Century."

196. Land issues are generally the basis of disputes in the *Anales.* A similar pattern emerges in *Titulo Pantzay* of struggles over milpa and land rights. The historical conflicts that Kaqchikel recognize in their oral histories are analogous to the earliest colonial documents.

Chapter 2

1. Kaqchikel use the term *contratistas* for labor brokers for the coast, while Ladinos and Western scholars generally use the term *habilitadores.* I will use *contratistas* to avoid confusion.

2. Wo'o' Kame, 5/29/98, Tecpán.

3. Hill, *Colonial Cakchiquels,* 48–52.

4. Carol Smith, "Labor and International Capital in the Making of a Peripheral Social Formation: Economic Transformations of Guatemala, 1850–1980" (Washington, D.C.: Latin American Program, Wilson Center, 1984), 6; Woodward, *Central America,* 98–105, 114–15; Hazel Ingersoll, "The War of the Mountain: A Study of Reactionary Peasant Insurgency in Guatemala, 1837–1873" (Ph.D. diss., University of Maryland, 1972); Keith Miceli, "Rafael Carrera: Defender and Promoter of Peasant Interests in Guatemala, 1837–1848," *The Americas* 31, no. 1 (1974): 72–95; Smith, *Indian Class and Class Consciousness,* 29; Ralph Lee Woodward, Jr., "Changes in the Nineteenth-Century Guatemalan State," in *Guatemalan Indians and the State,* ed. Carol Smith (Austin: University of Texas Press, 1990), 67–68; Robert A. Naylor, "Guatemala: Indian Attitudes toward Land Tenure," *Journal of Inter-American Studies* 9, no. 4 (1967): 626–29; Julio Castellanos Cambranes, *Coffee and Peasants: The Origins of the Modern Plantation Economy in Guatemala 1853–1897* (South Woodstock, Vt.: CIRMA, 1985), 53–55, 81–119; Marilyn M. Moors, "Indian Labor and the Guatemalan Crisis: Evidence from History and Anthropology," in *Central America: Historical Perspectives on the Contemporary Crisis,* ed. Ralph Lee Woodward, Jr. (New York: Greenwood, 1988), 67–68; Guillermo Náñez Falcón, "Erwin Paul Dieseldorff, German Entrepreneur in the Alta Verapaz of Guatemala, 1889–1937" (Ph.D. diss., Tulane University, 1970), 82. For assertions that adeptly stress the continuities between liberal and conservative governments in the nineteenth century see Lowell Gudmonson and Hector Lindo-Fuentes, *Central America, 1821–1871: Liberalism before Liberal Reform* (Tuscaloosa: University of Alabama Press, 1995) and David McCreery, "State Power, Indigenous Communities, and Land in Nineteenth-Century Guatemala, 1820–1920," in *Guatemalan Indians and the State,* ed. Carol Smith (Austin: University of Texas Press, 1990), 96–115.

5. McCreery, *Rural Guatemala 1760–1940* (Stanford: Stanford University Press, 1994), 1–3, 148, 294, 308, 326–33; Oliver La Farge, "Maya Ethnology: The Sequence of Cultures," in *The Maya and Their Neighbors,* ed. C. L. Hay (New York: 1940), 282–91; Náñez Falcón, "Erwin Paul Dieseldorff," 323; Richard Adams, "La población

indígena en el estado liberal," in *Historia General de Guatemala,* ed. Jorge Luján Muñoz, (Guatemala: Asociación de Amigos del País, Fundación para la Cultura y Desarollo, 1996), 5: 176; John Early, "Population Increase and Family Planning in Guatemala," *Human Organization* 34, no. 3 (1975), 276.

6. *Recopilación de las Leyes de la República de Guatemala* (Guatemala: Tipografía Nacional), 1: 457.

7. Ciro Flamarión Santana Cardoso, "Historia económica del café en Centroamérica," *Estudios Sociales Centroamericanos* 4, no. 10 (1975), 28–30; Robert Carmack, "State and Community in Nineteenth-Century Guatemala," in *Guatemalan Indians and the State,* ed. Carol Smith (Austin: University of Texas Press, 1990), 126–27; Moors, "Indian Labor and the Guatemalan Crisis," 68; Náñez Falcón, "Erwin Paul Dieseldorff," 83.

8. Carmack, *Historia Social de los Quichés,* 248; McCreery, "Coffee and Class," 457.

9. Handy, *Gift of the Devil,* 68.

10. J. C. Méndez Montenegro, *444 años de legislación agraria, 1513–1957* (Guatemala: Imprenta Universitaria, 1958); Handy, *Gift of the Devil,* 60–61, 68–69; McCreery, "State Power, Indigenous Communities, and Land," 106; Woodward, *Central America,* 154, 174; Carmack, *Historia Social de los Quichés,* 248; Robert Carmack, "Barrios y los indígenas: el caso de Santiago, Momostenango," *Estudios Sociales* 6 (1972): 52–73.

11. Wo'o' Iq', 12/2/97, Panicuy, Comalapa. A manzana is 1.73 acres.

12. Ka'i' Kame, 4/29/98, Saqirtacaj, Poaquil; Ka'i' Aq'ab'al, 6/7/98, Tecpán; Kaji' Kej, 11/12/97, Aguas Calientes; Jun Kan, 9/3/98, Comalapa; Junlajuj K'at, 7/9/98, Comalapa; Junlajuj Ajpu', 8/2/98, Comalapa.

13. Waqi' Iq', 4/22/98, Comalapa; Ixiq', 1/12/98, Comalapa; Jun Kan, 9/3/98, Comalapa.

14. AGCA, legajo 28734, expediente 2511.

15. AGCA, sección de tierras, paquete 8, expediente 2, 73.

16. Oxlajuj Kan, 10/17/97, Comalapa; Junlajuj Imox and Wo'o' Imox, 5/23/98, Comalapa; Wo'o' B'atz' and Waqi' B'atz', 7/9/98, Comalapa.

17. B'eleje' Ey, 11/23/97, Poaquil.

18. AGCA, sección de tierras, paquete 8, expediente 2.

19. AGCA, sección de tierras, paquete 10, expediente 11, 1.

20. AGCA, sección de tierras, paquete 6, expediente 12, 108b.

21. Oxi' Kame has the title for his land in Chi Chalí, Comalapa, that his grandfather signed on May 18, 1891.

22. Oxi' Imox, 2/11/98, Comalapa.

23. Oxlajuj Ajpu', 1/19/98, Panabajal, Comalapa; Wuqu' K'at, 4/5/98, Comalapa; Junlajuj Imox and Wo'o' Imox, 5/23/98, Comalapa; Wo'o' B'atz' and Waqi' B'atz', 7/9/98, Comalapa.

24. Waqxaqi' Kej, 5/24/98, Comalapa.

25. Wo'o' Iq', 12/2/97, Panicuy, Comalapa.

26. Oxi' Ajpu', 12/2/97, Panicuy, Comalapa. A cuerda is 4,810 square yards.

27. *Memoria de las labores del Ejecutivo en el Ramo de Agricultura 1938* (Guatemala: Tipografía Nacional), 460.

28. *Recopilación de las Leyes de la República de Guatemala,* 2: 69–75; *Recopilación de las Leyes de la República de Guatemala* 12: 402–6, 535–59; Woodward, *Central America,* 174–75; Carmack, "State and Community," 120, 123; McCreery, *Rural Guatemala,* 266–67, 328, 336; Ruth Bunzel, *Chichicastenango: A Guatemalan Indian Village* (Seattle: University of Washington Press, 1972); Moors, "Indian Labor and the Guatemalan Crisis," 73–74; Náñez Falcón, "Erwin Paul Dieseldorff," 312–40.

29. Ka'i' Imox, 4/14/98, Panabajal, Comalapa.

30. Kab'lajuj Imox, 11/5/97, Comalapa; Wuqu' Tz'i', 1/11/98, Comalapa; Ixsu't, 5/4/98, Comalapa; Ka'i' Ey, 7/11/98, Comalapa; Wuqu' Kawoq, 1/29/98, Comalapa; Oxi' Tz'ikin, 8/8/98, Comalapa; Oxi' No'j, 3/15/98, Poaquil; Oxi' Ajmaq, 3/27/98, Hacienda Vieja, Poaquil; Ka'i' Ajmaq, 11/23/97, Tecpán; Waqi' Imox, 5/3/98, Tecpán; Wo'o' Q'anil, 6/7/98, Tecpán; Kaji' Aq'ab'al, 6/8/98, Tecpán; Wuqu' B'atz', 2/10/98, Pawit, Comalapa; Ixb'alam, 12/17/97, Xiquín Sanahí, Comalapa.

31. *Memoria de las labores del Ejecutivo en el Ramo de Agricultura 1938,* 459–60.

32. Vera Kelsey and Lilly de Jongh Osborne, *Four Keys to Guatemala* (New York: Funk and Wagnalls, 1939), 62; Jim Handy, "Revolution and Reaction: National Policy and Rural Politics in Guatemala" (Ph.D. diss., University of Toronto, 1985), 60; William Krehm, *Democracies and Tyrannies of the Caribbean* (Westport, Conn.: Lawrence Hill, 1984), 40; Handy, *Gift of the Devil,* 95; Moors, "Indian Labor and the Guatemalan Crisis," 68.

33. Clayton Maxwell, "Selective Hybridity and Development in San José Poaquil, Guatemala" (Master's Thesis, University of Texas, Austin, 1998), 49.

34. Ka'i' Kame, 4/29/98, Saqirtacaj, Poaquil.

35. "Diagnóstico de salud, Distrito San José Poaquil, Chimaltenango," 16.

36. Luisa Frank and Philip Wheaton, *Indian Guatemala: The Path to Liberation* (Washington, D.C.: EPICA Task Force, 1984), 39; Handy, *Gift of the Devil,* 221–24; Moors, "Indian Labor and the Guatemalan Crisis," 75–76; Adams, "La población indígena en el estado liberal," 176.

37. Junlajuj Kawoq, 11/17/97, Poaquil; Ixche', 11/22/97, Poaquil; Ix'ajmaq, 11/29/97, Poaquil; Jun Tojil, 12/1/97, Barahona; Oxi' Kame, 3/4/98, Chi Chalí, Comalapa. The school year in Guatemala begins in January, offers a fifteen-day interim in July, and concludes at the end of October.

38. "Diagnóstico de salud, Distrito San José Poaquil, Chimaltenango," 25.

39. *Memorias de la Dirección General de Agricultura 1902* (Guatemala: Tipografía Nacional), 7.

40. Sol Tax, *Penny Capitalism: A Guatemalan Indian Economy* (Washington, D.C.: Smithsonian Institution, Institute of Social Anthropology, 1953); McCreery, "State Power, Indigenous Communities, and Land," 111.

41. Ka'i' Tz'i', 5/26/98, Tecpán; Ixmes and Ixch'op, 1/18/98, Aguas Calientes; Kab'lajuj Ajpu', 5/5/98, Comalapa; Oxi' Aq'ab'al, 10/26/97, Comalapa.

42. Santana Cardoso, "Historia económica del café en Centroamérica," 28–30; Carmack, "State and Community in Nineteenth-Century Guatemala," 126–27;

Smith, "Labor and International Capital," 7; Carol Smith, "Beyond Dependency Theory: National and Regional Patterns of Underdevelopment in Guatemala," *American Ethnologist* 5, no. 3 (1978): 589–90; Smith, *Indian Class and Class Consciousness,* 29–30; Moors, "Indian Labor and the Guatemalan Crisis," 68.

43. Ka'i' Tz'i', 5/26/98, Tecpán; Ixmes and Ixch'op, 1/18/98, Aguas Calientes; Kab'lajuj Ajpu', 5/5/98, Comalapa; Oxi' Aq'ab'al, 10/26/97, Comalapa.

44. Junlajuj K'at, 7/9/98, Comalapa; Kaji' No'j, Waqxaqi' B'atz', Lajuj Q'anil, 3/25/98, Ojer K'ayb'al, Poaquil; Oxlajuj Kawoq, 3/18/98, Poaquil; Oxi' Kame, 3/4/98, Chi Chalí, Comalapa; Wuqu' Tz'i', 1/11/98, Comalapa.

45. Iximnik'te', 5/30/98, Tecpán.

46. Junlajuj Aq'ab'al, 4/10/98, Comalapa; Wuqu' Imox, 11/12/97, Aguas Calientes; Ka'i' Aj (Jun Tojil interview), 1998, Barahona; Ix'ajmaq, 3/22/98, Poaquil; Oxi' Aj, 4/15/98, Simajulew, Comalapa; Ixk'aj, 12/17/97, Xiquín Sanahí, Comalapa; Jun Ajpu', 12/20/97, Comalapa; Waqxaqi' Q'anil, 3/21/98, Nueva Esperanza, Poaquil; P'ot, women's weaving cooperative, 2/7/98, Barahona.

47. B'eleje' Ey, 11/23/97, Poaquil; Wuqu' Q'anil, 3/21/98, Poaquil; Wo'o' Iq', 12/2/97, Panicuy, Comalapa.

48. Ka'i' Imox, 1/21/98, Panabajal, Comalapa.

49. McCreery, *Rural Guatemala,* 267.

50. Oxi' Tijax, 1/13/98, Paraxaquen, Comalapa.

51. Ix'aj, 2/9/98, Comalapa; Ka'i' Kej, 11/5/97, Comalapa; Ix'ajmaq, 11/29/97, Poaquil; Ix'aj, 11/26/97, Tecpán.

52. Ka'i' B'atz', 11/26/97, Tecpán; Ix'umül, 4/15/98, Simajulew, Comalapa; Jun Imox, 12/9/97, Xenimaquín, Comalapa; Ixb'alam, 12/17/97, Xiquín Sanahí, Comalapa; Ixya', 4/11/98, Comalapa; Jun Kan, 8/19/98, Comalapa; B'eleje' Ey, 4/28/98, Poaquil; Ixpo't, 11/17/97, Poaquil; Waqxaqi' Aq'ab'al, 3/17/98, Hacienda María, Poaquil.

53. *Memoria de la Secretaría de Gobernación y Justicia presentada a la Asamblea Nacional Legislativa en sus sesiones ordinarias, 1932* (Guatemala: Tipografía Nacional, 1932), 100.

54. Ibid.; Bunzel, *Chichicastenango,* 143.

55. Ixch'oy, 11/21/97, Tecpán.

56. Oxi' Ey, 11/28/97, Aguas Calientes.

57. B'eleje' Tz'i', Junlajuj B'atz', Junlajuj Toj, 5/20/98, Xetonox, Comalapa.

58. Kab'lajuj Kawoq, 3/23/98, Poaquil; Kab'lajuj K'at, 6/27/98, Comalapa; Kaji' Iq', 11/18/97, Tecpán; Waqi' Imox, 5/3/98, Tecpán; Kaji' No'j, Waqxaqi' B'atz', Lajuj Q'anil, 3/25/98, Ojer K'ayb'al, Poaquil; P'ot, women's weaving cooperative, 2/7/98, Barahona; Kab'lajuj Kan, 2/15/98, Barahona; Ixkan, 3/29/98, Poaquil; B'eleje' Kame, 10/17/97, Panabajal, Comalapa; Ixkawoq, 4/17/98, Pamumus, Comalapa; Wuqu' Aq'ab'al, 11/25/97, Tecpán.

59. Oxlajuj K'at, 3/10/98, Poaquil. During the time of Ubico, the quetzal was equal to the U.S. dollar. From 1994 to 1998, the exchange rate was six quetzals to one U.S. dollar. A quintal is one hundred kilograms, but Kaqchikel also use it as a unit of volume.

60. Wuqu' Q'anil, 3/21/98, Poaquil. Coastal wages have increased to fifteen to

twenty quetzals a day, compared to a daily wage of ten to fifteen quetzals in the highlands.

61. Waqxaqi' Ajpu' (Jun Tojil interview), 1998, Barahona. One quetzal equals one hundred cents.

62. Oxi' Kame, 3/4/98, Chi Chalí, Comalapa; Ixkawoq, 4/17/98, Pamumus, Comalapa; Ixmukane', 11/26/97, Tecpán; Ka'i' Tz'i', 5/26/98, Tecpán; Kaji' Ey, 5/4/98, Kojol Juyu', Comalapa; Kaji' Kej, 11/12/97, Aguas Calientes; Wuqu' Iq', 12/17/97, Xiquín Sanahí, Comalapa; Waqxaqi' Ajpu' (Jun Tojil interview), 1998, Barahona.

63. Ixq'anil, 3/3/98, Comalapa; Kaji' Q'anil, 11/19/97, Tecpán; Oxi' Tojil, 3/21/98, Nueva Esperanza, Poaquil; Waqxaqi' Imox, 2/7/98, Barahona; Oxi' Kame, 3/4/98, Chi Chalí, Comalapa; Ixkawoq, 4/17/98, Pamumus, Comalapa; Ixmukane', 11/26/97, Tecpán; Ka'i' Tz'i', 5/26/98, Tecpán; Kaji' Ey, 5/4/98, Kojol Juyu', Comalapa; Kaji' Kej, 11/12/97, Aguas Calientes; Wuqu' Iq', 12/17/97, Xiquín Sanahí, Comalapa; Waqxaqi' Ajpu' (Jun Tojil interview), 1998, Barahona.

64. Ka'i' Kan, 11/24/97, Chuwatz'unuj, Tecpán.

65. Oxi' Kawoq, 9/4/98, Pamumus, Comalapa; Ixpop, 5/20/98, Comalapa; Junlajuj Kej, 5/22/98, Paquixic, Comalapa; Wuqu' Imox, 11/12/97, Aguas Calientes; Ixtojil, 2/7/98, Barahona; Waqxaqi' Kej, 2/7/98, Barahona; Waqxaqi' Ajpu' (Jun Tojil interview), 1998, Barahona; Junlajuj Kan, 4/24/98, Simajulew, Comalapa; Wo'o' No'j, 4/22/98, Xenimaquín, Comalapa; Kaji' Tijax, 4/28/98, Patzaj, Comalapa; Lajuj Tz'i', 3/8/98, San Martín; Ix'ulew, 12/10/97, Rosario Canajal, San Martín Jilotepeque; Junlajuj Aq'ab'al, 12/10/97, Rosario Canajal, San Martín Jilotepeque; Wo'o' Kawoq and Waqi' Kawoq, 3/3/98, Kojol Juyu', Comalapa; Kaji' Ey, 5/4/98, Kojol Juyu', Comalapa; Oxi' No'j, 3/15/98, Poaquil; Waqxaqi' Aq'ab'al, 3/17/98, Hacienda María, Poaquil; Ka'i' Kame, 4/29/98, Saqirtacaj, Poaquil; Ka'i' Kawoq, 2/7/98, Aguas Calientes; Ka'i' Tzinik'an, 6/13/98, Comalapa.

66. Oxi' Kan, 8/19/98, Comalapa.

67. B'eleje' Iq', 6/4/98, Tecpán.

68. Ixk'at, 1/7/98, Comalapa.

69. Jun Tijax, 3/8/98, Panabajal, Comalapa.

70. Ka'i' Kame, 4/29/98, Saqirtacaj, Poaquil; Junlajuj Kej, 3/22/98, Poaquil; Lajuj Ajpu', 3/29/98, Poaquil; Waqi' Iq', 4/22/98, Comalapa; Kaji' Ey, 5/4/98, Kojol Juyu', Comalapa; Wo'o' No'j, Xenimaquín, Comalapa; Wuqu' Kan, 6/5/98, Tecpán.

71. Wo'o' Ey, 3/28/98, Panimacak, Comalapa.

72. Waqi' Ey, 4/24/98, Simajulew, Comalapa.

73. Ixsu'm, 6/1/98, Tecpán; Kab'lajuj Iq', 5/31/98, Tecpán; Lajuj Kame, 2/14/98, Comalapa; Kab'lajuj Tijax, 4/7/98, Comalapa; Oxi' B'atz', 4/26/98, Comalapa; Junlajuj Imox, 5/23/98, Comalapa; Junlajuj K'at, 7/9/98, Comalapa; Junlajuj Ajpu', 8/2/98, Comalapa.

74. Kab'lajuj Q'anil, 5/19/98, Comalapa; Ixtuctuc, 4/16/98, Comalapa; Waqxaqi' Q'anil, 3/21/98, Nueva Esperanza, Poaquil; Oxi' Ajmaq, 3/27/98, Hacienda Vieja, Poaquil; Ixtz'ib', 3/27/98, Paley, Poaquil; B'eleje' Ey, 4/18/98, Poaquil; B'eleje' Iq', 6/4/98, Tecpán; Waqi' Ey, 4/24/98, Simajulew, Comalapa.

75. B'eleje' Kej, 3/19/98, Poaquil; Jun Tzinik'an, 5/26/98, Tecpán; Ixtzinik'an,

6/2/98, Tecpán; Wo'o' Q'anil, 6/7/98, Tecpán; Iximnik'te', 5/30/98, Tecpán; Kaji' Ey, 5/4/98, Kojol Juyu', Comalapa; Ka'i' Imox, 8/5/98, Panabajal, Comalapa.

76. Jun Kame, 5/1/98, Agua Caliente, Comalapa.

77. Ka'i' Aq'ab'al, 6/7/98, Tecpán.

78. Ka'i' Kame, 4/29/98, Saqirtacaj, Poaquil; Junlajuj Kej, 3/22/98, Poaquil; Lajuj Ajpu', 3/29/98, Poaquil; Waqi' Iq', 4/22/98, Comalapa; Kaji' Ey, 5/4/98, Kojol Juyu', Comalapa; Wo'o' No'j, 4/22/98, Xenimaquín, Comalapa; Wuqu' Kan, 6/5/98, Tecpán.

79. Kab'lajuj Ajpu', 5/5/98, Comalapa.

80. Waqi' Iq', 4/22/98, Comalapa.

81. Kab'lajuj K'at, 6/27/98, Comalapa; Waqxaqi' Iq', 1/6/98, Comalapa; Ka'i' Aq'ab'al, 6/7/98, Tecpán; Kaji' Ajmaq, 3/28/98, Poaquil; Kaji' No'j, Waqxaqi' B'atz', Lajuj Q'anil, 3/25/98, Ojer K'ayb'al, Poaquil; Lajuj Kawoq, 3/16/98, Poaquil; Ix'ajmaq, 3/22/98, Poaquil; Oxi' Kej, 6/14/98, Comalapa; Wo'o' B'atz' and Waqi' B'atz', 7/9/98, Comalapa.

82. Kab'lajuj Kej, 4/26/98, Comalapa.

83. Ka'i' K'at, 5/16/98, Comalapa.

84. Smith, "Labor and International Capital," 9; Susanne Jonas, "Guatemala: Land of Eternal Struggle," in *Latin America: The Struggle with Dependency and Beyond,* ed. Ron Chilcote and Joel Edelstein (Cambridge: Schenkam, 1974), 151–69; Consejo Superior Universitario Centroamericano (CSUCA), *Estructura agraria, dinámica de población y desarrollo capitalista en Centroamérica* (San José, Costa Rica: EDUCA, 1978); Lester Schmid, *Papel de la mano de obra migratoria en el desarrollo económico de Guatemala* (Guatemala City: Universidad de San Carlos, 1973).

85. Moors, "Indian Labor and the Guatemalan Crisis," 71.

86. Jim Handy, *Revolution in the Countryside* (Chapel Hill: University of North Carolina Press, 1994), 66, 72, 153, 202–4; Jim Handy, "National Policy, Agrarian Reform, and the Corporate Community during the Guatemalan Revolution, 1944–54," *Comparative Studies in Society and History* 30 (Oct. 1988): 705; Handy, *Gift of the Devil,* 110, 116; Richard Adams, *Crucifixion by Power* (Austin: University of Texas Press, 1970), 185. For a concise assessment of Arbenz's land reform program and an insightful analysis of how it affected K'ichee's and Ladinos in Quetzaltenango and its environs see Grandin, *The Blood of Guatemala,* 198–219.

87. Jorge Skinner-Klee, *Legislación indigenista de Guatemala* (México, D.F.: Instituto Indigenísta Interamericano, 1954), 134–35; Handy, *Revolution in the Countryside,* 93, 146; Jim Handy, "The Corporate Community, Campesino Organizations, and Agrarian Reform, 1950–1954," in *Guatemalan Indians and the State: 1540–1988,* ed. Carol Smith (Austin: University of Texas Press, 1990), 165–69; Robert Wasserstrom, "Revolution in Guatemala: Peasants and Politics under the Arbenz Government," *Comparative Studies in Society and History* 17 (Oct. 1975), 474; Adams, *Crucifixion by Power,* 396; Handy, "National Policy," 708.

88. Wasserstrom, "Revolution in Guatemala," 474; Handy, "National Policy," 723; Handy, *Revolution in the Countryside,* 69–71, 205; Handy, *Gift of the Devil,* 129; Adams, *Crucifixion by Power,* 444–46.

89. Jim Handy, "The Most Precious Fruit of the Revolution," *Hispanic American*

Historical Review 68, no. 4 (1988): 695, 704–5; Handy, *Gift of the Devil,* 129–30; Handy, *Revolution in the Countryside,* 149.

90. Wasserstrom, "Revolution in Guatemala," 475.

91. Handy, *Revolution in the Countryside,* 197; Handy, "Most Precious Fruit," 687–88; Leo A. Suslow, *Aspects of Social Reform in Guatemala, 1944–1949: Problems of Social Change in an Underdeveloped Country* (Hamilton, N.Y.: Colgate University Press, 1949), 152; Wasserstrom, "Revolution in Guatemala," 459–60; Roland H. Ebel, "Political Modernization in Three Guatemalan Indian Communities," in *Community Culture and National Change,* ed. Richard Adams, Middle American Research Institute Series, publication no. 24 (New Orleans: Tulane University, 1972), 194; John Gillen, "San Luis Jilotepeque: 1942–1955," in *Community Culture and National Change,* ed. Richard Adams, Middle American Research Institute Series, publication no. 24 (New Orleans: Tulane University, 1972), 26.

92. Oxi' Kame, 3/4/98, Chi Chalí, Comalapa; Jun Tz'i', 7/12/98, Pamumus, Comalapa; Wo'o' Tijax, 4/24/98, Simajulew, Comalapa; Wo'o' No'j, 4/22/98, Xenimaquín, Comalapa; Kab'lajuj Imox, 9/28/98, Comalapa; Ixiq', 1/12/98, Comalapa; Waqxaqi' Iq', 6/23/98, Comalapa; Wuqu' Kawoq, 1/29/98, Comalapa; Kaji' No'j, Waqxaqi' B'atz', Lajuj Q'anil, 3/25/98, Ojer K'ayb'al, Poaquil; Wuqu' Kan, 6/5/98, Tecpán; Oxi' Tz'i', 5/29/98, Tecpán.

93. Oxlajuj K'at, 3/10/98, Poaquil; Wo'o' Kame, 5/29/98, Tecpán; Jun Ey, 11/12/97, Aguas Calientes; Ka'i' Kawoq, 2/7/98, Aguas Calientes.

94. Piero Gleijeses, "Agrarian Reform of Arbenz," *Journal of Latin American Studies* 21 (Oct. 1989): 472–73; Nathan L. Whetten, *Guatemala: The Land and the People* (New Haven: Yale University, 1961), 158; Handy, "National Policy," 712; Gillen, "San Luis Jilotepeque," 26.

95. Handy, "National Policy," 715; Handy, *Revolution in the Countryside,* 152.

96. Handy, *Revolution in the Countryside,* 167.

97. Oxlajuj Ajpu', 1/19/98, Panabajal, Comalapa.

98. Waqi' Ey, 4/24/98, Simajulew, Comalapa.

99. Ka'i' Imox, 1/21/98, Panabajal, Comalapa.

100. Jun Tz'i', 7/11/98, Pamumus, Comalapa; Oxi' Tz'ikin, 8/1/98, Comalapa.

101. Warren, *Symbolism of Subordination,* 89; Handy, "National Policy," 704; George Britnell, "Problems of Economic and Social Change in Guatemala," *Canadian Journal of Economic and Political Sciences* 17 (1951): 468–81; Samuel Guy Inman, *A New Day in Guatemala: A Study of the Present Social Revolution* (Wilton, Conn.: Worldover, 1954), 16.

102. Waqi' Amaq, Waqi' Tijax, and Kaji' Tzinik'an, 11/11/97, Paya, Comalapa; Oxi' Ajpu', Jun Imox, Ka'i' Ajpu', 12/2/97, Panicuy, Comalapa; Junlajuj Ajpu', 8/2/98, Comalapa; Kab'lajuj K'at, 6/27/98, Comalapa; Ixxokoq'a', 3/14/98, Poaquil; Oxi' K'at, 6/5/98, Tecpán; Waqxaqi' Imox, 2/7/98, Barahona; Oxi' Kawoq, 10/31/97, Pamumus, Comalapa.

103. For further description and analysis of the 1954 military coup in Guatemala see chapter 6.

104. Jun Kej (Jun Tojil interview), 1998, Barahona.

105. B'eleje' K'at, 11/5/97, Comalapa.

106. Oxi' Kame, 3/4/98, Chi Chalí, Comalapa.

107. Kab'lajuj Ajpu', 5/5/98, Comalapa; Ix'aq'om, 11/5/97, Comalapa; B'eleje' Ey, 11/23/97, Poaquil; Ix'aq'ab'al, 3/17/98, Hacienda María, Poaquil; Waqi' Imox, 5/3/98, Tecpán; Kab'lajuj Aq'ab'al, 11/19/97, Tecpán; Oxi' Kawoq, 10/31/97, Pamumus, Comalapa; Jun Imox, 12/9/97, Xenimaquín, Comalapa; Oxlajuj Ajpu', 1/19/98, Panabajal, Comalapa; Lajuj Kan, 10/15/97, Pachitur, Comalapa; Ixk'aj, 12/17/97, Xiquín Sanahí, Comalapa; Ixchiköp, 12/17/97, Xiquín Sanahí, Comalapa; Wo'o' No'j, 4/22/98, Xenimaquín, Comalapa; Ixkame, 8/17/98, Comalapa; Wuqu' B'atz', 2/10/98, Pawit, Comalapa; Ixmanik, 11/17/97, Poaquil.

108. Waqi' Iq', 4/22/98, Comalapa

109. B'eleje' K'at, 11/5/97, Comalapa.

110. A vara is a measurement of about thirty-three inches long; a costal is a large sack used to transport goods.

111. Lajuj Kan, 12/20/97, Pachitur, Comalapa.

112. Adams, "La población indígena en el estado liberal," 177; John Watanabe, "Enduring yet Ineffable Community in the Western Periphery of Guatemala," in *Guatemalan Indians and the State,* ed. Carol Smith (Austin: University of Texas Press, 1990), 188; Falla, *Quiché rebelde,* 82.

113. Junlajuj K'at, 7/9/98, Comalapa. The date of chemical fertilizer's arrival in oral histories ranged from as recently as thirty years ago (Jun Iq', 4/17/98, Comalapa; Oxlajuj Ajpu', 1/19/98, Panabajal, Comalapa) to as far back as sixty years ago (Oxi' Kawoq, 10/31/97, Pamumus, Comalapa).

114. Ixwatzik', 1/12/98, Xiquín Sanahí, Comalapa.

115. Wuqu' K'at, 4/5/98, Comalapa; Kab'lajuj Tijax, 4/7/98, Comalapa; Waqi' Kame, 5/17/98, Pamumus, Comalapa; Wo'o' Ey and Kab'lajuj B'atz', 3/28/98, Panimacak, Comalapa; Kaji' No'j, Waqxaqi' B'atz', Lajuj Q'anil, 3/25/98, Ojer K'ayb'al, Poaquil; Ka'i' Kan, 11/24/97, Chuwatz'unuj, Tecpán; B'eleje' Iq', 6/4/98, Tecpán.

116. Oxi' Kawoq, 10/31/97, Pamumus, Comalapa.

117. "La doctrina de los abonos químicos," *Boletín de Agricultura, Revista Mensual* (Guatemala, Apr. 1903), 246.

118. *Memoria del Ministerio de Agricultura* (Guatemala: Tipografía Nacional, 1922), 10–11.

119. Annis, *God and Production,* 44.

120. Ricardo Falla, *Quiché rebelde,* 82–83; Smith, *Indian Class and Class Consciousness,* 32. Also see Falla, "Hacia la revolución verde: Adopción y dependencia del fertilizante químico en un Municipio del Quiché, Guatemala," *Estudios Sociales* 6 (1972).

121. Wuqu' K'at, "Libreta de Apuntes."

122. Sotz O., "Monografía de Comalapa, Diagnóstico Comunitario," 9.

123. Santiago Xet, "Campos de Ensayos y de Demostraciones, Prácticas del Programa de Fertilización de 'FAO-SFEI' en San Juan Comalapa, Chimaltenango," *Comalapan,* Sept. 1966, 6.

124. "Técnica sobre la agricultura: Servicio de Fomento de Economía Indígena cuenta con programas de ensayo sobre fertilización," *Comalapan,* Sept. 1966, 7.

125. Junlajuj Tz'i', 10/24/97, Xiquín Sanahí, Comalapa.

126. Jun Kame, 5/1/98, Agua Caliente, Comalapa; Jun Tz'i', 7/11/98, Pamumus, Comalapa; Jun Iq', 4/17/98, Comalapa; Jun Kan, 8/19/98, Comalapa; Waqi' K'at, 5/3/98, Comalapa.

127. Oxi' Kame, 3/4/98, Chi Chalí, Comalapa. Oral accounts of these men and women from the United States did not associate them with any group affiliation. The implication is that these U.S. citizens came as individuals and acted of their own accord, not on behalf of an organization.

128. Menchú, *Crossing Borders,* 219.

129. Watanabe, "Enduring yet Ineffable Community," 188; Falla, *Quiché rebelde,* 82.

130. Wuqu' Imox, 11/12/97, Aguas Calientes; Lajuj Aq'ab'al, 11/12/97, Aguas Calientes; Ka'i' B'atz', 11/26/97, Tecpán; Waqi' K'at, 5/3/98, Comalapa; Wo'o' Kan, 4/26/98, Comalapa; Oxlajuj Kan, 3/8/98, Comalapa; Oxlajuj Iq', 4/17/98, Simajulew, Comalapa; Wuqu' Iq', 12/17/97, Xiquín Sanahí, Comalapa; Ixchel, 2/12/98, Comalapa; Ixsamaj, 9/6/98, Comalapa; Ixsu'm, 6/1/98, Tecpán. Unfortunately, Kaqchikel assertions about the deleterious health effects of chemical fertilizer ingested through agricultural products are not as yet supportable by scientific evidence. Nonetheless, agricultural and environmental studies in other regions of Guatemala and the world have posited similar assertions. See Sonia I. Arbona, "Commerical Agriculture and Agrochemicals in Almolonga, Guatemala," *Geographical Review* 88 no. 1 (Jan. 1998), 47–63; AVANSCO (Asociación para el Avance de las Ciencias Sociales en Guatemala), *Impacto ecológico de los cultivos hortícolas no-tradicionales en el altiplano de Guatemala* (Guatemala: Instituto AVANSCO, 1994); Angus Wright, *The Death of Ramón González: The Modern Agricultural Dilemma* (Austin: University of Texas Press, 1990), 205; Robert Repetto and Sanjay Baliga, *Pesticides and the Immune System: The Public Health Risks* (Washington, D.C.: World Resources Institute, 1996); Lori Ann Thrupp, Gilles Bergeron, and William Walters, *Bittersweet Harvests for Global Supermarkets: Challenges in Latin America's Agricultural Export Boom* (Washington, D.C.: World Resources Institute, 1995); Dennis D. Weisenburger, "Human Health Effects of Agrichemical Use," *Human Pathology* 24, no. 6 (June 1993): 571–76; Prabhu L. Pingali and Pierre A. Roger, *Impact of Pesticides on Farmer Health and the Rice Environment* (Boston: Kluwer, 1995); Douglas L. Murray, *Cultivating Crisis: The Human Cost of Pesticides in Latin America* (Austin: University of Texas Press, 1994); David Pimentel, "Green Revolution Agriculture and Chemical Hazards," *Science of the Total Environment* 188, no. 1 (1996), S86–S98.

131. Wo'o' Ajpu', 11/11/97, Comalapa.

132. Ixche', 11/22/97, Poaquil; Lajuj Kame, 2/14/98, Comalapa; Junlajuj Kej, 3/22/98, Poaquil; Wuqu' Ey, 3/26/98, Hacienda Vieja, Poaquil; Ixtz'ib', 3/27/98, Paley, Poaquil; Waqxaqi' Kej, 2/7/98, Barahona; Ixmukane', 11/26/97, Tecpán; Ka'i' Tz'i', 5/26/98, Tecpán; Junlajuj Kame, 4/12/98, Pachitur, Comalapa; Jun Q'anil, 2/9/98, Patzaj, Comalapa; Jun Imox, 12/9/97, Xenimaquín, Comalapa; Oxi' Kej, 6/14/98, Comalapa.

133. Wuqu' Kawoq, 4/7/98, Comalapa.

134. Junlajuj Imox and Wo'o' Imox, 5/23/98, Comalapa; Jun Iq', 4/6/98, 4/17/98, Comalapa; B'eleje' Kan, 11/9/97, Aguas Calientes; Oxi' Tz'i', 5/29/98, Tecpán; Waqi'

No'j, 3/15/98, Poaquil; Jun Kame, 5/1/98, Agua Caliente, Comalapa; Kaji' Aj, 3/8/98, Simajulew, Comalapa.

135. Kaji' Kej, 11/12/97, Aguas Calientes.

136. Wuqu' Iq', 12/17/97, Xiquín Sanahí, Comalapa.

137. Wuqu' Kej, 5/30/98, Tecpán; Kab'lajuj Iq', 5/31/98, Tecpán; Oxi' Tojil, 3/21/98, Nueva Esperanza, Poaquil; Waqi' K'at, 9/6/98, Comalapa; Wuqu' K'at, 4/5/98, Comalapa; Ixnum, 4/29/98, Comalapa.

138. Waqi' Kame, 5/17/98, Pamumus, Comalapa.

139. Jun Ey, 11/12/97, Aguas Calientes; Oxlajuj Imox, 1/13/98, Paraxaquen, Comalapa; Kab'lajuj Ajpu', 11/14/97, Comalapa; B'eleje' Iq', 6/4/98, Tecpán.

140. Wuqu' Iq', 12/17/97, Xiquín Sanahí, Comalapa

141. Oxi' Kame, 3/4/98, Chi Chalí, Comalapa.

142. Ja C'Amabal I'b, "La primera gran confrontación: El movimiento campesino indígena del altiplano guatemalteca," paper presented to the United Nations Subcommission on Ethnic Minorities, Geneva, August 1984.

143. Arturo Arias, "Changing Indian Identity: Guatemala's Violent Transition to Modernity," in *Guatemalan Indians and the State,* ed. Carol Smith (Austin: University of Texas Press, 1990), 235, 238, 240.

144. Ixb'oq', 5/31/98, Tecpán; Ixb'utz', 6/20/98, Comalapa.

145. Jun Ey, 11/12/97, Aguas Calientes.

146. Waqxaqi' Kej, 2/7/98, Barahona; Waqi' No'j, 3/15/98, Poaquil; Waqxaqi' Q'anil, 3/21/98, Nueva Esperanza, Poaquil; Wuqu' Kej, 5/30/98, Tecpán; Kaji' Aq'ab'al, 6/8/98, Tecpán; Kab'lajuj K'at, 6/27/98, Comalapa; Kaji' Tojil, 3/2/98, Palima, Comalapa; Jun Imox, Ka'i' Ajpu' and Oxi' Ajpu', 12/2/97, Panicuy, Comalapa; Wuqu' Kawoq, 1/29/98, Comalapa; Ixk'echelaj, 1/19/98, Comalapa.

147. Ka'i' Kame, 4/29/98, Saqirtacaj, Poaquil.

148. Waqxaqi' Q'anil, 3/21/98, Nueva Esperanza, Poaquil; Ixtz'ib', 3/27/98, Paley, Poaquil; Ixmanik, 11/17/97, Poaquil; Waqi' No'j, 3/15/98, Poaquil; Junlajuj Ajpu', 8/2/98, Comalapa; Wuqu' Tijax, 3/2/98, Palima, Comalapa; Waqxaqi' Iq', 6/23/98, Comalapa.

149. Smith, *Indian Class and Class Consciousness,* 2; Smith, "Labor and International Capital," 12; Smith, "Beyond Dependency Theory," 605–6.

150. Junlajuj Kawoq, 11/17/97, Poaquil; Ixche', 11/22/97, Poaquil; Ix'ajmaq, 11/29/97, Poaquil; Jun Tojil, 12/1/97, Barahona; Oxi' Kame, 3/4/98, Chi Chalí, Comalapa.

151. Smith, "Local History in Global Context"; Smith, "Does a Commodity Economy Enrich the Few while Ruining the Masses?" *Journal of Peasant Studies* 11, no. 3 (1984); Smith, *Indian Class and Class Consciousness,* 11.

152. Wuqu' Kame (Jun Tojil interview), 1998, Barahona; Waqxaqi' Kawoq, 11/8/97, Aguas Calientes; Lajuj Aq'ab'al, 11/12/97, Aguas Calientes; Wuqu' Imox, 11/12/97, Aguas Calientes.

153. Waqxaqi' Kej, 2/7/98, Barahona.

154. Ixkej, 11/9/97, Aguas Calientes.

155. Nelson, *Finger in the Wound,* 359–60. Nelson points to studies that show that over 80 percent of the employees in Guatemala's *maquiladora* factories are women, most of whom are Maya. The pattern of exploitation of female labor in *maquiladoras*

is common throughout the Caribbean and Mexico. The literature on *maquiladoras* is extensive; see Leslie Sklair, *Assembling for Development: The Maquila Industry in Mexico and the United States* (San Diego: Center for U.S.–Mexican Studies, University of California, 1989); Claudia Dary, *Mujeres tradicionales y nuevos cultivos* (Guatemala City: FLACSO, 1991); Patricia A. Austin, *Exports and Local Development: Mexico's New Maquiladoras* (Austin: University of Texas Press, 1992); Kurt Peterson, *The Maquiladora Revolution in Guatemala* (New Haven: Orville H. Schell, Jr., Center for International Human Rights at Yale Law School, Occasional Paper Series, 1992); Miriam Davidson, *Lives on the Line: Dispatches from the U.S.-Mexico Border* (Tucson: University of Arizona Press, 2000); Fatemi Khosrow, ed., *The Maquiladora Industry: Economic Solution or Problem?* (New York: Praeger, 1990); Devon Gerardo Peña, *Terror of the Machine: Technology, Work, Gender, and Ecology on the U.S.–Mexican Border* (Austin: Center for Mexican American Studies, University of Texas, 1997).

156. Jun Ey, 11/12/97, Aguas Calientes; Kaji' Kej, 11/12/97, Aguas Calientes; Wo'o' Aj (Ix'ey interview), 1998, Aguas Calientes; Ka'i' Kawoq, 2/7/98, Aguas Calientes; Waqi' Kan (Ix'ey interview), 1998, Aguas Calientes; P'ot, women's weaving cooperative, 2/7/98, Barahona; Wuqu' Ajpu' (Jun Tojil interview), 1998, Barahona.

157. Jun Tojil, 12/1/97, Barahona.

158. Jun Kej (Jun Tojil interview), 1998, Barahona.

159. Oxlajuj Ajmaq, 9/24/97, Tecpán.

160. Ixte and B'eleje' Imox family, Comalapa, author's observation.

161. Personal communication to the author from Walter Little, Oct. 14, 1997.

Chapter 3

1. Ixtoj, 8/21/98, Comalapa (I have paraphrased this quote to condense it).

2. Waqi' K'at, 9/6/98, Comalapa.

3. K'ayb'il B'alam, 10/5/97, Tecpán.

4. Jun Ajpu', 9/26/97, Comalapa; Kab'lajuj K'at, 9/9/98, Comalapa; Ixiq', 1/12/98, Comalapa; Kab'lajuj Tijax, Comalapa; Jun Tojil, 4/8/98, Barahona; Ixmes and Ixch'op, 1/18/98, Aguas Calientes; Waqxaqi' Aq'ab'al, 3/17/98, Hacienda María, Poaquil.

5. MacLeod, *Spanish Central America*, 20, 98; George Lovell, "Surviving the Conquest: The Maya of Guatemala in Historical Perspective," *Latin American Research Review* 23 (1988): 25–58.

6. Recinos, *Memorial de Sololá*, 119–21.

7. Sherburne F. Cook and Woodrow Borah, *Essays in Population History: Mexico and the Caribbean*, 3 vols. (Berkeley: University of California Press, 1971–79); Nathan Wachtel, "Indian and the Spanish Conquest," in *Cambridge History of Latin America*, ed. Leslie Bethell (Cambridge: Cambridge University Press, 1984), 1: 213; Eric Wolf, *Sons of the Shaking Earth* (Chicago: University of Chicago Press, 1959), 195–201; Fuentes y Guzmán, *Recordación Florida*, 348; Gall, *Diccionario Geográfico de Guatemala*, 4: 50. For recent research on the pre- and postcontact indigenous civilizations

in Latin America see William M. Denevan, *Native Population of the Americas in 1492* (Madison: University of Wisconsin Press, 1992).

8. Ralph Lee Woodward, Jr., *Rafael Carrera and the Emergence of the Republic of Guatemala, 1821–1871* (Athens: University of Georgia Press, 1993), 54; Miriam Williford, "Las Luces y La Civilización: The Social Reforms of Mariano Gálvez," in *Applied Enlightenment: Nineteenth Century Liberalism,* ed. Margaret A. L. Harrison and Robert Wauchope, Middle American Research Institute Series, publication no. 24 (New Orleans: Tulane University, 1972), 37–40; Pedro Tobar Cruz, *Los Montañeses* (Guatemala: Ministerio de Educación Pública, 1959), 54–57; McCreery, *Rural Guatemala,* 23, 56; Miceli, "Rafael Carrera"; Ingersoll, "War of the Mountain," 45.

9. Ixsamaj, 9/6/98, Comalapa.

10. Kab'lajuj Tijax, 4/7/98, Comalapa.

11. P. Molina F., "1918," *Diario de Centro América,* Jan. 7, 1919, 2; Woodward, *Rafael Carrera,* 295; M. Y. Arriola, "La epidemia reinante," *Diario de Centro América,* Jan. 18, 1919, 6; McCreery, *Rural Guatemala,* 148–49; Robert Carmack, "Los Indígenas," in *Historia General de Guatemala,* ed. Jorge Luján Muñoz (Guatemala: Asociación de Amigos del País, Fundación para la Cultura y el Desarrollo, 1995), 349.

12. Ix'aq'om, 9/13/98, Comalapa; Oxi' Imox, 2/11/98, 9/14/98, Comalapa; Junlajuj Imox, 5/23/98, Comalapa; Waqxaqi' Aq'ab'al, 3/17/98, Hacienda María, Poaquil; Jun Kej (Jun Tojil interview), 1998, Barahona; Ix'ajmaq, 6/2/98, Tecpán.

13. *Recopilación de las Leyes de la República de Guatemala,* 36: 205.

14. The tendency to eat lemon to prevent cholera may also be a result of the widespread and incorrect idea that lemon kills bacteria, although none of my oral sources cited this as a reason for its use.

15. Ixno'j and Waqi' Aq'ab'al, 2/16/98, Comalapa; Wo'o' Ajpu', 11/11/98, Comalapa.

16. Alfred Crosby, *Epidemic and Peace, 1918* (Westport, Conn.: Greenwood, 1977); Richard Adams, "Estado e Indígenas durante la epidemia de influenza de 1918–1919 en Guatemala," *Mesoamérica* 34 (1997): 484–85.

17. McCreery, "Guatemala City," in *The 1918–1919 Pandemic Influenza: The Urban Impact in the Western World,* ed. Fred R. van Hartesveldt (New York: Edwin Mellen, 1992), 164.

18. Woodward, *Central America,* 172, 200–201; Handy, *Gift of the Devil,* 88; Adams, "Estado e Indígenas," 547–48.

19. *Memoria de la Secretaría de Gobernación y Justicia presentada a la Asamblea Nacional Legislativa en sus sesiones ordinarias* (Guatemala: Minerva centro editorial, 1919), 20.

20. Luis Gaitán and Julio Roberto Herrera, "II día PanAméricano de la Salud en Guatemala," *Boletín Sanitario de Guatemala, órgano de la Dirección General de Sanidad Pública de Guatemala* 12, no. 49 (1941): 7–10. Their statistics reveal that 3.09 and 3.02 percent of the population died in 1918 and 1919, respectively; in contrast, only 1.72 percent of the population died in 1920.

21. McCreery, "Guatemala City," 161–83; Adams, "Estado e Indígenas," 495.

22. "Salubridad," *Diario de Centro América,* Jan. 9, 1919, 3; McCreery, *Rural Guatemala,* 277–78.

23. "Grippe," *La República,* Dec. 2, 1918, 2.

24. "Por telégrafo-por correo," *La República,* Dec. 18, 1918, 2.

25. Molina Flores, "Apunte Científico El Rayado," *La República,* Jan. 22, 1919, 2.

26. "Cuestiones de la peste," *La República,* Jan. 27, 1919, 1; *La República,* Jan. 23, 1919, and Feb. 3, 1919.

27. "Cuestiones de la peste," *La República,* Jan. 27, 1919, 1.

28. "De Chimaltenango," *La República,* Feb. 5, 1919, 4.

29. "Año Nuevo," *Díario de Centro América,* Jan. 1, 1919, 5.

30. "1918," *Díario de Centro América,* Jan. 7, 1919, 2.

31. *Díario de Centro América,* Dec. 18, 1918, 1.

32. *Díario de Centro América,* Jan. 11, 1919, 2.

33. Wuqu' Kan, 6/5/98, Tecpán.

34. Kaji' Aq'ab'al, 6/8/98, Tecpán; Ka'i' Aq'ab'al, 6/7/98, Tecpán; Waqi' No'j, 3/15/98, 8/30/98, Poaquil; Wuqu' Ey, 3/26/98, 8/12/98, Hacienda Vieja, Poaquil.

35. *Memoria de la Secretaría de Gobernación y Justicia,* 1919, 53; Ed Aguirre Velásquez, "Respuestas a la orden," *La República,* Dec. 26, 1918, 1.

36. *Memoria de la Secretaría de Gobernación y Justicia,* 1919, 54.

37. Ibid., 58.

38. "Noticias de Chimaltenango," *La República,* Jan. 4, 1919, 3.

39. Ixtijax, 8/17/98, Comalapa.

40. "De Chimaltenango," *La República,* Feb. 3, 1919, 2.

41. Kaji' Kan, 8/15/98, Comalapa; Jun Kan, 8/19/98, 9/3/98, Comalapa; Junlajuj Imox, 8/29/98, Comalapa; Ixnum, 4/29/98, Comalapa; Jun Iq', 4/18/98, Comalapa; Junlajuj Ajpu', 8/2/98, Comalapa; Ixya', 4/11/98, Comalapa; Oxi' Tz'i', 5/29/98, Tecpán; Wuqu' No'j, 11/10/97, Comalapa; Ix'aj, 2/9/98, Comalapa; Ka'i' Tz'i', 5/26/98, Tecpán; Wo'o' Aq'ab'al, 11/24/97, Chuwatz'unuj, Tecpán.

42. Ixq'anil and Iztz'i', 4/28/98, Comalapa.

43. Asturias de Barrios, *Mano de Mujer,* 204.

44. Ix'imox, 8/23/98, Comalapa; Ixtz'i', 9/9/98, Comalapa.

45. Kab'lajuj Tijax and Ixpo't, 7/19/98, Comalapa.

46. A proper burial is an important aspect of the Kaqchikel culture. Menchú refers to the significance of this tradition for the K'ichee' culture in *Crossing Borders,* 159. Grandin also notes that "mourning rituals were particularly fertile grounds for conflict" between Maya and government officials; see *Blood of Guatemala,* 94–96.

47. Patzún is a Kaqchikel town that borders Patzicía and Tecpán.

48. "Noticias de Chimaltenango," *La República,* Jan. 8, 1919, 4. Two days later, on January 10, *La República* reported that they had been told the story about Samayoa was incorrect, but in the article the author left some doubt as to the veracity of the negation; see "Diversas noticias de Chimaltenango," *La República,* Jan. 10, 1919, 2. Live burials were not just perceptions but documented incidents. Heather L. McCrea discovered a similar phenomenon in the Yucatán during the Cholera epidemic. Prisoners assigned to dig graves and inter the dead buried people who were still alive; see McCrea, "Burial and Cemetery Rights in Nineteenth-Century Yucatán," paper given at American Society for Ethnohistory Conference, Minneapolis, Nov. 12, 1998.

49. *Memoria de la Secretaría de Gobernación y Justicia,* 1919, 68–69, 60.

50. Ixte, 9/10/98, Comalapa.

51. *Memoria de la Secretaría de Gobernación y Justicia*, 1919, 57.

52. "Dos Problemas de urgente Resolución," *La República*, Jan. 29, 1919, 1.

53. "La influenza en los departamentos," *Diario de Centro América*, Jan. 4, 1919, 3.

54. "Resumen de los informes enviados al comite nacional de salubridad," *Diario de Centro América*, Jan. 28, 1919, 5; "Por telégrafo," *Diario de Centro América*, Nov. 29, 1918, 3; Adams, "Estado e indígenas," 551; *Memoria de la Secretaría de Gobernación y Justicia*, 1919, 57.

55. *Memoria de la Secretaría de Gobernación y Justicia*, 1919, 57–58.

56. *Memoria de la Secretaría de Gobernación y Justicia*, 1919, 54.

57. "El estado sanitario de los departamentos," *Diario de Centro América*, Jan. 8, 1919, 2.

58. "La epidemia reinante," *Diario de Centro América*, Jan. 18, 1919, 6.

59. Carlos Catalán Prem, "El tifus exantemático en Chimaltenango," *Boletín Sanitario de Guatemala, órgano de la Dirección General de Sanidad Pública de Guatemala* 11, no. 48 (1940): 138.

60. "Causas de la enfermedad en la clase indigena," *Diario de Centro América*, Jan. 25, 1919, 7.

61. "La epidemia reinante," *Diario de Centro América*, Jan. 18, 1919, 6.

62. *Memoria de la Secretaría de Gobernación y Justicia*, 1919, 9. In his study of the effects of influenza in San Marcos, Adams points out that one of the main Ladino concerns was the decrease in production of agricultural goods, especially coffee, and the construction of roads ("Estado e indígenas," 504–20).

63. *Diario de Centro América*, Dec. 27, 1918, 8.

64. *Diario de Centro América*, Feb. 8, 1919, 6.

65. SADINOEL, "Año Nuevo," *El Impulso*, Jan. 1, 1919, 1–2.

66. *Memoria de la Secretaría de Gobernación y Justicia*, 1919, 10, 17.

67. Adams, "Estado e indígenas," 551.

68. *Salubridad y Asistencia: órgano del Ministerio de Salud Pública y Asistencia Social*, Apr. 1951 (Guatemala, 1948–51), 4: 7.

69. Britnell, "Problems of Economic and Social Change," 474–75; Inman, *New Day in Guatemala*, 28–29; Suslow, *Aspects of Social Reform in Guatemala*, 104–6; "Resumen de los trabajos y actividades realizadas por Sanidad Pública en el año por la Redacción," *Boletín Sanitario de Guatemala, órgano de la Dirección General de Sanidad Pública de Guatemala*, 15 (1945): 69–70. Francisco Salazar, "Sanidad Public," *Salubridad y Asistencia: órgano del ministerio de salud pública y asistencia social*, Oct. 1948, 1: 5–6.

70. Lajuj Kan, 10/15/97, Pachitur, Comalapa; Ixpo't, 11/17/97, Poaquil; Kaji' Imox, 8/2/98, Comalapa; Jun Tz'i', 7/11/98, Pamumus, Comalapa; Ix'umül, 4/15/98, Simajulew, Comalapa; Wuqu' Iq', 12/17/97, Xiquín Sanahí, Comalapa; Ka'i' Aq'ab'al, 6/7/98, Tecpán.

71. Wo'o' Iq', 12/2/97, Panicuy, Comalapa.

72. Jun Kan, 8/19/98, Comalapa.

73. Isidro Cabrera and Manuel López Selva, "Campana contra el tifo," *Salubri-*

dad y Asistencia: órgano del ministerio de salud pública y asistencia social (Guatemala), Dec. 1948, 1: 46.

74. Ibid., 44–49; "Control de Tifo," *Salubridad y Asistencia,* June 1950, 3: 7; "Sección control de Tifo," *Salubridad y Asistencia,* Oct. 1950, 3: 4; Luís F. Galich, "Informe de la labor realizada por la Dirección General de Sanidad Pública en 1950," *Salubridad y Asistencia: Órgano del ministerio de salud pública y asistencia social,* Jan. 1951, 4: 19; Isidro Cabrera, "Trabajos realizados por la sección de control de tifo en 1950," *Salubridad y Asistencia: órgano del ministerio de salud pública y asistencia social,* Apr. 1951, 4: 7–9, 14. Cabrera and López Selva, "Campana contra el tifo," 38–43, shows photographs of medical personnel disinfecting a building with DDT and vaccinating people in Chimaltenango's central park.

75. *Díario de Centro América,* Jan. 29, 1919, 1, 5, 7, and Feb. 28, 1919, 1, 2. For other accounts of the effects of influenza in Sacatepéquez see "La influenza en Sacatepéquez," *Díario de Centro América,* Jan. 13, 1919, 2; "La situación sanitaria en el país," *Díario de Centro América,* Jan. 21, 1919, 1, 6.

76. *Memoria de la Secretaría de Gobernación y Justicia,* 1919, 20.

77. Lajuj Aq'ab'al, 11/12/97, Aguas Calientes; Ixkej, 11/9/97, Aguas Calientes; P'ot, women's weaving cooperative, 2/7/98, Barahona.

78. AGCA, Documentos de Jefetura Política de Sacatepéquez, Feb. 17, 1927; Annis, *God and Production,* 14.

79. "Encontrose en la Laguna de San Antonio Aguas Calientes una mina," *El Día, Díario Independiente,* May 20, 1927, 1–2.

80. Letters from Santiago Zamora municipality signed DSO, May 12, Feb. 11, June 9, 1928, AGCA, Documentos de Jefetura Política de Sacatepéquez, 1928.

81. Most oral accounts date the drying of the lake to the late 1920s or early 1930s; the majority say it happened during Lázaro Chacón's presidency.

82. Jun Ey, 11/12/97, Aguas Calientes; Kab'lajuj Tz'i', 9/1/98, Aguas Calientes; Waqxaqi' Kawoq, 11/8/97, Aguas Calientes; Waqxaqi' Ajpu' (Jun Tojil interview), 1998, Barahona; B'eleje' Ajpu' (Jun Tojil interview), Barahona; Lajuj Aq'ab'al, 11/12/97, Aguas Calientes; Wuqu' Imox, 11/12/97, Aguas Calientes; Ixtojil 2/7/98, Barahona; Jun Kej (Jun Tojil interview), Barahona; Waqxaqi' K'at, 11/8/97, Aguas Calientes; Wuqu' Ajpu' (Jun Tojil interview), 1998, Barahona.

83. Ix'ey, 10/6/97, Aguas Calientes.

84. Chacón to Jefe Político de Antigua, Jan. 12, 1927, AGCA, Documentos de Jefetura Política de Sacatepéquez, 1927; Secretaría de Estado en el despacho de Fomento, a Jefes políticos, Jan. 29, 1927, AGCA, Documentos de Jefetura Política de Sacatepéquez, 1927.

85. Chacón to Jefe Político de Sacatepéquez, Apr. 8, 1927, AGCA, Documentos de Jefetura Política de Sacatepéquez, 1927.

86. Fidel Castillo to Jefe Político de Sacatepéquez, May 28, 1927, AGCA, Documentos de Jefetura Política de Sacatepéquez, 1927.

87. "Encontrose en la Laguna de San Antonio Aguas Calientes una mina," *El Día, Díario Independiente,* May 20, 1927, 2.

88. Telegram from Manuel J. Velásquez to Jefe Político de Chimaltenango, Apr. 30, 1927, AGCA, Documentos de Jefetura Política de Sacatepéquez, 1927.

89. Castillo to Jefe Político de Antigua, Apr. 22, 1927, AGCA, Documentos de Jefetura Politíca de Sacatepéquez, 1927.

90. Telegram from Jefe Político de Chimaltenango, Apr. 23, 1927, AGCA, Documentos de Jefetura Politíca de Sacatepéquez, 1927.

91. "Encontrose en la Laguna de San Antonio Aguas Calientes una mina," *El Día, Díario Independiente,* May 20, 1927, 2.

92. Letter to Jefe Político de Sacatepéquez, July 26, 1927, AGCA, Documentos de Jefetura Politíca de Sacatepéquez, 1927.

93. "Encontrose en la Laguna de San Antonio Aguas Calientes una mina," *El Día, Díario Independiente,* May 20, 1927, 2.

94. Telegram from Jefe Político de Chimaltenango, June 29, 1927, AGCA, Documentos de Jefetura Politíca de Sacatepéquez, 1927. Manuel Salazar mentioned that Magdaleno Par and Feliciano Chang should be watched carefully lest they return early to their hometown of Tecpán (Telegram from Jefe Político de Chimaltenango, June 20, 1927, AGCA, Documentos de Jefetura Politíca de Sacatepéquez, 1927).

95. Telegram from Jefe Político de Chimaltenango, June 29, 1927, AGCA, Documentos de Jefetura Politíca de Sacatepéquez, 1927.

96. Letter from Jefe Político de Chimaltenango, Mar. 21, 1927, AGCA, Documentos de Jefetura Politíca de Sacatepéquez, 1927.

97. Dirección General de Obras Públicas (Public Works Department) to Jefe Político de Sacatepéquez, July 13, 1927, AGCA, Documentos de Jefetura Politíca de Sacatepéquez, 1927; telegram from Jefe Político de Guatemala, July 12, 1927, AGCA, Documentos de Jefetura Politíca de Sacatepéquez, 1927.

98. S. Reyes López, Memoria del Pueblo de San Antonio Aguas Calientes, correspondiente al año 1927 (San Antonio Aguas Calientes Annual Report, 1927), Dec. 31, 1927, 2, AGCA, Documentos de Jefetura Politíca de Sacatepéquez, 1927.

99. Ka'i' Kawoq, 2/7/98, Aguas Calientes.

100. Lajuj Aq'ab'al, 11/12/97, Aguas Calientes; Kaji' Kej, 11/12/97, Aguas Calientes; Wo'o' Aj (Ix'ey interview), 1998, Aguas Calientes; Waqi' Aj, 2/28/98, Aguas Calientes. Some oral accounts attribute the gift of the marimba to President José María Orellana, President Estrada Cabrera, or General Jorge Ubico, but the majority claim President Chacón; see Jun Ey, 11/12/97, Aguas Calientes; Lajuj Aq'ab'al, 11/12/97, Aguas Calientes. Archival evidence shows that Ubico did have a role in drying the lake. In 1934, during Ubico's reign, another outbreak of malaria occurred, and the government once again had to focus its efforts on drying the lake; see *Memoria de los trabajos realizados por la Dirección General de Sanidad Pública,* 1934 (Guatemala: Tipografía Nacional), 372–73.

101. Chacón to Jefe Político de Sacatepéquez, Dec. 8, 1927, AGCA, Documentos de Jefetura Politíca de Sacatepéquez, 1927; accord of Feb. 23, 1928, *Recopilación de las Leyes de la República de Guatemala,* 46: 758–59.

102. Jun Ey, 11/12/97, Aguas Calientes.

103. Annis, *God and Production,* 42.

104. Santiago Zamora, June 1, 1929, AGCA, Documentos de Jefetura Politíca de Sacatepéquez, 1927; *Memoria de los trabajos realizados por la Dirección General de Sanidad Pública,* 1934, 372–73.

105. Ka'i' Tojil, 6/12/98, Barahona; Wuqu' Ajpu' (Jun Tojil interview), 1998, Barahona. The municipal document in Barahona indicates that ownership of the lake has been disputed for hundreds of years (Santa Catarina Barahona municipal document, "Certificación Extendida," 5).

106. Kab'lajuj Kan, 2/15/98, Barahona.

107. VERA, "A los indios muertos," *La República,* Jan. 30, 1919, 3.

Chapter 4

1. *Memoria de la Secretaría de Gobernación y Justicia,* 1919, 9; "Noticias de Chimaltenango," *La República,* Jan. 4, 1919, 3.

2. Junlajuj Imox, 9/14/98, Comalapa.

3. Waqi' K'at, 9/6/98, Comalapa.

4. Kab'lajuj Ajpu', 11/14/97, Comalapa.

5. Oxi' Kej, 6/14/98, Comalapa.

6. Ixq'anil, 3/3/98, Comalapa.

7. *El Gráfico,* Feb. 16, 1976, 4. The next closest department to Chimaltenango in terms of deaths was Guatemala, with 3,240 dead and 15,927 injured. About a week after the earthquake struck, without final statistics tabulated, the *Díario de Centro América,* estimated 10,170 dead and 18,523 injured in Chimaltenango (*Díario de Centro América,* Feb. 13, 1976, 6).

8. Saul David Oliva, "Ruina, dolor y muerte: cauda tragica del fenomeno Telurico," *Díario de Centro América,* Feb. 9, 1976, 4.

9. *La Hora,* Feb. 9–13, 1976, reported the calculations of the National Meteorological Observatory to be as high as an additional 716 tremors.

10. Miguel Angel Rayo, "5,000 muertos en Chimaltengo departamento: espactacules indescriptibles en Comalapa, San Martín Jilotepeque, Zaragoza, Patzicía, Chimaltenango, Poaquil, Balanya, Acatenango, Parramos, Yepocapa, y Tejar," *La Hora,* Feb. 7, 1976, 1.

11. "5 son las cuidades con mayor destrozo," *La Hora,* Feb. 7, 1976, 1.

12. Ibid.

13. Rayo, "5,000 muertos en Chimaltengo departamento," *La Hora,* Feb. 7, 1976, 1. Fuego (fire) is the name of one of the volcanoes in the department of Sacatepéquez.

14. Oxlajuj Kan, 10/17/97, Comalapa.

15. Waqi' K'at, 9/6/98, Comalapa.

16. Kaji' Kawoq, Patzicía (phone conversation), 12/10/98.

17. Wuqu' Ajmaq, 4/6/98, Comalapa.

18. Kab'lajuj Tz'i', 9/1/98, Aguas Calientes; Waqxaqi' Kawoq, 11/8/97, Aguas Calientes; Kab'lajuj Kan, 2/15/98, Barahona; Waqxaqi' K'at, 11/8/97, Aguas Calientes; Jun Ey, 11/12/97, Aguas Calientes; Wuqu' Imox, 11/12/97, Aguas Calientes; Ixkej, 11/9/97, Aguas Calientes; Waqi' Kan (Ix'ey interview), 1998, Aguas Calientes; B'eleje' Ajpu' (Jun Tojil interview), 1998, Barahona.

19. Ixtojil, 2/7/98, Barahona.

20. Kaji' Kej, 11/12/97, Aguas Calientes; Oxi' Ey, 11/28/97, Aguas Calientes.

21. Waqxaqi' No'j, 10/3/98, Poaquil; Ix'ajmaq, 3/15/98, Poaquil; Lajuj Kawoq, 3/16/98, Poaquil; Waqxaqi' Tijax, 4/18/98, Poaquil.

22. Ixb'atz', 3/10/98, Poaquil.

23. B'eleje' Ey, 4/28/98, Poaquil.

24. Handy, *Gift of the Devil,* 173; "Integrado un comite para Comalapa," *La Hora,* Feb. 11, 1976, 1; "Generosa ayuda internacional," *Díario de Centro América,* Feb. 10, 1976, 5. See the Feb. 13 issue of the *Díario de Centro América* for evidence of Israel's aid, 3. For an account of how aid arrived in the communities see, Ricardo Gatica Trejo, "Fluye la ayuda a las poblaciones afectadas," *El Gráfico,* Feb. 14, 1976, 3.

25. Ix'ichaj, 5/29/98, Tecpán.

26. For an examination of the Protestant movement throughout Latin America see David Stoll and Virginia Garrard-Burnett, eds., *Rethinking Protestantism in Latin America* (Philadelphia: Temple University Press, 1993). For Protestantism in Guatemala see Garrard-Burnett, *Protestantism in Guatemala* and Zapata Arceyuz, *Historia de la iglesia evangelica in Guatemala.*

27. Walter Lafeber, *Inevitable Revolutions: The United States and Central America* (New York: W. W. Norton and Company, 1984), 258–59; Robert G. Williams, *Export Agriculture and the Crisis in Central America* (Chapel Hill: University of North Carolina Press, 1986), 175; Shelton H. Davis, "State Violence and Agrarian Crisis in Guatemala: The Roots of the Indian-Peasant Rebellion," in *Trouble in Our Backyard: Central America and the United States in the Eighties,* ed. Martin Diskin (New York: Pantheon, 1983), 164; Arias, "Changing Indian Identity," 242, 252–53; Susanne Jonas, *The Battle for Guatemala: Rebels, Death Squads, and U.S. Power* (Boulder: Westview, 1991), 124–27; Frank and Wheaton, *Indian Guatemala,* 51; Carol Smith, "Class Position and Class Consciousness in an Indian Community: Totonicapán in the 1970s," in *Guatemalan Indians and the State: 1540–1988,* ed. Carol Smith (Austin: University of Texas Press, 1990), 225; Rigoberta Menchú, *I, Rigoberta Menchú: An Indian Woman in Guatemala* (New York: Verso, 1984), 135.

28. Flora and Torres Rivas, "Sociology of Developing Societies: Historical Bases of Insurgency in Central America," in *Sociology of Developing Societies: Central America,* ed. Jan L. Flora and Edelberto Torres Rivas (New York: Monthly Review, 1989), 38.

29. Kaji' Iq', 11/18/97, Tecpán.

30. Annis, *God and Production,* 3. See Sheldon Annis, "A Story from a Peaceful Town," in *Harvest of Violence: Guatemala's Indians and the Counterinsurgency War,* ed. Robert Carmack (Norman: University of Oklahoma Press, 1988), for more details about the civil war's effects on Aguas Calientes.

31. Recinos, *Memorial de Sololá,* 105.

32. Ibid., 118.

33. Oxlajuj Ajmaq, 9/24/97, Tecpán; Ixch'oy, 11/21/97, Tecpán.

34. Ix'ajpu', 9/23/97, Comalapa.

35. *Memoria de la Secretaría de Gobernación y Justicia,* 1915, 3, 214; McCreery, *Rural Guatemala,* 148, 294, 308.

36. M. Vargas Ortíz, "Situación Penosa," *El Impulso,* Feb. 28, 1915, 2.

37. I established a range from the 1920s to the 1930s by compiling oral accounts. Most Kaqchikel provided a more concise time frame.

38. Oxi' Tz'i', 5/29/98, Tecpán; Wuqu' Kej, 5/30/98, Tecpán; Ixb'oq', 5/31/98, Tecpán; Oxi' K'at, 6/5/98, Tecpán; Jun Aj and Ix'ik', 6/6/98, Tecpán; Lajuj Ajpu', 6/6/98, Poaquil.

39. *Memoria del Ministerio de Agricultura, 1934,* 473.

40. Ixsamaj, 9/6/98, Comalapa; Ixq'anil, Comalapa; Ixb'utz', 6/20/98, Comalapa; Oxi' Ajmaq, 3/27/98, Hacienda Vieja, Poaquil; Kab'lajuj Tijax, 4/7/98, 7/19/98, Comalapa.

41. "Informe Anual," *Memoria del Ministerio de Agricultura,* 1923, 28.

42. Ibid., 65; *Memoria del Ministerio de Agricultura,* 1924, 57–59.

43. *Memoria del Ministeria de Agricultura,* 1923, 189; *Recopilación de las Leyes de la República de Guatemala,* decree no. 810, Jan. 24, 1923, vol. 42. See *Recopilación de las Leyes de la República de Guatemala,* decree no. 852, Jan. 18, 1924, vol. 43 for a similar law the following year.

44. Ixkuk, 10/30/97, Comalapa; Junlajuj Ajpu', 8/2/98, Comalapa; Ixsamaj, 9/6/98, Comalapa; Kab'lajuj Kawoq, 3/23/98, Poaquil; Ixtz'i', 9/9/98, Comalapa.

45. *Memoria del Ministerio de Agricultura,* 1926, 11–12, 105; *Memoria del Ministerio de Agricultura,* 1927, 14–16, 111; *Memoria del Ministerio de Agricultura,* 1929, 6; *Memoria del Ministerio de Agricultura,* 1930 to 1935, 1937, and 1938; *Memoria del Ministerio de Agricultura,* 1931, 37.

46. *Memoria del Ministerio de Agricultura,* 1935, 707; *Memoria del Ministerio de Agricultura,* 1938, 458.

47. *Memoria del Ministerio de Agricultura,* 1935, 628.

48. Ixkinäq', 11/23/97, Tecpán; Ixkuk, 10/30/97, Comalapa; Junlajuj Ajpu', 8/2/98, Comalapa; Ixsamaj, 9/6/98, Comalapa; Kab'lajuj Kawoq, 3/23/98, Poaquil; Ixtz'i', 9/9/98, Comalapa.

49. *Memoria del Ministerio de Agricultura,* 1938, 458–59.

50. Oxi' Imox, 9/14/98, Comalapa; B'eleje' Iq', 6/4/98, Tecpán; Ixtijax, 2/9/98, Comalapa.

51. *Memoria del Ministerio de Agricultura,* 1957, 27, 120.

52. B'eleje' Iq', 6/4/98, Tecpán; Wuqu' Kan, 6/5/98, Tecpán; Ixkuk, 10/30/97, Comalapa; Junlajuj K'at, 7/9/98, Comalapa; Wuqu' K'at, "Libreta de Apuntes."

53. Price, *First Time,* 12.

Chapter 5

1. Kab'lajuj Kawoq, 3/23/98, Poaquil.

2. Skinner-Klee, *Legislación indigenísta de Guatemala,* 20.

3. Smith, "Indian Class and Class Consciousness," 31; Woodward, *Central America,* 102–3, 172–73; Carlos González Orellana, *Historia de la educación en Guatemala* (México, D.F.: Coleción Científico Pedagógica, 1960), 195–98; Carol Smith, "Origins of the National Question in Guatemala: A Hypothesis," in *Guatemalan Indians and the State: 1540–1988,* ed. Carol Smith (Austin: University of Texas Press,

1990), 78; Julia Becker Richards and Michael Richards, "Maya Education: A Historical and Contemporary Analysis of Mayan Language Education Policy," in *Maya Cultural Activism in Guatemala,* ed. Edward Fischer and R. McKenna Brown (Austin: University of Texas Press, 1996), 209–10.

4. Woodward, *Central America,* 211; González Orellana, *Historia de la educación en Guatemala,* 237–38, 247, 282; *Recopilación de las Leyes de la República de Guatemala,* decree no. 131, Jan. 2, 1875, 319–40.

5. Wuqu' Kan, 6/5/98, Tecpán; Kab'lajuj Ajpu', 5/5/98, Comalapa; Kab'lajuj Tz'i', 9/1/98, Aguas Calientes; Ixche', 11/22/97, Poaquil; Ix'ey, 10/20/97, Aguas Calientes.

6. Lajuj Iq', 12/9/97, Xenimaquín, Comalapa.

7. Oxlajuj K'at, 3/10/98, Poaquil; Jun Tijax, 3/8/98, Panabajal, Comalapa.

8. Kab'lajuj Imox, 11/5/97, Comalapa.

9. *Recopilación de las Leyes de la República de Guatemala,* decree no. 1959, May 10, 1937, 56: 89–102; Kenneth J. Grieb, *Guatemalan Caudillo: The Regime of Jorge Ubico, Guatemala 1931–1944* (Athens: Ohio University Press, 1979), 175; Chester Lloyd Jones, *Guatemala: Past and Present* (Minneapolis: University of Minnesota Press, 1940), 174; Erna Fergusson, *Guatemala* (New York: Alfred A. Knopf, 1938), 225, 292; Flavio Rodas N., Ovidio Rodas C., and Lawrence F. Hawkins, *Chichicastenango: The Kiche Indians* (Guatemala: Union Tipografía, 1940), 95; Whetten, *Guatemala: The Land and the People,* 260–65, 269–71.

10. González Orellana, *Historia de la educación en Guatemala,* 305.

11. *El Imparcial,* May 18, 1938; Handy, *Gift of the Devil,* 97; González Orellana, *Historia de la educación en Guatemala,* 306; Federíco Hernández de León, *Viajes presidenciales: breves relatos de algunas expediciones administrativos del General D. Jorge Ubico, presidente de la República* (Guatemala: Tipografía Nacional, 1940), 1: 19, 143; Warren, *Symbolism of Subordination,* 150; Whetten, *Guatemala: The Land and the People,* 269–71; Fergusson, *Guatemala,* 225.

12. Smith, "Indian Class and Class Consciousness," 31–32, 42n40; Sam Colop, "Discourse of Concealment," 111–12; Severo Martínez Paláez, *La patria del criollo: ensayo de interpretación de la realidad colonial guatemalteca* (Guatemala: Editorial Universitaria Centroamericana, 1973).

13. "Monografía del Municipio de San Juan Comalapa, Chimaltenango, Area Urbana, Ciclo Escolar 1994, Supervisión educativa no. 95–18," San Juan Comalapa Administration of Education Office (typescript, ca. 1994), 3.

14. R. McKenna Brown, "The Mayan Language Loyalty Movement in Guatemala," in *Maya Cultural Activism in Guatemala,* ed. Edward Fischer and R. McKenna Brown (Austin: University of Texas Press, 1996), 175; Demetrio Cojtí Cuxil, "The Politics of Maya Revindication," in *Maya Cultural Activism in Guatemala,* ed. Edward Fischer and R. McKenna Brown (Austin: University of Texas Press, 1996), 39–40. Alfredo Tay Tocoy, who was appointed minister of education in 1993, was Guatemala's first Mayan Cabinet member.

15. An ajq'ij, or Mayan daykeeper, is a Mayan priest who can read, interpret, and divine the 260-day Mayan calendar, interpret signs and dreams, and cure people. For an excellent description and analysis of their duties and role in Mayan communities

see Tedlock, *Time and the Highland Maya,* 47–85. Also see Benjamin N. Colby and Lore M. Colby, *The Daykeeper: The Life and Discourse of an Ixil Diviner* (Cambridge: Harvard University Press, 1981).

16. B'eleje' Kawoq, 6/9/98, Tecpán.

17. Waqi' Kan (Ix'ey interview), 1998, Aguas Calientes.

18. Ka'i' K'at, 5/16/98, Comalapa; Jun Q'anil, 2/9/98, Patzaj, Comalapa; Jun Kan, 8/19/98, Comalapa; B'eleje' Ey, 11/23/97, Poaquil; Ixkan, 3/29/98, Poaquil; Junlajuj Kej, 3/22/98, Poaquil; Lajuj Aq'ab'al, 11/12/97, Aguas Calientes; Kaji' Kej, 11/12/97, Aguas Calientes; Jun Aj and Ix'ik', 6/6/98, Tecpán.

19. Wo'o' Imox, 5/23/98, Comalapa.

20. Ixpaläj, 8/19/98, Comalapa.

21. Waqxaqi' Tijax, 4/18/98, Poaquil; Ixmuxu'x, 3/21/98, Hacienda María, Poaquil; Jun Kan, 8/19/98, Comalapa; Junlajuj Imox, 5/23/98, Comalapa; Ixtoj, 8/21/98, Comalapa; Wuqu' Kej, 5/30/98, Tecpán.

22. Oxi' Iq', 12/2/98, Comalapa.

23. Díaz, "Sacatepéquez," *Diario de Centro América,* July 10, 1912, 1.

24. Luis Gaitán, Julio Roberto Herrera, Carlos Martínez Durán, and Hernán Martínez Sobral, "Contribución al estudio del tifus exantemático en Guatemala," *Boletín Sanitario de Guatemala, órgano de la Dirección General de Sanidad Pública de Guatemala* 11, no. 48 (1940): 34.

25. González Orellana, *Historia de la educación en Guatemala,* 305.

26. Waqi' Kan (Ix'ey interview), 1998, Aguas Calientes. Ironically, this man requested that the interview be conducted in Spanish. In some cases, Kaqchikel intellectuals are proof of the loss of knowledge and language that many Kaqchikel fear, because they speak about ideas in Spanish, not Kaqchikel.

27. Ix'ey, 10/6/97, Aguas Calientes; Waqxaqi' K'at, 11/8/97, Aguas Calientes; Ixtz'i', 9/9/98, Comalapa; Ka'i' Imox, 8/5/98, Panabajal, Comalapa; Ixkej, 11/9/97, Aguas Calientes; Ixmusmut, 5/18/98, Santiago Zamora, Aguas Calientes; Waqxaqi' Aq'ab'al, 3/17/98, Hacienda María, Poaquil; Wuqu' Aj, 3/26/98, Hacienda Vieja, Poaquil; Ixtz'ib', 3/27/98, Paley, Poaquil; Oxlajuj K'at, 3/10/98, Poaquil; Ix'ichaj, 5/29/98, Tecpán; Ka'i' Tz'i', 5/26/98, Tecpán; Ka'i' Ajmaq, 11/23/97, Tecpán.

28. Goubaud Carrera, *San Antonio Aguas Calientes,* 47.

29. Kab'lajuj Kawoq, 3/23/98, Poaquil.

30. Ixb'atz', 3/10/98, Poaquil.

31. Junlajuj Ey, 5/22/98, Comalapa.

32. Ixsanik (Ix'ajpu' interview), 1998, Comalapa; Ixwatzik', 1/12/98, Xiquín Sanahí, Comalapa; Ix'ik', 6/6/98, Tecpán; Ixpop, 5/20/98, Comalapa; Ixtijax, 8/17/98, Comalapa; Iximnik'te', 4/13/99, Tecpán.

33. Ix'ajmaq, 6/2/98, Tecpán.

34. Ka'i' Ey, 7/11/98, Comalapa.

35. Ixno'j and Waqi' Aq'ab'al, 2/16/98, Comalapa. The generational divergence of attitudes toward school is evident in other regions. For example, Carlsen notes that a Tz'utujil boy was repeatedly punished by his father for surreptitiously attending school; see Carlsen, *War for the Heart and Soul,* 140.

36. Waqi' Kame, 5/3/98, Pamumus, Comalapa; Lajuj Iq', 12/9/97, Xenimaquín,

Comalapa; Junlajuj Ajpu', 8/2/98, Comalapa; B'eleje' Kame, 10/17/97, Panabajal, Comalapa.

37. Ixkawoq, 4/17/98, Pamumus, Comalapa.

38. Waqxaqi' Kawoq, 11/8/97, Aguas Calientes; Wuqu' Iq', 12/17/97, Xiquín Sanahí, Comalapa; Waqxaqi' Aj, 4/15/98, Simajulew, Comalapa.

39. Jun Kej (Jun Tojil interview), 1998, Barahona.

40. Náñez Falcón, "Erwin Paul Dieseldorff," 344.

41. Junlajuj Kan, 4/24/98, Simajulew, Comalapa.

42. Oxi' Tojil, 3/21/98, Nueva Esperanza, Poaquil.

43. Oxi' Tz'ikin, 8/5/98, Comalapa; Kab'lajuj Ajpu', 11/14/97, Comalapa; Oxlajuj Kan, 9/12/98, Comalapa; Waqi' K'at, 9/6/98, Comalapa; Oxi' Kawoq, 9/4/98, Pamumus, Comalapa; Kab'lajuj Tijax, 4/7/98, Comalapa; Waqxaqi' Kej, 5/24/98, Comalapa; Ixkik', 6/21/98, Comalapa; Junlajuj Ajpu', 8/2/98, Comalapa; B'eleje' Aj, 8/5/98, Comalapa.

44. González Orellana, *Historia de la educación en Guatemala*, 282.

45. Jun Kan, 8/19/98, Comalapa; Wuqu' K'at, 4/6/98, Comalapa; Ix'imox, 8/23/98, Comalapa; Ix'umül, 4/15/98, Simajulew, Comalapa; Ixchel, 2/12/98, Comalapa; B'eleje' Imox, 1/11/98, Comalapa; Oxi' B'atz', 4/26/98, Comalapa; Ixtz'i', 2/14/98, Comalapa; Waqi' No'j, 3/15/98, Poaquil; Waqxaqi' Tijax, 4/18/98, Poaquil; Oxi' Iq', 12/2/98, Comalapa.

46. *Dirección General de la Policía Nacional, Memoria de sus trabajos realizados en el año 1924, rendida al ministerio de gobernación y justicia,* (Guatemala: Tipografía Nacional, 1925), 45.

47. Ibid., 162, 181; *Memoria del cuerpo de Policía Nacional de la República, rendida al Ministerio de Gobernación y Justicia* (Guatemala: Tipografía Nacional, 1927), 88–89, 113; *Memoria del cuerpo de Policía Nacional de la República, rendida al Ministerio de Gobernación y Justicia,* 1928, 98–99; *Memoria del cuerpo de Policía Nacional de la República, rendida al Ministerio de Gobernación y Justicia,* 1929, 45; *Memorias de Secretaría de Gobernación y Justicia,* 1932, 330.

48. "La Reforma de la Constituticion de la República de Guatemala, decretada 11 julio 1935," in *Las Constituciones de Guatemala,* ed. Luis Marinas Otero (Madrid: Instituto de Estudios Políticos, 1958), 581, 590–91.

49. *Boletín sanitario de Guatemala, órgano de la Dirección General de Sanidad Pública de Guatemala* 6 (1935): 152.

50. Jun Kan, 8/19/98, Comalapa; Wuqu' K'at, 4/6/98, Comalapa; Ix'imox, 8/23/98, Comalapa; Ix'umül, 4/15/98, Simajulew, Comalapa; Ixchel, 2/12/98, Comalapa; B'eleje' Imox, 1/11/98, Comalapa; Oxi' B'atz', 4/26/98, Comalapa; Ixtz'i', 2/14/98, Comalapa; Waqi' No'j, 3/15/98, Poaquil; Waqxaqi' Tijax, 4/18/98, Poaquil; Oxi' Iq', 12/2/98, Comalapa; Junlajuj Imox and Wo'o' Imox, 5/23/98, Comalapa; Jun Iq', 4/18/98, Comalapa.

51. Wo'o' No'j, 4/22/98, Xenimaquín, Comalapa; Ka'i' Imox, 1/21/98, Panabajal, Comalapa; Wo'o' Q'anil, 6/7/98, Tecpán; Ka'i' Ajmaq, 11/23/97, Tecpán; Lajuj Ajpu', 4/19/98, Poaquil; Junlajuj Ajpu', 8/2/98, Comalapa.

52. González Orellana, *Historia de la educación en Guatemala,* 336, 353–37, 362, 368–69; *El Imparcial,* Mar. 18 and Mar. 22, 1948; Handy, *Revolution in the Country-*

side, 51; Handy, *Gift of the Devil,* 107–8; Suslow, *Aspects of Social Reform in Guatemala,* 24, 26–27, 30–32; Woodward, *Central America,* 234; Cojtí Cuxil, "Politics of Maya Revindication," 40.

53. Oxi' Kawoq, 9/4/98, Pamumus, Comalapa; Waqi' Kame, 5/3/98, Pamumus, Comalapa; Ixpo't, 11/17/97, Poaquil; Oxi' K'at, 6/5/98, Tecpán; Wo'o' Kame, 5/29/98, Tecpán; Oxlajuj K'at, 3/10/98, Poaquil; Ka'i' Kawoq, 2/7/98, Aguas Calientes.

54. Handy, *Revolution in the Countryside,* 51; Suslow, *Aspects of Social Reform in Guatemala,* 24; Handy, *Gift of the Devil,* 107–8; González Orellana, *Historia de la educación en Guatemala,* 336, 338, 354; Inman, *New Day in Guatemala,* 22.

55. Oxi' Iq', 12/2/98, Comalapa.

56. Kab'lajuj Kawoq, 3/23/98, Poaquil.

57. *Recopilación de las Leyes de la República de Guatemala,* accord of Aug. 12, 1920, 39: 703.

58. Oxi' Tz'ikin, 8/5/98, Comalapa; Jun Kan, 8/19/98, Comalapa; B'eleje' Aj, 8/5/98, Comalapa.

59. "Monografía del Municipio de San Juan Comalapa, Chimaltenango," 11.

60. Oxi' Tz'ikin, 8/5/98, Comalapa.

61. Junlajuj Imox, 6/23/98, Comalapa.

62. The first Kaqchikel teachers from Comalapa were Benjamín Otzoy, Máximo Otzoy, Cayetano Otzoy, Edwardo Otsoy, Pedro Calel, and Trinidad Velásquez (Waqi' K'at, 9/6/98, Comalapa).

63. Jun Kan, 8/19/98, Comalapa.

64. Wuqu' K'at, 7/25/98, Comalapa.

65. Ixtijax, 8/17/98, Comalapa; Junlajuj Ajpu', 8/2/98, Comalapa; Ixtoj, 8/21/98, Comalapa; Lajuj Kame, 5/22/98, Comalapa; Ka'i' Aq'ab'al, 6/7/98, Tecpán; B'eleje' Kawoq, 6/9/98, Tecpán. *Indio* and *ixto* are pejorative terms used to describe members of Guatemala's Mayan population. See chapter 9 for further discussion of the use of these terms by Ladinos.

66. Kaji' Iq', 11/18/97, Tecpán.

67. Lajuj Iq', 12/9/97, Xenimaquín, Comalapa.

68. *Memoria de la Secretaría de Fomento, presentada a la Asamblea Nacional Legislativa en sus sesiones ordinarias* (Guatemala: Tipografía Nacional, 1917), 39.

69. *Memoria de la Secretaría de Fomento,* 1921, 83.

70. Waqxaqi' Ajmaq, 12/13/97, Comalapa.

71. Wo'o' No'j, 4/22/98, Xenimaquín, Comalapa; Jun Tz'i', 7/11/98, Pamumus, Comalapa; Wuqu' Tijax, 3/2/98, Palima, Comalapa.

72. Ministerio de Educación de Guatemala, *Primer seminario sobre problemas de la educación rural guatemalteca* (Guatemala City: Ministerio de Educación de Guatemala, 1964), 180.

73. For an excellent analysis of the development and goals of these schools see Becker Richards and Richards, "Maya Education."

74. Wuqu' Kawoq, 1/29/98, Comalapa; Jun Kan, 9/3/98, Comalapa; Ka'i' Tijax, 10/13/97, Comalapa; Oxi' No'j, 3/15/98, Poaquil; Ixk'at, 1/7/98, Comalapa; B'eleje' Ajmaq, 8/21/98, Comalapa; Iximnik'te', 4/13/99, Tecpán.

75. Oxi' Imox, 2/11/98, Comalapa.

76. Kab'lajuj Imox, 9/28/97, Comalapa.

77. Jun Aq'ab'al, 5/2/98, Tecpán.

78. Oxi' Tz'ikin, 8/17/98, Comalapa.

79. Ix'ey, 10/20/97, Aguas Calientes; Ixb'atz', 3/10/98, Poaquil; Wuqu' Q'anil, 3/21/98, Poaquil; Waqxaqi' Q'anil, 3/21/98, Nueva Esperanza, Poaquil.

80. Jun Q'anil, 2/9/98, Patzaj, Comalapa.

81. Jun Kej (Jun Tojil interview), 1998, Barahona; Kaji' Tijax, 4/28/98, Patzaj, Comalapa; Kaji' Kame, 3/4/98, Comalapa; Oxi' B'atz', 4/26/98, Comalapa; Lajuj Ajmaq, 8/21/98, Comalapa.

82. Jun Ajmaq, 9/4/98, Mixcolabaj, Comalapa.

83. Ixtz'i', 9/9/98, Comalapa.

84. Jun Q'anil, 2/9/98, Patzaj, Comalapa; Jun Kame, 5/1/98, Agua Caliente, Comalapa; Junlajuj Kej, 5/22/98, Paquixic, Comalapa; Lajuj Ajpu', 6/6/98, Poaquil; Kab'lajuj Kan, 2/15/98, Barahona; Oxlajuj Kawoq, 3/18/98, Poaquil; Ixchiköp, 12/17/97, Xiquín Sanahí, Comalapa.

85. Ix'ey, 10/20/97, Aguas Calientes; Waqxaqi' Ajpu' (Jun Tojil interview), 1998, Barahona; Waqxaqi' Aq'ab'al, 3/17/98, Hacienda María, Poaquil; Oxi' Aq'ab'al, 10/26/97, Comalapa.

86. Kaji' Kej, 11/12/97, Aguas Calientes.

87. Kaji' Kej, 11/12/97, Aguas Calientes; Ixkej, 11/9/97, Aguas Calientes; Kaji' Aq'ab'al, 6/8/98, Tecpán.

88. Warren, *Symbolism of Subordination,* 160–61. Also see Warren, *Indigenous Movements,* 51, 68.

89. Lajuj Kame, 2/14/98, Comalapa.

90. Waqi' Kame, 5/17/98, Pamumus, Comalapa.

91. Ixkawoq, 4/17/98, Pamumus, Comalapa; Pachitur primary school graduation ceremony, 10/29/97, Pachitur, Comalapa; Kab'lajuj Kej, 4/26/98, Comalapa.

92. Ix'aj, 2/9/98, Comalapa.

93. Kab'lajuj Iq', 5/31/98, Tecpán.

94. Waqxaqi' Iq', 6/23/98, Comalapa. At the same time, this man also knows the limits of the Peace Accords, as he had to withdraw his mayoral candidacy in 1998 because of death threats against him and his family.

95. Junlajuj Iq', 5/31/98, Tecpán; Lajuj Ajpu', 8/30/98, Poaquil.

96. B'eleje' Ey, 8/30/98, Poaquil.

97. Kaji' Kej, 11/12/97, Aguas Calientes.

98. Waqi' K'at, 9/6/98, Comalapa.

99. *CERIGUA,* Mar. 18, 1999.

100. Warren, *Indigenous Movements,* 37.

101. Cojtí Cuxil, "Politics of Maya Revindication," 39–41.

Chapter 6

1. Woodward, *Central America,* 114; Richard Adams, *Etnicidad en el ejército de la Guatemala Liberal (1870–1915)* (Guatemala: FLACSO, 1995), 14.

2. Handy, *Gift of the Devil*, 63; Woodward, *Central America*, 114, 154, 166.

3. Wuqu' Kawoq, 1/29/98, Comalapa; Ka'i' Imox, 1/21/98, Panabajal, Comalapa; Wuqu' Q'anil, 3/21/98, 4/29/98, Poaquil.

4. Woodward, *Central America*, 169–70; Handy, *Gift of the Devil*, 70.

5. *Recopilación de las Leyes emitidas por el Gobierno Democrático de la República de Guatemala, desde el 3 de junio de 1871, hasta el 30 de junio de 1881* (Guatemala: Tipografía de "el progreso," 1881) decree no. 65, June 8, 1872, 115–18; decree no. 81, Dec. 7, 1872, 143–45; and decree no. 83, Jan. 11, 1873, 151.

6. Adams, *Etnicidad en el ejército*, 16–17.

7. Ibid., 30; Carmack, "State and Community in Nineteenth-Century Guatemala," 121; McCreery, *Rural Guatemala*, 180, 236–64.

8. Carmack, *Historia Social*, 277; Carmack, "Los Indígenas," 4: 344.

9. Jun Kawoq, 5/1/98, Agua Caliente, Comalapa; Ka'i' Kawoq, 2/7/98, Aguas Calientes; Wo'o' Kawoq and Waqi' Kawoq, 3/3/98, Kojol Juyu', Comalapa; Oxi' Kawoq, 10/31/97, Pamumus, Comalapa; Ixkawoq, 4/17/98, Pamumus, Comalapa.

10. *El amigo del soldado* (Guatemala: Tipografía Nacional, 1904), 66.

11. Waqxaqi' Kawoq, 11/8/97, Aguas Calientes; Junlajuj Kawoq, 11/17/97, Poaquil; Lajuj Kawoq, 3/16/98, Poaquil; Wuqu' Kawoq, 1/29/98, Comalapa; B'eleje' Kawoq, 6/9/98, Tecpán.

12. Kab'lajuj Kawoq, 3/23/98, Poaquil.

13. Wuqu' Ajpu' (Jun Tojil interview), 1998, Barahona; Oxlajuj Kawoq, 3/18/98, Poaquil; Wo'o' Ajpu', 11/11/97, Comalapa; Oxi' Ajpu', Ka'i' Ajpu', and Jun Imox, 12/2/97, Panicuy, Comalapa; Waqi' Ajpu', 2/28/98, Aguas Calientes.

14. McCreery, *Rural Guatemala*, 181.

15. Adams, *Etnicidad en el ejército*, 22, 57.

16. Carmack, *Historia Social*, 278.

17. Waqxaqi' Kawoq, 11/8/97, Aguas Calientes.

18. Junlajuj Ajpu', 8/2/98, Comalapa; Oxlajuj Ajpu', 1/19/98, Panabajal, Comalapa; Kab'lajuj Ajpu', 11/14/97, Comalapa; Waqxaqi' Ajpu' (Jun Tojil interview), 1998, Barahona; B'eleje' Ajpu' (Jun Tojil interview), 1998, Barahona; Lajuj Ajpu', 4/19/98, Poaquil.

19. Woodward, *Central America*, 78, 169–70; Adams, *Etnicidad en el ejército*, 11.

20. Carmack, *Historia Social*, 278.

21. Waqi' Imox, 5/3/98, Tecpán; Jun Imox, 12/9/97, Xenimaquín, Comalapa; Wo'o' Imox, 5/23/98, Comalapa; Ixtijax, 8/17/98, Comalapa; Ix'imox, 8/23/98, Comalapa; Jun Ajpu', 12/20/97, Comalapa; Wuqu' Imox, 11/12/97, Aguas Calientes; Oxi' Imox, 2/10/98, Comalapa; Wuqu' Kan, 6/5/98, Tecpán; Ka'i' Imox, 1/21/98, Panabajal, Comalapa; Kaji' Imox, 8/12/98, Comalapa; Jun Imox, 12/9/97, Xenimaquín, Comalapa.

22. Ka'i' Imox, 1/21/98, Panabajal, Comalapa.

23. Adams, *Etnicidad en el ejército*, 24; Carmack, *Historia Social*, 288.

24. Waqxaqi' Imox, 11/28/97, Aguas Calientes.

25. B'eleje' Imox, 9/20/97, Comalapa; Lajuj Imox, 12/20/97, Comalapa; Kaji' Imox, 8/2/98, Comalapa.

26. Ixiq', 1/12/98, Comalapa.

27. Oxi' Imox, 11/9/97, Comalapa; Junlajuj Imox, 5/23/98, Comalapa; Lajuj Imox, 1/18/98, Comalapa; Ixk'at, 1/7/98, Comalapa.; Oxlajuj Imox, 1/13/98, Paraxaquen, Comalapa; Kab'lajuj Imox, 11/5/97, Comalapa; Junlajuj Ajpu', 8/2/98, Comalapa; Wuqu' Imox, 11/12/97, Aguas Calientes. Scholars also note that the military provided instruction for Maya men and that as a result few deserted; see Adams, *Etnicidad en el ejército*, 24, and Carmack, *Historia Social*, 288.

28. Junlajuj Ajpu', 8/2/98, Comalapa.

29. Ka'i' Kawoq, 2/7/98, Aguas Calientes.

30. Kab'lajuj Tijax, 9/13/97, Comalapa; Ixkawoq, 4/17/98, Pamumus, Comalapa; Jun K'at, 2/11/98, Comalapa; Wuqu' Ajpu' (Jun Tojil interview), 1998, Barahona.

31. Oxi' K'at, 6/5/98, Tecpán; Ka'i' K'at, 5/16/98, Comalapa; Ka'i' Imox, 8/5/98, Panabajal, Comalapa.

32. Junlajuj Imox, 5/23/98, Comalapa.

33. Oxi' Tz'ikin, 8/5/98, Comalapa.

34. Waqi' K'at, 9/6/98, Comalapa.

35. Carmack, *Historia Social*, 277.

36. Junlajuj Ajpu', 8/2/98, Comalapa.

37. Jun Kawoq, 5/1/98, Agua Caliente, Comalapa; Ka'i' Kawoq, 2/7/98, Aguas Calientes; Wo'o Kawoq and Waqi' Kawoq, 3/3/98, Kojol Juyu', Comalapa; Oxi' Kawoq, 10/31/97, Pamumus, Comalapa; Ixkawoq, 4/17/98, Pamumus, Comalapa.

38. Wuqu' K'at, 4/5/98, Comalapa; Waqxaqi' K'at, 11/8/97, Aguas Calientes. Xerka is a knee-length cloth traditionally worn by Kaqchikel males.

39. B'eleje' K'at, 11/5/97, Comalapa.

40. Jun Kan, 8/19/98, Comalapa.

41. Junlajuj Ajpu', 8/2/98, Comalapa.

42. Jun Kawoq, 5/1/98, Agua Caliente, Comalapa; Ka'i' Kawoq, 2/7/98, Aguas Calientes; Wo'o' Kawoq and Waqi' Kawoq, 3/3/98, Kojol Juyu', Comalapa; Oxi' Kawoq, 10/31/97, Pamumus, Comalapa; Ixkawoq, 4/17/98, Pamumus, Comalapa.

43. Oxlajuj Ajpu', 1/19/98, Panabajal, Comalapa.

44. Wuqu' Imox, 11/12/97, Aguas Calientes; Ka'i' Kawoq, 2/7/98, Aguas Calientes.

45. Kab'lajuj Imox, 11/5/97, Comalapa.

46. Hernández de León, *Viajes presidenciales*, 2: 17.

47. Adams, *Etnicidad en el ejército*, 58; McCreery, *Rural Guatemala*, 320; Adams, "La Población Indígena en el Estado Liberal," 188; Woodward, *Central America*, 217–18; Grieb, *Guatemalan Caudillo*, 47–48; Handy, *Gift of the Devil*, 99.

48. Guillermo Kuhsiek A., "La importancia del indio para el ejército de Guatemala," *Revista Militar Ilustrada; órgano de la Academia Military del Ejército de la República. Memoria de Labores, Municipalidades Chimaltenango* 1, no. 2–3 (1916): 4–6; Adams, *Etnicidad en al ejército*, 25.

49. Gaitán, et al., "Contribución al estudio del tifus exantemático en Guatemala," 34; "El Ejército y los indios," *Revista Militar Ilustrada; órgano de la Academia Militar del Ejército de la República*, Sept. 15, 1911, 9–11; Adams, *Etnicidad en al ejército*, 26.

50. "El Ejército y los indios," 9–11.

51. *El Imparcial,* July 10, 1940.

52. *El Imparcial,* Jan. 2, 1940, July 10, 1940.

53. *Liberal Progresista,* Feb. 14, 1941.

54. Fergusson, *Guatemala,* 317.

55. Ixkan, 3/29/98, Poaquil.

56. Jun Kan, 8/19/98, Comalapa; Lajuj K'at, 8/23/98.

57. Lajuj Kan, 10/15/97, Pachitur, Comalapa; B'eleje' Kan, 11/9/97, Aguas Calientes; Jun Iq', 4/18/98, Comalapa; Oxi' Imox, 2/10/98, Comalapa; Kab'lajuj Imox, 11/5/97, Comalapa; Waqxaqi' Kan, 3/18/98, Poaquil. Carmack asserts that military superiors recognized the inherent ability of K'ichee' men to be good soldiers and promoted a few to officer ranks. He concludes: "The indigenous people who remember that period [early twentieth century] sustain almost unanimously that, yes they were exploited by the military, but they were respected nevertheless as soldiers." See Carmack, *Historia Social,* 288.

58. Junlajuj Imox, 5/23/98, Comalapa.

59. Oxlajuj Kawoq, 3/18/98, Poaquil; Ixkame, 8/17/98, Comalapa.

60. Junlajuj K'at, 7/9/98, Comalapa.

61. Kab'lajuj K'at, 6/27/98, Comalapa.

62. Oxlajuj K'at, 3/10/98, Poaquil.

63. Ka'i' Kan, 11/24/97, Chuwatz'unuj, Tecpán.

64. Oxi' Kan, 8/19/98, Comalapa.

65. Ixiq', 1/12/98, Comalapa.

66. Ka'i' Aj (Jun Tojil interview), 1998, Barahona.

67. Ka'i' Kawoq, 2/7/98, Aguas Calientes; Ixkej, 11/9/97, Aguas Calientes.

68. For accounts of these uprisings see *El Imparcial,* Oct. 22, Nov. 2, and Nov. 8, 1944.

69. *El Imparcial,* Oct. 24, 1944.

70. *El Imparcial,* Oct. 24, Nov. 30, 1944.

71. Handy, *Revolution in the Countryside,* 55. For an excellent study of the 1944 Patzicía massacre coauthored by a Kaqchikel scholar see Esquit and Rodas, *Élite ladina-vanguardia indígena de la intolerancia a la violencia, Patizicia 1944.* Richard Adams, "Las masacres de Patzicía de 1944," *Revista Winak Boletín Intercultural 7,* no. 1–4 (1992): 3–40, is also very insightful.

72. B'eleje' Iq', 6/4/98, Tecpán; Wuqu' Kan, 6/5/98, Tecpán; Oxi' B'atz', 4/26/98, Comalapa.

73. Ixya', 4/11/98, Comalapa.

74. Woodward, *Central America,* 237.

75. Ibid., 238–40.

76. Junlajuj K'at, 7/9/98, Comalapa.

77. Jun Imox, 12/9/97, Xenimaquín, Comalapa; Kaji' Tz'i', 7/12/98, Comalapa.

78. Lajuj Kame, 2/14/98, Comalapa.

79. Oxlajuj Kawoq, 3/18/98, Poaquil.

80. Ixtijax, 8/17/98, Comalapa.

81. Lajuj K'at, 4/11/98, Comalapa; Lajuj Ajpu', 4/19/98, Poaquil; B'eleje' Kawoq, 6/9/98, Tecpán; Ixtojil, 2/7/98, Barahona; Ka'i' K'at, 5/16/98, Comalapa; Lajuj Kan, 10/15/98, Pachitur, Comalapa.

82. Kab'lajuj Tijax, 4/7/98, Comalapa; Kab'lajuj Kej, 4/26/98, Comalapa; Waqi' Iq', 4/22/98, Comalapa; Kab'lajuj Ajpu', 11/14/97, Comalapa; Ix'ajmaq, 3/15/98, Poaquil; Wuqu' Aq'ab'al, 11/25/97, Tecpán; Wuqu' Kej, 5/30/98, Tecpán.

83. Woodward, *Central America,* 237–41; Warren, *Symbolism of Subordination,* 154; Jonas, *Battle for Guatemala,* 28–39; Handy, *Gift of the Devil,* 133; Jim Handy, "Resurgent Democracy and the Guatemalan Military," *Journal of Latin American Studies* 18 (Nov. 1986): 391; For an analysis of the UFCO's role in the 1954 invasion see Stephen Schlesinger and Stephen Kinzer, *Bitter Fruit: The Untold Story of the American Coup in Guatemala* (New York: Doubleday and Anchor, 1982). A new edition of *Bitter Fruit* was published by the David Rockefeller Center Series on Latin American Studies, Harvard University Press, 1999. For the role of the Cold War, the CIA, and President Dwight Eisenhower in the coup see Nick Cullather, *Secret History: The CIA's Classified Account of Its Operations in Guatemala, 1952–1954* (Stanford: Stanford University Press, 1999); Richard H. Immerman, *The CIA in Guatemala* (Austin: University of Texas Press, 1982); John McCamant, "Intervention in Guatemala," *Comparative Political Studies* 13, no. 1 (1984): 373–407; Gordon L. Bowen, "U.S. Foreign Policy toward Radical Change: Covert Operations in Guatemala, 1950–1954," *Latin American Perspectives* 36 (winter 1983): 88–102; and Blanche Wiesen Cook, *The Declassified Eisenhower: A Divided Legacy* (New York: Doubleday, 1981), 217–92. A number of studies show that internal unrest, in some cases caused by the agrarian reform itself, had as much to do with Arbenz's downfall as external factors; see Handy, *Revolution in the Countryside.* For a look at the inner workings of the Arbenz government from a Guatemalan perspective see Piero Gleijeses, *Shattered Hope: The United States and the Guatemalan Revolution, 1944–1954* (Princeton: Princeton University Press, 1991).

84. Adams, *Etnicidad en el ejército,* 11.

85. Junlajuj Ajpu', 8/2/98, Comalapa.

86. Kaji' Kan, 9/6/98, Comalapa; Wo'o' Kan, 4/26/98, Comalapa.

87. Waqi' Kan (Ix'ey interview), 1998, Aguas Calientes.

Chapter 7

1. Grieb, *Guatemalan Caudillo;* Jones, *Guatemala Past and Present,* 74, 351; Kelsey and de Jongh Osborne, *Four Keys to Guatemala,* 60. For praise for Ubico from a contemporary Latin American author see Santiago Arguello, *Barrios y Ubico: la obra creadora de dos constructores de naciones* (Havana: Cia Tipografía, S.A., 1937), 33–34.

2. Hernández de León, *Viajes presidenciales,* vols. 1 and 2; Grieb, *Guatemalan Caudillo,* 35–37.

3. Skinner-Klee, *Legislación indigenísta de Guatemala,* 117.

4. Hernández de León, *Viajes presidenciales,* 2: 60.

5. Paul Thomas Lokken, "The Challenge of Reform: Pluralism and Repression in Guatemala, 1920–1944" (Master's thesis, University of Saskatchewan, 1989), 112.

6. Handy, *Gift of the Devil*, 93; James Dunkerley, "Guatemala since 1930," in *Cambridge History of Latin America*, ed. Leslie Bethell (Cambridge: Cambridge University Press, 1984), 7: 214–16; Whetten, *Guatemala: The Land and the People*, 333.

7. Waqi' Kan (Ix'ey interview), 1998, Aguas Calientes.

8. Wuqu' K'at, 4/5/98, Comalapa.

9. Lajuj Kan, 1/30/98, Pachitur, Comalapa; Jun Tijax, 3/8/98, Panabajal, Comalapa; Oxi' Kawoq, 10/31/97, Pamumus, Comalapa; Jun K'at, 2/11/98, Comalapa; Ka'i' Ajmaq, 11/23/97, Tecpán; Ixkej, 11/9/97, Aguas Calientes; Wo'o' Kej (Ix'ey interview), Aguas Calientes; Ka'i' Kawoq, 2/7/98, Aguas Calientes.

10. Grieb, *Guatemalan Caudillo*, 39–40.

11. Kaji' Kej, 11/12/97, Aguas Calientes.

12. The currency at the time was the peso. In 1915 the government set the minimum daily wage at six pesos and in 1923 raised it to eight pesos. The devalued state of the peso (about sixty pesos to the U.S. dollar in 1928, and as high as two hundred pesos to the U.S. dollar) prompted the government to change the currency to the quetzal and peg it to the U.S. dollar. For a good description of these fluctuations see Náñez Falcón, "Erwin Paul Dieseldorff," 324–28.

13. *Diario de Centro América*, Feb. 22, 1919, 1.

14. Warren, *Symbolism of Subordination*, 149.

15. Ibid., 144–49.

16. Ix'ey, 7/25/98, Aguas Calientes.

17. Oxi' Kame, 3/4/98, Chi Chalí, Comalapa.

18. B'eleje' Iq', 6/4/98, Tecpán; Ka'i' Tijax, 10/13/97, Comalapa; Oxi' Iq', 12/2/98, Comalapa; B'eleje' Ey, 11/23/97, Poaquil; Oxi' Tojil, 3/21/98, Nueva Esperanza, Poaquil; Kaji' Aq'ab'al, 6/8/98, Tecpán.

19. Kab'lajuj Tijax, 4/7/98, Comalapa; Ixkame, 8/17/98, Comalapa; Oxi' Aq'ab'al, 10/26/97, Comalapa; Ixk'at, 1/7/98, Comalapa.

20. Waqxaqi' Iq', 6/23/98, Comalapa.

21. Kab'lajuj Ajpu', 11/14/97, Comalapa.

22. Waqxaqi' Q'anil, 3/21/98, Nueva Esperanza, Poaquil; Kaji' No'j, Waqxaqi' B'atz', Lajuj Q'anil, 3/25/98, Ojer K'ayb'al, Poaquil; Waqxaqi' Ajmaq, 4/5/98, Comalapa; Waqxaqi' K'at, 11/8/97, Aguas Calientes; Wo'o' Aq'ab'al, 11/24/97, Chuwatz'unuj, Tecpán.

23. *Recopilación de las Leyes de la República de Guatemala*, 52: 363–64; Jones, *Guatemala: Past and Present*, 247; *Memoria de las labores del Ejecutivo en el Ramo de Agricultura* from 1931 to 1940; *Memoria del Ministerio de Agricultura*, 1922, 22; *Memoria de la Secretaría de Fomento*, 1914, 57; "Carreteras," *El Impulso*, Jan. 31, 1916, 6; *Memoria del Ministerio de Agricultura*, 1926, 6; *Memoria de las labores del Ejecutivo en el en el Ramo de Agricultura*, 1932, 263–64; Krieb, *Guatemalan Caudillo*, 40; Lokken, "Challenge of Reform," 110.

24. "Caminos de Guatemala," *Seis años del progreso, 1931–37* (Guatemala: Tipografía Nacional, 1937); "Resena historica de los caminos de Guatemala," *Boletín de Ministerio de Comunicaciones y Obras Públicas*, Nov. 1956, 14, 52.

25. Grieb, *Guatemalan Caudillo,* 132–34; Jones, *Guatemala: Past and Present,* 73–74; Joseph Apolonio Pitti, *Jorge Ubico and Guatemalan Politics in the 1920s* (Ann Arbor, Mich.: Xerox University Microfilms, 1975), 491.

26. Warren, *Symbolism of Subordination,* 144–50.

27. Oxi' Kawoq, 9/4/98, Pamumus, Comalapa.

28. Jun Ajmaq, 9/4/98, Mixcolabaj, Comalapa.

29. Junlajuj Kame, 4/12/98, Pachitur, Comalapa; Jun Kame, 5/1/98, Agua Caliente, Comalapa; Wo'o' B'atz' and Waqi' B'atz', 7/9/98, Comalapa; Oxi' Ajmaq, 3/27/98, Hacienda Vieja, Poaquil; Kaji' No'j, Waqxaqi' B'atz', Lajuj Q'anil, 3/25/98, Ojer K'ayb'al, Poaquil; speech, president of Quizaya Road Committee, 4/15/98, Quizaya, Comalapa. See *El Imparcial,* Apr. 24, 1934, for an example of leaders from Sacapulas and other neighboring municipalities in the K'ichee' department petitioning the government to have a road built to serve their communities. The government responded favorably and provided technical and material support. In turn, the petitioning communities provided the labor and some economic resources.

30. Jun No'j, 12/12/97, Comalapa

31. Ixkotz'i'j, 4/26/98, Pamumus, Comalapa. In many areas of Guatemala, improved roads facilitated the movement of the military to previously less accessible areas. This connection was especially detrimental during the civil war and led to increased violence in some communities. Nonetheless, few Kaqchikel cited this consequence as a reason to retard road development.

32. Oxi' Aq'ab'al, 10/4/97, Comalapa.

33. Kab'lajuj Ajpu', 11/14/97, Comalapa.

34. B'eleje' Ey, 4/19/98, Poaquil.

35. Ixkawoq, 4/17/98, Pamumus, Comalapa;

36. Waqi' Ey, 4/15/98, Simajulew, Comalapa; Oxi' Imox, 2/10/98, Comalapa; Ka'i' Aq'ab'al, 6/7/98, Tecpán.

37. Jun Imox, 12/9/97, Xenimaquín, Comalapa.

38. *Recopilación de las Leyes de la República de Guatemala,* decree no. 1995, 53: 69–70; *Memoria de las labores del Ejecutivo en el Ramo de Agricultura,* 1936, 16; Dunkerley, "Guatemala since 1930," 214; Handy, *Gift of the Devil,* 83.

39. *Recopilación de las Leyes de la República de Guatemala,* 53: 71–75.

40. Oxi' Kawoq, 10/31/97, Pamumus, Comalapa; Jun Tz'i', 7/11/98, Pamumus, Comalapa; Wo'o' Iq', 12/2/97, Panicuy, Comalapa; Ixmukane', 11/26/97, Tecpán; Jun Tzinik'an, 5/26/98, Tecpán; Lajuj Aq'ab'al, 11/14/97, Aguas Calientes; Iximnik'te, 2/23/99, Tecpán (interview performed in New Orleans, La.).

41. B'eleje' Kawoq, 6/9/98, Tecpán.

42. Jun Ey, 11/12/98, Aguas Calientes.

43. "Mensaje que el Presidente de la República General Jorge Ubico dirige a la Asamblea Nacional Legislativa al abrir su período de sesiones ordinarias, 10 de marzo de 1937," *Recopilación de las Leyes de la República de Guatemala* 56: 94–95.

44. Whetten, *Guatemala: The Land and the People,* 120–21; Handy, *Gift of the Devil,* 98; Frank Griffith Dawson, "Labor Legislation and Social Integration in Guatemala," *American Journal of Comparative Law* 14 (1965): 124–42; Adams, *Crucifixion by Power,* 178; Grieb, *Guatemalan Caudillo,* 39.

45. *Diario de Centro América,* June 4, 1936.

46. *Memorias de la Dirección General de Agricultura,* 1938, 464; Handy, *Gift of the Devil,* 98; Grieb, *Guatemalan Caudillo,* 163–73; Ebel, "Political Modernization," 163.

47. Grieb, *Guatemalan Caudillo,* 35.

48. Skinner-Klee, *Legislación indigenísta de Guatemala,* 119–20.

49. Ix'aj, 2/9/98, Comalapa.

50. Walter Little, "Home as a Place of Exhibition and Performance: Mayan Household Transformations in Guatemala," *Ethnology* 39, no. 2 (2000): 165–66. Little adeptly argues that Ubico was more concerned with creating a sense of national identity than with providing an economic venue for Maya.

51. Skinner-Klee, *Legislación indigenísta de Guatemala,* 118; McCreery, *Rural Guatemala,* 317–18.

52. Skinner-Klee, *Legislación indigenísta de Guatemala,* 119.

53. Oxi' Tojil, 3/21/98, Nueva Esperanza, Poaquil.

54. Ixxokoq'a', 3/14/98, Poaquil; Junlajuj Kawoq, 11/17/97, Poaquil; Wuqu' Kame (Jun Tojil interview), 1998, Barahona.

55. Jun Kawoq, 5/1/98, Agua Caliente, Comalapa.

56. Waqxaqi' K'at, 11/8/97, Aguas Calientes; Kaji' Imox, 12/13/97, Comalapa.

57. Jun B'atz', 11/4/97, Panabajal, Comalapa.

58. Richard Adams, "Ethnic Images and Strategies in 1944," in *Guatemalan Indians and the State: 1540–1988,* ed. Carol Smith (Austin: University of Texas Press, 1990), 42. For an excellent example of Ubico's hands-on approach in favoring Maya over local officials in La Union, Zacapa, see *El Imparcial,* Jan. 28, 1941.

59. Waqi' Amaq, Waqi' Tijax, and Kaji' Tzinik'an, 11/11/97, Paya, Comalapa; Ixmes and Ixch'op, 1/18/98, Aguas Calientes.

60. Jun Ajpu', 12/20/97, Comalapa.

61. Jun Aj and Ix'ik', 6/6/98, Tecpán.

62. Wuqu' B'atz', 2/10/98, Pawit, Comalapa.

63. Wuqu' Ey, 3/26/98, Hacienda Vieja, Poaquil.

64. Warren, *Symbolism of Subordination,* 144–49.

65. Ixiq', 1/12/98, Comalapa.

66. Jun Kan, 8/19/98, Comalapa.

67. Lajuj Kan, 10/15/97, Pachitur, Comalapa.

68. Jun Ajpu', 12/20/97, Comalapa; Ixtzinik'an, 6/2/98, Tecpán

69. Ixsu't, 5/4/98, Comalapa.

70. Kaji' Aq'ab'al, 6/8/98, Tecpán; Oxi' K'at, 6/5/98, Tecpán; Wuqu' Kan, 6/5/98, Tecpán; Kaji' Ajmaq, 3/28/98, Poaquil; Ixche', 11/22/97, Poaquil; Ixya', 4/11/98, Comalapa; B'eleje' No'j, 8/8/97, Santa María de Jesús; Wuqu' K'at, 4/5/98, Comalapa.

71. B'eleje' Kan, 11/9/97, Aguas Calientes.

72. Jun Tzinik'an, 5/26/98, Tecpán.

73. Ixya', 4/11/98, Comalapa.

74. Ixkej, 11/9/97, Aguas Calientes; Wo'o' Aj (Ix'ey interview), 1998, Aguas Calientes; Wuqu' Imox, 11/12/97, Aguas Calientes; Kab'lajuj Kan, 2/15/98, Barahona; Ka'i' Ajmaq, 10/20/97, Tecpán; Ka'i' Kame, 4/29/98, Saqirtacaj, Poaquil; Ka'i' Imox, 8/5/98, Panabajal, Comalapa.

75. Ix'ey, 7/25/98, Aguas Calientes.

76. Kab'lajuj Tijax, 4/7/98, Comalapa.

77. Jun Ey, 11/12/97, Aguas Calientes; Oxi' Ey, 11/28/97, Aguas Calientes; B'eleje' Q'anil (Ix'ey interview), 1998, Aguas Calientes; Wo'o' Kawoq and Waqi' Kawoq, 3/3/98, Kojol Juyu', Comalapa; Oxi' Kej, 6/14/98, Comalapa; Ixkik', 6/21/98, Comalapa.

78. Ixkej, 11/9/97, Aguas Calientes; Lajuj Ajpu', 3/29/98, Poaquil; Oxi' Aq'ab'al, 10/26/97, Comalapa; P'ot, women's weaving cooperative, 2/7/98, Barahona; Wuqu' Aq'ab'al, 11/25/97, Tecpán.

79. Ixxokoq'a', 3/14/98, Poaquil; Junlajuj Kawoq, 11/17/97, Poaquil; Iximnik'te', 9/24/97, Tecpán, Oxlajuj Ajmaq, 9/24/97, Tecpán; Waqxaqi' Imox, 2/7/98, Barahona; Wuqu' Kame (Jun Tojil interview), 1998, Barahona; Waqi' Ajpu', 2/28/98, Aguas Calientes; Wuqu' Kawoq, 1/29/98, Comalapa; B'eleje' Kej, 3/19/98, Poaquil; Wuqu' Aq'ab'al, 11/25/97, Tecpán; Wo'o' Kawoq and Waqi' Kawoq, 3/3/98, Kojol Juyu', Comalapa.

80. Waqxaqi' Kej, 2/7/98, Barahona.

81. Waqi' Kan (Ix'ey interview), 1998, Aguas Calientes.

82. Hernández de León, *Viajes presidenciales,* 2: 49.

83. *El Imparcial,* Oct. 14, 1940.

84. *Memoria de la Secretaría de Gobernación y Justicia,* 1941, 113.

85. B'eleje' Kawoq, 6/9/98, Tecpán; Ixmes and Ixch'op, 1/18/98, Aguas Calientes; Junlajuj Kame, 4/12/98, Pachitur, Comalapa; Wo'o' Iq', 12/2/97, Panicuy, Comalapa; Kab'lajuj Ajpu', 11/14/97, Comalapa.

86. Oxi' Kame, 3/4/98, Chi Chalí, Comalapa.

87. Oxi' Kawoq, 10/31/97, Pamumus, Comalapa.

88. Kab'lajuj Kan, 2/15/98, Barahona.

89. B'eleje' Ey, 8/21/98, Poaquil.

90. Oxi' Kawoq, 10/31/97, Pamumus, Comalapa; Lajuj Kan, 10/15/97, Pachitur, Comalapa; Kaji' Tojil, 3/2/98, Palima, Comalapa; Ka'i' Imox, 9/12/98, Panabajal, Comalapa; Wo'o' No'j, 4/22/98, Xenimaquín, Comalapa.

91. Wuqu' Kan, 6/5/98, Aguas Calientes.

92. Road crew, 10/29/97, Pachitur, Comalapa.

93. Oxlajuj K'at, 3/10/98, Poaquil.

94. Lajuj Aq'ab'al, 11/12/97, Aguas Calientes; Ixtzinik'an 6/2/98, Tecpán; Wo'o' Aq'ab'al, 11/24/97, Chuwatz'unuj, Tecpán; Kab'lajuj Ajpu', 11/14/97, 5/5/98, Comalapa; B'eleje' Imox, 9/20/97, Comalapa; Lajuj Kan, 10/15/97, Pachitur, Comalapa.

95. Ixk'u'x (Ix'ajpu' interview), 1998, Comalapa.

96. Jun Q'anil, 2/9/98, Patzaj, Comalapa.

97. Hernández de León, *Viajes presidenciales,* 2: 60.

98. Hernández de León, *Viajes presidenciales,* 1: 19, 143, 416; Grieb, *Guatemalan Caudillo,* 36–37; Adams, "Ethnic Images and Strategies in 1944," 42; Dunkerley, "Guatemala since 1930," 215; Adams, *Crucifixion by Power,* 182; Handy *Gift of the Devil,* 97; Lokken, "Challenge of Reform."

99. Ka'i' Imox, 9/12/98, Panabajal, Comalapa.

100. *Recopilación de las Leyes de la República de Guatemala,* 1935–36, decree no. 1692, July 22, 1935, 54: 389; Dunkerley, "Guatemala since 1930," 216; Krehm, *Democracies and Tyrannies,* 39; Handy, *Gift of the Devil,* 97–99; Adams, *Crucifixion by Power,* 176.

101. Junlajuj Ajpu', 8/2/98, Comalapa.

102. Ka'i' Tz'i', 5/26/98, Tecpán; Wuqu' Q'anil, 3/21/98, Poaquil; Kab'lajuj Imox, 1/5/98, Comalapa; Wo'o' No'j, 4/22/98, Xenimaquín, Comalapa; B'eleje' Tz'i', Junlajuj B'atz', Junlajuj Toj, 5/20/98, Xetonox, Comalapa; Ka'i' Kej, 11/5/97, Comalapa; Waqxaqi' Ajmaq, 4/5/98, Comalapa.

103. Ka'i' Kej, 11/5/97, Comalapa.

104. Kab'lajuj Ajpu', 5/5/98, Comalapa.

105. For examples of the effects of the intendente system and its resultant tensions in Mayan communities see Robert Ewald, "San Antonio Sacatepéquez, 1932–53," in *Community Culture and National Change,* ed. Richard Adams, Middle American Research Institute Series, publication no. 24 (New Orleans: Tulane University, 1972), 18; Morris Siegel, "San Miguel Acatán: 1938–53," in *Community Culture and National Change,* ed. Richard Adams, Middle American Research Institute Series, publication no. 24 (New Orleans: Tulane University, 1972), 40–41; Ebel, "Political Modernization," 164, 180, 195–97; and Charles Wisdom, *The Chorti Indians of Guatemala* (Chicago: University of Chicago Press, 1940), 232–24.

106. Ixtzinik'an, 6/2/98. Tecpán.

107. Wuqu' Kan, 6/5/98, Tecpán; Kaji' Tijax, 4/28/98, Patzaj, Comalapa;

108. Oxi' Kawoq, 9/4/98, Pamumus, Comalapa.

109. Oxi' Kej, 6/14/98, Comalapa.

110. Dunkerley, "Guatemala since 1930," 216–17; Adams, *Crucifixion by Power,* 179; Náñez Falcón, "Erwin Paul Dieseldorff," 327; Wisdom, *Chorti Indians,* 233–34, 238–40; Rodas, et al., *Chichicastenango: The Kiche Indians,* 87.

111. Oxi' Kawoq, 10/31/97, Pamumus, Comalapa; Lajuj Imox, 1/18/98, Comalapa; Kaji' Kame, 3/4/98, Comalapa; Kab'lajuj Ajpu', 5/5/98, Comalapa; Oxi' Tz'ikin, 8/8/98, Comalapa; Kab'lajuj Kan, 2/15/98, Barahona.

112. Oxi' Kawoq, 10/31/97, Pamumus, Comalapa; Lajuj Imox, 1/18/98, Comalapa; Kaji' Kame, 3/4/98, Comalapa; Kab'lajuj Ajpu', 5/5/98, Comalapa; Oxi' Tz'ikin, 8/8/98, Comalapa; Kab'lajuj Kan, 2/15/98, Barahona.

113. Ix'ajpu', 9/23/97, Comalapa; Ixkawoq, 4/17/98, Pamumus, Comalapa; Ka'i' Q'anil, 12/12/97, Comalapa; Ka'i' B'atz', 11/2/97, Tecpán.

114. *Memoria de la Secretaría de Gobernación y Justicia,* 1932, 360.

115. Lokken, "Challenge of Reform," 107–17; Grieb, *Guatemalan Caudillo,* 282–84.

116. Dunkerley, "Guatemala since 1930," 217; Lokken, "Challenge of Reform," 110–17; Richard Adams, "Changing Political Relationships in Guatemala," in *Political Changes in Guatemalan Indian Communities, A Symposium,* Middle American Research Institute Series, publication no. 24 (New Orleans: Tulane University, 1957), 48–49.

117. Wo'o' Kame, 5/29/98, Tecpán; Kaji' Kej, 11/12/97, Aguas Calientes.

Chapter 8

1. B'eleje' Ey, 4/19/98, Poaquil.

2. Ix'aq'ab'al, 3/17/98, Hacienda María, Poaquil.

3. Ix'ajmaq, 3/15/98, Poaquil.

4. Ka'i' Kame, 4/29/98, Saqirtacaj, Poaquil.

5. Jun B'atz', 11/4/97, Panabajal, Comalapa; Ka'i' Kej, 11/5/97, Comalapa; Junlajuj Kan, 4/24/98, Simajulew, Comalapa; Ka'i' K'at, 5/16/98, Comalapa; Oxi' Iq', 12/2/98, Comalapa; Ixte, 10/27/97, Comalapa.

6. Oxi' Imox, 2/11/98, Comalapa.

7. Smith, *Indian Class and Class Consciousness,* 29; Carmack, *Historia social de los Quichés.*

8. B'eleje' Imox, 9/20/97, Comalapa

9. Oxi' Tz'i', 5/29/98, Tecpán; Wuqu' Kej, 5/30/98, Tecpán; Wuqu' Kan, 6/5/98, Tecpán.

10. Lajuj Iq', 12/9/97, Xenimaquín, Comalapa.

11. John B. Rae, *The American Automobile: A Brief History* (Chicago: University of Chicago Press, 1965), 7–15.

12. "Reseña historica de los caminos de Guatemala," *Boletín de Ministerio de Comunicaciones y Obras Públicas,* Nov. 1956, 10; Woodward, *Central America,* 161–65; McCreery, *Rural Guatemala,* 179–80; Thomas Herrick, "Economic and Political Development in Guatemala during the Barrios Period, 1871–1885" (Ph.D. diss., University of Chicago, 1967), 130–31, 225; Paul Dosal, *Power in Transition: The Rise of Guatemala's Industrial Oligarchy, 1871–1994* (Westport, Conn.: Praeger, 1995), 21, 23; Paul Burgess, *Justo Rufino Barrios* (San José, Costa Rica: Editorial Universitaria Centroamericana, 1972), 347.

13. Oxi' Kawoq, 10/31/97, Pamumus, Comalapa; Jun Imox, 12/9/97, Xenimaquín, Comalapa; B'eleje' Tz'i', Junlajuj B'atz', Junlajuj Toj, 5/20/98, Xetonox, Comalapa; Kab'lajuj Tz'i', 9/1/98, Aguas Calientes; Kab'lajuj Kawoq, 3/23/98, Poaquil.

14. B'eleje' Kan, 11/9/97, Aguas Calientes; Kab'lajuj Kan, 2/15/98, Barahona; Junlajuj Ajpu', 8/2/98, Comalapa; Wuqu' K'at, 4/5/98, Comalapa; Wo'o' Tojil, Waqi' Tojil, and Wuqu' Tojil, 10/21/97, Paquixic, Comalapa; Kaji' Tz'i', 6/7/98, 7/12/98, Comalapa.

15. Justo Rufino Barrios, "Mensaje y memoria dirije a la Asamblea Nacional Constituyente," Sept. 11, 1876, quoted in Jorge Mario García Laguardia, *El pensamiento liberal de Guatemala* (San José, Costa Rica: Editorial Universitaria Centroamericana, 1977), 68–71.

16. H. J. Miller, "Positivism and Education in Guatemala," in *Positivism in Latin America, 1850–1900: Are Order and Progress Reconciliable?* ed. Ralph Lee Woodward, Jr. (Lexington, Mass.: Health, 1971), 109; Handy, *Gift of the Devil,* 62–63; Woodward, *Central America,* 169.

17. B'eleje' Ey, 4/19/98, Poaquil; Oxlajuj Kan, 10/17/98, Comalapa; Ka'i' K'at, 5/16/98, Comalapa; Jun Tojil, 12/1/97, 7/8/98, Barahona; Iximnik'te, 11/25/97, Tecpán; Ixmukane', 11/26/97, Tecpán.

18. Oxi' Aq'ab'al, 10/26/97, Comalapa.

19. Ka'i' Tojil, 6/12/98, Barahona.

20. John A. Booth and Thomas W. Walker, *Understanding Central America* (Boulder: Westview, 1993), 42–43; Handy, *Gift of the Devil,* 105; Jorge Luján y Muñoz, interview, July 23, 1994, Guatemala City.

21. Handy, *Revolution in the Countryside,* 25; Handy, *Gift of the Devil,* 106.

22. Adams, *Crucifixion by Power,* 184–85; Wasserstrom, "Revolution in Guatemala"; Handy, "National Policy," 704.

23. For an example of Mayan assertions of a better life under Ubico see Warren, *Symbolism of Subordination.*

24. "Constitución 1945," Article 83, Article 137. par. 15, in Marinas Otero, *Las Constituciones de Guatemala,* 635, 655.

25. *Diario de Centro América,* May 18, 1945.

26. Handy, "National Policy," 703.

27. Waqi' Imox, 5/3/98, Tecpán; Wuqu' Kame (Jun Tojil interview), 1998, Barahona.

28. B'eleje' Tz'i', Junlajuj B'atz', Junlajuj Toj, 5/20/98, Xetonox, Comalapa.

29. B'eleje' K'at, 11/5/97, Comalapa.

30. Oxi' Tz'i', 5/29/98. Tecpán.

31. Waqi' Iq', 12/12/97, Comalapa.

32. Junlajuj Kej, 5/22/98, Paquixic, Comalapa; Ka'i' Q'anil, 12/12/97, Comalapa.

33. Handy, *Gift of the Devil,* 124; Skinner-Klee, *Legislación indigenísta de Guatemala,* 121–22; Handy, *Revolution in the Countryside,* 24; Adams, *Crucifixion by Power,* 185. The Arévalo government passed a new vagrancy law that continued some control over rural labor but did not specify punishment.

34. Jun Kawoq, 5/1/98, Agua Caliente, Comalapa; Oxi' Kame, 3/4/98, Chi Chalí, Comalapa; Wo'o' Kawoq and Waqi' Kawoq, 3/3/98, Kojol Juyu', Comalapa; Waqi' Kame, 5/3/98, Pamumus, Comalapa; Waqxaqi' Imox, 2/7/98, Barahona; Kab'lajuj Kan, 2/15/98, Barahona; Kaji' Tz'i', 7/12/98, Comalapa; Lajuj Kame, 2/14/98, Comalapa; Ixkan, 3/29/98, Poaquil. Ubico eliminated local mayoral representation because he viewed it as a system of spoils based on reciprocal patronage. The demand from fictive kin ties resulted in unequally distributed favors and goods. Kaqchikel do not mention the effect of this change on the spoils system; rather, they focus on renewed representation by their own people.

35. Handy, *Revolution in the Countryside,* 24, 43–44, 52, 131; Rubén E. Reina, "Chinautla: A Guatemalan Indian Community, 1944–53," in *Community Culture and National Change,* ed. Richard Adams, Middle American Research Institute Series, publication no. 24 (New Orleans: Tulane University, 1972); Adams, *Crucifixion by Power,* 187–89; Handy, "National Policy," 703, 706; Handy, "Corporate Community," 147, 178–79; Handy, *Gift of the Devil,* 167–71.

36. Kalman H. Silvert and Arden R. King, "Cobán: 1944–53." In *Community Culture and National Change,* ed. Richard Adams, Middle American Research Institute Series, publication no. 24 (New Orleans: Tulane University, 1972), 44–47; Ebel, "Political Modernization," 189–90.

37. Adams, *Crucifixion by Power,* 188–89, 427–34; Britnell, "Problems of Economic and Social Change," 470; Handy, *Gift of the Devil,* 27; Handy, *Revolution in the Countryside,* 107.

38. Waqi' Kame, 5/3/98, Pamumus, Comalapa; Ix'ajmaq, 3/15/98, Poaquil; Waqxaqi' Kan, 3/18/98, Poaquil.

39. Kaji' Kej, 11/12/97, Aguas Calientes.

40. Oxi' Kame, 3/4/98, Chi Chalí, Comalapa; Jun Imox, 12/9/97, Xenimaquín,

Comalapa; Ka'i' Aq'ab'al, 6/7/98, Tecpán; Jun Ey, 11/12/97, Aguas Calientes; Ka'i' Kawoq, 2/7/98, Aguas Calientes; Oxi' Tojil, 3/21/98, Nueva Esperanza, Poaquil; Oxlajuj Kawoq, 3/18/98, Poaquil; Junlajuj Imox, 5/23/98, Comalapa.

41. Kab'lajuj Imox, 9/28/97, Comalapa.

42. Lajuj Kan, 1/30/98, Pachitur, Comalapa; Oxlajuj Ajpu', 1/19/98, Panabajal, Comalapa; Wo'o' Ey and Kab'lajuj B'atz', 3/28/98, Panimacak, Comalapa; Jun Tijax, 3/8/98, Panabajal, Comalapa; Jun Q'anil, 2/9/98, Patzaj, Comalapa; Ixxokoq'a', 3/14/98, Poaquil.

43. Wuqu' Ajpu' (Jun Tojil interview), 1998, Barahona.

44. Ixwa'in, 12/17/97, Xiquín Sanahí, Comalapa; Ixwatzik', 12/17/97, Xiquín Sanahí, Comalapa; Ka'i' Kan, 11/24/97, Chuwatz'unuj, Tecpán; Jun Imox, 12/9/97, Xenimaquín, Comalapa; Wuqu' Tijax, 3/2/98, Palima, Comalapa; Lajuj Kan, 10/15/97, Pachitur, Comalapa; Jun K'at, 2/11/98, Comalapa; Ka'i' B'atz', 11/26/97, Tecpán; B'eleje' Kej, 3/19/98, Poaquil; Lajuj Ajpu', 4/19/98, Poaquil.

45. K'ayb'il B'alam, 10/5/97, Tecpán.

46. Jun Tz'i', 7/11/98, Pamumus, Comalapa; Ix'umül, 4/15/98, Simajulew, Comalapa; Wuqu' Iq', 12/17/97, Xiquín Sanahí, Comalapa; Ka'i' Aq'ab'al, 6/7/98, Tecpán; Wo'o' Iq', 12/2/97, Panicuy, Comalapa; Lajuj Kan, 10/15/97, Pachitur, Comalapa; Ixpo't, 11/17/97, Poaquil; Kaji' Imox, 8/2/98, Comalapa; Jun Kan, 8/19/98, Comalapa.

47. Wo'o' No'j, 4/22/98, Xenimaquín, Comalapa; Oxi' Kawoq, 9/4/98, Pamumus, Comalapa; Waqi' Kame, 5/3/98, Pamumus, Comalapa; Ixpo't, 11/17/97, Poaquil; Oxi' K'at, 6/5/98, Tecpán; Wo'o' Kame, 5/29/98, Tecpán; Oxlajuj K'at, 3/10/98, Poaquil.

48. B'eleje' Kawoq, 6/9/98, Tecpán.

49. Oxi' Tz'ikin, 8/8/98. Comalapa.

50. Kab'lajuj Ajpu', 11/14/97, Comalapa.

51. Kab'lajuj K'at, 6/27/98, Comalapa; Kab'lajuj Tijax, 4/7/98, Comalapa; Kaji' Kame, 3/4/98, Comalapa; Kaji' Kan, 9/6/98, Comalapa.

52. Wo'o' No'j, 4/22/98, Xenimaquín, Comalapa; Lajuj Ajpu', 4/19/98, Poaquil; Ixxokoq'a', 3/14/98, Poaquil.

53. Wuqu' Kan, 6/5/98, Tecpán; Ixkej, 11/9/97, Aguas Calientes; Kab'lajuj Kan, 2/15/98, Barahona; Ixxokoq'a', 3/14/98, Poaquil.

54. Handy, "Corporate Community," 180; Adams, *Crucifixion by Power,* 106–7, 191; Gleijeses, "Agrarian Reform of Arbenz," 470.

55. Smith, "Labor and International Capital," 9. For analysis of the emergence of a strong peasant class in Guatemala see Smith, "Does a Commodity Economy Enrich the Few?"

56. Jun Kawoq, 5/1/98, Agua Caliente, Comalapa; Kaji' Ey, 5/4/98, Kojol Juyu', Comalapa; Waqi' No'j, 3/15/98, Poaquil. Oral accounts credit Matzer with two to five mayoral terms. Municipal documents show that Matzer served as mayor in 1955 and 1958, but information before 1932 is unavailable (Comalapa Municipal Documents). I was unable to locate information concerning Matzer's mayoral terms in the AGCA.

57. Jun Tz'i', 7/12/98, Pamumus, Comalapa.

58. Lajuj Ajpu', 4/19/98, Poaquil.

59. Kaji' Kan, 9/6/98, Comalapa.

60. Wuqu' Tijax 3/2/98, Palima, Comalapa; Jun Kawoq, 5/1/98, Agua Caliente, Comalapa; Oxi' Kawoq, 10/31/97, Pamumus, Comalapa; Oxlajuj Ajpu', 4/14/98, Panabajal, Comalapa; Jun Tijax, 3/8/98, Panabajal, Comalapa; Waqxaqi' Kej, 5/24/98, Comalapa; Ixsu't, 5/4/98, Comalapa.

61. Ka'i' Imox, 8/5/98, Panabajal, Comalapa; Oxi' Imox, 2/11/98, Comalapa; Oxi' Kan, 8/19/98, Comalapa.

62. Lajuj Kan, 1/30/98, Pachitur, Comalapa; Kab'lajuj Ajpu', 5/5/98, Comalapa.

63. Junlajuj Imox, 5/23/98, 6/23/98, Comalapa. Most people date the road to the early Ubico administration; see Oxlajuj Tz'i', 8/20/98, Comalapa.

64. Wo'o' Tijax, 4/24/98, Simajulew, Comalapa; B'eleje' Tz'i', Junlajuj B'atz', Junlajuj Toj, 5/20/98, Xetonox, Comalapa.

65. Junlajuj Kan, 4/24/98, Simajulew, Comalapa; Junlajuj Ajpu', 8/2/98, Comalapa.

66. Tz'ikin is a pseudonym for the family surname.

67. More accurately, Jun Tz'ikin was one of the first Mayan mayors of Comalapa after Guatemala's independence in 1823. Comalapa had indigenous mayors during the colonial period.

68. Junlajuj Ajpu', 8/2/98, Comalapa; B'eleje' Aj, 8/5/98, Comalapa.

69. Cayetano Otzoy, "Breve reseña biográfica del ciudadano Ka'i' Tz'ikin" (Typescript, n.d.); Juan Val Curruchich to Oxi' Tz'ikin, Apr. 28, 1975.

70. Jun Kan, 8/19/98, Comalapa.

71. Otzoy, "Breve reseña biográfica."

72. Jun Kan, 8/19/98, Comalapa; Cayetano Otzoy, "Breve reseña biográfica."

73. Val Curruchich to Oxi' Tz'ikin, Apr. 28, 1975.

74. Otzoy, "Breve reseña biográfica."

75. Ibid. A chicharía is a local drinking establishment where they serve *chicha,* a homemade alcoholic concoction made from fermented fruit.

76. Lajuj Ajmaq, 8/21/98, Comalapa.

77. Ixsanik (Ix'ajpu' interview), 1998, Comalapa.

78. Ixpop, 5/20/98, Comalapa; Jun Kawoq, 5/1/98, Agua Caliente, Comalapa.

79. Ixno'j, 2/16/98, Comalapa.

80. Oxlajuj Kan, 4/11/98, Comalapa; B'eleje' Tz'i', Junlajuj B'atz', Junlajuj Toj, 5/20/98, Xetonox, Comalapa.

81. Oxi' Tz'ikin, 8/1/98–9/11/98 (seven different interviews, quote from 8/17/98), Comalapa.

82. Lajuj K'at, 8/23/98, Comalapa.

83. Lajuj K'at, 8/1/00, Comalapa.

84. It is important to note that Kaqchikel praise other members of the younger Tz'ikin generation. For example, another of Oxi' Tz'ikin's daughters works for a development organization in Guatemala and uses her position there to aid her compatriots on a national and local level.

85. As will be explored in the final chapter, these precepts are not limited to clothing or language as identity markers. In fact, for many Kaqchikel it is sufficient to self-identify as Kaqchikel/Maya, but one must stand behind this decision and uphold Kaqchikel values. Vacillation or capitulation are not viewed lightly by

Kaqchikel. For an insightful analysis of generational changes and distinct approaches to Mayan activism in a Kaqchikel family from San Andrés Semetabaj see Warren, *Indigenous Movements,* 163–93.

86. Kab'lajuj Kej, 4/26/98, Comalapa.

87. Oxlajuj Kan, 3/7/98, Comalapa.

88. Ixno'j and Waqi' Aq'ab'al, 2/16/98, Comalapa; Kaji' Tz'i', 7/12/98, Comalapa; Wo'o' Kawoq and Waqi' Kawoq, 3/3/98, Kojol Juyu', Comalapa; Wo'o' No'j, 4/22/98, Xenimaquín, Comalapa; Ixb'atz', 3/10/98, Poaquil; Lajuj Ajpu', 4/19/98, Poaquil; Ix'ajmaq, 3/15/98, Poaquil; Ka'i' Aj (Jun Tojil interview), 1998, Barahona; Ixb'oq', 5/31/98, Tecpán.

89. Ixkik', 6/21/98, Comalapa.

90. Wuqu' Kawoq, 2/7/98, Comalapa.

91. Ixchel, 2/12/98, Comalapa; Ixkame, 8/17/98, Comalapa; Wo'o' Tijax, 4/24/98, Simajulew, Comalapa. Clearly, the strategy of military officials to brand people like Tuyuc and Menchú as guerillas because of their outspoken criticism against the military has affected Kaqchikel perceptions.

92. Oxlajuj Ajpu', 1/19/98, Panabajal, Comalapa.

93. Kaji' Kan, 9/6/98, Comalapa; Wo'o' Kan, 4/26/98, Comalapa.

94. Ixkik', 6/21/98, Comalapa; Jun Ajpu', 4/26/98, Comalapa; Oxlajuj Kan, 3/7/98, Comalapa; Ka'i' K'at, 5/16/98, Comalapa; Kab'lajuj Ajpu', 5/5/98, Comalapa.

95. Lajuj K'at, 4/11/98, Comalapa. The PAN was the ruling party in Guatemala under President Alvaro Arzú from 1996 to 2000.

96. Junlajuj Ajpu', 8/2/98, Comalapa

97. Ixtoj, 8/21/98, Comalapa.

98. Kab'lajuj K'at, 6/27/98, Comalapa; Jun Kame, 5/1/98, Agua Caliente, Comalapa; Oxi' Aj, 4/15/98, Simajulew, Comalapa; Ixkan, 3/29/98, Poaquil; Junlajuj Kej, 3/22/98, Poaquil; Lajuj Kawoq, 3/16/98, Poaquil.

99. Ixkawoq, 4/17/98, Pamumus, Comalapa.

100. Junlajuj Imox and Wo'o' Imox, 5/23/98, Comalapa; Oxlajuj Kan, 3/7/98, Comalapa; Jun Tojil, 9/2/98, Barahona; Kab'lajuj Kan, 2/15/98, Barahona.

101. Oxlajuj Kawoq, 3/18/98, Poaquil.

Chapter 9

1. For examples of Kaqchikel efforts to contribute their historical perspectives and worldviews to Guatemala's national record, see Demetrio Cojtí Cuxil, *Ub'aniik ri una'ooj uchomab'aal ri Maya' tinamit: Configuración del pensamiento político del pueblo Maya, segundo parte* (Guatemala: Editorial CHOLSAMAJ, 1995); Demetrio Cojtí Cuxil, *Ri Maya' moloj pa Iximulew: El movimiento Maya en Guatemala* (Guatemala City: Editorial CHOLSAMAJ, 1997); Consejo Nacional de Educación Maya, *Análisis del proceso de paz desde la perspectiva indígena* (Chimaltenango, Guatemala: Editorial Maya Nojib'sa, 1998); Demetrio Rodríguez, *Las ONGs y las relaciones interétnicas* (Guatemala: Editorial CHOLSAMAJ, 1995); Victor M. Racancoj, *Socioeconomía Maya precolonial* (Guatemala: Editorial CHOLSAMAJ, 1994); Mesa nacional Maya

de Guatemala, *Plan Nacional de desarrollo del pueblo Maya de Guatemala. Programa de las Naciones Unidas para el desarrollo* (Guatemala: Q'uq'kumat-MENMAGUA, 1999); Juan Yool Gómez and Juan Kaqjay, *Tzijonik kan qate' qatata'* (Guatemala: Universidad Rafael Landivar, 1990). Younger Kaqchikel authors such as Ronal Simón and Audelino Sacbin write in Guatemalan periodicals, including *Kaqchi Wuj* and *Kukuy.*

2. It is important to note that in some nations, such as Mexico, indigenous people are taking this term back and revaluing it. Therefore, in Mexico it is not exclusively a derogative term but one of ethnic pride. Nonetheless, out-group use of the term remains suspect.

3. Lajuj Aj, 6/4/00, Chimaltenango (interview conducted in San Francisco, Calif.).

4. For example, not sharing your own food when having lunch at work is considered a kaxlan practice.

5. In his book *The Blood of Guatemala,* Grandin adeptly argues for a history of multiethnic alliances between K'ichee's and Ladinos. He also points out the division between urban and rural K'ichee's of Quetzaltenango. His analysis (as he notes) contributes to a more holistic understanding of Guatemala's history, one that moves away from the dichotomy of the Maya versus the state.

6. B'eleje' Ey, 6/28/99, Poaquil; Lajuj K'at, 6/25/99, Comalapa; Jun Aq'ab'al, 6/28/99, Tecpán; Kaji' K'at, 6/28/99, Tecpán. For an insightful analysis of the 1999 popular referendum see Jonas, *Of Centaurs and Doves,* 189–216.

7. Lajuj Aj, 6/4/00, Chimaltenango (interview conducted in San Francisco, Calif.). Zapeta received his graduate degree from the State University of New York under the direction of Robert Carmack. His columns, which regularly appear in the Guatemalan newspaper *Siglo Veintiuno,* tend to be controversial partly because of his confrontational manner and strong ties to the political right.

8. For an excellent analysis of divisions in a Mayan community developing along religious lines (including Catholic and Protestant opposition to traditional Mayan religions) see Carlsen, *War for the Heart and Soul.*

9. Oxlajuj Kan, 10/17/98, Comalapa; Ka'i' K'at, 5/16/98, Comalapa; Jun Tojil, 12/1/97, 7/8/98, Barahona; Iximnik'te, 11/25/97, Tecpán; Ixmukane', 11/26/97, Tecpán.

10. *Recopilación de las Leyes Emitidas por el Gobierno Democrático de la República de Guatemala desde 3 de junio 1871, hasta el 30 de junio 1881,* Oct. 13, 1876, decree no. 165, 453; Skinner-Klee, *Legislación indigenista de Guatemala,* 117. Menchú asserts that while Barrios rescinded their nominal identification, these residents maintained their Mayan identity and continue to distinguish themselves as Maya today; see Menchú, *Crossing Borders,* 17.

11. Castellanos Cambranes, *Coffee and Peasants,* 302.

12. Jun Kan, 8/19/98, Comalapa.

13. *Historia del himno nacional,* 11–16, 25.

14. Ixya', 4/11/98, Comalapa.

15. Jun Kan, 9/3/98, Comalapa.

16. Oxi' Imox, 2/11/98, Comalapa.

17. Ixkawoq, 4/17/98, Pamumus, Comalapa; Ka'i' Imox, 1/21/98, Panabajal, Co-

malapa; Wo'o' Ey and Kab'lajuj B'atz', 3/28/98, Panimacak, Comalapa; Lajuj Kame, 2/14/98, Comalapa.

18. Lajuj K'at, 4/11/98, Comalapa; Ixtijax, 8/17/98, Comalapa.

19. B'eleje' Tz'i', Junlajuj B'atz', Junlajuj Toj, 5/20/98, Xetonox, Comalapa; Kab'lajuj Kej, 4/26/98, Comalapa; Ixiq', 1/12/98, Comalapa.

20. Ixb'utz', 6/20/98, Comalapa. Wo'o' B'atz' and Waqi' B'atz', 7/9/98, Comalapa; Jun Ajpu', 12/20/97, Comalapa, also made similar observations.

21. Oxi' Imox, 2/11/98, Comalapa; Kab'lajuj Tijax, 7/25/98, Comalapa; Oxi' Kej, 6/14/98, Comalapa; Kab'lajuj K'at, 6/27/98, Comalapa; Wuqu' B'atz', 2/10/98, Pawit, Comalapa.

22. *Historia del himno nacional,* 24–29, 55–58.

23. Ibid., 25–29, 55–66.

24. Junlajuj Ajpu', 8/2/98, Comalapa.

25. Otzoy, "Breve reseña biográfíca," 1.

26. Kab'lajuj Ajpu', 11/14/97, Comalapa.

27. *Historia del himno nacional,* 13, 60–61.

28. This resistance was also evident when Menchú, a Maya-K'ichee', won the 1992 Nobel Peace Prize. Many Ladinos were upset and argued that Guatemalan president Marco Vinicio Cerezo Arévalo (1986–91) should have won the award.

29. Certainly, that a Cuban, Joaquin Palma, wrote the words to the national anthem intensifies the competition over who can claim responsibility for the music.

30. Otzoy, "Breve reseña biográfíca."

31. An important distinction must be made here. Kaqchikel from Comalapa and Poaquil were less likely to hear these epithets than were people from Aguas Calientes, Barahona, Tecpán, and Chimaltenango. In Comalapa and Poaquil, Kaqchikel control many aspects of the towns, and in many ways this results in greater respect from and egalitarian interaction with Ladinos. In contrast, other towns that either retain a strong Ladino presence or are closely connected to Ladino power centers retain more overt expressions of ethnic tension. In general, the greater the Ladino influence in a town the more likely the use of racist terms.

32. Solares, *Derechos humanos,* 61–62, 67.

33. Adams, "Ethnic Images and Strategies in 1944," 148–51.

34. Handy, *Revolution in the Countryside,* 56–57. For an example of ethnic conflict in Rabinal, Baja Verapaz, see *El Imparcial,* May 11, 1945.

35. Asturias, *El problema social del indio,* 72, 101–13.

36. Lajuj Ajpu', 4/19/98, Poaquil.

37. Smith, *Indian Class and Class Consciousness;* Eric Wolf, "Closed Corporate Peasant Communities in Mesoamerica and Central Java," *Southwestern Journal of Anthropology* 13 (1957): 1–18.

38. Sam Colop, "Discourse of Concealment," 113.

39. Lajuj Aj, 6/4/00, Chimaltenango (interview conducted in San Francisco, Calif.).

40. Story told to me by Judith Maxwell, 3/17/97.

41. Cojtí Cuxil, *Políticas para la reivindicación,* 65–66.

42. Wilson, "Educating America," 47.

43. Ibid., 46.

Sources

Kaqchikel Oral Accounts

Unless otherwise indicated, I conducted the interview; and unless otherwise indicated, the interview was conducted in the informants hometown or aldea.

INFORMANT'S NAME	TOWN (AND ALDEA)	DATES
	Acatenango	
Ixmaq'uq'		12/12/97
	Chimaltenango	
Ixspa'ch		12/5/95 (interview conducted in New Orleans, La.)
Ixtuktuk		4/16/98
Kab'lajuj Kame		5/4/98
Lajuj Aj		4/30/00, 6/4/00, 7/30/00 (interviews conducted in San Francisco, Calif.)
Oxlajuj Q'anil		5/28/98
Oxlajuj Raxche'		7/30/00 (interview conducted in San Francisco, Calif.)
Waqxaqi' Maq'uq'		6/4/00 (interview conducted in San Francisco, Calif.)
Wo'o' Kot		1/23/98, 3/26/98
	Comalapa	
B'eleje' Aj		8/5/98
B'eleje' Ajmaq		8/21/98

B'eleje' Imox	9/20/97, 1/11/98, 4/17/98, 4/26/98, 5/19/98, 5/25/98, 8/1/98, 8/9/98
B'eleje' K'at	11/5/97
B'eleje' Tijax	5/23/98, 9/14/98
Ix'aj	10/10/97, 2/9/98
Ix'ajpu'	9/23/97, 10/23/97, 1/18/98, 8/29/98
Ix'ak'wal	8/21/98, 8/29/98
Ix'aq'	5/19/98
Ix'aq'om	11/5/97, 9/13/98
Ixb'utz'	5/14/98, 6/20/98
Ixcha'im	4/13/98
Ixchel and Ixraxchel	2/12/98
Ixch'i'p	10/24/97, 11/16/97
Ixch'ok	1/19/98
Ix'ija'tz	10/20/97
Ix'imox	8/23/98, 9/6/98
Ixiq'	1/12/98, 7/9/98
Ixjo'q	11/6/97
Ixkame	8/17/98, 8/22/98
Ixk'at	1/7/98, 2/9/98, 4/7/98, 4/20/98, 4/26/98, 8/15/98
Ixk'ayil	11/5/97, 4/26/98, 5/5/98, 5/19/98
Ixk'echelaj	1/19/98
Ixkik'	11/4/97, 6/21/98, 9/12/98
Ixkot	3/1/98, 9/19/98
Ixkuk	10/30/97
Ixk'u'x	Ix'ajpu' interview, 1998
Ixmi'al and Ixximoj	8/18/98, 8/20/98
Ixno'j and Waqi' Aq'ab'al	1/16/98, 2/16/98, 3/3/98, 3/23/98
Ixnum	4/29/98
Ixpop	5/20/98
Ixpo't	10/23/97, 7/19/98
Ixq'anil	9/21/97, 9/29/97, 10/27/97, 11/4/97, 12/21/97, 1/11/98, 1/14/98, 1/19/98, 1/28/98, 2/3/98, 2/9/98, 3/1–3/98,

	3/8/98, 3/23/98, 4/7/98, 4/10/98, 4/16/98, 4/20/98, 4/23/98, 4/28/98, 4/29/98, 5/5/98, 5/17–18/98, 5/20/98, 5/23/98, 6/10/98, 6/20/98, 6/25/98, 6/27/98, 7/12/98, 8/16–19/98, 8/30–31/98, 9/3/98, 9/9/98
Ixsamaj	9/6/98
Ixsanik	Ix'ajpu' interview, 1998
Ixsokaj	11/30/97
Ixsotz'	6/27/98
Ixsu't	5/4/98
Ixte	10/27/97, 5/21/98, 6/10/98, 9/10/98
Ixtijax	2/9/98, 2/14/98, 4/22/98, 8/17/98
Ixtoj	8/21/98
Ixtz'i'	2/14/98, 4/28/98, 5/5/98, 9/9/98, 9/12/98
Ixtz'ite'	10/12/97
Ixtz'unun	8/29/98
Ixxajan and Jun Toj	9/5/98
Ixxajo	3/1/98
Ixya'	4/11/98
Junlajuj Aq'ab'al	4/10/98, 4/13/98
Jun Ajpu'	9/26/97, 10/21/97, 10/24/97, 10/27/97, 12/20/97, 1/14/98, 4/7/98, 4/10/98, 4/13/98, 4/26/98, 5/1/98, 5/25/98, 6/11/98, 9/7/98
Jun Iq'	4/6/98, 4/17/98
Jun Kan	8/15/98, 8/19/98, 9/3/98, 9/14/98
Jun K'at	2/11/98
Jun Kot	9/21/98
Jun No'j	12/12/97
Junlajuj Aj	10/13/97

Junlajuj Ajpu'	8/2/98
Junlajuj Ey	5/22/98
Junlajuj Imox	5/23/98, 6/23/98, 7/11/98, 8/29/98, 9/14/98, 9/15/98
Junlajuj K'at	3/20/98, 7/9/98
Junlajuj No'j	12/12/97, 12/16/97, 12/19/97, 1/20/98, 4/27/98
Junlajuj Tijax	4/5/98
Kab'lajuj Ajpu'	11/14/97, 5/5/98
Kab'lajuj Ey	12/13/97
Kab'lajuj Imox	9/28/97, 10/23/97, 11/5/97, 1/5/98
Kab'lajuj Kej	4/26/98, 8/2/98
Kab'lajuj K'at	6/27/98, 7/11/98, 7/18/98, 8/1/98, 9/9/98
Kab'lajuj Maq'uq'	9/28/97, 3/2/98
Kab'lajuj No'j	10/17/97, 1/28/98, 3/6/98, 4/14/98, 9/12/98
Kab'lajuj Q'anil	5/18–19/98
Kab'lajuj Tijax	9/13/97, 9/28/97, 4/7/98, 7/12/98, 7/19/98, 7/25/98
Ka'i' Ey	7/11/98
Ka'i' Iq'	6/28/98, 7/25/98, 8/22/98, 8/31/98
Ka'i' K'at	2/12/98, 4/5/98, 5/16/98
Ka'i' Kej	11/5/97
Ka'i' Kot	5/27/98
Ka'i' Q'anil	12/12–13/97
Ka'i' Tijax	10/12/97, 10/16/97, 10/22/97, 5/5/98
Ka'i' Toj	3/1/98
Ka'i' Tzinik'an	6/13/98
Kaji' Imox	12/13/97, 4/12/98, 8/2/98
Kaji' Kame	3/4/98
Kaji' Kan	8/16/98, 9/6/98
Kaji' Kot	9/26/97, 4/26/98
Kaji' Toj	1/13/98
Kaji' Tz'i'	6/7/98, 7/12/98, 8/29/98

K'at Family	10/21/97
Kot Family	4/9/98
Lajuj Ajmaq	8/22/98
Lajuj Ey	9/14/97, 9/19/98
Lajuj Imox	12/20/97, 1/18/98, 3/3/98
Lajuj Kame	2/14/98, 5/22/98
Lajuj K'at	4/10–11/98, 5/6/98, 5/20/98, 8/23/98, 10/5/99, 8/1/00
Lajuj Tijax	4/27/98
No'j, women's organization	11/97
Oxi' Aq'ab'al	10/4/97, 10/26/97, 5/25/98
Oxi' B'atz'	4/26/98
Oxi' Imox	11/13/97, 2/10–11/98, 5/1/98, 8/11/98, 9/14/98
Oxi' Iq'	12/2/98
Oxi' Kan and Ixpaläj	8/19/98
Oxi' Kej	6/14/98
Oxi' Kot	9/13/97
Oxi' Q'anil	6/26/99
Oxi' Toj	10/25/97
Oxi' Tz'ikin	8/1/98, 8/5/98, 8/8/98, 8/11/98, 8/17–18/98, 9/11/98
Oxlajuj Aj	8/16/98
Oxlajuj B'atz'	10/30/97, 11/10/97
Oxlajuj Ey	6/21/98
Oxlajuj Kame	10/3/98
Oxlajuj Kan	10/17/97, 10/29/97, 12/10/97 (Rosario Canajal), 12/19/97, 3/7–8/98, 4/11/98, 4/14/98, 9/12/98
Oxlajuj Kej	6/26/98
Oxlajuj Tz'i'	8/20/98
Waqi' Iq'	12/12/97, 4/22/98
Waqi' K'at	5/3/98, 8/21–22/98, 9/6/98, 9/19/98
Waqi' Kot	6/20/98
Waqi' Toj	10/27/97
Waqi' Tzinik'an	3/1/98
Waqxaqi' Ajmaq	12/13/97, 2/13/98, 4/5/98

Waqxaqi' Ey	5/19/98
Waqxaqi' Iq'	1/6/98, 6/23/98,
	7/7/98,
Waqxaqi' Kej	5/24/98
Waqxaqi' Tojil	4/6/98
Wo'o' B'atz', Waqi' B'atz', and Oxlajuj Aq'ab'al	7/9/98
Wo'o' Imox	5/23/98
Wo'o' Kan	4/26/98
Wo'o' Ajpu'	11/6/97, 11/11/97,
	1/20/98, 1/31/98,
	4/21/98

Wo'o' Toj	4/5/98
Wo'o' Tzinik'an	12/13/97
Wuqu' Ajmaq	4/6/98
Wuqu' K'at	4/5/98, 4/6/98,
	7/25/98
Wuqu' Kawoq	1/6/98, 1/10/98,
	1/29/98, 2/7/98,
	4/7/98, 4/14–15/98,
	5/15/98
Wuqu' No'j	11/10/97
Wuqu' Toj	4/6/98
Wuqu' Tz'i'	10/23–24/97,
	11/9/97, 1/11/98
Wuqu' Tzinik'an	8/21/98

Ladinos

Felipe	9/23/97, 10/29/97

Comalapa Aldeas

Agua Caliente
Jun Kame	5/1/98
Jun Kawoq	5/1/98, 8/10/98
Oxlajuj No'j	5/1/98
Wuqu' Kot	5/1/98

Chi Chalí
B'eleje' Tojil	3/4/98
Ixq'aq'	3/9/98
Oxi' Kame	3/4/98
Oxlajuj Tijax	3/3/98

Kojol Juyu'
Kaji' Ey	5/4/98
Wo'o' Kawoq and Waqi' Kawoq	3/3/98

Mixcolabaj

B'eleje' Tzinik'an	4/24/98
Jun Ajmaq and Ixsu'm	9/4/98

Pachitur

Junlajuj Kame	4/12/98
Lajuj Kan	10/12/97, 10/15/97, 10/29/97, 12/20/97, 1/30/98
Primary school graduation ceremony	10/29/97
Road crew	10/29/97
Tijoxela (students)	9/23/97

Palima

Jun Juyu'	3/2/98
Kaji' Tojil	3/2/98
Lajuj Tzinik'an	3/2/98
Waqxaqi' Kot	3/2/98
Waqxaqi' Toj	3/2/98
Wuqu' Tijax	3/2/98

Pamumus

Ixjuyu', Ix'achb'il, Ix'abäj,	9/4/98
Ixkotz'i'j	4/26/98
Ixkawoq	4/17/98
Jun Tz'i'	7/11–12/98
Oxi' Kawoq	10/31/97, 9/4/98
Waqi' Kame	5/3/98, 5/17/98, 9/13/98

Panabajal

B'eleje' Kame	10/17/97
Ixti'oj	11/4/97
Jun B'atz'	11/4/97
Jun Tijax	3/8/98
Jun Ulew	11/4/97
Ka'i' Imox	1/21/98, 4/14/98, 8/5/98, 9/12/98
Ka'i' Juyu'	1/23/98
Lajuj Tzinik'an	3/6/98
Oxlajuj Ajpu'	1/19/98, 4/14/98, 4/17/98

Panicuy

Jun Imox, Ka'i' Ajpu', and Oxi' Ajpu'	12/2/97
Wo'o' Iq'	12/2/97

Panimacak

Oxi' Juyu'	3/28/98
Wo'o' Ey and Kab'lajuj B'atz'	3/28/98

Paquixic

Junlajuj Kej and Ixtinamit	5/22/98
Ka'i' Ulew	10/21/97
Wo'o' Tojil, Waqi' Tojil, and Wuqu' Tojil	10/21/97

Paraxaj

Ixti'ij, Kaji' Juyu', and Wo'o' Juyu'	10/27/97

Paraxaquen

Oxlajuj Imox	1/13/98, 8/17/98, 9/1/98
Oxi' Tijax	1/13/98

Patzaj

Jun Q'anil	2/9/98, 3/9/98, 3/18/98, 9/4/98
Kaji' Tijax	4/28/98
Oxi' Ulew	9/4/98
Waqi' Juyu'	2/9/98

Pawit

Wuqu' B'atz'	2/10/98

Paya

Waqi' Amaq, Waqi' Tijax, and Kaji' Tzinik'an	11/11/97

Quizaya

B'eleje' Kot	4/15/98

Simajulew

Ix'umül	4/15/98, 8/10/98
Junlajuj Kan	4/24/98
Junlajuj Tzinik'an	4/25/98
Kaji' Aj	3/8/98
Kaji' Ulew	4/25/98
Lajuj Tojil	4/12/98, 4/25/98
Oxi' Aj	4/15/98, 4/24/98, 5/16/98
Oxlajuj Iq'	4/17/98
Waqi' Ey	4/15/98, 4/24/98
Waqi' Q'anil, Wo'o' Tz'i', and Kaji' B'atz'	4/24/98
Waqxaqi' Aj	4/15/98, 8/10/98
Waqxaqi' Juyu'	4/25/98
Wo'o' Tijax	4/24/98
Wuqu' Juyu'	4/24/98

Xenimaquín

Ak'wala (students)	9/30/98
Ixtulül	1/30/98
Jun Imox	12/9/97
Lajuj Iq'	12/9/97
Waqi' Tz'i'	4/22/98
Wo'o' No'j and Waqxaqi' Tzinik'an	4/22/98
Wo'o' Ulew	4/22/98

Xetonox

B'eleje' Tz'i', Junlajuj B'atz', Junlajuj Toj	5/20/98

Xiquín Sanahí

Ixb'alam	12/17/97
Ixchiköp	12/17/97
Ixk'aj	12/17/97
Ixkumätz	1/12/98
Ixwa'in	12/17/97
Ixwatzik'	1/12/98
Junlajuj Tz'i'	10/24/97
Waqi' Ulew	10/22/97
Wuqu' Iq'	12/17/97

Zaragoza Aldea

Ixpoy	9/5/98

Guatemala City

Ixq'ij	9/12/98
Jun Raxche'	12/19/97, 4/13/98, 6/17/98
Kab'lajuj Tzinik'an	8/7/98

Patzicía

Kaji' Kawoq	3/20/98 (Clayton Maxwell interview), 4/15/98, 5/14/98, 5/20/98, 5/23/98, 6/11/98, 6/18/98, 6/25/98, 12/10/98 (phone conversation)
Lajuj Kot	4/30/98, 5/13/98

Poaquil

B'eleje' Aq'ab'al	3/14/98, 4/1/98, 8/30/98

B'eleje' Ey	10/3/97, 11/15/97, 11/23/97, 1/23/98, 3/10–11/98, 3/14/98, 3/17–18/98, 3/23/98, 3/26–27/98, 3/29/98, 4/1–2/98, 4/18–19/98, 4/28/98, 8/12/98, 8/30/98
B'eleje' Kej	3/19/98
B'eleje' Juyu'	3/15/98, 3/17/98
B'eleje' Toj	3/2/98
Ix'ajmaq	11/29/97, 3/15/98, 3/22/98, 4/2/98
Ixb'atz'	12/4/97, 3/10/98
Ixche'	11/22/97, 4/28/98
Ixkach'	3/11/98
Ixkan	3/29/98
Ixk'ayb'al	3/11/98
Ixmanik	11/17/97
Ixpo't	11/17/97
Ixq'ayïs	4/20/98
Ixqitzij	3/9/98, 3/15/98, 3/23/98
Ixxokoq'a'	3/11/98, 3/14/98, 8/30/98
Ixyuq'	3/10/98
Junlajuj Kawoq	11/17/97
Junlajuj Kej	3/22/98, 3/24/98
Kab'lajuj Kawoq	3/23/98, 8/30/98
Kab'lajuj Tzinik'an	3/15/98
Ka'i' Raxche'	4/19/98
Kaji' Ajmaq	3/28/98
Lajuj Ajpu'	3/29/98, 4/19/98, 6/6/98, 8/30/98
Lajuj Kawoq	3/16/98, 4/1/98
Oxi' No'j	11/22/97, 3/15/98
Oxi' Raxche'	3/27/98
Oxlajuj K'at	3/10/98
Oxlajuj Kawoq	3/18/98, 4/19/98, 8/30/98
Oxlajuj Tzinik'an	3/27/98
Tijax women's cooperative	3/11/98
Waqi' No'j	3/11/98, 3/15/98, 8/30/98
Waqxaqi' Kan	3/18/98

Waqxaqi' No'j	10/3/97
Waqxaqi' Tijax	4/18–19/98
Waqxaqi' Ulew	11/15/97
Wuqu' Q'anil	3/21/98, 4/1/98,
	4/29/98
Wuqu' Ulew	3/14/98

Other Interviews

Kathy Gilroy (Peace Corps worker)	3/9/98

Poaquil Aldeas

Hacienda María

Ix'aq'ab'al	3/17/98
Ixmuxu'x	3/21/98
Junlajuj Tojil	3/21/98
Waqxaqi' Aq'ab'al	3/17/98

Hacienda Vieja

Oxi' Ajmaq	3/27/98
Wuqu' Aj	3/26/98
Wuqu' Ey	3/26/98, 8/12/98

Nueva Esperanza

Ix'i'x	8/12/98
Ixjeb'ël	3/20/98
Oxi' Tojil	3/21/98
Waqxaqi' Q'anil	3/21/98

Ojer Caibal (Ojer K'ayb'al)

Kaji' No'j, Waqxaqi' Tz'i', Waqxaqi' B'atz'	3/25/98
B'eleje' B'atz', and Lajuj Q'anil	

Palama

Junlajuj Kot	1/24/98

Paley

Ixtz'ib'	3/27/98

Panimacak

Kaji' Raxche'	3/11/98

Saqirtacaj

Kab'lajuj Tojil	3/25/98
Ka'i' Kame	4/29/98

San Antonio Aguas Calientes (Aguas Calientes)

B'eleje' Kan	11/9/97
B'eleje' Q'anil	Ix'ey interview, 1998

B'eleje' Ulew	2/8/98
Ix'ey	10/6/97, 10/20/97, 11/3/97, 11/8/97, 11/28/97, 1/18/98, 5/14/98, 5/23/98, 7/25/98, 9/1/98
Ix'is	2/8/98
Ixkej	11/9/97
Ixmes and Ixch'op	1/18/98, 2/8/98
Jun Ey	11/12/97, 1/18/98
Kab'lajuj Tz'i'	10/6/97, 9/1/98
Ka'i' Kawoq	2/7/98
Kaji' Kej	11/12/97
Lajuj Aq'ab'al	11/12/97
Lajuj Juyu'	5/15/98
Oxi' Ey	11/28/97
Waqi' Aj	2/28/98
Waqi' Ajpu'	2/28/98
Waqi' Kan	Ix'ey interview, 1998
Waqxaqi' K'at	11/8/97, Jun Tojil interview, 1998
Waqxaqi' Kawoq	11/8/97, 11/28/97
Wo'o' Aj	Ix'ey interview, 1998
Wo'o' Kej	Ix'ey interview, 1998
Wo'o' Raxche'	6/12/98
Wuqu' Imox	11/12/97

Aguas Calientes Aldeas

Santiago Zamora

Ixmusmut	5/18/98

San Antonio Polopó

Lajuj Toj	2/2/98

San Martín Jilotepeque

Lajuj Tz'i'	3/8/98
Waqi' Raxche'	3/8/98

San Martín Jilotepeque Aldeas

Chi Jolom

Junlajuj Juyu'	3/8/98

Chuwatablon

Lajuj Ulew	3/8/98

Rosario Canajal

Ix'ixtutz'	3/7/98
Ix'ulew	12/10/97
Jun Maq'uq'	12/10/97
Junlajuj Aq'ab'al	12/10/97
Junlajuj Toj	3/7/98
Junlajuj Ulew	3/7/98
Kab'lajuj Kot	3/7/98
Kab'lajuj Juyu'	3/7/98
Oxlajuj Juyu' and Kab'lajuj Ulew	12/10/97
Oxlajuj Kot	12/10/97
Oxlajuj Tojil	3/9/98
Waqxaqi' Raxche'	3/7/98
Wuqu' Raxche'	3/7/98

Santa Catarina Barahona (Barahona)

B'eleje' Ajpu'	Jun Tojil interview, 1998
B'eleje' Raxche'	4/8/98
Ixjut	Jun Tojil interview, 1998
Ixko'öl	4/8/98
Ixtojil	2/7/98, 5/23/98, 9/2/98
Jun Kej	Jun Tojil interview, 1998
Jun Tojil	12/1/97, 1/17/98, 1/19/98, 2/7/98, 2/15/98, 2/28/98, 4/8/98, 5/15/98, 5/23/98, 6/15/98, 7/8/98, 9/2/98
Kab'lajuj Kan	2/15/98, 6/20/98
Ka'i' Aj	Jun Tojil interview, 1998
Ka'i' Maq'uq'	6/12/98
Ka'i' Tojil	6/12/98, 6/20/98
Oxi' Maq'uq'	6/12/98
Po't, women's weaving cooperative (including Ixkol, Ixxar, Ixweqoj, Ixxajab')	2/7/98
Waqxaqi' Ajpu'	Jun Tojil interview, 1998
Waqxaqi' Imox	2/7/98
Waqxaqi' Kej	2/7/98, 6/12/98

Wuqu' Ajpu'	Jun Tojil interview, 1998
Wuqu' Kame	Jun Tojil interview, 1998

Santa Catarina Polopó

Ixb'aq	7/13/98
Ixch'ich'	7/16/98
Ixjik	7/14/98
Ixkemon	7/15/98
Kaji' Maq'uq'	7/13/98, 7/16/98
Lajuj Raxche'	7/14/98
Wo'o' Maq'uq' and Ixjuku'	7/15/98

Santa Cruz Balanya

Ix'echa'	9/9/98
Junlajuj Raxche'	9/9/98, 9/18/98
Waqi' Maq'uq'	9/18/98

San Jorge de la Laguna

Ixtob'al and Ixtew	1/17/98 (interview conducted in Antigua)

Santa María de Jesús

B'eleje' No'j	8/8/97, 12/19/97
Wuqu' Maq'uq'	3/1/98

Sumpango

Kab'lajuj Raxche'	8/22/98

Tecpán

B'eleje' Iq'	6/4/98
B'eleje' Kawoq	6/9/98
Ix'aj	11/26/97
Ix'ajmaq	6/2/98
Ixb'oq'	5/31/98
Ixch'oy	11/21/97
Ix'ichaj	5/29/98
Iximnik'te'	9/25/97, 11/18/97, 11/21/97, 11/24–25/97, 5/3/98, 5/29–31/98, 8/28/98, 9/8/98, 2/23/99, 4/13/99

Ixkinäq'	11/23/97
Ixmukane'	11/22/97, 11/26/97
Ixsu'm	6/1/98
Ixtzinik'an	6/2/98
Ixwuj	6/1/98
Jun Aj and Ix'ik'	6/6/98
Jun Aq'ab'al	5/2/98, 6/28/98
Jun Tzinik'an	5/26/98
Junlajuj Iq'	5/31/98
Kab'lajuj Aq'ab'al	11/19/97
Kab'lajuj Iq'	5/31/98
Ka'i' Ajmaq	10/20/97, 11/23/97
Ka'i' Aq'ab'al	6/7/98
Ka'i' B'atz'	11/26/97
Ka'i' No'j	6/4/00 (interview conducted in San Francisco, Calif.)
Ka'i' Tz'i'	5/26/98, 6/10/98
Kaji' Aq'ab'al	6/8/98
Kaji' Iq'	11/18/97
Kaji' K'at	5/2/98
Kaji' Q'anil	11/19/97
K'ayb'il B'alam	10/5/97, 6/5–6/98, 6/10/98, 7/8/98
Lajuj B'atz'	7/8/98, 9/9/98
Oxi' K'at	6/5/98
Oxi' Tz'i'	5/29/98
Oxlajuj Ajmaq	9/24/97, 7/8/98, 9/9/98
Oxlajuj Ulew	6/2/98
Waqi' Imox	5/3/98
Waqi' Kej	6/5/98, 6/7/98
Wo'o' Kame	5/26/98, 5/29/98
Wo'o' Q'anil	6/7/98
Wuqu' Aq'ab'al	11/25/97
Wuqu' Kan	6/5/98
Wuqu' Kej	5/30/98

Ladinos

Mardo Keoho	5/29/98

Tecpán Aldeas

Chuwatz'unuj

Ka'i' Kan	11/24/97
Wo'o' Aq'ab'al	11/24/97

Ladino Interviews

Lujan y Muñoz, Jorge. Guatemala City, Guatemala, 7/23/94.
Pellecer, Carlos Manuel. Antigua, Guatemala, 6/27/94.

Primary Sources

Kaqchikel Written Accounts

Kaji' Kan. "Chixot y Desde 1541 Asta Hoy San Juan Comalapa." In possession of Kaji' Kan. Typescript, ca. 1980.
Otsoy, Edwardo. "Breve Historia del Antiguo Nombre de Comalapa." *Comalapan,* October 1966: 10.
Otzoy, Cayetano. "Breve reseña biográfica del ciudadano Ka'i' Tz'ikin." Typescript, n.d. In possession of Oxi' Tz'ikin.
Val Curruchich, Juan. Letter to Oxi' Tz'ikin, April 28, 1975. In possession of Oxi' Tz'ikin.
Wuqu' K'at. "Libreta de Apuntes." Personal document, n.d.

Monographs

APAOP (Asociación de Pequeños Agricultores Orgánicos Poaquileños). "Proyecto Caficultura Orgánica." San José Poaquil, Chimaltenango. Grant proposal, ca. 1998.
"Centro de Salud Monografía." San Juan Comalapa Health Center. Typescript, December 1994.
"Diagnóstico de Salud, Distrito San José Poaquil, Chimaltenango." San José Poaquil Health Center. Typescript, 1980.
Gómez Sálazar, Jerson Alexis M., and Epifanio Sálazar Bal. "Municipalidad de San Juan Comalapa, Departamento de Chimaltenango." San Juan Comalapa Municipal Building. Typescript, ca. 1996.
Ministerio de Educación, "Mapa Escolar, Marzo 1996, San José Poaquil, Chimaltenango." Dirección Técnica Regional Central V, Supervisión Educativa No. 95–16. San José Poaquil Municipal Building. Typescript, ca. 1996.
"Monografía de San Antonio Aguas Calientes." *El Pueblo,* Sacatepéquez, June 1968.
"Monografía de San José Poaquil." San José Poaquil Municipal Building. Typescript, n.d.
"Monografía del Municipio de San Juan Comalapa, Chimaltenango, Area Urbana, Ciclo Escolar 1994, Supervisión educativa no. 95–18." San Juan Comalapa Administration of Education Office. Typescript, ca. 1994.
"Monografía de San Juan Comalapa, Chimaltenagno." Escuela Urbana Mixta, Cantón 8. San Juan Comalapa Administration of Education Office. Typescript, 1997.
"Monografía del Municipio de Tecpán, Guatemala, Departamento de Chimaltenango." Tecpán Municipal Building. Typescript, ca. 1987.

Sotz O., Miguel Angel. "Mongrafia de Comalapa, Diagnóstico Comunitario 1994." Proyecto 2439 Chuwi' Tinamït. San Juan Comalapa. Typescript, n.d.

Sut Cristal, Pablo. "Monografía de San José Poaquil." San José Poaquil Municipal Building. Typescript, n.d.

Government Documents

I have identified the AGCA sources by their general catalog numbers. They are cataloged by docket numbers (legajo—in most cases a bundle of papers) and a specific proceeding or action (expediente) number. In the case of separate sections in the AGCA, I have listed the name of the section (e.g., sección de tierras) followed by package (paquete) and proceeding numbers. Documents that are not cataloged in this manner are listed simply by the title of their package (e.g., Documentos de Jefetura Política de Sacatepéquez) and date.

(AGCA) Archivo General de Centro América, Guatemala City, Guatemala. Documentos de Jefetura Politíca de Sacatepéquez. 1927–28.

(AGCA) Archivo General de Centro América, Guatemala City, Guatemala. Documentos de Jefetura Politíca de Chimaltenango, 1838–1946.

(AGCA) Archivo General de Centro América, Guatemala City, Guatemala. Sección de Tierras. 1807–1913

(AGCA) Archivo General de Centro América, Guatemala City, Guatemala. Secretaría de gobernación y justicia, 1860–95.

Boletín de Agricultura, Revista Mensual, Guatemala, 1901–3.

Boletín de Agricultura y Caminos, Guatemala, 1929–30.

Boletín de Ministerio de Comunicaciones y Obras Públicas. Guatemala, 1955–56.

Boletín Sanitario de la Dirección General de Salubridad Pública. Guatemala, 1927.

Boletín Sanitario de Guatemala, órgano de la Dirección General de Sanidad Pública de Guatemala. 15 vols. Guatemala, 1927–45.

Comalapa Municipal Documents. Municipal Building in Comalapa, Chimaltenango.

Dirección General de Policía de la República: Memoria de sus trabajos realizados en el año 1924, rendida al ministerio de gobernación y justicia. Guatemala: Tipografía Nacional, 1925.

Guerra, Viviano. *Recopilación de las leyes en todos por el supremo gobierno de la República de Guatemala desde 10 enero 1886 a último día de este año.* Vol. 5. Guatemala: Tipografía de P. Arenales, 1893.

Instituto Nacional de Estadística X Censo Nacional de Población y V de Habitación. Guatemala: Instituto Nacional de Estadística, 1996. (Departments of Chimaltenango, Sacatepéquez, Sololá)

Land Title of Fernando Chalí. In possession of Junlajuj Juyu'. 1889–1891.

Memoria del cuerpo de Policía Nacional de la República, rendida al Ministerio de Gobernación y Justicia. Guatemala: Tipografía Nacional, 1927–49.

Memoria de las labores del Ejecutivo en el Ramo de Agricultura. 15 vols. Guatemala: Tipografía Nacional, 1931–44, 1957.

Memoria del Ministerio de Agricultura. 11 vols. Guatemala: Tipografía Nacional, 1922–31.

Memoria de la Secretaría de Fomento, presentada a la Asamblea Nacional Legislativa en sus sesiones ordinarias. Guatemala: Tipografía Nacional, 1914–22.

Memoria de la Secretaría de Gobernación y Justicia presentada a la Asamblea Nacional Legislativa en sus sesiones ordinarias. Guatemala: Minerva centro editorial, 1919.

Memoria de la Secretaría de Gobernación y Justicia presentada a la Asamblea Nacional Legislativa en sus sesiones ordinarias. Guatemala: Tipografía Nacional, 1909–17, 1922–43.

Memoria de los trabajos realizados por la Dirección General de Sanidad Pública. Guatemala: Tipografía Nacional, 1913–38.

Memorias de la Dirección General de Agricultura. Guatemala: Tipografía Nacional, 1902.

Ministerio de Educación de Guatemala. *Primer seminario sobre problemas de la educación rural guatemalteca.* Guatemala City: Ministerio de Educación, 1964.

Plan de estudios y programas para las escuelas rurales de la República. Guatemala, 1933.

Recopilación de las Leyes Emitidas por el Gobierno Democrático de la República de Guatemala desde 3 de junio 1871, hasta el 30 de junio 1881. Guatemala: Tipografía de "el progreso," 1881.

Recopilación de las Leyes de la República de Guatemala. Guatemala: Tipografía Nacional. 21 vols. 1917–37.

"La Reforma de la Constitución de la República de Guatemala, decretada 11 de julio 1935." In *Las Constituciones de Guatemala,* ed. Luis Marinas Otero. Madrid: Instituo de Estudios Políticos, 1958.

Revista Caminos de Guatemala, Guatemala, 1940.

Revista Militar Ilustrada; órgano de la Academia Militar del Ejército de la República. Publicación mensual. Guatemala, 1911–16.

Salubridad y Asistencia: órgano del Ministerio de Salud Pública y Asistencia Social. 4 vols. Guatemala, 1948–51.

Santa Catarina Barahona, Sacatepéquez, municipal document. "Certificación extendida a favor de la Municipalidad de Santa Catarina Barahona del Sacatepéquez." January 5, 1950. Office of the mayor, Santa Catarina Barahona.

Seis años de gobierno presidido por el General Jorge Ubico. Guatemala: Tipografía Nacional, 1937.

Seis años del progreso, 1931–37. Guatemala: Tipografía Nacional, 1937.

Newspapers and Magazines

Guatemala

CERIGUA Weekly Briefs, 1998–99
El Chimalteco, 1974
Comalapan, 1966
El Día, Diario Independiente, 1927
Diario de Centro América, 1890–1976

Díario Exito, 1935
La Gaceta de Guatemala, 1870
El Gráfico, 1968–76
La Hora, 1967–86
El Imparcial, 1944–67
El Impulso, 1910–19
El Liberal Progresista, 1934–41
Mercurio, 1944
Nuestro Díario, 1944
Prensa Libre, 1967–68, 1999
La República, 1908–44
Revista de la Cruz Roja Guatemalteca, 1942
Revista Franciscana, 1948
Rutzijol: Periódico Maya Independiente, por la autogestión del Pueblo Maya, 1993–98

United States

Boston Globe, 1999
New York Times, 1999

Secondary Sources

Adams, Richard. "Changing Political Relationships in Guatemala." In *Political Changes in Guatemalan Indian Communities, A Symposium,* 48–52. Middle American Research Institute Series, publication no. 24, New Orleans: Tulane University, 1957.
———. *Crucifixion by Power.* Austin: University of Texas Press, 1970.
———. "Estado e Indígenas durante la epidemia de influenza de 1918–1919 en Guatemala." *Mesoamérica* 34 (1997): 481–558.
———. "Ethnic Images and Strategies in 1944." In *Guatemalan Indians and the State: 1540–1988,* ed. Carol Smith, 141–62. Austin: University of Texas Press, 1990.
———. *Etnicidad en el ejército de la Guatemala Liberal (1870–1915).* Guatemala: FLACSO, 1995
———. "Las masacres de Patzicía de 1944." *Revista Winak Boletín Intercultural* 7, no. 1–4 (1992): 3–40.
———. "La población indígena en el estado liberal." In *Historia General de Guatemala,* ed. Jorge Luján Muñoz, 173–98. Vol. 5. Guatemala: Asociación de Amigos del País, Fundación para la Cultura y Desarollo, 1996.
El amigo del soldado. Guatemala: Tipografía Nacional, 1904.
Anderson, Benedict. *Imagined Communities.* London: Verso, 1991.
Annis, Sheldon. *God and Production in a Guatemalan Town.* Austin: University of Texas Press, 1987.
———. "A Story from a Peaceful Town." In *Harvest of Violence: Guatemala's Indians*

and the Counterinsurgency War, ed. Robert Carmack, 155–73. Norman: University of Oklahoma Press, 1988.

Arbona, Sonia I. "Commercial Agriculture and Agrochemicals in Almolonga, Guatemala." *Geographical Review* 88, no. 1 (1998): 47–63.

Archila Serrano, Ligia. "La penetración evangélica en San Antonio Aguas Calientes, municipio de Departamento de Sacatepéquez." Guatemala, Universidad de San Carlos de Guatemala, escuela de historia, área de antropología, 1989.

Arguello, Santiago. *Barrios y Ubico: la obra creadora de dos constructores de naciones.* Havana: Cia Tipografía, S.A., 1937.

Arias, Arturo. "Changing Indian Identity: Guatemala's Violent Transition to Modernity." In *Guatemalan Indians and the State,* ed. Carol Smith, 230–57. Austin: University of Texas Press, 1990.

Asturias, Miguel Angel. *El problema social del indio y otros textos.* Paris: Centre de recherches de l'institut d'etudes hispaniques, 1971.

Asturias de Barrios, Linda. *Comalapa: el traje y su significado.* Guatemala: Museo Ixchel del Traje Indígena de Guatemala, 1985.

———. "Mano de Mujer, Mano de Hombre: Produción artesanal textil en Comalapa Guatemala." Ph.D. diss., State University of New York, Albany, 1994.

Austin, Patricia A. *Exports and Local Development: Mexico's New Maquiladoras.* Austin: University of Texas Press, 1992.

AVANSCO (Asociación para el Avance de las Ciencias Sociales en Guatemala). *Impacto ecológico de los cultivos hortícolas no-tradicionales en el altiplano de Guatemala.* Guatemala: Instituto AVANSCO, 1994.

Axtell, James. "Ethnohistory: An Historian's View." In *The European and the Indian: Essays in the Ethnohistory of Colonial North America,* 3–15. Oxford: Oxford University Press, 1981.

Bancroft, Hubert Howe. *History of the Pacific States of North* America. Vol. 2: *Central America, 1530–1800.* San Francisco: A. L. Bancroft, 1883.

Batres Jáuregui, Antonio. *Los Indios, su historia y su civilización.* Guatemala: La Unión, 1894.

Becker Richards, Julia, and Michael Richards. "Maya Education: A Historical and Contemporary Analysis of Mayan Language Education Policy." In *Maya Cultural Activism in Guatemala,* ed. Edward Fischer and R. McKenna Brown, 208–21. Austin: University of Texas Press, 1996.

Bernard, H. Russel. *Research Methods in Anthropology: Qualitative and Quantitative Approaches.* London: Altamira, 1994.

Booth, John A., and Thomas W. Walker. *Understanding Central America.* Boulder: Westview, 1993.

Bowen, Gordon L. "U.S. Foreign Policy toward Radical Change: Covert Operations in Guatemala, 1950–1954." *Latin American Perspectives* 36 (winter 1983): 88–102.

Bricker, Victoria Reifler. *The Indian Christ, the Indian King: The Historical Substrate of Maya Myth and Ritual.* Austin: University of Texas Press, 1981.

———. *Ritual Humor in Highland Chiapas.* Austin: University of Texas Press, 1973.

Britnell, George. "Problems of Economic and Social Change in Guatemala." *Canadian Journal of Economic and Political Sciences* 17 (1951): 468–81.

Brown, R. McKenna. "Language Maintenance and Shift in Four Kaqchikel Towns." Ph.D. diss., Tulane University, 1991.

———. "The Mayan Language Loyalty Movement in Guatemala." In *Maya Cultural Activism in Guatemala,* ed. Edward Fischer and R. McKenna Brown, 165–77. Austin: University of Texas Press, 1996.

Bunzel, Ruth. *Chichicastenango: A Guatemalan Indian Village.* Seattle: University of Washington Press, 1972.

Burgess, Paul. *Justo Rufino Barrios.* San José, Costa Rica: Editorial Universitaria Centroamericana, 1972.

Busto, Inocencio del. "San Juan Comalapa." *Antropología e Historia de Guatemala* 13, no. 2 (1961): 27–36.

Cabrera, Isidro. "Trabajos realizados por la sección de control de tifo en 1950." *Salubridad y Asistencia: órgano del ministerio de salud pública y asistencia social.* Vol. 4. April 1951. Guatemala.

Cabrera, Isidro, and Manuel López Selva. "Campana contra el tifo." *Salubridad y Asistencia: órgano del ministerio de salud pública y asistencia social.* Vol. 1. December 1948. Guatemala.

Carey, David, Jr. "*Indigenísmo* and Guatemalan History in the Twentieth Century." *Revista Interamericana de Bibliografía* 48, no. 2 (1998): 379–408.

Carlsen, Robert. *The War for the Heart and Soul of a Highland Maya Town.* Austin: University of Texas Press, 1997.

Carmack, Robert. "Barrios y los indígenas: el caso de Santiago, Momostenango." *Estudios Sociales* 6 (1972): 52–73.

———. *Historia Social de los Quichés.* Guatemala: Editorial "José de Pineda Ibarra," Ministerio de Educación. 1979.

———. "Los Indígenas." In *Historia General de Guatemala,* ed. Jorge Luján Muñoz, 4: 339–52. Guatemala: Asociación de Amigos del País, Fundación para la Cultura y el Desarrollo, 1995.

———. *The Quiché Mayas of Utatlán: The Evolution of a Highland Guatemala Kingdom.* Norman: University of Oklahoma Press, 1981.

———. *Rebels of Highland Guatemala: The Quiché-Mayas of Momostenango.* Norman: University of Oklahoma Press, 1995.

———. "State and Community in Nineteenth-Century Guatemala." In *Guatemalan Indians and the State,* ed. Carol Smith, 116–36. Austin: University of Texas Press, 1990.

Carrasco, Davíd. "Religions of Mesoamerica: Cosmovision and Ceremonial Centers." In *Religious Traditions of the World: A Journey through Africa, Mesoamerica, North America, Judaism, Christianity, Islam, Hinduism, Buddhism, China, and Japan,* ed. H. Byron Earhart, 107–253. New York: Harper and Row, 1993.

Castañeda, Ester S. *Estudios Sociales (primer curso).* Guatemala City: Tallers Imprel, 1962.

Castellanos Cambranes, Julio. *Café y campesinos en Guatemala, 1853–1897.* Guatemala: Editorial Universitaria, 1985.

Castellanos Cambranes, Julio. *Coffee and Peasants: The Origins of the Modern Plantation Economy in Guatemala 1853–1897.* South Woodstock, Vt.: CIRMA, 1985.

Catalán Prem, Carlos. "El tifus exantemático en Chimaltenango." *Boletín Sanitario de Guatemala, órgano de la Dirección General de Sanidad Pública de Guatemala* 11, no. 48 (1940): 138–41.

Cavender Wilson, Angela. "Educating America: The Historian's Responsibility to Native Americans and the Public." *Perspectives* 38, no. 5 (2000): 46–47.

Cervantes, Fernando. *Devil in the New World: The Impact of Diabolism in New Spain.* New Haven: Yale University Press, 1994.

Champagne, Duane. "American Indian Studies Is for Everyone." In *Natives and Academics, Researching and Writing about American Indians,* ed. Devon A. Mihesuah. Lincoln: University of Nebraska Press, 1998.

Chávez, Adrián Ines. *K'iche' Tz'ib': escritura K'iche' y otros temas.* Guatemala: Libreria, ca. 1991.

Chinchilla Aguilar, Ernesto. "Tecpán, Guatemala." *Antropología e Historia de Guatemala* 13, no. 1 (1961): 9–14.

Coe, Michael D. *The Maya.* New York: Thames and Hudson, 1999.

Cohen, David William. *Womunafu's Bunafu: A Study of Authority in a Nineteenth Century African Community.* Princeton: Princeton University Press, 1977.

Cojtí Cuxil, Demetrio. *Políticas para la reivindicación de los Mayas de hoy: (fundamento de los derechos específicos del pueblo maya).* Guatemala City: Editorial CHOLSAMAJ, SPEM, 1994.

———. "The Politics of Maya Revindication." In *Maya Cultural Activism in Guatemala,* ed. Edward Fischer and R. McKenna Brown, 19–50. Austin: University of Texas Press, 1996.

———. *Ri Maya' moloj pa Iximulew: El movimiento Maya en Guatemala.* Guatemala City: Editorial CHOLSAMAJ, 1997.

———. *Ub'aniik ri una'ooj uchomab'aal ri Maya' tinamit: Configuración del pensamiento político del pueblo Maya, segundo parte.* Guatemala: Editorial CHOLSAMAJ, 1995.

Colby, Benjamin N., and Lore M. Colby. *The Daykeeper: The Life and Discourse of an Ixil Diviner.* Cambridge: Harvard University Press, 1981.

Consejo Nacional de Educación Maya. *Análisis del proceso de paz desde la perspectiva indígena.* Chimaltenango, Guatemala: Editorial Maya Nojib'sa, 1998.

Consejo Superior Universitario Centroamericano (CSUCA). *Estructura agraria, dinámica de población y desarrollo capitalista en Centroamérica.* San José, Costa Rica: EDUCA, 1978.

Contreras R., J. Daniel. *Una rebelión indígena en el partido de Totonicapán en 1820: El indio y la independencia.* Guatemala: Imprenta Universitaria, 1951.

Cook, Blanche Wiesen. *The Declassified Eisenhower: A Divided Legacy.* New York: Doubleday, 1981.

Cook, Sherburne F., and Woodrow Borah. *Essays in Population History: Mexico and the Caribbean.* 3 vols. Berkeley: University of California Press, 1971–79.

Crosby, Alfred. *Epidemic and Peace, 1918.* Westport, Conn.: Greenwood, 1977.

Cullather, Nick. *Secret History: The CIA's Classified Account of Its Operations in Guatemala, 1952–1954.* Stanford: Stanford University Press, 1999.

Dalton, Roque. *Miguel Marmol.* Willimantic, Conn.: Curbstone, 1982.

Dary, Claudia. *Mujeres tradicionales y nuevos cultivos.* Guatemala City: FLACSO, 1991.

———. *Relatos de los Antiguos: Estudios de la tradición oral de Comalapa, Chimaltenango.* Guatemala: Universidad de San Carlos de Guatemala, 1992.

Davidson, Miriam. *Lives on the Lines: Dispatches from the U.S.–Mexico Border.* Tucson: University of Arizona Press, 2000.

Davis, Shelton H. "State Violence and Agrarian Crisis in Guatemala: The Roots of the Indian-Peasant Rebellion." In *Trouble in Our Backyard: Central America and the United States in the Eighties,* ed. Martin Diskin, 155–72. New York: Pantheon, 1983.

Dawson, Frank Griffith. "Labor Legislation and Social Integration in Guatemala." *American Journal of Comparative Law* 14 (1965): 124–42.

Denevan, William M. "Native American Populations in 1492: Recent Research and a Revised Hemispheric Estimate." In *The Native Population of the Americas in 1492,* xvii–xxix. Madison: University of Wisconsin Press, 1992.

———, ed. *The Native Population of the Americas in 1492.* 2nd. ed. Madison: University of Wisconsin Press, 1992.

Dosal, Paul. *Power in Transition: The Rise of Guatemala's Industrial Oligarchy, 1871–1994.* Westport, Conn.: Praeger, 1995.

Dunkerley, James. "Guatemala since 1930." In *Cambridge History of Latin America,* ed. Leslie Bethell, 7: 211–51. Cambridge: Cambridge University Press, 1984.

Early, John. "Population Increase and Family Planning in Guatemala." *Human Organization* 34, no. 3 (1975): 275–87.

Early, John, Christopher Lutz, and Robert Carmack, eds. *The Historical Demography of Highland Guatemala.* Institute for Mesoamerican Studies, no. 6. Albany: State University of New York Press, 1982.

Ebel, Roland H. "Political Modernization in Three Guatemalan Indian Communities." In *Community Culture and National Change,* ed. Richard Adams, 131–206. Middle American Research Institute Series, publication no. 24. New Orleans: Tulane University, 1972.

"El Ejército y los indios." *Revista Militar Ilustrada.* September 15, 1911.

Esquit Choy, Edgar. "El impacto del movimiento cafetalero en la vida cotidiana del municipio de Patzicía a finales del siglo XX." Tésis de grado, Escuela de Historia, Universidad de San Carlos de Guatemala, 1994.

———. "Proyecto político Maya y reconstructora de la historia." Unpublished paper, ca. 1998.

———. "Relaciones de poder en Patzicía, 1871–1944." *Estudios Interetnicos: Revista del Instituto de Estudios Interetnicos* 4, no. 5 (1996): 55–75.

Esquit Choy, Edgar, and Carlos Ochoa García. *Yiqalil q'anej kunimaaj tziij niman tzij: el respeto a la palabra.* Guatemala: Centro de estudios de la cultura maya, 1995.

Esquit Choy, Edgar, and Isabel Rodas, *Élite ladina-vanguardia indígena de la intolerancia a la violencia, Patzicía 1944.* Guatemala: Caudal, S.A., 1997.

Edmonson, Munro. *The Ancient Future of the Itza: The Book of Chilam Balam of Tizimin.* Austin: University of Texas Press, 1982.

Estrada Monroy, Agustín. *Historia de la Catedral.* Guatemala: Editora La Sagrada Familia, 1977.

Ewald, Robert. "San Antonio Sacatepéquez, 1932–53." In *Community Culture and National Change,* ed. Richard Adams, 18–22. Middle American Research Institute Series, publication no. 24. New Orleans: Tulane University, 1972.

Falla, Ricardo. "Hacia la revolución verde: Adopción y dependencia del fertilizante químico en un Municipio del Quiché, Guatemala." *Estudios Sociales* 6 (1972): 16–51.

———. *Masacres en la selva: Ixcán, Guatemala (1975–82).* Guatemala City: Editorial Universitaria de Guatemala, 1992.

———. *Quiché rebelde: estudio de un movimiento de conversión religiosa rebelde a las creencias tradicionales en San Antonio Olotenango, Quiché, 1948–70.* Guatemala: Editorial Universitaria, 1978.

Farris, Nancy. *Mayan Society under Colonial Rule.* Princeton: Princeton University Press, 1984.

Fergusson, Erna. *Guatemala.* New York: Alfred A. Knopf, 1938.

Fischer, Edward F., and R. McKenna Brown, eds. *Maya Cultural Activism in Guatemala.* Austin: University of Texas Press, 1996.

Flora, Jan L., and Edelberto Torres Rivas. "Sociology of Developing Societies: Historical Bases of Insurgency in Central America." In *Sociology of Developing Societies: Central America,* ed. Jan L. Flora and Edelberto Torres Rivas, 32–55. New York: Monthly Review, 1989.

Frank, Luisa, and Philip Wheaton. *Indian Guatemala: The Path to Liberation.* Washington, D.C.: EPICA Task Force, 1984.

Freidel, David, Linda Schele, and Joy Parker. *Maya Cosmos: Three Thousand Years of the Shaman's Path.* New York: Quill William Morrow, 1993.

Fuentes y Guzmán, Francisco Antonio de. *Recordación Florida: Discurso Historial y Demostración natural, material, militar y política del Reino de Guatemala.* 1690. Vol. 1. Guatemala: Tipografía Nacional, 1932–33.

Galich, Luís F. "Informe de la labor realizada por la Dirección General de Sanidad Pública en 1950." *Salubridad y Asistencia: órgano del ministerio de salud pública y asistencia social.* Vol. 4. January 1951.

Gall, Francis, *Diccionario Geográfico de Guatemala.* 4 vols. Guatemala: Instituto Geográfico Nacional, 1976.

García Añoveros, Jesús María. *Población y estado sociorreligioso de la diócesis de Guatemala en el último tercio del siglo XVIII.* Guatemala City: Editorial Universitaria, Universidad de San Carlos de Guatemala, 1987.

García Laguardia, Jorge Mario. *El pensamiento liberal de Guatemala.* San José, Costa Rica: Editorial Universitaria Centroamericana, 1977.

García López, Daniel. "Historia de la ciudad de Tecpán Guatemala." *Revista Tecpán Guatemala* (1997): 14–15.

———. "Valiosa Historia." *Revista Tecpán Guatemala* (1997): 12–13.

García Peláez, Francisco de Paula. *Memorias para la Historia del Antiguo Reino de Guatemala*. Vol. 1, 3rd ed. Guatemala: Tipografía Nacional, 1968.

Garrard-Burnett, Virginia. *Protestantism in Guatemala: Living in the New Jerusalem*. Austin: University of Texas Press, 1998.

Gaitán, Luis, and Julio Roberto Herrera. "II día PanAméricano de la Salud en Guatemala." *Boletín Sanitario de Guatemala, órgano de la Dirección General de Sanidad Pública de Guatemala* 12, no. 49 (1941): 7–10.

Gaitán, Luis, Julio Roberto Herrera, Carlos Martínez Durán, and Hernán Martínez Sobral. "Contribución al estudio del tifus exantemático en Guatemala." *Boletín Sanitario de Guatemala, órgano de la Dirección General de Sanidad Pública de Guatemala* 11, no. 48 (1940): 27–35.

Gillen, John. "San Luis Jilotepeque: 1942–1955." In *Community Culture and National Change*, ed. Richard Adams, 23–27. Middle American Research Institute Series, publication no. 24. New Orleans: Tulane University, 1972.

Gleijeses, Piero. "The Agrarian Reform of Arbenz." *Journal of Latin American Studies* 21 (October 1989): 453–80.

———. *Shattered Hope: The United States and the Guatemalan Revolution, 1944–1954*. Princeton: Princeton University Press, 1991.

González Orellana, Carlos. *Historia de la educación en Guatemala*. México, D.F.: Coleción Científico Pedagógica, 1960.

Gordillo Barrios, Gerardo. *Guatemala historia gráfica*. Guatemala City: Editorial Piedra Sanata, 1987.

Gossen, Gary H. "The Chamula Festival of Games: Native Macroanalysis and Social Commentary in a Maya Carnival." In *Symbol and Meaning beyond the Closed Community: Essays in Mesoamerican Ideas,* ed. Gary Gossen, 227–54. Institute for Mesoamerican Studies. Albany: State University of New York Press, 1986.

Goubaud Carrera, Antonio. *San Antonio Aguas Calientes, Síntesis socio-económica de una comunidad indígena Guatemalteca*. Guatemala: Instituto Indigenísta Nacional, Ministerio de Educación Pública, 1948. Publicaciones Especiales del Instituto Indigenísta Nacional, no. 6.

Grandin, Greg. *The Blood of Guatemala: A History of Race and Nation*. Durham: Duke University Press, 2000.

Grieb, Kenneth J. *Guatemalan Caudillo: The Regime of Jorge Ubico, Guatemala 1931–1944*. Athens: Ohio University Press, 1979.

Gudmonson, Lowell, and Hector Lindo-Fuentes. *Central America, 1821–1871: Liberalism before Liberal Reform*. Tuscaloosa: University of Alabama Pres, 1995.

Guillemín, Jorge. "The Ancient Cakchiquel Capital of Iximche'." *Expedition: Bulletin of the University Museum of University of Pennsylvania* 9, no. 2 (1967): 22–35.

———. "Un entierro señorial en Iximche'." *Anales de la Sociedad de Geografía e Historia* 34 (1961): 89–105.

———. *Iximche'*. Guatemala: Tipografía Nacional, 1965.

Haley, Alex. "Black History, Oral History, and Genealogy." In *Oral History: An Interdisciplinary Anthology,* ed. David K. Dunaway and Willa K. Baum, 257–78. London: Altamira, 1996.

Handy, Jim. "The Corporate Community, Campesino Organizations, and Agrarian Reform, 1950–1954." In *Guatemalan Indians and the State: 1540–1988,* ed. Carol Smith, 163–82. Austin: University of Texas Press, 1990.

———. *Gift of the Devil: A History of Guatemala.* Boston: South End, 1984.

———. "The Most Precious Fruit of the Revolution." *Hispanic American Historical Review* 68, no. 4 (1988): 675–705.

———. "National Policy, Agrarian Reform, and the Corporate Community during the Guatemalan Revolution, 1944–54." *Comparative Studies in Society and History* 30 (Oct. 1988): 698–724.

———. "Resurgent Democracy and the Guatemalan Military." *Journal of Latin American Studies* 18 (Nov. 1986): 383–408.

———. *Revolution in the Countryside.* Chapel Hill: University of North Carolina Press, 1994.

———. "Revolution and Reaction: National Policy and Rural Politics in Guatemala." Ph.D. diss., University of Toronto, 1985.

Hendrickson, Carol. *Weaving Identities: Construction of Dress and Self in a Highland Guatemalan Town.* Austin: University of Texas Press, 1995.

Henige, David. *The Chronology of Oral Tradition: Quest for a Chimera.* Oxford: Clarendon, 1974.

———. *Oral Historiography.* London: Longman, 1982.

Hernández de León, Federico. *Viajes presidenciales: breves relatos de algunas expediciones administrativos del General D. Jorge Ubico, presidente de la República.* Vols. 1 and 2. Guatemala: Tipografía Nacional, 1940.

Herrick, Thomas. "Economic and Political Development in Guatemala during the Barrios Period, 1871–85." Ph.D. diss., University of Chicago, 1967.

Hill, Robert M., II. "Chinamit and Molab: Late Postclassic Highland Maya Precursors of Closed Corporate Community." *Estudios de Cultura Maya* 15 (1984): 301–27.

———. *Colonial Cakchiquels: Highland Maya Adaptations to Spanish Rule 1600–1700.* New York: Harcourt Brace Jovanovich, 1992.

———. "Land, Family, and Community in Highland Guatemala: Seventeenth-Century Cakchiquel Maya Testaments." In *Dead Giveaways: Indigenous Testaments of Colonial Mesoamerica and the Andes,* ed. Susan Kellogg and Matthew Restall. Salt Lake City: University of Utah Press, 1998.

———. *The Pirir Papers and Other Colonial Period Cakchiquel-Maya Testamentos.* Vanderbilt University Publications in Anthropology, no. 37. Nashville: Vanderbilt University, 1989.

Hill, Robert M., II, and John Monaghan. *Continuities in Highland Maya Social Organization: Ethnohistory in Sacapulas, Guatemala.* Philadelphia: University of Pennsylvania Press, 1987.

Hinojosa, Servando. "Spiritual Embodiment in a Highland Maya Community." Ph.D. diss., Tulane University, 1999.

Historia del himno nacional. Guatemala: Tipografía Nacional, 1997.

Hymes, Dell. "Language, Memory, and Selective Performance: *Cultee's 'Salmon's Myth'* as Twice Told to Boas." *Journal of American Folklore* 98, no. 390 (1985): 391–434.

Immerman, Richard H. *The CIA in Guatemala.* Austin: University of Texas Press, 1982.

Ingersoll, Hazel. "The War of the Mountain: A Study of Reactionary Peasant Insurgency in Guatemala, 1837–1873." Ph.D. diss., University of Maryland, 1972.

Inman, Samuel Guy. *A New Day in Guatemala: A Study of the Present Social Revolution.* Wilton, Conn.: Worldover, 1954.

Ja C'Amabal I'b. "La primera gran confrontación: El movimiento campesino indígena del altiplano guatemalteca." Paper presented to the United Nations Subcommission on Ethnic Minorities, Geneva, August 1984.

Jonas, Susanne. *The Battle for Guatemala: Rebels, Death Squads, and U.S. Power.* Boulder: Westview, 1991.

———. "Guatemala: Land of Eternal Struggle." In *Latin America: The Struggle with Dependency and Beyond,* ed. Ron Chilcote and Joel Edelstein, 151–69. Cambridge: Schenkam, 1974.

———. *Of Centaurs and Doves: Guatemala's Peace Process.* Boulder, Co.: Westview, 2000.

Jones, Chester Lloyd. *Guatemala: Past and Present.* Minneapolis: University of Minnesota Press, 1940.

Jones, Oakah L., Jr. *Guatemala in the Spanish Colonial Period.* Norman: University of Oklahoma Press, 1994.

Juarros, Domingo. *Compendio de la Historia del Reino de Guatemala 1500–1800.* Guatemala: Editorial Piedra Santa, 1981.

Kan B'alam. "Reflexión sobre la historia y la actualidad." *Rutzijol: Periódico Maya Independiente, por la autogestión del Pueblo Maya,* Oct. 16–31, 1993, 5.

Kelsey, Vera, and Lilly de Jongh Osborne. *Four Keys to Guatemala.* New York: Funk and Wagnalls, 1939.

Khosrow, Fatem, ed. *The Maquiladora Industry: Economic Solution or Problem?* New York: Praeger, 1990.

Krehm, William. *Democracies and Tyrannies of the Caribbean.* Westport, Conn.: Lawrence Hill, 1984.

Kuhsiek A., Guillermo. "La importancia del indio para el ejército de Guatemala." *Revista Militar Ilustrada; órgano de la Academia Military del Ejército de la República. Memoria de Labores, Municipalidades Chimaltenango* 1, no. 2–3 (1916).

La Farge, Oliver. "Maya Ethnology: The Sequence of Cultures." In *The Maya and Their Neighbors,* ed. C. L. Hay, 281–91. New York: 1940.

Lafeber, Walter. *Inevitable Revolutions: The United States and Central America.* New York: W. W. Norton and Company, 1984.

León Pérez, José Alejandro de, ed. *Memoria de Labores, Municipalidades Chimaltenango.* Guatemala: Editora Educativa, 1984.

———. "Tecpán Guatemala." In *Memoria de labores, municipalidades de Chimaltenango,* 36–38. Guatemala: Editora Educativa, 1984.

Little, Walter. "Home as a Place of Exhibition and Performance: Mayan Household Transformations in Guatemala." *Ethnology* 39, no. 2 (2000): 163–81.

Lokken, Paul Thomas. "The Challenge of Reform: Pluralism and Repression in Guatemala, 1920–1944." Master's thesis, University of Saskatchewan, 1989.

Lovell, George. "Surviving the Conquest: The Maya of Guatemala in Historical Perspective." *Latin American Research Review* 23 (1988): 25–58.

Lunn, Joe. *Memoirs of a Maelstrom: A Senegalese Oral History of the First World War.* Portsmouth, N.H.: Heinemann 1999.

Lutz, Christopher. *Historia sociodemográfica de Santiago de Guatemala 1541–1773.* La Antigua, Guatemala: CIRMA, Monograph series no. 2, 1984.

———. "Population History of the Parish of San Miguel Dueñas, Guatemala, 1530–1770." In *The Historical Demography of Highland Guatemala,* ed. Robert M. Carmack, John Early, and Christopher Lutz, 121–35. Institute for Mesoamerican Studies, no. 6. Albany: State University of New York, 1982.

———. *Santiago de Guatemala, 1541–1773, City, Caste y Colonial Experience.* Norman: University of Oklahoma Press, 1994.

MacLeod, Murdo. *Spanish Central America: A Socioeconomic History, 1520–1700.* Berkeley: University of California Press, 1973.

Marinas Otero, Luis, ed. *Las Constituciones de Guatemala.* Madrid: Instituto de Estudios Políticos, 1958.

Martínez Paláez, Severo. *La patria del criollo: ensayo de interpretación de la realidad colonial guatemalteca.* Guatemala: Editorial Universitaria Centroamericana, 1973.

Maxwell, Clayton. "Selective Hybridity and Development in San José Poaquil, Guatemala." Master's Thesis, University of Texas, Austin, 1998.

Maxwell, Judith M. "Three Tales—Two and a Half Linguistic Systems." Paper presented at the American Anthropological Association Conference, Philadelphia, 1986.

Maxwell, Judith M., and Robert M. Hill, II. *Kaqchikel Chronicles.* New Orleans: MesoAmerican Research Institute, forthcoming.

McCamant, John. "Intervention in Guatemala." *Comparative Political Studies* 13, no. 1 (1984): 373–407.

McCrea, Heather L. "Burial and Cemetery Rights in Nineteenth-Century Yucatán." Paper given at American Society for Ethnohistory conference, Minneapolis, November 12, 1998.

McCreery, David J. "Coffee and Class: The Structure of Development in Liberal Guatemala." *Hispanic American Historical Review* 56, no. 3 (1976): 438–60.

———. "Guatemala City." In *The 1918–1919 Pandemic Influenza: The Urban Impact in the Western World,* ed. Fred R. van Hartesveldt, 161–83. New York: Edwin Mellen, 1992.

———. *Rural Guatemala 1760–1940.* Stanford: Stanford University Press, 1994.

———. "State Power, Indigenous Communities, and Land in Nineteenth-Century Guatemala, 1820–1920." In *Guatemalan Indians and the State,* ed. Carol Smith, 96–115. Austin: University of Texas Press, 1990.

Menchú, Rigoberta. *Crossing Borders.* London: Verso, 1998.

———. *I, Rigoberta Menchú: An Indian Woman in Guatemala.* New York: Verso, 1984.

Méndez Montenegro, J. C. *444 años de legislación agraria, 1513–1957.* Guatemala: Imprenta Universitaria, 1958.

Mesa nacional Maya de Guatemala. *Plan Nacional de desarrollo del pueblo Maya de Guatemala. Programa de las Naciones Unidas para el desarrollo.* Guatemala: Q'uq'kumat-MENMAGUA, 1999.

Miceli, Keith. "Rafael Carrera: Defender and Promoter of Peasant Interests in Guatemala, 1837–1848." *The Americas* 31, no. 1 (1974): 72–95.

Milla y Vidaurre, Jose. *Historia de la América Central.* Guatemala: Tipografía Nacional, 1937.

Miller, H. J. "Positivism and Education in Guatemala." In *Positivism in Latin America, 1850–1900: Are Order and Progress Reconciliable?* ed. Ralph Lee Woodward, Jr. Lexington, Mass.: Health, 1971.

Milroy, Lesley. *Observing and Analysing Natural Language: A Critical Account of Sociolinguistic Method.* Oxford: Basil Blackwell, 1987.

Montejo, Víctor. *Testimony: Death of a Guatemalan Village,* ed. Víctor Perera. Willimantic, Conn.: Curbstone, 1987.

Moors, Marilyn M. "Indian Labor and the Guatemalan Crisis: Evidence from History and Anthropology." In *Central America: Historical Perspectives on the Contemporary Crisis,* ed. Ralph Lee Woodward, Jr., 67–83. New York: Greenwood, 1988.

Murray, Douglas L. *Cultivating Crisis: The Human Cost of Pesticides in Latin America.* Austin: University of Texas Press, 1994.

Náñez Falcón, Guillermo. "Erwin Paul Dieseldorff, German Entrepreneur in the Alta Verapaz of Guatemala, 1889–1937." Ph.D. diss., Tulane University, 1970.

Naylor, Robert A. "Guatemala: Indian Attitudes toward Land Tenure." *Journal of Inter-American Studies* 9, no. 4 (1967): 619–39.

Nelson, Diane. *Finger in the Wound: Body Politics in Quincentennial Guatemala.* Berkeley: University of California Press, 1999.

Nosotros conocemos nuestra historia: 500 años de resistencia indígena, negra y popular. 2nd ed. Guatemala: Iglesia Guatemalteca en el Exilio, 1992.

Ortner, Sherry. "Resistance and the Problem of Ethnographic Refusal." *Comparative Studies in Society and History* 137, no. 1 (1995): 173–93.

———. "Theory in Anthropology since the Sixties." *Comparative Studies of Society and History* 26 (1984): 126–66.

Paret-Limardo de Vela, Lise. "Original del baile del torito." *Guatemala Indígena* 3, no. 2 (1963): 93–118.

Peña, Devon Gerardo. *Terror of the Machine: Technology, Work, Gender, and Ecology on the U.S.–Mexican Border.* Austin: Center for Mexican American Studies, University of Texas, 1997.

Peñalosa, Fernando, ed. *Tales and Legends of the Q'anob'al Maya.* Rancho Palos Verdes, Calif.: Yax Te', 1995.

Peterson, Kurt. *The Maquiladora Revolution in Guatemala.* Orville H. Schell, Jr., Center for International Human Rights at Yale Law School, Occasional Paper Series. New Haven: Yale University. 1992.

Peterson, Marshall N. *The Highland Maya in Fact and Legend.* Lancaster, Calif.: Labyrinthos, 1999.

Petrich, Perla. *Memoria de Mi Pueblo: Santa Catarina Palopó.* Guatemala: IRIPAZ Publicaciones, 1992.

Pimentel, David. "Green Revolution Agriculture and Chemical Hazards." *Science of the Total Environment* 188, no. 1 (1996): S86–S98.

Pingali, Prabhu L., and Pierre A. Roger. *Impact of Pesticides on Farmer Health and the Rice Environment.* Boston: Kluwer, 1995.

Pitti, Joseph Apolonio. *Jorge Ubico and Guatemalan Politics in the 1920s.* Ann Arbor, Mich.: Xerox University Microfilms, 1975.

Polo Sifontes, Francis. *Los Cakchiqueles en la conquista de Guatemala.* 2nd ed. Guatemala: Editorial José de Pineda Ibarra, 1980.

Price, Richard. *First Time: The Historical Vision of an Afro-American People.* Baltimore: Johns Hopkins University Press, 1983.

Racancoj, Víctor M. *Socioeconomía Maya precolonial.* Guatemala: Editorial CHOLSAMAJ, 1994.

Rae, John B. *The American Automobile: A Brief History.* Chicago: University of Chicago Press, 1965.

Ramírez Arroyo, Rafael. "Tecpán." *Revista Franciscana* 1, nó. 1 (1948): 2–3.

Recinos, Adrián. *Cronicas Indígenas de Guatemala.* Guatemala: Editorial Universitaria, 1957.

———. *Memorial de Sololá, Anales de los Cakchiqueles.* México, D.F.: Fondo de Cultura Económica, 1950.

———. "Títulos de la casa Ixquin-Nehaib, señora del territorio de Otzoya." In *Crónicas indígenas de Guatemala,* ed. Adrián Recinos, 71–94. Guatemala City: Editorial Universitaria, 1957.

Recinos, Adrián, and Delia Goetz. *The Annals of the Cakchiqueles.* Norman: University of Oklahoma Press, 1953.

(REMHI) Recovery of Historical Memory Project. *Guatemala, Never Again!: The Official Report of the Human Rights Office, Archdiocese of Guatemala.* Maryknoll, N.Y.: Orbis, 1999.

Repetto, Robert, and Sanjay Baliga. *Pesticides and the Immune System: The Public Health Risks.* Washington, D.C.: World Resources Institute, 1996.

Rodas N., Flavio, Ovidio Rodas C., and Lawrence F. Hawkins. *Chichicastenango: The Kiche Indians.* Guatemala: Union Tipografía, 1940.

Rodríguez, Demetrio. *Las ONGs y las relaciones interétnicas.* Guatemala: Editorial CHOLSAMAJ, 1995.

Rodríguez Rouaret, Francisco. *Diccionario Municipal de Guatemala.* Guatemala: Instituto de Estudios y Capacitación Cívica, 1996.

Rojas Lima, Flavio. *Etnicidad: teoría y práxis: la revolución cultural de 1990.* Guatemala: Editorial Cultura, 1990.

———. *La simbología del lenguaje en la cofradía indígena.* Guatemala: Seminario de Integración Social Guatemalteca, 1984.

Saberwal, Satish. "The Oral Tradition, Periodization, and Political Systems: Some East African Comparisons." *Canadian Journal of African Studies* 1 (1967): 155–62.

Sahil ch'oolej sa'li hoonal (momentos alegres) leyendas Q'echi'es de El Estor, Izabal. Rancho Palos Verdes, Calif.: Yax Te', 1995.

Salazar, Francisco. "Sanidad Public." *Salubridad y Asistencia: órgano del ministerio de salud pública y asistencia social.* Vol. 1. October 1948.

Sam Colop, Luis Enrique. "The Discourse of Concealment and 1992." In *Maya Cultural Activism in Guatemala,* ed. Edward Fischer and R. McKenna Brown, 107–13. Austin: University of Texas Press, 1996.

Santana Cardoso, Ciro Flamarión. "Historia económica del café en Centroamérica." *Estudios Sociales Centroamericanos* 4, no. 10 (1975): 9–55.

Schlesinger, Stephen, and Stephen Kinzer. *Bitter Fruit: The Untold Story of the American Coup in Guatemala.* New York: Doubleday and Anchor, 1982.

Schmid, Lester. *Papel de la mano de obra migratoria en el desarrollo económico de Guatemala.* Guatemala City: Universidad de San Carlos, 1973.

Scott, James C. *Weapons of the Weak: Everyday Forms of Resistance.* New Haven: Yale University Press, 1985.

Sexton, James D., ed. *Mayan Folktales: Folklore from Lake Atitlán, Guatemala.* New York: Anchor Books, Doubleday, 1992.

Sherman, William. *Forced Native Labor in Sixteenth-Century Central America.* Lincoln: University of Nebraska Press, 1979.

Shopes, Linda. "Using Oral History for a Family History Project." In *Oral History: An Interdisciplinary Anthology,* ed. David K. Dunaway and Willa K. Baum. London: Altamira, 1996.

Siegel, Morris. "San Miguel Acatán: 1938–53." In *Community Culture and National Change,* ed. Richard Adams, 40–43. Middle American Research Institute Series, publication no. 24. New Orleans: Tulane University, 1972.

Sifontes, Francis Polo. *Los Cakchiqueles en la conquista de Guatemala.* Guatemala: Editorial "José de Pineda Ibarra," 1980.

Silvert, Kalman H., and Arden R. King. "Cobán: 1944–53." In *Community Culture and National Change,* ed. Richard Adams, 44–47. Middle American Research Institute Series, publication no. 24. New Orleans: Tulane University, 1972.

Skinner-Klee, Jorge, ed. *Legislación indigenísta de Guatemala.* México, D.F.: Instituto Indigenísta Interamericano, 1954.

Sklair, Leslie. *Assembling for Development: The Maquila Industry in Mexico and the United States.* San Diego: Center for U.S.–Mexican Studies, University of California, 1989.

Smith, Carol. "Beyond Dependency Theory: National and Regional Patterns of Underdevelopment in Guatemala." *American Ethnologist* 5, no. 3 (1978): 574–617.

———. "Class Position and Class Consciousness in an Indian Community: Totonicapán in the 1970s." In *Guatemalan Indians and the State: 1540–1988,* ed. Carol Smith, 205–29. Austin: University of Texas Press, 1990.

———. "Does a Commodity Economy Enrich the Few while Ruining the Masses?" *Journal of Peasant Studies* 11, no. 3 (1984): 60–95.

———. *Indian Class and Class Consciousness in Prerevolutionary Guatemala.* Washington, D.C.: Latin American Program, Wilson Center, 1984.

———. "Introduction: Social Relations in Guatemala over Time and Space." In *Guatemalan Indians and the State 1540–1988,* ed. Carol Smith, 1–30. Austin: University of Texas Press, 1990.

——. "Labor and International Capital in the Making of a Peripheral Social Formation: Economic Transformations of Guatemala, 1850–1980." Washington, D.C.: Latin American Program, Wilson Center, 1984.

——. "Local History in Global Context: Social and Economic Transitions in Western Guatemala." *Comparative Studies in Society and History* 26, no. 2 (1984): 193–228.

——. "Origins of the National Question in Guatemala: A Hypothesis." In *Guatemalan Indians and the State: 1540–1988,* ed. Carol Smith, 72–96. Austin: University of Texas Press, 1990.

——, ed. *Guatemalan Indians and the State 1540–1988.* Austin: University of Texas Press, 1990.

Solares, Jorge. *Derechos humanos desde la perspectiva indígena en Guatemala.* Guatemala: FLACSO, 1995.

Stoll, David, and Virginia Garrard-Burnett, eds. *Rethinking Protestantism in Latin America.* Philadelphia: Temple University Press, 1993.

Suslow, Leo A. *Aspects of Social Reform in Guatemala, 1944–1949: Problems of Social Change in an Underdeveloped Country.* Hamilton, N.Y.: Colgate University Press, 1949.

Tax, Sol. "April Is This Afternoon: Correspondence of Robert Redfield and Sol Tax, 1933–44." *Collection of Manuscripts on Cultural Anthropology Series* 63:330. Microfilm. University of Chicago Library, 1980.

——. *Penny Capitalism: A Guatemalan Indian Economy.* Washington, D.C.: Smithsonian Institution, Institute of Social Anthropology, 1953.

Tedlock, Barbara. *Time and the Highland Maya.* Albuquerque: University of New Mexico Press, 1992.

Tedlock, Dennis. *Popol Vuh: The Mayan Book of the Dawn of Life.* New York: Simon and Schuster, 1996.

——. *Spoken Word and the Work of Interpretation.* Philadelphia: University of Pennsylvania Press, 1983.

Thompson, Eric. *The Rise and Fall of Maya Civilization.* Norman: University of Oklahoma Press, 1975.

Thrupp, Lori Ann, Gilles Bergeron, and William Walters. *Bittersweet Harvests for Global Supermarkets: Challenges in Latin America's Agricultural Export Boom.* Washington, D.C.: World Resources Institute, 1995.

Tobar Cruz, Pedro. *Los Montañeses.* Guatemala: Ministerio de Educación Pública, 1959.

United Nations Human Rights Report (on-line). *Guatemala: Memoria del Silencio.* Comisión para el Esclaracimiento Histórico (CEH). *Http://hrdata.aaas.org/ceh/mds/spanish.* 1999.

Vansina, Jan. *Living with Africa.* Madison: University of Wisconsin Press, 1994.

——. *Oral Tradition as History.* Madison: University of Wisconsin Press, 1985.

Vansina, Jan, and Carolyn Keyes Adenaike, eds. *In Pursuit of History: Fieldwork in Africa.* Portsmouth, N.H.; Heinemann, 1996.

Vásquez, Fray Francisco. *Crónica de la Provincia del Santísimo Nombre de Jesús de Guatemala.* Vol. 1. Guatemala: Tipografía Nacional, 1937.

Villacorta Calderón, José Antonio. "Conquista de los Sacatepéquez." *Anales de la Sociedad de Geografía e Historia* I, no. 3 (1927): 182–87.

———. *Curso de Geografía de la América Central para uso de los Institutos y Escuelas Normales.* Guatemala: Tipografía Sánchez y de Guise, 1928.

———. *Prehistoria e historia antigua de Guatemala.* Guatemala: Impreso en la Tipografía Nacional, 1938.

Wachtel, Nathan. "The Indian and the Spanish Conquest." In *Cambridge History of Latin America,* ed. Leslie Bethell, vol. 1: 207–48. 11 vols. Cambridge: Cambridge University Press, 1984.

Warren, Kay. *Indigenous Movements and Their Critics: Pan-Maya Activism in Guatemala.* Princeton: Princeton University Press, 1998.

———. *The Symbolism of Subordination: Indian Identity in a Guatemalan Town.* Austin: University of Texas Press, 1978.

———. "Transforming Memories and Histories: The Meaning of Ethnic Resurgence for Mayan Indians." In *Americas: New Interpretive Essays,* ed. Alfred Stephan, 189–219. New York: Oxford University Press, 1992.

———. *The Violence Within: Cultural and Political Opposition in Divided Nations.* Boulder: Westview, 1993.

Wasserstrom, Robert. "Revolution in Guatemala: Peasants and Politics under the Arbenz Government." *Comparative Studies in Society and History* 17 (October 1975): 443–78.

Watanabe, John. "Enduring yet Ineffable Community in the Western Periphery of Guatemala." In *Guatemalan Indians and the State,* ed. Carol Smith, 183–204. Austin: University of Texas Press, 1990.

———. "From Saints to Shibboleths: Image, Structure, and Identity in Maya Religious Syncretism." *American Ethnologist* 17, no. 1 (1990): 131–50.

Wauchope, Robert. "Las edades de Utatlán e Iximche'." *Revista de Antropología e Historia de Guatemala* I, no. 1 (1949).

Weisenburger, Dennis D. "Human Health Effects of Agrichemical Use." *Human Pathology* 24, no. 6 (1993): 571–76.

Whetten, Nathan L. *Guatemala: The Land and the People.* New Haven: Yale University Press, 1961.

Williams, Robert G. *Export Agriculture and the Crisis in Central America.* Chapel Hill: University of North Carolina Press, 1986.

Williford, Miriam. "Las Luces y La Civilización: The Social Reforms of Mariano Gálvez." In *Applied Enlightenment: Nineteenth Century Liberalism,* ed. Margaret A. L. Harrison and Robert Wauchope. Middle American Research Institute Series, publication no. 24. New Orleans: Tulane University, 1972.

Wisdom, Charles. *The Chorti Indians of Guatemala.* Chicago: University of Chicago Press, 1940.

Wolf, Eric. "Closed Corporate Peasant Communities in Mesoamerica and Central Java." *Southwestern Journal of Anthropology* 13 (1957): 1–18.

———. *Europe and the People without History.* Berkeley: University of California Press, 1982.

———. *Sons of the Shaking Earth.* Chicago: University of Chicago Press, 1959.

Woodward, Ralph Lee, Jr. *Central America: A Nation Divided.* Oxford: Oxford University Press, 1985.

———. "Changes in the Nineteenth-Century Guatemalan State." In *Guatemalan Indians and the State,* ed. Carol Smith, 52–71. Austin: University of Texas Press, 1990.

———. *Rafael Carrera and the Emergence of the Republic of Guatemala, 1821–1871.* Athens: University of Georgia Press, 1993.

Wright, Angus. *The Death of Ramón González: The Modern Agricultural Dilemma.* Austin: University of Texas Press, 1990.

Xet, Santiago. "Campos de Ensayos y de Demostraciones, Prácticas del Programa de Fertilización de 'FAO-SFEI' en San Juan Comalapa, Chimaltenango." *Comalapan,* September 1966, 6.

Yool Gómez, Juan, and Juan Kaqjay. *Tzijonik kan qate' qatata'.* Guatemala: Universidad Rafael Landivar, 1990.

Zapata Arceyuz, Virgilio. *Historia de la iglesia evangelica en Guatemala.* Guatemala City: Genesis Publicidad, 1982.

Index

DDT, 127, 128

Debt peonage, 87, 92, 107, 196, 199, 203–5, 218

Díaz, Victor Miguel, 73, 159

Díaz de Castillo, Bernal, 47–48, 51

DIGEBI (Dirección General de Educación Bilingüe), 158

Discrimination, 115, 254–55; administrative, 234, 285 (n. 43); legal, 26; political, 23, 27–28, 68, 85, 137–38, 242, 244; in schools, 22, 165, 172. *See also* Education: discrimination in; Military, Guatemalan: and discrimination

Disease, x, 90–91, 108, 115–16, 121; and chemical fertilizer, 104–5; and hygiene, 125, 137. *See also* AIDS; Alcoholism; Cancer; Cholera; Coast, Pacific; Influenza, Spanish; Leprosy; Malaria; Measles; Pneumonia; Smallpox; Typhoid; Typhus; Yellow Fever

Doctors, 91, 119, 120, 121, 122, 129, 130, 131, 132, 136, 137, 159, 230; and community tensions, 124–25, 127, 129, 264, 267; and language barrier, 13. *See also* Catalán Prem, Carlos; Gaitán, Luis; Molina Flores, P.; Robles, Rodolfo

Dress, 4, 7, 27, 40, 56, 58, 67, 90, 147, 160, 183, 235, 238, 241, 242, 245, 248, 256, 257, 260, 282 (n. 15). See also *Güipil*

Dulles, John Foster, 189

Earthquake, 1917, 139–40, 142

Earthquake, 1976, xi, 5, 16, 19, 115, 139–46, 152, 168; and *la violencia,* xi, 145–46, 254; and National Reconstruction Committee, 144

Earthquakes, xi, 151, 260; and relief workers, xi, 143–46

Education: vs. agriculture, 170–71; discrimination in, 48, 172, 175, 260; and employment, 169–71, 173, 174, 262; gender and, 9, 160, 161; informants' levels of, 4, 6, 9, 12; liberal approach to, 155–57, 196; Ministry of, 158, 168,

174; and power, 169–70, 171–72, 175, 207, 215, 218, 231, 239, 241, 245, 260, 262; unequal, x. *See also* Arbenz Guzmán, Jacobo: and education; Arévalo Bermejo, Juan José: and education; Barrios, Justo Rufino: and education; Schools; Tz'ikin, K'ai'; Ubico, Jorge: and education

Elections, 196; 1999, 23

Electrification, 205, 222, 230

El Salvador, 189, 190

Employment: perceptions of, 13; self-, 27; types of, 4, 6, 13, 15, 24, 59, 82, 89, 93, 133. *See also* Labor

England, 143–44

Entrepreneurs, Mayan, 89, 103, 108, 109, 112–14, 205–6, 265, 270. *See also* Matzer Tuwac, Nemesio

Epidemics, 115–38, 266. *See also* Disease

Ermita, Valley of, 45

Escuela Politécnica, 165, 187

Esquit Choy, Edgar, 18

Estrada Cabrera, Manuel, 119, 128, 191, 199, 237, 245, 258

Ethnic relations, 25, 31, 32, 78, 101, 112, 164, 165, 166–67, 226–27, 231, 232, 273, 337 (n. 5); and discrimination, x, 23, 251; improved, 167, 169–70, 173, 175, 181, 182–83, 192, 194, 201, 207–8, 236, 238–39, 240, 247–48, 261, 263, 267; among Maya, 30, 46, 48, 58–77, 79, 80, 95–96, 99, 134–35, 147, 252, 254; and shifting tensions from Maya to Ladinos, 45, 48, 68, 80; and tensions, xi, 22–23, 29–30, 46, 48, 52, 68, 72, 79, 99, 137–38, 142, 162–63, 177, 182, 187–88, 214, 215, 228, 237–39, 249–52, 255–59, 265–66, 272, 338 (n. 31). *See also* Discrimination; Kaqchikel; Ladinos; Racism

Ethnohistory, xi

Europe, 117, 119

Factories, 108–9, 110, 113, 260–61

Family, 14, 254